Godden's Guide to

# IRONSTONE

STONE & GRANITE WARES

Godden's Guide to

# IRONSTONE

## STONE & GRANITE WARES

Geoffrey A. Godden.

F.R.S.A.



ANTIQUE COLLECTORS' CLUB

ISBN 1 85149 278 X



British Library Cataloguing-in-Publication Data
A catalogue record for this book is available from the British Library.

FRONTISPIECE: *A superb quality Charles Meigh hand-painted 'Opaque Porcelain' plate of 1851 Exhibition type (see Colour Plate 43)*

Printed in England
by the Antique Collectors' Club Ltd., Woodbridge, Suffolk,
on Consort Royal Satin paper
supplied by the Donside Paper Company, Aberdeen, Scotland.

# Contents


| | | |
|---|---|---|
| Preface | | 8 |
| Introduction | | 11 |
| Colour Plates | | 17 |
| Chapter I | The Pre-Ironstone period. | 57 |
| Chapter II | The Introduction of Mason's Patent Ironstone China. | 71 |
| Chapter III | Mason's Patent Ironstone China and Marks. | 79 |
| Chapter IV | Mason's 1818 and 1822 auction sales. | 107 |
| Chapter V | The Later Ironstone and Granite Wares. | 157 |
| Chapter VI | Identification. An alphabetical list of British manufacturers. | 174 |
| Chapter VII | The non-British manufacturers. | 361 |
| Appendix I | Check-list of manufacturers' initials and trade names. | 369 |
| Appendix II | Registered Marks, Patterns or Forms. | 374 |
| Appendix III | The Silber & Fleming trade catalogues. | 385 |
| Notes | | 390 |
| Bibliography | | 391 |
| Acknowledgements | | 395 |
| Index | | 396 |

## Other books by Geoffrey Godden

*Victorian Porcelain*
*Encyclopaedia of British Pottery and Porcelain Marks*
*Illustrated Encyclopaedia of British Pottery & Porcelain*
*The Handbook of British Pottery and Porcelain Marks*
*Minton Pottery and Porcelain of the First Period*
*Caughley and Worcester Porcelains 1779 -1800*
*Coalport and Coalbrookdale Porcelains*
*The Illustrated Guide to Lowestoft Porcelains*
*The Illustrated Guide to Ridgway Porcelains*
*Jewitt's Ceramic Art of Great Britain, 1800-1900*
*British Porcelain. An Illustrated Guide*
*British Pottery. An Illustrated Guide*
*Godden's Guide to English Porcelain*
*Oriental Export Market Porcelain and its Influence on European Wares*
*Godden's Guide to Mason's China and the Ironstone Wares*
*Chamberlain-Worcester Porcelain, 1786-1852*
*Staffordshire Porcelain*
*English China*
*Lowestoft Porcelain*
*Ridgway Porcelain*
*Eighteenth-century English Porcelain –a selection from the Godden Reference Collection*
*Encyclopaedia of British Porcelain Manufacturers*
*Davenport China, Earthenware & Glass 1794-1887 (with T.A. Lockett)*
*Collecting Lustreware*
*The Concise Guide to British Pottery and Porcelain*
*Godden's Guide to European Porcelain*
*Collecting Picture Postcards*
*The Concise Guide to European Porcelain*

# Antique Collectors' Club

THE ANTIQUE COLLECTORS' CLUB was formed in 1966 and quickly grew to a five figure membership spread throughout the world. It publishes the only independently run monthly antiques magazine, *Antique Collecting*, which caters for those collectors who are interested in widening their knowledge of antiques, both by greater awareness of quality and by discussion of the factors which influence the price that is likely to be asked. The Antique Collectors' Club pioneered the provision of information on prices for collectors and the magazine still leads in the provision of detailed articles on a variety of subjects.

It was in response to the enormous demand for information on 'what to pay' that the price guide series was introduced in 1968 with the first edition of *The Price Guide to Antique Furniture* (completely revised 1978 and 1989), a book which broke new ground by illustrating the more common types of antique furniture, the sort that collectors could buy in shops and at auctions rather than the rare museum pieces which had previously been used (and still to a large extent are used) to make up the limited amount of illustrations in books published by commercial publishers. Many other price guides have followed, all copiously illustrated, and greatly appreciated by collectors for the valuable information they contain, quite apart from prices. The Price Guide Series heralded the publication of many standard works of reference on art and antiques. *The Dictionary of British Art* (now in six volumes), *The Pictorial Dictionary of British 19th Century Furniture Design*, *Oak Furniture* and *Early English Clocks* were followed by many deeply researched reference works such as *The Directory of Gold and Silversmiths*, providing new information. Many of these books are now accepted as the standard work of reference on their subject.

The Antique Collectors' Club has widened its list to include books on gardens and architecture. All the Club's publications are available through bookshops world wide and a full catalogue of all these titles is available free of charge from the addresses below.

Club membership, open to all collectors, costs little. Members receive free of charge *Antique Collecting*, the Club's magazine (published ten times a year), which contains well-illustrated articles dealing with the practical aspects of collecting not normally dealt with by magazines. Prices, features of value, investment potential, fakes and forgeries are all given prominence in the magazine.

Among other facilities available to members are private buying and selling facilities and the opportunity to meet other collectors at their local antique collectors' club. There are over eighty in Britain and more than a dozen overseas. Members may also buy the Club's publications at special pre-publication prices.

As its motto implies, the Club is an organisation designed to help collectors get the most out of their hobby: it is informal and friendly and gives enormous enjoyment to all concerned.

*For Collectors — By Collectors — About Collecting*

ANTIQUE COLLECTORS' CLUB
5 Church Street, Woodbridge Suffolk IP12 1DS, UK
Tel: 01394 385501 Fax: 01394 384434
or
Market Street Industrial Park, Wappingers' Falls, NY 12590, USA
Tel: 914 297 0003 Fax: 914 297 0068

# Preface

The British, or more precisely the English, potters have much to be proud of in introducing to the world at large several new basic types of ceramic bodies that can with good reason be said to have revolutionized the ceramic industry and to have made our tables, or life in general, more enjoyable.

Porcelain was not invented in Britain but in the early part of the eighteenth century British potters certainly did introduce and perfect a refined type of earthenware that came very near to porcelain and marketed it widely. Indeed that type of earthenware had some important advantages over porcelain; it was lighter in weight, less troublesome to produce and it was less expensive. To its low cost we could also add another commercial consideration – novelty. These qualities will be discussed repeatedly in this book.

But I have, of course, been referring to creamware or, as Josiah Wedgwood christened the body in the mid-1760s, 'Queen's Ware', a pleasant, light, reasonably durable body that could be produced in remarkably fancy shapes with little apparent difficulty. By the 1770s it was being produced in very many potteries, large and small, all over the British Isles, not just in Staffordshire.

A contemporary French report stated that in every inn from Calais to Moscow one ate off English creamware and, reputedly, the Continental potters producing their tin-glazed earthenwares were being put out of business or were being forced to emulate British creamwares. Not only were creamwares selling internationally but some potters were also migrating to help manufacture British-style creamware in foreign lands.[1]

To Josiah Wedgwood we also owe the introduction, in or about 1779, of 'pearl white' or 'pearl ware'. In essence this was a whiter version of the standard creamware, the white appearance being said to have been achieved by adding a very little cobalt blue to the glaze. This works well – as does washing blue – but it is probably an over-simplification of the improvement in the basic earthenware body initially achieved by Wedgwood.

Pearlware like creamware was again copied by all and sundry and was widely marketed as 'china glaze' or 'china glazed ware'. One great advantage of this whiter body was that, apart from appearing closer to the ever-popular Oriental porcelains, it took the underglaze blue Chinese-style decoration so effectively. Much of this was hand-painted in a rather naïve manner but soon underglaze-blue printed patterns were being applied in a mass-production manner. These well-engraved British printed designs (Plate 1) very closely emulated the popular hand-painted Chinese porcelains (Plate 2). They were light, pleasant to use, reasonably durable, and at least were fit for their purpose and quite moderately priced. In the nineteenth century engraving skills improved noticeably and truly beautiful underglaze-blue prints were added to British standard earthenwares, which like the earlier creamwares were exported to all overseas markets. Particularly important was, of course, the rapidly expanding North American market.

To the list of British ceramic innovations can surely be added 'Bone China'. This was introduced, reputedly, by Josiah Spode, in about 1800. The exact date is open to question but there is documentary backing for December 1800. Spode's new type of body quickly superseded all other British porcelain mixes and again became a staple line which manufacturers shipped all over the world. It was pleasing to the

PLATE 1. *A Staffordshire blue printed pearlware dinner service plate, with potter's (Heath) impressed initials. Produced to rival the Chinese porcelain imports. 9½in. (24.13cm) diameter. c.1790-1800.*

eye and touch, it was translucent, relatively stable in the various manufacturing processes and all importantly in the firing. It served as a beautiful canvas for all forms of ceramic decoration. It has been referred to as the 'evergreen bone china'. For some hundred and fifty years the British porcelain manufacturers held a world monopoly on its production but in recent years its manufacture has spread to several other countries.

When Josiah Spode the Second introduced the new body he termed it 'Stoke Porcelain'; the present-day description 'Bone China' was applied much later. Spode and his illustrious father before him were earthenware manufacturers, but like most go-ahead potters they set their sights on becoming porcelain manufacturers. Josiah Spode achieved this by inventing a new body, one that combined the two basic ingredients of hard-paste or true porcelain, China clay and China Stone, with a proportion of calcined (that is burnt) animal bones. The bones had been added to earthenware bodies well before 1800 but Spode's 'Stoke China' added them to a porcelain mix and in quite high proportions. The proportion varied from manufacturer to manufacturer and on the type of article being produced but in general terms the amount of added calcined bones varied between 25 and 50 per cent. The calcined bones are deemed to have strengthened the body, made it whiter and more translucent than former mixes and to have added to its ease of manufacture – it was a near-perfect ceramic body.[2]

What is not clear is what this earthenware potter, Josiah Spode, hoped to achieve when he added burnt bones to a very well known basic porcelain mix. He was probably seeking to produce a strong white economical body that could be fired at earthenware temperatures in his existing kilns. True or hard-paste porcelain required a higher temperature that gave rise to many expensive problems and high firing losses. He was most probably also seeking to produce a white body that would emulate the much praised Oriental porcelains and enable him to help fill the great void that opened up when the English East India Company ceased its bulk importations of Chinese porcelains. He succeeded on all counts.

Yet, as you will learn, he was not alone in seeking to produce a white, durable, ceramic body to emulate Chinese porcelains at this period. Furthermore, perhaps inspired by Spode's success with the 'ever green' bone china, other potters sought to experiment further in order to produce a durable highly vitrified earthenware body to imitate the costly and now much sought-after porcelains.

This book is concerned with those nineteenth century durable wares which we call 'Ironstone China', 'Stone China' or later 'Granite'. Different manufacturers were to coin various other trade names[3] for what we can from now on term for convenience 'Ironstone China'.

The production of these novel ceramic bodies further stimulated the industry and prolonged the British hold on all overseas markets. The world wanted such strong but good-looking table wares for they were more than poor man's porcelain and achieved their purpose of everyday use by all. Thus Ironstone and the Stone Chinas furnished the world in the nineteenth century as creamware had done in the eighteenth.

British ironstones have also proved universally popular for their decorative merits. Arthur Hayden in his 1904 book, *Chats on English China* (T. Fisher Unwin, London), rightly noted that Mason ironstone 'on account of its handsome decorative effect is rapidly rising in value'. A photograph of my grandfather's antique shop at the same period features a so-popular (but not expensive) Mason's ironstone jug in the window. Today there are specialist dealers who stock only Mason's and other decorative and highly collectable ironstone-type wares. Their shops or displays at antique fairs are breathtakingly colourful and varied.

The ultimate compliment has been paid to the humble yet homely Mason jugs by the production of these strangely popular angular vessels in the East complete with very close copies of an old Mason's back-stamp. Meanwhile in the Staffordshire Potteries British manufacturers are still producing useful table wares in 'Classic English Ironstone'. The Masons' early nineteenth century advertisements are now updated but have much the same meaning and appeal: 'Dishwasher and microwave safe, this charming ironstone pottery will bring a touch of distinction to every meal'.

# Introduction

The emphasis of English manufacturers during the all important eighteenth century was on the production of white-bodied ceramics. The basic intention, of course, was to make wares that imitated the Oriental porcelains which were white-bodied, translucent and, in most cases, embellished with patterns that were colourful, then novel and interesting. Even the simple Chinese landscape motifs painted in blue under the glaze (Plate 2) were extremely popular and were imported into England and most other European countries by the ton!

The availability of Chinese porcelains in England in ever-increasing quantities during the eighteenth century until the early 1790s changed domestic habits to a major degree. Obviously it took time for the fashions of the rich to work their way down to the middle classes but, by the end of the century, most folk would have been eating from ceramic plates and partaking of tea or coffee from ceramic teapots, cups and saucers.

Admittedly, not all would enjoy porcelain utensils. Many would make do with the less expensive earthenwares but these would nearly always have been of white or light-coloured bodies. The main types of earthenwares made on an almost nationwide basis were creamware or, slightly later, pearlware – originally termed 'Pearl-white' by Josiah Wedgwood. The emphasis was on the light colour and the use of attractive descriptions which tended to suggest to the buyer that the ware was in some way superior to ordinary pottery – as indeed it was – while the cost was still quite reasonable.

The increasing importations of Oriental porcelains into Europe also increased domestic requirements and added to the delights of table setting. An obvious example is the introduction of tea into Europe and the Oriental vessels for its consumption, ranging from the teapot to the tea bowl. Many other Eastern foods and spices added culinary requirements and new vessels to kitchens and tables. This is a large and interesting subject that may not yet have been studied fully.

The great and traditional skills of the Chinese and other Eastern potters also meant that from the latter part of the seventeenth century onwards many articles that had previously been produced in pewter and other metals, in stoneware, glass or even wood, could now be manufactured in Chinese porcelain to special order. In time, as the eighteenth century progressed, such originally novel Chinese export-market porcelains became accepted as the norm and were in turn copied by European potters and porcelain manufacturers. My (now out of print) book, *Oriental Export Market Porcelain* (Granada Publishing, London, 1979), explains at length the development and large scale of these imports from the East. Just a few quotations from the original orders that went out to China on the vessels chartered to the English East India Company will show how originally non-ceramic articles were sent out as samples or models to be copied by the Chinese porcelain makers; also how non-Chinese utensils and objects were ordered to suit European tastes and fashions:

> Procure chocolate cups...to be made higher and narrower than what have usually been bought that the more of them may stand on a salver (1700).

> 12,000 boats for the tea spoons (such spoon-trays were not used by the Chinese) (1709).

> 2,000 hollow-cut fruit dishes, three sizes...according to the patterns you will receive... (1709).
>
> 8,000 small cups with one handle, fit for coffee or chocolate (1709).
>
> 3,000 small deep plates to bake in (1709).
>
> 300 boats three in a nest, as Pattern 1 (1709).
>
> 2,000 milk pots, the glass pattern, 1000 blue and white, 1000 coloured (1713).
>
> 2,000 cups in colours to be painted after the Japanese pattern (1713).
>
> 50,000 coffee cups with a blue flowers at the bottom within side and blue rims also within and without such as are used in Garroways Coffee House (1719).
>
> ...a parcel of china tyles for Chimneys like the pattern now sent and at encouraging prices – buy as far as one hundred thousand of them... (1719).[1]

Plates by the thousand variously listed as 'pewter fashion', 'English fashion' or more clearly 'brim-plates' show that these standard objects were to have condiment brims. This was in contrast to the Oriental-fashion plates which were like an enlarged saucer, without a flat brim.

In addition English records show that wooden pattern-pieces for required new Chinese porcelains, made to suit local fashions and requirements in about 1710, were carved in London by Joshua Bagshaw.

In 1712 a locked box of chinaware patterns was sent out to China, to show what shapes and styles sold best in London. Many other pattern pieces were sent out to China in subsequent seasons.

Apart from English glass wares and wooden models being sent to China as samples, other orders show that English salt-glaze stoneware was also sent so that the Chinese could copy the forms. It is also clear that European metal goods such as candlesticks were carried to China as samples of shapes required to be made in porcelain.

As the taste for Oriental porcelain table ware and household ornaments such as sets of vases, jars, bowls or more rarely figures became general, British potters and, from the mid-1740s onwards, the new porcelain manufacturers sought to trade upon the demand. They commenced to produce similar or more elaborate articles, being influenced also by the many Continental manufacturers, several of which enjoyed Royal or State support. Yet always the emphasis was on white (or near-white) bodied wares that looked like the ever-popular Oriental porcelains.

The other great appeal, one which became more and more important, especially as overseas markets were developed, was durability. What riches could be gained if one could produce a reasonably priced, porcelain look-alike body that would stand up to rough usage, yet could be decorated in an attractive colourful manner. To

PLATE 2. *A Chinese hard-paste porcelain hand-painted dinner service plate. This type of European market plate was imported in vast quantities and was very variable in quality. Later English copies were often superior and less prone to chipping.* 8¾in. (22.22cm). c.1705.

PLATE 3. *A British tin-glazed earthenware blue painted soup plate, emulating in an inferior body the imported Chinese porcelains.* 8½in. (21.59cm). c.1760.

these obvious and basic requirements the manufacturers sought ease of production, low kiln losses and reasonably priced ingredients. One might well have had to experiment and search out new materials to add strength to the mix.

The old tin-glazed clay-coloured bodies, variously called Delft, Faience or Maiolica, had sold for well over a hundred years in most European countries because the tin glaze gave a white, porcelain-like, surface-appearance which could be painted in blue (or other colours) to emulate in a general fashion Chinese porcelain (Plate 3). These opaque tin-glazed earthenwares were, however, certainly not durable and were especially liable to chip at the edges, so exposing the underlying, porous, clay-coloured earthenware body.

The tin-glazed wares were superseded by the superior British cream-coloured earthenwares or creamware (perfected and well marketed by Josiah Wedgwood under the name 'Queen's ware') and later by the whiter-looking pearlware, although some potters continued to produce tin-glazed wares into at least the 1780s. Looking onwards the standard cream-coloured wares, abbreviated by potters to 'C C', remained in favour but towards the end of the nineteenth century this was renamed 'Ivory' by most potters.

The greatest need, however, was to introduce a new type of reasonably priced, porcelain-like, durable ceramic body which could be made to emulate the so-popular Oriental porcelains.

This need became all the more important and commercially attractive when in the early 1790s the great English East India Company ceased its bulk importations of Chinese porcelains, leaving the market to be serviced by the relatively small quantity of 'Private Trade' importations permitted for the benefit of the ships' officers and crew.[2]

Yet even with the cessation of the massive bulk imports of the English East India Company, the British potters were still very greatly affected by the traditional popularity of the Chinese porcelains and their low prices which were difficult to match.

Their points were put to the Government in the summer of 1803 when it was proposed to cut the rate of import duty from the war-tax rate of over a hundred per cent to a mere (!) £59.8s.6d per hundred pound value.[3] One would have thought that a tax on competition of over fifty per cent would have satisfied any home manufacturer but it was deemed to spell ruin for the British potters, so popular and relatively inexpensive were the Oriental imports.

I quote below from the 'Case of the Manufacturers of Porcelain and Earthenware' as preserved in Enoch Wood's scrap book preserved in the Stoke-on-Trent City Museum and Art Gallery. The potters' case included the observations:

> ...The kinds of Porcelain manufactured in greatest quantity and in universal use, are the Blue and White, such as are imported from China under the names of Nankeen and Common.
>
> The Potteries of Staffordshire have also for some years made imitations of these Oriental Porcelains, and they are become at length staple articles at those extensive manufactories, from which so much National benefit is derived, not only by the employment of many thousands, but also from the considerable Tonnage they afford to Coasting Vessels, carrying their raw materials, and the advantages they give to Commerce by furnishing a cheap and bulky article.
>
> These manufactories, both of Porcelain and Earthenware, through the Protection of a wise Government, and the Ingenuity and persevering Industry of Individuals, having attained a Degree of Prosperity, unknown in any other Country of Europe, may seem now in a state to bid Defiance to Rival-ship; but if it be considered that the Prices of Labour and of all the materials they use, are advanced from thirty to forty per cent within the last five years, and that the public contributions and the Expense of Living are also much increased, they will be found to send[4] in need of the same fostering system as in a less advanced state...
>
> The Directors of the East India Company have for a period of years [since 1792], discontinued the importation of Porcelain on their own account, leaving it to the Private Trade of their servants; and the manufacturers of England, have, during that period, considerably enlarged their Works, with a view to fill up the European markets...
>
> In former periods when the East India Company carried on a Trade in Porcelain to the greatest extent, the market was frequently overstocked by extraordinary arrivals, and as uniformly happens in Commerce under such circumstances, the prices were reduced. In the event then of this Trade being re-established with the aforesaid reduction of Duty, a very prejudicial fluctuation in the Price of English manufacturers will be occasioned, because their prices must fall with those of this powerful Competition, without the means on the part of the manufacturers to reduce the charges of labour or raw materials...

To put their Fears to the Test of Calculation, the manufacturers have carefully compared the average Prices of Oriental Porcelain at the sales of the East India Company adding thereto the reduced Duty of fifty per cent with the Prices at which they can render their own wares to the Retailers, and they find the difference so small, as by no means to counter balance the strong Prejudices of the public mind in Favour of the rival manufacture, and the advantages which it may possess in point in texture. The superiority, however, in this one respect, they trust, will gradually disappear, if the Legislature should see fit to continue its Protection of a Body of manufacturers who produce the value of their merchandise from the Soil of the Country and the Labour of its inhabitants.

June 1st 1803.

The British potters were not content only to appeal for higher import duties on the popular importations from China, as they had always sought to improve their own products and closely to emulate the Oriental forms and patterns. Yet obviously they had to produce wares that were less expensive to manufacture than porcelain which ideally were strong and durable and capable of being formed into larger objects than could then be made in porcelain. Large dishes and vases were obviously in demand but were in general terms the monopoly of the Chinese potters.

The main section of this book, therefore, will tell the story of the introduction of such durable, Oriental-style British ceramic bodies that were to be aptly called 'Ironstone', 'Stone China' or 'Granite' and illustrates and explains the very large range of such wares which were produced to grace home tables as well as those of the world. It is a success story evidence of which is still seen in every hotel or café we might visit. The durable so-called 'Hotel Wares' and kitchen wares are related to the nineteenth century ironstone china as introduced by the Masons in 1813.

But first we must further set the scene, for Mason's Patent Ironstone China was by no means the first attempt to produce strong table wares, nor was it the first to employ a clever descriptive name to underline its strength. It has proved, however, the one to last to the present day and the one which introduced a new description into the international ceramic world.

# Colour Plates

COLOUR PLATE 1. *A Chinese hard-paste porcelain hand-painted dinner service plate. This type of European market plate was imported in vast quantities and was very variable in quality. Later English copies were often superior and less prone to chipping. Diameter 8¾in. (22.22cm). c.1785.*

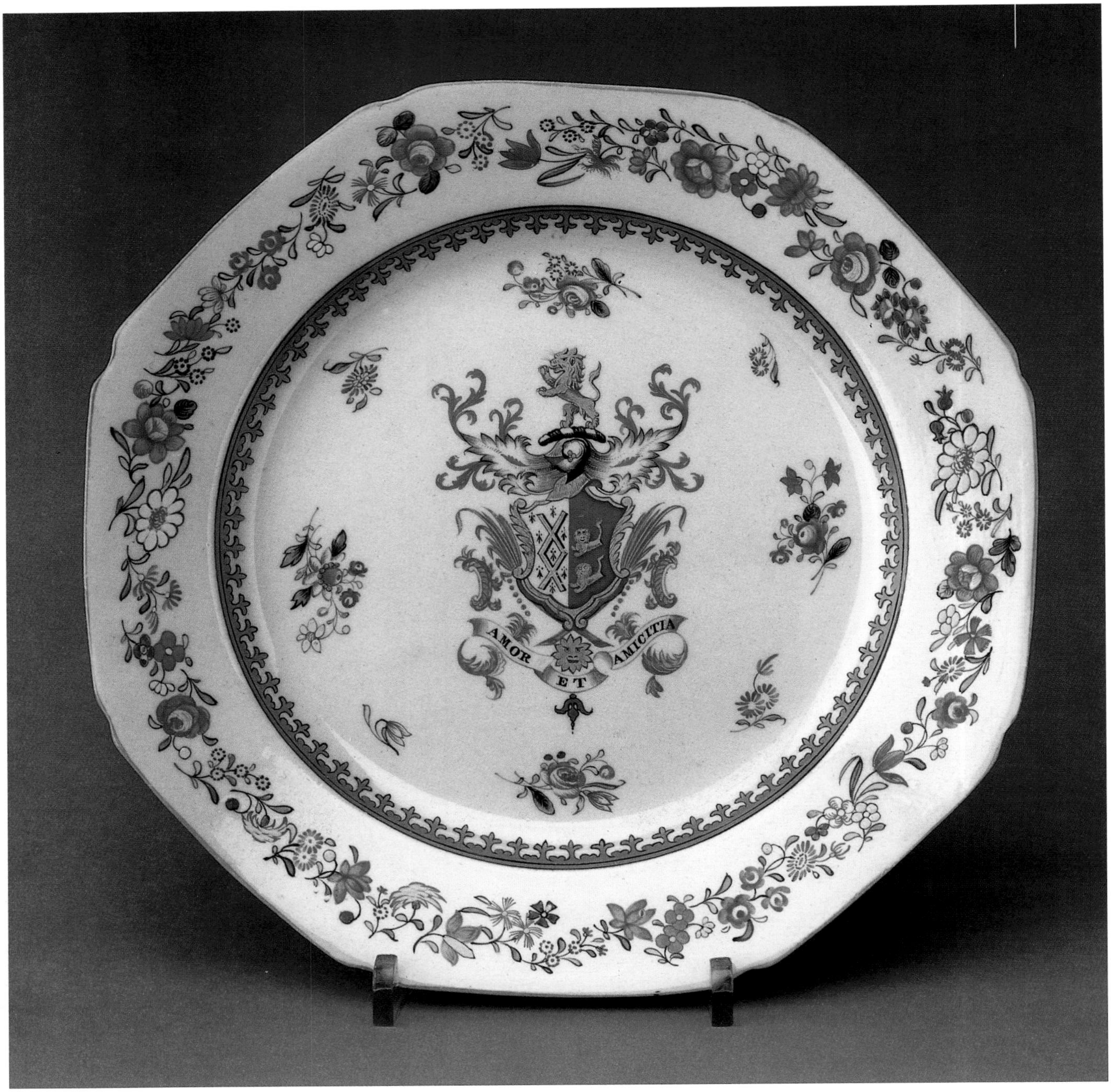


COLOUR PLATE 2. *A superb quality, marked 'Spode Stone China' plate in the style of, or a replacement to, a Chinese export-market armorial dinner service of c.1780. 8¾in. (22.22cm) diameter. c.1815-20. Mr and Mrs G. Fisk.*

COLOUR PLATE 3. *Representative pieces from an impressed marked 'Mason's Patent Ironstone China' dessert service, painted with a typical 'Old Japan' pattern. Centrepiece 14¼in. (36.19cm) long. c.1815-20.*

COLOUR PLATE 4. *An early 'Mason's ironstone dinner service tureen, cover and stand. Transfer printed in underglaze-blue with the 'blue pheasants' or 'birds and flowers' pattern purchased by Chamberlains in December 1814. This example has some gold trim. Printed crown mark. 11in. (27.94cm) high. c.1820. Mason's Factory collection. Reproduced by Courtesy of the Trustees of The Wedgwood Museum, Barlaston, Stoke-on-Trent.*

COLOUR PLATE 5. *A superb quality, impressed marked 'Mason's Patent Ironstone China' dessert dish from a complete service (see Plate 55). The centre almost certainly painted by Samuel Bourne – as mentioned in the 1822 auction sale catalogue. Inscribed on reverse: 'Interior of the Hall at Kenilworth Castle, Warwickshire'. 10¼in. x 9in. (26.03cm x 22.86cm). c.1820-22.*

COLOUR PLATE 6. *A superb quality and very colourful marked 'Mason's Patent Ironstone China' dinner service showing some of the differing shapes and sizes of objects found in such services. All different pieces would require separate engraved copper plates for the outlines – see Plate 20 Printed crowned mark. c.1815-20. Messrs Phillips.*

COLOUR PLATE 7. *A superb quality, impressed marked Mason's Patent Ironstone Italian style ewer of the 'most noble, splendid and magnificent' type. The front and rear panels painted by Samuel Bourne – see page 117. 27in. (68.58cm) high. c.1818-22. Messrs Christie's.*

COLOUR PLATE 8. *The reverse side of the 'Mason's Patent Ironstone China' 1851 Exhibition vase shown in Plate 32. A classic eighteenth century Chinese export-market vase shape still deemed saleable in 1851. 17½in. (44.45cm) high. c.1851. Photograph by courtesy of the Trustees of the Wedgwood Museum, Barlaston, Stoke-on-Trent.*

COLOUR PLATE 9. *A typical, marked 'Mason's Patent Ironstone China' 'Hydra'-shape jug. These popular jugs were made in various sizes or in sets of graduated sizes and adorned with many different designs. 6½in. (16.51cm) high. c.1840-51. N.B. This Mason shape has been much copied and reproduced.*

COLOUR PLATE 10. *A Mason's ironstone jug decorated in a hasty, inexpensive, manner with coloured-in printed outline design of ever-popular Chinese figures. 9in. (22.86cm) high. c.1840-51. Messrs Phillips.*

COLOUR PLATE 11. *A standard underglaze-blue printed Mason's Patent Ironstone China soup plate from a dinner service. In form and pattern this closely follows standard Chinese export-market porcelains. This design was, perhaps, the 'Blue Chinese landscape' dinner service pattern included in the 1818 sale catalogue. Diameter 9½in. (24.13cm). c.1813-25.*

COLOUR PLATE 12. *Another Mason underglaze-blue printed Chinese landscape design used on dinner services. This plate has unusual relief-moulded design and the edge was gilt. Diameter 9½in. (24.13cm). c.1825-35.*

COLOUR PLATE 13. *A further superb quality large size Mason's ironstone 'Neapolitan' vase with rich gilding and landscape panels painted by Samuel Bourne – see page 117. Such splendid vases were included in the London auction sales. 27½in. (69.85cm) high. c.1818-22. Messrs Valerie Howard, London.*

COLOUR PLATE 14. *A very large marked C.J. Mason & Co. Granite China hall or alcove vase and cover, rivalling in size some of the massive vases imported from China. The printed mark incorporates a view of the Company's 'Stone China Works' at Fenton. 59in. (149.86cm) high. c.1845. Messrs Bonhams.*

COLOUR PLATE 15. *A fine ornate Italian-style vase as featured in the London auction sales but here decorated with a rich blue ground with well painted and gilt flowers and birds – a typical Mason decorative style. See also Plate 45. 27in. (68.58cm) high. c.1820. Messrs Christie's.*

COLOUR PLATE 16. *A selection of Mason Ironstone blue-ground wares with typical gilt decoration – a popular style, if rather heavy looking. Pair Mitre loving cups. 14in. (35.56cm) high. c.1825-35. Messrs Bonhams.*

COLOUR PLATE 17. *A rare, impressed marked 'Mason's Patent Ironstone China' pot-pourri bowl, complete with its inner cover. A rare ground colour and unusual decoration. Diameter 14½in. (36.83cm). c.1825-35. Messrs Bonhams.*

COLOUR PLATE 18. *A selection of miniature or 'toy' pieces made in the Mason's ironstone body. Similar 'cabinet pieces' were included in the 1818 auction sale. Largest vase 8in.(20.3cm) high. c.1818-22.*

COLOUR PLATE 19. *Representative pieces from a marked 'Mason's Patent Ironstone China' dessert service showing rare forms of the 1820s. Coloured-in printed outline Oriental figure subject pattern – possibly the 'Mogul' pattern of the London auction sales. Centrepiece 12½in. (31.75cm) long. c.1802-30.*

COLOUR PLATE 20. *A rare ironstone Japan pattern dough or bread-bin, one of many useful objects made in the ironstone body. 15½in. (39.37cm) high. c.1820s. Messrs Valerie Howard, London.*

COLOUR PLATE 21. *A large heavily-potted covered jar decorated with an Oriental-inspired printed outline floral design. Printed 'Fenton Stone Works' mark. 16½in. (41.91cm) high. c.1825-35. Messrs Phillips.*

COLOUR PLATE 22. *A standard blue printed pheasant pattern, impressed marked 'Mason's Patent Ironstone China' 'Antique' or 'Hydra'-shape jug. This pattern was favoured for toilet services – see Lots 2, 37, etc. in the 1822 sale. 6½in. (16.51cm) high (various sizes were made). c.1822-25.*

COLOUR PLATE 23. *A rare and finely decorated pair of Mason's ironstone card racks. Such fine decoration rivals in quality much contemporary and more costly porcelains. 6¾in. (17.14cm) high. c.1818-22. Messrs Valerie Howard, London.*

COLOUR PLATE 24. *Representative pieces from an impressed marked 'Mason's Patent Ironstone China' dessert service showing typical shapes of the 1820s.*

COLOUR PLATE 25. *Representative pieces from a Mason's Patent Ironstone dinner service of the approximate period 1835-45. The missing soup tureen would have been of the shape shown in Plate 121. Messrs Christie's South Kensington.*

COLOUR PLATE 26. *A printed outline dragon pattern 'Mason's Patent Ironstone China' tureen, cover and stand from a dessert service, with gilt enrichments. Tureen 7½in. (19cm) high.* c.1820-30.

COLOUR PLATE 27. *A very decorative marked 'Mason's Patent Ironstone China' dinner service plate. A coloured-in printed outline design but one of the most colourful produced by any manufacturer. Diameter 10in.* (25.4cm). c.1840s. Mrs Y. Eldridge.

COLOUR PLATE 28. *Representative parts of a Mason's Patent Ironstone China dinner service – typical of the long, colourful and durable table services produced in the ironstone body. Diameter of meat plates 10in. (25.4cm). c.1840s. Messrs Sotheby's.*

COLOUR PLATE 29.
*An American-market platter, registered by Clementson & Young in 1845. This 'Columbia' pattern shows the flow-blue effect although some examples have 'flown' very much more. Arnold Kowalsky.*

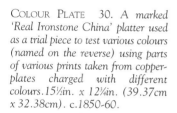

COLOUR PLATE 30. *A marked 'Real Ironstone China' platter used as a trial piece to test various colours (named on the reverse) using parts of various prints taken from copper-plates charged with different colours. 15½in. x 12¾in. (39.37cm x 32.38cm). c.1850-60.*

COLOUR PLATE 31. *A marked 'Ashworth Real Ironstone China' plate of pattern 'B 1876' showing the reuse of earlier designs, in this case a Hicks & Meigh pattern. Diameter 11in. (27.94cm). c.1870-80.*

COLOUR PLATE 32. *Colourful and good quality Ashworth ironstone dinner wares, bearing both printed and impressed marks. Impressed potting devices for September 1892, although the pattern (3623) and shapes were introduced at an earlier period. Tureen 11½in. (29.21cm) high. c.1892.*

COLOUR PLATE 33. *A colourful, hand-painted ironstone dinner service of good quality but by an as yet unattributed maker. Pattern number 106, mark as shown on page 220. Messrs Christie's South Kensington.*

COLOUR PLATE 34. *A Hicks, Meigh & Johnson 'Stone China' soup plate, part of a large order from the Skinners' Company, in London. Blue printed DuCroz retailer's name over a standard Hicks mark, with pattern number '51' added below, see page 235. Diameter 10¼in. (26.03cm). c.1827.*

COLOUR PLATE 35. *A printed outlined Stephen Folch 'Improved Ironstone China' plate, bearing the ornate Royal Arms – Prince of Wales feather device, as shown on page 243. Diameter 8in. (20.32cm). c.1819-29.*

COLOUR PLATE 36. *The reverse side of a typical Hicks & Meigh plate (as shown in Plate 197) displaying the Chinese-style trimmed (and tinted) footrim and a typical Hicks Royal Arms mark. The painter's initial mark is added near the footrim, to the right.*

COLOUR PLATE 37. *A typical Hicks & Meigh Chinese export-market form plate, decorated with a popular Japan-type pattern. Hicks pattern '5'. Printed Crown and 'Ironstone Warranted' mark. Diameter 9in. (22.86cm). c.1813-22.*

COLOUR PLATE 38. *A standard, indented-edged, Hicks & Meigh 'Ironstone Warranted' dinner service plate. Printed outline, coloured-in Hicks pattern '5'. Diameter 9¾in. (24.76cm). c.1813-22.*

COLOUR PLATE 39. *A Hicks & Meigh 'Stone China' soup plate from a dinner service. The typical outline design can be seen in Plate 194. Hicks' pattern '8'. Painter's initial or tally mark 'M' added in enamel. Diameter 9½in. (24.13cm). c.1813-22.*

COLOUR PLATE 40. *A Hicks & Meigh 'Stone China' Royal Arms marked soup plate bearing the largely hand-painted Hicks pattern number '13'. Diameter 9½in. (24.13cm). c.1815-22.*

COLOUR PLATE 41. *A rare footed cheese stand from a Hicks & Meigh dinner service. Printed Royal Arms 'Stone China' mark with pattern number '23' below. The printed outline pattern is neatly coloured in by hand. Diameter 12in. (24.13cm). 2½in. (6.35cm) high. c.1815-22.*

COLOUR PLATE 42. *A superbly engraved underglaze-blue printed Hicks, Meigh & Johnson meat platter from a dinner service. Royal Arms 'Stone China' mark, with '61' added below. 13in. x 10¼in. (33.02cm x 26.03cm). c.1822-35.*

COLOUR PLATE 43. *A superb quality Charles Meigh hand-painted 'Opaque Porcelain' plate of 1851 Exhibition type and standard. Impressed mark overprinted with Royal Arms and 'Ironstone' mark, see page 286. Diameter 10¼in. (26.03cm).* c.1850-55.

COLOUR PLATE 44. *A hand-painted John Ridgway, initial marked 'Imperial Stone China' plate of pattern 5053. Diameter 9¾in. (24.76cm). c.1835-40.*

COLOUR PLATE 45. *A marked 'W.R.S. & Co. Granite China' William Ridgway, Son & Co. dinner service plate printed in brown. Pattern number 1471. Diameter 10in. (25.4cm). c.1838-45.*

COLOUR PLATE 46. *An initial-marked Robinson, Wood & Brownfield 'Opaque Stone China' dinner service platter decorated with coloured-in printed pattern number 24. Printed crowned mark. 19½in. x 15½in. (49.53cm x 39.37cm).* c.1836-41.

COLOUR PLATE 47. *A marked 'Spode Stone China' blue printed Chinese export-market style dinner service plate. Messrs Spode specialized in fine blue printed designs. Diameter 10¼in. (26.03cm).* c.1815-25.

COLOUR PLATE 48. *A marked 'Spode Stone China' part dessert service decorated with a very popular Chinese-style printed outline pheasant design – Spode's pattern 2118. This pattern can also occur on Spode porcelains. Fruit cooler 12¼in. (31.11cm) high.* c.1815-20.

CHAPTER I

# The Pre-Ironstone Period

The term 'Stone-China', which is generally associated with the durable rather heavy ironstone-type earthenwares produced in the first quarter of the nineteenth century, was in fact employed in the eighteenth century. Rather surprisingly the term was used by the knowledgeable and much travelled Dr Richard Pococke on the occasion of his visit to the first Bristol porcelain works in October 1750. This manufactory, he noted, had been founded by 'one of the principal manufacturers at Limehouse, London which failed'. Apparently in 1750 the Bristol porcelains, as then made by Benjamin Lund and William Miller, could be divided into two types:

> One called stone china – which has a yellow cast, both in the ware and the glazing, that I suppose is made of Pipe clay and calcined flint...

and secondly:

> That called 'old china' that is whiter and I suppose this is made of calcin'd flint and the soapy rock at Lizard Point, which 'tis known they use...

Clearly by 1750 the term 'Stone China' was used to describe a near-white body which was slightly inferior and no doubt cheaper than the Chinese-style porcelains. However, at least one standard type of eighteenth century imported Chinese porcelain was also generally known in England as 'Stone China'. Josiah Wedgwood's Common Place Book in 1775 contains an account of the Chinese method of manufacture and reference is made to 'blue Stone China...'. This probably refers to the blue-painted Chinese table wares which were heavily potted and durable but not necessarily translucent! I return to the Chinese 'Stone China' or 'Stone Wares' on page 60. The term 'Stone China' or 'Stone Ware' had also at least four different meanings from that used in this chapter for the decorative British nineteenth century wares.

First, the Staffordshire salt-glaze wares of the types shown in Arnold Mountford's standard book, *The Illustrated Guide to Staffordshire Salt-Glazed Stoneware* (Barrie & Jenkins, London, 1971), were termed 'stone-wares' or more exactly 'Staffordshire white stone-ware' to quote from an advertisement in the Scottish *Caledonian Mercury* of 22 April 1769.

One could fill many pages with contemporary eighteenth century quotations relating to British white-bodied salt-glaze stonewares (Plate 4). I will,

PLATE 4. *Mid-eighteenth century relief-moulded salt-glaze stonewares. Superior predecessors to the later white durable granite wares. Jug 6in. (15.24cm) high. c.1740. City of Stoke-on-Trent Museum & Art Gallery.*

however, content myself with a few extracts from Mr Christie's May 1767 sale catalogue of the stock of 'Mr Steuart at his China, Glass and Staffordshire Warehouse' in Oxford Road (now Oxford Street). Mr Stuart or Steuart's stock 'consists of upwards of three thousand white stone dishes and plates...china, glass and green stone ware...'. Individual lots included:

Eighteen white stone dishes, 2 dozen of plates, 6 sallad dishes, a tureen, 4 sauceboats, 6 baking dishes and 2 fruit baskets.

Twelve round stone dishes, a tureen, 24 plates, 4 sauceboats, 6 baking dishes, 3 sallad ditto.

Seventy-six stone dishes, a chamber pot, a bottle and basin.

Forty-two stone dishes in proper sizes.

Seventy-two pieces of white stone ware, as butter cups, etc.

Thirteen stone-dishes, a dozen of plates, 6 fruit dishes, a tureen, a punch pot and four sauceboats.

Twenty stone dishes, soup and flat, four sallad dishes, a tureen, two fruit baskets and stands, two dozen of plates, four sauce boats, six baking dishes and a cullendar.

Two stone wash hand basons and 6 dozen blomange cups.

All these and many similar lots were durable, white-bodied, Staffordshire salt-glazed stonewares, as shown in Plate 4. Other lots were variously described as 'Chinese', 'Delf', 'Nottingham Ware' or 'black ware'. The description 'stoneware' was obviously a standard one indicating durability. These and many other lots from this mid-eighteenth century dealer's stock were undecorated but were standard lines (both for home and overseas markets) because they were durable, inexpensive and of required forms. These attributes were repeated with the later decorative nineteenth century ironstone wares.

Second, but rather rarely, the widely produced so-popular cream-coloured earthenware or 'Queen's Ware', of the type perfected by Josiah Wedgwood was on occasions referred to as stoneware, presumably to increase its sales. Hence, the Scottish retailer Thomas Mills in Edinburgh in 1774, advertised: 'Royal cream-coloured Staffordshire stone-ware'. This description was possibly a continuation of the 'stone-ware' designation as applied to the salt-glaze stonewares just mentioned.

Thirdly, we find that the close-grained creamy-white body that we now associate with John Turner of Lane End, and which he and other potters used so effectively for jugs, mugs and tea wares, was contemporarily known at the time as 'Stone', 'New Stone' or 'Stone

PLATE 5. *A late 18th century Chinese export-market dinner service tureen of traditional form. Painted in underglaze blue. 8in. (20.32cm) high. c.1780.*

PLATE 6. *Typical underglaze blue painted Chinese porcelain meat-dishes representing standard export-market patterns, later copied by British potters. Such dishes vary greatly in size from 8in. (20cm) upwards. c.1780s.*

Ware'.[1] Simeon Shaw, writing in his 1829 book *History of the Staffordshire Potteries*, stated:

> About 1780 he (John Turner) discovered a vein of fine clay on the land at Green Dock… From this he obtained all his supplies for manufacturing his beautiful and excellent Stone Ware Pottery, of a cane colour; which he formed into very beautiful jugs with ornamental designs, and the most tasteful articles of domestic use.

Typical, contemporary, descriptions of the 1790s included, for example, 'Pint new Stone figd Jug. Archery. 4/-'. The Quart size Turner moulded archery subject jugs were priced at 5/-, the three-pint size 7/-, in April 1793.

This Turner-type stone body was almost entirely employed for attractive, relief-decorated hollow-ware jugs, mugs and similar articles. It is therefore unrelated to the stone chinas and ironstone-type, mainly flat, table wares that are the subject of this study.

However, another class of eighteenth century 'Stone China' does have a distinct likeness in form and added patterns to the nineteenth century Staffordshire earthenwares and ironstone wares. For some of the Chinese porcelain imports, particularly the dinner services, were described as 'Stone China'. I quote from the original eighteenth century accounts:

> China-ware Bot. of Synchong in Canton 3 Table [dinner] sets of Best Blue and White Stone China, scolloped border gold edge and landscape pattern consisting of 170 pieces packed in 5 half-chests.

The make-up of such typical late eighteenth century Chinese dinner-services made for the European and North American market is remarkably similar to the English post-1813 Mason's Ironstone China dinner-services. In many cases the English potters were copying the earlier and even contemporary Chinese forms and styles because they were so popular. These three blue and white Chinese landscape pattern dinner services for example, comprised:

2 Large tureens, covers and stands [Plate 5]
2 small tureens, covers and stands
4 sauceboats & stands
4 salts
8 sallad dishes
2 dishes [platters or meat dishes] of 18 ins [45.72cm]
2 ditto. 16 ins [40.64cm]
2 ditto. 14 ins [35.56cm]
4 ditto. 12 ins [30.48cm]
4 ditto. 10 ins [25.4cm]
4 ditto. 8 ins [20.32cm] [Plate 6]
72 Flat [or meat] plates
24 soup plates
24 small desert plates.

This should add up to 170 pieces including the covers and stands. The cost of these hand-painted, gilt-edged dinner services in Canton was 52 tales or approximately £17. Mason and other English potters closely copied standard Oriental blue scenic designs although the English copies were usually printed in underglaze-blue rather than being painted by hand.

It would also seem that more delicate objects imported from Canton were sometimes described as being 'Stone' or 'Stone China' instead as we might expect as 'porcelain' or 'china'. For example the private-trade imports of Captain John Wordsworth, the Commander of the *Earl of Sandwich*, East Indiaman, in the 1783-4 season included:

10 Stone blue tea sets
12 Pint stone blue basons
4 Coffee pots stone blue
5 sets mugs stone blue
144 Stone coffee cups and saucers
144 Breakfast ditto.

The complete blue-painted tea services were invoiced at a pound per set. It seems to me, having considerable experience in dealing in eighteenth century Oriental export-market ceramics, that these articles were in reality translucent Chinese standard hard-paste porcelain. Even in the early years of the nineteenth century the Chinese blue and white dinner and teasets were described as 'best blue and white stone'.

Why one may ask was it termed 'Stone' or 'Stone China'? The simple answer of course is that it underlined the durability of the Chinese export-market wares – the point the British potters were later making with their 'Stone China', 'Ironstone' or 'Granite' descriptions and marks.

The description 'Stone' or 'Stone China' was obviously well known to the English dealers and probably also to the British potters because these Chinese services were their main competition. However, the stone chinas and ironstone-type wares discussed in this book are purely English, are earthenware rather than porcelain (although when thinly potted they can display some translucency) and are purely of nineteenth century date.

Yet in general the English stone china and the ironstone-type wares were produced to emulate the saleable Chinese export-market porcelains, chiefly the heavily potted but durable Chinese dinner services (Plate 7), see in my book *Oriental Export Market Porcelains* (Granada Publishing, London, 1979).

That work also explained the circumstances that led to the discontinuation of the English East India Company's bulk importation of Chinese porcelains in the early 1790s. This was to have vital repercussions for the British manufacturers of both porcelain and earthenware. A great void occurred in the market for middle-range table wares of the type previously met by the Chinese imports. However, some Chinese porcelains were still imported as 'Private Trade'. Such relatively small imports continued into the nineteenth century.

The new British bodies which are to be discussed in this chapter very closely followed the Oriental forms and their styles of decoration. It is strange how the market for Chinese porcelains of the 1780s and 1790s was extended by the British potters well into the nineteenth century and in some cases right up to the period of the 1851 Exhibition! In fact the taste is still to be found in today's productions of the seemingly ageless willow pattern or some of the more colourful productions of the present Mason company, see Plates 215-217.

I have just discussed the late eighteenth century Chinese forms and patterns being emulated in the nineteenth century by British potters but the large Christie's sale held in Amsterdam in March 1995[2] shows that the Chinese were still producing and selling

PLATE 7. *Representative Chinese export-market dinner service shapes of the type copied by Mason in Ironstone from 1813. Tureen 8½in. (21.59cm) high. c.1780. Messrs Christie's.*

what we consider to be pure eighteenth century tableware forms and designs in 1816 and perhaps even later. The Mason ironstone dinner services were in effect copying contemporary Chinese exports.

It is vitally important, when considering the British stone china and ironstone-type wares, especially the dinner and dessert services, to remember the very great popularity in the markets of the Chinese porcelains. In June 1803, the duty on the Chinese imports was reduced from a crippling £109.8s.6d. per £100 value to 80 per cent. One would have thought that this still large import duty would have well satisfied the interests of the British manufacturers but, in fact, they were up in arms, addressing two memoranda to the Government Committee in protest. The first has been quoted in part on page 14, the second dated 2 June 1803 is here given to show the esteem enjoyed by the Oriental imports and their low cost in relation to the home-produced porcelains and the more decorative earthenwares. The potters' address read:

> MORE REASONS FOR THE ALARM TAKEN BY THE MANUFACTURERS OF PORCELAIN & EARTHENWARE &c &c.
>
> Taking then the average of twenty years previous to establishing the duty of £109-8-6d per centum, and during the time the duty was no more than 45 to 52 per cent, it will be found that Table [dinner] services, consisting of 180 pieces, were generally sold at the Company's sales, including duty, more than sixty per centum under the sum for which the same number of pieces of similar nature can be delivered at the manufactories of English Porcelain

and twenty per centum under the price of the imitations in earthenware, without adding to either the expense and risk of conveying to market.

For Home consumption there is a clear and great advantage in favour of Oriental against English Porcelain, even if the duty had been one hundred per centum and a difference in respect of earthenware too small to leave any hope that it can stand a chance of extensive sale.

For exportation the case is still more fatal to the British trade, because the Oriental Porcelain pays only a bonus of three to five per centum for warehouse room and no duty when exported to the West Indies or to Ireland, both great marts for the sale of English Porcelain and earthenware.

So far the comparison has been upon similar manufacturers but there are still important branches to be considered, upon which the effect of great importations of Oriental Porcelain will be quite as ruinous. These are the enamelled and higher finished services of Porcelain and earthenware, for the painting of which alone, there is very often as much paid to the artist – and sometimes a great deal more, than the former [the imported Chinese wares] may be purchased for at the Chinese sales. The manufacturers in these branches have uniformly found, for the last twenty years, that the smaller the importations of Oriental Porcelain, the greater the number of persons they were enabled to employ...

The Potters partly lost the day for, from 5 July 1803 the new lower rates came into force:

> Duties payable on goods wares and merchandise imported into Great Britain by the United Company of Merchants of England trading to the East Indies (The Honourable East India Company). China Ware for every £100 of the value £80.

One must never forget the great influence that the imported Chinese porcelains had on the buying public and consequently on British manufacturers. These draft appeals to the Government show how the Chinese true porcelains decorated with hand-painted designs undersold not only home-produced porcelains but also earthenwares such as underglaze-blue painted or printed Chinese-style pearlwares or 'china glaze'; 'china glazed blue'; 'china glazed wares, painted with blue', to use contemporary descriptions.

In fact this high rate of import duty – over three-quarters of the London sale value being added again in duty – did much to limit the imports of the Chinese porcelains, especially in respect of the large dinner services. The British manufacturers sought to copy the popular Oriental imports and reduce the price of their own products. In so striving to emulate the Chinese imports they naturally tended to copy both the established and popular Chinese export-market shapes and the saleable Oriental designs.

The all important buying public required British wares that were more vitrified than the standard earthenwares, approaching in texture and appearance the Chinese porcelains but not as costly as the English porcelains then available.

We do not know for certain who first filled this need but early contenders for the honour must be the Staffordshire potters William and John Turner of Lane End who, in January 1800, applied for a Patent for:

> ...our new method or methods of manufacturing Porcelain and Earthenware by the introduction of a material not heretofore used in the manufacture of these articles...

This new material was described in the 1800 specification as 'Tabberner's Rock or Little Rock'. For the production of the new porcelain calcined Cornish Stone and flint was added to the mix as explained in Chapter 6 of my *Staffordshire Porcelain* (Granada Publishing, London, 1983).

When Turner's specifications were first published some of the other Staffordshire potters showed great concern and meetings were arranged to object to the proposed Patent. Thomas Byerley at Etruria recorded in letters to Josiah Wedgwood (then in residence at Clifton, Bristol) the general unrest regarding the new Patent. If the Turners succeeded in obtaining a Patent for their new wares, the other potters would be prevented from using the all important raw materials – a clay that should be available to all.

Byerley himself was interested, for in a letter to Josiah Wedgwood dated 17 January 1800, he noted:

> ...I send you in this box a piece of clay lately discovered by W & J Turner and a cup which I have had made of it and fired in the B O (Biscuit Oven).

On 9 March 1800 Byerley further reported to Josiah Wedgwood:

> Mr Spode has called a meeting of the Potters about W & J Turner's Patent which gives to them exclusive use of a certain stone called by the name of Tabberners Mine Rock... it is of a ash or greyish colour but when dry becomes white...
>
> I am told that Spode frankly told them they will contest the thing with them... Mr Perry of

Keelings, Lane End, declares he made ware of this material 15 years ago but abandoned the use of it on account of the expense of grinding it.

William Adams of Tunstall says when he was apprenticed to John Brindley they made use of it and I believe others would say the same thing.

In reporting the result of this local meeting Thomas Byerley wrote:

This notice was sent to 80 persons, only about 25 attended and these seemed very indifferent about the matter.

Some are of the opinion that the Patent cannot be supported and others that the quantity of the Stone is so inconsiderable [this word is indistinct, perhaps – inconsistent] as to be an objection [to others using the material?].

Mr Spode alone appears anxious and could not conceal his extreme desire from the first that a small party only of the manufacturers – say 6 or 8 – might join together and purchase the Patent right...

Certainly, of all the later makers of Stone China-type bodies Spode made the best quality examples. His specimens mark the high water mark of this type of ceramic. It is here seen that his interest in a new trouble-free and therefore inexpensive body dates back to at least 1800. Whilst the Patent was entered on 9 January 1800, experiments in the use of the new ingredients must have been carried out prior to this date. Nevertheless the use of the 'Turner's Patent' painted mark will date from 1800.

It is interesting to note that in April 1799, the London auctioneer Harry Phillips held a sale at his Great Room, no. 67, New Bond Street, comprising 'Part of the genuine stock in Trade of a respectable china merchant in the city whose successful improvements in the manufacture of English porcelane has induced him wholly to decline the sale of Foreign china of every description'. The auctioneer's catalogue for this sale gives two names, Mortlock and 'A & N'. The latter would be Abbott & Newbury of 82 Fleet Street. This partnership formerly traded as Turner, Abbott & Newbury and the firm retained a prime interest in stocking the Turners' Staffordshire goods. They were also leading stockists of Chinese porcelains in the 1790s. Did the early experiments in the pre-patented new bodies bode such success that their foreign goods were sold off by Mr Phillips in 1799. On the other hand the reference to the success of new English wares may relate to the Coalport 'British Nankin' porcelain supplied to Mortlock in London (see page 68).

Returning to the Turners, the Patent specification in William and John's names (no. 2367, dated 9 January) reads, in part:

The manner in which we prepare and use the said material in the manufacturing of earthenware after being ground as before directed is by mixing it with ground Flint or other silicious earth, previously calcined, in different proportions according to the kind or sort of earthenware intended to be made and the degree of heat which the same may require...

From the potter's point of view one of the great advantages of the new body was the relative ease of manufacture and therefore of a lower production cost and, ultimately, a cheaper price to the buying public. To quote from the original 1800 Patent, it was claimed that:

...because of its great durability larger pieces of that ware are more easily formed than theretofore and also less liable to accident in the Kiln from the moderate degree of heat required in the burning thereof as the same may be burnt in the same Kiln and at the same time with Cream Colour or Queen's Ware and also by the raw material being found in the same place with the fuel and various kinds of Fire Clay used in the manufactory a great expense is saved and the English manufactory of Porcelain and Earthenware is thereby less liable to be rival'd by foreign manufactories...

It seems that the production of Turner's new china-like body was now economically viable. It would also appear that the Turners were willing to supply the new Patent mix to other potters. The Wedgwood archives, now in the care of Keele University, show that the Wedgwood firm purchased half a ton in August, 1801. The account reads:

Messrs. Wedgwood & Byerley Lane End, 3 Aug. 1801
Bot. of Wm & Joh Turner.
½ ton best Patent China stone £2- 2- 0
Grinding 6/-
Drying 1/-
Carriage from the pits 1/-

This totals £2.10s.0d. (£2.50) or £5 per ton delivered.

The new 1800 Turner wares (Plates 8 and 9) must have attracted considerable attention, helped by the fact that a clear special mark was boldly printed or painted on the bottom of the objects. This simple mark read 'Turner's Patent' – a novel form of mark for the period.

The Turner's Patent wares were made over a relatively short period. Simeon Shaw writing in his 1829 privately printed book, *History of the Staffordshire Potteries*, recorded his view that 'at the time when most benefit might have accrued to Mr Turner, in consequence of the celebrity which his Porcelain had acquired, the late Mr Harwood of Newcastle, steward of the late Marquis of Stafford, interdicted any further supplies of the stone indispensably requisite, under the pretext that the Marquis was offended at the Patent having been obtained, and would not encourage any monopoly'. The Turner brothers were declared bankrupt in July, 1806.

It is now very difficult to distinguish between the two different bodies which could have been made under the 1800 Patent, part of which related to porcelain and part to earthenware. Most pieces bearing this mark are nearer in appearance to an earthenware, or rather to the later stone-chinas, than they are to porcelain. On the other hand, they show some translucency.

The Turner's Patent marked vegetable dish (Plate 8), presumably from a large dinner service, probably represents the new earthenwares. In its angular plan and handle-form it is in the style of the Chinese imports, as is the added underglaze-blue printed design.

It is to be expected that other potters would have tried to copy the new Turner wares or sought to purchase the ingredients and produce similar articles under licence. It is, however, by no means certain what happened after the Turners' bankruptcy in 1806. James Mist, the London dealer (formerly of Messrs Abbott & Mist, *c*.1802-9), advertised on his printed bill-heads used as late as 1810 that he was sole agent for 'Turner's Strong Patent China'. Mist was a leading retailer in Fleet Street, London and with his earlier partner had enjoyed close commercial links with the Turners although the Mists obviously also stocked other makes of porcelain and earthenwares. The Mist bill-heads are, however, interesting as they feature especially Turner's post-1800 body and mention its special properties – 'Strong Patent China'. Mason was later to trump this description with his well-known sales pitch 'Patent Ironstone China'.

If Turner's new patented bodies (for earthenware and china) were commercially successful other potters could certainly have purchased the Patent-rights and produced similar wares, but I do not know of any evidence indicating that Turner's patented body was being used by others. Yet the Turners became bankrupt in July 1806 and they would no doubt have been very happy to sell their rights to anyone making a reasonable offer. It is, however, possible that Spode's 'Stoke China' of *c*.1795-1810 was a form of new durable earthenware, not a true porcelain, see *Staffordshire Porcelain*, Plate 152.

Simeon Shaw writing in or before 1829 of events that should have been in his memory, noted: 'The late J. Spode Esq., purchased the right to manufacture this [Turner's] patent stone porcelain...' – a statement copied by many later writers.

Josiah Spode, of Stoke-on-Trent, certainly produced a rather similar heavy durable but superior earthenware body, but the exact date of its introduction is in doubt. Leonard Whiter, in his excellent 1970 book on Spode ware, suggests that the Spode stone china body was not introduced until 1813 or 1814, to compete with the newly patented Mason ironstone china. Spode called his ware 'Stone China' to emphasize its strength; a later variation was known as 'New Stone'. Spode did not follow, or emulate, Mason's use of the word patent which he might have done if he had purchased the patent and or its rights from the bankrupt Turner brothers. On the other hand he may not have been able to patent his body as it did not include any new features, no novel materials nor firing technique. It was simply an improvement over existing ceramic bodies, employed basically to produce dinner services in the style of the largely discontinued importations of Chinese porcelain.

The Spode ware is of the finest quality, neatly potted, thinly turned and, in general, well produced. Again, the painted or printed designs show strong Chinese influence, occasioned by the popular Chinese export porcelain they were imitating. Fine large dinner and dessert services were made, as well as a host of other articles (see Plates 10-12, 252-256; Colour Plates 2, 47 and 48). We know from contemporary commons that Spode's 'Stone China' table wares were available and popular from at least the spring of 1814 (see page 74), but we urgently seek evidence to show that such wares were made before Mason's Patent Ironstone China hit the market in 1813. No dated examples are recorded.

I have republished elsewhere[3] a trade-card relating to Elizabeth Ring, the Bristol dealer in earthenwares, china and glass. Under an engraving of her shop-front at 8 High Street, Bristol, she listed the basic types of ceramics in stock – 'Services of Earthenware, China & Glass to pattern, also of the newly invented Stone China...' Alas, we do not have a way of precisely dating this trade-card, although the local directories do not list Mrs Ring at this High Street address before 1814. Perhaps one day a dated bill-head will be discovered with the description 'newly invented Stone China'.

Another tantalising non-precise reference to the

introduction of 'stone china' as opposed to ironstone china, occurs in Samuel Parkes' *Chemical Essays, principally related to the Arts and Manufactures of the British Dominions*, volume III. This five-volume work was published by Baldwin, Cradock & Joy of London in 1815 but we have no evidence as to when the following reference to stone china in volume three was written. On page 307 Samuel Parkes (1761-1825) noted:

> The great durability of the oriental china is its main excellence. We make porcelain in this country which is equally beautiful... although it possesses a less degree of tenacity and hardness. We have, indeed, lately noticed the introduction of what is called stone china, which is made very thick and clumsy to imitate some of the best productions of the East...

Alas, Parkes did not give a precise date for noticing the introduction of the new body. Rodney Hampson informs me that the author of this work came to Stoke in 1793 but left for London in 1803, where he practised as a manufacturing chemist and writer on chemistry subjects. He probably saw the new stone china being offered for sale in London and, if that is the case, it is likely to have been Spode's essays in this new ceramic body.

At this stage I must show (Colour Plate 2 and Plate 11) a really superb Spode stone china plate, painted with English armorial bearings in the manner of so many Chinese dinner services made for European families. The Spode factory made and proudly marked many such examples as replacements or additions to old Chinese porcelain services. The armorial bearings, crest and Latin motto on this plate relate to Chinese porcelains attributed to c.1745 and described by David Sanctuary Howard[4] as relating to Mills of Harscomb of Gloucestershire and Clapham in Surrey and Hatch of Clabery Hall in Essex. The Spode replacement plate is of the correct Oriental export-market form and has the correct type of trimmed (glaze-free) footrim. Whilst it may not be translucent, the stone china body is surely stronger than the oriental original and is not so prone to chipping at the edge.

It has the high quality and neatness of potting that one would expect the early Mason *porcelains* to have had. Miles Mason had advertised as early as October 1804 that he would 'renew or match' oriental table wares.

The Spode stone china matchings are, however, more plentiful than the earlier Mason porcelain replacement pieces. Alas, we have as yet no accurate dating of the Spode efforts or indeed of the introduction of English 'stone china'.

A surprisingly early reference to Staffordshire 'stone ware' dinner services, seemingly printed in underglaze-blue, appeared as an advertisement in the *Aberdeen Journal* of 9 September 1801. This reads:

> SALE OF BLUE STONEWARE TABLE SERVICES
>
> YATES & CO. Stoneware manufacturers, Staffordshire... have sent from their manufactory, an elegant assortment of RICH SAXON BLUE STONEWARE table services which will be exposed to sale in Mrs Taylor's Auction Hall, Broad Street [Aberdeen] on Monday the 21st inst [September 1801]...
>
> Printed catalogues of the goods will be

PLATE 8. *The base of a blue printed vegetable dish marked 'Turner's Patent'. Oriental-style pattern and basic form. 13¼in. (33.65cm) long. c.1800.*

PLATE 9. *A dessert service marked 'Turner's Patent', showing typical forms, painted in a popular Oriental-style pattern. Centrepiece 13¼in. (33.65cm) long. c.1800.*

published, specifying the particular articles contained in each set...

As Blue table ware is now become all the fashion among genteel families, in most parts of the kingdom, it is hoped that the above collection will be found worthy of the attention of the public.

This is a most important but again tantalising announcement, first quoted in *Aberdeen Ceramics* (published by the Aberdeen Art Gallery and Museums, 1981). No marked Yates & Co. stone china or indeed any Yates wares are recorded. We can assume at this period that the dinner services – then termed 'Table Services' – were printed in underglaze-blue and that the basic designs were Oriental in general style – mock Chinese landscape designs. The shapes too may well have followed the very popular standard Chinese export-market forms.

PLATE 10. *A selection of table wares marked 'Spode. Stone China' decorated with typical Oriental-inspired designs, usually printed and coloured in. Handled dessert dish 9½ in. (24.13cm) c.1813-20.*

We are, however, in the dark as to the body. The wares are not described as having a Patent body, so they should not relate directly to Turner's Patent wares introduced in 1800. They are also not described as a durable porcelain or likened to the well-known Chinese porcelains, as were the Coalport efforts in the Chinese style. We can only conclude that they were of a superior type of durable or thickly potted earthenware, called 'Stoneware' by Yates & Co. or their agents.

We are likewise in the dark regarding the manufacturer Yates & Co. We have John and William Yates of Shelton working in the approximate period 1794-1808. They may have traded as Yates & Co. We also have the little-known Hanley partnership between John Yates and Thomas Baggeley. These earthenware manufacturers certainly traded as Yates & Co. up to the time of the dissolution of this partnership on 12 March 1803. This official notice also mentioned 'Table

PLATE 11. *A plate of superb quality marked 'Spode Stone China' in the style of, or a replacement to, a Chinese export-market armorial dinner service of c.1780. 8¾in. (22.22cm) diameter. c.1815-20. Mr and Mrs G. Fisk.*

plates'. Other Yates were connected with the manufacture of porcelain – see my *Encyclopaedia of British Porcelain Manufacturers* (Barrie & Jenkins, London, 1988). However, it looks as if the first recorded reference to Staffordshire blue-printed 'Stone China' dinner wares relates to the partnership between John Yates and Thomas Baggeley, a firm we only know from the 1803 dissolution notice!

Certainly in that period various manufacturers strove to fill the huge market for Oriental-style dinner services that opened up when the English East India Company ended the import of such porcelains in bulk. In March 1802 Thomas Brocas of the 'Coalport China Warehouse', Castle Street, Shrewsbury, reported in the local *Salopian Journal* that:

> he has just received from Coalport Table services of an entire new article called BRITISH NANKEEN, so exactly like the foreign, both as to shape, colour etc. that few can distinguish it from Foreign Blue and white china, and if there is any difference it will be found the BRITISH NANKEEN excells both as to beauty and strength.
>
> He has two kinds of it, one an exact imitation of

PLATE 12. *A tureen of Chinese export-market form marked 'Spode. Stone China' with a printed outline decorative Oriental-style coloured-in pattern of typical type and high quality. Pattern 2054. 13½in. (34.29cm) long. c.1820.*

PLATE 13. *Left, a Chinese hand-painted small tureen with, right, a blue-printed early Coalport copy of 'British Nankin' type.* 7¾in. (19.68cm) *long.* c.1802.

India blue and white china, of a pale colour which he offers at 18 guineas the Table Service, manufacturer's price; the other exactly like the old fine dark blue stone ware, or Nankeen at 25 guineas... it is considered the above ware will be equally durable with the Foreign, more beautiful and comes at less than half the price...

Thomas Brocas, the Shrewsbury retailer and local agent for Coalport porcelain, of course was comparing the 'entire new article' with Chinese porcelain when he was referring to the foreign or to India blue and white. I believe that these table or dinner wares as we would now call them were of John Rose's porcelain, but were particularly thickly potted to give durability and to resemble Chinese export-market dinner wares as nearly as possible. I show in Plate 13 a blue transfer-printed Coalport covered tureen of the type I believe was called British Nankeen (for good commercial reasons) along with a slightly earlier Chinese hand-painted example. The Coalport examples, however, seem to be completely unmarked, as were the Chinese originals. I do not know of any British wares of the early 1800s which bear a British Nankeen or British

Nankin descriptive mark.

It is interesting to observe in this 1802 Brocas advertisement the use of the term 'Blue Stone Ware' in relation to the so-called Nankin blue and white Chinese porcelains. I have earlier noted the same description being used in the East India Company records. There are further references to Brocas and ironstone-type bodies on page 76 and one must also recall that Miles Mason in 1804 was referring to his 'British Nankin' porcelain body (see below), using a slightly different spelling but with the same intent.

The make-up of an early nineteenth century 'British Nankin' porcelain dinner service is shown by one such set sold by Mr Christie on 6 July 1804, as lot 378. This was described as:

> A Table service of blue & white china, British Nankin, containing 18 dishes in sizes, 2 soup tureens and stands, 4 sauce tureens and stands, 1 salad dish, 4 sauce boats, 4 vegetable dishes with covers, 4 baking dishes, 6 dozen meat plates, 2 dozen soup plates, 2 dozen pie-plates and 2 dozen cheese plates.

This seemingly new and complete dinner service with its hundred and forty-four plates fetched £15.4s.6d.

There is, however, difficulty in identifying this 'British Nankin', its maker and the type of body used. Thomas Brocas had advertised the ware in 1802 as being 'just received from Coalport'. However, Miles Mason, the former London 'Chinaman' and now a manufacturer in Staffordshire, at Lane Delph, advertised in a London newspaper in October 1804 his own chinaware similar to the Chinese wares but even stronger and more durable. He too used the term 'British Nankin'. This newspaper announcement or advertisement reads in part:

> MASON'S CHINA
>
> ...Miles Mason, late of Fenchurch Street, London, having been a principal purchaser of Indian Porcelain, till the prohibition of that article by heavy duties, has established a Manufactory at Lane Delph, near Newcastle-under-Line [*sic*] upon the principle of the Indian [Chinese] and Sève China. The former is now sold at the principal shops only in the City of London, and the Country as British Nankin. His article is warranted from the manufactory to possess superior qualities to Indian [Chinese] Nankin China, being more beautiful as well as more durable, and not so liable to snip at the edges, more difficult to break, and refusable or unitable by heat, if broken. Being aware that to combat strong prejudices with success, some thing superior must be produced: he, therefore, through the medium of his Wholesale Friends, proposes to renew or match the impaired or broken services of the Nobility and Gentry, when by a fair trial or conjunction with foreign china, he doubts not that these fears will be removed...
>
> N.B. The articles are stamped on the bottom of the large pieces to prevent imposition.

The stamp on the larger pieces was seemingly the impressed name 'M. MASON', for I have not noted a 'British Nankin' mark. This being so the 1804-plus Mason British Nankin table wares were of a porcelain body as would also have been the Coalport examples.

In the main these would have been thickly potted articles based on popular Chinese export-market shapes and often decorated in underglaze-blue with Chinese landscape designs. These patterns were either direct copies of traditional Oriental designs or were close copies of much marketable patterns.

These porcelains certainly filled the great void left by the ending of the English East India Company importations in the 1790s, at a time when the market for such porcelains was increasing. The demand had been established and it now had to be satisfied.

Good copies as the 'British Nankin' and other porcelains may have been, I believe they did not match the Oriental originals in price. A less expensive durable body was urgently required – a porcelain look-alike.

CHAPTER II

# The Introduction of Mason's Patent Ironstone China

We have seen in the previous chapter the commercial need for the British potters to emulate the long-popular and even contemporary Chinese porcelains. In particular large dinner services were so difficult and expensive to produce in English porcelain so a completely new durable and inexpensive body was urgently required to compete with the Chinese wares. Over the years several attempts had been made to introduce such an ideal.

Turner's Patent China of 1800 (pages 62 and 344) was undoubtedly an important step forward. The basic Turner standard patterns (Plates 8 and 9) were greatly influenced by the Chinese importations and the potting was neat. The Turner Patent covered new types of both porcelain and earthenware, but their wares were rather too expensive for the mass market – or perhaps Shaw was correct in stating that the Turners' bankruptcy in 1806 was due to the supply of the special clay being cut off. Yet the seed had been sown and perhaps was to mature later as the popular 'Stone China'.

Nevertheless, if the various makes of stone china were introduced in succession to Turner's Patent, they were launched in a very tentative and modest manner and apparently without publicity. This was certainly not the case with Mason's Patent Ironstone China in 1813. It became almost instantaneously popular, helped, of course, by the fact that the firm was well known and its porcelains and earthenwares were already much respected and well placed in the market. The china dealers would have been ready and willing to stock, display and advertise a novel new type of ware produced by such a manufacturer.

PLATE 14. *Representative units from a dinner service impressed marked 'Mason's Patent Ironstone China', decorated with a typical 'Japan' pattern, with areas of underglaze-blue. c.1813-20. Messrs Phillips.*

Mason's choice of name for the new body was also a masterly stroke that did much to popularise his new ware and outsell any rivals. Each word has significance: 'Patent' suggesting a new, unique discovery; 'Ironstone' suggesting great strength and durability; 'China' suggesting a delicate ware capable of gracing any table or home and, although this 'Ironstone China' is normally regarded as earthenware today, some thinly potted pieces do in fact show a slight translucency. It would be difficult to find an adult in the civilised world who has not heard the term 'Ironstone', firmly placed in the ceramic vocabulary by Charles James Mason in July 1813, which is a tribute to its lasting qualities. The abstract of the patent reads:

> A process for the improvement of the manufacture of English porcelain, this consists of using the scoria or slag of Ironstone pounded and ground in water with certain proportions, with flint, Cornwall stone and clay, and blue oxide of cobalt.

The details are given more fully in the full patent specification (3724 of July 1813), after the usual written preliminaries:

> ...The Ironstone which contains a proportion of argil and silex is first roasted in a common biscuit kiln to facilitate its trituration, and to expel sulphur and other volatile ingredients which it may contain. A large earthen crucible is constructed after the exact model of an iron forge, a part of the bottom of which is filled with charcoal or coaks [sic]; these, having been previously strewed with ore and about one third part of lime, are raised to an intense heat by a strong blast of air introduced under the coaks at the bottom.
>
> By this heat ore is fused, and the fluid iron drops through the fuel to the bottom, then follows the scoria, which floats upon the top of the fluid iron. This latter scoria, or as the workmen call it slag, is the material used in the manufacture of china, and is much impregnated with iron, and of a compact and dense structure. The slag is next let off by a hole through the forge into a clean earthen vessel, where it cools... The scoria is next pounded into small pieces and ground in water to the consistence of a fine paste at the flint mills of the country. This paste is next evaporated to dryness, it is used with the other ingredients to the following proportions, viz:

| | Cwts. |
|---|---|
| Prepared Iron Stone | 3 |
| Ground Flint | 4 |
| Ground Cornwall Stone | 4 |
| Cornwall Clay | 4 |
| Blue Oxide of Cobalt | 1 lb. |

> These, having been mixed together with water by the slip maker, are again evaporated in the slip kiln to the proper consistency for use...

Some authorities have stated that the materials mentioned in the patent would not, on their own (without perhaps Ball Clay), make a workable ceramic body, and that the patent specification was a misleading front. It might well be thought that iron was the least likely of all materials to be added to a ceramic mix, for manufacturers of white-bodied wares go to great pains to exact any trace of staining iron from the clays. However, I find that the surplus slag is essentially a calcium aluminium silicate and that large quantities are used in the manufacture of Portland cement.

Be this as it may, from 1813 the brothers George and Charles James Mason produced a durable, heavy earthenware bearing the trade name 'Patent Ironstone China' with or without the Mason name preceding the new descriptive title.

It must be stated, however, that Mason's apparent use of ironstone was not new in 1813. The Breeze grinding-mill accounts list several instances of grinding ironstone for firms such as Knight, Sproston & Knight of Tunstall in 1807 and in 1809. One such entry even dates back to 1801 and reads: 'To Grinding 360 lbs. Ironstone, 3/- £10-10-0.'

I return on page 74 to the question of the earlier use of 'ironstone' but it should be mentioned that George Bernard Hughes in his 1959 book, *Victorian Pottery & Porcelain* (Country Life Ltd., London), suggests that 'Prepared ironstone' or 'Patent Ironstones' was available from Wolverhampton, from where it was transported to the Staffordshire Potteries by canal, so saving the potters the troublesome process outlined in the Mason Patent. In view of the controversy over the workable qualities of Mason's patent specification, I asked the Director of the Ceramic Testing Laboratory at the North Staffordshire College of Technology at Stoke to analyse an early impressed marked 'Mason's Patent Ironstone China' plate. The result was:

| | % |
|---|---|
| Silica ($SiO_2$) | 76.00 |
| Alumina ($Al_2O_3$) | 18.87 |
| Potash ($K_2O$) | 1.77 |
| Lime (CaO) | 1.31 |
| Soda ($Na_2O$) | 0.75 |
| Ferric Oxide ($Fe_2O_3$) | 0.41 |
| Titanic Oxide ($TiO_2$) | 0.40 |
| Magnesia (MgO) | 0.25 |
| Loss (Calcined at 950°C) | 0.44 |

PLATE 15. *Representative dessert service pieces impressed-marked 'Mason's Patent Ironstone China' decorated with typical early 'Japan' patterns. Centrepiece 14¼in. (36.19cm) long. c.1813-20.*

As a comparison, I also sent a marked example of Ridgway's 'Stone China' of about 1820. The resulting analysis read:

| | % |
|---|---|
| Silica ($SiO_2$) | 72.71 |
| Alumina ($Al_2O_3$) | 21.48 |
| Potash ($K_2O$) | 2.02 |
| Lime ($CaO$) | 1.15 |
| Soda ($Na_2O$) | 1.08 |
| Ferric Oxide ($Fe_2O_3$) | 0.43 |
| Titanic Oxide ($TiO_2$) | 0.40 |
| Magnesia ($MgO$) | 0.20 |
| Loss (Calcined at 950°C) | 0.35 |

Dr W.L. German, the Director of the Ceramic Testing Laboratory, comments that the small amount of iron [ferric oxide ($Fe_2O_3$)] found in the marked Mason sample indicated that the body was not prepared in accordance with the published patent specification.

Mason's patent of 1813 was granted for an initial period of fourteen years, taking the coverage up to 1827. It was not then renewed, probably as very similar bodies were then in general use. William Evans, in his *Art and History of the Pottery Business* (1846), published several recipes for ironstone bodies. One of these was:

| | |
|---|---|
| 350 lbs Cornwall stone | 300 lbs Cornwall clay |
| 160 lbs Blue clay | 60 lbs Flint |
| Fritt for ironstone body: | 14 oz Blue Calx |
| 90 lbs Cornwall stone | 20 lbs Salts of soda |

Glaze: 33 lbs of above fritt 33 lbs Cornwall stone
35 lbs whiting, 80 lbs white lead

William Evans also quoted two other recipes for the ironstone body:

200 parts Cornish stone
150 parts Cornish clay
200 blue or brown clay
100 of flint
1 of calx

Another variant, read:

175 parts Cornish stone
150 of Cornish clay
90 of blue or brown clay
35 of flint
5 of fritt (number 30)
½ of calx

There is no mention of 'ironstone' in any of these recipes but, in another part of the book, Evans states:

> The ironstone china is formed by introducing ground clay from the smelting furnace in the proportion of 28 [parts] for 72 [parts] of No. 3 or 8 [other recipes listed] carefully blunging [mixing] the fluids together.

While writing of ironstone it is interesting to note that the term had at least one other meaning. Under the date Saturday, 14 May 1796, the knowledgeable Charles Hatchett noted in his diary:

> To the east of the Town are some rocks on the shore which on their upper strata consist of a schorl intimately mixed with quartz forming what in Cornwall is called Iron Stone...

Very many other recipes for British Ironstone China were published. Sheridan Muspratt in 1860, noted:

> That class called Ironstone china is made from a mixture of plastic clay, kaolin, Cornish stone in excess and silica.

He then lists six different mixes. His first and last, read:

| | | | |
|---|---|---|---|
| Cornish Stone | 180 parts | Cornish Stone | 400 |
| China Clay | 120 | China Clay | 250 |
| Blue Clay | 60 | Blue Clay | 150 |
| Flint | 80 | Flint | 75 |

(from Sheridan Muspratt, *Chemistry, Theoretical, Practical and Analytical*, W. MacKenzie, Glasgow, 1860).

Dr. F. Knapp in Volume 11 of his 1848 *Chemical Technology*,[1] noted:

> That which is called ironstone china is made from a mixture of plastic clay and kaolin, with a clay containing borax; similar ware is made on the Continent, and is known by the name of semi-porcelain (Halb Porzelan) or Opaque Porcelain.

It should be noted, however, that whilst many British marks incorporate these descriptions the wares can be of a standard earthenware, not a high-fired ironstone or stone china.

The new Mason ironstone china body was in production within months of the patent being granted, for the following announcement appeared in *The Times* in December 1813:

> Patent Ironstone-China
>
> The great importance of this article is well worth the attention of the nobility, gentry and the Public, the durability of the composition is beyond any other yet produced, and not being so liable to chip or break, which, together with its being much lower in price than any other china, it is presumed will prove a recommendation for its general utility...

The appealing virtues of durability combined with cheapness were placed to the fore, in this and other advertisements or notices. Obviously Miles Mason and his sons had carried out experiments and perhaps placed similar wares on the market before the Patent was applied for in Charles James Mason's name in July 1813. Nevertheless, the standard form of early impressed or printed mark incorporating the word 'Patent' must indicate a period subsequent to its granting.

It should be noted that the patent claimed to be for 'improvements in the manufacture of English Porcelain', not earthenware. Some of the early Mason's thinly-potted examples show some slight translucency. Some porcelain forms were copied and, more importantly, colourful china designs were often employed, especially the so-called 'Japan' patterns. These Imari-style patterns were broadly painted with overglaze-red, green and gold in conjunction with underglaze-blue, see typical examples in Colour Plates 3 and 20 and Plates 14-16, 25, 29, 47-50, 60-62, 69-72, 75, 83, 92, 93, 100-102, 105-109.

Rather strangely, such obviously popular Oriental-style coloured designs were not usually applied to the pre-ironstone standard pearlwares – or to other white earthenwares. They were reserved for the expensive porcelains and the new compact-bodied ironstone and stone china wares, both of which were on the market by the spring of 1814, as is shown by a letter preserved in the Wedgwood archives. The note is dated 19 March 1814, and is additionally interesting because it shows that Spode's stone china was also popular and was linked with the new Mason Patent Ironstone china:

> Every one enquires for the stone china, made by Spode and Mason and it has a very great run. I presume you know what it is – it is a thick coarse china body, not translucent, with china patterns but in texture similar to old stoneware.

The description 'china patterns' is relevant for much of the early Mason ironstone wares. The single Mason cup shown in Plate 16 has a gilt handle and a very meticulously painted 'Japan' pattern. In quality of potting and of decoration this ironstone cup would not disgrace any porcelain manufacturer.

Some Mason ironstones were very well decorated in a porcelain-like manner with landscape and figure compositions painted by Samuel Bourne (b.c.1789)

PLATE 16. *The front and side view of a delicately potted Mason's ironstone cup, well painted with a typical colourful, if simple, 'Japan' pattern. 2¾in. (6.98cm) high. c.1815-20*

who had been apprenticed to Messrs Wood & Caldwell and who later joined Minton's where he became Art Director in the 1840s. This Mason artist is mentioned several times in the 1822 sale catalogue of Mason wares (see Chapter IV), one such lot reading:

> A costly dessert service exquisitely painted in select views by S. Bourne, enriched with burnished gold. (Sold for £31.10s.0d.).

A superb dish from such a service is shown in Plate 17. While later ironstone wares may have been produced to cut costs, this was certainly not always the case.

The reader may well be interested in the contemporary prices of Mason's ironstone dinner wares. The following list relates to a service of the 'Birds and flowers' pattern supplied in December 1814 by 'G. & C. Mason' to Messrs Chamberlain's, the Worcester porcelain manufacturers. Fortunately the pieces are separately priced and even the different sizes of dishes are detailed:

| | | |
|---|---|---|
| 2 Tureens (with covers) & stands @ | 11/- | £1. 2s. 0d. |
| 4 Sauce tureens & Stands | 4/- | 16s. 8d. |
| 4 Square covered (vegetable) dishes | 5/- | £1. 0s. 0d. |
| 1 Salad | 5/6 | 5s. 6d. |
| 1 20-inch Gravy (dish with well) | | 13s. 0d. |

PLATE 17. *A superb quality dessert dish from a complete service, impressed marked 'Mason's Patent Ironstone China' (see Plate 55). The centre is almost certainly painted by Samuel Bourne – as mentioned in the 1822 auction sale catalogue. Inscribed 'Interior of the Hall of Kenilworth Castle, Warwickshire'. 10¼ x 9in. (26.03cm x 22.86cm). c.1820-22.*

PLATE 18. *A Chinese export-market-shaped Mason's ironstone dinner service tureen, bearing a standard Oriental-style printed outline design which may relate to Chamberlain's 'birds and flowers' pattern received for resale in December 1814. Printed and impressed marks. 10in. (25.4cm) high. c.1814-20.*

| | | | |
|---|---|---|---|
| 1 20-inch dish | | | 10s. 6d. |
| 2 18-inch dishes | | 7/6 | 15s. 0d. |
| 1 [pierced] Drainer to 18-inch dish | | | 7s. 6d. |
| 2 16-inch dishes | | 4/6 | 9s. 0d. |
| 1 [pierced] Drainer to 16-inch dish | | | 4s. 8d. |
| 2 14-inch dishes | @ | 3/6 | 7s. 0d. |
| 4 12-inch dishes | | 2/- | 8s. 0d. |
| 4 10-inch dishes | | 1/3 | 5s. 0d. |
| 1 12-inch Baker [deep oval baking dish] | | | 2s. 8d. |
| 1 10-inch Baker | | | 1s. 4d. |
| 60 Table [dinner] plates | | 6½d. | £1.12s. 6d. |
| 24 Twifflers [middle-size plates] | | 5½d. | 11s. 0d. |
| 24 6-inch plates | | 5d. | 10s. 0d. |

The complete set totals £10.1s.4d., but this was probably the trade price as quoted between fellow manufacturers. The retail price would have been lifted by at least a third giving a selling price of just over £13. This service is, however, rather larger at 155 pieces – if we include the covers – than most included in Mason's subsequent auction sales, which were listed as being of 142 pieces. The make-up may also have been slightly different to suit varying orders. The auction reserve prices ranged up to £35 for Mason's Ironstone dinner services but such high bids were not always forthcoming! Other contemporary non-Mason listings and prices are given in my specialist books on other factories.

Mason's Patent Ironstone wares were not, however, introduced without opposition from some retailers who claimed to have been selling ironstone china before its introduction by the Masons. Eddowe's *Salopian Journal* of 29 March 1815 contains the following two announcements. The first is under the name and address of T. Brocas[2] of the 'Original China Warehouse', Raven Street, Shrewsbury:

> ...T. Brocas thinks it right here particularly to speak of iron-stone china because an idea has been conveyed that he never sold the article, whereas he was the first that ever sold it in these parts, and has sold it for many years. And when about a dozen years back, the chief material of which it is composed was first found out it was shewn to him, and he was actually consulted by the father of the present manufacturer of PATENT IRON-STONE CHINA as to what kind of ware or china could best be made out of it. Time alone must determine whether or not it will be more durable than COALPORT CHINA. But the finest kind which, in Shropshire, is only sold by Thomas Brocas. The table services are nothing inferior in beauty or strength to the Coalport or to fine old India China.

PLATE 19. *Another early Mason's ironstone standard tureen form – probably not directly related to a Chinese shape. Perhaps the 'blue pheasants' as mentioned in the sale catalogue or 'birds and flowers' as purchased by Chamberlains in December 1814. Printed crowned Mason's mark. 7in. (17.78cm) high. c.1820-25. Victoria & Albert Museum (Crown Copyright).*

*If* Thomas Brocas was correct in his claim that 'the father of the present manufacturers of Patent Ironstone China' consulted him about a dozen years ago (that is about 1803!) about the ceramic merits of ironstone, it shows that Miles Mason was himself experimenting with this ingredient several years before his son took out the patent in 1813.

But the Masons replied to Brocas' claim in the following manner:

> The Patentees of the Patent Ironstone China do hereby contradict the bare-faced assertion of Mr. Brocas, china dealer, Shrewsbury, wherein he affirms that he was consulted some years since in the possibility of manufacturing china from Ironstone, Ironstone China being totally a new invention. All china purporting to be ironstone is spurious and a mere imitation which is not printed at the back Patent Ironstone China under a crown...

These last few lines are most important as they show that by March 1815 the Mason ironstone china bore a printed mark with a crown, whereas I once believed that the printed mark with crown was not used for several years after 1813. Such a basic mark is here shown.

I should record that Thomas Brocas and the Masons seem to have worked closely together at the time of the March 1815 statement that Brocas had been instrumental in introducing ironstone. He was also advertising that he had in stock near twenty full (complete) table services of Patent Ironstone China. This trade with Mason seemingly continued for in a November 1816 advertisement, he featured: 'Patent Ironstone china this they continue to sell... in very large table services, dessert ditto, chamber ware, etc, with several sets of Masons finest tea china'. This advertisement underlines the essence of the ironstone market, large dinner services, dessert services and bedroom toilet wares, whilst the more delicate tea wares were still best served by porcelains.

As we have seen Mason's Patent Ironstone China had truly 'arrived' within a very short time of its introduction in the summer of 1813. This we should remember was at a difficult time when Britain was at war with the United States of America and with

PLATE 20. *The printed outline as used for the base of a particularly fine and detailed Mason dinner service pattern. This outline would be coloured in by female paintresses or even children – but the results could be superb. Messrs Mason's Ironstone Ltd.*

France, and there were great hardships and commercial problems at home – not the best of times to introduce a new ceramic body and to 'retool' a factory to produce new forms suitable for the novel body. Yet this is what the Masons undertook in a very big way, perhaps even stimulated by the difficulties experienced by the other firms producing standard earthenwares.

Soon, however, 'Ironstone' had truly entered the national and probably the international language and was to be widely emulated, just as Mason's Ironstone wares closely emulated earlier Chinese porcelains. It was, however, to become a generic term, associated with a very strong durable ceramic body, not necessarily linked with the Mason family name of its originating Staffordshire manufacturer.

As Wedgwood's chief London salesman noted in regard to the new ironstone and stone china wares, 'a dealer cannot be without it and a great deal is sold' and in December 1816 '...Spode, Davenport & Mason are the best makers'. Obviously, many other makers had joined in the rush to produce this highly saleable type of earthenware, which was largely sold on the reputation of the simple names 'ironstone' and 'stone china'. Indeed the rush to manufacture the new ware was remarked upon in April 1819:

> ...Stone China is repeatedly enquired for but it appears from the great quantity of this ware made and making by several manufacturers, and selling by auction and otherwise advertised for sale, that the competition... must be unprofitable...[3]

The new ironstone china and the related stone chinas in the main comprised useful wares. Dinner services which were both colourful, durable and less expensive than porcelain formed the main trade for at least the major Staffordshire manufacturers. Such services included various plates for meat, soup, sweet and cheese. Each of these plates had to show the same often intricate design well laid out across the surface.

It follows that to achieve this variety and to keep down production costs, most designs were at least partly printed. The border and main central design would therefore be printed in outline (Plate 20) – that is the guide lines or 'colour me in' print would be applied. Inexpensive child labour would then add the colours. The quality and extent of the print would vary; some were merely guides, others would include much detail and shading – which would show through the semi-translucent enamel colours. The prints also served to sharpen up the design. Even heavy Japan-style patterns were probably first laid out with the help of a pounced outline which later was completed, first with the underglaze-blue areas and then after glazing and refiring, the overglaze enamels were added.

As late as 1838 Minton & Boyle was still receiving orders to replace old, presumably eighteenth century Chinese dinner services and was stating that their ironstone body best matched the true, or hard-paste, Chinese porcelain. Even with minor replacement orders they recommended that copper-plates be specially engraved to give the outline design, later to be filled-in or coloured-up by hand, see page 290.

Before I proceed to discuss and list the very many manufacturers, large and small, which produced Mason-style ironstone-type wares and the related 'Granite' wares, I must devote a special chapter to 'the founder of the feast' (to quote from Charles Dickens), the Mason dynasty. That is an admittedly strong description of a relatively modest Staffordshire firm that, nevertheless, was to enjoy lasting fame because it marketed an improved and durable earthenware under those so well-chosen words 'Mason's Patent Ironstone China'.

CHAPTER III

# Mason's Patent Ironstone China and Marks

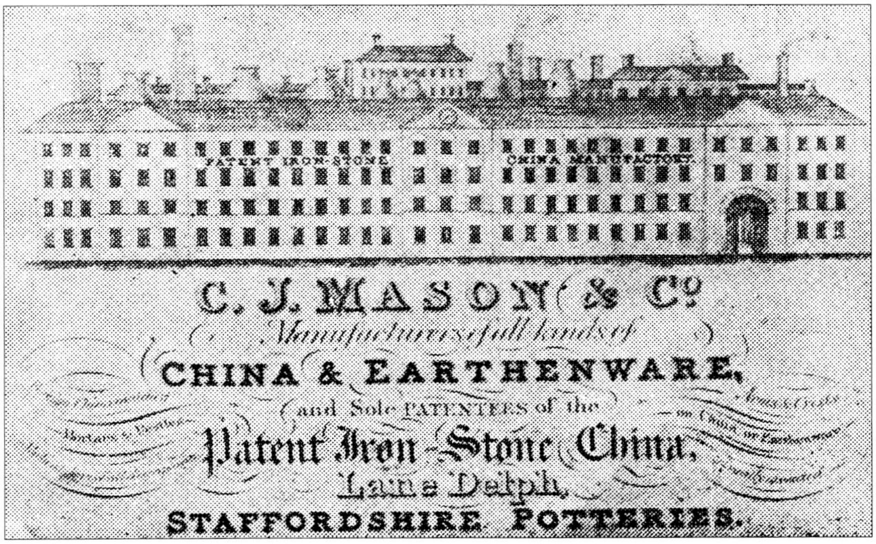


*The works of Charles James Mason & Co., standing obliquely to the turn-pike road, and on the line of the Canal Company's railway, present an extensive front of four stories in height, inscribed in large letters, 'Patent Iron Stone China Manufactory.'*

*For this article of trade, which Messrs. G and C.J. Mason introduced some years ago, they obtained extensive public favour and an almost exclusive sale, on account of its resemblance to porcelain, and its very superior hardness and durability...*

(John Ward's *The Borough of Stoke-upon-Trent...* 1843)

We have in the previous chapters outlined the circumstances that led to the introduction of Mason's Patent Ironstone China in July 1813, as witnessed by the Patent granted to Miles Mason's eldest son, Charles James Mason.

The novel new patented ceramic body which the 'inventors' always referred to as 'china' was evidently soon on the market and was initially aimed at the higher end of the trade. It was featured in *The Times* in December 1813 as being well worth the attention of the nobility and gentry (see page 74). It was not intended to be a variation on the standard earthenware bodies (which continued in general production) but something quite superior and well decorated in the porcelain fashion.

Before discussing the Mason products it would be relevant to mention again the dire financial and trading difficulties being experienced in the potting industry and indeed in all trades at the period when the Masons were planning to introduce their novel ceramic body. For Great Britain was at war with the potters' main customer – the United States of America, as well as with France and her allies.[1]

The Staffordshire potters went so far as to petition the Prince Regent, the future George IV, in 1812. They stated, in part:

> ...it is with the most painful anxiety, we find ourselves compelled to represent the present depressed and alarming state of our Trade. The number of Bankruptcies is unprecedented. More than one fifth of our manufacturers are unoccupied and falling into decay; and the remainder employed to little more than half their usual extent. Great numbers of workmen are without employment and they and their families are dependent upon our daily increasing Poor Rates for subsistence...

PLATE 21. *A Mason's blue printed earthenware (not ironstone) tureen and ladle. Such wares were less expensive than the ironstone wares but not as durable. Printed mark 'Semi China Warranted'. Similar pieces have 'Mason's' added to the mark. 14in. (35.56cm) long. c.1810-15).*

On 27 January 1813 a Peace meeting was held in Hanley Town Hall to consider 'the propriety of Petitioning the Legislature, to adopt such measures as in this wisdom they shall think fit, for bringing about a General Peace, on terms consistent with the safety and honour of the Country'. Sixty-nine leading Staffordshire potters signed the request for this peace meeting. The Treaty of Ghent ending the war with America was not, however, signed until 24 December 1814, representing the best of Christmas presents for the potters.

In February 1813 Thomas Brocas, the Shrewsbury 'Chinaman', recorded, 'what misery is now felt in the Potteries, not more than half employment for the people and what goods are got up, the masters really do not know what to do with. It appears as though more than half the dealers in glass, china and earthenware in London were breaking [*sic*], their bills being returned...' In April 1813 he further noted 'Trade almost at an end, an amazing stock and no one coming to look at table services of China and Staffordshire ware...'

Such a period of war would not have been the best in which to introduce a new ceramic body and effectively to drop the production of the well-tested standard blue-printed and other earthenwares (as Plate 21) and Mason's very good quality porcelains.

Yet the Masons' bold move did, to a large degree, revolutionize the industry, at least in the Staffordshire Potteries. Non-porcelain bodies – ironstone and stone china – were decorated with colourful porcelain-style designs, often for ease of production based on printed outlines or base-designs (Plate 20). The novel durable, decorative and relatively inexpensive wares, table services as well as decorative articles caught the public's fancy. Earthenwares were represented with a splash of colour.

As a result there was a great expansion in the industry, amongst porcelain manufacturers as well as amongst the earthenware potters. Work-forces were enlarged, more raw materials were required. Factories were in effect re-tooled as new forms were introduced to take advantage of the new and enlarging market. Thousands of new moulds were required, masses, even tons, of new copper plates had to be engraved with the new outline patterns, one plate for each different size or shape of article. The earlier introduction of white salt-glaze stoneware, of cream-coloured 'Queen's ware' or even of bone china probably did not cause such a general upsurge in the ceramic industry as did the early ironstone-type bodies in the 1813-1825 period. The rather later popularity of the related granite-type bodies in the vast export trade added to the general growth in the British ceramic industry. In a time of peace this overseas demand was soon to outstrip the home trade's requirements.

While the Mason firm introduced the new patented ironstone china in 1813 primarily to emulate and undersell the Chinese porcelain table wares, it is remarkable how the body was soon used to produce a wealth of fancy and decorative articles. The descriptions in the auction sale catalogues of 1818 and 1822, which are quoted in Chapter IV, show how this body, so heavy and durable when thickly potted, could be trimly turned to produce even toy or miniature pieces of porcelain-like delicacy. Some pieces were sold with protective glass-shades, others were accurately described as 'cabinet pieces'. Mason's new child turned out to be both robust and beautiful, able to turn its hand to very many uses and to adapt itself to almost any task. No wonder it was universally popular.

But in our study of the post-1813 ironstone china we are not concerned with Miles Mason, the founder of the family business, but rather with his sons, who continued to run the business after their father's retirement. Even if they did not invent or improve the patented body from earlier essays, it was the young Masons who successfully marketed the wares and enlarged the factory's output, ensuring that other large firms were all but forced to produce similar durable earthenwares – the stone chinas, in order to compete commercially with the so-successful Mason wares.

The original makers of Mason's Patent Ironstone China were the brothers Charles James Mason and George Miles Mason. Charles, the youngest son of Miles and Ruth Mason, was born in London on 14 July 1791. Little is known of his early life, but he must have assisted his father and elder brother in the potting business because he was only twenty-one when he took out the all-important patent for 'Ironstone China'. It is open to some doubt whether he alone invented the body; and it is more probable that it was the result of experiments carried out by Miles Mason and his sons over several years. Nevertheless, the patent was in Charles James Mason's name. A month before the patent, Miles Mason had formerly transferred the business to his two sons, George Miles and Charles James, who henceforward traded as G. & C. Mason or as G & C Mason & Co.

Charles' brother George Mason was born on 9 May 1789. Besides being an Oxford graduate and a man of

Plate 22. *A well-potted and colourful Mason's ironstone jardinière, on separate base. Such a pair of useful and ornamental objects were superior to many makes of contemporary porcelain. Printed crowned mark. 5¼in. (13.33cm) high.* c.1815-20.

Plate 23. *A superb, celadon-ground, marked Mason's ironstone letter or note rack, matching in style and quality contemporary porcelains. Impressed mark. 6in. (15.24cm) long.* c.1815-20.

cultivated taste, he was to be a prominent figure at Stoke, being responsible in part for establishing both a mail coach route through the Potteries as well as a police force, and introducing several other improvements – listed by Reginald C. Haggar in his excellent book, *The Masons of Lane Delph* (1952).

From 1813 to November 1830,[2] George and Charles traded in partnership together with Samuel Bayliss Faraday (the '& Co.' in the firm of G & C Mason & Co.), George looking after the administrative side of the large, thriving concern. After retiring from active participation, George remained in the district and may even have retained a financial stake in the pottery, for Charles James Mason's bankruptcy in February 1848 seems to have affected George also, a fact that would, however, be explained if George had stood security for his brother on the factory premises or on any loans. George Miles Mason died on 31 August 1859.

Apart from Miles Mason's two sons, Charles James Mason and George Miles Mason, there was a third son – the eldest – named William. Little is known about William, but at one period he had his own factory and a retail shop in Manchester. He was born on 27 January 1785. On coming of age, in 1806, he seems to have joined his father, which accounts for the style M. Mason & Son, although the standard impressed mark on porcelain remained 'M. Mason' up to 1813.[3] Two meetings of his creditors were held in 1828 but apparently he continued as an auctioneer and was still living in 1860.

Miles Mason seems to have retired from active participation in the manufacturing of ceramics in 1813, leaving the business to his sons, who henceforth concentrated on the production of the new durable ironstone body. Miles Mason died on 26 April 1822, but meetings of his creditors were still being held late in 1828, suggesting again that the Mason family and business was short of funding.

Mason's Ironstone China was first produced at Miles Mason's former porcelain factory known as the Minerva Works at Lane Delph, Fenton. The brothers William, George Miles and Charles James Mason bought the Fenton Stone Works at Lane Delph, Fenton from Sampson Bagnall. This factory had earlier been let to Josiah Spode under a lease dated July 1805. The Fenton premises were depicted on several printed marks (see page 101) and are described in two contemporary accounts:

> The manufactory of Messrs. G. & C. Mason, for Patent Iron Stone China, is commodious. Here is a steam engine of some peculiarity in its construction by Holford of Hanley... The front warehouse is four stories high, is fire proof, and has the most beautiful facade of any in the district. (S. Shaw, *History of the Staffordshire Potteries*, 1829.)

and later:

> The works of Charles James Mason & Co., standing obliquely to the turnpike road, and on the

PLATE 24. *Representative parts of an Oriental-style English form dessert service. Printed marks, washed over in green. Centrepiece 14in. (35.56cm) long. c.1815-20. Messrs Phillips.*

PLATE 25. *Representative parts of a Japan pattern Mason's ironstone dinner service. A complete set of this general type sold for £15.5s.0d. in 1827. Tureen 12¼in. (31.11cm) high. c.1815-25. Messrs Christie's.*

> line of the Canal Company's Railway, present an extensive front of four stories in height, inscribed in large letters 'Patent Iron Stone China Manufactory'. ...A Steam engine is employed here in aid of manual labour, and for the other uses of the trade. (John Ward, *History of the Borough of Stoke-upon-Trent*, 1843.)

The elevation is also depicted in the trade card reproduced at the beginning of this chapter.

These 'Fenton Stone Works' were retained until Mason's bankruptcy in 1848, when they were taken by Samuel Boyle (1849-52) and then by E. Challinor & Co., whose successors worked them until *c*.1896. For many years, however, the Masons also managed Sampson Bagnall's works in Lane Delph, Fenton, just below the Minerva Works. From 1811-22, these premises were in the name of William Mason but were probably worked by his brothers, as William was then dealing in pottery at Manchester. From 1822-25, the rate records show the executors of Miles Mason as tenants. The works were then purchased by George and Charles Mason; but in the March 1827 rate records they are shown as 'void' or empty. Since the changes in the various Mason premises are rather difficult to follow they are set out at the end of this chapter.

Whereas sale catalogues of household goods sold in the pre-1810 era include a good proportion of Chinese export porcelain, especially dinner services, by the late 1820s these had often been replaced by ironstone table wares. In a sale held in January 1827, Christie's sold:

> A dinner service of blue and white iron-stone china, with gilt edges, consisting of two soup tureens, covers and dishes, six sauce ditto and stands, four vegetable dishes and covers, a salad bowl, nineteen dishes in sizes, two fish plates, 60 table plates, 18 soup and 48 pie plates. [Sold for £12.12s.]
>
> A dessert service of iron-stone china, in imitation of Oriental burnt-in, consisting of centre piece,

two cream bowls and stands, 12 dishes and 24 plates. [Sold for £2.12s.6d.]

In May 1827, the contents of Clarence Lodge, Roehampton, were sold and contained:

A dinner service of iron-stone china, in imitation of Japan, consisting of 2 tureens, covers and stands, 2 vegetable dishes, 7 corner dishes, 6 covers, 3 sauce tureens and stands, 22 dishes in sizes, 49 table plates, 19 soup, 18 pie and 11 cheese plates. Some pieces imperfect. [Sold for £15.5s.]
A pair of handsome octagonal iron-stone jars, in imitation of Oriental. [Sold for £5.5s.]
A pair of smaller ditto. [Sold for £3.]
A vase of iron-stone china with rams heads and the companion, broken and 2 ditto bowls. [Sold for £3.3s.]
A pair of very handsome bottles of iron-stone china, pencilled with gold upon mazarine blue ground, and painted with landscapes and bouquets in compartments. [Sold for £3.10s.]

The best evidence we have of the great variety of Mason ironstone wares being produced and available within ten years of its introduction is contained in the original catalogues of London sales held in December 1818 and June 1822. Selected extracts from these important sales are given in Chapter IV. The 1822 sale was particularly important and ran to nearly two thousand lots, for it comprised the stock of the firm's London showrooms. Apart from these large London auction sales, Messrs Mason held a series of auction sales in various cities and towns around the country. These were being held by at least the beginning of 1818 for on 12 January an Edinburgh china dealer, wrote to his supplier John Davenport in Staffordshire:

At last Masons have open'd out their forty hhds [hogsheads] stoneware and china here and are selling by auction, which circumstances of course for ever closes our Account with them...[4]

It is interesting to note that this Scottish china dealer – Child & Co. – called Mason's Ironstone 'Stoneware' and that the selection of Mason wares being sold included 'china', being in the main, I assume, porcelain tea services.

While Child, like other 'chinamen' whose trade had been cut by Mason's direct sales to the public by way of auctions, was understandably upset, he did in this same letter advise John Davenport that 'we must now cry down the Ironstone, at least the patent and it will warrant any one to do so as in fact it is now bad earthenware'.

Bad earthenware indeed by 1818! Surely this overstates the case against the flood of ironstone which Mason was releasing on to the market, yet this 1818 letter does show us the reaction of the china dealers who, in many cases, sought to find alternative sources of supply for colourful, oriental-looking, durable table wares, perhaps marked with new trade-descriptions. Of course, the auction sales were not the only means by which the Mason goods were sold. Most would have been sold in the normal way, via china dealers or wholesalers. Much was also exported and the firm had at least representatives in other countries. A French trade card has survived, relating to Charles James Mason & Cie., 'Manufacture de Porcelaine Fine de Porcelaine Opaque. Breveté du Roi'. Five per cent discount was allowed for cash payments.

Nevertheless the Mason auctions do provide us with a most helpful source of information on the types of ironstone being produced by Masons at the period of the various sales, ranging onwards from the large 1818 London sale (Chapter IV). Although the catalogues of the provincial sales do not seem to have survived, the local press announcements list the main contents.

One such sale, that conducted by Mr Wise of Oxford, in November 1826, is particularly interesting. The announcement published in Jackson's *Oxford Journal* of 25 November 1826 reads:

EXTENSIVE SALE OF CHINA
at WISE'S Room, in St. Clements.

In consequence of the dissolution of the Partnership of Messrs GEORGE and CHARLES MASON, Proprietors of the extensive Works at Lane Delph, Staffordshire, Patentees of the IRON STONE CHINA, and late of No. 11, Albemarle Street, London, Mr. WISE begs most earnestly to assure the Nobility and Gentry of Oxford and its environs, that he has been especially appointed to dispose of the whole of this truly elegant and useful STOCK by PUBLIC AUCTION; and that his Room will be opened for the view of part of this grand assemblage of China on Monday next, Nov. 27th, and on Tuesday the 28th. On WEDNESDAY, Nov. 29th, at Eleven o'clock, the Sale will commence, and continue at the same hour each following day of business, till the whole is disposed of. As it may be necessary to enumerate part of the Stock, W.W. begs to point out the great variety of Enamel and Gilt Table Sets, with the usual additions in fashionable Society of Yacht Club Finger Bowls; Ice Pails, Wine Coolers, Stilton Cheese Tubs, Custards and Covers, Celery Vases, Salts and Pickle Saucers; Dessert Services,

PLATE 26. *A massive blue ground relief-moulded ironstone jardinière or 'fish-globe' of the type featured in auction sale announcements. Diameter 42in. (106.68cm) c.1820-30.*

Punch Bowls, Hydra Jugs, Egyptian Mugs, Broth Basins &c. in corresponding patterns. Breakfast Services, with the addition of Honey Pots, Egg Pipkins, Tea and Coffee Sets &c; also a supply of Unmerapoora Tea Extractors, which have entirely superseded the Rockingham Tea Pot. Complete Chamber Services with additional pieces, such as Foot Pails, Slop Jars &c. &c.

In matters of taste and ornament a selection will be seen peculiarly meriting attention. The Neapolitan Ewer rivals the best Work of Dresden manufactory; Fish Pond Bowls, of extraordinary magnitude; Siamese Jardinieres and Plateaux, adopted by the Horticultural Society, for the culture of Bulbous Roots &c; a general and extensive variety of Jars, Beakers, Ornaments for the Cabinet and Mantel Piece, from French, Italian, Spanish, Chinese, Japanese, Berlin and Saxon Originals. The Blue Printed Table Services comprise a variety of this year's patterns. All other Earthenware in use will be found in the Stock.

Catalogues may be had, and the Property viewed, at the Room.

The Sale will commence each day at Eleven o'clock.

Packers from the Manufactory will attend, for the accommodation of Country Purchasers.

It is interesting to read a candid letter written by this auctioneer within a fortnight on his sale:

St. Clements,
Oxford,
December 11th, 1826.

...I have recently held a sale of china for the manufactory of Mason & Co., Lane Delph, it is of a very inferior quality and they have been attack'd by the Trade here since the sale and put to some expense in Penalties. They are about attempting another sale in Oxford, but I have declined officiating for them...

Wm. Wise.

Other Mason sales were held in London and were featured in the leading papers. Samuel Bayliss Faraday, Charles Mason's partner and London retailer, advertised from a fashionable Regent Street address. His advertisements give helpful information on their products. Those of 1828 include:

Mr. Faraday, 190 Regent Street, has certainly collected the finest stock of china ever seen in the metropolis, and has caused the art of Potting to be carried to its highest pitch in the higher branches

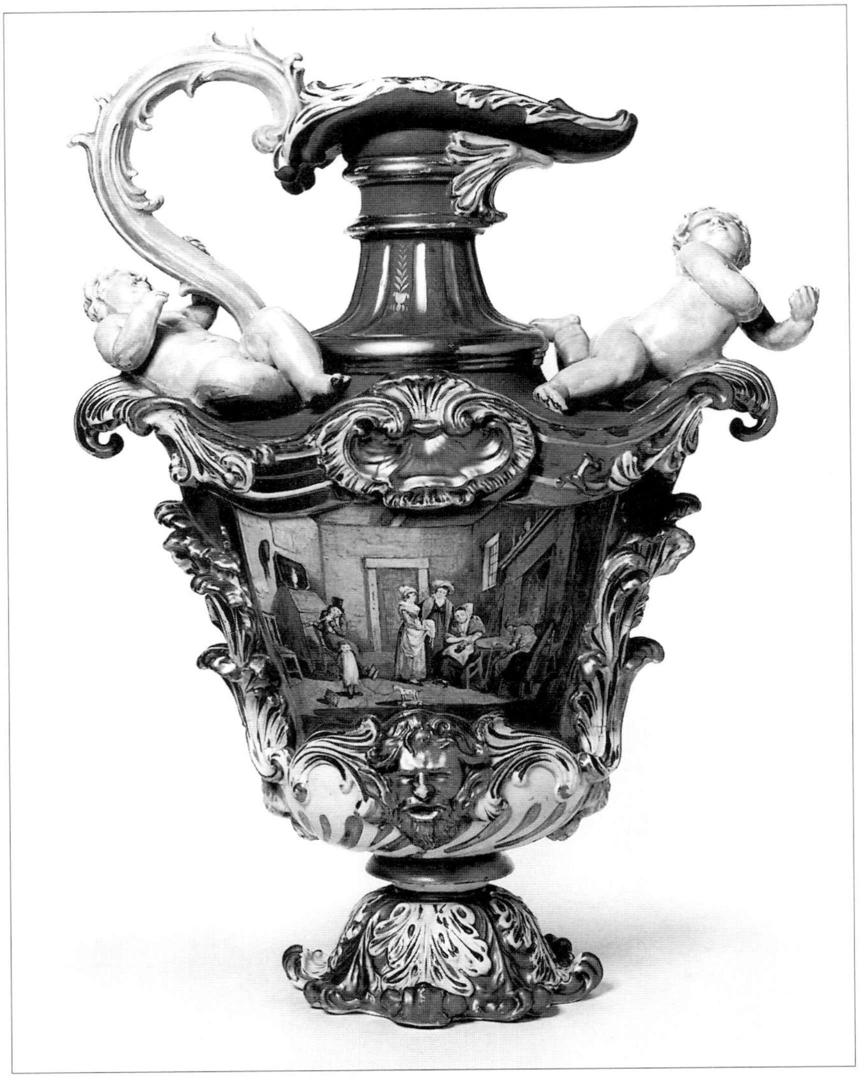

PLATE 27. *A massive and fine Mason's 'Italian' or 'Neapolitan' ewer stated to 'rival the best work of the Dresden manufactory'. Green ground, richly gilt and with fine quality figure painting, perhaps by Samuel Bourne. 26in. (66.04cm) high. c.1825-35. Messrs Phillips.*

of that interesting manufacture. The set of fine jars of English make are the finest we ever saw, and are superior to foreign productions; we understand the models cost five hundred pounds...

[*John Bull*, 23 March 1828.]

...splendid, extensive, and unique Stock of Porcelain and... comprising, richly gilt table [dinner] and dessert services... a variety of earthenware table sets, gadroon and plain edges, in light and full patterns of the newest make, rivalling China in delicacy of colour and elegance of patterns... The Stock further embraces drawing room and vestibule vases, pot pouries, pastile burners, fine flower and scent jars, capacious fish globes, Italian urns, delicate diminutive specimens, etc.... [*The London Morning Herald*, 1st April 1828.]

Many hundred table services of modern earthenware, breakfast and tea ware, toilet and chamber sets, many hundred dozen of baking dishes, flat dishes, broth basins, soup tureens, sets of jugs, and numerous other articles. The china is of the most elegant description, and embraces a great variety of splendid dinner services, numerous dessert services, tea, coffee, and breakfast sets of neat and elegant patterns, ornaments of every description that can be manufactured in china from the minutest article calculated to adorn pier

PLATE 28. *A further impressed marked Mason's Italian ewer of the 'most noble, splendid and magnificent' type. The model was stated to have cost some £500. Green ground, richly gilt and enamelled panel-painted by Samuel Bourne. 27in. (68.58cm) high. c.1818-22. (See also Colour Plate 7.) Messrs Christie's.*

> table and cabinet, to the most noble, splendid and magnificent jars some of which are near five feet high. [*The London Morning Herald*, 21st April 1828.]

Messrs Masons were well ahead of their rivals in producing decorative ornamental ironstone wares. Other firms, except perhaps Spode, restricted their ironstone and stonewares to table services.

Large auction sales of Mason's ironstone china also continued to be held at various provincial centres. One such lengthy sale was held by Vaile of Leeds early in June 1829 and was announced in the *Leeds Mercury* at various dates in April and May of that year. Mr Ron Morley of Leeds has kindly supplied me with details of Vaile's advertisements which show the extent of the Mason output or stock at this period, some fifteen or sixteen years after the Patent Ironstone body had been introduced. I was excited to receive details of this large Leeds sale of Mason's Ironstone but it turned out that Vaile's 1829 press-announcement was an almost exact replica of Wise's 1826 Oxford notice. Again 'the whole of the manufactured stock' was being disposed of by auction in 'consequence of a Dissolution of Partnership.'

There were, however, a few new lines including 'Oatlands and Trentham vases, hexagonal flower pots, dolphin bowls, Etruscan inks, violet baskets and pot-pouries in sets of three and five'. Miniature novelties were included 'For the cabinet, boudoir and console table, every little essential will appear, such as diminutive pitchers, ewers and basins, tripods, watering cans, lily cups, lavender bottles, tapers (small candle or taper sticks), tea kettles, coffee pots, sauce pans, tubs, jugs and mugs, square scent bottles, etc, etc, etc.' But such delightful 'toy' miniature pieces had been included in the 1818 London sale.

Sales by auction are bad in the long term as the temptation is to include slightly faulty ware which floods the market, encouraging the buyers to obtain cheap examples and leave the more expensive perfect articles. The local auctions also destroy the trade of the retailers (the manufacturer's main and long-term link with the buying public), who are then less inclined to reorder from the manufacturer who has stolen their trade. In general, disposal of china by auction is a good expedient when one is closing a concern and has stock to clear. It is bad when the firm wishes to continue. Many faulty specimens of Mason's Ironstone China may be found. Large tears in the body or chips (caused in the manufacture, as they are often glazed over) are relatively common and were, I believe, finished for the auction sales rather than rejected, as they should have been. Such faulty or plain bad quality 'seconds' or 'thirds' certainly found a market at a low price but they were not good for the long-term reputation of the factory or indeed for ironstone in general. The management even sank to glazing and decorating a jug, the handle of which had come adrift in the first firing. They sold a handleless jug.

The 1829 Leeds auction had been advertised as being held in consequence of a dissolution of partnership but in fact this took place some three years earlier. It is generally believed that George Miles Mason retired from the firm of G. & C. Mason & Co. in 1826, but the official notice of such a change is dated 22 November 1830 and was not published in *The London Gazette* until May 1832 (see Appendix I). It must be recorded that the long series of auction sales held by or for Charles Mason caused general unrest and on some occasions the Law or local by-laws were invoked to stop the practice. Reginald Haggar and Elizabeth Adams give good details of such troubles in their 1977 book.

After George Miles Mason retired from the partnership of G. & C. Mason, Charles James Mason continued the concern, trading as Charles J. Mason & Co., the '& Co.' referring to Samuel Bayliss Faraday (who died in 1844). Some rate records and *Pigot's Directory* of 1841 refer to a firm called Mason & Faraday. There is a great divergence of opinion regarding Charles Mason as an employer. Some regard him as an enlightened employer keen on improving the working conditions and pay of his work-people.

There are, as is often stated, two sides to most questions and evidently Charles Mason provoked wrath among the workers for his efforts to introduce machinery into his works. The workers' side is well stated in various issues of William Evans' weekly newspaper *The Potters Examiner and Workman's Advocate* of the mid-1840s.[5] The main and continual complaints were low wages, high rates of interest for borrowing, being paid only for perfectly formed items 'good from the oven' (articles that had survived the firing processes), and also Mason's efforts to introduce machinery into the manufactory. One might have thought that machinery would aid the workers' lot, but they dreaded it and the consequent risk of unemployment or at best lower rates of pay.

I can only quote here a few of the complaints and worries that troubled the workers who wrote to the Editor of *The Potters' Examiner*. It is interesting to note that, at a period when many Staffordshire manufacturers signed official documents with a cross, the workers complaining in *The Potters' Examiner* were extremely literate. As they, including the Editor, William Evans, wrote under pen-names, such as 'Mentor', it is now impossible to tell the true names or positions of these contributors. Still, their writings are of interest. Here are quotations from a few issues of November and December 1844:

> ...that curse of the working man – science – may have descended on our trade, and may have robbed us of the power which we now possess. Now is the time! Let us use it, then to secure ourselves against the evil that is pending; a fearful progressive evil!
>
> The curse is stealing in amongst us. The anticipated mechanical appliances are being silently introduced. Mr C.J. Mason, of Fenton, is now in possession of machines for making flatware (plates etc.). Be alive, then, men of the Potteries and prepare for the worst. Master potters are only waiting for one successful experiment, and the mischief is accomplished. Let a gap be once made, and they will all rush through to the use of machinery with all the eagerness of the cotton lords of Lancashire. Your doom will then be sealed; and the present opportunity will have passed for ever. Get funds, then, funds, funds...
>
> 'Mentor' (2 November 1844).

The funds were not only required to give backing to the new unions, in case strike action was needed but as the very next newspaper column related there was much plotting amongst the workers to form an 'Emigration Society' under which Staffordshire workers and their families would be shipped off to find their

PLATE 29. *Contrasting sizes. The Mason's ironstone wares varied from giant vases to miniature or 'toy' pieces. Impressed marked. Vase 15in. (38.1cm) high.* c.1815-25.

fortunes in the New World.

In the following Saturday's issue of *The Potters' Examiner,* 'Mentor' returned at great length to address the 'United branches of operative potters' on Charles Mason's dreaded machinery. Mentor's 'Friends, Brothers and Fellow-Workmen' were addressed in terms that would do credit to a modern Union leader! In an inserted extra letter we learn something of the small extent to which Mason's new machinery had affected work which, after all, had always been assisted by a form of machinery – the potter's wheel. The November 1844 letter reads, in part:

> ...as far as I understand its construction, I have not the least doubt but that it will, in a very short period of time, supersede, if not wholly, to a very considerable extent, adult manual labour in the Flat-pressing branch of our trade.
>
> It is constructed, to make plates, dishes, cups, bowls and saucers; and is constructed well; it will make them, and it will make them well; and, so far as I understand it, there is no human labour

> required in the working of it, but what may be equally as well done by boys and women, as by adult men.
>
> The machine, is, at present only experimenting upon saucers; it is furnished with two jigger heads, which may be multiplied; and on each head, there may be made sixty to one hundred dozens per day... a man, that has never seen a potworks in his life, I believe, in the course of a day would do the work as efficiently as the most skilful potter in the district. Thus, skilled labour will be of no value...

Of course Charles Mason did not invent the machines, nor was he the first to introduce them, the same November 1844 writer noted:

> ...In Stockton they have had a machine for making inside [*sic*] cups for several years and in Sunderland and Newcastle they have got some of the same kinds. One of these machines, with the assistance of two women, or boys of fourteen years of age, will do as much work as six middling workmen. One woman for about two shillings [10p], will make sixty dozen of cups, for which we should receive, at most places, from fifteen to seventeen shillings [75p to 85p]. Now, the machine introduced at Mr Mason's works, is a great improvement upon these, and will not only do a greater variety of work, and a great deal better, but will also make a greater quantity...
>
> Up, the, potters and be doing! Now is the time!... come to the rescue of your trade! Machinery is your foe, your mortal enemy. Battle with it, as you love your wives and children... Machinery is your foe, your mortal foe!...

And so on, and on and on!

The Union called a public meeting for 12 November 1844, the hand-bill notice of which read in part:

> Men of the Potteries, a crisis has arrived... Mr. C.J. Mason of Fenton, is now in the possession of machinery for the making of all kinds of Flat Ware, which may be worked either by steam or hand power and the principles of which may be extended to the other branches. Arise and prepare for the worst...

The Union was pressed to raise funds to enable Mason's work-force to be withdrawn and paid by the Union's funds but, in the event, by the middle of December 1844, Mason withdrew the new machinery – which apparently was prone to producing faulty articles – and the advance of the pottery industry was stilled, at least for the time being. It should be noted, however, that the Mason factory boasted a steam engine from at least 1829 and this presumably assisted the workers in some of their labours. Not all machinery would have been considered an evil, only that which threatened to replace the workers.

Tedious, and perhaps overstated, as the workers' lengthy letters may appear today, their difficulties were undoubtedly very real to them and their families. From the historian's point of view one letter in particular is still of interest. This appeared in *The Potters' Examiner* of 23 December 1845, under the pen-name 'Timothy Scribble'. The writer noted under the heading 'Grievances of Mr Mason's workmen', the various wages or prices for work then being paid at Mason's Fenton manufactory:

> In 1840, earthenware salads and sauce tureens and stands were 3/6d per dozen. In 1843, they were 2/8d. Comports, that were at the former period 1/6d, were at the latter 9d per dozen. Large square jars, that were 10d each, are now 4d. Bear in mind, that of what I now write is all best ware.
>
> The prices generally are one-fourth or more, under what are given at other manufactories. What do you think of 4½d being the price given for best tureen and stand in earthenware and 6d in ironstone (Patent ironstone, I should have said) or of earthenware covered dishes being made at 1/10d, ewers 1/5½, chambers 1/3d, soap boxes 1/10, *per dozen*...
>
> In most things apprentices and journeymen have but one price... let a lad of seventeen be set to make teapots, he shall be paid 1/6d per dozen for them, a man of forty may do the same work, and not receive a fraction more...
>
> ...It is generally after work is made, and fired, that reductions [for faults] take place... all the socalled 'bad ware' or in other words, all the ware that his agents think fit to place to the master's sole account, is taken away to the dipping house... so that the workmen have not the slightest chance of seeing whether the ware be really bad or not. By these means, in addition to the extremely low rates of payment... the men often and grievously suffer, from entirely losing far more of their work than can be satisfactorily accounted for...
>
> The *liberal* C.J. Mason has a steam machine for printing, and two printers that work at it, are so advantageously situated that if they work very hard and make long days, they can, perhaps, earn 12/- or 14/- in a whole week. But the transferers, beat this hollow! Some of them, after coming several miles to their work, (women, recollect,) march off home

PLATE 30. *The later Mason's ironstone products include a wonderful range of rococo designed large fireplaces. This example, one of several in the same house, had a blue ground. Large printed 'China Chimney Piece' mark (page 155). 72in. (182.88cm) wide. c.1835-45. L.J. Allen, Esq.*

on the Saturday night, with two, three or perhaps four shillings, for their week's earnings. At first they had to pay their paper-cutters out of their own earnings...

Returning to discuss the Mason ironstone wares themselves, evidence of the undoubted early commercial success of the ironstone body and the colourful durable wares produced from it can be seen, to some degree, in the prohibition of imports of the British ironstone into France. This may be the explanation for the not infrequent lack of marks. Non-designated 'Ironstone' might have escaped this embargo while 'Stone-China' and other similar names might perhaps also have proved acceptable, as would unmarked and undescribed earthenwares.

The Masons over the years obviously endeavoured to retain their lead in the ironstone market, producing an amazing array of articles from minute toy pieces to giant vases and even huge fire-surrounds and mantelpieces

PLATE 31. *A rare marked Mason's ironstone plate, still similar to 18th century Chinese export forms but with a well-engraved central design of* Britannia – *the first steam Cunarder which was launched in 1840. Printed crowned mark.* c.*1840-45.*

(Plates 30 and 115-116). Apart from new forms and designs they also amended the basic body from time to time, to cut costs or improve the standard or appearance of the wares. William Evans in his 1846 privately published work, *Art & History of the Potting Business* gave the recipe for 'Mason's newly improved stone body':

| | | |
|---|---|---|
| 12½ | cwt | china clay |
| 12½ | " | flint |
| 10 | " | (china) stone |
| 2½ | " | blue clay-stained with 2 lbs 7 oz of Zaffre |

The glaze for this amended body was made up from 50 lbs. borax, 15 lbs. flint, 25 lbs. stone, 30 lbs. spar – all fired in the glost oven and finely ground.

By this period the Mason body would have been little different from the mixes employed by their trade rivals but they still traded on the now out-of-date magical description Mason's Patent Ironstone China, not now covered by a patent and seemingly devoid of any ironstone!

In August 1846 Charles Mason announced his forthcoming retirement, at a period when the Mason firm owed the bank the then very considerable sum of two thousand pounds. This debt was seemingly entirely the responsibility of Charles, for his partner Samuel Faraday had died in February 1844.

The auction sales continued to afford some financial relief, or at least enable unsaleable old stock to be sold. The auctions were not confined to England. A large sale was held in New York in 1847 consisting entirely of Mason's ironstone wares. It seems likely that similar sales were held in other places but records of these have not been preserved. It must be stated, however, that Mason was not alone in selling surplus stock by auction. It was a convenient long-established, method of turning goods into cash.

Yet, the Masons, dogged by lack of funds, troubles with the workforce and ever-increasing competition in their chosen field of production – ironstone-type wares – continued for over thirty years, from 1813 to 1846, producing a vast quantity of ironstone china. Some now rare earthenware and stoneware moulded jugs etc., were also made, but these probably represent less than five per cent of the total production. It was almost inevitable that the ironstone market became saturated. The novelty had worn off. Vast amounts were on the market, and to some extent, by the late 1840s, the traditional Chinese-style designs were outmoded. It is also probable that the ironstone proved too durable, reducing the demand for replacements or new dinner and dessert services. It was also unfortunate that most buyers preferred their tea wares to be made in the more delicate and whiter-bodied bone-china. Dinner and dessert services were purchased less often than the fashionable tea and coffee services.

In view of these basic points it is not surprising that Charles James Mason was declared bankrupt in February 1848. Furthermore, as I shall shortly show, he was in great difficulties in 1846, and had then let his Fenton factory. The factories and private possessions were offered for sale by auction in March 1848 when the following notices appeared in *The Staffordshire Advertiser*:

FENTON
PATENT IRONSTONE CHINA
MANUFACTORY
–

MR. HIGGINBOTTOM
WILL SELL BY AUCTION
THE PATENT IRONSTONE CHINA
MANUFACTORY
FENTON
THE ENTIRE OF THE FIXTURES, UTENSILS,
MATERIALS, STOCK, & BELONGING TO
THE
ESTATE OF MR C.J. MASON, ON MONDAY
(to) FRIDAY, APRIL 3rd, 4th, 5th, 6th & 7th,
1848.

Further details of the factories' contents are given in other sale notices:

> The Patent Ironstone Manufactory, Fenton and the Patent Ironstone China Manufactory, Terrace Buildings, also at Fenton... the entire of the Fixtures, Utensils, Moulds, Green (unfired), Biscuit (once fired but unglazed) and Glossed (glazed) Stock, Materials, etc., a complete Patent Printing Machine by Pott, with 17 Engraved Rollers, and all necessary appliances for immediate work.
>
> Also, at the Ironstone China Manufactory, Terrace Buildings, Fenton, the whole belonging to the estate of Mr. C.J. Mason...

PLATE 32. *A Chinese form vase of eighteenth century form but shown by Mason at the 1851 Exhibition. Special printed exhibition mark, see page 100. 17½in. (44.45cm) high. c.1851.*

However, the story has recently been complicated by the researches of Mr Rodney Hampson as reported in newsletters of The Northern Ceramic Society. This authority's contribution on the fortunes (or rather the misfortunes) of Richard Daniel, as published in

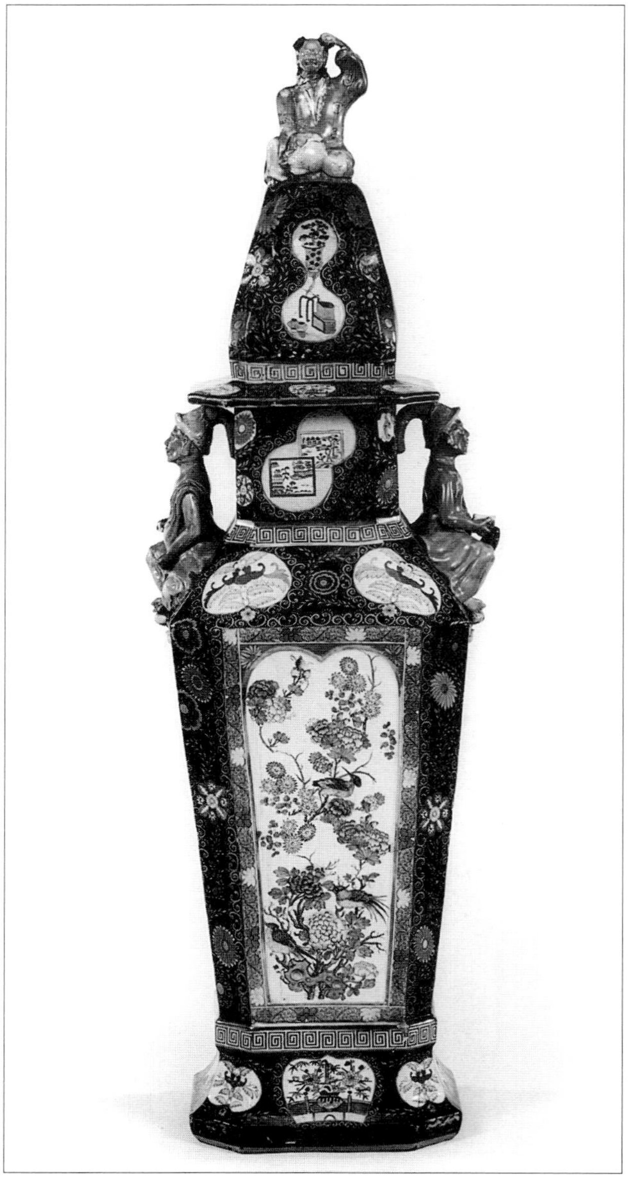

PLATE 33. *An unmarked ironstone vase of the ornate style associated with the 1851 Exhibition but most such forms were introduced at an earlier period. 52in. (132.08cm) high. c.1840-50. Messrs Neales.*

Newsletter number 22 of September 1976, included a quotation from the *Staffordshire Advertiser* of 1 May 1847, relating to the sale by auction of

> All the remaining valuable stock of Ironstone China, earthenware materials, saggars, moulds, marl, flint and other effects of Mr Richard Daniel... on the premises at Fenton.

Mr Hampson's second contribution on the subject appeared in the Northern Ceramic Society's Newsletter, number 68 of December 1987, in which it is stated on good evidence that 'Richard Daniel actually occupied one of Charles James Mason's factories at Fenton in 1846-47'. It was shown by Mr Hampson that a sale of Mason's stock advertised on 10 September 1846 stated that the sale was 'to make room for Mr Mason's successor'. A further auction notice of 31 October 1846 makes it clear that Daniel was the new tenant – 'Messrs Daniel having taken the extensive manufactory of Mr Mason at Fenton'.

This venture was unfortunately of very short duration as Richard Daniel was declared insolvent in March 1847 and his stock of ironstone china and other goods from the Fenton Works was sold in May 1847.

The brief transcripts from the now destroyed Rate Records confirm this change and Richard Daniel's brief occupation of the former Mason Patent Ironstone Works in Fenton. C.J. Mason is listed there in 1845, Richard Daniel in 1846 and Mason again in 1847.

It seems likely that either Richard Daniel only leased the works or that if a purchase was planned he was unable to complete the payment, so that on Daniel's insolvency the Fenton Patent Ironstone works reverted to Mason's ownership.

It is not known if Richard Daniel, when he took over the great Mason factory at Fenton in 1846, also purchased Mason's moulds, engraved copperplates etc., so that he could continue the Mason business under his own name. Possibly Mason retained his working materials for his own use but I cannot find any mention of a pottery in his own name in 1846. Whichever course was agreed the materials would have reverted to Mason with the factory on Daniel's bankruptcy in 1847. It must be remembered that at the time of Mason's sale in March 1848 there was included 'The entire of the fixtures, utensils, materials, stock and belonging to the estate of Mr C.J. Mason', at the Patent Ironstone China Manufactory, Fenton.

We can consider what, if anything, Daniel produced at the Mason Patent Ironstone Works during this brief spell in 1846-1847. Recently discovered items suggest two different possibilities. Following on from Rodney Hampson's contribution in The Northern Ceramic Society's Newsletter number 68, Betty Reed reported an ironstone plate with a near copy of the standard Mason printed ironstone mark with the crown device and a drape below and the initials 'H & R D'. She mentioned, 'To use such a mark with its close association with Mason's ironstone wares, Daniel must have been in actual occupation of the Mason factory with the use of all the factory moulds, etc. It is, therefore, possible to date my plate to 1846-47...'

I think it rather dangerous to deduce so much from the use of a Mason-type mark with totally different initials added, but Mrs Reed may well be correct in her belief. Certainly these initials fit only the partnership between

PLATE 34. *A colourful, marked Mason's Patent Ironstone China plate. The basic shape was registered on 16 April 1849, and was featured in the 1851 Exhibition. Printed crowned mark with design-registration diamond-shaped device. Diameter 10¼in. (26.03cm).* c.1849-51.

Henry and Richard Daniel and certainly Richard Daniel (alone) did occupy the Mason factory for a short period.

The other recent find, however, rather complicates the position. A large earthenware tea-pot (shown in Plate 163) and a matching cream jug, have been reported. Both these pieces bear the rather unclear impressed mark

DANIEL'S
IRONSTONE

Applied directly over this impressed Daniel mark, so as effectively to obliterate it, is a clear printed Mason Patent Ironstone China mark with the late angular crown above.

Three possibilities occur to me to explain this double Daniel and Mason name-marking. First, it could well be that Richard Daniel moved his remaining stock to the Mason factory at Fenton when he acquired these premises. He then made use of the available former Mason copper-plates to add the decoration and that to aid the sales he retained the Mason mark which formed part of the existing coppers.

Second, it could also have been the case that after Richard Daniel was bankrupt Mason took over Daniel's existing stock when he re-occupied his old factory. He needed to finish and make saleable the blanks and therefore added his designs and applied his own Mason mark over the top of the impressed Daniel mark.

Third, you may like to consider that at this difficult time Mason, in returning to the trade, was in effect a decorator rather than a manufacturer, that he purchased blanks from various sources and decorated these plus his own available stock using his own copper-plates and patterns.

All these possibilities arise from a teapot (Plate 163) and creamer (Plate 164) that should have been destroyed at birth. They are extremely faulty specimens; to use trade terms they are clearly 'Seconds', 'Thirds' or even 'Fourths'! Some chips have been glazed over and the large chip on the front of the pot has been accepted and the printed lower-border applied straight across this large blemish.

However, as I have already indicated Charles James

PLATE 35. *A further marked Mason's ironstone plate, showing the moulded April 1849 registered shape to advantage. This late shape can (like others) be embellished with different designs. Printed crowned mark with design-registration diamond-shaped device. Diameter 10¼in. (26.03cm). c.1849-51.*

Mason continued trading either as a manufacturer or as a decorator and was able to display a largish assortment of ironstone wares at the Great Exhibition in 1851. It is not clear whether these 1851 exhibits were new productions or old ware rescued from the bankruptcy or 'bought in' at the auction sales. On the evidence of the fine vase or jar 'with raised enamel mandarin figures and sea-dragon handles' shown in Plate 32, the Mason 1851 exhibits, or at least some of them, bore the printed inscription, in script letters, 'Exhibition 1851' as well as the standard mark including the angular-shaped crown which also occurs on the plate form registered in 1849. I reproduce this special 1851 Exhibition marking on page 100.

Charles Mason's stand at the 1851 exhibition in Hyde Park comprised the following 'specimens of Patent Ironstone China':

Garden Seats of mixed Anglo-Indian and Japanese pattern, representing an old dragon, in raised enamel on a gold ground. [The description 'Indian' or 'Anglo-Indian' relates to Chinese-based designs, the term 'Indian' being widely used in the eighteenth and nineteenth centuries for articles of Chinese origin.]

Garden seats of an Anglo-Chinese pattern, on a sea-green ground, with raised solid flowers and gilt panels.

Fish Pond bowls of Anglo-Indian pattern The Water Lily, an Anglo-Japanese pattern.

Jars with raised enamel Mandarin figures and sea-dragon handles. Large jars and covers of Anglo-Indian pattern. There are also some open jars. Jars covered: dragon handles of Anglo-Indian and Anglo-Japanese patterns,with raised solid flowers, etc.

Specimens of plates in the Oriental style of pattern, on registered shapes [see Plates 34 and 35] and Anglo-Japanese. Three jars and covers, with Anglo-Indian grounds. A plate, a dish, a tureen, a covered dish, a tall coffee cup and saucer, and a sugar-basin, made of the white patent ironstone china, as used in the United States of America.

Jugs of old Indian, Japanese and gold patterns of the original shape; also Anglo-Indian and melon pattern; with Oriental figures and gold ornaments.
Ewer and basin, and mouth ewer and basin, with Oriental figures, and a rose border.
Jars: the old Indian crackle, with India red grounds. A breakfast cup and saucer.
A monumental tablet, made of ironstone, and lettered under the glaze. Jugs, showing various patterns in Bandanna ware. Toilet ewers and basins. Antique jugs of Japanese pattern and gold ornaments. Red and gold paint jars. Zigzag beakers, on bronze. Table ware of a Japanese pattern in blue, red and gold.

The Mason stand at the gigantic 1851 exhibition, at the 'Crystal Palace' in Hyde Park, was a small one situated between Copeland's seven-case display and John Rose's show of fine, richly decorated, Coalport porcelain. Charles Mason was in good company but perhaps too good to attract the large sales and valuable publicity that might have come to his rescue. The Mason's vases or jars in ironstone were singled out for mention, although the Jury's report made no mention of the Mason exhibits.

At the time of the 1851 census Charles James Mason, then a widower living at Daisy Bank, stated that he was a manufacturer of 'Patent Ironstone China' and that he was then employing 31 men, 24 women, 16 boys and 14 girls. This was a surprisingly large workforce for someone who had sought to retire in 1846, and who had been bankrupt and had to sell his works, home and its contents in 1848. Perhaps the merits of Mason's Patent Ironstone China were still enough to attract backers willing to provide funds to continue the Mason venture.

After the sale of the old Fenton works to Samuel Boyle, C.J. Mason took a presumably smaller pottery at Mill Street, Longton, although the description 'Fenton Patent Ironstone Works' was seemingly retained. Longton was the address when the new plate shape was registered on 16 April 1849. During the approximate period 1851-1853 Charles Mason took Richard Ray's Daisy Bank Pottery, which later passed into the hands of Messrs Hulse, Nixon & Adderley. The revival of the business and Mason's show at the 1851 exhibition, however, does not seem to have been successful for in 1852 a supplier of raw materials took Charles Mason to court over a mere £33 debt. He died on 5 February 1856, aged sixty-five. It is interesting that Charles Mason had married Samuel Spode's daughter, Sarah, but she had died in May 1842. He later remarried. At least one post-1848 mark, includes the late place-name Longton.

PLATE 36. *A typical Chinese form and patterned garden seat, several of which were included in Mason's display at the 1851 Exhibition. 20in. (50.8cm) high. c.1845-51.*

Now, after the 1851 Exhibition and Charles James Mason's death early in 1856 we can trace the subsequent movements of the all-important Mason patterns and copper-plates and also the succeeding ownership of the Mason Ironstone trade-name.

The majority of these former Mason moulds, engraved copper-plate designs and other working materials were apparently purchased by Francis Morley of High Street, Shelton. The name MORLEY was added below Mason's former standard crown mark on ware made to Mason's designs. Francis Morley was an experienced potter, first in partnership as Ridgway, Morley, Wear & Co. in the 1836-42 period and then as Ridgway & Morley around 1842-45. From 1845 to 1858 he traded under his own name, '& Co.' being added on most marks to cover his partner Samuel Asbury.

The next partnership, that between Francis Morley and George Leach Ashworth during the 1858-60 period, is most important as it explains how the firm of G.L. Ashworth & Bros. (Ltd.), retitled 'Mason's

Ironstone China Ltd.' in 1968, acquired the original Mason shapes and patterns. On 4 August 1860, the Morley & Ashworth partnership was dissolved, with G.L. Ashworth continuing the firm and finding himself in possession of valuable old Mason copper plates and trade-marks which were used to great advantage by Ashworths over a long period, from 1860 until 1968.

George L. Ashworth traded under his own name although he used the old Mason printed trade mark on his ironstone ware. He also produced a wide range of earthenware which was plainly marked with his own name or initials – 'A. Bros' or 'G.L.A. & Bros' – or with the Ashworth name. Some, but not all, 'Mason' printed marked Ashworth ware also bore Ashworth's name added under the old Mason printed device or the name Ashworth can be impressed into the body. The words

REAL
IRONSTONE
CHINA

also occur, even on otherwise unmarked Ashworth wares.

The Ashworth reissues of Mason's original shapes and decorative patterns are often difficult to distinguish from the earlier originals, especially now that some reissues are themselves antique. In general the later body is not quite as compact or heavy as the original, although it is whiter – a floury white rather than a creamy tint. The underglaze-blue parts of the design are normally lighter in tint than the dark blue original. Impressed numerals indicate a late nineteenth or twentieth century date and, in fact, they give the month number and the last two digits of the year in which the piece was manufactured, e.g. 7.06, but this practice has now been discontinued (see page 191).

For over a century George L. Ashworth & Bros. Ltd. sold, in both home and export markets, vast quantities of their Mason's-type ware decorated with traditional Oriental-style patterns. The tradition continues. Mason's number one pattern, the Grasshopper design – now called 'Regency' or 'Regency Ducks' – is still proudly displayed in most china shops and stores, and there can be few homes in the British Isles that cannot boast a specimen of 'Mason's Ironstone'. Indeed, two leading collectors of antique Mason owe their interest to the happy purchase of a modern Mason dinner service which took their fancy! In 1968, the firm of G.L. Ashworth & Bros. Ltd. took the new title 'Mason's Ironstone China', so the wheel has turned full circle (see page 279).

## MASON IRONSTONE MARKS

Given that Charles James Mason patented 'Mason's Patent Ironstone China' just after his father Miles Mason had retired from the firm, it follows that the impressed standard mark 'M. MASON' and the rare variation 'MILES MASON', do not apply to ironstone china. This mark occurs only on pre-1814 porcelain and perhaps on some rare earthenwares.

The new firm of G. & C. Mason or G. & C. Mason & Co., in advertising their newly introduced body and its brilliant trade-name or description, obviously sought to use a special mark to help sales and further publicise the novel wares.

It appears that the earliest form of mark comprised simply the words 'MASON'S PATENT IRONSTONE CHINA' or surprisingly 'PATENT IRONSTONE CHINA'. These descriptive marks usually took a circular impressed form but the words could also be arranged in a straight line, or more rarely in two lines. These impressed marks were seemingly introduced with the new body, and therefore can be dated from the middle of 1813. These indented or impressed name marks appear to have been discontinued after about 1830. Unfortunately they are often indistinct and certainly do not reproduce well from a photograph. The wording should read 'MASON'S PATENT IRONSTONE CHINA', impressed in circular form or in line.

A very rare early painted mark, 'P$^{t}$. Iron$^{e}$ China', has been reported in red on a pair of hexagonal covered vases. These vases were very well decorated with a typical Japan pattern. It is unusual but not unique to find a Mason mark that does not include the Mason surname. It must be borne in mind that not all Mason products bore a mark. It can also happen that an impressed name mark was placed in an unexpected place, inside a lid or on the exterior of a rim or edge and can be easily missed especially when the mark was glazed over or over-painted.

Undoubtedly the best-known Mason ironstone mark is the crowned-ribbon (or drapery) name mark which occurs in a printed form usually, but by no means always, printed in underglaze-blue. This mark can occur washed over with a semi-translucent enamel colour. The printed crowned Patent Ironstone mark was certainly in use by the spring of 1815, for in March of that year Mason advertised 'all china purporting to be ironstone is spurious and a mere imitation which is not printed at the back Patent Ironstone China under a crown' (see page 77).

Whilst the early marks just cited include in the description 'Patent' (in this rare case misspelt 'PAENT'), as would be expected, some rare examples, particularly of pattern 1, bear a blue printed name-mark that does not include this word and therefore lacks a little sales impact. This mark, as seen on two examples in Valerie Howard's 1995 exhibition, reads:

IRONSTONE CHINA
WARRANTED

The off-centre wording suggests that the word 'Patent' was originally engraved to the left of 'Ironstone'. It is now difficult to suggest why this rare and unusual uncrowned printed mark was employed. Was it engraved on the copper-plates of pattern 1 dinner services before the Patent had been granted? Perhaps such sets were made for other manufacturers who were not yet producing their own ironstone wares but wished to make a profit on selling Mason's wares, without letting the public know the real maker. Certainly it is rather unlike the Masons to shun publicity and to delete their own name and 'Patent' from their marks.

To return to the standard printed crowned Mason's Patent Ironstone China mark, one can see that this printed mark (which can occur with the impressed mark, or alone) takes many forms. Most standard Mason tableware designs were based on a printed outline which was subsequently coloured in. Each engraved copper-plate would have a mark added in the corner, the later paper impression being cut off and applied to the back of the plate or other article.

It therefore follows that the Mason factory at any one time was using not one version of the mark but as many as the various patterns then in production. The position was even more complicated because to decorate a dinner-service, for example, twenty or thirty engraved copper-plates were required for the different sizes or shapes of objects. Each copper-plate would have an individually engraved Mason's ironstone mark. Slight differences in engraving can therefore be disregarded and there is no point in illustrating such minor variations. It must, however, be remembered that this basic mark has been used up to the present time – for more than a hundred and eighty years!

There are, however, several major differences. It is thought that the earliest versions did not include the name 'MASON'S' over the crown. I am not sure that this is a wholly reliable guide to dating, but certainly the Mason name is missing from some examples. Some retailers also painted or blinded out the Mason's name and included their own name and address.

A more certain guideline relates to the form of the crown. A rather flat, angular version seems to have been used in the 1840s and was current at the period when new dinner-ware shapes were registered in April 1849. I here show such a version, with the diamond-shape registration device added below. It will also be noticed that the crown is depicted in simple elevation, without any three-dimensional effect. It must be understood that this angular mark of the late 1840s and early 1850s was not always used on later copies of the Mason mark, such as the Ashworth marks from 1862 onwards into the present century.

Apart from the late angular crown used on new[6] designs in the 1840s, there are two earlier basic variations. I believe the earliest of these was what we may term the jewelled curved crown, where representations of pearls or other jewels are included on the curved side-pieces. I show two of several variations of this basic type. Some examples, particularly on jugs, may have the pattern number printed below the main mark, for example 'no 311'.

The top part of the standard Mason device, the crown plus the word 'Mason's' above, can rarely occur on their own, especially on the so-called Bandana wares, of the 1840s.

Another basic form of Mason crown mark does not show the jewels but the outline of the crown appears to be made of ribbons. I show a single example of the ribbon crown device.

Another basic variation of the standard Mason's crown and drapery mark, has the revised wording 'Improved Ironstone China' within the drape. This may date from the early or mid-1840s but this version is quite scarce and never fully superseded the standard 'Patent Ironstone China' wording. Note the word 'Patent' was included in marks, long after the patent had officially expired – it was a description to be traded upon.

The Mason exhibits at the 1851 exhibition bore a special mark. The one reproduced here occurs, in a large size, on the splendid Chinese-style ironstone vase shown in Colour Plate 8 and Plate 32. This standard type of mark will also be found on Mason-type ironstone produced by subsequent firms, including Ashworths, and in modern times the present firm of Mason's Ironstone China Ltd. (see page 279).

In general terms the early Mason ironstones do not bear hand-written pattern numbers; the standard patterns were probably known by names, rather than by numbers. This factory practice seems to have continued possibly into the early 1830s. Mason pattern numbers in excess of a hundred probably post-date 1840. Numbers above a thousand, or having a letter prefix such as 'B' or 'C', relate to present century Ashworth reissues of Mason designs and shapes. Likewise, impressed month and year potting numerals denote a post-Mason period (see page 191. Printed marks from 1952 onwards have a point or dot added for each year. These new year marks normally appear in line under the main device.

The addition of the word 'England' to a standard apparently Mason mark denotes a date after 1891. The fuller description 'Made in England' indicates a period after about 1920. Design (or shape) registration numbers will also show a date of introduction after 1883 (see page 377). It must be remembered that these pointers only work in a positive manner – their inclusion will indicate a late date but such indicators do not always occur and their absence does not prove an early dating!

From about 1960 the word 'China' was correctly dropped from newly engraved marks – as the body is earthenware, not china. Obviously such additional wording, to the standard crowned mark, as 'Printed and Hand-Painted' or 'Dish Washer Proof' indicate a recent product although the pieces may well bear a version of an early nineteenth century Mason mark. Likewise, recent marks from the 1970s onwards include registered trade name and copyright signs in the form of an 'R' and an 'C' enclosed in a circle. I reproduce the mark found on a 'Mandalay' pattern dish purchased new in January 1996. This piece and other articles then on sale did not include impressed month and year numbers; they, or the standard designs, were designated by a name rather than a pattern number. Modern Trade Description Acts may also have prompted the description – 'printed and handpainted' – to correctly describe the hand-tinted printed outline design – the traditional technique used from the earliest days of Mason's ironstone.

These two marks are typical of the modern post-1973 Wedgwood Group marks. For a short note on the present Mason's Ironstone China Ltd. company see page 279.

The various crowned drapery marks previously discussed include only the single word Mason's (and sometimes even this was not used) but several other rather rarer marks incorporate the initials of the partnership, between G.M. and C.J. Mason. Marks incorporating the initials or names 'G.M. & C.J. Mason' or 'G. & C. Mason' should pre-date 1830. Several authorities suggest that this partnership ceased in 1826 but see page 88.

Christmas 1976
The second of a series of plates specially produced to celebrate Christmas.
MASON'S
PATENT IRONSTONE
MADE IN ENGLAND
Holyrood House
Holyrood, the ancient royal palace at Edinburgh, dates from the 15th century. Formerly the residence of many Scottish sovereigns, it has since become known as Holyrood House and is still used for State purposes.

PLATE 37. *A 1976 Mason's Ironstone Christmas plate decorated with a print of Holyrood Palace. The colourful border design, however, relates to Mason products made some hundred and fifty years earlier. The crowned mark is of traditional type but with 'Made in England' added. Diameter 10in. (25.4cm).*

Most usually the initials and name marks relate to the succeeding firm of C.J. Mason & Co, giving rise to several 'C.J.M. & Co.' initial marks.

The simple address mark

FENTON
STONE WORKS

occurs in various printed marks, normally enclosed within an octagonal double-lined frame, sometimes with a hand-painted pattern number added below. This mark, probably used from about 1825 onwards, usually occurs on utilitarian wares decorated with inexpensive Japan-style patterns.

It will have been noticed that the elaborate marks just reproduced include the description 'Granite China', rather than ironstone china. Another extremely rare impressed mark has been recorded by Mrs Jennifer Moody. This mark comprises the words 'Mason's Granite China', in circular form within a leaf or rather Star of the Garter surround. This impressed Granite China mark can occur with standard printed ironstone China marks.

Another 'C J M & Co.' initial mark is reproduced below. This example is found on printed dinner and other wares bearing various views in the 'British Lakes' series, the mark incorporating this general title and the name of each view – 'Loweswater', etc. This mark also incorporates the description 'NEW STONE CHINA' but in truth the body appears to be a standard earthenware, rather than heavy, compact, ironstone or stone china, still the near magical description new stone china is boldly featured to assist sales.

I would date this C.J. Mason & Co. mark to about 1840-4 but any C.J.M & Co. mark will post-date the November 1830 dissolution of the partnership between George and Charles James Mason and most will pre-date C.J. Mason's bankruptcy in February 1848, although he later had a brief come-back, *c*.1849-53 (see page 96).

Various marks also occur incorporating the wording 'Royal Terra Cotta Porcelain', sometimes with a Royal crown and lion device. These marks are difficult to explain as the body appears to be a standard ironstone. The wares bearing these marks appear to be of Mason's manufacture.

Some rare marks can occur, the following of which are believed to relate to Mason's. The finely engraved Royal Arms mark here shown includes the key wording 'Patent Iron Stone China Warranted' on the drapery or curtains, *c*.1820-30.

Much the same elaborate printed Royal Arms device also occurs on the superb 'Chimney Pieces', as shown in Plates 30, 115 and 116.

An impressed Royal Arms device also occurs, with the word 'Patent' in the central shield. This is a rare mark but it does occur in association with standard overglaze printed marks and can probably be dated *c*.1820-30.

Another very rare Royal Arms mark takes the form shown below. It is probably an early device, *c*.1815-1825.

Some special types of Mason products bear marks individual to that family. Apart from the chimney pieces mentioned above, the 'Patent Yacht Club' finger bowl (see page 84), the Unmerapoora Tea Extractor (Plate 118), Mason's Siamese Jardinier and the Patent Butter Frigefacter, bear special printed marks. Other special printed marks appear on Mason Bandana Ware of the late 1840s and early 1850s and on the rare Bronzed Metallic Wares made by C.J. Mason in 1850.

Over the years, I have been astounded to discover how high a proportion of apparent Mason Ironstone ware does not bear a factory mark. In some services, only a few pieces are marked. Consequently, when the services are divided, many individual pieces may be found unmarked. Many vases and other ornamental articles are also without marks, and yet other pieces are marked in unusual and easily overlooked positions such as inside covers and inside the top flange of vases. This is not to say that all unmarked ironstone-type wares were made by Mason – that would be very wide of the mark, for well over a hundred other British firms made this popular type of ceramic and many of their productions were also unmarked. However, study of the illustrations in this book should enable the reader to distinguish Mason shapes and designs from those of the many imitators.

Whilst writing of imitations I am prompted to cite the ever popular rather angular eight-sided Anglo-Oriental 'HYDRA' jugs that are understandably forever linked with Mason's Ironstone. A photograph of my

PLATE 38. *A set of five standard shape Mason's ironstone Hydra jugs. Decorated in a colourful, yet broadly painted 'Japan' pattern design. 3½ to 7½in. (8.89cm to 19.05cm) high (much larger examples exist). Printed crowned Mason marks. c.1830-50. Messrs Woolley & Wallis.*

Grandfather's first antique shop in Worthing in about 1900 shows such a jug prominently displayed in the window.

A fellow dealer of the same period, P.W. Phillips of Hitchin, issued a 'Catalogue of old china offered for sale at The Manor House, Hitchin' (privately published, 1901). This included a good array of a typical Edwardian dealer's stock of ceramics, including 'Mediaeval and Early English Pottery', 'English Delft', 'Whieldon Ware', 'Wedgwood', 'School of Wedgwood' plus Bow, Chelsea, Derby, Swansea and Worcester porcelains as well as porcelains from the major Continental factories. Also included we find:

> A complete set of seven jugs, graduated in height from 3 ins up to 10 ins high, with green lizard-handles, and rich colouring, marked Mason's Patent Ironstone China. £5 - 5 - 0.

Mr Phillips was also pleased to offer a single six-inch Mason jug for a mere 14/6d (70p). In my period in the trade from the late 1940s into the 1990s I have purchased and sold hundreds of such Mason jugs. Today in retirement we have two on the kitchen dresser, examples that are brought into use for daffodils or other flowers. The number produced by Mason over the years from 1813 is incalculable – they are still in production nearly two hundred years later. They have probably never been out of production. At the end of the twentieth century close copies of these Mason, Oriental-inspired jugs are being made in the East and shipped to Europe. We have gone full circle!

After more than fifty years' study and research I have no idea if Charles Mason directly copied the Mason's Jug from a Chinese or even Japanese original. I think not as I have never seen an oriental example. I think that like most Mason pieces – ornamental vases and the like – the design was more English than oriental but that the basic shape was intended to display a Chinese origin. They were nineteenth century Chinoiserie. The strange jugs with their dragon-like handles were, like most of the contemporary Mason shapes, obviously commercially successful. Success, of course, brings with it the problem of imitation.

Several other manufacturers copied this popular basic form. The major firms include Davenport (Plate 178) and Spode. Spode and Chamberlain-Worcester produced this pattern in porcelain. Several smaller firms also emulated the Mason's ironstone jugs (Plate 218), simply because they were in demand. For the same reason Mason's successors have continued the tradition and very many jugs found today would have been produced in the Ashworth period (see Plate 148). These post-1860 examples are in a softer body than the dense, heavy, early ironstone examples, some of which will bear impressed Mason name-marks.

The Mason jugs may not have been featured in the 1818 auction. The June 1822 sale, advertised as Mason's London stock, included several lots, various catalogued as, for example:

| | | |
|---|---|---|
| Four antique shape jugs | (Reserve price | 14/-) |
| Five jugs from the antique | ( ditto | 16/-) |
| Six jugs, pheasant and flowers from the antique | (pattern) ( ditto | 14/-) |
| Three jugs from the antique, fancy pattern | ( ditto | 30/-) |
| Four antique form jugs, grasshopper pattern | ( ditto | 11/-) |
| Six jugs, gold jar (pattern) and four ditto grasshopper (pattern) | ( ditto | 26/-) |
| Ten jugs from the antique | ( ditto | 23/-) |

These Mason 'Antique' shape jugs can be found in a variety of sizes, from two or three inches (5cm) to giant examples well over a foot (30cm) in height. From at least the mid-1820s they were available in sets in graduating sizes, although single jugs were always available. In the 1851 Exhibition catalogue the Mason 'antique' shape jugs were featured as being of the 'original shape' – 'Jugs of old India, Japanese and gold pattern; with Oriental figures and gold ornaments'. In the eighteenth and nineteenth century the description India was often used when Chinese was meant, a practice that possibly arose from the naming of the East India Company trading to China.

Whilst most examples found today were painted with colourful but broadly painted Japan patterns, practically every repetitive pattern ever made by Mason and his successor were applied to these traditional jugs. The dragon-like handles are often enhanced with an iron-type lustre effect. These Japan patterns vary greatly in quality, and some are very slap dash! With the standard Japan patterns the underglaze blue portions may well have been printed or the main aspects set by the use of a pounced outline. They were mass-produced standard objects with a variety of uses. Note the auction sale description did not include any restricting name, they were not called beer or cider jugs. Many in later years at least were used purely for decoration.

These remarks on the long period of popularity, the variety of sizes and available patterns, apply equally to many traditional Mason ironstone articles. The jugs sold originally for a few shillings have given succeeding generations much visual pleasure and use. They have a timeless quality.

## MASON FACTORIES AND SUBSEQUENT OWNERS

Italics are used to indicate that a factory owner (or owners) was a member of the Mason family

### VICTORIA POTTERY

### LANE DELPH, FENTON

| | |
|---|---|
| c.1800 | *Miles Mason* & George Wolfe |
| c.1800-06 | *Mason & Co.* |
| c.1806-43 | Samuel Ginder & Co. |
| c.1844-45 | Samuel & Henry Ginder |
| c.1847-57 | James Floyd |
| c.1860 | Wathen & Hudden |
| c.1862-64 | Wathen & Lichfield |
| c.1864-69 | James Bateman Wathen |
| c.1870-1948 | James Reeves |

### MINERVA WORKS LANE DELPH, FENTON

| | |
|---|---|
| c.1800-05 | John Lucock |
| c.1806-16 | *Miles Mason* |
| c.1818-26 | Felix Pratt & Co. |
| c.1826-34 | Pratt, Hassall & Gerrard |
| c.1834-47 | Green & Richards |
| c.1848-59 | Thomas Green (died 1859) |
| c.1860-75 | Mary Green & Co. |
| c.1876-90 | T.A. & S. Green |
| c.1891 to recent years | Crown Staffordshire Porcelain Co. Ltd. |

### SAMPSON BAGNALL' S WORKS at angle of the road below MINERVA WORKS

| | |
|---|---|
| c.1811-22 | *William Mason* (works probably run by George and Charles Mason while William was dealing in china, see page 82) |
| c.1822-25 | *Miles Mason* (executors of) |
| c.1825-26 | *George & Charles Mason* |
| c.1827 | Void (or empty according to rate records; |

works may have been dismantled and combined with the Fenton Stone Works).

FENTON STONE WORKS
PATENT IRONSTONE MANUFACTORY
HIGH STREET
LANE DELPH, FENTON

| | |
|---|---|
| c.1780-1805 | Sampson Bagnall |
| c.1805-15 | Josiah Spode |
| c.1815-29 | *George & Charles Mason* |
| c.1829-39 | *Charles James Mason* |
| c.1841-43 | *Mason & Faraday* (or C.J. Mason & Co.) |
| c.1845-48 | *Charles James Mason* (bankrupt February 1848) |
| c.1849-52 | Samuel Boyle (& Son) |
| c.1853-60 | E. Challinor & Co. |
| c.1862-91 | E. & C. Challinor |
| c.1891-96 | C. Challinor & Co. |
| c.1897-1932 | William Baker & Co. (Ltd.) |

DAISY BANK WORKS
LONGTON

| | |
|---|---|
| c.1797-1802 | Samuel Hughes |
| c.1803-11 | Peter & Thomas Hughes |
| c.1812 | Drury & Co. |
| c.1815-17 | John Drury (or Drury & Co.) |
| c.1818-30 | Thomas Drury & Son |
| c.1831-37 | Ray & Tideswell |
| c.1838-40 | Richard Tideswell |
| c.1851-53 | *Charles James Mason* |
| c.1853-68 | Hulse, Nixon & Adderley |
| c.1869-73 | Hulse and Adderley |
| c.1876-85 | William Alsager Adderley |
| c.1886-1905 | William Alsager Adderley & Co. |
| c.1906-47 | Adderley's Ltd. |

## CHECKLIST OF MASON-RELATED DISSOLUTION OF PARTNERSHIP NOTICES

Although details of new partnerships did not have to be published it was necessary or extremely prudent for retiring partners or ceasing partnerships to publish the basic facts as *A Dissolution of Partnership Notice*. Such notices which were normally drawn up by a solicitor or lawyer to a traditional pattern should have been published in local newspapers. As these were not necessarily read by all creditors (or debtors), it was usual to publish such notices in the official *London Gazette*. This was deemed sufficient public notice of the change and permitted creditors to identify the continuing partners and Company. It also cleared the responsibilities of the retiring partner or partners. The *London Gazette* dates back to 1665-6 and an 1712 Act required debtors, etc., to publish details in that twice weekly newspaper.

I have checked issues from the mid-1750s, extracting those Dissolution of Partnership notices which relate to potters. The following few relate to Miles Mason or his sons.

*London Gazette*. 13990. March 7 1797.
*LIMPUS & MASON*.

February 28th 1797.

Whereas the partnership carried on between James Green and Charles Limpus of Upper Thames Street [London], Potters and Glasssellers was by mutual consent dissolved on the 31st day of December last and the Business has since that time been carried on by the said James Green on his own account and whereas the said James Green hath assigned to the said Charles Limpus and Miles Mason all the said Partnership Debts and effects and also the Debts due to the said James Green, all Persons indebted to the said partnership and also to the said James Green on account of the said Business are required to pay the said Debt to Messrs Limpus & Mason who are intitled to receive the same, and all Debts owing by the Partnership and by the said James Green, on account of the said business will be discharged by Messrs Limpus & Mason.

Ja. Green, Charles Limpus, Miles Mason.

*London Gazette*. 15267. June 14th 1800.
*THOMAS WOLFE & CO*.
Notice is hereby given that the Partnership heretofore subsisting between Thomas Wolfe, Miles Mason and John Luckcock and established at Islington, Liverpool in the County of Lancaster in the China Manufactory under the firm of Thomas Wolfe & Co, is this Day dissolved by mutual consent.

Witness the Parties hands this 7th Day of June 1800.

Thomas Wolfe, Miles Mason, J. Luckcock.

*London Gazette*. 15274. July 8th 1800.
*MASON & WOLFE*.
Whereas the Partnership between us Miles Mason of Fenchurch Street, in the City of London, China-merchant and George Wolfe of Fenton Culvet, otherwise Lane Delph in the Parish of Stoke-upon-Trent in the County of Staffordshire, trading under the Firm of Mason & Wolfe of Lane Delph, as manufacturers of Earthenware, is this day

dissolved by mutual consent and all Debts due to the concern are to be paid into the Hands of the said Miles Mason, who will discharge every just demand against the said Co-partnership. As witness our Hands this 5th Day of July 1800.

Miles Mason, George Wolfe.

*London Gazette*. 15393. September 1st 1801.
*LIMPUS & MASON.*

London July 31st 1801.

The Partnership between Charles Limpus and Miles Mason of Upper Thames Street, Wholesale Potters and Glass Warehousemen was mutually dissolved the 17th Day of February last past. All Debts due and owing to the said estate will be received and paid by the said Miles Mason at the warehouse.

Charles Limpus. Miles Mason.

*London Gazette*. 15435. December 12th 1801.
*MILES MASON & CO.*

London. Dec 12th 1801.

The Partnership between Miles Mason and Robert Elliot of Fenchurch Street, London, Chinaman and Glass Seller under the Firm of Miles Mason & Co. was dissolved by mutual consent on the 1st Day of December instant.
All Debts due to the said Partnership to be paid to the said Robert Elliot, who will discharge all demands on the same and carry on the Business for the future on his own account.

Miles Mason, Robert Elliot.

*London Gazette*. 18938. May 22nd 1832.
*G & C MASON (& Co.) ?*
Notice is hereby given that the Co-partnership between us the undersigned George Miles Mason, Charles James Mason and Samuel Bayliss Faraday as China and Earthenware manufacturers at Lane Delph in the Parish Stoke-upon-Trent was dissolved by mutual consent on the 11th day of November instant, so far as regards the said George Miles Mason. As witness our hands this 22nd day of November 1830.

George Miles Mason. Chas James Mason.
Samuel Bayliss Faraday.

N.B. This notice is dated November 1830 rightly or wrongly, although it was not published until the *London Gazette* of 22 May 1832.

No further Mason-related Dissolution of Partnership notices were published in the *London Gazette*.

PLATE 39. *An unusual and fine quality dessert plate impressed marked 'Mason's Patent Ironstone China' and with moulded floral relief work in the porcelain manner. Diameter 9½in. (24.13cm). c.1815-25. R.G. Austin.*

CHAPTER IV

# The 1818 and 1822 London Auction Sales

Two of the most important documents relating to the products of Mason's Patent Ironstone China are undoubtedly the catalogues of auction sales held in London by leading auctioneers in December 1818 and in June 1822, that is some five and nine years after the ironstone body was first introduced.

The first sale of December 1818 conducted by Mr Christie importantly comprised articles consigned direct from the manufacturers in Staffordshire, not the left-over stock of a retiring retailer. The selection therefore may be regarded as a fair sampling of the Mason factory's products at that period and is therefore of the greatest interest.

The second held by Mr Phillips is equally interesting in that it reputedly comprised the stock of Mason's London showroom at 11 Albemarle Street and was held in those premises.

From the manufacturer's point of view, however, these sales were not a great success, for very many of the lots did not reach the reserve and were 'bought in'. Indeed, the totals for the first twelve days of the 1822 sale of the London stock auctioned by Mr Phillips show the gross amount sold totalled only £1,093.18s.6d., whilst the unsold lots totalled £3,762.12s.0d. Some of the unsold lots were no doubt included in other Mason auction sales which were later held in various other cities and towns (see pages 84-88).

Some failed lots might well have been sold at a reduced price to various retailers or perhaps found their way to foreign markets. But even so they show what was being produced and stocked by Messrs Mason.

It must be stated that Mason was by no means the first potter or porcelain manufacturer to have offered large selections of their current productions at auction.

PLATE 40. *A Mason's ironstone tureen and cover of conventional form copied from late eighteenth century Chinese export-market shapes. Printed outline design, coloured in by hand. 13in. (33.02cm) high. c.1813-20. Messrs Woolley & Wallis.*

PLATE 41. *A standard underglaze-blue printed Mason's Patent Ironstone China soup plate, in form and pattern closely following standard Chinese export-market porcelains. This basic blue printed pattern remained in production for well over a hundred years. It was perhaps the 'Blue Chinese landscape' dinner service included in the 1818 sale catalogue, Diameter 9½in. (24.13cm). c.1813-25.*

PLATE 42. *A rare blue printed Chinese export-market-style landscape design used on Mason's ironstone dinner services, in this case added to a relief-moulded plate shape with gilt edging – an unusual feature. Impressed 'Mason's Patent Ironstone China' mark. Diameter 9½in. (24.13cm). c.1820-30.*

In the eighteenth century the Chelsea, Derby, Bristol and Worcester factories marketed at least some of their products in this manner.

In reproducing later in this chapter the meat of Mr Christie's 1818 sale catalogue (by kind permission of the present Directors), I have retained the original lot numbers and the reserve prices given in the auctioneer's master copy, as well as the original spelling. I have,

PLATE 43 *A thickly potted Mason's ironstone salad bowl from a dinner service. One of several willow pattern-style designs which closely emulated the popular but earlier importations from China. Blue printed crowned mark. c.1825-35.*

however, deleted the several duplicated lots or articles. These included, for example, many lots of several jugs or mugs. I have also deleted from this listing various tea and breakfast services as these were seemingly of bone china, rather than ironstone.

Confining first our attention to the 1818 sale, we can clearly see what progress the Mason firm had made in five years. Before the 1813 patent for the new ironstone body they, or rather Miles Mason, produced mainly porcelains, at first of a compact type of hybrid hard-paste porcelain and later a soft-bodied bone china mix.[1] Such porcelains were in the main useful table wares such as tea, and dessert services, with a relatively few large dinner sets. The ornamental wares were very restricted being mainly confined to a few simple vase forms, of a relatively small size.

The introduction of the ironstone body enabled very much larger objects to be produced; although they may be thickly potted and therefore heavy, this was not judged a fault. Indeed it underlined the strength and durability of the pieces which, from the manufacturers' point of view, were made from a less costly material than the porcelain mix.

Not all the new pieces were large, however, and some were extremely small, even miniature or 'toy' objects, made as novelties to grace a cabinet. These small pieces, which opened the 1818 sale, serve to show how versatile was the early ironstone china. It might not possess the delicacy of china, but it could be neatly turned or moulded. It is also obvious that great care was taken in producing and decorating the early ironstone pieces. The large Mason pottery really concentrated on the new Patent Ironstone China and, having established the market, it strove to build upon its firm base, determined not to allow others to steal the market. The exception was its continued production of tea-services in the more delicate bone china, although some ironstone sets were certainly produced.

Generally speaking the inspiration was the traditional Chinese export-market lines, shapes and patterns that dated back to the later part of the previous century, c.1770-1790 – rich, so-called Japan patterns (which are also termed 'Imari'), with their broad areas of underglaze-blue with overglaze enamels of red or green. Some examples were also enriched with gilding, emulating not only Oriental examples but also various makes of English porcelain. They were cheap and cheerful and therefore sold well.

Now the firm's products are probably more associated with Ironstone than with the earlier porcelain prototypes. Typical Mason's 'Japan' patterns are shown in Plates 14-16, 26, 29, 47-50, 60-62, 69-72, 75, 83, 92-93, 100-102, 195-109.

Also prominently featured in the 1818 auction were conventional Chinese export-market style designs, the blue-printed Oriental landscape designs popular over a very long period (see Colour Plate 11 or Plate 41). These blue printed dinner services had previously been produced in Miles Mason's more costly porcelain. Now in ironstone, tureens and large dishes were easier

PLATE 44. *An impressed marked Mason's Patent Ironstone ornate, neatly potted, teapot. Well painted, perhaps in the Dresden style. 5¼in. (13.33cm) high. c.1815-20. Messrs Sotheby's.*

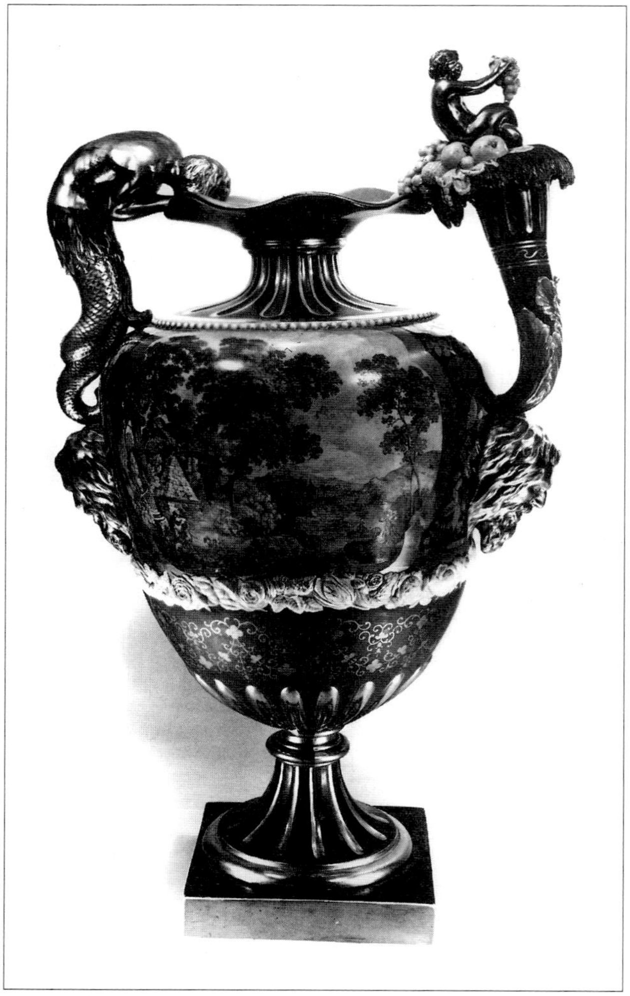

PLATE 45. *A superb quality impressed marked Mason's Patent Ironstone ewer in the Continental style showing the high standard reached within ten years of the introduction of this ironstone body. 27in. (68.58cm) high. c.1820. Messrs Sotheby's.*

PLATE 46. *A superb quality, deep blue 'mazarine' ground Mason's ironstone large 'hall jar' with rich gilding. 21in. (53.34cm) high. c.1820. Messrs Sotheby's.*

to produce and the price for such sets was drastically reduced. Chinese figure-subject patterns such as 'Mogul' were in most cases enamelled over a printed outline design (see page 78). Several lots, or rather the patterns, are described as 'Indian'. As mentioned before, such pieces were, I believe, of Chinese inspiration, the two descriptions Chinese and Indian being interchangeable in the eighteenth and nineteenth centuries – as with the *East India* Company itself or the 'East Indiamen' vessels which brought the porcelains home from China.

It would be a mistake, however, to regard all early Mason patterns, or indeed forms, to be based on Oriental prototypes. We find listed various European-style designs which included objects described as 'Dresden': 'Two Dresden pattern jars', 'Two tall candlesticks, Dresden pattern' or 'Two Dresden cans and stands'. It is now difficult to say what was meant by Dresden-style designs. If added painted patterns were in mind these would probably have been floral patterns, perhaps as Plate 44.

Perhaps, the most ornate and superb production included in the 1818 London sale, was lot 39:

> One Italian formed jar or vase, biscuit [unglazed] of elegant workmanship.

Other large and ornate items of the type we now readily associate with Mason's Ironstone were the hall vases:

> Lot 200. One costly Hall jar, elegant Chinese design.
> Lot 256. One fine hexagonal Hall jar and cover, enamelled in compartments and sumptously gilt.

Various large bowls were also included: 'One very large

PLATE 47. *An oval dinner service tureen, cover and stand of unusual form, impressed marked Mason's Patent Ironstone and decorated with a superior quality 'Japan' pattern of the type described as 'rich Japan'. 12½in. (31.75cm) high. c.1820-25.*

dolphin-headed bowl richly embellished in colours and gold'. Many objects, large and small were described as 'mazarine'. That is they had a rich, glossy, deep-blue ground, a treatment associated with so many pre-1830 pieces. Examples auctioned in 1818 include:

233. Two beakers and covers, rich in mazarine, enamel and gold.

257. Two Pan's head ornaments, landscapes in compartments of mazarine and gold.

272 One richly executed jar, Chinese subjects, on mazarine ground (Plate 46).

The most important aspect of this first London auction sale was surely the high proportion of ornate and mainly decorative articles made in ironstone within some five years of its introduction. Initially the idea

PLATE 48. *A standard form impressed Royal Arms marked Mason's Ironstone dinner service tureen. Decorated with a middle-range design. Such complete sets of 142 pieces were selling for prices in the mid-£20s. 13½in. (34.29cm) long. c.1820.*

must have been to produce Oriental-style durable dinner wares but soon the commercial success of the body dictated that Mason at least produced high quality, richly decorated fancy articles in the new porcelain-like ironstone body.

The June 1822 sale was larger than the 1818 auction. This second assortment was auctioned by Mr Phillips of New Bond Street, but at the Mason shop or warehouse at 11 Albemarle Street, London W.1. It was claimed that this sale comprised the 'entire assemblage' of the stock. This was probably the case for Masons were soon to vacate the premises. The impression is also given that the sale was held because of the recent death[2] of 'the late Mr Mason', indeed it was stated in the catalogue of the remaining portion that it was held 'by order of the executors, without reserve'. This last claim is contradicted by the auctioneer's own marked catalogue, which included reserve prices.

The reason for the sale by auction of the London stock was probably because the executors needed funds to pay off bank, or other, loans granted to Miles Mason or to fulfil wishes contained in Miles Mason's will. Mason or his sons owned stock but seemingly not cash. Indeed, they were to be continually plagued by a shortage of ready funds – an all too familiar story in the Potteries.

The June 1822 auction sale took place over nine days and comprised very nearly twelve hundred lots. In addition there was a further three-day sale held by Mr Phillips on Thursday, Friday and Saturday 20-22 June 1822, comprising 389 more lots. The catalogue described this selection as 'The remainder of the stock of china of the late Mr Mason, Patentee and Manufacturer of the Iron Stone China' and finished the main summary with 'A great variety of Cabinet Ornaments, of the most Tasteful and elegant forms. The extent, variety and great value of this stock afford the most advantageous opportunity to the public to provide themselves with porcelane of every class and of peculiar strength, for which the Iron Stone China has long been distinguished'.

Mr Phillips held yet another sale on the Mason premises on 28-29 June 1822, described as 'The Last Part of the Stock of the late Mr Mason...' This included a further[3] 257 lots, giving a total of 1836 lots for the June 1822 sale of Mason's London stock. Many of the lots included many items, the dinner services were listed as containing 87 or 142 pieces. Dessert services comprised 43 pieces and jugs or mugs were offered in various numbers up to twelve per lot. In total the stock of Mason's goods held at the Albemarle Street premises must have numbered tens of thousands of pieces.

In printing the original descriptions from the 1818 and 1822 catalogues I have included the original reserve prices. These were most probably fixed by Mason's staff and will reflect to some degree the original wholesale price. These reserve prices also help us to gauge the relative quality or degree of decoration on the various items, for the reserves will have been set

PLATE 49. *A standard form, impressed marked Mason's ironstone dinner service tureen, rather broadly painted in a manner that could be described as 'common Japan'. Such a complete service was reserved at £14 in the 1822 sale of stock. 12½in. (31.75cm) long. c.1820.*

PLATE 50. *A rare Mason's Ironstone dejeune tray for a two-person tea service with impressed Royal Arms mark, . Note the neatly potted moulded basketwork border. 16¾in. x 13¼in. (33.65cm). c.1820.*

by a single person having knowledge of the various patterns, the factory cost and the market, or Mason's shop price, bearing in mind the similar patterns produced by rival firms.

Taking as a simple example the 142-piece Mason Ironstone dinner services included in the first day's sale, Tuesday 4 June 1822, we find the lowest priced services were the printed designs, some at least which would have been coloured up by hand. The hand-painted richly decorated sets were some three times the price of the common standard printed patterns. The design with the lowest reserve was 'Dragon' at nine guineas, followed by 'Blue birds & flowers' and 'Tourney sprigs' at eleven guineas. We then jump to presumably hand-painted 'Dresden sprig' floral groups at twenty-five guineas and to a gilt-and-flower painted set at thirty guineas. Top reserve of the day was thirty-five pounds for a dinner service described as 'rich japan pattern, sumptuously gilt'. This was obviously a London-market set and one doubts if all Japan pattern services were so highly priced, or so highly finished.

In fact the 142-piece dinner services, decorated with the colourful Japan patterns, bore various reserve prices, obviously depending on the quality of the decoration. For example Lot 348, sold on 6 June 1822, was a dinner service ornamented in 'gilt japan' reserved at £26 (against £35 for the earlier 'rich japan' pattern) but the next lot, simply described as 'common japan', was reserved at a mere £14, just over half the price of the gilt-enriched set.

The mid-1822 sale of the contents of Mason's London showroom included several types of ware that did not appear in the 1818 sale. Such new lines included toilet or chamber services:

Lot 2 Two blue and white pheasant [pattern] toilet suites, 16 pieces.

Lot 151 Two Chamber sets, japan, with [glass?] caraft and tumblers.

PLATE 51. *Impressed marked Mason's ironstone, small size tea wares probably from a dejeune or early morning teaset. Teapot 5¼in. (13.33cm) high. c.1820. Messrs Phillips.*

Lot 278 Two new form blue chamber sets with carafts and tumblers.

By 1822 some at least of the dinner services were being produced with hexagonal shape tureens:

Lot 69. A dinner service, hexagonal shape, blue birds and flowers, 142 pieces.

This new, higher, form of tureen would be similar to that illustrated in Plates 19 and 25.

Other newly listed articles include 'dejeunes', that is small-scale two-party tea services on a matching tray (Plate 50). One also finds 'Stilton cheese stands and covers' – this 1822 reference to a covered cheese dish was to a very early one. In a few cases we cannot now be sure if the described articles were made in ironstone or in bone china. For example, the sectional supper services included as lot 36, 'A supper service, centre and 4 quadrants and covers, japanned flowers, gilt (Reserve price £4), could have been either but these useful sets were certainly made in the ironstone body (see Plate 52).

While the majority of pieces sold from the London

PLATE 52. *A rare complete Mason's ironstone 'supper service' decorated in underglaze-blue with the 'blue birds and flowers' design. Printed crowned name mark. Diameter of set 22in. (55.88cm). c.1822. Mason's Works Collection.*

PLATE 53. *A rare good quality impressed marked Mason's ironstone plate with green border and owner's crest to centre. Plates with arms and crests were included in the 1822 sale. Diameter 9in. (22.86cm). c.1820.*

PLATE 54. *A fine quality Mason's ironstone 'Italian formed vase superbly gilt and burnished', almost certainly painted by Samuel Bourne. Such magnificent pieces were featured in the 1822 sale of London stock. 28in. (71.12cm) high. c.1820-25. Mason's Works Collection.*

showroom in 1822 were undoubtedly made of ironstone, the stock-clearing auction sales certainly included other wares such as porous wine-coolers and high-fired stoneware relief-moulded jugs and mugs:

| | |
|---|---|
| Six hunting jugs and 5 mugs | 24/- |
| Five stone jugs and 6 mugs | 25/- |

The last sale, described as containing the 'remainder of the stock', also included various earthenwares, often printed in underglaze blue in the traditional Staffordshire style. These earthenwares may have been truly remainder items, left about unsold in the showrooms for some years. But there is still the possibility that the Masons continued to produce such low-priced earthenwares at the period well after the introduction of the new ironstone china in 1813. Sample earthenwares that were in the 1822 sale included:

PLATE 55. *Part of a 'costly dessert service, exquisitely painted in select views by S. Bourne, enriched with burnished gold' – to quote from the 1822 sale catalogue. This set is of porcelain quality. See Colour Plate 5. Diameter of plates 9in. (22.86cm). c.1820. Messrs Phillips.*

| | |
|---|---|
| 50 | A dinner set, blue and white earthenware 142 pieces. 6 guineas. |
| 387 | Twenty-four tea-cups and saucers, dragon, (pattern), earthenware. 8/-. |
| 389 | Twelve jugs, blue earthenware, 121/. |

Various other lots, included towards the end of the series of sales, were described as 'Blue ironstone'. Such articles may well have been slightly tinted, so that the whole body appeared to be light-blue, rather than white. Samples include:

| | |
|---|---|
| 112 | Two punch bowls, blue ironstone. 15/-. |
| 115 | Two punch and 2 pudding bowls, blue ironstone. 11/-. |

Such objects were I believe otherwise undecorated, as would have been the dessert service listed on 29 June 1822, as lot 171:

A white ironstone dessert set, 43 pieces. 40/-.

The stock of the London showroom included ironstone (or perhaps porcelain) plates variously painted with armorial bearings. These plates were perhaps samples of the types of personalized designs that could be produced in complete services in the manner of the well-known Chinese export-market armorial decorated porcelains. These sample plates were included as lot 737, sold on 5 June 1822:

Twelve plates, richly painted, with various arms and crests.

Unfortunately, I must emphasize that armorial Mason's china is extremely rare. Most wares were of stock patterns and not made to an individual order.

The Mason showroom in London's Albemarle Street during the 1820-22 period must have been a feast of

PLATE 56. *These superb quality impressed marked Mason's ironstone vases have rich gilding. The landscapes are almost certainly painted by Samuel Bourne, 11½in. and 7¾in. (29.21cm and 19.68cm) high. Messrs Sotheby's.*

colour and contained large-size objects, the like of which were not produced by any other British manufacturer. Who could rival, for example, lot 55 sold on 4 June 1822, with a reserve of nine guineas:

> A noble lofty jar and cover, surmounted with griffins and blue ground, beautifully enamelled in birds and flowers.

The richness of the decoration on Mason's ironstone china by 1833 is best typified by the various lots catalogued as being painted by Samuel Bourne:

329. A very beautiful Italian formed vase, painted by S. Bourne, superbly gilt and burnished. 35 guineas.
837. A costly dessert service, exquisitely painted in select views, by S. Bourne, enriched with burnished gold. 35 guineas
866. A noble vase, formed from the antique, beautifully painted in landscapes and figures, in Bourne and sumptuously gilt. 20 guineas.
1016. A handsome Neapolitan vase, formed from the antique, beautifully painted in landscapes, enriched with burnished gold, by S. Bourne. 15 guineas.

Such rich goods may well have been largely produced for the London market and were undoubtedly outnumbered by the more standard but still colourful traditional Oriental-style designs, which were obviously much less expensive than the articles painted by Samuel Bourne. This artist's work is featured in my Colour Plates 5, 7 and 13 and Plates 17, 27, 28, 54-56, but his painting on Mason ironstone was not signed – as this practice was not permitted during this period. As stated on page 74, Samuel Bourne was born in about 1789 and was apprenticed to Enoch Wood. He then from approximately 1818 (or earlier) worked for Mason before moving on to Minton where he acted as Art Director. His best-known work is found on important and costly Mason ironstone wares of the approximate period 1818 into perhaps the early 1830s.

I now quote the introduction to Mr Christie's first sale of Mason's goods offered in December 1818.

A
CATALOGUE
OF
A MOST VALUABLE AND EXTENSIVE STOCK
OF
ELEGANT AND USEFUL
CHINA
SUITED FOR DOMESTIC PURPOSES
OF ENGLISH MANUFACTURE

Recently consigned from the Manufactory for actual sale, and highly deserving the attention of Persons of Fashion and Private Families.

It comprises
a large assortment of complete Table and Dessert services, composed of strong and serviceable material, painted in imitation of the rich Japan and other Oriental Patterns; Breakfast, Tea and Coffee equipages, ornamental Dejeunes and Vases for flowers and essence, including about Twelve of noble size, suited to fill niches or Recesses in Drawing Rooms, superbly ornamented.

Which will be sold by Auction
BY MR. CHRISTIE
at his Great Room, Pall Mall,
on Tuesday, December 15th, 1818
and two following Days, at one o'clock
FIRST DAY'S SALE
TUESDAY, DECEMBER 15th, 1818
punctually at one o'clock

1 Two taper candlesticks, coloured and gilt, and 2 cabinet pitchers
2 One toy ewer, bason jug, and mug, and 2 tall taper candlesticks, roses and gilt
3 Two toy cups and saucers, japanned and gilt
4 Two Dresden pattern jars, 2 square essence burners; and 2 toy jars
5 One table service, India pheasant pattern, viz. 18 dishes in sizes, 2 soup tureens, covers and stands, 4 sauce ditto, 4 square vegetable dishes, 1 sallad ditto, 1 fish ditto, 72 table plates, 24 ditto soup and 24 pie ditto
6 Two square Chinese jars and covers. £1.3.0.
7 One coffee pot, antique pattern and shape
8 Two hexagonal antique beakers
9 Two handsome tulip cups and saucers, and 2 match pots
10 Two tall jars and covers, richly ornamental and gilt
11 Two elegant mitre shaped jars and covers, sumptuously gilt
12 One desert service, Mogul pattern, viz. 1 centre piece, 12 fruit dishes, 2 cream tureens and stands, and 24 plates. £5.18.0.
14 One toy ewer, bason, jug and mug for a cabinet
15 Two chimneypiece jars. 16/-
16 One table service, exact quantity as Lot 5, Chinese landscape pattern
17 Two cabinet cups and saucers, a toy ewer, bason, jug and mug
18 One Dejeune service, antique forms and ornamented. £3.8.0.
19 One desert service, old Japan pattern, blue, red, and gold, exact quantity as Lot 12
20 Two costly beakers, à la Chinoise
21 Two jars and covers, Chinese forms, richly enamelled and gilt
22 One table service, exact quantity as Lot 5, blue and gold border
23 One handsome sideboard jar, dragon handles and sumptuously gilt
24 Two rose and apple jars and covers, octagonal bronze and gold
25 Two square caddies
26 Two ornamental groups of flowers and gold

PLATE 57. *A marked Mason's ironstone dinner service tureen, probably the 'India pheasant pattern' as included in the 1818 auction sale. The description 'India' usually meant Chinese! 13½in. (34.29cm) long. c.1818.*

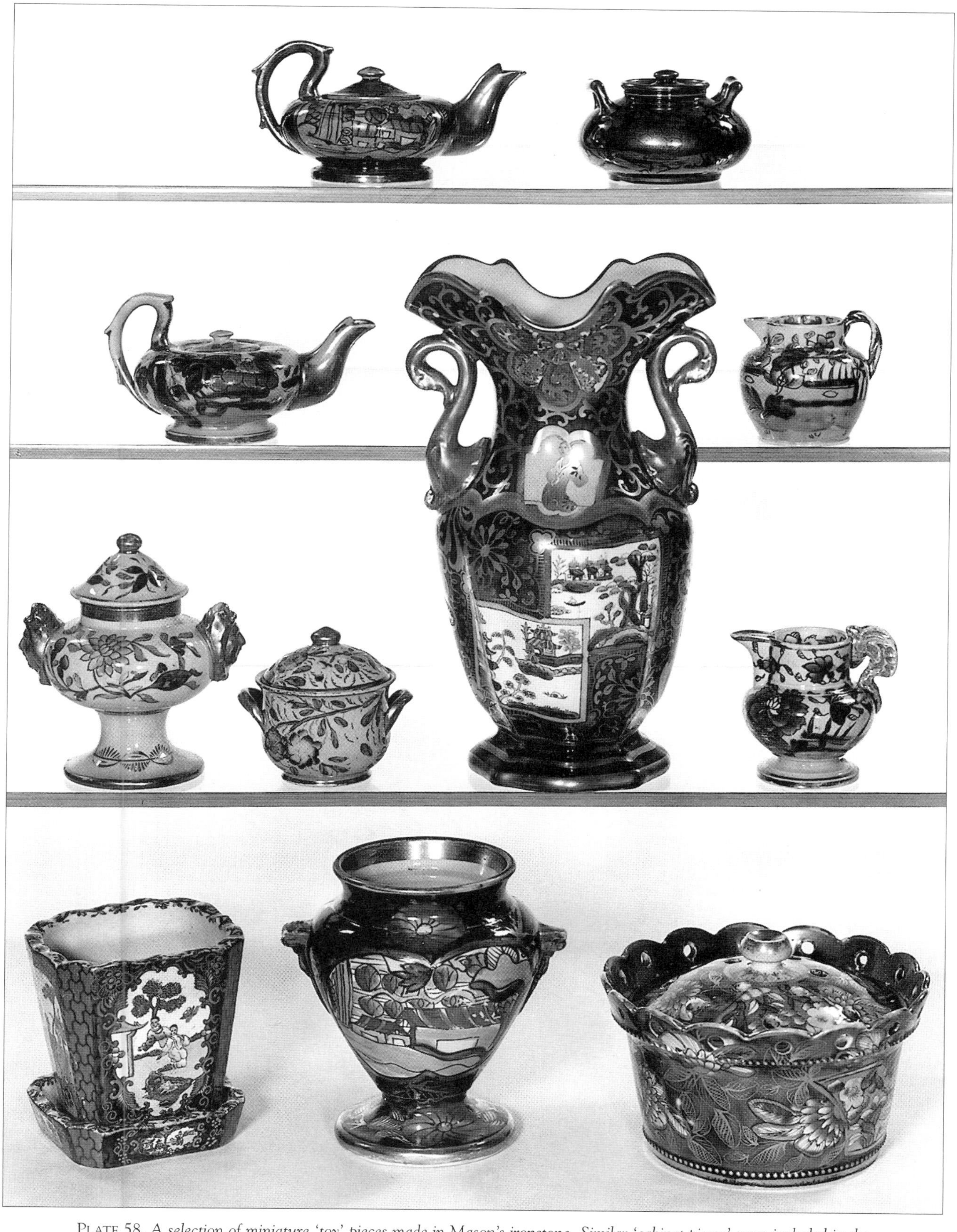

PLATE 58. *A selection of miniature 'toy' pieces made in Mason's ironstone. Similar 'cabinet pieces' were included in the 1818 auction sale. Large vase 8in. (20.32cm) high.c.1818-22.*

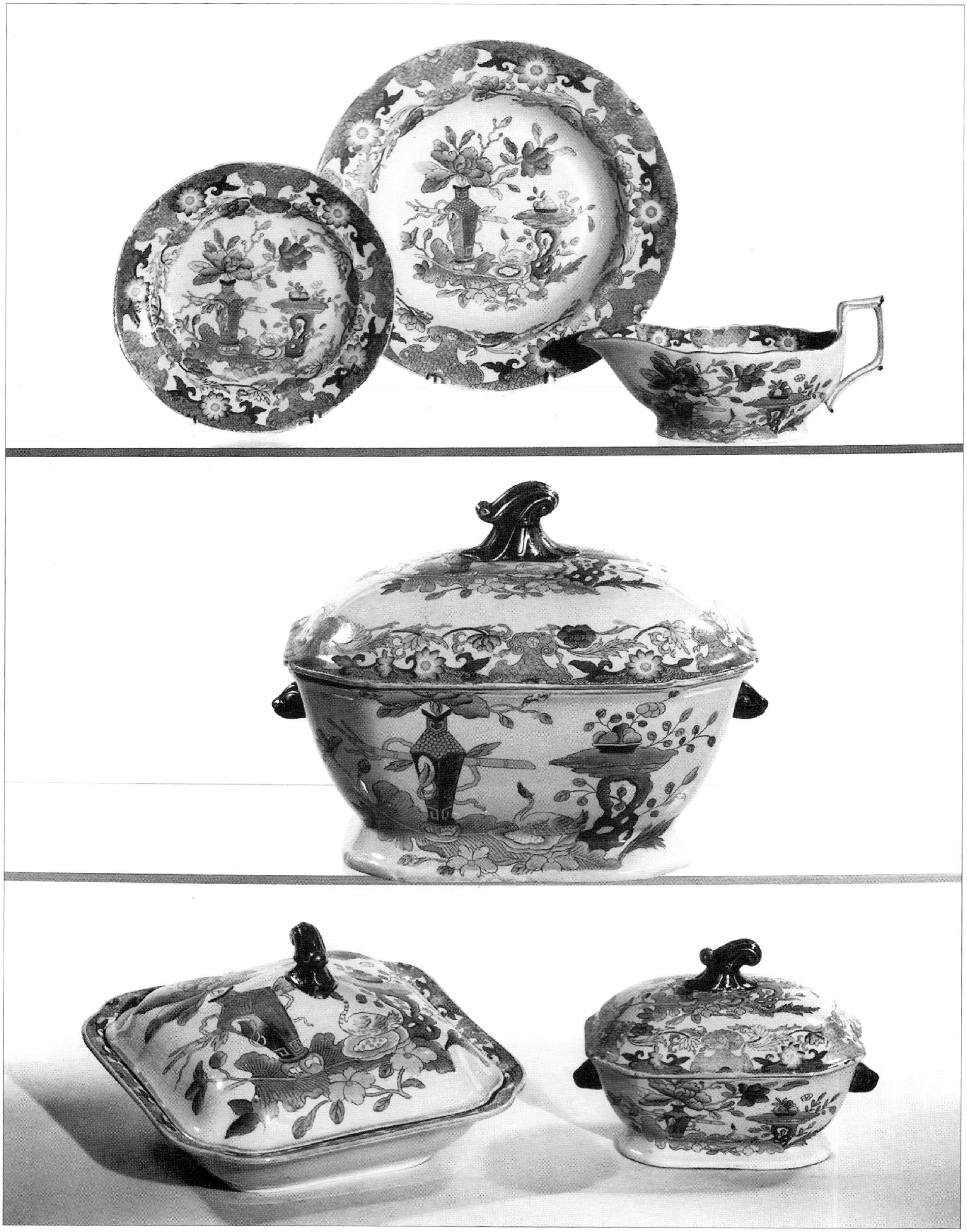

PLATE 59. *Representative pieces from a Mason's ironstone dinner service. Almost certainly the 'table and flower pot' pattern, as sold in 1818 (Lot 29). Tureen 13½in. (34.29cm) long. c.1818.*

PLATE 60. *Representative pieces from a Mason's Patent Ironstone dinner service with impressed, and printed, marks. The tureen shapes are different and probably rather later than those shown in Plate 59. Tureen 13½in. (34.29cm) high. c.1820-25. Messrs Phillips.*

27 One antique coffee pot
28 Two tulips and stands, cabinet, and two square scent boxes. £1.4.0.
29 One table set, exact quantity as Lot 5, table and flower pot pattern
30 Two costly jars, à la Chinoise, beautifully pencilled, and gilt
31 One desert service, exact quantity as Lot 12, gold rose japanned and gilt, antique forms
33 Two tea caddies, groups of flowers and gold lace border
34 One table service, exact quantity and pattern as Lot 5
36 Two taper candlesticks, toy ewer, bason, jug and mug. 2 lavender bottles, 2 flower beakers, and 1 cabinet teapot. £2.12.6.
37 Two dragon octagonal beakers
38 One desert service, plain Japan, exact quantity as Lot 12. £12.12.0.
39 One Italian formed jar, or vase, biscuit of elegant workmanship
40 One table service, exact quantity as Lot 5, old Japan pattern, in green, pink, mazarine, red, and richly gilt
42 One Trentham bowl
43 One splendid dragon jar, à la Chinoise
44 Two costly beakers
45 One watering can and 2 flat formed bottles. £1.2.0.
46 Two Chinese jars. £1.3.0.
47 One desert service, gold rose, exact quantity as Lot 12
48 One table service, blue and gold
49 One octagonal rose and apple jar
51 One table service, exact quantity and pattern as Lot 5
52 Two cabinet jugs and mugs and 2 flower beakers
53 One foot pail. £1.1.0.
54 Ditto and slop jar. £2.2.0.
55 One table service, exact quantity as Lot 5, basket Japan
56 Two bell jars, lion's heads
57 Two 3-handled fluted vases
58 Two hexagonal tea caddies. £2.10.0.
60 Two low fluted jars
61 One fine octagon vase, à la Chinoise
62 One Table service, exact quantity as Lot 5, India gold jar pattern
64 Two card candlesticks, 2 tall ditto, Dresden pattern, and 2 baskets
65 Two tall hexagonal embossed jars and covers
66 Two small griffin octagonal jars
67 Two cabinet jugs and mugs
68 One table service, richly japanned in red, blue, green, and gold, exact quantity as Lot 5
70 Two low bat-head ornaments. 18/-
71 Two hexagonal beakers
72 Two lavender bottles, 2 low bat-head ornaments, 2 beakers, and 2 cabinet coffee biggins. £2.5.0.
73 Two antique jars and covers
75 Two sugar caddies
76 One desert service, gold thorn, exact quantity as Lot 17
78 Two pot pourri jars. £1.1.0.

PLATE 61. *Representative pieces from a Mason's ironstone dinner and dessert service having one of several early well painted designs that could be described as 'Landscape Japan', see Lot 81 in the 1818 auction sale. Tureen 12¾in. (32.38cm) high. c.1818-25. Messrs Sotheby's.*

80 Two small antique bottles
81 One table service, landscape, Japan, slightly gilt, exact quantity as Lot 5
82 Two lavender bottles, 2 ranunculus pots, and 2 card candlesticks

PLATE 62. *A large, Japan pattern, foot bath or 'foot pail' as sold for £1.1s.0d. in the 1818 auction sale. 15in. (38.1cm) long. c.1818-25.*

PLATE 63. *A superb quality blue-ground Mason's ironstone jar, perhaps similar to Lot 83 'Two round jars, of rich pattern', included in the 1818 auction sale. 9¼in. (23.49cm) high. c.1818-20. Messrs Sotheby's.*

PLATE 64. *Representative pieces from a large Mason's ironstone dinner service, perhaps the 'India figure pattern' of the 1818 auction sale. Tureen 12in. (30.48) high. c.1818-25. Messrs Phillips.*

83 Two rounds jars, of rich pattern
85 Two toy churns, 2 Dresden pattern jars, and 2 toy cups and saucers
86 Two tripods, 2 coffee biggins
88 Two flower vessels, colour and gold. 10/-.
89 Two tall Roman shaped jars. £1.0.0.
90 Two toy churns, 3 Lavender bottles, 2 candlesticks

SECOND DAY'S SALE
WEDNESDAY, DECEMBER 16th, 1818
at one o'clock precisely

91 One cabinet ewer, bason, jug and mug, 2 ditto, coffee biggins
92 Two Chinese beakers
93 Two three-handled dragon jars, fluted, richly coloured and gilt
94 One desert service, Indian figure pattern, exact quantity as Lot 12. £4.14.6.
95 One table service, India pheasant, japan, slightly gilt, exact quantity as Lot 5
96 Two dolphin-head bowls, rich in colours and gold
97 Two pot pourries
98 Two cabinet teapots
100 Two rose-handled bell-shaped jars, bronze and gold
101 One table service, exact quantity as Lot 5, richly coloured figure pattern
102 Two three-handled jars
103 Two watering cans, 2 low bottles and stoppers. £1.7.0.
104 Two octagon jars. 14/-
105 Two curiously formed vases, of antique shape, elegantly enamelled and gilt. £3.7.0.
106 One desert service, landscape Japan as Lot 12
107 Two small antique bottles, 2 toy cups and saucers
108 One table service, blue pheasants with gold border, exact quantity as Lot 5
109 One elegant sideboard jar, damaged
110 Two ink stands, 2 tulip cups and stands
111 Two Dresden cans and stands, 2 ditto cups, etc.
112 One table service, blue Chinese landscapes, exact quantity as Lot 5
113 Two large beer jugs. 9/6.
114 Two small Dresden pattern cups
115 Two garden flower pots and stands

PLATE 65. *An early form of Mason's ironstone inkstand decorated with typical, if broadly painted, Japan pattern. 6¾in. (17.14cm) long. c.1818-25.*

116 Two small octagon jars, 4 card candlesticks, 2 ink stands
117 Two elegant beakers and covers, à la Chinoise
118 Two antique coffee pots
119 Two Trentham bowls, highly finished
120 Two 3-handled Dragon vases. £3.8.0.
121 One table set, richly finished in colour and gold, exact quantity as Lot 12
122 One desert set, rock and rose japan and gilt, exact quantity as Lot 12
124 Two bell shaped jars
125 Two lavender bottles , cabinet ewer, bason, jug and mug
126 Two watering cans
127 Two tall covered jars
128 Two low open jars
129 A table service, mandarin pattern in colours and gold, exact quantity as Lot 5. £15.15.0.
130 Two beer jugs
131 One desert service, pheasants, in colours and gold, exact quantity as Lot 12
132 One table service, red mazarine, and richly gilt, exact quantity as Lot 5
133 Two Dresden pattern tulips and stands, 2 ditto, cans and stands, and 2 flat formed bottles. £1.4.0.
134 Two large bottle-shaped perfume jars. £6.6.0.
136 Two small hexagonal bottles. 9/-
137 Two beer jugs
138 Two tall octagonal embossed Chinese covered jars
139 Two low fluted open jars, à la Chinoise
140 Two low jars and covers. 9/-
141 Two small octagonal jars and covers, red, blue and gold
142 Two Lizard-handled vases. 18/-
143 One table service., of costly manufacture, in colours, mazarine and gold, exact quantity as Lot 5
144 Two fine large bottles, ornamented, à la Chinoise
146 One desert service, gold rose pattern as Lot 12
147 Two essence burners, 2 lavender bottles, and 4 paint cups
148 Two open jars
149 Two singularly formed jars, à la Chinoise
150 Two low Dolphin vases
151 One table set, old India Japan pattern, exact quantity as Lot 5
153 Ditto, blue, red, and gold, ditto
155 Two beakers
156 Two tall hexagonal beakers
157 Two curiously formed beakers, à la Chinoise
158 Two small round jars and covers. 10/-.
159 Two ditto octagon jars and covers
161 Ditto, rich Japan pattern, in colours and gold, as Lot 9
163 One Dejeune set, red and gold
164 Two small round jars and covers, and 2 cabinet cups and saucers
165 Two porter mugs
166 Two sugar caddies
167 One ewer and bason, and 2 cabinet cups and saucers
168 One table service, India grass-hopper pattern, in colours, and slightly gilt, exact quantity as Lot 5

PLATE 66. *Two views of a superb quality Mason's jar, perhaps the 'low open jars' of the 1818 auction sale. Diameter 13in. (33.02cm). c.1818-25. R. and Z. Taylor Collection.*

PLATE 67. *Two mazarine blue ground mugs with superb quality gilding, perhaps the 'porter mugs' of the 1818 sale. 5½in. and 3¼in. (13.97cm and 8.25cm) high. c.1818-22. The late Mrs M. Symes Collection.*

PLATE 68. *A tureen of the printed outline Mason's pattern number 1. Probably the 'India grasshopper design' of the 1818 auction sale catalogue. Printed mark 'N 1' and printed warranted mark. 12½in. (31.75cm) long. c.1815-25.*

169 One desert service, Japan, red purple and gold, exact quantity as Lot 12
171 One drawing room lions head perfume jar, and 4 toy Dresden pattern cups and saucers. 12/-.
175 Two jars, colours and gold
176 Two jardiniers and stands. 13/-.
177 Two antique formed coffee pots
178 Two watering cans, rich pattern, 2 small round jars and covers
179 Two rich lizard-handled jars. 18/-.
180 Two Etruscan jars
181 Four chamber candlesticks
182 Two square scent boxes, 2 toy churns
183 Two perforated jars
184 Two lizard jars. 10/6.
185 One desert service, India gold vase pattern, as Lot 12
186 Four jugs for beer. 17/-.
187 One fine perfume jar, à la Chinoise

PLATE 69. *Representative plates from an early Mason's ironstone dessert service. The colourful design is an unusual one, perhaps the 'rose and rock' pattern of the 1818 auction sale (Lot 216). Centrepiece 7½in. (19.05cm) high. c.1815-25.*

PLATE 70. *A selection of early Mason spill vases or 'match-pots', decorated with standard colourful Japan patterns. 5¾in. to 2¼in. (14.6cm to 5.71cm) high. c.1818-25.*

PLATE 71. *A rare pair of Mason's cornucopia decorated with a colourful Japan pattern, probably the 'flower horns' of the 1818 auction sale catalogue. Printed mark. 8in. (20.32cm) high. c.1818-30.*

PLATE 72. *Two Mason's ironstone miniature or toy jugs. Lots such as 'Two toy pitchers' were included in the 1818 auction. 5¾in. and 2½in. (14.6cm and 6.35cm) high.* c.1815-25. *A.M. Broad.*

THIRD DAY'S SALE
THURSDAY, DECEMBER 17th, 1818
at one o'clock precisely

189 Two match pots, 2 Lizard handled vases, 2 ink stands
190 Two rich beakers, 2 toy pitcher jars, 2 handled embossed essence burners
192 Two handsome ornaments, à la Chinoise
193 Two rich tea caddies
194 Desert service, India flower basket Japan exact quantity as Lot 12
198 A table service, of rich Mogul pattern in colours and gold border, exact quantity as Lot 5
199 One desert service, gold rose Japan in colours and gold, exact quantity as Lot 12
200 One costly Hall jar, elegant Chinese designs
202 One table service, pattern and quantity as Lot 5
203 Two caddies, flowers and gold
204 Two pot pourris, small
205 Two Lizard-handled jars
206 One table service, Pagoda pattern in mazarine and gold, as Lot 5
207 Two fluted open jars
208 Two coffee biggins, toy size
209 Three handsome octagonal jars
210 Two small octagonal dragon-handled bottles
211 Two beakers, handsome patterns
212 One desert service, India grasshopper pattern
214 Two vase-shaped ink stands
215 Two elegant Trentham bowls
216 One table service, rose and rock pattern, à la Chinoise, richly gilt, quantity as Lot 5
217 Two caddies, mazarine colours and gold
218 Two flower horns
219 Four wafer cups
220 Two square essence boxes
221 Two toy churns
222 One elegant toilet ewer and bason, antique forms and patterns
224 One table service, old Japan pattern, red purple and gold, quantity as Lot 5
225 One very large dolphin-headed bowl, richly embellished in colours and gold, damaged
226 Two watering cans, colours and gold
227 Two toy pitchers
228 One sideboard jar, dragon handles, sumptuously gilt
229 One desert set, Chinese thorn pattern, in colours and gold
230 Two rose and apple handled octagonal perfume jars
231 Two dolphin-headed bowls
232 One table service, India water-melon Japan, and richly gilt, quantity as Lot 5
233 Two beakers and covers, rich, in Mazarine, enamel and gold

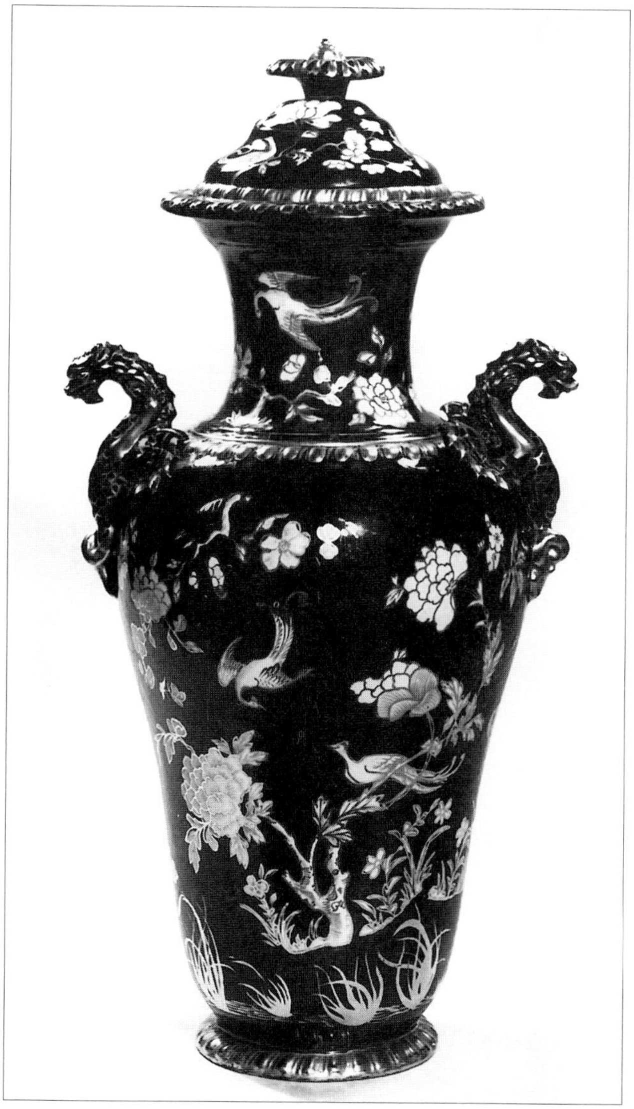

PLATE 73. *A large embossed, blue-ground vase and cover. This form could relate to 1818 sale items such as 'griffin-handled vases' or 'embossed jars and covers' (Lots 277 and 278). 21in. (53.34cm) high.* c.1818-25.

234 Two handled open top fluted jars
235 Two lizard-handled vases
236 Two flat bottles
238 One table service, Mogul pattern, enamelled and gilt, quantity as Lot 5
240 One table service, blue India pheasant (pattern and quantity as Lot 5)
241 Two antique pattern coffee pots
242 Two cabinet ink stands
243 One table set, gold jar pattern, gold border, quantity as Lot 5
244 Four card candlesticks
245 Two handsome vase inkstands
246 Two cabinet tea kettles
247 Two cabinet coffee biggins
248 Two flower horns
249 One table set, India figure pattern, as Lot 5
250 One breakfast tea and coffee set, grasshopper pattern, 85 pieces (perhaps bone china, not ironstone).
251 Two open perfume bowls
252 Two Etruscan jars for pastiles
253 One desert set, flower basket pattern
254 One table service, richly finished in mazarine, green and gold; quantity as Lot 5
255 Two strawberry jars and covers
256 One fine hexagonal hall jar and cover, enamelled in compartments, and sumptuously gilt
257 Two Pan's head ornaments, landscapes in compartments of Mazarine, and splendidly gilt
258 Two cabinet tea pots
259 One desert service, Chinese subject, in compartments of Mazarine and gold
260 Two scollopt scent jars
261 Two three handled fluted jars
262 Two water bottles
264 Two watering pots
265 Two elegant dragon head octagonal jars
266 Two octagonal embossed jars and covers
267 One table set, India pheasant pattern in colours
268 Two round jars and covers
270 Two Chinese beakers, richly ornamented
271 Two oak-leaf low vases and covers
272 One richly executed jar, Chinese subjects, on Masarine ground

PLATE 74. *A standard blue printed pheasant pattern 'Antique-shape' jug, impressed marked 'Mason's ironstone'. This pattern was much used for toilet services, see Lots 2, 37 etc. in the 1822 sale. 6¼in. (15.87cm) high (various sizes were produced). c.1822-25.*

274 Four toy cream stands
275 Two cabinet pitchers
277 Two griffin-handled vases
278 Two embossed jars and covers

281 Two octagonal rose and apple jars for perfume
282 Two curious antique formed jars, handsomely gilt
283 Two octagonal jars and covers
284 One ditto embossed jar and cover

PLATE 75. *A well decorated Japan pattern pair of impressed marked 'card racks', perhaps as Lot 13 in the 1822 sale. 6in. (15.24cm) high. c.1820-25. Messrs Lawrence, Crewkerne.*

We can now move forward three and a half years to learn something of the stock held in Mason's London showroom as evidenced by Phillips' auction sales held in June 1822

**1822 SALE CATALOGUE**
**THE VALUABLE AND EXTENSIVE**
**STOCK OF CHINA**
**OF THE LATE**
**MR. MASON,**
**PATENTEE AND MANUFACTURE OF THE**
**IRON STONE CHINA,**
**AT NO. 11, ALBEMARLE STREET.**

**A**
**CATALOGUE**
**OF THE**
**ENTIRE ASSEMBLAGE OF USEFUL & DECORATIVE**
**PORCELAIN**
**OF RICH AND ELEGANT PATTERNS;**
**comprising**
**SEVERAL HUNDRED**
**DINNER, DESSERT, BREAKFAST AND TEA**
**SERVICES;**
**JUGS, EWERS, BASINS,**
**DISHES IN SETS, BOTH OPEN AND COVERED:**
**PLATES IN DOZENS, OF EVERY SIZE:**
**NOBLE ORNAMENTAL JARS & EWERS,**
**superbly gilt and beautifully enamelled:**
**AND**
**GREAT VARIETY OF CABINET ORNAMENTS,**
**OF THE MOST TASTEFUL AND ELEGANT FORMS.**
**WHICH WILL BE SOLD BY AUCTION**
**BY MR. PHILLIPS,**

**ON THE PREMISES**
**AT NO. 11, ALBEMARLE STREET**
**ON FRIDAY, the 14th day of JUNE, 1822,**
**And following Day, at Twelve for One precisely,**
**BY ORDER OF THE EXECUTORS,**
**WITHOUT RESERVE.**
**FIRST DAY'S SALE**
**TUESDAY, the 14th Day of JUNE, 1822**
**commencing at one 'clock precisely**

The Description of the various Pieces composing the Dinner, Dessert and Tea Services, will be found on the largest or principal Piece in each Service.

| Lot | | |
|---|---|---|
| 1 | Twenty-four jars and covers | 12/- |
| 2 | Two blue and white pheasant toilet suites, 16 Pieces | 10/- |
| 3 | Six ditto jugs, and a toilet suite, dragon pattern | 10/- |
| 5 | A tea and breakfast set, 56 pieces | 16/- |
| 6 | Four antique shape jugs | 14/- |
| 7 | A tea service, 43 pieces | 20/- |
| 8 | Two match boxes and 3 paper cases, mazarine ground | 30/- |
| 9 | A dejeune, gold edge, japan | 42/- |
| 10 | Two broth basins, covers and stands and 2 porus wine coolers | 24/- |
| 11 | Five jugs from the antique and 5 kitchen jugs | 16/- |
| 13 | Two card racks and 2 violet baskets | 30/- |
| 14 | A dinner service, dragon pattern, 142 pieces, as per label on tureen | |

PLATE 76. *A small oval covered flower-holder, perhaps the 'violet baskets' as included in the 1822 sale. Such delicate objects are more usually found in true porcelain rather than ironstone. Impressed marked. 3¾in. (9.52cm) long. c.1820-25.*

| | | |
|---|---|---|
| 15 | A pair of wine coolers, gilt mask heads and ornaments | 42/- |
| 17 | A pair of jars, Chinese landscape and figures | 25/- |
| 18 | A pair of essence jars, gilt and painted in birds and flowers faulty | 30/- |
| 21 | Two large jars, gold plaid and flowers | 30/- |
| 22 | Eleven meat, 12 soup and 5 pie plates | 42/- |
| 23 | A Stilton cheese stand and cover, and 3 trays | 20/- |
| 24 | A pair of hexagon vases, gilt Chinese building, figures, flowers and moths | 55/- |
| 25 | A pair of ice pails, covers and liners, gilt and painted in flowers | 60/- |
| 26 | Six basins, covers and stands, painted in flowers | 42/- |
| 27 | A DINNER SERVICE, in boquet, 142 pieces, as per description on tureen | 12gns. |
| 28 | A wine cooler, gilt and japanned flowers | 30/- |
| 29 | A breakfast service, dragon pattern, 69 pieces | 90/- |
| 30 | Two ink stands, green ground and flowers, gilt | 24/- |
| 31 | Six jugs, formed from the antique | 16/- |
| 32 | Four basins, covers and stands, gilt edge | 20/- |
| 33 | A ewer and basin, Indian sprig, gilt edge | 20/- |
| 35 | A pair of jars and covers, japanned flower and gilt ram's heads and edges | 70/- |
| 36 | A supper service, centre and 4 quadrants and covers, japanned flowers, gilt | 80/- |
| 37 | Six jugs, pheasant and flowers from the antique | 14/- |
| 38 | A ditto toilet suite, 8 pieces, and a tea set painted in flowers | 30/- |
| 39 | A dessert service, gilt and painted in flowers, centre, 12 compotiers and 24 plates | 150/- |
| 40 | A large chamber jar and cover, blue landscape and a foot pan | 30/- |
| 41 | A pair shaped jars and covers, japanned and gilt flower | 100/- |
| 42 | Three jugs from the antique, fancy pattern | 30/- |
| 44 | A pair of hand candlesticks with extinguishers and glass shades | 42/- |
| 45 | A pair of biscuit vases, with bandeau of flowers and glass shades | 35/- |

PLATE 77. *Representative pieces from a basket-moulded Mason's ironstone breakfast service, including large size cups and saucers, eggcups, covered muffin dishes and such rare objects. Impressed marks. Plate 7in. (17.78cm) diameter. c.1815-25.*

46 A suite of three ditto with shades 45/-
47 A DINNER SERVICE, gilt and ornamented with flowers, 142 pieces, as described 30gns.
49 A toilet suite in flowers, 8 pieces and a glass caraft and tumbler, fluted 55/-
50 A small ewer, basin and pair of candlesticks with glass shades 30/-
51 A DINNER SERVICE, rich japan pattern; sumptuously gilt, 142 pieces £35.
52 A pair of Grecian form essence bowls, with handles £6.
53 A pair of blue essence bottles , 2 inkstands, wafer cup and cover and 4 glass shades 35/-
54 A pair of handsome urns on pedestals, richly gilt and glass shades 40/-
55 A NOBLE LOFTY JAR with cover, surmounted with griffins and blue ground, beautifully enamelled in birds and flowers 9gns.
56 An essence cup and cover, pair of square bottles and a breakfast and tea set, blue border 65/-
57 A chamber slop pail and cover, painted in flowers, gilt edges and ornaments 40/-
58 A porous wine cooler and 9 jugs, formed from the antique 16/-
60 A lofty ESSENCE JAR and cover dragon handles and top painted in flowers 63/-
62 A dessert service, blue and gold flower border 190/-

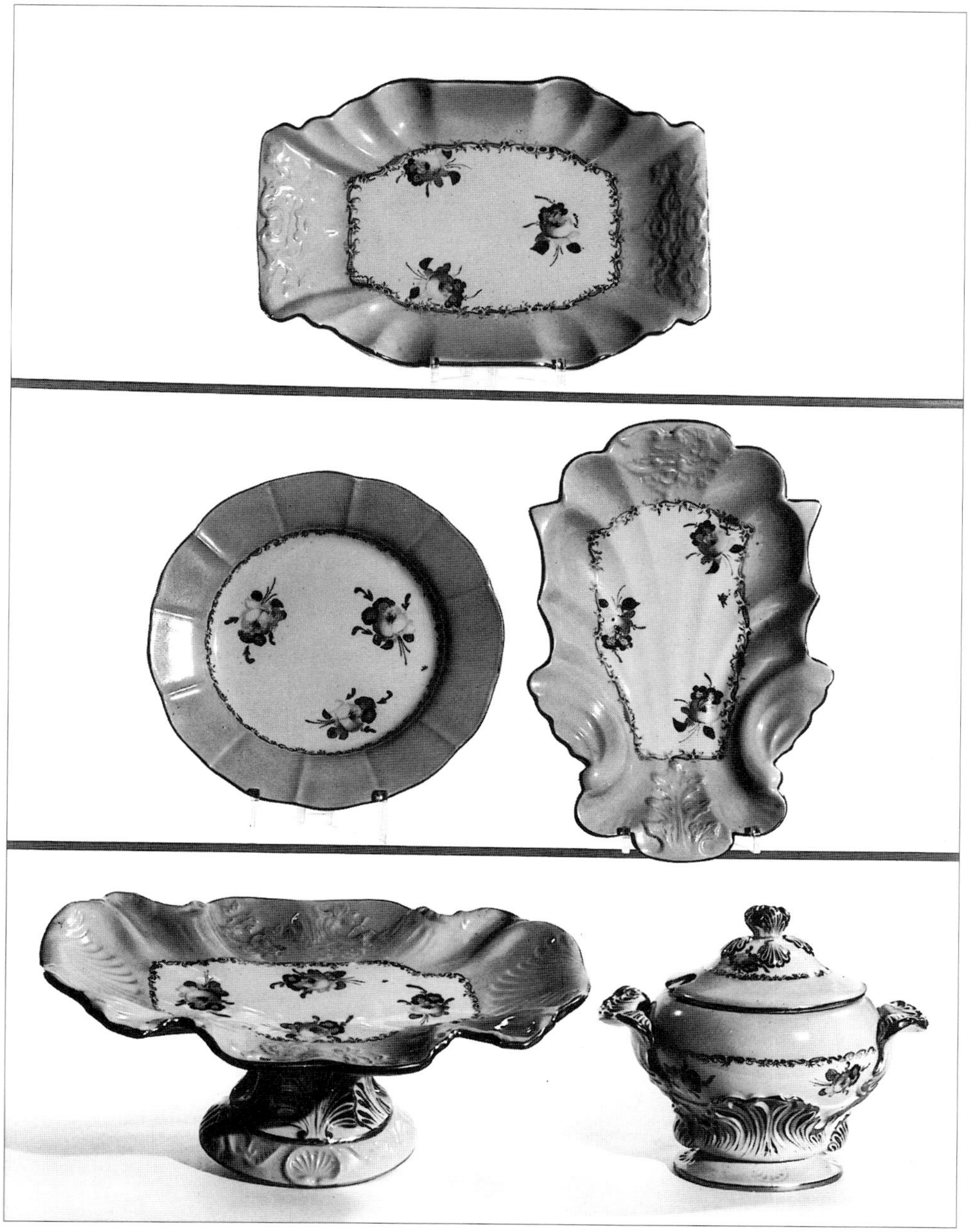

PLATE 78. *Representative pieces from a green bordered dessert service, perhaps matching the 'Handsome dessert service, painted in bouquets, relieved by sea-green and gold' (Lot 855, 1822 sale). Impressed marks. Centrepiece 12½in. (31.75cm) long. c.1815-25.*

| | | |
|---|---|---|
| 63 | A chamber suite of 9 pieces, caraft and tumbler | 50/- |
| 64 | A DINNER SERVICE, peacock and flowers, 142 pieces | £14. |
| 65 | A suite of 4 jugs in flowers | 30/- |
| 68 | A dessert service, blue birds and flowers, 43 pieces | 130/- |
| 69 | A DINNER SERVICE, hexagon shape, blue birds and flowers, 142 pieces | 11gns. |
| 70 | A pair of shaped jars and covers, gilt and painted flowers | 40/- |
| 71 | A pair of flower urns, richly gilt and painted and 2 glass shades | 35/- |
| 72 | A pair of handsome essence jars and covers, large hexagonal, gold plaid | 30/- |
| 73 | A pair of blue sprinklers, gilt handles, embossed figures and glass shades | 40/- |
| 74 | A DINNER SERVICE, rich old japan pattern, containing 142 pieces, as described | 25gns. |
| 75 | A ditto DESSERT SERVICE, 43 pieces | 6gns. |
| 76 | A pair of jars with dragon handles | 35/- |
| 80 | A pair of match cases, Dresden flower and glass shades | 20/- |
| 81 | A centre piece, fruit basket, radish tray, 2 sallad bowls, mustard, pepper, argyle and egg beater | 26/- |
| 82 | Two chamber services, 16 pieces | 32/- |
| 83 | A DINNER SERVICE, Dresden sprig, 142 pieces, as described | 25gns. |

PLATE 79. *A selection of Mason's ironstone jugs. The 1822 sale included a large array of such pieces, in various shapes, sizes and designs. These were produced over a long period. The late Mrs M. Symes Collection.*

84 A ewer and basin, enamelled moths and flowers, and 8 jugs, blue bird and flower 30/-

85 A set of five Grecian shape urns, painted in birds and flowers, sumptuously gilt and 5 shades 130/-

87 Twenty-two meat, soup and dessert plates, Dresden flower and gold edge & 40/-

88 A DINNER SERVICE, blue bird and flower, containing 142 pieces, as described 190/-

89 A dessert service, blue sprig, 43 pieces, ditto 5gns.

90 Four jugs from the antique, enamelled border and flowers 10/-

92 A dejeune, festoon flowers and sprig 15/-

93 Two pink jars and covers 20/-

94 A DINNER SERVICE, blue birds and flowers, contents, 142 pieces, as described 190/-

96 A tea set, same pattern, 45 pieces (probably bone china) 7gns.

97 A pair of broth basins, covers and stands, japanned blue compartments 30/-

98 A pair of hexagon FLOWER POTS and stands, mazarine ground and gold edge 5gns.

99 Two jugs from antique designs 16/-

100 A breakfast service, painted sprig, 30 pieces and 12 plates, melange 40/-

101 A ragout dish, cover and liner, a steak ditto, an ice butter tub, butter tub, and a pickle stand 50/-

102 A supper service, richly gilt, 10 pieces 70/-

103 Two ice pails, covers and liners, grasshopper and flowers, gilt edge 42/-

105 Twelve jugs and covers, blue birds, etc. 30/-

107 A chamber slop pail and cover, blue birds and flowers 16/-

108 Four antique form jugs, grasshopper pattern 11/-

109 Two fruit baskets, on feet 40/-

110 Three mugs, gold plaid, and shaving box, red rose, etc. 20/-

111 Five large jugs, embossed flower 15/-

112 Two japanned jars, dolphin handles 35/-

113 A DINNER SERVICE, dragon pattern, contents, 143 pieces, as described 9gns.

114 A rich japan DESSERT SERVICE, 43 pieces 8gns.

117 A DINNER SERVICE, hexagon shape, grasshopper pattern, 143 pieces, as described 15 ? gns.

119 Pair of rich jars and covers, sumptuously gilt 30/-

120 Twelve melange plates 18/-

121 Twelve ditto, various rich patterns 18/-

122 A rich gilt and japan toilet service, 8 pieces 63/-

PLATE 80. *A rare impressed marked Mason's ironstone two-division dish. Such items as 'ragout dishes and covers and liners' were included in the 1822 sale. This may lack the larger bottom unit. 11in. (27.94cm) long. c.1815-25.*

123 A DINNER SERVICE, Tourney sprig, 143 pieces, as described — 11 gns.

124 Two ewers, gilt and japan flower, formed from the antique — 20/-

125 A breakfast service, white and gold, 30 pieces — 30/-

126 A broth basin, cover and stand and chamber slop pail and cover — 24/-

127 A handsome essence jar, green ground and flowers and 2 match cases in landscapes — 63/-

128 Two blue and white chamber sets, 16 pieces — 35/-

130 A potatoe dish and cover, 5 potting pots and an eggstand with 6 cups

PLATE 81. *A rare impressed marked pot-pourri bowl. Perhaps similar to Lot 127 in the 1822 sale, 'A handsome essence jar, green ground and flowers...' 14in. (35.56cm) high. c.1820-25.*

**SECOND DAY'S SALE**
**WEDNESDAY, the 5th Day of JUNE, 1822**
**commencing at One o'Clock precisely**

| Lot | | Reserve |
|---|---|---|
| 131 | Thirteen blue jugs, in sizes | 30/- |
| 132 | Two blue chamber sets with carafts and tumblers | 40/- |
| 134 | Twelve white preserving jars and covers | 32/- |
| 135 | A dejeune, Bourbon sprig | 30/- |
| 138 | Two Stilton cheese stands and 2 fluted-top wine coolers, willow | 40/- |
| 141 | Six coloured jugs and 12 mugs | 27/- |
| 142 | Two ice pails, richly gilt (1 cover faulty) | 37/- |
| 143 | A table set, willow | 190/- |
| 146 | Three paper cases and 2 scent pots, mazarine | 20/- |
| 147 | Three rich India pattern jugs | 25/- |
| 148 | Two wine coolers, elegantly gilt | 42/- |
| 149 | A breakfast service, 42 pieces | 70/- |
| 151 | Two chamber sets, japan, with caraft and tumbler | 60/- |
| 152 | A table set, grasshopper, gold knobs | £16. |
| 153 | A ditto, flower pattern (not Ironstone) | £7. |
| 154 | Two porous wine coolers, 2 ditto butter tubs and 24 glass wines | 36/- |
| 156 | A dessert service, japan | 105/- |
| 160 | A supper set, rich japan, gold edge | 38/- |
| 161 | Three jars, mazarine and gold chased figures, with shades | 105/- |
| 162 | A breakfast set, Chinese sprig, 77 pieces | 60/- |
| 163 | Two chamber sets, white, with carafts and tumblers | 28/- |
| 164 | Two large flower pots and stands, mazarine | 80/- |
| 166 | A set of lunch plates, Tourney sprig, gold edge | 30/- |
| 167 | A pair of ice pails, japan | 60/- |
| 168 | A table service, Chinese figures, gold edge | £18. |
| 169 | A very richly gilt tea service | 190/- |
| 172 | Six hunting jugs and 5 mugs | 24/- |
| 173 | Three jugs, japan | 20/- |
| 174 | Two antique coffee pots, with glass shades | 35/- |
| 175 | One fine hexagonal hall jar | 150/- |
| 176 | Six broth bowls, covers and stands | 35/- |
| 177 | Twenty-four rich melange plates | 50/- |
| 178 | Two antique jars | 42/- |
| 180 | Two pastille burners, with glass shades | 55/- |
| 181 | A breakfast set, coloured flowers, 61 pieces | 75/- |
| 182 | A table service, japan, richly gilt | 23gns. |
| 183 | A blue supper set | 25/- |
| 190 | One superb square very large hall jar, mazarine and Indian devices | 17gns. |
| 191 | A tea set, japan, 57 pieces | 84/- |
| 192 | A chamber set, green border, enamelled, with caraft and tumbler | 15/- |
| 193 | A Trentham plaid jar | 35/- |
| 194 | Seven mugs, hunting, and 24 glass tumblers | 25/- |
| 195 | Two toy ewers and basins, mazarine with shades | 27/- |
| 196 | Two shell pen trays, 2 hand candlesticks and 2 glass shades | 24/- |
| 197 | A dessert service, roses and gold edge, 41 pieces | 6gns. |
| 198 | Two porous wine coolers and 2 butter tubs | 20/- |
| 202 | Forty-eight lunch plates | 30/- |
| 203 | Two chamber sets, blue, with carafts and tumblers | 40/- |
| 204 | A supper set, blue | 30/- |
| 205 | A table service, blue | 190/- |
| 206 | A dessert service, Dresden flowers, 37 pieces | 7gns. |
| 207 | Two ice pails, flowers in compartments, on blue border, richly gilt | |
| 208 | Two elegant vases, with shades | 40/- |
| 209 | Two flower pots and stands, japan, with shades | 31/6 |
| 210 | Three ragout dishes, pans and covers, white | 60/- |
| 211 | A breakfast set, Indian dragon, gold edge, 94 pieces | 110/- |
| 212 | A table service, white | 6gns. |
| 216 | Eight jugs, blue, and 4 covered ditto | 30/- |
| 217 | Six jugs, gold jar pattern | 25/- |
| 218 | Twelve breakfast cups and saucers, white and gold | 30/- |
| 219 | An elegant chamber service, with caraft and tumbler | 60/- |
| 220 | Six very rich plates | 52/- |
| 221 | Two elegant griffin jars, painted in fruit and flowers, sumptuously gilt | 6gns. |
| 224 | Forty-eight lunch plates, various | 30/- |
| 225 | Two broth basins, covers and stands, japan, and 4 soup plates, rich melange | 30/- |
| 226 | A table service, japan, gold edge | £25. |
| 227 | A dessert set, japan, ungilt | 6gns. |
| 228 | An oval set, japan, gilt, with mahogany tray | 52/- |
| 235 | A chamber service, Chinese figures, with caraft and tumbler | 25/- |
| 237 | Twelve plates, richly painted, with various arms and crests | 60/- |
| 239 | Seven handsome dessert plates, melange | 35/- |
| 240 | A splendid Neapolitan vase, painted by S. Bourne [see Plate 27] | £30 |
| 241 | Two hexagon vases, mazarine (1 faulty) | 10/- |
| 244 | Twelve blue mugs and 12 horns | 25/- |
| 246 | Five club top jugs and 6 stone mugs | 25/- |
| 247 | Twelve lunch plates, blue bell japan, and dish and cover | 25/- |
| 248 | Two vegetable dishes for hot water | 60/- |
| 249 | Four chocolate cups and stands, and 4 odd dishes | 20/- |
| 250 | Twenty-two lunch plates, gilt Japan | 25/- |
| 251 | A lunch set, of basket pattern, gold edge, 68 pieces (plates not gilt) | 96/- |
| 252 | Two chimney vases, Chinese pattern | 20/- |
| 253 | Two ditto, japanned | 25/- |

**THIRD DAY'S SALE**
**THURSDAY, the 6th Day of JUNE, 1822**
**Commencing at One o'Clock precisely**

| Lot | | Reserve |
|---|---|---|
| 262 | One foot tub and 1 slop jar, blue | 20/- |
| 263 | Two ice pails, blue, and 2 wine coolers, white | 25/- |
| 266 | Two blue large flower pots and stands | 40/- |
| 268 | A breakfast set, Tourney sprig, gold edge, 54 pieces | 63/- |
| 269 | A ditto, japan, 22 pieces | 35/- |
| 270 | Two bottles, mazarine, white figures with shades, and 1 centre jar | 63/- |
| 271 | Nine hunting mugs | 12/- |
| 272 | Two vegetable dishes, japan | 30/- |
| 273 | A table service, white | 6gns. |
| 274 | A ditto, blue | 9½gns. |
| 275 | A ditto, blue japanned | 12gns. |
| 277 | Three cheese stands and 1 vegetable dish for hot water, japan | 42/- |
| 278 | Two new form blue chamber sets with carafts and tumblers | 40/- |
| 281 | One large sideboard bowl, Indian pattern | 105/- |
| 282 | Two richly gilt ice pails | 80/- |
| 283 | Three jugs, japan | 25/- |
| 284 | A supper set, richly gilt | 60/- |
| 288 | A set of three vases, fruit and green ground, with shades | 75/- |
| 289 | Two match pots, roses on black ground and 1 antique coffee pot, with shades | 32/- |

PLATE 82. *A richly gilt blue-ground small ewer and basin, perhaps the 'toy ewer and basins' of the 1822 sale. Printed circular Royal Arms marks. Diameter of bowl 3⅛in. (7.93cm). c.1815-25. Dr M. Tanner Collection.*

290 A japanned table service, grasshopper £14.
292 Thirty-five lunch plates, rich brown and gold border 90/-
294 A very rich ragout dish and cover 50/-
295 A table service, blue £9.10.0d.
296 A breakfast service, blue, 87 pieces 40/-
298 A large hydra top jar, mazarine birds and flowers 9gns.
299 Two Chinese jars and covers no price
300 Four toy spouted mugs, rich japan, and 2 candlesticks, tourney and shade 35/-
301 Two candlesticks, flowers and orange ground, with shades 40/-
308 A rich japan table service £25.
309 A very beautifully painted landscape dessert service,

PLATE 83. *A rather crudely painted dessert service dish, perhaps relating to 'dessert set, Japan, ungilt' of the 1822 sale. 15½in. (39.37cm) c.1820-30.*

PLATE 84. *Two marked Mason's ironstone mugs of basic shapes and differing styles of decoration. The 1822 auction sale included many mugs. 4¾in. and 3in. (12.06cm and 7.62cm) high. c.1820-30. Mrs G. Allbright.*

| | | |
|---|---|---|
| | by S. Bourne [see Plate 55] | £30. |
| 311 | A breakfast service, green scroll and gold border, 77 pieces | 5gns. |
| 312 | A dejeuner, Indian garden | 50/- |
| 313 | Two chamber sets, green leaf border, with carafts and tumblers | 35/- |
| 314 | A ragout dish and cover, and 2 vegetable dishes for hot water, gold jar pattern | 42/- |
| 316 | Six beautiful plates | 35/- |
| 317 | Four hexagon jugs, mazarine and gold bands | 50/- |
| 318 | Six broth basins and stands, grasshopper japan | 24/- |
| 319 | A blue table service, willow | 9½gns. |
| 320 | Twelve species of useful articles, willow | 18/- |
| 324 | A richly gilt table service, gold tops | £25. |
| 325 | A table set, Tourney sprig | £20. |
| 326 | Two vases, mazarine, and 1 centre ditto, with shades | 63/- |
| 327 | Two vases, Views in Rome | 4gns. |
| 329 | A very beautiful Italian formed vase, painted by S. Bourne, superbly gilt and burnished [see Plate 54] | 35gns. |
| 330 | Sixty-nine sundry pieces, peacock japan | 90/- |
| 332 | Two large myrtle pots and stands, mazarine | 84/- |
| 333 | Two candlesticks, buff ground, with shades | 40/- |
| 341 | A Chinese jar, white, figures on mazarine | 30/- |
| 344 | A breakfast service, green ground, gold edge, 52 pieces | £5. |
| 345 | Five stone jugs and 6 mugs | 25/- |
| 348 | A table service, gilt japan | £26. |
| 349 | A ditto, common japan | £14. |
| 351 | A tea set, Bourbon sprig, 45 pieces | 25/- |
| 353 | Two hexagon tall jars and covers, japan | 42/- |
| 354 | Eight mugs and 7 ditto japan | £6.16.0d. |
| 355 | Three jugs, corbeau grounds | 32/- |
| 356 | Two ice pails, peacock japan | 40/- |

PLATE 85. *A good quality Chinese style punch bowl decorated with printed outline mogul(?) pattern (see Plate 20). Diameter 13in. (33.02cm). c.1815-25.*

PLATE 86. *A colourful Chinese style Mason's ironstone punch bowl, of an ever popular type. Diameter 12½in. (31.75cm). c.1820-30.*

| | | |
|---|---|---|
| 359 | Eight jugs, blue, and 6 mugs | 25/- |
| 360 | Two wine coolers and 2 ice pails, blue | 25/- |
| 361 | Five punch bowls, blue | 30/- |
| 362 | A table set, enamelled sprigs | 14gns. |
| 363 | A table service, Chinese characters on mazarine ground | £40. |
| 364 | A breakfast service, dragon pattern, 70 pieces | 55/- |
| 367 | Three small vases with shades | 35/- |
| 368 | A pagoda vase, japan | £5.10.9d. |
| 377 | Two card racks, mazarine | 20/- |
| 378 | Four rich broth basins, covers and stands | 32/- |
| 379 | Two very rich chocolate cups and stands | 30/- |
| 380 | Three cheese stands and 6 bakers, rich japan | 40/- |
| 381 | Eight hunting jugs | 24/- |
| 382 | Two chamber sets, gold jar, with carafts and tumblers | £2.10.9d. |
| 387 | Two fruit baskets, japan | 42/- |
| 388 | Six jugs, gold jar and 4 ditto grass-hopper | 26/- |
| 389 | Six mortars | 30/- |
| 390 | Seventeen ice plates, japan | 50/- |

**FOURTH DAY'S SALE**
**FRIDAY, the 7th Day of June, 1822**
**commencing at One o'Clock precisely**

| Lot | | Reserve |
|---|---|---|
| 391 | Two vegetable dishes for hot water, 2 cheese stands and 6 bakers, grass-hopper japan | 28/- |
| 392 | One ragout dish and cover and 2 vegetable dishes for hot water, japan | 30/- |
| 394 | Nine jugs and 4 covered ditto, blue | 30/- |
| 395 | Two small hexagon bottles, mazarine, with shades, and 2 small candlesticks, red ground, with ditto | 27/- |
| 396 | A breakfast set, bourbon sprig, 54 pieces | 30/- |
| 407 | Two chamber sets, green border, with carafts and tumblers | 45/- |
| 410 | Two soup tureens and stands, rich brown and gold border | 70/- |
| 412 | A Trentham jar, japan | 25/- |
| 413 | A set of 5 vases, painted shells and landscape, | 8gns. |
| 414 | A table service, japan | 11gns. |
| 415 | A ditto, peacock japan | 12gns. |
| 416 | A dessert service, gold jar japan | 80/- |
| 418 | A square supper set, rich japan | 50/- |
| 420 | One chamber set, Indian paintings, with caraft and tumbler | 30/- |
| 422 | Two vegetable dishes and 4 bakers, rich japan | 63/- |
| 426 | One dragon jar | 84/- |
| 427 | A splendid hall jar, mazarine and Oriental device | 12gns. |
| 428 | Four cabinet pieces | 12/- |
| 429 | Two rich toilet ewers and basins | 63/- |
| 430 | Four broth bowls and stands | 28/- |
| 435 | A table service, very richly japanned hexagon tureens, gold burnished tops | £26. |
| 443 | Nine stone jugs and 12 goblets | 24/- |
| 446 | A dessert service, rich japan, gold edge | 7gns. |
| 447 | Six beautiful plates | 30/- |
| 449 | Two fruit baskets and stands, japan | 30/- |
| 450 | Three Indian sprig jugs | 63/- |
| 452 | A pair of ice pails, very richly japanned | 63/- |
| 453 | Twenty-four lunch plates, enamelled | 12/- |
| 454 | Six bakers, rich japan | 15/- |
| 455 | Two hexagon vegetable dishes for hot water and 6 bakers nosegay | 30/- |
| 459 | Two tall Chinese jars | 15/- |
| 460 | Two small Indian pattern tea pots, pair vases, and glass shades | 30/- |

PLATE 87. *A rare covered jug, perhaps for hot punch, decorated with a standard Mason's printed outline Chinese-style design. Covered jugs are unusual but were included in the 1822 auction sale. 10in. (25.4cm) high.* c.*1820-30. S. O'Toole Collection.*

| | | |
|---|---|---|
| 461 | An Italian formed vase, superior painting, richly burnished and finely modelled | 18gns. |
| 462 | A breakfast set, Indian coloured sprigs, 70 pieces, gold edge | 35/- |
| 463 | A chamber service, very richly japanned, with carafts and tumblers | 42/- |
| 466 | A tea service, red and gold border | 30/- |
| 467 | A small breakfast service, japanned, 33 pieces | 105/- |
| 468 | A ditto, ungilt, 68 pieces | 63/- |
| 470 | Two foot pans, blue | 20/- |
| 471 | Two ditto | 20/- |
| 474 | A rose and apple jar | 42/- |
| 475 | Five two-handle vases, enamel sprig, on masarine ground | 50/- |
| 476 | Six beautiful plates | 40/- |
| 480 | Two ice pails, japan | 42/- |
| 481 | A hexagon temple jar | 28/- |
| 482 | Six bakers and 3 cheese stands | 25/- |
| 483 | Two vegetable dishes for hot water and a 22-inch dish, japan | 63/- |
| 484 | A coloured table service | 12gns. |
| 485 | A handsome table service, rich Indian devices, hexagon tureens | £21. |
| 486 | A table service, bourbon sprig | 12gns. |
| 488 | A pot pouri, ram's head, mazarine | 42/- |
| 489 | Two Indian flower jars, mazarine | 42/- |
| 492 | Three paper cases, beautifully painted | 42/- |
| 493 | A tea set, brown and gold border | 80/- |

494 A ditto coloured wreath, gilt, and 12 breakfast cups and saucers 73/-
503 Two white ice pails and 2 blue coolers 20/-
504 Six jugs and 3 covered ditto, blue, and 24 liquere glasses 35/-
505 A shell ink stand, red ground, 1 toy watering can, and 2 tea pots 32/-
506 Four square canisters, japan, with shades 40/-
507 Two ditto and a shell ink stand 20/-
509 A shaving box and 2 violet baskets, Dresden flower 20/-
511 A ditto, willow, japanned and richly gilt (only one tureen) 16gns.
514 Thirty-three preserving jars, white 50/-
518 Two hexagonal jars and covers, japan 21/-
519 A tea set, white, 45 pieces [perhaps of bone china] 15/-
520 A ditto, yellow and gold border, 45 pieces [ditto] 25/-

**FIFTH DAY'S SALE**
**SATURDAY, the 8th Day of JUNE, 1822**
**Commencing at One o'Clock precisely**

| Lot | | Reserve |
|---|---|---|
| 523 | Two mantle jars, masarine | ?40/- |
| 524 | One soup tureen, 4 bakers and 2 vegetable dishes for hot water, Mogul japan | ?40/- |
| 526 | One tea set, gilt japan, 49 pieces | 50/- |
| 537 | A table service, japan | no price |
| 538 | Two jars, sprigs, on mazarine | no price |
| 539 | A fine hall jar, Oriental design | no price |
| 540 | Four baskets, Dresden flowers, and 2 square bottles | 25/- |
| 544 | One chamber set, basket japan, with caraft and tumbler | 20/- |
| 545 | Two sets, green leaf border | 30/- |
| 546 | Six bakers, 4 boats and stands and 2 cheese stands, jar pattern | 28/- |
| 548 | A dessert, richly gilt Indian pattern | 147/6 |
| 551 | A breakfast service, blue, 100 pieces | 30/- |
| 552 | A chamber service, japanned and gilt, with caraft and tumbler | 25/- |
| 554 | A table service, birds, gilt | 7gns. |
| 558 | A dragon vase and cover, Indian devices | 73/6 |
| 567 | Eleven jugs, Indian form | 22/- |
| 568 | A large sideboard bowl | 4gns. |
| 570 | Two paper cases, raised figures on mazarine | 15/- |
| 571 | Two Indian-formed jars and shades | 4gns. |
| 567 | A very rich dessert service, Oriental style | 10gns. |
| 569 | A breakfast service, after the Chinese manner, 94 pieces | 6gns. |
| 576 | Two match cases, delicately finished, with shades | £3.10.0d. |
| 577 | Two beautiful antique coffee pots, withshades | £3.13.6d. |
| 580 | Eighteen preserving jars, white | 20/- |
| 582 | A dinner service, nosegay pattern | £12. |
| 584 | A toilet ewer and basin, rich pattern | 20/- |
| 585 | A flower bowl, ma'zarine and delicate sprigs | 30/- |
| 586 | Two exquisitely painted satyr goblets | £5. |
| 599 | Five rich mugs, various | 20/- |
| 600 | Twenty lunch plates | 20/- |
| 602 | Two potatoe dishes and covers, and 1 vegetable dish for hot water, japan | [no price] |
| 603 | A rich dessert service | £9.19.6d. |
| 606 | A table service, highly gilt, etc. | £22.10.0d. |
| 611 | Two wine coolers, richly japanned | £2. |
| 612 | A small lunch service, blue and gold edge, 27 pieces | [no price] |
| 613 | Two octagonal jars, Chinese | [no price] |
| 614 | A conservatory bowl | [no price] |
| 615 | Two Indian bottles with shades | [no price] |
| 616 | A mazarine toilet, ewer and basin, with shades | [no price] |
| 617 | Four small flower pots and stands, mazarine and delicate sprigs | [no price] |
| 625 | A hall jar, lion head handles | £2.10.0d. |

PLATE 88. *A neatly potted Mason's ironstone inkstand, perhaps as the 'shell inkstands' included in the 1822 sale of stock, Lots 505, 507 or 805. 3in. (7.62cm) high. c.1820-25.*

PLATE 89. *A very rare double inkstand with loose ink containers impressed marked 'Mason's Ironstone'. Perhaps the 'shell escritoire' (Lot 805). Another example of porcelain quality ironstone objects. 5¼in. (13.33cm) long. c.1820-25. R.G. Austin Collection.*

| | | |
|---|---|---|
| 626 | A table service, enamelled and gilt in the Oriental manner | £22.10.0d. |
| 627 | A very highly japanned chamber service | 45/- |
| 628 | A breakfast service, Chinese coloured sprigs, 116 pieces | 90/- |
| 631 | Twelve white jugs | [no price] |
| 632 | A two-handled Etruscan formed flower vase highly finished in flowers and gold, with shade | [no price] |
| 641 | A pagoda vase, for vestibule | [no price] |
| 642 | Two very rich water jugs | [no price] |
| 643 | Four mugs, richly gilt | [no price] |
| 644 | A Trentham bowl | [no price] |
| 647 | Two very rich chocolate cups and covers | [no price] |
| 648 | Three large and 2 small dishes, and 1 drainer, coloured | [no price] |
| 649 | Twelve stone jugs, of two shapes | [no price] |
| 650 | Two chamber sets, jar pattern | [no price] |

**SIXTH DAY'S SALE**
**MONDAY, the 10th Day of JUNE, 1822**
**Commencing at One o'Clock precisely**

| Lot | | Reserve |
|---|---|---|
| 655 | Four mortars and 2 porous wine coolers | 30/- |
| 660 | Two chamber services, gold jar pattern | 35/- |
| 661 | Twelve melange breakfast cups and saucers | 18/- |
| 666 | Two chocolate cups and saucers and 7 useful pieces of table ware | 27/- |
| 669 | Two fruit baskets and stands, Oriental designs | 35/- |
| 670 | Three paper cases, rich, with shades | 35/- |
| 671 | Two octagon jars | 63/- |
| 672 | Twelve beautifully finished plates, various | 80/- |
| 673 | Two serpent handled jars | 42/- |
| 674 | Two vases, green ground, fruit and shades | 84/- |
| 678 | A table service, richly coloured and gilt, hexagon tureens | £26. |
| 680 | A square supper service, finished japan | 70/- |
| 681 | A small breakfast set, 30 pieces | 30/- |
| 682 | A chamber service, richly gilt | 35/- |
| 684 | A table service, green ground, Dresden border | 15gns. |
| 686 | Two handsome jars and covers | 50/- |
| 689 | A table service, blue | 9gns. |
| 691 | A splendid hall jar, from an improved Indian model | 16gns. |
| 692 | Two delicate vases, with shades | 24/- |
| 693 | Four japan candlesticks, mazarine | 16/- |
| 694 | A very richly finished tea set, 45 pieces | 8gns. |
| 695 | An Indian pattern breakfast service, 77 pieces | 30/- |
| 701 | Four candlesticks and extinguishers, mazarine japan | 15/- |
| 702 | Two large flat candlesticks, masarine, with shades | 42/- |
| 703 | Two handsome mantle jars, with shades | 45/- |
| 704 | Four rich jugs | 35/- |
| 705 | A table service, coloured hexagon tureens | 17gns. |

PLATE 90. *A rare Mason's ironstone Oriental-patterned sauce or gravy boat. These, like the Chinese export-market examples, had stands. 6¾in. (17.14cm) long. c.1820-30.*

PLATE 91. *Representative pieces of a Mason's ironstone dessert service, showing typical forms of the 1815-25 period. Centrepiece 14in. (35.56cm) long. Mason's Works Collection.*

| | | |
|---|---|---|
| 706 | A small breakfast service, 28 pieces | 42/- |
| 709 | A dessert service, blue foliage | 3gns. |
| 710 | Two beautiful painted goblets | 4gns. |
| 711 | Four delicate cabinet pieces | 24/- |
| 716 | Two porous coolers and 4 mortars | 30/- |
| 720 | A table service, blue | 9gns. |
| 721 | A ditto, rich japan | 25gns. |
| 722 | Two toilet ewers and basins, and 2 chocolate cups, rich | 30/- |
| 723 | Seven dishes, rich japan | 30/- |

PLATE 92. *A colourful, impressed marked Mason's Japan pattern chamber-pot. Various 'Chamber sets' or toilet wares were included in the 1822 sale. 6in. (15.24cm) high. c.1815-25.*

PLATE 93. *A very rare impressed marked Mason's Japan pattern bourdalou or lady's chamber-pot. 8¼in. (20.95cm) long. c.1815-25.*

| | | |
|---|---|---|
| 728 | Six highly wrought plates | 60/- |
| 729 | Six soup ditto | 50/- |
| 730 | Two fruit baskets and stands, rich | 35/- |
| 731 | Two sugar bowls, covers and stands, japanned | 24/- |
| 738 | An elegant flower vase, with shade | 42/- |
| 740 | A chamber service, green leaf border | 20/- |
| 741 | A table service, nosegay pattern, hexagon tureens | 12gns. |
| 743 | Six compotiers | 20/- |
| 744 | Seven bakers, rich japan | 30/- |
| 745 | Two vegetable dishes for hot water, a ragout dish and cover and 2 bakers, coloured | 40/- |
| 746 | One 20-inch gravy dish, 1 cheese stand and 1 vegetable dish for hot water | 25/- |
| 750 | Two two-handled low vases, with shades | 40/- |
| 751 | One toilet ewer and basin | 21/- |
| 752 | Five scent jars and covers | 42/- |
| 753 | Two large flat candlesticks, mazarine with shades | 42/- |
| 754 | A hall bowl | 42/- |
| 756 | A table set, plaid japan, richly gilt | £30. |
| 758 | A breakfast service, japan, 54 pieces | 105/- |
| 760 | A square supper set, Indian pattern with border | 40/- |
| 761 | Two chamber services and gold jar | 40/- |
| 762 | A small melange breakfast set, 31 pieces | 23/- |
| 763 | Two cream bowls and covers, gold thorn | 18/- |
| 771 | A table set, brown border | 73/- |
| 772 | A dessert set ditto, 4 chamber sets ditto, with carafts and tumblers | 70/- |

**SEVENTH DAY'S SALE**
**TUESDAY, the 11th Day of June, 1822**
**commencing at One o'Clock precisely**

| Lot | | Reserve |
|---|---|---|
| 781 | Twelve jars and covers | 16/- |
| 783 | Two porous wine coolers and 2 butter tubs | 15/- |
| 785 | Ten jugs from the antique | 23/- |
| 793 | Two sprinkling bottles, 2 cups and covers, moth on mazarine ground with glass shades | 30/- |

PLATE 94. *A rare, well-decorated pair of deep blue-ground Mason's ironstone square section tall vases, richly enamelled and gilt. 13½in. (34.29cm) high. c.1815-25.*

PLATE 95. *Two rich blue-ground dessert dishes, the ground 'enriched by moths, flowers and gilt decoration' – a description used in the 1822 sale catalogue, 10in. and 9in. (25.4cm and 22.86cm) long. c.1820-25. The late Mrs M. Symes Collection.*

PLATE 96. *An impressed marked Mason's ironstone dessert dish with deep blue borders very richly gilt with leafage with hand-painted floral sprays to centre. 10½in. x 9in. (26.67cm x 22.86cm). c.1815-25.*

PLATE 97. *An unusual form of impressed marked jug with rich blue ground, with enamel and gilt decoration. 5¾in. (14.6cm). c.1815-25.*

PLATE 98 (left). *A standard 'antique' or 'Hydra' jug well decorated with rich blue ground and good quality over-gilding. Impressed mark. 8¾in. (22.22cm) high. c.1815-25.*

795 A pair of toy chamber candlesticks and 2 buckets with glasses 23/-
796 A breakfast set, dragon, 43 pieces 50/-
801 Two chamber suites, blue and white 30/-
803 A dessert service, painted and gold flower, 43 pieces 8gns.
805 A shell escritoire and pair of match cases, blue and gold 32/-
806 Ten mugs, embossed hunting figures 20/-
807 Twelve broth basins and stands 30/-
808 Six punch bowls 25/-
809 A pair of toy hand candlesticks, a pen tray, and sprinkling pot, gold edges and flowers 25/-
813 A chamber suite, blue and gold edge 20/-
814 A DINNER SERVICE, blue and white 9gns.
815 Twelve fruit dishes 12/-
816 A pair of blue bottles, raised flower, an ink cup and canister and 4 glass shades 28/-
817 A pair of ice pails and 2 baskets and stands 25/-
819 A chamber set, japan gold edge 30/-
826 Two vegetable dishes and covers and a steak ditto 25/-
827 Two blue essence bottles, 2 wax hand candlesticks, gilt and painted flower, 2 inkstands and 4 glass shades 35/-
828 A chamber suite, japan flower 25/-
829 Eight broth basins and stands 20/-
831 A pair of handsome vases, richly gilt and painted in flowers, and 2 blue bottles in birds and glass shades 30/-
837 A costly DESSERT SERVICE, exquisitely painted in SELECT VIEWS, by S. Bourne, enriched with burnished gold[Plate 55] 35gns.
838 Ten jugs, embossed flowers and figures 23/-
839 A handsome DINNER SERVICE, painted in roses 18gns.
840 A DESSERT DITTO, japan and gilt flowers, 43 pieces £8.
842 Two neat essence bottles, gold sprig, and 2 jugs with glass shades 35/-
850 A handsome japan and gilt DINNER SERVICE £21.
851 A dessert service, blue and gold border 9gns.
852 Two blue essence bottles, small sprig, 2 hand candlesticks,a pot pouri and cup and cover 25/-
855 A handsome DESSERT SERVICE, painted in boquets, relieved by sea green and gold devices [Plate 78] 15gns.
856 A pair of handsome jars, with glass shades 28/-
857 An ice pail, japan, and 1 ditto barbeaux 30/-
858 Two vegetable dishes and covers, 2 cheeses stands and 4 bakers 25/-
859 A handsome escritoire and 2 essence bottles 25/-
862 A pair of toy jars, gilt and painted in flowers, and a violet basket painted in landscapes 25/-
863 A pair of handsome ice pails 37/-
866 A NOBLE VASE, formed from the antique. Beautifully painted in landscapes and figures, by Bourne, and sumptuously gilt £21.
867 A pair of ornaments in the style of the Portland vase and shades 50/-
868 A pair of neat jars and covers 40/-
872 A violet basket, painted in a landscape, a toy jug, an ink stand and sprinkler 20/-
873 A pair of handsome candlesticks, painted in flowers and glass shades 30/-
875 A pair of jars, neat sprig, on blue ground 63/-
878 A pair of jars, painted in landscapes and glass shades 40/-

PLATE 99. *A large blue ground Mason's vase, superbly decorated in a typical style favoured in the 1820s. 24in. (60.96cm) high. c.1820-25. Messrs Bonhams.*

879 A handsome TABLE SERVICE, japanned 13gns.
880 A pair of beakers, painted in flowers, and a japan vase 20/-
881 A NOBLE ESSENCE JAR, painted in flowers, on celests ground, relieved by burnished gold 20gns.
882 A pair of reading candlesticks, Dresden flower, a pen tray and an ink stand with glass shade 30/-
883 A handsome jug, painted in landscapes and hunting subject 42/-
887 A handsome ESSENCE URN, blue ground, enriched by moths, flowers and gilt decorations 84/-
888 A ditto, its companion 84/-
889 Two ice pails, rich japan 84/-
894 A coffee ewer, richly gilt, from the antique, and glass shade 25/-
896 A breakfast set, India sprig, 44 pieces 50/-
897 A pair of flower pots and stands, painted in moths, and an accurate sun dial with glass shades 25/-
898 Six handsome dessert plates, sumptuously gilt 36/-
899 A pair of neat reading candlesticks, with glass shades 25/-
901 Two violet baskets, 2 hand candlesticks, gilt and painted in flowers and 2 sprinkling pots 30/-

PLATE 100. *A simple impressed marked Mason's ironstone Japan-pattern candlestick, perhaps described as the 'japan reading candlestick' (Lot 989). 6in. (15.24cm) high. c.1820-25.*

903 A pair of blue jars, raised figures, on blue ground and glass shades
904 Two toy jugs and a sprinkler, a japan flower, 3 glasses and 4 toy candlesticks 40/-
905 A toy ewer and basin, painted in landscapes, 2 pair of candlesticks and glass shades 25/-
907 Six punch bowls 20/-
908 A breakfast set, 41 pieces, blue flower 35/-
909 Three japan jugs, gilt edge 24/-
910 Twelve breakfast cups and saucers, small sprig 20/-
919 A soup tureen and cover, Japan 12/-
920 Four delicate cabinet pieces and shades 27/-
925 Four plaid Japan dishes and drainers 105/-

### EIGHTH DAY'S SALE
### FRIDAY, the 14th Day of JUNE, 1822
### commencing at One o'Clock precisely

Lot — Reserve
932 Two vegetable dishes and steak ditto with covers and liners, for hot water 28/-
933 Two chamber suites, blue and white 30/-
941 An ewer basin and slipper, japan 15/-
952 Nine jugs, 4 covered ditto and 3 mugs 35/-
957 Twenty-one hexagon shape blue jugs 45/-
958 A pair of vases and covers, masarine, 1 faulty 30/-
959 A dessert service, colour japan 4gns.
960 Two chamber suites, blue and white 30/-
964 A pair of hexagon essence jars, painted in flowers, and a glass shade 3gns.
967 A japan vase and shade 30/-
968 Two vegetable dishes and steak ditto, with covers and liners 28/-
970 A DINNER SERVICE, coloured japan 14gns.
972 Two rich cabinet cups, covers and stands, painted in landscapes and shades 70/-
973 A japan ewer and basin, soap and brush trays 20/-
975 Two pastil burners with glass shades, and 2 match cases, mazarine 42/-
978 A sprinkling can, 2 shell candlesticks and 3 egg cups 20/-
981 An essence jar, painted in flowers on green ground, and glass shades 31/6
984 Five ornamental vases 46/-
986 Three handsome paper vases with glass shades 40/-
987 Two vegetable dishes, covers and liners, and a steak ditto 28/-
989 A pair of japan reading candlesticks and 2 paper cases, birds on green ground 42/-
991 A vase and 2 match cases, mazarine, and glass shades 46/-
995 Two candlesticks, 2 vases, and 2 paper cases, masarine glass shades 40/-
997 A lofty ESSENCE JAR, dragon handles, japan flower and gilt ornaments 70/-
1001 An essence bottle, 2 vases, 2 scent pots, and 3 glass shades 46/-
1004 Two scent bottles, 2 candlesticks, 2 hexagon bottles, and 4 glass shades 35/-
1007 A scent bottle, 2 ditto pots, and 2 paper cases and glass shade 25/-
1008 A noble square ESSENCE JAR and COVER, Masarine ground, enriched with flowers, etc. 20gns.
1010 A TABLE SERVICE, green border 15gns.
1012 Two hexagon jugs, 2 ditto bottles and 2 taper candlesticks,and 4 glass shades 40/-
1016 A handsome NEAPOLITAN VASE, formed from the antique, beautifully painted in landscapes, enriched with burnished gold, by S. Bourne [as Plate 28] 15gns.
1017 Six essence bottles and covers, 2 paper cases, in landscapes, and 6 shades 40/-
1018 A NOBLE CISTERN, japan flowers and gilt dolphin handles 10gns.
1022 Five scent bottles, 3 match cases, painted in landscapes, with 2 shades 52/6
1024 Two vegetable dishes and steak ditto, with covers and liners 28/-
1028 Two essence bottles, toy tea pot, 2 ink stands, 2 paper cases in landscapes, and 7 glass shades 50/-
1029 A pair of handsome vases 46/-
1030 A DINNER SERVICE, coloured japan £20.
1033 Two match cases, birds on green ground, 2 jars and covers, a bottle and 2 vases, with glass shades 46/-
1038 Three paper cases, landscapes, a bottle, an inkstand, and 4 shades 50/-
1039 A LOFTY JAPAN ESSENCE JAR AND COVER, with gold enrichments 8gns.
1043 Two wafer baskets in landscapes, 2 bottles and shades, 3 cups and saucers, and 2 glass shades 40/-
1044 Two vegetable and 1 steak dishes, with covers and liners 28/-

PLATE 101. *Representative pieces from a large impressed marked Mason's ironstone dinner service of the type sold each day in the 1822 auction sale of stock. Tureen 11¾in. (29.84cm) long. c.1820-30. Messrs Sotheby's, New York.*

| | | |
|---|---|---|
| 1046 | Two ewers and basins, japan | 35/- |
| 1049 | Three ornamental vases and covers | 60/- |
| 1057 | Two toy jugs and shades, 3 paper cases and shades | 35/- |
| 1058 | A toy ewer and basin, and 3 flat candlesticks and 3 shades | 28/- |
| 1059 | A handsome ewer and basin, India sprig | 20/- |

**NINTH DAY'S SALE**
**SATURDAY, the 15th Day of JUNE, 1822**
**Commencing at One o'Clock**

| Lot | | Reserve |
|---|---|---|
| 1063 | Three vegetable dishes and a steak ditto, with covers and liners | 30/- |
| 1071 | A steak dish and 2 vegetable dishes, with covers and liners for hot water | 23/- |
| 1073 | Four large beakers, green dragon | 25/- |
| 1074 | A pair of reading candlesticks and shades | 40/- |
| 1076 | Three violet baskets, a wafer box, vase and 2 churns | 15/- |
| 1077 | A roll tray, potatoe dish, 2 nappies, and bowl | 14/- |
| 1078 | Two jars and covers, and 2 vases, green dragon (1 faulty) | 40/- |
| 1079 | Six ewers and basins, and 6 slippers, blue | 30/- |
| 1080 | A DINNER SERVICE, Tourney sprig | 13gns. |
| 1081 | A ditto, blue and white (1 soup tureen) | £6. |
| 1082 | Two jars and covers, a cup and saucer, and 3 vases | 30/- |
| 1086 | A DINNER SERVICE, embossed, blue foliage (no soup tureens) | 15gns. |
| 1089 | Two japan vases, and a paper case | 25/- |
| 1095 | Two mummy Jars, and 2 octagon vases | 40/- |
| 1096 | An ink stand, 2 wafer baskets, and 2 candlesticks and shades | 30/- |
| 1097 | Two card racks, and 2 incense burners, mazarine | 46/- |
| 1098 | Two vases and covers, and 2 jars and covers | 40/- |
| 1099 | Four large bottles, dragon | 40/- |
| 1102 | Four vegetable dishes and 3 small ewers and basins | 40/- |
| 1104 | An ink stand, 2 canisters, 2 candlesticks and shades | 35/- |
| 1107 | Six ewers and basons, and 6 slippers, white | 60/- |
| 1108 | Two vases and 4 bottles, dragon | 40/- |
| 1112 | Two jars and covers, and 2 vases | £2. |
| 1113 | Pair of ice pails, rich japan | 3½gns. |
| 1114 | Forty-eight cups and saucers and 24 basins, blue | 28/- |
| 1115 | Six ewers and basins, and six slippers; blue | 30/- |
| 1119 | Six ewers and basins, and 12 mugs and jugs | 23/- |
| 1123 | Forty-eight cups and saucers and 24 basins, blue | 30/- |
| 1124 | A rich japan DINNER SERVICE | £21. |
| 1130 | Six ewers and basins, and 6 slippers | 30/- |
| 1133 | A handsome TABLE SERVICE, blue, enamel and gold border | £20. |
| 1139 | A pair of ice pails, richly coloured and gold border | 90/- |
| 1140 | Two hexagon soup tureens, 4 sauce ditto, 4 dishes and covers, rich japan, and 2 salad bowls, flower and gold decoration | 25gns. |
| 1143 | Two card racks and 2 incense burners, masarine | 30/- |
| 1146 | A pair of ice pails, rich japan | 70/- |
| 1147 | Four vegetable dishes, and 3 small ewers and basins | 35/- |
| 1148 | Two vases and covers, and 2 jars and covers | 40/- |
| 1150 | A splendid japan DINNER SERVICE | £42. |
| 1153 | Six ewers and basins, and 4 slippers, white | 42/- |
| 1173 | A table service, blue birds | £9. |
| 1189 | Six handsome chimney ornaments | 60/- |
| 1190 | A DINNER SERVICE, blue and white | £9. |

THE REMAINDER OF THE
STOCK OF CHINA
OF THE LATE
MR. MASON
PATENTEE AND MANUFACTURER OF THE IRON
STONE CHINA
AT NO. 11, ALBEMARLE STREET.
A
CATALOGUE
OF THE
ENTIRE ASSEMBLAGE OF USEFUL & DECORATIVE
PORCELANE,
OF RICH AND ELEGANT PATTERNS:
COMPRISING
SEVERAL HUNDRED
DINNER, DESSERT, BREAKFAST, & TEA SERVICES;
JUGS, EWERS, BASINS,
DISHES IN SETS, BOTH OPEN AND COVERED;
PLATES IN DOZENS, OF EVERY SIZE;
NOBLE ORNAMENTAL JARS & EWERS,
**Superbly Gilt and beautifully Enamelled;**
AND
A GREAT VARIETY OF CABINET ORNAMENTS,
OF THE MOST TASTEFUL AND ELEGANT FORMS,
**The extent, Variety, and great Value of this Stock afford the most advantageous opportunity to the public to provide themselves with Porcelane of every class, and of peculiar strength, for which the Iron Stone China has long been distinguished.**
WHICH WILL BE SOLD BY AUCTION
BY MR. PHILLIPS,
ON THE PREMISES,
AT NO. 11, ALBEMARLE STREET,
**On THURSDAY, the 20th day of JUNE, 1822,**
**And Two following Days, at Twelve for ONE PRECISELY,**

BY ORDER OF THE EXECUTORS
WITHOUT RESERVE
FIRST DAY'S SALE
**THURSDAY, the 20th day of JUNE, 1822**
**Commencing at Twelve for One o'Clock precisely**

| Lot | | Reserve |
|---|---|---|
| 1 | Twelve breakfast cups and saucers and 12 tea ditto, earthenware | 10/- |
| 2 | Twenty-four breakfast cups and saucers and 2 milks, earthenware | 12/- |
| 4 | Five hunting jugs, stone | 12/- |
| 5 | Twelve mugs, iron stone | 14/- |
| 6 | Seven ditto, stone | 12/- |
| 8 | Six antique jugs, iron stone | 15/- |
| 9 | A pair of Chinese formed jars | 52/- |
| 10 | A fine pot pourie | 30/- |
| 13 | A table service, blue, iron stone, 142 pieces (2 soup tureens, covers and stands, 4 sauce ditto, 18 dishes, 1 drainer, 4 ragout dishes, 1 salad, 60 plates, 18 soup, 18 dessert) | £9. |
| 14 | Two rich fruit baskets and stands | 30/- |
| 17 | Two match cases, an antique coffee pot and 2 shades | 36/- |
| 18 | Five jugs from a beautiful Chinese original | 30/- |
| 19 | Two chocolate cups and stands, very rich | 18/- |
| 20 | Two pair of Chinese beakers | 36/- |
| 26 | A pair of well painted vases | 42/- |
| 29 | Two highly finished candlesticks and shades | 24/- |
| 31 | Two match cases, and shades, mazarine | 22/- |
| 32 | A breakfast service, japan colours and gold, 22 pieces | £8. |
| 33 | A pair of rich ice pails | £3.10.0d. |
| 36 | Two rich caddies and shades | 42/- |

PLATE 102. *Representative pieces from a Japan pattern tea or breakfast service, showing rare cup forms. Plate 8½in. (21.59cm) in diameter. c.1820-30.*

| | | |
|---|---|---|
| 37 | A pair of beautiful hexagon flower pots and stands | £3.10.0d. |
| 42 | A beautiful flower bowl, mazarine | 18/- |
| 48 | A breakfast set, 52 pieces | 40/- |
| 49 | A lofty hall jar | 7gns. |
| 50 | A dinner set, blue and white earthenware, 142 pieces | 6gns. |
| 51 | A set of 3 vases and shades | 36/- |
| 54 | Two vases, landscapes, and crimson grounds | 30/- |
| 55 | Two khan dragon beakers | 30/- |
| 56 | A pair of rich chamber candlesticks and shades | 30/- |
| 59 | A pair of card cases, mazarine and white embossed figures | 24/- |
| 64 | A fine dragon jar | 4gns. |
| 65 | A table service, basket pattern, 142 pieces | 14gns. |
| 66 | A set of 5 jars | 50/- |
| 68 | Four jugs and 5 mugs, stone | 18/- |
| 69 | Four antique jugs, corbeau | £1. |
| 72 | Two very rich vases | £3.10.0d. |
| 77 | A pair of essence burners, masarine | 32/- |
| 79 | Three handsome vases, painted in landscape, and shades | 4gns. |
| 80 | Two vases, flies, on mazarine (ground) and shades | 28/- |
| 84 | One handsome japan vase and shade | £1. |
| 85 | Five vases and covers, japan | £2. |
| 92 | A handsome japan bowl | 30/- |
| 93 | Two vegetable dishes and 1 steak dish | 38/- |
| 102 | Two vegetable dishes, rich japan | 50/- |
| 103 | Six beakers and 3 cheese stands, ditto | 50/- |
| 106 | Two vases and covers, green dragons | 30/- |
| 107 | Four rich jugs, corbeau | 20/- |
| 108 | Three paper cases, rich landscapes | 30/- |
| 109 | Two ewers and basins, and 2 slippers, blue | 25/- |
| 110 | Two bottles, mazarine, and shades, and 2 baskets, landscapes | 27/- |
| 112 | A pair of ice pails, rich border | £4.10.0d. |
| 113 | One essence pot, masarine, and 3 cabinet cups and saucers | 28/- |
| 120 | Two vegetable dishes and 1 steak ditto, blue | 28/- |
| 122 | Two paper cases, landscape, and 2 essence bottles and 4 shades | 30/- |
| 123 | One toy tea pot, 2 inks and 3 shades | 24/- |
| 124 | A dragon pattern earthenware breakfast set, 92 pieces | 37/- |

End of the First Day

**SECOND DAY'S SALE**
**FRIDAY, the 21st Day of JUNE, 1822**
**Commencing at One o'Clock precisely**

| Lot | | Reserve |
|---|---|---|
| 131 | Three ewers and basins, and 3 slippers, white | 30/- |
| 133 | Two foot pans, white | 25/- |
| 134 | Two dozen blue earthenware cups and saucers, 2 tea pots, 4 basins, and 2 milks | 15/- |
| 137 | A square supper set, 8 pieces, snipe pattern | 40/- |
| 139 | Two vegetable dishes, and 1 steak ditto, blue | 25/- |
| 141 | A dessert service, India landscape, 43 pieces | £4. |
| 145 | Eight baking dishes in sizes, peacock | 16/- |
| 147 | Two candlesticks, japan, and 2 paper cases, birds | 25/- |
| 148 | Three paper cases, painted birds, and shades | 40/- |
| 152 | A pair of vases and covers, mazarine | 35/- |
| 153 | Two hexagon bottles, 2 ditto jugs, and 2 taper candlesticks and 4 shades | 36/- |
| 155 | Two hexagon vases and covers, dragon | 30/- |
| 161 | A square supper set, willow japan, 12 pieces | 78/- |
| 162 | Two bottles, and 2 scent pots, enamelled | 22/- |
| 163 | Two vegetable dishes and 1 steak ditto, blue | 25/- |
| 167 | Two handled vases, mazarine, and shades | 24/- |
| 168 | Two vases, mazarine, and 2 essence bottles, japan and glass shades | 30/- |
| 174 | Two Spanish vases and covers, japan | 44/- |
| 181 | A dessert set, red and gold rose, 43 pieces | £8.10.0d. |
| 184 | Two small bottles and 2 essence ditto, mazarine and shades | 27/- |
| 188 | A handsome antique jug | 23/- |
| 190 | A very rich coloured and gilt table service, 142 pieces | £35. |
| 194 | A rich antique vase | 35/- |
| 195 | Two Spanish vases, coloured and gilt | 30/- |
| 196 | A paper case, and 2 small jugs, mazarine and shades | 20/- |
| 198 | A pair of vases and covers, green dragon | 15/- |
| 199 | A handsome antique jug | 20/- |
| 202 | Two baskets and stands, japan | 50/- |
| 203 | Two tall hexagonal bottles, mazarine | 35/- |
| 204 | Four flower pots and stands, mazarine | 63/- |
| 206 | Two bottles, India figures and landscape | 30/- |
| 207 | Two three-handled vases, mazarine | 60/- |
| 208 | Two vases, views in Rome | 80/- |
| 209 | Three vases, fainted in landscape | 70/- |
| 211 | A vase, painted in shells | 50/- |
| 212 | A tea set, rock pattern, 41 pieces | 50/- |
| 213 | Two tall jars and covers, dragon | 15/- |
| 214 | Twelve custard cups and covers, basket pattern | 14/- |
| 217 | An ewer and basin, and brush tray, handsome japan | 46/- |
| 219 | A shell ink stand, and 2 paper cases, flower border | 23/- |
| 220 | A table service, peacock, japan, 87 pieces | £8.10.0d. |
| 221 | A dessert set, japan, 43 pieces | 8gns. |
| 225 | A handsome antique ewer, japanned and gilt | 25/- |
| 226 | A pair of flat candlesticks and extinquishers, mazarine | 25/- |
| 227 | A tea set, gold border, 44 pieces | 50/- |
| 231 | Two vases and 2 beakers, green dragon | 30/- |
| 232 | A large essence jar, jappaned and gilt | 42/- |
| 234 | Two bottles, 2 vases, and a watering pot, mazarine | 30/- |
| 236 | Two buckets, 2 ink stands, and 2 flat candlesticks | 23/- |
| 237 | Two handsome vases and shades | 28/- |
| 239 | A dejeune, coloured sprigs | 35/- |
| 245 | Five punch bowls, blue | 30/- |
| 246 | A breakfast set, blue, 54 pieces | 23/- |
| 247 | Four broth basins, 3 pudding ditto, 5 mugs, and 2 boats, blue | 23/- |
| 248 | Four candlesticks, 2 small ewers and basins, and 2 broth basins, blue | 23/- |
| 249 | Two vegetable dishes and 1 steak ditto, blue | 25/- |
| 250 | Three small vases, and an essence pot, flowers | 18/- |
| 251 | A caddy, candlestick, jug, mazarine, and ink stand | 15/- |
| 252 | Six ewers and 6 basins, blue earthenware | 23/- |
| 257 | Two vegetable dishes, 2 small ewers and basins, and 4 mugs, white | 23/- |

**THIRD DAY'S SALE**
**SATURDAY, the 22nd Day of JUNE, 1822**
**Commencing at One o'Clock precisely**

| Lot | | Reserve |
|---|---|---|
| 262 | One potato dish, 3 hot water plates, 7 bakers, and 3 pudding basins, white | 22/- |
| 263 | Six ewers and basins, blue earthenware | 15/- |
| 266 | Two vegetable dishes, and 1 steak dish, blue | 24/- |

| | | |
|---|---|---|
| 268 | Three jugs, japan flowers and gold edge | 21/- |
| 269 | One chamber set, gold jar | 31/- |
| 270 | A table service, blue, 87 pieces (1 soup tureen, cover and stand, 2 sauce ditto, 2 covered vegetable (or ragours), sallad, 13 dishes, 36 meat plates, 12 soups, 12 sweets) | £5.0.0d. |
| 271 | Twelve jugs, blue earthenware, and 12 cups and saucers | 14/- |
| 281 | Twelve custard cups and covers, grasshopper | 14/- |
| 285 | Three beakers, mazarine sprigs | 16/- |
| 286 | Two bottles, ditto and white flowers | 24/- |
| 287 | Two Grecian shape vases, flowers and green ground with shades | 63/- |
| 289 | A handsome two-handle vase, mazarine and shade | 42/- |
| 292 | Two handsome satyr vases, painted in landscape and shades | 90/- |
| 295 | Two candlesticks, green, and flowers with shades | 28/- |
| 296 | A handsome one handled vase, fruit and green ground | 30/- |
| 297 | Two hexagon vases, japan, with shades (1 faulty) | 42/- |
| 298 | A handsome japan dessert set, 43 pieces | 14gns. |
| 299 | A pair of ice pails, ditto | 90/- |
| 300 | A table service, blue, 87 pieces | £5.0.0d. |
| 302 | Two rich vases, fruit and green grounds | 50/- |
| 305 | A handsome Trentham bowl | 24/- |
| 307 | A small ewer and basin, 2 toy watering cans and 2 shell candlesticks | 27/- |
| 311 | A pair of four-handled vases, mazarine | 42/- |
| 312 | Two Spanish vases, mazarine | 42/- |
| 314 | A pair of urns, beautifully painted in landscapes and glass shades | 48/- |
| 315 | A pair of vases, mazarine, and shell escretoire and 2 glass shades | 48/- |
| 316 | A pair of flower pots and stands, painted in birds, with glass shades and two match cases | 28/- |
| 317 | A pair of jars, japanned, flower and dragon handles | 24/- |
| 319 | A pair of green dragon beakers | 21/- |
| 321 | A dessert service, japan, birds and flowers, 43 pieces | £5.0.0d. |
| 323 | Four jars and beakers, green dragon | 60/- |
| 324 | Pair of hand candlesticks and extinguishers, and 2 bottles flowers on mazarine ground | 28/- |
| 326 | A rich blue and gold ewer and basin with glass shade | 38/- |
| 327 | A pair of ditto essence burners, and 2 cups and covers | 30/- |
| 329 | A blue and gold coffee ewer and 2 tea canisters | 26/- |
| 332 | Two flat candlesticks and extinguishers, 1 toy ewer and basin, 2 essence bottles and 5 shades | 38/- |
| 333 | A chamber set, rich japan | 70/- |
| 336 | Two broth basins, covers and stands, rich japan | 28/- |
| 337 | Two hexagon vases and covers, mazarine | 42/- |
| 338 | Two rich candlesticks and extinguishers, and 1 small vase, japan | 28/- |
| 339 | A dejeune, rich japan | 50/- |
| 341 | Six plates, birds and shells on gold border | 30/- |
| 342 | Two match cases, mazarine, and shades | 18/- |
| 344 | Two Satyr vases, flowers and red ground | 63/- |
| 345 | Two beakers and covers, Chinese pattern | 20/- |
| 346 | Pair of ice pails, flowers and blue border | 5gns. |
| 347 | A table service, blue sprig and gold edge, 142 pieces | 15gns. |
| 349 | Two bottles and 1 beaker, green dragon | 20/- |
| 354 | Two coolers, plaid Japan | 50/- |
| 357 | A supper set, 5 pieces, and tray, rose japan | 21/- |
| 360 | Two candlesticks, japan, and 1 antique vase | 26/- |
| 364 | A rich flat candlestick and extinguisher, and a pair small bottles, mazarine | 12/- |
| 368 | Four oval dishes and covers, blue | 22/- |
| 369 | Four antique jugs, corbeau | 20/- |
| 377 | A supper set, blue, 9 pieces | 21/- |
| 380 | A table service, blue, 87 pieces | £5. |
| 381 | A breakfast set, dragon, 62 pieces | 48/- |
| 384 | Two vegetable dishes, peacock pattern | 42/- |
| 386 | Eight beakers, blue | 16/- |
| 387 | Twenty four tea cups and saucers, dragon, earthenware | 8/- |
| 388 | Twenty-four ditto, blue earthenware | 8/- |
| 389 | Twelve jugs, blue earthenware | 12/- |

THE LAST PART OF THE
STOCK OF CHINA
OF THE LATE
MR. MASON
PATENTEE AND MANUFACTURER OF THE IRON
STONE CHINA
AT NO. 11, ALBEMARLE STREET

A
CATALOGUE
OF
THE REMAINING STOCK
OF USEFUL & DECORATIVE
PORCELANE,
OF RICH AND ELEGANT PATTERNS:
COMPRISING
DINNER, DESSERT, BREAKFAST, & TEA SERVICES;
JUGS, EWERS, BASINS,
DISHES IN SETS, BOTH OPEN AND COVERED;
PLATES
AND A
VARIETY OF CABINET ORNAMENTS,
OF THE MOST TASTEFUL AND ELEGANT FORMS.

**The extent, Variety, and great Value of this Stock affords the most advantageous opportunity to the public to provide themselves with Porcelane of every class, and of peculiar strength, for which the Iron Stone China has long been distinguished.**

WHICH WILL BE SOLD BY AUCTION
BY MR. PHILLIPS.
ON THE PREMISES,
AT NO. 11, ALBEMARLE STREET,
**ON FRIDAY, the 28th day of JUNE, 1822**
**And following Day, at Twelve for ONE precisely,**
BY ORDER OF THE EXECUTORS

**May be Viewed One Day preceding the Sale, and Catalogues had on the premises; at the Auction Marts; and at Mr. PHILLIPS', 73, New Bond Street.**

FIRST DAY'S SALE
**FRIDAY, the 28th Day of JUNE, 1822**
**Commencing at One o'Clock precisely**

| Lot | | Reserve |
|---|---|---|
| 1 | Twelve white jars | 24/- |
| 4 | Twelve ditto mugs | 7/- |
| 5 | Two ditto ice pails | 16/- |

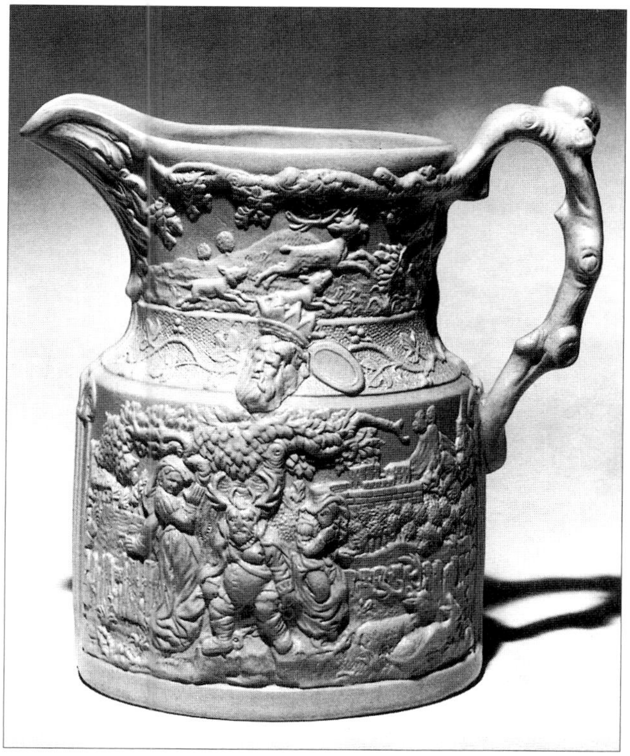

PLATE 103. *A moulded jug marked 'Mason's Patent Ironstone China'. The 1822 auction sale included various lots of 'stone figured jugs' but such drab-bodied articles are not always regarded as ironstone. 7¾in. (19.68cm) high. c.1820-30. Worthing Museum.*

| | | |
|---|---|---|
| 7 | Twenty-four cups and saucers, 2 pint and 2 half pint basins, blue earthenware | 10/- |
| 8 | Six jugs, blue ironstone | 18/- |
| 9 | Twelve ditto, blue earthenware | 13/- |
| 12 | A breakfast set, 36 pieces | 28/- |
| 13 | Eight stone figured jugs | 20/- |
| 15 | Two porous wine coolers and 2 butter tubs | 18/- |
| 16 | A Stilton cheese stand | 44/- |
| 17 | A pair of fruit baskets, rich japan | 18/- |
| 21 | A pair of Indian beakers | 28/- |
| 22 | A pair of blue iron stone coolers | 14/- |
| 25 | A pair of mantle ornaments | 28/- |
| 28 | A dessert service, Indian landscape | 4gns. |
| 30 | A table set, blue, 87 pieces | 6gns. |
| 32 | A breakfast set, japan, 22 pieces | 48/- |
| 33 | A pair of vases, painted in landscapes, and shades | 42/- |
| 38 | A very finely japanned jug | 31/- |
| 39 | A pair of mazarine myrtle pots and stands | 84/- |
| 41 | A rich pot pourie | 36/- |
| 46 | Seven stone figured mugs | 18/- |
| 47 | A pair of ice pails, blue iron stone | 36/- |
| 48 | A pair of chinese flower vases | 60/- |
| 50 | A table set, 142 pieces, Tournay, gold edge | 28gns. |
| 51 | Four rich jugs | 28/- |
| 53 | Two chamber sets, blue, iron stone | 30/- |
| 56 | A pair of water jugs, mazarine and broad gold edge | 32/- |
| 57 | Two green beakers | 36/- |
| 58 | A rich pagoda formed hall jar | 6gns. |
| 60 | A table set, 142 pieces, Tournay | 12gns. |
| 63 | A pair of elegant vases | 120/- |

| | | |
|---|---|---|
| 65 | Two vegetable dishes and a steak dish, blue iron stone | 25/- |
| 67 | A pair of fruit baskets and stands, japan | 32/- |
| 68 | A pair of mantle jars | 34/- |
| 75 | Two card racks and a pen tray | 30/- |
| 77 | A set of 5 ornaments | 44/- |
| 78 | One flower bowl and shade | 30/- |
| 79 | A supper set, richly japanned and gold edge, 12 pieces | £3.10.0d. |
| 82 | A rich toilet ewer and basin with shade | 34/- |
| 83 | A pair of ice pails, japanned | £3.10.0d. |
| 84 | One water jug, neatly pencilled | 36/- |
| 86 | A pair of wine coolers, rich japan | 50/- |
| 87 | One pot pourie, rich japan | 36/- |
| 88 | A dessert service, beautifully painted in flowers and green ground | 18gns. |
| 89 | Twenty-four plates, carnation, gold edge | 36/- |
| 93 | Twelve custard cups | 18/- |
| 95 | A pair of flower jars and shades | £3.10.0d. |
| 97 | Two ewers and basins, green border | 26/- |
| 103 | A chamber set, green border | 27/- |
| 107 | Two mantle jars | 63/- |
| 108 | Twelve jugs, blue earthenware | 14/- |
| 109 | Twenty-four breakfast cups and saucers, 2 pint basins, cream, 1 tea pot, dragon earthenware | 21/- |
| 112 | Two punch bowls, blue iron stone | 15/- |
| 114 | Two broth basins and stands | 10/- |
| 115 | Two punch and 2 pudding bowls, blue iron stone | 11/- |
| 116 | Six ewers and basins, blue earthenware | 24/- |

PLATE 104. *A well-painted green bordered dessert dish, impressed marked 'Mason's Ironstone', perhaps sold as Lot 88 on 28 June 1822, 'A dessert service, beautifully painted in flowers and green ground'. 9¾in. x 8¼in. (24.76cm x 20.95cm) c.1815-25. Victoria and Albert Museum, Crown copyright.*

PLATE 105. *One of several forms that would fit 1822 catalogue descriptions such as 'pot-pourri, rich Japan'. Impressed mark. Diameter 4½in. (11.43cm). c.1820-30. E.H. Chandler Collection.*

PLATE 106. *A well-decorated Mason's Japan-pattern covered bowl, of the type often described as pot-pourris. They were, however, more probably flower-holders, such as the violet baskets described in the sale catalogue. Printed marks. Diameter 4¾in. (12.06cm). c.1815-25.*

PLATE 107. *A Japan-pattern pot-pourri bowl, impressed marked 'Mason's Ironstone' complete with its inner liner. 9½in. (24.13cm) high. c.1815-25.*

PLATE 108. *Three impressed marked Mason's ironstone vases of forms that are impossible to link accurately with the brief sale catalogues. 11in. and 10¾in. (27.94cm and 27.3cm) high. c.1820-30. Messrs Sotheby's.*

**SECOND DAY'S SALE**
**SATURDAY, the 29th Day of JUNE, 1822**
**Commencing at One o'Clock precisely**

| Lot | | Reserve |
|---|---|---|
| 133 | A breakfast set, 55 pieces, dragon, iron stone | 30/- |
| 140 | Four composition mortars and pestles | 10/- |
| 141 | A table set, 87 pieces, blue, iron stone | £5.10.0d. |

PLATE 109. *A rare relief-moulded Mason's ironstone teacup, over-painted with a simple Japan pattern. As the Masons were still producing porcelains in the post-1813 ironstone period most tea services would have been in the more expensive porcelain. 2in. (5.08cm) high. c.1813-20.*

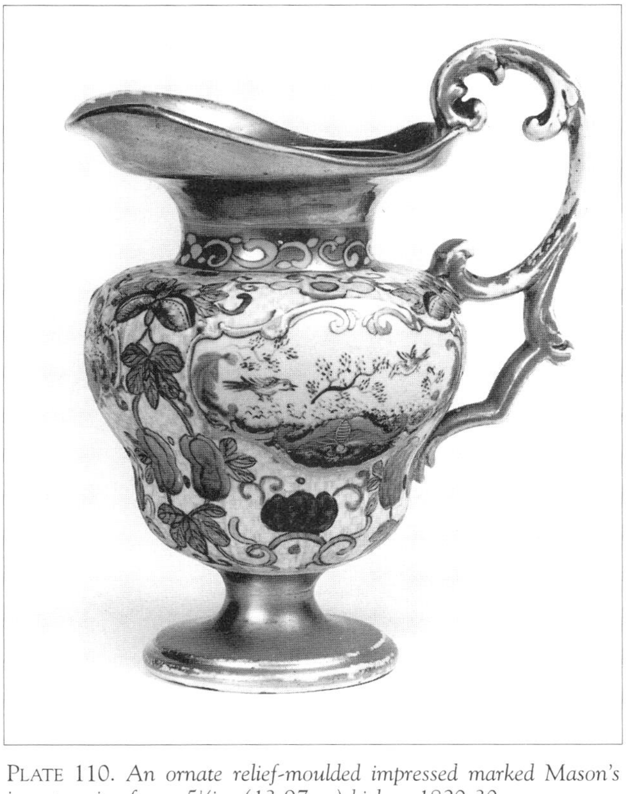

PLATE 110. *An ornate relief-moulded impressed marked Mason's ironstone jug form. 5½in. (13.97cm) high. c.1820-30.*

PLATE 111. *A very rare Mason's ironstone bulb-pot, in the manner of porcelain examples. This ironstone example probably pre-dates the 1818 auction. 9in. (22.86cm) long. c.1813-18.*

PLATE 112. *An unusual blue-printed Mason's ironstone design, coloured in by hand with overglaze enamels. One of the many now rare patterns that seemingly did not prove popular with the buying public. Impressed and printed mark. Diameter 9¾in. (24.76cm). c.1815-25.*

PLATE 113. *A superb quality green ground and richly gilt Mason's ironstone part dessert service, of porcelain quality. Tureen 6¼in. (15.87cm) high. c.1825-35. James II Galleries, New York.*

PLATE 114. *Representative pieces from a relief-moulded Mason's ironstone dessert service. These forms also occur in the bone china body. These ornate shapes seemingly post-date the 1822 sale of stock. Impressed Royal Arms and 'Patent' mark. Centrepiece 14in. (35.56cm) long. c.1825-35.*

| | | |
|---|---|---|
| 145 | A chamber set, green border | 27/- |
| 147 | A chamber service, green border | 27/- |
| 149 | Two vegetable dishes, and 1 steak ditto, blue, iron stone | 25/- |
| 152 | Six ewers and basins, blue earthenware | 24/- |
| 160 | A table set, 87 pieces, blue iron stone | 6gns. |
| 163 | Two vegetable dishes and 1 cheese stand, richly japanned | 60/- |
| 164 | Two beautiful caudle cups and shades | 84/- |
| 165 | A dessert service, Indian flowers, rich | £8.10.0d. |
| 166 | A set of 3 rich jars | 58/- |
| 167 | Two bottles and 2 match cases, ditto | 30/- |
| 170 | A table set, 142 pieces | 15gns. |
| 171 | A white iron stone dessert set, 43 pieces` | 40/- |
| 172 | An ink stand and 2 wafer cups with 2 shades | 28/- |
| 173 | Two vegetable dishes and 1 steak dish, blue iron stone | 25/- |
| 176 | Three match cases and shades | 30/- |
| 178 | Two richly painted flower baskets and 2 lavender bottles and shades | 27/- |
| 189 | A breakfast set, enamelled, 31 pieces | 18/- |
| 190 | A table set, 142 pieces, rich Japan pattern | 21gns. |

PLATE 115. *Another magnificent moulded Mason's ironstone fireplace surround, with hand-painted floral panels. Large printed 'China Chimney Piece' mark (see page 155). 54in. (137.16cm) high. c.1835-45. L.J. Allen, Esq.*

| | | |
|---|---|---|
| 191 | A pair of candlesticks, Japan | 16/- |
| 192 | A chamber service, ditto | 24/- |
| 193 | Six very rich dessert plates | 30/- |
| 195 | A dessert service, Pekin sprigs | 10gns. |
| 196 | Three jugs and 2 mugs, figured stone | 10/- |
| 197 | Three flower baskets, enamelled china | 16/- |
| 198 | A pair of Chinese vases and covers | 63/- |
| 199 | A very fine hall jar, mazarine hydra top | 9gns. |
| 207 | A pair of Chinese jars | 50/- |
| 210 | A table set, 87 pieces, grasshopper, hexagonal tureens | £9.10.0d. |
| 215 | Three cabinet pieces | 17/- |
| 216 | A rich chamber service | £3.10.0d. |
| 218 | Eighteen tea cups and saucers, blue earthenware | 8/- |
| 220 | A table set, 87 pieces, rich japan | 12gns. |
| 221 | Two wine coolers, blue iron stone | 20/- |
| 225 | A handsome mantle jar, beautifully painted in shells | 50/- |
| 226 | Twenty-four cups and saucers, blue earthenware | 11/- |
| 230 | A table set, 87 pieces, mandarine | £9.10.0d. |
| 231 | A pair of very richly painted goblets | £4.10.0d. |
| 232 | A pair of candlesticks and shades | 48/- |
| 233 | A pair of cabinet jars and a vase | 18/- |
| 234 | Eight rich plates, arms | 40/- |
| 242 | Two beautifully painted candlesticks | 28/- |
| 243 | A fine flower bowl and shade | £3.10.0d. |
| 246 | Four broth basins and stands, blue iron stone | 20/- |
| 253 | A pair of rich broth basins and stand | 12/- |
| 255 | Two toilet ewers and basins, and a candlestick, ditto | 24/- |
| 256 | Two vegetable dishes, blue | 20/- |
| 257 | A pair of porous wine coolers | 16/- |

PLATE 116. *A simpler Oriental-style Mason's ironstone chimney piece. This model was produced in various sizes and was embellished in different ways. Large printed 'China Chimney Piece' mark on underside of the top slabs – as shown. 50in. (127cm) high. c.1825-35.*

PLATE 116A. *Finely engraved special mark found on units of the fireplaces or 'chimney pieces' produced by Masons (see Plates 30, 115 and 116). Mark 2¾in. (6.98cm) long.*

PLATE 117. *A rare form of Mason's ironstone large size teapot with blue-printed, seemingly ever popular, Broseley or Pagoda design. 10½ in. (26.67cm) long. c.1820-30. R.G. Austin.*

PLATE 118. *The vast assortment of Mason's ironstone ranges from large hall vases and the chimney pieces to small table wares such as this 'Unmerapoora tea extractor' mentioned in an 1826 advertisement. 7¼ in. (18.41cm) high. c.1825-35. R. and Z. Taylor Collection.*

My 1980 specialist book on Mason wares – *Godden's Guide to Mason's China and the Ironstone Wares* published by the Antique Collectors' Club – contains between page 144 and 191 an alphabetically arranged list of the different objects included in these 1818 and 1822 auction sales – an amazing range of colourful and varied useful and ornamental items. It has not been thought right to duplicate this section in the present work which is not concerned primarily with Mason's products but with the whole field of ironstone, stone china and granite wares.

The illustrations included in this chapter on the two major London auction sales held in 1818 and in 1822, do not by any means represent all the shapes or added patterns employed by Mason's in this period. Indeed, no book could do justice to the variety of colourful objects produced in ironstone within ten years or so of its introduction in 1813.

I show in Plates 107-118 just a very few of the objects known to me that I have not linked with sale-catalogue entries. Very many more were produced after 1822 – a few of these are shown in the later illustrations – associated with the 1830s or 1840s. Other interesting forms and patterns are featured in Wedgwood's publication *Mason's The First Two Hundred Years* by Gaye Blake Roberts (Merrell Holberton Publishers Ltd., London. 1996).

CHAPTER V

# The Later Ironstone and Granite Wares

I have detailed the circumstances that led to the successful introduction of Patent Ironstone China in 1813 and its subsequent development by the market leaders, Masons. The Mason firm continued to produce its various ironstones into the 1840s and again at the 1851 exhibition, but it must not be thought, however, that Masons had this profitable market to itself. Chapter VI contains the names of over three hundred manufacturers of ironstone-related bodies. Most of these were quite small concerns and many relate to a post-1850 period.

While details are also given in that chapter on early and important manufacturers, I should state again that Mason's main rivals in the growing trade for durable table wares – mainly quite costly and decorative dinner services – were Davenport, Hicks & Meigh, Ridgway and Spode, all situated like Mason in the Staffordshire Potteries.

In general their productions were superior to Mason's, in quality of potting and of decoration. This is most certainly true of Spode's essays which included fine dessert services. Yet Spode and the other manufacturers did not enjoy the commercial advantage of being able to use the description 'Patent Ironstone China', nor did they advertise the durable qualities of their wares to the extent that Mason did in order to publicise his own products. Also they did not produce as many ornamental shapes as Masons. The rival firms who were greater in size and no doubt enjoyed better bank-balances than Mason, usually marketed their own ironstone-type wares as 'Stone China', rather than as ironstone.

PLATE 119. *An ornate Mason's ironstone inkstand. This, like all basic models, could be decorated in various colours and styles. 13½in. (34.29cm) long. c.1834-45. Messrs Bonhams.*

PLATE 120. *A highly decorative pair of Mason's cornucopia vases, typical of that form and of a type not produced by the other ironstone manufacturers. Printed mark. 8½in. (21.59cm) high. c.1835-45. Messrs Sotheby's, New York.*

PLATE 121. *Representative pieces from a Japan-pattern dessert service of the 1830s or early 1840s. The same design was also applied to dinner wares. Printed mark. Centrepiece 14in. (35.56cm) long. c.1835-45. Messrs Phillips.*

PLATE 122. *Representative pieces from a Japan-pattern dessert service of the 1830s or early 1840s. These shapes are rare and were originally unpopular! Printed mark. Centrepiece 6¼in. (15.87cm). high. c.1835-45.*

Details of the Davenport, Hicks & Meigh, Ridgway and Spode stone chinas are given in alphabetical order in Chapter VI, but the reader should bear in mind that their products can date back to the earliest days of the ironstone story, around 1813-15, and that they rival or can even excel the quality of the better known, universally respected Mason Ironstones.

The British ironstones and related durable ceramic bodies remained deservedly popular for a century or more and were widely favoured at home and indeed world-wide. Not only did the British potters export on a grand scale, some manufacturers seemingly being entirely engaged in producing ironstone-type wares for the American market, but many foreign manufacturers reproduced British-style ironstone wares because they were universally popular.

Obviously, with a ceramic body that was in production for over a hundred years and being produced by over three hundred different firms, there were going to be wide variations in design, form, quality and price. Today these differences add to the interest the ironstones give to collectors. Remember that the articles we collect today and place in museums or collectors' cabinets were originally made and purchased for every-day use.

PLATE 123. *A typical and popular Mason's Oriental-inspired pattern shown on a dinner service tureen shape of the 1830s or early 1840s. Printed mark. 14¼in. (36.83cm) long. c.1835-45. Messrs Sotheby's.*

The earliest ironstone chinas, produced in the approximate period 1813-1830, represent the highwater mark regarding quality. The examples produced by the leading Staffordshire manufacturers were usually superbly potted, well decorated and often enhanced with gold. They were of porcelain-like appearance. Masons in particular produced in its Patent Ironstone China shapes that other firms made only in costly porcelain. The delightful range of toy or miniatures articles (Plates 57, 72 and 82) underlines the delicacy to which the ironstone body could be worked.

PLATE 124. *A 'C.J. Mason & Co.' marked dinner plate bearing a 'British Lakes' design 'Loweswater'. The printed mark also incorporates the, unusual for Mason's, body description, 'New Stone China'. Diameter 9in. (22.86cm). c.1835-48.*

Yet in regard to these charming pieces, the use of the ironstone body does seem inappropriate. It had been introduced as a new durable body to emulate the Chinese-style dinner services and other useful wares. Yet Mason's later use of ironstone to produce porcelain-like ornamental articles underlines the working qualities of the body and its relatively low cost, compared with the whiter bodied bone china. Mason's ability also to produce massive vases shows the merits of the body from the manufacturer's point of view.

Finely produced as the ironstones could be it must be remembered that the majority of the later, post-1830, manufacturers were producing utilitarian ironstone table wares to a low price. The mass-produced ironstones made by a host of small manufacturers, often for the export markets, reflected the low price demanded in such markets. Initial prices were of course increased by middleman, shipping and other transport charges and by various customs duties and taxes. Yet, those British ironstones proved astoundingly popular, not only in North America but on a truly world-wide basis. It was the durability of ironstone that was to prove the great attraction, rather than the colourful decoration that attracted most British buyers, who were mainly of a higher social class – if I may still use such a term.

## WHITE IRONSTONE

The wholely undecorated wares known as 'White Ironstone' proved highly popular overseas. Large and small Staffordshire potteries produced thousands of tons of such white ironstone useful wares. The appeal was largely based on durability and low price, coupled with novel European forms. Many Staffordshire firms introduced new moulded shapes specifically for the American market which were registered at the Patent Office (see Plate 125). We even have an American authority writing of British ironstones in the 1850s: 'We see the emergence of improved white ironstone as the English export ware *par excellence*.'

This was praise indeed as the North American markets were vast and ever-growing and the dealers and the individual buyers had the world's suppliers to draw upon. The Chinese were still producing their traditional heavily potted inexpensive porcelains. The Germans and the French potters, large and small, were also looking to supply North America. Porcelain and earthenware factories were also being set up in America. Some of these were owned, managed and largely staffed by British potters who had emigrated during difficult times from the old country.[1] The American firms obviously had a great advantage in

Plate 125. A T. & R. Boote *white ironstone tea-coffee pot of 'Sydenham' registered shape, with an 'Atlantic' moulded form soap-dish.* Pot 8¼in. (20.95cm) high. c.1853-6. Jean Wetherbee.

Plate 126. *A selection of Staffordshire white ironstone of the type shipped to North America in vast quantities in the 1840-60 period. Jug 12in. (30.48cm) high. Jean Wetherbee.*

PLATE 127. *Two typical Staffordshire white ironstone jugs and basins from bedroom toilet services. Many of these are of registered moulded forms. Jugs 12in. and 13¼in. (30.48cm and 33.65cm) high (but variable). c.1845-55. Jean Wetherbee.*

supplying their home trade with duty-free ceramics that had not to be transported from Europe. Yet Great Britain, or perhaps the Staffordshire potters, all but monopolized the vast American market for everyday useful articles which had the appearance of white porcelain, without the high cost of the finer wares.

The term 'White Granite' is also entirely used in America, probably as these wares were purely an export line. The abbreviation 'W. G.' was and is also used in invoices, receipts and export documents. George L. Miller, the noted American authority, stated in *Historical Archaeology* (Vol. 25. no. 1, 1991), that the term was selected because it 'avoids the confusion of these plain white wares with the highly decorated stone chinas or early ironstones'. He further stated that 'From the invoices and price lists examined for this study, it is clear that white Granite became the dominant type in use from the 1850s until the end of the 19th century'.

The thickly potted, often relief-moulded, white granite or undecorated ironstone wares, which rather surprisingly included tea wares, were probably introduced in the late 1830s. I have to say 'probably', because we now have no record of its introduction, if it was formally introduced as a basic type. Possibly the undecorated ironstones were at first simply the most inexpensive lines available or ordered by price-conscience buyers, as the British wares undercut the popular white French porcelains produced by Haviland and other Limoges or Paris makers. As noted above, the British white wares were dominant in the American market by the 1850s. A great advantage was that matching sets could easily be built up by the home owner. The shapes or moulded motifs were relatively few and were produced in bulk and the buyer did not have to choose one from thousands of designs. Life was easier for the retailer also; he could, for example, stock only one popular pattern, perhaps 'Ceres' or wheat, and all his customers would be buyers of his sole stock-line.

The concept of supplying such undecorated ceramics was, of course, no new idea. In the earlier part of the eighteenth century undecorated British salt-glazed stonewares formed a large part of home and export markets and mid-eighteenth century white salt-glaze plates are even now not all that uncommon. They were produced in huge quantities (see page 57). Later in the century and indeed into the nineteenth century, undecorated British creamwares were universally popular and were again produced in vast quantities, at most British ceramic centres.[2] White ironstone was a continuation of an established trade, with the added advantage of its great strength and durability.

The white ironstone obviously varied slightly from one manufacturer to another, according to quality and price. It would also appear that two distinct varieties were made for different aspects of at least the important American market. The whitest body was mainly required for city buyers, whereas the slightly blued wares were in demand in rural areas. The trade description 'Pearl' or 'Pearl White' was often used for

PLATE 128. *Two typical Staffordshire (Anthony Shaw) moulded tea or coffee pots decorated with the popular and originally inexpensive tea leaf design in lustre. 9½in. (24.13cm) high. c.1850-60. Dale Abrams.*

such wares. However, the basic ceramic term 'Pearl' or 'Pearl ware' dates back to the eighteenth century when the cream-coloured earthenwares were whitened by adding small quantities of blue to the mix or glaze. History was repeating itself in the nineteenth century regarding ironstone.

It is perhaps a pity that the white ironstone-type wares were almost wholely made for the export market. They are all but unknown in the country of their origin or to British collectors.[3] Consequently any research on these socially interesting ceramics has been left to the American collectors, dealers and researchers. They certainly have the advantage of having the ceramics to research but these were very often unmarked. The American authorities do not have the advantage of readily available design registers, the Staffordshire directories, rate records, etc. In some instances often repeated American statements and dates will vary from those contained in Chapter VI of this British study.

## TEA LEAF IRONSTONE

One simple step from the all-white, undecorated, ironstone, is represented by what is termed in North America 'Tea Leaf Ironstone'. Again articles mainly comprised standard, useful, table wares but they were embellished with variations of a three-leaf and bud design, usually framed within a single line edge-trim

PLATE 129. *A selection of Alfred Meakin's Bamboo moulded-shape toilet ware with simple tea leaf motifs. Typical of a long and popular North American market type. Jug 12in. (30.48cm) high. c.1870-80. Jean Wetherbee.*

PLATE 130. *A Joseph Clementson moulded dolphin-handled form tureen decorated with simple lustre trim – in the manner of the tea leaf design. Impressed name mark.* c.1840-50. *Private American Collection.*

(Plates 128-129). This leaf motif and edging was normally painted in a form of copper lustre, giving rise to such American descriptions as 'Tea Leaf Lustre' or 'Copper Tea Leaf'. The simple central sprig motif, however, hardly looks like a tea-leaf. This name probably came later than the basic much-copied design, so popular in North American markets from about 1850 onwards.

Staffordshire tea leaf wares were apparently sent overseas in standard large barrels or circular wicker crates, which were easily transhipped across the vast areas of North America, without the need for unpacking the crates. They contained a standard saleable commodity – like flour or sugar – which could be sold merely by description. Indeed much was sold from late nineteenth century mail-order catalogues.

However, as far as the British records are concerned, these 'tea leaf' ironstone and granite-bodied wares do not exist! The home trade required entirely different types. Even the less discriminating end of the home market demanded inexpensive bone china, as was supplied by a host of Longton manufacturers, or quite well decorated earthenwares of traditional types. Perhaps for the British the place for tea-leaves was in the teapot!

Nevertheless, very many British potters earned their bread and butter, or even their cakes, from producing vast quantities of simple tea leaf crockery for exportation. It seems so common that the manufacturers failed to feature it in their advertisements in the trade journal, *The Pottery Gazette*. Even painstaking researchers and ceramic historians such as Llewellynn Jewitt failed to mention this aspect of British potters' output in his comprehensive work, *The Ceramic Art of Great Britain*, published in 1878 with a revised edition in 1883 – during the height of the tea-leaf era! The American specialist collectors and dealers believe that the first major manufacturer of the tea leaf wares was Anthony Shaw (& Co., also & Son), a Burslem firm that is practically unknown to British collectors.

A good American specialist reference book on these wares is *Grandma's Tea Leaf Ironstone, A History and Study of English and American Potteries* by Annise Doring Heaivilin (Wallace-Homestead Book Company, Iowa, 1982).

## FLOW BLUE

Much the same position obtains in regard to the misty so-called 'Flow blue' or 'Flown blue' printed earthenwares (Plates 131 and 132) so liked in North America. The basic body on which the indistinct and often uninspired designs were printed can be ironstone, rather than pearlware or other standard comparatively soft-bodied earthenwares, but such flow, or flown, blue designs are very little known or found in the British Isles. They were mid-nineteenth century export wares. Again American collectors and writers have studied these highly desirable (and often highly priced) wares and have published several works on this facet of British ceramics. Perhaps, the fullest British contribution to the literature is contained in *Davenport*

*China, Earthenware & Glass 1794-1887* by Terence A. Lockett and Geoffrey A. Godden (Barrie & Jenkins, London, 1989). A contemporary quote of mid-1844 serves to underline the British dislike of such 'prevailing abomination, the floating blue', at least in the more high-class circles. In America the same effect was described as 'the much admired Flowing Blue'.

Certainly, not all contemporary writers disdained the blurred printed designs. One finds the following unbiased notes contained in Sheridan Muspratt's *Chemistry, Theoretical, Practical and Analytical* (W. Mackenzie, Glasgow, 1860):

> of late a manufacture has been introduced of a flowing blue and other colours, giving a softness to the colouring upon fine earthenware, which has been much exteemed. This is produced by what is termed a *flow*, introduced into the seggar or fire-case.

Musspratt then gives four recipes for the flow, the first being:

| | |
|---|---|
| Quicklime | 5 parts |
| Salt | 2 " |
| Nitre | 3/4 " |
| Borax | 3/4 " |

These ingredients were to be 'well mixed together and sprinkled carefully round the bottom edge of the seggar'. He also made the important point that the blue printing pigment was of a special type. His standard recipe for 'Blue for flowing' comprised:

PLATE 131. *An impressed marked 'J & G. Alcock, Oriental Stone' teapot decorated with the popular 'Scinde' print which normally occurs – as in this example – in 'flow blue' – a self-explanatory description! 9in. (22.86cm) high. c.1838-48.*

| | |
|---|---|
| Black prepared oxide of cobalt | 12lbs |
| Flint glass | 4lbs |
| Oxide of Zinc | 2lbs |

All were to be calcined in the glazing oven. If a lighter tone was desired a flux composed of equal parts flint glass and flint was added.

PLATE 132. *A marked American market Clementson & Young registered (1845) dinner service platter of the Columbia pattern. In this example the flow blue has not run or flown as much as in some examples. 10⅝in. x 8in. (27cm x 20.32cm) c.1845-7. Arnold Kowalsky.*

Robert Copeland's specialist book on British blue printed earthenwares, *Spode's Willow Pattern* (Studio Vista, London, 1980), makes some interesting, modern professional comments on flow blue designs. Several American books cover these wares as found and collected in the States. A helpful recent book is Jeffrey B. Snyder's *Historic Flow Blue, with Price Guide* (Schiffer Publishing Ltd., Atglen, PA, USA, 1994). This pleasantly written well-illustrated book gives a good historical and social background to the development of these popular wares. The same author's 1997 book on the same American collecting subject is *Fascinating Flow Blue* (Schiffer Publishing Ltd., Atglen, USA). The reader of the present book on ironstone-type wares should bear in mind, however, that relatively little flow blue was printed on ironstone bodies.

It could be stated, in passing, that the flow-blue printed designs made mainly for export markets were rather more costly than the standard British sharply defined printed designs. Messrs Alfred Meakin Ltd's bowls, sold wholesale in warehouse-dozens, and ranged from 57d. (old pence) in the white, 78d. for standard printed, and 84d. for flow colours (not blue) to 90d. for flow blue designs. Flow blue bowls with a gilt edge were 108d. All these prices were for warehouse-dozens, with the count varying according to the size, and ranging from four large size to forty-two for the smallest size to the dozen.

## MULBERRY IRONSTONE

Having written of flow blue or flown blue designs, which were mainly produced for export markets, I should mention another North American line, called 'Mulberry Ironstone'. I probably cannot do better than quote the definition suggested by Ellen R. Hill, the author of the specialist publication *Mulberry Ironstone. Flow Blue's best kept little secret* (Mulberry Hill, Madison, NJ, USA, 1993). Mrs. Hill stated:

> Mulberry Ironstone is ironstone china made primarily in England between 1840 and 1870 transfer printed or hand-painted in any of several colorations: dark grays, browns or purplish-black – the design can flow.

This American authority shows illustrations of a very good and long range of mid-Victorian earthenware table wares decorated with non-blue printed designs and lists the main makers of such wares. These names are all included in my all-embracing list (Chapter VI) of makers of ironstone china. Some Mulberry-coloured designs can be found in the British Isles but mainly such wares were produced for export markets. Like flow blue, not all the so-called Mulberry designs were produced on the ironstone type bodies.

The most modern American specialist book on the export-market wares discussed in this chapter is Dawn Stoltzfus and Jeffrey Snyder's *White Ironstone. – A Survey of its many Forms – Undecorated, Flow-Blue, Mulberry, Copper-lustre* (Schiffer Publishing Ltd., USA, 1997).

## COLOUR PRINTING

Progressing from the so-called mulberry-coloured prints it can be stated that the British potters were able to produce underglaze printed designs in many colours. Simeon Shaw, writing in his 1829 work, *History of the Staffordshire Potteries*, noted:

> Very recently several of the most eminent Manufacturers have introduced a method of ornamenting Table (dinner) and Dessert services, similarly to Tea services, by the Black printers using red, brown and green colours… This Pottery has a rich and delicate appearance and owing to the Blue printing having become so common, the other is now obtaining a decided preference in most genteel circles.

Quite soon after this colour printing spread to the export-market goods and, by at least the 1850s, printing in various colours (or combination of colours) seemingly presented no difficulties. The platter shown in Colour Plate 30 represents a factory trial or perhaps a sample piece showing the different colours and shades that could be produced by one factory. It appears too that each print in its different colour could be fired at the same time, each tint maturing at much the same temperature. This procedure resulted in reduced trouble and lower production costs.

Yet this generally accepted attitude is not by any means the full story – it is a very complicated business. Let us for a moment consider Thomas Potter's unpublished 1839 manuscript ceramic recipe book in which he detailed various bodies, glazes and colours then in general use. He listed the following recipes for underglaze printing colours:

Common underglaze Mulberry colour

| | |
|---|---|
| 4 parts of | Prepared Manganese |
| 2 parts | Blue Calx of Zaffre |
| 1 part | Nitre |
| ½ | part Borax |

mix well together
when calcined add 2 parts glass and
1 part of calcined flint, grind together.

PLATE 133. *An initial-marked W. Adams & Sons teapot of the 1840s. The mark incorporates the body description 'Granite'. In most cases, however, granite and ironstone was indistinguishable one from the other. 8in. (20.32cm) high. c.1840-50.*

Better colour of purple

| | |
|---|---|
| ½ oz | Manganese |
| ¼ oz | Printing blue |
| ½ oz | Red Lead |
| ½ oz | Flint. |

An Olive Brown
24 parts of Antimony
7 parts of Manganese
6 parts of Terdescena. [*sic*]

Another Brown for Printing
24 parts of Manganese
33 parts of Antimony
35 parts Litharge of Lead.

Underglaze Brown
5 oz Litharge of Lead
3 oz Crude Antimony
1 oz Manganese
4 oz Zaffre Blue.

Underglaze Orange
9 parts Red Lead
9 parts Litharge
12 parts Crude Antimony
2 parts glass of Antimony
6 parts Salts of Steel.

These and other colour recipes are here quoted only in their basic forms. Other complicated preparation processes were involved before the mix was ready to use. To quote the advice for the common brown, as an example:

> All pounded together and well mixed, then spread on flinted dish ½in thick. Press the colour...put it in easy part of the glost hovel under the bungs of saggers....then give the cakes a hard fire in biscuit oven. Pound and grind for use.

Even some of the named ingredients had themselves to be prepared, for example:

Blue smalts to make Green with
2 lbs Glass
10 oz of Cornwall stone
6 oz of flint
6 oz of Nitre
6 oz Litharge
4½ oz Blue Calx.

Put in deep dish or bowl, flint it first then put it in the glost oven to calcine or run together, then chip off the flint. Pound it for use. Then 4 parts of this smalts to 3 of yellow calx to 3 of Naples yellow.

The saga continues!

How to make Naples Yellow
12 of white Lead
2 of Diphoretic Antimoney
1 of Crude Salamonic
½ of Alumn

Pound all fine and mix well together put in a crucible over a slow fire. Then stir it up all the time with an iron rod – about 3½ hours – then powder it into an iron morter and let it cool. Then take out the contents pound and grind it.

I have quoted only some of the complicated recipes for printing colours. Others relate to printing oils and, of course, the all important glazes – quite apart from the basic bodies and the firing processes.

We should certainly have a great respect for even the humblest printed earthenwares and for the men, women, boys and girls who made and applied the transferred patterns. It is amazing how the finished articles were produced at such a low cost – the success was due to team work, a large team, each with his or her part to play. The result can be delightful – but we see only the successes, not the many failures that must have occurred.

## GAUDY IRONSTONE

This term is of American origin, relating to mid-nineteenth century wares which were usually hand-painted in a broad manner.

Larry Freeman, in his 1954 book *Ironstone China*, describes typical Gaudy Ironstones as having 'hand-applied polychrome – chiefly blue and lustre decoration of the 1850 era. Said to have been made for the Pennsylvania Dutch market... various decorative patterns are found...'.

Of course, such so-called Gaudy patterns which were usually produced for the lower-priced end of the market occur on ordinary earthenware bodies, as well as on some ironstone.

## GRANITE etc.

I can now proceed to mention a highly important British ceramic body, very closely related to ironstone in its durable qualities although it was perhaps introduced to vie with the popular and relatively inexpensive white or sparsely decorated French porcelains being shipped to North America. I refer to ceramics variously called 'Granite ware', 'Granite China' or merely 'Granite'.

The description 'Pearl White Granite' was used by the Staffordshire potters' January 1840 new increased price list relating to the American market. The price range for 'Pearl White Granite' was naturally higher than the standard cream-coloured earthenwares, being of superior quality and fired to a higher temperature.

We have no idea, I believe, when this clever descriptive name 'Granite' was introduced or by whom. It was a brilliant choice, for not only is granite closely associated with the basic raw materials of porcelain, decomposed granite, but also in the public's mind granite is clearly associated with great strength and durability. It may be assumed that the term 'Granite' was dreamt up as an alternative to ironstone by a manufacturer who did not want his wares to be associated with Mason's then perhaps old-hat ironstone.

Unfortunately it seems the description granite was neither introduced with the same fanfare as the Patent Ironstone, nor was any patent applied for or any recipe published, until years later. Indeed I think the novelty was in the name, not the body. Léon Arnoux, Minton's French-born Art Director, writing in *British Manufacturing Industries* published in 1876, noted:

> Granite Ware
>
> ...The name of ironstone remained to that class of pottery which is strong and resistive. Since then, however, earthenware has so much improved that ironstone has gone out of fashion; the nearest to it is the ware called *White Granite*, used in the American market, which is richly glazed, and made thick to compete with the French hard porcelain, that is also exported to the United States for the same class of customer. About fifty manufactories are specially engaged in producing this ware; and those in the occupation of Messrs Meakin, Shaw, Bishop and Powell, and G. Jones, may be considered the largest...

The American Department of Commerce published an interesting report on 'The Pottery Industry' in 1915. The material on English manufacturers and their products was entirely gathered within the Staffordshire Potteries. This deeply researched report includes definition of the various types of ceramics, 'Jet ware', 'Samian Ware' etc. In this section ironstone and white granite are grouped together:

> These names are used indistriminately by the trade... They are made of a superior quality of

> materials, the body being slightly stained by a solution of cobalt, which gives it a bluish-white cast.

The next grouping included 'white earthenware, semi-porcelain and pearl granite'. It would appear from the following explanation that 'pearl granite' was a superior variety – as has previously been explained in regard to the term 'pearl white'. Of 'pearl granite' the American report stated:

> These terms are used for the best quality of white earthenware. The names indicate to some extent that the object of the manufacturer is to produce an article resembling porcelain or chinaware. This ware, however, is opaque and the body porous. The finest qualities of materials are used in this mixture with generally a little larger percentage of feldspar, thus producing a closer body and in very thin places a slight translucency....

The American report recorded that:

> White ware varies in porosity. The white and better grades – white granite – may absorb from 3 to 8 per cent of their weight of water in an unglazed state. Inferior ware, on the other hand, may show an absorbtion as high as 14 per cent. The white granite pottery is usually shaped into thinner ware than the C.C. [cream coloured] ware and hence requires some attention in making. Both classes, as a rule, require two burns, the biscuit firing, in which the unglazed ware is burned, and the glost firing, in which the glaze is fused to the body... for the white granite the temperature [of the biscuit firing] is about cone 7 to 9 or 1,155, 1,190°C. The glost burn is usually carried to cones 1-4 or 1,100-1,130°C....

Minton's Art Director Léon Arnoux wrote that 'in time of prosperity the United States market might take as much as £800,000 of granite ware'. Considering that in general these wares were of the less expensive kinds this export market would have amounted to thousands of tons of granite ware; the demand was truly enormous.

One of the attractions of the English white granite wares, apart from the all important low cost, was that in general terms it competed with the so popular French porcelains – which were often supplied to the American market in the white. American trade advertisements often featured the durable English granite wares side by side with their stock of French porcelains.

Taking just one example of many cited by Neil Ewins, we find Cortlan & Co. of Baltimore in the 1860s featuring pure white French china dinner, tea and dessert services, with 'English White Granite Table and Toilet sets... equal in whiteness to the French'.

The British potters often copied fashionable French shapes, perhaps on the suggestion of their American trade customers, but the French also copied or adopted some British forms. Ceramic forms and decoration tended to be international. The manufacturers were in business to make a living and they had to produce wares that the buying public wanted. French designs always enjoyed a certain cachet; the British potters likewise enjoyed a great reputation for the quality of their products. A happy marriage often resulted, to the benefit of all.

It should be noted that some British manufacturers used misleading French-sounding terms to describe their durable granite type earthenwares. 'Porcelaine Opaque' was a contradiction in terms but with the final 'e' it gave a French aire!

An interesting contemporary account of the later Victorian granite wares appeared in *The Staffordshire Times* of 13 January 1877:

> It is very interesting to watch the movement that is now going on in the Potting Trade. Many fresh models are being introduced in dinners and toilets. Messrs. Meakin, the most extensive American manufacturers, are bringing out a new shape in dinner ware, which promises to be a great success. We are glad to find that some spirit is being manifested among the granite manufacturers, and we hope that it will lead to an increase in trade. It has been said before in our columns that our Pottery masters are too tame in respect to the American market, and do not sufficiently take advantage of their position in introducing new shapes. It would appear that there was no such thing as an improvement on the old heavy forms which have for the last quarter of a century continued to be made for that country. The native potters of America have with very good taste, endeavoured to reform this old and barbarous style, and such American pottery as is made possesses both good form and lightness. Granite is a body which, in the hands of, such potters as Mr. Hughes, Burslem, has shown itself capable of sustaining the highest decoration, and it only needs that form should be in keeping. For fineness of body and china-like whiteness nothing can excel the granite ware of Messrs. Edwards, of Fenton. The goods are light and beautiful, and we are made to see what can be done in this class of ceramics. But here again form has not received that attention which it was bound to, if full justice is to be done to it as an important department in pottery. When this body

> was first introduced great things were promised and expected, and had it not been initiated at the commencement in the dull, heavy forms in which it was made up, we have no doubt but it would have attained all that was hoped. As a body it is well adapted for utile pottery, and if thorough reform in the models could take place it would even now redeem itself... We shall notice some new models in the home trade at the earliest moment.

*The Staffordshire Times* in the mid-1870s also carried a series of articles on local firms and on wares destined for display at the 1876 Philadelphia Exhibition. The following reviews relate to American market granite wares:

> T. HUGHES, Waterloo Road, Burslem. July 1876.
> There are certainly a greater variety of shapes than would have been supposed, considering the market to which the goods are sent. And while often there is an absence of taste in American granite goods, or taste peculiarly displayed, it is pleasing to find that such is not the case at this firm, but that good style has been as much sought after as a good body. The ware has also a very clean look and is free from exterior blemishes than much of this class of pottery. There is also a hardness and ring about it, which shows a high quality and a severe fire.
>
> The class of ware manufactured may be divided into light and heavy granite, the latter being much more to the taste of the writer. The light granite is exceedingly artistic and when decorated would not lose much by a comparison with the best specimens of semi-china...
>
> The Flores shape has many good points that will recommend it and as a piece of embossed ware, is free from that heavy and cumbrous look which too often spoils the beauty of this class of pottery. Of teas a very choice variety are manufactured, of both heavy and light granite and without doubt there would be little difficulty in satisfying the taste of such as love the American market shapes. The Flores shape makes a very handsome teapot and the Roman shape jugs, both the round and the oval form are good specimens of articles of general utility...
>
> (*The Staffordshire Times*, 22 July 1876)

> HOPE & CARTER, Burslem. August 1876.
> Messrs. Hope & Carter of Burslem, have a fair show of ornamental and printed earthenware. Their specimens of 'white granite' are wonderfully pure in colour and perfect in shape.
>
> (*The Staffordshire Times*, 12 August 1876).

> POWELL & BISHOP, Hanley. March 1876.
> ...The white granite offered have the [high] qualities alluded to, and are in every respect the same in character, minus the decoration
>
> (*The Staffordshire Times*, 11 March 1876).

Leonard Forester's manuscript recipe book of the 1880s gives very full information on the make up of 'White Granite bodies' as made up by Messrs Powell & Bishop, J.W. Pankhurst & Co., Meakin, A. Shaw, Turner & Tomkinson, Messrs Boote and John Edwards. The standard ingredients in decreasing amounts were Ball slip, China clay, Flint and Stone.

Each of the seven manufacturers cited employed slightly different mixes. Those recorded for Powell & Bishop and for J.W. Pankhurst & Co, illustrate standard mixes, the given figures represent parts per hundred.

| | **Powell &Bishop** | **Pankhurst** |
|---|---|---|
| Ball slip | 34 3/16 | 40 8/16 |
| China clay | 31 6/16 | 32 7/16 |
| Flint | 19 15/16 | 16 4/16 |
| Stone | 14 8/16 | 10 13/16 |

To which would be added special body-stains.

It should be noted that these ingredients formed the body for other types of earthenware including creamware and stone bodies for jugs, although of course the proportions vary slightly according to the body required.

The glaze used for the granite bodies was seemingly more complicated than the basic body mix. Messrs Powell & Bishop's granite ware glaze comprised boracic acid, soda crystals, stone, flint, whiting, china clay, feldspar, and white lead. Again various manufacturers would employ slightly different proportions in their glaze mix to suit their slightly different bodies and the temperatures employed.

Visually, at least, granite ware is similar to the ironstone bodies but it tended to be more thickly potted and its use restricted to useful table wares. It tended to be very modestly decorated – in fact much of it was sold in an undecorated state, being widely known as 'White Granite'.

This term is important, for not only were most export wares white in the sense that they were undecorated, but also the material itself was white and porcelain-like. This was a great sales point for inferior or slightly off-white lower-fired earthenwares, included the long popular creamwares which were still widely available. The granite wares with their white surface appear highly vitrified, having been possibly higher fired by the 1860s than the contemporary ironstone wares.

The strong granite wares produced in relatively simple forms and sold with little or no decoration were obviously inexpensive to mass-produce, a fact that led to their popularity, especially in overseas markets. Granite wares can almost be said to have been introduced specifically for the North American market. Evidence for the introduction of granite ware will have to come from research in America, from newspaper advertisements, from market export reports or from datable sites.

In Britain, Simeon Shaw in his *History of the Staffordshire Potteries*, which he published privately in 1829, does not mention granite wares although he discusses ironstone china and other post-1800 improvements in the Staffordshire pottery industry.

Whilst the names 'ironstone' and 'stone china' are very often included in factory marks, with other trade descriptions such as 'Opaque China', the word 'Granite' seldom appears. Early exceptions include Joseph Clementson's printed marks associated with the 'Lucerne' and 'Rustic Scenery' patterns both of which were registered on 2 December 1842. These marks included the body-names 'Granite Ware' and 'Granite Opaque Pearl'.

Some Ridgeway, Morley & Wear printed marks which pre-date 24 June 1842 also included the description 'Improved Granite China' suggesting that the description Granite China was then well established and was already being improved upon. It is also rather surprising that Messrs C.J. Mason & Co., within the working period 1829-1845, employed some marks that included the description 'Granite China', rather than their 'Patent Ironstone China'. It is possible that the term granite was favoured only for export-market wares. It is also possible that the ironstone wares attracted a higher duty when exported to some countries and it is said that ironstone was even totally prohibited from export to France. This difficulty may have been avoided by the subtle change in name.

The official catalogue of the 1851 exhibition includes only one British pottery firm which included granite ware in the basic list of its productions. This was Thomas Till & Son of the Sytch Pottery, Burslem:

Albany shape dishes, baker and plates – pearl white granite.
Virginia shape set, teapot, sugar, cream, cup and saucer, in pearl white granite.
Set of jugs, pearl white granite, Virginia shape; bowls of the same. Coffee pot of the same; Boston shape.
Albany shape soup tureen and sauce tureen complete, white granite, gold bands.
Virginia shape, set tea cup and saucer and teapot, white granite, ,gold bands.

These goods were obviously especially destined and made for the American market, a fact that may account for the rare use of the terms 'pearl white granite' and 'white granite', descriptions particularly associated with export-market wares. However, not all manufacturers used this term. C.J. Mason, in his 1851 display of Mason's Patent Ironstone China, retained that description of what other manufacturers might well have described as granite – 'a plate, a dish, a tureen, a tall coffee cup and saucer and a sugar-basin, made of the white Patent ironstone china, as used in the hotels of the United States of America'.

Unfortunately, the official catalogue does not provide a detailed description of the exhibits. The types of ironstone or stone-china articles displayed by the important Staffordshire firm of John Ridgway & Co. were described only as: 'Specimens of earthenware for the United States market'. Messrs Ridgway's own fuller listing of their show at the 1851 Exhibition includes:

One flat dish, one table plate, one dish and cover, one handled cup and saucer.
Montpelier shape, light blue Palestine.
One table plate
Flowering Mulberry, Berlin vase.
One Boston teapot, one ditto jug, five plates, in sizes, one tureen, cover and stand.
White china glaze ware.

There was a selection of fifteen ewers and basins that may also have been in a granite type body. The 'Fine Vitreous Earthenware for the United States Market' dinner and dessert wares are listed on page 306.

## SPATTER WARE

While writing mainly of standard British export-market lines supplied to North America I should mention briefly Spatter and Sponged designs although certainly these naïve, inexpensive, patterns are by no means confined to ironstone. Indeed, most was applied to lower-fired earthenwares.

Sam Laidacker writing in *The American Antiques Collector* (see below) noted: 'Spatter is a type or method of decoration... It refers to that spotted or splash type of decoration made with a sponge instead of a brush...' The result is a series of child-like renderings of simple motifs such as a bird in the branches of a tree, primitive houses in a landscape or floral designs. The coloured border is often dappled, as applied with a coarse sponge. Such pieces undoubtedly have charm and look fine in a country kitchen type setting. They were decorated down to a price – hence their original appeal. They never have gilding and the decoration is kept to a minimum. Shapes too are basic, simple table wares, cups were often made and sold without handles, even after the 1850s. These wares very seldom bear a maker's mark. Much was made in the Staffordshire Potteries, Adams being a known maker, but much of the sponge-decorated pottery was made in Scotland. The Glasgow firm of Bell & Co. included in their large and varied display at the 1851 Exhibition 'common stoneware, in dipt, sponged and painted', this very basic description being all but hidden away in a mass of more elaborate other types of ceramic articles. This wording 'sponged and painted' serves to make the point that not all the design may have been applied by a colour-charged small cut-to-shape sponge. Other parts of the pattern could be brushed on in the normal manner.

The basic designs are broad but effective. These Spatterware and sponged designs are typical of the less expensive export lines, the decoration being seemingly added by low-paid labour, young boys or girls.

There is a miniature library of reference books on this facet of our ceramic art. Such specialist works known to me are:

*The American Antiques Collector*, Vol 111, no. 8 by Sam Laidacker (Privately printed, West Bristol, P., USA, 1952).

*Spatterware and Sponge. Hardy Perennials of Ceramics* by Earl F. and Ada F. Robacker (A.S. Barnes & Co., Inc. Cranbury, NJ, USA, 1978).

*Spongeware and Spatterware* by Kevin McConnell (Schiffer Publishing Ltd., West Chester, PA, USA, 1990).

*Scottish Sponge Printed Pottery* by Henry E. Kelly (Lomondside Press, Glasgow, 1993).

I should perhaps state that I do not agree with all the details or dates given in the American books although the illustrations are highly interesting.

## HOTEL WARE

Mason's 1851 Exhibition catalogue reference to his white ironstone china, 'as used in the hotels of the United States of America', prompts me to mention an important but as yet little researched aspect of British ceramics – Hotel Wares, to use modern parlance. In fact in recent years several large firms have concentrated on this important aspect of the trade. Names such as Churchill Hotel or Grindley Hotelware Co. Ltd. illustrate their speciality. Nowadays hotel wares can be very decorative, modern and tasteful, even showing some delicacy in design and potting, as far as the basic requirement of durability will permit. Indeed, some current hotel ware is made to a very high standard. High-class establishments may have their own unique designs. Some modern hotel wares may even be regarded as leading the domestic market in their clean designs. Hotel ware is no longer the poor relation and the better aspects of durable hotel table ware is spreading to the home, to the kitchen, if not the drawing room.

However, the manufacture of relatively inexpensive mass-produced strong wares for hotels, caterers, shipping lines and so on, is not new. The Staffordshire salt-glazed stonewares would have graced the tables of the larger eighteenth century hostelries. A little later many of these white stonewares might have been replaced by the cream-coloured earthenwares, variously termed creamware or Queen's ware. This is the type of British ceramic that so impressed an eighteenth century French traveller to record:

> ...in travelling from Paris to St, Petersburg, from Amsterdam to the farthest point of Sweden, and from Dunkirk to the extreme south of France one is served at every inn with British ware.

In the nineteenth century the traveller may well have been able to observe that he ate and drank from British ironstone or granite-type wares, not only throughout Europe but wherever ship, train or coach would take him.

Initially hotel-owners or others catering for travellers might well have been ready customers for slightly faulty wares, the 'seconds' or 'thirds' which the manufacturers were happy to sell at reduced prices, but clearly, as the century progressed and hotels and inns were improved, there arose a large market for strong table wares which would not easily chip or crack when used to excess and washed by low-paid casual staff. Apart from table wares, decent hostelries might well have aspired to ironstone or stone china toilet wares in the bedrooms.

By at least the 1870s the hotel-ware aspect of the trade was in full flood. In a review of T. Hughes' current products a writer in *The Staffordshire Times* of July 1876, noted:

> Among the special ware manufactured here may be mentioned several classes. The Hotel ware is extra heavy and may be safely dropped from the table to the floor... without sustaining the slightest

damage. It is in quality as hard and almost as durable as bell metal and rings like mortar ware. This result is produced by a special body and extra hard firing...

Another class which may come under the head of a speciality is the Steamship Ware. The design of this ware is exceedingly good and looks very handsome with printed centre, badges of different characters, among which may be mentioned the chain and cable, the anchor, the crown and trident, etc., all printed in clean and effective colours. The rims of the plates and soups are grooved so as to hold any condiment that may be used. There cannot be two opinions about the character of this ware, it is of the highest order of its class, and really deserves to be styled super- excellent.

Or whilst reviewing the products of James Edwards & Son:

Messrs. James Edwards & Son of Dalehall, Burslem, have a very useful assortment of goods. Chief amongst their exhibits are articles of the 'white ware' description, designed for the somewhat rough service of hotels, steamships, &c. This includes goods known as 'vitreous', on account of their capability of withstanding great heat...

The heat-withstanding capabilities of the compact ironstone and granite-type bodies had always been welcomed and, of course, such plates and dishes retained their heat for far longer than would the softer-bodied earthenwares. Many old Mason's ironstone plates and dishes were seemingly put in the hot oven and have lived to tell the tale! In this respect, as with several others, the durable British nineteenth century table wares were the forerunners of today's 'oven to table' ceramics which are certainly not a modern phenomenon.

## EXPORT MARKETS

My concern in previous pages with the United States market reflects the importance of Britain's main export market, as is underlined by the two references just quoted from the official catalogue of the 1851 Exhibition – 'as used in the hotels of the United States of America' and 'specimens for the United States market'. Indeed, in earthenware terms (rather than finer porcelains) the sales to America probably exceeded home sales! However, the general remarks made in relation to inexpensive, sparsely-decorated, American-market wares also apply to other markets, in both the northern and southern hemispheres. Pleasing, durable, inexpensive earthenwares were supplied throughout the nineteenth century. As Messrs Ashworth's advertisements stated – 'no climate affects this ware'.

Llewellynn Jewitt's *Ceramic Art of Great Britain* (Virtue & Co. London, 1878, revised edition 1883 and later reprints) is helpful regarding the export markets catered for by the many nineteenth century firms which he listed.

Good and competitively priced as the Staffordshire and other British wares undoubtedly were, manufacturers in other countries obviously sought to emulate British goods and to supply their own home markets. It is interesting to note that of the marked wares or shards discovered on excavated sites in Sacramento, British articles far outnumbered all others. Out of 103 manufacturers represented 79 were British, fifteen were home American products, whilst three were French and two German. Four were unattributed (California Archeological Reports, no 22. State of California Dept of Parks & Recreation, 1983).

It must be admitted that whilst the British ironstone and granite-type heavy durable wares were of great importance in the vast export trade as well as in the home market, by no means all post-1813 earthenwares were of this type. Large amounts were in the less expensive lightweight but less durable standard earthenware bodies – sometimes termed in marks 'Semi-China'. Jeffrey B. Snyder's *Romantic Staffordshire Ceramics* (Schiffer Publishing Ltd., USA, 1997) illustrates this point well for relatively few of his decorative printed designs of the approximate period 1820-1850 can be regarded as on ironstone-type bodies. Most are on the less expensive lower-fired earthenwares. Both types, of course (with other styles) had their following. English ironstone was the innovator, sharing a new durability with its decorative merits in forms and in the added patterns.

# CHAPTER VI

# Identification

## An Alphabetical List of British Manufacturers of Ironstone-Type Wares

As this chapter heading suggests, the following section contains an alphabetically arranged list of the many British pottery firms that are known to have produced the durable ironstone-type bodies, granite, etc., under various names from 1813 to the present day.

While the products of many of the smaller firms were not marked in any way, a surprisingly large number of potters did on occasions use impressed or printed marks. Such marked examples can be identified, and usually dated to quite close limits, by reference to the following list.

Some marks include the full name or names of the manufacturer or partnership. Many others include only the initial or initials of the manufacturing firm. Single initial marks such as 'B', however, are very difficult to attribute to one firm as such common initials fit several manufacturers. In general, the more initials included in a mark the more certain can be the attribution. The index will show the firm of partnership associated with any set of initials. It should be noted that a final 'S' will in most cases indicate 'Son' or 'Sons', especially when preceded by an ampersand. However, '& Co.' or 'Ltd.' are usually rendered in this form, not by '& C' or 'L'.

The final initial in a set can also indicate the location of the firm, rather than a surname. Within the Staffordshire Potteries the following initials will relate to the various separate townships:

| | | | |
|---|---|---|---|
| B | Burslem | C | Cobridge |
| F | Fenton | H | Hanley |
| L | Longton | S | Stoke |
| T | Tunstall | | |

These initials, when used, obviously help to suggest or confirm the correct identification of the maker.

It will certainly be found that the majority of the firms listed in this section were situated in the different towns that make up the Staffordshire Potteries. It should be borne in mind, however, that the influence of this centre of the British ceramic industry was even greater than it would appear. The relatively few non-Staffordshire firms often closely copied Staffordshire forms and patterns, even to the extent of obtaining their sets of engraved copper-plates from specialist Staffordshire engravers, and some master-models would also have been obtained from Staffordshire modellers and designers. Some at least of their workforce may well also have been trained in Staffordshire. This influence also extended to non-British factories which would order specialist materials, tools, engravings or models.

The date of manufacture can also materially help to tie down the identity of the maker. A piece can occasionally be accurately dated by discovering the impressed year numbers that were sometimes imprinted into the body during the potting process. Such date markings usually only occur after about 1860. They may take the form of month and year numerals, for example, 1.81, 2.81 for January or February 1881. Or the month may be indicated by a letter, such as J.81, F.81 for the same dates. The arrangement may also be in fractional form with the month number or letter appearing above the year. Remember, these impressed dates relate to the period of potting and the piece may well have been decorated rather later, but not earlier! A few basic rules for the dating of marks should be kept in mind.

1. The word 'Ironstone' will not occur before 1813 when Mason patented the body and introduced the description Ironstone or 'Patent Ironstone' as a mark.

2. Amended descriptions. such as 'Improved Ironstone', obviously post-date the introduction of the first ironstones in 1813, and in general terms they seem to post-date 1830.

3. Terms such as 'Stone China' when used as part of the mark also seem to post-date at least 1810 and probably post-date Mason's Patent Ironstone body of 1813. It was an alternative term used by many manufacturers who did not wish their durable bodies to be confused in any way with the Mason firm.

4. Marks comprising or incorporating the British Royal Arms in a simple quartered central area – as shown below – will be post-1837.

5. Marks incorporating the name of a pattern will be post-1830 and are often very much later.

6. Marks incorporating the diamond shape design-registration device will be post-1842, or if the year letter is in the right-hand segment, after 1867 (see page 376.

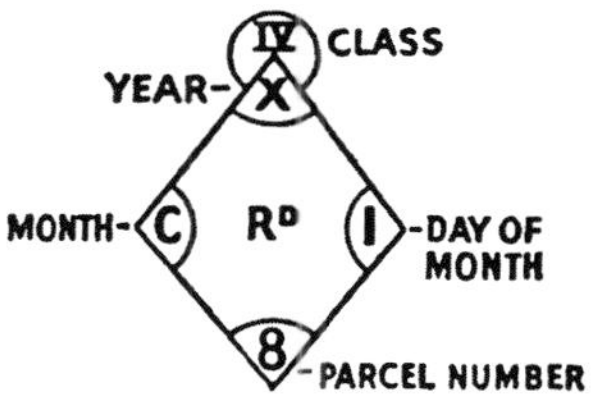


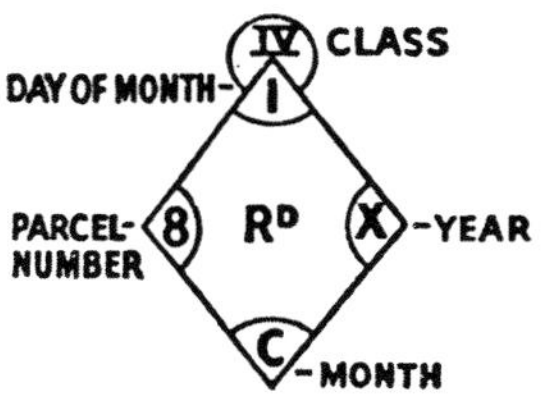


7. Pattern numbers painted on ironstone-type wares will suggest a post-1825 date, certainly if the number is above a hundred or is in a fractional form.

8. Printed, garter-type marks incorporating the maker's name or initials, etc., were popular from about 1840.

9. Marks incorporating the word 'Royal' tend to have been used after about 1850.

10. Marks incorporating the abbreviations 'Ltd'. etc., relate to the 1861 *Limited Liability Act* and cannot predate this event.

11. Marks incorporating the words 'Trade Mark' relate to the 1862 *Trade Mark Act* and will not predate this event.

12. The addition of the word 'England' in a mark indicates a date after 1880 and in general after 1891 when the American *Tariff Act* came into force. However, the absence of such a designation does not necessarily show that the piece is of an earlier date!

Whilst 'England' was the usual description, as it included all the Staffordshire wares, alternative country names were occasionally used. Scottish firms did not use 'England', preferring 'Scotland' or the earlier name 'North Britain' or 'Britain'.

The abbreviation 'U.K.' or 'United Kingdom' is usually only found on late twentieth century productions.

13. Marks incorporating a registration number, which is usually prefixed 'R$^{D}$N$^{o}$.' will post-date 1883. The key to these numbers is given on page 377.

14. The wording 'Made in England' (etc.) tends to occur on marks after about 1910. However, this is far from being an inflexible rule and many post-war marks do not include 'Made in …'

15. Marks incorporating the word 'Copyright' will post-date *c.*1920.

16. Marks incorporating the letter 'R' (usually within a small circle) post-date 1955.

17. Marks incorporating the initials 'P.L.C.' post-date the mid-1970s.

18. Marks or pattern descriptions incorporating the word 'old' or 'olde' are generally reasonably modern reissues of nineteenth century designs or are based on such former patterns. They are nostalgic efforts in salesmanship!

19. Marks incorporating the initials 'BS' followed by a number denote a 'British Standard' quality or performance standard showing that the object or the body has passed tests. A BS number again denotes a late twentieth century date for that mark or product.

Obviously marks incorporating references to detergents or dish-washers are of post-war period and any pieces incorporating a bar-code device will be relatively modern.

Having recorded these helpful Godden guides to dating, it should be remembered that age in itself is not a virtue. Do not worship age alone!

Various Chinese-style square marks occur printed in underglaze-blue. These normally occur on the so-called Broseley Willow pattern type patterns of the approximate period 1815-45. Some of these marks incorporate the body description 'STONE CHINA'. In the absence of fuller impressed name or initial marks it is difficult, or impossible, to attribute them to

individual factories, although various collectors are endeavouring to identify the different versions of these generally unhelpful standard marks.

Remember that many marks relate to the retailer, wholesaler or agent, not to the manufacturer. Such name or initial marks that include the name of a non-pottery-producing city or town, will fall into this category. Typical non-ceramic place names include, London, Birmingham, Manchester, Dublin, although most towns had their own retailers who might include in their orders the requirement to include their own name, rather than that of the maker. The interested reader can sometimes carry out their own research on individual retailers and their working period by consulting local directories. If, however, you seek to take a short cut and write to the local Reference Librarian seeking such facts, do enclose a stamped-addressed envelope and do not expect a reply by return. Often lengthy research is needed by already overworked personnel!

I have been writing of marks and marked examples but the reader should always bear in mind that unmarked examples are not necessarily early and no pieces bearing the name 'ironstone' will predate 1813. There is a natural tendency to worship early examples but an interesting printed pattern of the 1860s or an unusual or rare shape may well be more desirable to many collectors than a standard pattern plate of 1815.

It should also be noted that whilst it is good to be able to attribute a given example, the end result will not necessarily greatly affect its commercial value. An attribution to a given potter will make the piece rather more desirable or saleable from a dealer's point of view, yet it matters little if the piece is made by one small, uncollected, firm or by another largely unknown manufacturer. It is, however, helpful if a piece can be attributed to a large, well-known, popular, collectable firm. But such attributions should be based on fact rather than pure fancy!

The following lengthy list of manufacturers gives in alphabetical order details of those who produced ironstone-type wares, often in conjunction with more costly porcelains or with the less expensive lower-fired standard earthenwares.

It may well be found that the dates given for any listed potter or partnership differ from those given in other works or indeed from my 1971 book on Mason's Ironstone, or its 1980 revised edition. I have gone to great trouble to recheck all the facts and I believe the information provided in the following list is not only the most complete but also the most accurate.

Briefly the basic British source material which gives rise to such dating, includes:

Rate-records,
Land-tax returns,
Census returns,
Directories,
Bankruptcy notices,
Dissolution of Partnership notices,
Invoices and receipts,
Newspaper announcements or reports,
Trade advertisements and listings
(*Pottery Gazette* yearly diary).

Nevertheless, few of these available sources represent a complete picture. The helpful rate-records cover only a limited period and not all towns. We do not have a yearly run of local directories and have no guarantee of their accuracy! It therefore follows that some given dates are approximate and carry the prefix 'c.' for *circa*, indicating that no precise record is available for the commencement or ending of that firm.

## THE ORDER OF LISTING

The basic order is in alphabetical sequence within the following sub-divisions:

A. First single name firms, i.e.
  A. Brown
  B. Brown, etc.

B. Secondly multi-named firms with the same surname, i.e.
  A & B Brown
  W & X Brown

C. Other relationships, i.e.
  A. Brown & Son.
  B. Brown & Co.

D. Partnerships, as
  Brown & Black
  Grey & Green

However, in practice such clear-cut sub-sections tend to become complicated as firms progress from one division to another as they grow, and in some cases such later amendments are added in brackets, as for example, A. Brown & Co. (Ltd.).

PLATE 134. *A rare marked W. Adams & Sons hot water plate, blue-printed with the 'Cyrene' pattern on a stone china body – all details given in the decorative mark. Very many different name or initial marks were employed, most being unique to an individual pattern. Diameter 10½in. (26.67). c.1840-50.*

**JOHN ADAMS & Co., Hanley, c.1865-71.**
John Adams & Co. is listed at St. James's Street and at the Victoria Pottery, Broad Street, Hanley from the mid-1860s.

The partnership comprised John Adams, John Bromley and Henry Cartledge but the last named retired in November 1871 and the main partners continued under the style Adams & Bromley.

Although the firm is mainly known for majolica and jasper-type goods, it seemingly also produced some granite type wares.

The marks normally include the simple style Adams & Co.

**WILLIAM ADAMS, WILLIAM ADAMS & Co.**
**WILLIAM ADAMS & Son(s)**
**WILLIAM ADAMS & Sons (Potters) Ltd., Tunstall and Stoke, 1769-present day**
**(a division of the Wedgwood Group since 1966).**
This well-known succession of firms produced a wide range of good quality ceramics: basalt, jasper, creamware, parian, porcelain and standard earthenware as well as ironstone and granite wares. Various printed or impressed marks were used on the ironstone-type ware from about 1830 onwards. These normally comprise or incorporate the name 'ADAMS' or the initials 'W.A. & S.' or 'W.A. & Co.' However, the firm changed its title from time to time and from c.1866 to 1899 traded as William & Thomas Adams, during which period the marks usually incorporated the name 'W. & T. Adams' or the initials 'W. & T.A.' Printed 'Adams, Stone China' marks are rare and could be quite early c.1820-30. 'Granite' marks appear later, some late marks incorporating the description 'Real English Ironstone'.

However, most Adam marks use the simple name 'Adams' or 'William Adams & Son', or 'William Adams & Sons'. Several, mainly printed, marks incorporate the Royal Arms and supporters, although from about 1920 onwards new marks use a mock Royal Arms with three lions in the central shield, a boar's head crest above and a cat and stag replacing the lion and unicorn supporters. The addition of England on any Adams mark (or other mark) normally signifies a date after 1891. The date '1657' incorporated in several Adams' marks is merely the claimed date of the firm's establishment and has no relation to the date of the object. Indeed this 1657 date indicates a late dating, after about 1880! The trading name of the Adams firms changed several times but as the marks do not necessarily reflect these amendments little importance can be given to the name or initials – W. Adams, W. Adams & Co. or W. Adams & Son. could be used at much the same period.

The Adams' factories have always been very large producers of ironstone-type wares, particularly for overseas markets. The output has however tended to comprise mainly useful wares of standard patterns, in contrast to the more varied output of Masons.

In the present century the Adams company has reissued many traditional old nineteenth century printed designs. Often the mark on such reissues closely follows the original style. The reader should therefore watch for the tell-tale addition of the word 'England' or amended descriptions such as 'Old English Rural Scenes'. When first issued such designs or names were contemporary and were not described as 'old'.

In 1851 William Adams was employing 165 men, 75 women, 65 boys and 26 girls. The firm did not, however, show at the Great Exhibition, a regrettable fact that might well underline the general utilitarian nature of the products.

Llewellynn Jewitt (*The Ceramic Art of Great Britain*, 1878) noted:

> White granite, or ironstone china, of an excellent quality is also made for the American and other markets, some of the raised patterns, as, for instance, the Dover, being remarkably good and the forms of the pieces – side dishes with covers – being faultless. Transfer printing is much used and is by this firm judiciously combined with sponged patterns with good effect.

This aspect of the trade is again emphasised in James Lidstone's 1866 resumé of the output, as reflected in his poem included in that author's privately printed *Thirteenth Londoniad*. The Adams firm then traded as 'William & Thomas Adams, Manufacturers of General Earthenware, Granite, etc. etc.' Our poet singled out 'White Iron Stone China', 'Flown Blue... the best in the Potteries', 'Sponged and Dipt... by the eminent House of Adams, who supply the world'. James Lidstone also noted that this firm produced 73,000 dozen plates a week, that is over three-quarters of a million (876,000) plates alone each week.

Moving forward nearly a hundred years, Messrs Adams introduced an especially strong ironstone-type body in 1963, under the trade name MICRATEX. Some nineteenth century-style Royal Arms 'Real English Ironstone' marks have been reused but the inclusion of the post-1962 Micratex trade name should be noted. The firm became part of the Wedgwood Group in 1966 and most later marks record this fact.

*Sample Adams printed marks*

A dedicated group of researchers is interested in all aspects of the Adams history and productions. Privately circulated 'Adams Notes' are published by David Furniss of 14 Leadhall Grove, Harrogate, Yorkshire, HG2 9ND.

**G. ADAMS & Sons.**

Some American authorities list this firm as being a branch of the main Adams family of potters. The British records do not however list a Staffordshire Adams firm with the initial G.

**WILLIAM & THOMAS ADAMS, Tunstall, 1866-1892.**

William & Thomas Adams potted together at Greenfield, Tunstall, in succession to William Adams, senior. The partnership was dissolved on 31 December 1890, but William continued under the old style probably until 1892.

Various ironstone-type wares were made and various printed or impressed name marks occur, 'W & T Adams', etc. 'W & T A' initial marks may occur.

**ALBION** – See Bell Bros.

**JOHN ALCOCK, Elder Road, Cobridge, c.1848-61.**

John Alcock made a good range of ironstone and white granite wares including registered shapes. He succeeded from the John and George Alcock partnership from 20 January 1848. Examples are normally clearly marked. The description 'Imperial Ironstone China' was often used and the firm seemingly enjoyed a good export trade in white and other ironstone types. In 1855 one Boston importer alone sold by auction 175 crates of John Alcock 'best white granite' and other earthenwares.

Henry Alcock & Co. succeeded John at the Elder Pottery.

**JOHN & GEORGE ALCOCK, Cobridge, c.1838-48.**

This partnership produced good quality ironstone-type ware from June 1838 until the dissolution of partnership on 20 January 1848. The impressed mark 'ORIENTAL/STONE/J. & G. ALCOCK' occurs. Other printed marks incorporate the initials 'J. & G.A.'

**JOHN & SAMUEL ALCOCK (Junr.), Cobridge, c.1848-49.**

This firm seemingly succeeded John & George Alcock (see previous entry) and continued the old lines and patterns which included 'flowing blue' designs. John Alcock continued the works on his own account as from 6 June 1849. Marks include 'J. & S. Alcock Jr.' and the description 'Oriental Stone' was favoured.

**HENRY ALCOCK & Co. (Ltd.), Elder Pottery, Cobridge, c.1861-1910.**

Jewitt, writing of Henry Alcock & Co. in the revised 1883 edition of his *Ceramic Art of Great Britain*, noted:

> At these extensive works, which have recently been much enlarged (formerly carried on by John Alcock) Henry Alcock & Co. manufactures white Granite ware, under the names of 'Ironstone China' and 'Parisian porcelain', exclusively for the American markets, and also the common description of printed wares.

The Henry Alcock ware bears marks incorporating the initials 'H.A. & Co.', 'H. Alcock & Co.' or the name in full. The descriptions 'Imperial Ironstone China', 'Royal Ironstone China', 'Best Ironstone China' etc. occur as part of various Henry Alcock marks. Post-1890 versions usually have 'England' added and sometimes the wording 'Royal Warranted'. From 1910-35 the firm was retitled the Henry Alcock Pottery and the marks include this new title.

**RICHARD ALCOCK, Burslem, c.1870-82.**

Richard Alcock worked the Central Pottery, Market Place, Burslem, from c.1870 to 1882.

Fragments of ironstone plates discovered on an 'archaeological' site in California have borne marks relating to Richard Alcock. Indeed, fragments of Alcock's durable ironstone wares have been reported from several excavated sites in America, suggesting a large trade to that part of the world.

Standard marks include an impressed device in circular form reading: 'RICHARD ALCOCK /BURSLEM' with 'Staffordshire' below and the numerals '76' which almost certainly relate to the date of manufacture. In conjunction with this impressed mark appears the printed mark incorporating the Royal Arms device with the wording 'ROYAL PATENT/ IRONSTONE/RICHARD ALCOCK/BURSLEM. ENGLAND'. This is an example of the word 'England' appearing in marks before 1891. The description 'Imperial Ironstone China' also occurs on Richard Alcock Royal Arms marks.

**SAMUEL ALCOCK & Co., Cobridge and Burslem, c.1826-59.**

Samuel Alcock & Co. manufactured a large range of decorative and fine quality porcelain and earthenware from August 1826. The name has not, in the past, been associated with ironstone but recent finds on the factory site include fragments marked 'ALCOCK'S INDIAN IRONSTONE' with, in some cases, other standard Alcock marks which incorporate the initials 'S.A. & Co' or the name in full. Some printed marks incorporate the description 'Stone Ware'. Several such marks incorporate an ornate armorial bearing (Plate 135). One site fragment bearing the impressed 'Alcock's Indian Ironstone' mark has also the date '1839'. A general review of Samuel Alcock's porcelains and history is given in *Staffordshire Porcelain*. However, whilst the pattern numbers for porcelain usually run into the thousands, a separate lower series seems to have been used for the stonewares and ironstone pieces.

An undated price list of Samuel Alcock & Co's table wares in both earthenware and ironstone shows the difference in prices. Assuming that similar patterns were applied to each body, the stoneware prices were almost double those for the same size standard earthenware dinner service. Ironstone dinner services for twenty-four persons ranged in price from £9.6s.8d. to £29.16s.0d. according to the amount and type of decoration applied. The prices for earthenware sets were between £5.3s.9d. and £15.5s.1d.

The make-up of such a dinner service for twenty-four persons was considerable; even for under £10 one obtained:

| | |
|---|---|
| 2 | soup tureens, covers and stands, |
| 4 | smaller sauce tureens, covers and stands, |
| 4 | covered vegetable dishes, |
| 1 | salad bowl, |
| 1 | cheese stand, |
| 4 | gravy boats, |
| 4 | pickle dishes, |
| 1 | gravy or drainer dish (20 inches – 50.8cm), |
| 20 | platters from 20 to 9 inches (50.8cm to 22.86cm)long, |
| 2 | Fish drainers, 2 sizes, |
| 4 | pie dishes, 2 sizes, |
| 12 | dinner plates, |
| 24 | soup plates, |
| 48 | pie plates, |
| 24 | cheese plates. |

PLATE 135. *The reverse of a printed outline Oriental-styled 'Indian Flowers' plate found on the Alcock factory site. The armorial-styled 'Indian Iron Stone' mark occurs in various forms. Dated 1839. City Museum and Art Gallery, Stoke-on-Trent.*

Without counting covers or stands the buyer possessed 215 pieces! You could also purchase smaller sets, for eighteen persons (165 units) or for twelve persons (108 units). You could also purchase 'miscellaneous pieces', such as three-part root dishes, a beef-steak dish, muffin dishes, hot-water plates in two sizes, ladles and gravy-boat stands.

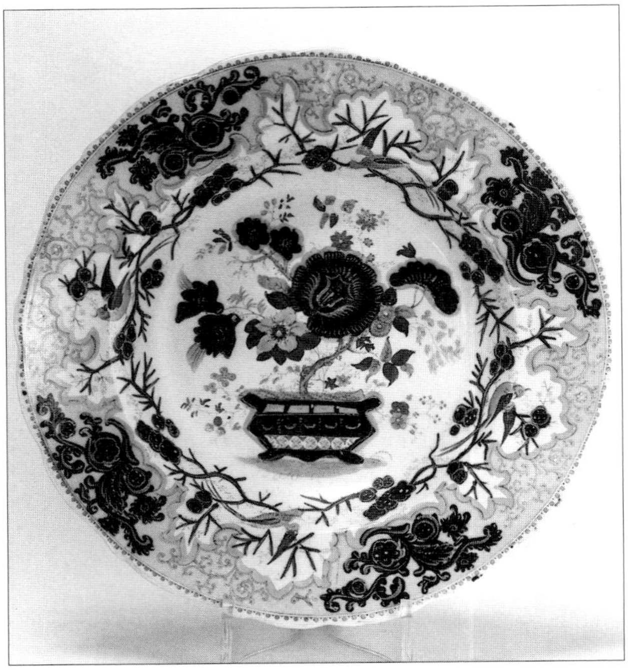

PLATE 136. *An 'Alcock's Indian Ironstone' impressed marked plate of typical printed outline type. This example also bears a printed initial mark 'Stone Ware. Japanese, S.A. & Co.' Diameter 10½n. (26.67). c.1845-55.*

It would seem that the standard sets and the pieces just quoted did not include gilding for the cost of gilding the knobs and handles on the major pieces, such as the tureens, was quoted separately – 2s.6d. per large tureen. Gold borders were also additional.

Alcock's ironstone dessert services comprised centrepiece, two cream bowls, covers and stands, twelve side dishes in three shapes and twenty-four plates. The prices for the standard sets ranged from £2.3s.6d. to £7.8s.0d. Gilt handles to the major pieces were extra. In addition one could purchase baskets and stands. Smaller 'short' dessert services were also available; these comprised centre dish, eight side dishes and eighteen plates. Like the dinner wares, all these dessert pieces were available in the less expensive earthenware as well as in the more durable ironstone body. The description 'Imperial Ironstone China' was used as part of some Samuel Alcock & Co. marks.

Much Alcock ironstone of the less expensive types was exported to North America. Such shipments included the white (undecorated) ironstone table wares.

Apart from ironstone table services and utilitarian objects this large and important Staffordshire firm also produced some decorative objects, such as vases. These can be very large and ornately decorated.

PLATE 137. *Representative parts of an impressed marked 'Alcock's Indian Ironstone' dinner service. Typical Oriental-style printed design, coloured in by hand. Most plates 10½in. (26.67). c.1845-55. Messrs Sotheby's.*

**ALLERTON, BROUGH & GREEN, Longton, c.1832-59.**

This partnership between Charles Allerton, Benjamin Singleton Brough and William Green was an important one. In 1840 they are recorded as working four separate potteries, but the main one was the Park Works, High Street, Longton.

This firm produced both earthenwares, including ironstone-type wares, and china. Various marks have been included, including a printed mark:

WARRANTED
STONE WARE
A.B. & G.

At a date before January 1860 both Brough and William Green had died and the partnership was continued by their executors with Charles Allerton, up to 31 December 1859 when the partnership was dissolved.

Charles Allerton & Sons succeeded.

For further information on this Longton firm the reader is referred to Rodney Hampson's specialist study 'Longton Potters 1700-1865' (*Journal of Ceramic History*, Vol. 14, City Museum and Art Gallery, Stoke-on-Trent, 1990).

**AMHERST.**
**AMHERST IRONSTONE.**
**AMHERST JAPAN.**

Various printed marks incorporate the name 'Amherst', generally reading 'Amherst Japan'.

These references do not relate to the manufacturer but rather to a formal Oriental inspired floral design mainly featuring a pot of flowers and foliage with various landscape backgrounds.

Like all Japan patterns the design in its standard form comprises both underglaze-blue sections with overglaze enamels – normally reds and greens. Some gilding can enhance the better quality examples.

Messrs Minton probably introduced this design or gave it the name 'Amherst Japan'. It is one of the earliest Japan patterns to have been given a name by the Staffordshire potters.

The design, which usually has an underglaze-blue printed base or outline, proved exceedingly popular and it was widely adopted by British potters as a standard Japan pattern. It can occur as a named pattern from at least 1826 but the same basic Oriental-style design was probably introduced prior to this period.

The name most probably relates to William Pitt (1773-1857), the British Envoy to Peking (1816-17), Governor-General of India (1823-28). He invaded Burma in 1824 and was created Earl Amherst in 1826, retiring home to England in 1828.

The Amherst marks illustrate that a name used in a mark is not necessarily that of the manufacturer and that many different firms produced popular patterns, often over a very long period – in this case into the present century.

**JON ANTON (Ltd.), Longton, c.1968-74.**
Jon Anton was known mainly for porcelains but ironstone wares were also made. The standard marks incorporate the name in full.

**'ASBESTOS CHINA'.**
This blue printed descriptive mark within an oval border design has been reported by a British collector, John Cockerill, on a blue printed earthenware saucer of perhaps the 1840s. The general appearance of this example does not suggest a Staffordshire source, rather a Yorkshire or northern factory that was seeking a new body description – perhaps suggesting a fire-proof durable product.

It is but one of several unhelpful descriptive marks that do not include the maker's name or initials. The fact that the only reported example was found in Belgium may well suggest a pottery in the north-east of England, perhaps around Stockton-on-Tees.

**G.L. ASHWORTH & Bros. (Ltd.), Hanley, 1860-1968.**
**(subsequently continued under the style 'Mason's Ironstone China Ltd.')**
Ashworth has been the largest producer of ironstone since August 1860. The firm acquired Mason's original moulds, patterns, etc., through the partnership between George Leach Ashworth and Francis Morley, the latter having purchased them, some on his own account and some through his later partnerships. The last of these, between Francis Morley and George Leach Ashworth (*c*.1858-60), led to the formation of G.L. Ashworth & Bros., as from August 1860. The Ashworths also had woollen and cotton interests at Rochdale.

The April 1861 Hanley census returns show that at that period Taylor Ashworth, a brother of George Leach Ashworth, employed 250 men, one hundred women, fifty boys and fifty girls. These figures may have been approximate, as the numbers are strangely even, but they do show that the Ashworth concern was large. The brothers in partnership with George Leach Ashworth were James Ashworth, Edmund Ashworth (who retired on 1 March 1866) and Taylor Ashworth.

An interesting early account of Ashworth's products is given in *The Staffordshire Advertiser's* review of local exhibits intended for the 1862 London Exhibition. The Ashworth consignment was initially shown in the firm's showrooms in March 1862 and excited much interest. The main display comprised 'their well known Ironstone China', but it must be remembered that Ashworths, as with other ironstone manufacturers, also produced different types of ceramics. In this case Ashworths showed:

> enamelled dinner, dessert and toilet services with other articles in richly decorated earthenware. They are, in addition manufacturing some beautiful specimens of ornamental jet [black-glazed pottery]... Two vases in jet with bold Roman scrolls in burnished gold, traced with delicate lines of colour. Another pair, in earthenware, have a maroon and green ground, richly decorated in

> gold, while a fifth has a wreath of water lilies, with ornamentation in gold on a chrome green ground. There is also a four-gallon punch bowl in earthenware, richly decorated in the Japanese style...

This last item, the large punch bowl and 'two covered jars or vases, 26 inches high in the Indian style...' would probably be classed as Ashworth's ironstone by collectors today, but at the time, or by this reviewer, many of the Ashworth products such as the 'sets of jugs in jet and cobalt blue, picked out in gold...' were simply described as 'earthenware'.

Ashworth's ironstone was not neglected but it was apparently only part of the firm's output and at this important exhibition took rather a back seat being related to the more commercial articles of a durable nature. *The Staffordshire Advertiser* of 29 March 1862 noted:

> In useful wares this firm attached great importance to its Ironstone goods, which are as a rule, decorated in the Oriental style in printing and pencil [painted] work. This ware is remarkable for its great weight and strength and is supplied in large quantities to the leading ship companies...

PLATE 138. *An impressed marked 'Real Ironstone China' blue printed plate, being an Ashworth's continuation of a popular Oriental pattern. This design first occurs hand painted on 18th century Chinese porcelains, then on English porcelains and earthenwares and after 1813 on Mason's Ironstones. Printed Mason's-type crowned mark. Diameter 8¾in. (22.22cm). c.1860-70.*

While discussing the Ashworth wares produced in the early 1860s, it is of interest to quote briefly from the 1863 government report on children employed in various industries, including pottery. John Lawton, who described himself as Ashworth's factory manager, had started work as a mould-runner at the age of eight and had worked his way up to foreman and then manager. In 1863 the average age of boy mould-runners and jigger-turners was between ten and eleven but they could be younger. They would earn (really earn!) their two shillings a week. They were employed in teams by the main workman. In other words the plate-maker would pay the child or children that turned his jigger and the boys that fetched and carried

PLATE 139. *An impressed marked 'Real Ironstone China' Oriental-style punch bowl of superb quality. It also bears the Royal Arms 'Ironstone China' mark with painted pattern number '3749'. Diameter 12½in. (31.75cm). c.1860-70.*

PLATE 140. *An impressed marked 'Real Ironstone China' Oriental-style plate with a printed copy of the former standard 'Mason's Patent Ironstone China' crowned mark with 'Ashworth's' added below. Diameter 10¼in. (26.03cm). c.1870-80.*

for him. The children also arrived at about six in the morning to light the fires but had an half an hour break for breakfast.

After describing the boy's traditional tasks, John Lawton continued: 'All the ordinary painting work is done by girls and women, Girls begin to learn to paint about 11 or 12. They are apprenticed about that age... It is nice work for women'. The girls also assisted the printer. Lawton recorded: 'The cutters begin cutting (the transfer paper) at an early age. There is one cutter to each printer. They become transferrers (applying the inked paper) as they get older. Their work as cutters initiates them into the others work...' As I have previously shown, Ashworth's employed about a hundred boys and girls at the time of the 1861 census. They were vital to the running of any pottery.

Messrs Ashworth continued to produce their Mason-style ironstone wares (as Plates 148 to 150) for the rest of the nineteenth century, often trading on the old, highly respected Mason name and tradition, from the preceding Morley & Ashworth partnership. Llewellynn Jewitt, in the 1878 edition of his monumental work *The Ceramic Art of Great Britain*, then stated:[1]

PLATE 141. *Two unusual blue printed Ashworth's ironstone plates depicting British views (Balmoral Castle and Osborne House) rather than Oriental designs. Impressed and printed 'Ashworth Bros.' name mark with potting dates '4-04' for April 1904. Diameter 9½in. (24.13cm).*

Mr Morley... having sold the entire business, moulds, copper-plates, &c, to the present owners, Messrs. Geo L. Ashworth and Taylor Ashworth (brothers), who continue to the fullest extent, the manufacture of the 'Patent Ironstone China', which they and their predecessor named the 'Real Ironstone China' (of which patented articles they are the only makers) on their marks, and produce all Mason's best patterns in services, vases, &c., made from his original models. They also manufacture Meigh's ironstone, from his old moulds, &c. This manufacture has been very largely developed by Mr Taylor Ashworth, who studied the process under Mr Morley, and is the resident acting partner... This gentleman married the grand-daughter of Mr Meigh, obtaining by that alliance a vast deal of valuable information about the working of the stoneware...

The Ironstone China, from its extreme hardness and durability is specially adapted, in its simpler styles of decoration, for services used by large steamship companies, hotels, clubs, colleges, and other places where hard usage has to be undergone; while in its more elaborate and rich styles – and it is capable of the very highest degree of finish – it is eminently fitted for families of the higher ranks. No climate affects this ware. The usual style of decoration for dinner services is imitations of Oriental patterns – Japanese and Indian[2] flowers, &c. – and the colours and gilding are rich in the extreme. In vases and jugs the handles are usually dragons and other grotesque animals. The Indian vases are of perfect form, of exquisite design, rich in their colours, and massive in gilding. They are priceless Art-treasures, and examples of Ashworth's make deserve to be in every 'home of taste'.

Jewitt would seem to have been quoting from a publicity hand-out or Ashworth catalogue for the wording is surely over-flowery in its complimentary tone, even for Jewitt! Still the descriptions are contemporary and of interest. Apart from the preceding references to Ironstone China, Jewitt also commented on the standard Ashworth earthenwares and noted that in general 'about one-third of the whole being exported. The ordinary classes are principally exported to Russia, India, &c., and the more rich and costly to Havana, Spain and other countries...'.

Writing in, or slightly before, 1878, Jewitt noted that the marks on Ashworth's wares took the following forms:

...a circular garter, bearing the words 'Real Ironstone China' and enclosing the Royal Arms

PLATE 142. *An impressed marked Ashworth's 'Real Ironstone China' plate of colourful Oriental type – see also Plate 285. Also marked with Royal Arms 'Ironstone China' mark and pattern number '8689'. Diameter 10¼in. (26.03cm).* c.1870-85.

and the name 'G L Ashworth & Bros, Hanley', Mason's mark Patent Ironstone China, on a scroll, under a crown with the addition of the word 'Ashworth's', a crown with the words 'Ashworth Bros' above and a ribbon bearing the words 'Real Ironstone China' beneath it; and the Royal Arms, with supporters, crest, motto, &c. and the words 'Ironstone China'.

Samples of Ashworth's ironstone dinner services of the early 1880s are shown in Plate 285 and discussed in Appendix III. Although the Ashworth trading title remained the same for the rest of the century, a change of ownership took place in December 1883, when John Hackett Goddard purchased the company from the Ashworths for his son John Shaw Goddard (1857-1939), by whom it was continued with the help of Ashworth's existing experienced manager, Charles Brock. After several changes the firm became a Limited Liability Company in 1914 but no change was made in the marks used.

The largest proportion of Ashworth's output comprises useful ware – dinner, dessert and tea services with some jugs, vases, etc. – decorated with traditional Mason-style designs.

*The Potteries Illustrated* in 1893 carried a review of Ashworth's wares which were apparently still enjoying a large market for the traditional ironstone wares introduced nearly eighty years previously by C.J. Mason, in 1814.

PLATE 143. *Representative parts of an attractive Ashworth dinner service of pattern 'B 1486'. The printed Royal Arms 'Ironstone China' mark includes the name of the American importer and retailer – Richard Briggs of Boston.* *See also Plate 285 for these shapes. Diameter of plate 10¼in. (26.03cm). c.1880-90. Messrs Dreweatt Neate.*

The ironstone, china and earthenware trades possess no better known names as manufacturers, than Messrs. George L. Ashworth & Bros, of the Broad Street Works, Hanley, and it can be honestly stated that the productions of the firm are known in the leading markets throughout the civilised world...

The firm at the present time gives employment to a large number of workers. The present proprietors are Mr John S. Goddard and Mr F.L. Johnson...

PLATE 144. *An imposing Ashworth Ironstone china tureen decorated with Oriental-style printed outline pattern number 'B 1834'. Printed Mason's-style crowned mark. 11in. high. (27.94cm). c.1870-80.*

PLATE 145. *A colourful Ashworth (Hicks & Meigh type) Japan-patterned dinner service plate. Printed crowned mark 'Ashworth Real Ironstone China' with painted pattern number 'B 1876'. Diameter 11in. (27.94cm). c.1870-80.*

*Plate 146. An impressed marked 'Ashworth Real Ironstone China' Oriental-style dinner service plate. Printed Royal Arms 'Ironstone China' mark, with painted pattern number 'B 1955'. Diameter 10½in. (26.67cm). c.1870-80.*

The London offices are in Hatton Garden.

...The firm are principally known for their exquisite productions from the designs of the late Mr Charles Mason, whose name will be long remembered. The firm purchased these designs and patterns...so that they are their exclusive property, and are used in the manufacture of dinner, tea and other services, Japan ware, domestic utensils and a vast array of articles in ironstone and earthenware. For their beauty and originality there is still nothing to beat them and they are in greater demand than ever... The firm ranks high in the industrial world and is worthy of the reputation it has so justly gained and so long maintained.

J.F. Blàcker, the author of *The A B C of Nineteenth Century English Ceramic Art* (Stanley Paul & Co. Ltd., not dated but c.1911), wrote to the major British firms that had been included in a 1900 list. Extracts from the replies were given in his Chapter XXI, with further points incorporated in the main text. Ashworth's reply or covering letter, read:

We beg to say that we are the sole reproducers of Mason's Real Ironstone China, and all his decoration and shapes, all the existing moulds and engravings being in our possession, and were purchased from the Mason firm by us when his business was closed. We enclose herewith a circular giving a few particulars, also a few illustrations, which may be of interest to you.

Mr Blacker then incorporated much of the information given in the Company's brochure, but this included large extracts from Jewitt's 1867 *Art Journal* article, which I have previously quoted. Blacker's post-1900

PLATE 147. *An Ashworth's Ironstone bowl decorated with a version of an early Mason's printed outline design – see Plates 29, 85 and 111. The crowned Mason's style of tradition mark has the later additional word 'England' added. Diameter 10in. (25.4cm). c.1892-1900.*

PLATE 148. *A selection of Ashworth-Mason jugs and basins showing traditional Oriental-style designs still being produced after 1900. Reproduced from Ashworth's publicity material, c.1910.*

illustrations, which were presumably supplied by the Company, comprised six traditional Mason jugs and large bowls, each decorated with a printed base Oriental-style design; six similarly styled plates and a group of two large covered vases, two smaller bottle-shape vases, a two-handled mug and a large jug and basin. A selection of post-1900 Ashworth ironstone is shown in Plates 148 to 150.

Mr Blacker's own comments are of a general nature. Writing of Ashworth's Mason-style productions, he continued:

and still the trade flourishes, and through the home and foreign markets there comes a constant demand for immense quantities in all qualities, from the simplest in decoration to the most elaborate, in which colours and gilding are applied with finished skill. Ashworth's vases, the Indian vases of fine form, are worthy of a high place. No doubt collectors in the future will think so, but for the decoration of a modern home scarcely any will be found of better design or richer colour; none will be equal in durability, which is, after all, a con-

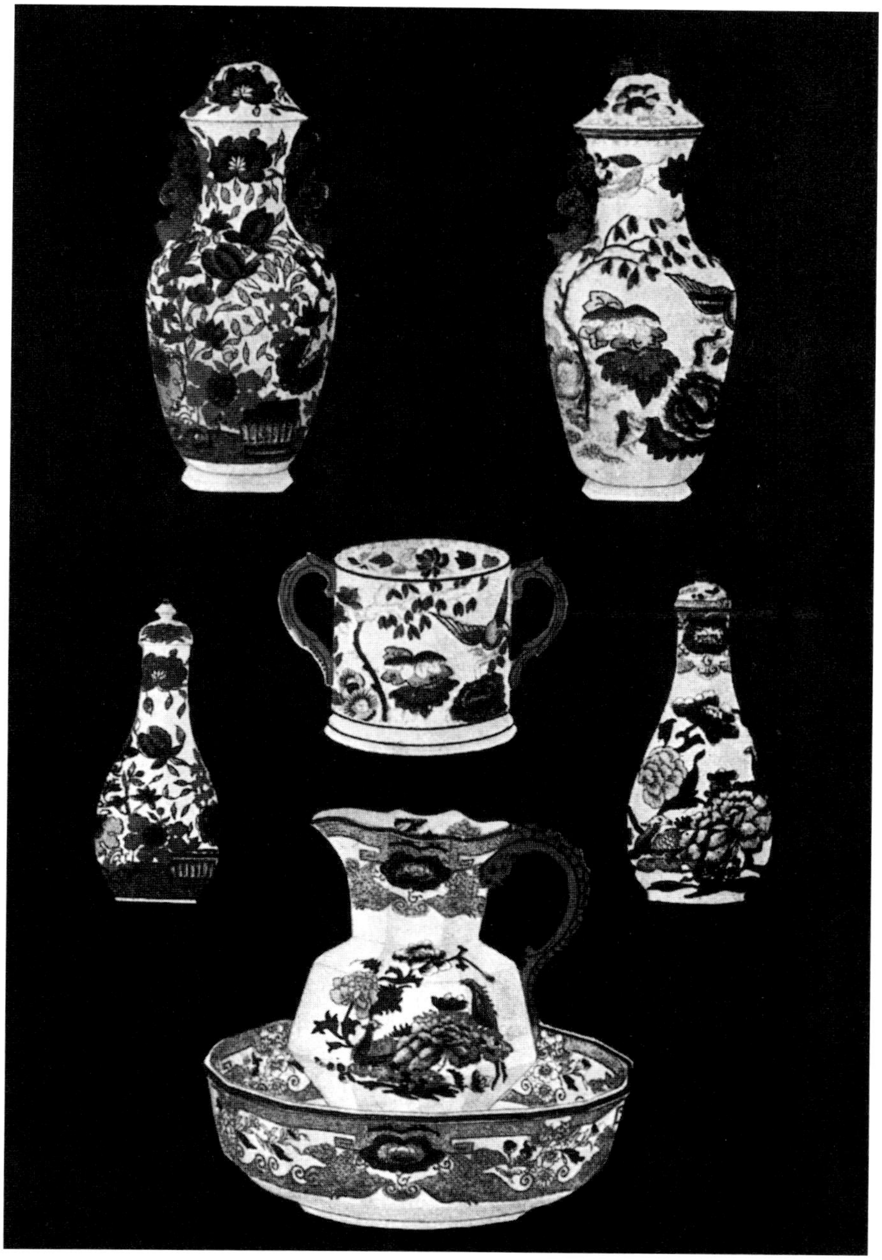

PLATE 149. *A selection of traditional Mason designs as featured in Ashworth's publicity material of the 1910 period.*

sideration worthy of the purchaser, who often buys cheap foreign goods because they are bright, even if they have no artistic qualities. It is not too much to say that English china and earthenware, such as are produced by the firm of Geo. L. Ashworth & Bros., have an immense superiority over the products of other countries. And they are much cheaper, because one service of ironstone china would outshine several of the fragile ones..., and in the first cost there is not a great difference.

The fame of Ashworth's products had naturally spread across the Atlantic and its products were available there. The American monthly magazine *Old China* of November 1901 carried an article on 'Mason's Patent Ironstone China' and noted:

> The Ashworth firm is in existence today and uses the same old Mason moulds, and the modern ware can be seen at the store of Edward Boote, 25 West Broadway, New York... As the modern firm has

PLATE 150. *A selection of Ashworth ironstone plates, as shown on Messrs Ashworth's c.1910 publicity material. The basic Oriental-style designs have hardly varied from the Mason's essays of the 1815-20 period!*

reproduced most of Mason's best pieces and has sometimes used the old Mason crown, collectors must be careful to distinguish between the real Mason and the Ashworth reproductions.

The original Mason engraved designs, incorporating the 'Mason's Patent Ironstone' printed marks, have been extensively used up to recent times. It can happen that wares bearing impressed marks such as 'ASHWORTHS. REAL IRONSTONE CHINA' also bear earlier printed marks not always relating to the Mason family, including Hicks & Meigh-type 'Stone China' marks, because these devices occur on the reused original copper plates. Various later marks have also been issued, but these still retain the original basic wording. The additions of the word 'England' to a Mason-style mark indicates an Ashworth parentage after 1891. The wording 'Made in England' is a twentieth century variation. Mason printed marks with these additions are obviously Ashworth productions.

PLATE 151. *A new style Ashworth dinner service design but retaining the traditional much favoured Oriental influence. Printed Mason's Patent Ironstone mark with 'England' added. Indistinct impressed year marks for 1930(?). Pattern (G?) '1659'. Diameter 10½in. (26.67cm).*

PLATE 152. *An Oriental-style printed outline Ashworth dinner service design. The traditional former Mason's crowned mark including 'England' and the 1915 registration number '652974'. Painted pattern number 'C 1859' of 1915. Diameter 10½in. (26.67cm).*

Some Ashworth-Mason wares from the 1880s into the twentieth century have month and year numerals impressed to show the date of potting. These date numerals take the form 6.98 for June 1898, or 7.09 for

July 1909, and so on. These impressed potting dates can be very helpful in determining the period of a reissued old Mason design because many of the traditional shapes were kept in production along with an assortment of more modern forms. William Scarratt, writing in or before 1906, noted in his local history book *Old Times in the Potteries* that Ashworth's decoration was 'maintained on the old lines as well as modern variations. The body is durable and of good quality and appearance.'

In fact to practised eyes the body does not appear so compact and as highly vitrified as the old Mason body. It is more open or floury and has not the great weight of the original. High four-figure pattern numbers, sometimes with a letter prefix, indicate a later Ashworth product. I have a plate for example with a Harrods retailer's printed mark with the Mason's crowned mark and the Ashworth's pattern number 'B 9799'. Also a Mason's and 'England' mark example of pattern 'C.1859' with a 1915 pattern registration number. Mason-style marks incorporating the name of a pattern, as the example here shown, obviously relates to the Ashworth period. This example further includes the present century wording 'Made in England' and reference to an American patent. Many other printed marks relating to individual patterns may be found.

The 'Mason's' Ashworth mark shown next is one of several used in the 1942-47 period, including a war-time 'Group' letter 'B'. This relates to the then Board of Trade requirements relating to different categories of domestic wares, classed as 'A' 'B' or 'C'. These letters were added to standard British marks in the period between 1942 and March 1947.

I reproduce below a sample selection of the various

types of old Ashworth printed marks that can occur. While most include the firm's name or initials, or simply 'A. Bros.', some (mainly reissues of earlier Mason or Meigh) marks are not so identified. A standard impressed mark comprising the wording 'REAL IRONSTONE CHINA', with or without the Ashworth name, can appear from 1860 onwards.

It should be borne in mind that Messrs Ashworth, as major manufacturers of ironstone wares, purchased and continued to produce the popular saleable patterns produced by several earlier firms – including Samuel Alcock's designs. The relevant earlier marks were often also used, not always with updated amendments, such as 'A Bros'.

John Goddard's son John Vivian Goddard succeeded his father in 1919. For a period in the 1920s Messrs Ashworth were part of Harold Robinson's large group of major pottery firms trading together as Cauldon Potteries Ltd. However, to outward appearances the old firm of G.L. Ashworth & Bros. continued to produce the traditional old Mason-style ironstone-type wares and the Mason's trade mark continued in use. On the bankruptcy of Harold Robinson in the early 1930s John Vivian Goddard repurchased the Ashworth company in its entirety and continued without further interruption.

In the past the Ashworth products have been neglected by many collectors but they are now, rightly, commanding respect. Some examples are extremely rich and decorative. Examples bearing marks without the *c.*1891 addition of the word 'England' should be 'antique' and indeed as old as were the true Mason ironstone wares when Jewitt and others were writing in such glowing terms of old Mason!

The old Ashworth firm adopted the new name of Mason's Ironstone China Ltd. in March 1968. In April 1973 the firm joined the Wedgwood Group and henceforth traded under the shortened title 'Mason's Ironstone'.

For further information the reader is referred to *Mason's. The First Two Hundred Years* by Gaye Blake Roberts (Merrell Holberton Publishers Ltd., London, 1996).

**BAGSHAW & MAIER (Meir?), Burslem, c.1802-8.**

This entry is occasioned by the attribution of a 'B & M' initial mark with the description 'Ironstone' to this partnership, which was dissolved in 1808.

It should be obvious that no ironstone mark can relate to a firm or partnership that had ceased trading before the introduction of the ceramic body description 'ironstone'! In practice this single word description is not normally found as part of a mark before the 1830s.

The 'B & M' ironstone mark referred to may relate to Booth & Meigh (*c*.1828-37.) or more probably to Brougham & Mayer of Tunstall (*c*.1853-60).

**J.D. BAGSTER,[3] High Street, Hanley, c.1823-27.**

John Denton Bagster produced various earthenwares, including ironstone-type wares. He succeeded Messrs Phillips & Bagster at the Church Works, High Street, Hanley, in April 1823, but the rate records mark the premises as void in 1827, after John Denton Bagster's death.

The marks incorporate or comprise the initials 'J.D.B.' Alternatively the initials 'I.D.B.' will also relate to Bagster.

Messrs Phillips, the London auctioneers, sold an interesting dessert service in December 1983. I illustrate the handled dish in Plate 153 The printed Prince of Wales three-feather crest mark incorporates the initials 'J.D.B.' and also the description 'Celtic China'. However, the body appears to be a type of ironstone rather than porcelain. The pieces were heavily potted and opaque, and were also very spotted and rather stained although the flower painting was of good quality. Most pieces, apart from the large printed mark, also bore an impressed Staffordshire knot.

PLATE 153. *A porcelain-like hand painted ironstone-type dessert service dish. Initial mark 'J.D.B.' of J.D. Bagster of Hanley. Mark includes the description 'Celtic China' with pattern number '300'. 9½ x 9in. (24.3cm x 22.86cm). Messrs Phillips.*

**W. & D. BAILEY (& Co.), Lane End, Longton. c.1828-29.**

This partnership between William and David Bailey produced china wares at their Flint Street pottery at Lane End in the approximate period 1828-29.

In 1829 they traded, with William Copestake, as W. & D. Bailey & Co., but on the death of David Bailey this partnership was dissolved on 19 October 1829. William Bailey seemingly continued but a William Bailey had potted under his name at Lane End from about 1798 to *c*.1832.

Although in the 1829 dissolution of partnership notice W. & D. Bailey & Co. were described as china manufacturers, the W. & D. Bailey name mark has been reported on earthenwares.

**BAILEY & BEVINGTON, Hanley, c.1866-68.**

This partnership between John Bailey and John Bevington at their Elm Street Works, Hanley is mainly known for their parian wares but their advertisement in an 1867 directory also mentions 'Stone and Granite etc'.

They may therefore have produced some granite-type wares such as jugs. It is doubtful if they produced standard table wares and no marked examples have as yet been reported.

The partnership also traded as Bailey, Bevington & Co., but Messrs Bevington & Bradley succeeded as from 31 January 1868.

**CHARLES BAKER, Burslem, c.1874-76.**

Charles George Baker, formerly a partner in Baker & Chetwynd, continued the Sylvester Pottery, Nile Street, Burslem, from 20 November 1874 for a year or so before the pottery was taken over by Holmes, Plant & Madew (*c*.1876-84).

Jewitt notes in the first edition of *The Ceramic Art of Great Britain* that 'Charles G. Barker[4] produces the ordinary white granite ware for the United States, Canadian and Foreign markets'.

Royal Arms, Charles G[5] Baker name marks have been recorded from the United States. Some examples include the country name 'England' (as well as 'Burslem'), an early use of this designation. The description 'Imperial Ironstone China' was continued from the Baker & Chetwynd period.

**BAKER & Son.**
Various 'B. & S.' printed marks have been attributed to Baker & Son – see Jeffrey B. Snyder's *Romantic Staffordshire Ceramics* (Schiffer Publishing Ltd., USA, 1997). However, I cannot trace any record of this firm in Staffordshire.

These initials occur with the British design registration mark of 5 June 1850, relating to the 'Missouri' pattern entered in the British records as Barker & Son of the Hill Works, Burslem. The firm of William Barker & Son traded there in the approximate period 1850-60.

Other Staffordshire firms that may have used 'B. & S.' initial marks include Booth & Son of Lane End, c.1830-35, and Broadhurst & Sons of Longton, c.1854-63. Several later partnerships also shared these initials.

[Price Lists on Application.] **BAKER & CO.,** [Price Lists Application.]
MANUFACTURERS OF
**WHITE GRANITE, PRINTED,**
AND ALL KINDS OF
**EARTHENWARE**
Suitable for Colonial and Foreign Markets.
FENTON POTTERIES, STAFFORDSHIRE, & 1, ORANGE COURT, CASTLE STREET, LIVERPOOL

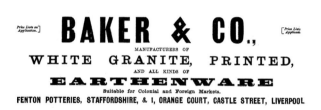

**(W.) BAKER & Co. (Ltd.), Fenton, c.1839-1932.**
The early ware of this firm was often unmarked although the marks 'W. Baker & Co.' or 'Baker & Co.' are sometimes found. A late printed mark of the post-1893 period, when 'Ltd.' was added to the firm's title, is reproduced. The firm was a large one employing over 500 people in 1851 and 650 in 1861. Printed and white ironstone, stone china and granite wares were produced for the colonial and foreign markets and the company had a shipping office in Liverpool.

**BAKER & CHETWYND, Burslem, c.1869-74.**
This partnership at the Sylvester Pottery, Nile Street, Burslem was originally between Charles George Baker, Elijah Chetwynd and David Chetwynd (see page 193) but Elijah retired in April 1872 leaving Charles Baker and David Chetwynd to continue until their partnership was dissolved on 20 November 1874. Charles Baker seemingly continued the Sylvester pottery alone until at least 1875. The Pottery was later owned by Holmes, Plant & Maydew (c.1876-84) and then by Holmes & Plant (c.1884-8).

The Baker & Chetwynd partnership registered teaware forms designated 'United States' on 6 April 1869. Local Directory entries state that the partnership produced ironstone china and earthenwares 'for foreign markets only'.

The description 'Imperial Ironstone China' was used with the Victorian Royal Arms, with the name 'Baker & Chetwynd' added below.

**BARKER Bros., Longton, 1876-82.**
Barker Bros. produced earthenwares and stonewares at their Gold Street Works at Longton from c.1876 to about 1882 when the trade style was changed to Barker Bros. Ltd. (see the following entry).

Various impressed or printed marks occur incorporating the name Barker Bros. or the initials 'B.B.', often with the name of the relevant body, 'Stone Ware', etc.

**BARKER Bros. Ltd., Longton, c.1882-c.1980s.**
This Limited Company succeeded Barker Bros. in about 1882. New or enlarged works were acquired and titled the Meir Works, at Burslem Street, Longton. The 'Meir' trade name was incorporated in several printed marks, as was also 'Tudor Ware' or 'Royal Tudor Ware'.

Various types of earthenware and ironstone-type wares were produced. Most marks incorporate the firm's name in full but the initials 'B.B.Ltd.' were also used.

**BARKER & Son, Burslem, c.1850-60.**
The impressed mark 'BARKER & SON' is recorded on ironstone-type ware, and the initial mark 'B. & S.' occurs on a printed design, 'Missouri', registered at the Patent Office on 5 June 1850, in the name of Barker & Son, Hill Works, Burslem. This relates to William Barker and his son. William Barker had been in partnership with Thomas Till up to 15 April 1850. The new firm was a large concern and employed 265 people.

A printed 'stoneware', 'Barker & Son' mark also occurs, of similar form to the preceding Barker Bros. mark. An impressed anchor mark has also been reported with this device but it is difficult to explain this mark unless it relates to another manufacturer of the bought-in blank purchased by Barker & Son.

Other firms could well have used 'B. & S.' initial marks – see Baker & Son.

**BARKER, SUTTON & TILL, Burslem, c.1834-42.**

This partnership between William Barker, James Sutton and Thomas Till worked the Sytch Pottery, Liverpool Street, Burslem, from *c*.1834 to 28 September 1842, when James Sutton retired.

The partnership produced the usual range of Staffordshire earthenwares including ironstone or stone china. Printed or impressed marks incorporate or comprise the three names or the initials 'B.S & T'.

Messrs Barker & Till succeeded – see the following entry.

**BARKER & TILL, Burslem, c.1842-50.**

William Barker and Thomas Till continued the Sytch Pottery, Liverpool Road, Burslem in succession to Barker, Sutton & Till (see preceding entry).

The usual range of earthenwares including ironstone-type wares were produced. Various printed marks incorporate or comprise the names in full or the initials 'B. & T.'

The partnership was dissolved on 15 April 1850, after which Thomas Till continued on his own account.

It should be noted that other Staffordshire partnerships could also have employed 'B & T' initial marks. These firms included:

| | | |
|---|---|---|
| Bethany & Tomlinson | Lane End | *c*.1843-44 |
| Barrow & Taylor | Hanley | *c*.1859 |
| Banks & Thorley | Hanley | *c*.1875-86 |
| Beech & Tellwright | Cobridge | *c*.1882-84 |

**THOMAS BARLOW, Fenton and Longton, 1835-93.**

This entry explains the difficulty of correctly identifying the maker of wares bearing single or double common initials. The poorly registered 'T.B. Stone China' mark here shown could have been used by several Staffordshire potters.

| | | |
|---|---|---|
| Thomas Bond | Lane End | *c*.1810-15 |
| Thomas Bagnall | Fenton | *c*.1818 |
| Thomas Brough | Lane End | *c*.1818-22 |
| Thomas Brown | Hanley | *c*.1824-25 |
| Thomas Birks | Lane End | *c*.1830 |
| Thomas Barker | Lane End | *c*.1834 |
| Thomas Beech | Hanley | *c*.1834 |
| Thomas Brunt | Lane End | *c*.1835-41 |
| Thomas Barlow | Fenton | *c*.1835-41 |
| Thomas Barlow | Longton | *c*.1849-93 |
| Thomas Birks | Longton | *c*.1854-73 |

plus several later potters.

Of the above 'T.B.' potters perhaps the most likely is Thomas Barlow, but even then we have two distinct periods and places of work perhaps representing two different potters of the same name. A third initial signifying the town would have helped identification but alas no such initial was added.

**T.W. BARLOW (& Son), (Ltd.), Longton, c.1856-1940.**

Having treated ourselves to a general entry on the several 'T.B.' potters, I should include a separate entry for the important firm of T.W. Barlow, succeeded by T.W. Barlow & Son and then by T.W. Barlow Ltd. These firms produced a good range of earthenwares at their Coronation Works, Commerce Street, Longton.

Thomas Waterhouse Barlow worked in partnership with William Cotton, under the trade name Cotton & Barlow prior to 11 November 1856. He traded under his own name until *c*.1882 when he took his son into the firm, then trading as T.W. Barlow & Son until *c*.1920 when 'Ltd' was added to the firm's style. A twentieth century trade name used on marks was 'Coronation Ware'.

**BARROW & Co., Longton or Fenton, c.1853-56.**

This firm, which was also listed as Barrow, Taylor & Pears of Market Street, Longton produced ironstone wares which bear an impressed or relief-moulded mark incorporating the Royal Arms with supporters and also the words 'IRONSTONE CHINA/BARROW & CO'.

Registrations were taken out for tableware and toiletware forms in October 1853 and August 1855 from a Fenton rather than a Longton address; this would be the Park Works. Seemingly this firm exported white ironstone or granite-type wares to North America. The moulded 'Adriatic Shape' is the most commonly found Barrow & Co. form.

**BATES, WALKER & Co., Burslem, c.1875-78.**

This partnership between William Bates and John Walker working the famous Dale Hall Works in succession to Bates, Elliott & Co. (1870-75) produced a good general selection of pottery, including ironstone china. One mark incorporates the kneeling boy with vase trade mark with the year '1790' and the initials 'B.W. & Co.'

**BATKIN, WALKER & BROADHURST, Lane End, c.1840-45.**
This partnership between W. Batkin, Thomas Walker and Job Broadhurst was dissolved on 21 November 1845, after which Thomas Walker continued alone. Good quality ironstone-type ware was made by this short-lived firm under the description 'Stone China'. Printed marks incorporate the initials 'B.W. & B.'

**BATES & BENNETT, Cobridge, c.1868-95.**
The printed mark here reproduced may have been used by this firm, but the initials could relate to any one of sixteen other Staffordshire partnerships of the 1820-80 period.

It will be observed that the basic form of this mark relates to that used by Barker Bros. in the 1876-82 period.

**BEARDMORE & Co., Staffordshire Potteries, c.1840-45.**
John Hackett Goddard's diaries record purchase of white granite wares for his American market from Beardmore & Co. However, I cannot trace a mid-nineteenth century Staffordshire firm of this brief title. It was, perhaps, a handy abbreviation for one of the following partnerships:

| | |
|---|---|
| Beardmore, Birks & Blood | Longton *c.*1850-54 |
| Beardmore & Edwards | Longton *c.*1856-58 |

**BEARDMORE & BIRKS, Longton, c.1832-43.**
It is possible that this partnership potting at St Gregory's Works, High Street, Longton produced some of the ironstone-type wares that bear various printed marks incorporating the initials 'B. & B.'

It should be noted, however, that these initials fit various other Staffordshire firms including the later partnership of Bates & Bennett, *c.*1868-95 – see the previous column.

The similarly titled Longton firm of Beardmore, Birks & Blood is of a later period, *c.*1850-54. For further information on this Longton firm the reader is referred to Rodney Hampson's specialist study 'Longton Potters 1700-1865' (*Journal of Ceramic History*, Vol. 14, City Museum & Art Gallery, Stoke-on-Trent, 1990)

**BEARDMORE & DAWSON, Longton, 1863.**
This partnership between Thomas Beardmore and James Dawson succeeded Messrs Newton & Beardmore at Commerce Street, Longton, from 10 June 1863, but was in turn dissolved on 10 October of that year, giving it a life of only four months. Yet the initial mark 'B. & D.' has been reported on ironstone-type wares.

For further information on this Longton firm the reader is referred to Rodney Hampson's specialist study 'Longton Potters 1700-1865' (*Journal of Ceramic History*, Vol. 14, City Museum & Art Gallery, Stoke-on-Trent, 1990).

**BEARDMORE & EDWARDS, Longton, c.1856-58.**
This partnership between Thomas Beardmore and Aaron Edwards was dissolved on 24 April 1858, after which Messrs Newton & Beardmore continued, then Beardmore & Dawson. The initial mark 'B. & E.' occurs, rarely, on blue printed ware. No other Staffordshire partnership used these initials before Bradbury & Emery of *c.*1889-1902.

It is possible that this partnership also traded as Beardmore & Co., q.v.

For further information on this Longton firm the reader is referred to Rodney Hampson's specialist study 'Longton Potters 1700-1865' (*Journal of Ceramic History*, Vol 14, City Museum & Art Gallery, Stoke-on-Trent, 1990).

**BECK, BLAIR & Co., Longton, 1879.**
This partnership between John Beck and William Blair (in succession to. Beck, Wild & Co.) worked the Beaconsfield Pottery in Anchor Road, Longton, from 13 January 1879 until an enlarged partnership was terminated on 19 November 1879. The pottery continued under the trade style Blair & Co.

These firms mainly produced china but the name mark has been reported apparently on ironstone-type earthenwares. The firm registered four printed designs – birds and foliage – on 29 March 1899.

**JAMES BEECH, Tunstall, c.1834-89.**
Several potters of this name worked at Tunstall and at Burslem, within the ironstone period. I am here concerned with James Beech of Tunstall who may have used 'J.B.' initial marks, such as those found on American market 'Texian Compaique' printed wares – see 'J.B.' (page 269).

James Beech of Newfield, Tunstall, is recorded from 1834. He had five kilns in use in 1836. In the 1890-59 period his address is given as High Street, Tunstall. In the period 1878-1889 a James Beech was working the Swan Bank Pottery at Tunstall. This was later continued by Beech & Hancock – see the following entry.

It is not certain that these directory entries relate to the same James Beech or if the occupation of the Tunstall works was continuous. A James Beech also potted at the Bell Works, Burslem, from the 1830s to at least the mid-1860s.

As stated above, 'J.B.' initial marks may relate to this potter.

**BEECH & HANCOCK (BEECH, HANCOCK & Co.), Burslem & Tunstall, c.1851-5 and 1862-76.**
Beech & Hancock, sometimes trading as Beech & Co., or Beech, Hancock & Co., worked the Swan Bank Pottery, Burslem, in the 1851-55 period and later at Swan Bank Pottery in Tunstall which the partnership continued to c.1876. James Beech continued under his own name up to 1889.

Beech & Hancock produced a range of earthenwares including ironstone-type wares. Printed or impressed marks can incorporate the names in full or the initials 'B. & H.' or 'B.H. & Co.'

**BELL BROS., Albion Pottery, Newcastle upon Tyne, c.1863+.**
Various printed marks occur incorporating or comprising the name 'Albion'. Such marks can include the British Royal Arms and a description of the body, such as 'Stone China'. The name 'Albion' will relate to the name of the pottery, rather than the name of the pattern.

The Bell Bros. renamed the Ouseburn Bridge Pottery at Ouseburn, Newcastle upon Tyne, the Albion Pottery in about 1863. Jewitt records that it was later worked by Atkinson & Galloway and then by W. Morris before it closed in 1872.

'Albion' marks probably relate to this pottery, within the period c.1863-72.

**J. & M.P. BELL & Co. (Ltd.), Glasgow, Scotland, c.1842-1928.**
This firm produced a very large range of earthenware and porcelain. Its exhibits at the 1851 Exhibition included:

> Dinner services in stoneware – blue printed landscape pattern, 'Italian lakes'
> Flowered ware, mulberry centre with azure border, 'Warwick vase' registered pattern. Pure white, gilt.
> Toilet services in stoneware – white basin and ewer, gilt antique shape; 'Diana' with registered ewer. Basin and ewer, printed and coloured. Large basin, flowered mulberry, convolvulus pattern, Footbath and jug marble pattern.
> Tea services and jugs in stoneware and porcelain. Common stoneware, in dipped, sponged and painted [patterns]....

The registered shapes or patterns were registered on

| | |
|---|---|
| 13 February 1850 | (parcel 3) 'Ionia' pattern, |
| 4 June 1850 | (parcel 1) 'Warwick Vase' pattern, |
| 16 September 1850 | (parcel 8) fluted forms, |
| 11 March 11th 1851 | (parcel 4) moulded jug shape, |
| 11 April 1851 | (parcel 4) ewer and basin shape, |
| 14 April 1851 | (parcel 7) dinner and tea service shapes. |

Most of Bell's ware bear marks incorporating the initials 'J.B.' or 'J. & M.P.B. & Co'. ('Ltd.' was added to the firm's style, and initial marks from 1881) or the name in full. The Royal Arms device was often used and most marks include the name of the body – 'Royal Stone China' etc. A bell device was also used as a mark, and it occurs impressed or printed.

Further information on this important firm may be found in Jewitt's *Ceramic Art of Great Britain* or in J.A. Fleming's *Scottish Pottery*, 1923. *Scottish Pottery, 16th Historical Review* (Scottish Pottery Society, Glasgow, 1994) is also of interest as it contains an important article 'The Export Trade of J. & M.P. Bell & Co ' by Henry E. Kelly.

**BELLEEK POTTERY Ltd., Belleek, Co.Fermanagh, N. Ireland, c.1863-present day.**
This Irish firm, originally titled The Belleek Pottery Works Co. Ltd., is mainly known for its delicate, thinly potted porcelain ware, often based on marine forms – objects vastly different from one's image of ironstone.

However, ironstone or granite-type ware was made and L. Jewitt in the first (1878) edition of his *Ceramic Art of Great Britain* especially notes:

> Besides the speciality of these works (the 'Belleek China') Messrs. McBirney & Armstrong manufacture to a large extent white granite ware services of every variety and of excellent quality both in body, in glaze, and in printed, painted, enamelled, and gilt decorations. Many of the patterns are of more than average excellence, and in every respect the Irish earthenware equals the ordinary commercial classes of Staffordshire wares...

Belleek earthenware is rare. It may be marked with the words 'BELLEEK Co. FERMANAGH' and a crowned harp device or with the standard hound, tower and harp mark with the name 'BELLEEK' below. A catalogue of Belleek ware, dated 1904, includes useful earthenware but no ironstone.

General books on the Belleek wares include *Belleek* by Richard K. Degenhardt (Portfolio Press, Huntington, USA, 1978, British 1994 revised edition, Batsford); *Belleek Porcelain and Pottery* by G.M. Smith (Toucan Press, St Peter Port, Guernsey, 1979) and *Belleek Irish Porcelain* by M. Langham (1992).

**R. BESWICK, Tunstall, c.1841-54.**
Robert Beswick succeeded Beswick & Lee at the Warwick Works, High Street, Tunstall, in 1841. He continued until *c.*1854, producing various types of earthenware useful wares including ironstone-type wares.

Printed and impressed 'R. Beswick' name marks have been reported, and it is probable that 'R B' initial marks were also employed.

**B. & H.**
Several printed marks occur on mid-nineteenth century earthenwares and ironstone-type wares, incorporating the initials B. & H. These initials can link with several Staffordshire partnerships, including the following:

| | | |
|---|---|---|
| Bailey & Harvey | Longton | *c.*1833-35 |
| Barker & Hall | Longton | *c.*1852-56 |
| Barker & Hill | Longton | *c.*1864-82 |
| Beech & Hancock | Tunstall | *c.*1860-76 |
| Bodley & Harold | Burslem | *c.*1863-65 |

**BIRKS BROTHERS & SEDDON (BIRKS BROTHERS), Cobridge, c.1878-88.**
This firm employed the Royal Arms device above the wording 'IMPERIAL IRONSTONE CHINA, BIRKS BROS. & SEDDON'. A trade review of July 1878 noted that the new firm was producing granite wares. White granite wares were supplied to the American market during at least the 1880s.

The short title Birks Brothers was also used, rather than the full name.

**BISHOP & STONIER, Hanley, c.1890-1939.**
This important partnership succeeded Powell, Bishop & Stonier (*c.*1880-90) and various types of earthenware, including ironstone, were produced. The marks incorporate the name 'Bishop & Stonier' or the initials 'B. & S.'

**BLAKENEY**
**BLAKENEY ART POTTERY**
**BLAKENEY POTTERY LTD, Stoke, c.1969 onwards**
This company situated at the Cauldon Works, Wolfe Street, Stoke-on-Trent, produces a range of mostly Victorian-style earthenwares. A mark on blue printed ironstone-type wares comprises versions of the British Royal Arms and supporters with the word 'Victorian' under the crown and the words 'Ironstone, Staffordshire, England' under the device. One mark comprises the 'Victorian' trade name across a crowned garter type mark.

Various other Victorian-style printed mark marks are used, several with close copies of the Royal Arms device. The initials 'M.J.B.' for Michael Bailey can also occur incorporated in the marks. Most Blakeney marks incorporate the word 'England' and all post-date 1969.

The pattern or style name 'Romantic' occurs as part of various old-fashioned-style marks. Many 'Flow Blue'-style printed wares are made for the American market. The initials 'T.M.' occur on some printed marks with the basic address 'Staffordshire-England'.

**EDWARD F. BODLEY & Co. (& Son), Burslem, c.1865-98.**
Edward F. Bodley & Co. worked the Scotia Pottery at Burslem from 1865 in succession to Messrs Bodley & Harrold. Various kinds of earthenware were produced and marked with the name or initials 'E.F.B. & Co.' The name 'Scotia Pottery' also occurs up to 1881. Much Bodley ironstone was exported, including the

popular American market 'Ceres' or moulded wheat pattern.

In 1881 the firm's style was amended to Edward F. Bodley & Son and the New Bridge Pottery at Burslem was taken over. Advertisements feature 'Genuine Ironstone China', which was manufactured between 1881 and 1898 and bore marks incorporating the initials 'E.F.B. & Son' or 'E.F.B. & S.' A further mark incorporates the address 'New Bridge Pottery' arranged in a Staffordshire knot.

**BODLEY & HARROLD (BODLEY & Co.), Burslem, c.1863-65.**
This partnership between Edward F. Bodley and William Harrold at the Scotia Pottery at Burslem produced a range of ironstone dinner wares etc.

The partnership registered an Oriental-style dinner service design on 12 May 1863 and examples bear a printed mark comprising 'B. & Co.' with a Staffordshire knot. This suggests that in about May 1863 the firm traded as Bodley & Co. However, other printed marks incorporate the full name Bodley & Harrold or the initials 'B. & H'. Their wares bear also the impressed description

Genuine
Ironstone

After the dissolution of partnership on 10 April 1865, Edward F. Bodley continued the Scotia Pottery.

**T. & R. BOOTE Ltd., Burslem, c.1845 into the present century as tile manufacturers.**
The date for the commencement of this partnership between Thomas and Richard Boote is open to question. The earliest reference I have traced relates to the joint registration on 26 April 1845 of octagonal dinner service shapes, with Edward Walley and Elijah Jones. A similar joint registration for a moulded jug with shooting subjects was entered on 10 May 1845. The firm's early products were featured in *The Art Journal* in 1848. The partnership worked several different factories, all at Burslem. The most important of these were the Kilncroft Works, the Newfields Pottery and the Waterloo Potteries. Tiles were always a major concern.

Messrs Boote made a wide selection of earthenware and parian ware in the middle of the nineteenth century but, by 1880, the firm had confined its attention to tiles and to ironstone or 'Granite Ware' marketed under the title 'Royal Patent Ironstone'. The printed marks incorporate the firm's name or the initials 'T. & R.B.' Much of Boote's ironstone and granite ware was for overseas markets and a great quantity was made for North America. The 'Sydenham' moulded shapes first registered on 3 September 1853 proved exceptionally popular in North America as did the 'Atlantic' shapes introduced in the 1850s.

**G. & W. BOOTH, Hanley, c.1821-54.**
It is difficult to date this partnership at Waterloo Place, Hanley, exactly but in August 1825 they supplied the Chamberlain management at Worcester with '8 Blue and white ironstone dishes at £1-4-0' less 4s.6d. discount. Various members of the family worked at Waterloo Place until at least 1854.

**THOMAS G. BOOTH, Tunstall, c.1878-83.**
Thomas Gimbert Booth succeeded Thomas Booth & Son at the Church Bank Pottery, High Street, Tunstall, from January 1878. His trade advertisements feature 'best Ironstone china for Hotels and Ship's use, suitable for Home, Foreign and Colonial markets'. Printed marks include the initials 'T.G.B.' or the fuller name.

The T.G. & F. Booth (q.v.) partnership succeeded in 1883.

T. G. & F. BOOTH,
TUNSTALL, STAFFORDSHIRE,
MANUFACTURERS OF
EARTHENWARE
SUITABLE for HOME, FOREIGN, & COLONIAL MARKETS.
BEST IRONSTONE-CHINA FOR HOTELS' AND SHIPS' USE.
ALSO TILES FOR GRATES, STOVES, AND WALL DECORATION.
LONDON SHOW ROOMS:—Mr. T. A. GREEN, 25, ELY PLACE, HOLBORN.
ILLUSTRATIONS, SAMPLES, AND PRICES ON APPLICATION.

**T.G. & F. BOOTH, Tunstall, c.1883-89.**
This partnership between Thomas G. Booth and Frederick Booth succeeded Thomas Booth at the Church Bank Pottery, Tunstall, in 1883. The partnership was dissolved on 1 January 1887, although the firm seems to have been continued under the old style by Thomas Booth into 1889, when the new style 'Booths' was adopted.

Various types of earthenware useful wares were produced including ironstone and granite-type wares. The trade name 'Parisian Granite' is included in some marks which usually incorporate the initials 'T G & F B'. Other initial marks incorporate the description 'Genuine Ironstone China'.

Messrs Booths (Ltd.) succeeded, producing its 'Royal

Semi Porcelain' and refined earthenware 'Silicon China' rather than granite-type wares. A slim book on the long Booth story was published in 1997 – *The Earthenwares of Booths. 1864-1948* by W.M. Parkin (The Keeling Collection, P.O. Box 65, Matlock, Derbyshire, DE4 35D). This work gives a good resumé of the Booth progression.

### THOMAS BOOTH & Co., Burslem or Tunstall, c.1868-72.

Thomas Booth & Co. produced earthenware and ironstone-type bodies in succession to Messrs Evans & Booth (1864-68) of Burslem. Initially the new partnership continued the Knowle Works. Thomas Booth (and his partner William Hales Turner) moved to the Church Bank Works, Tunstall, in 1870. This was rebuilt and continued by various Booth firms into the twentieth century.

Various initial marks 'T.P. & Co.' were used on a good range of earthenwares and ironstone type wares.

Thomas Booth & Son succeeded as from 11 November 1872.

### THOMAS BOOTH & Son, Tunstall, 1872-77.

Thomas Booth & Son (also Thomas) succeeded Thomas Booth & Co. as from 11 November 1872. Thomas Senior, however, died on 23 January 1873, but the firm continued using the same trade name.

As with preceding Booth firms a good varied range of useful earthenwares were produced. These may bear name or initial marks – 'T.B. & S.' or 'T.B. & Co.'

A further change of title (T.G. Booth) came into use on 1 January 1876, so it can be considered that Thomas Booth & Son ceased at the end of 1877.

### BOOTH & MEIGH, Lane End, c.1837-38.

The mark 'IRONSTONE/B. & M.' is recorded and has been attributed by some writers to Bagshaw & Meir (*c*.1802-08) although the name 'Ironstone' could not have been used at so early a period. These initials probably relate to Booth & Meigh (*c*.1837-38) or to Brougham & Mayer of Tunstall (*c*.1835-60).

### JOSEPH BOURNE.

American authorities cite an oval 'Joseph Bourne. Ironstone China' mark, seemingly appearing on mid-nineteenth century Staffordshire-type white-surfaced table wares. However, I have been unable to trace a Staffordshire potter of this name.

The name Joseph Bourne is associated with the Denby and other Derbyshire factories but those potteries produced traditional Derbyshire clay-coloured stoneware, not white bodied granite-type table wares.

There was also Joseph Bourne of the Pool Works at Woodville but the usual Woodville wares comprise the standard yellow Derbyshire ironstone utilitarian wares – mixing bowls, etc.

### W. BOURNE.

Various ironstone-type wares have been reported with name marks 'W. BOURNE'. Several potters of this name are recorded:

William Bourne, Bell Works, Burslem, *c*.1805-11. This pottery is too early to have produced ironstone but it was succeeded by:

William Bourne & Co., 1811-1818.

William Bourne of High Street, Longton, working in the period *c*.1856-1860, is the most likely contender.

### BOURNE, BAKER & BAKER, Fenton, 1833-35.

On the dissolution of the important and long-lived firms of Bourne, Baker & Bourne (see following entry) in November 1833, the surviving partner Ralph Bourne was joined by William Baker and John Baker, trading as Bourne, Baker & Baker. However, the senior partner Ralph Bourne died in November 1835 and the partnership was dissolved as from 9 December 1835.

It is possible that some 'B.B. & B.' initial marks relate to the products of this later partnership, rather than to the better known firm of Bourne, Baker & Bourne.

### BOURNE, BAKER & BOURNE[6], Fenton, 1796-1833.

I am not sure if the important partnership between Ralph Bourne, William Baker and John Bourne produced ironstone-type wares from *c*.1813 until the dissolution of the partnership in 1833. The firm certainly produced some superior quality printed earthenwares, often angled at the American market.

Some rare pieces are signed in the engraving. Other pieces attributed to Bourne, Baker & Bourne bear 'B.B. & B.' initial marks. It should be borne in mind, however, that these initials can also relate to the succeeding partnership of Bourne, Baker & Baker (q.v.) or to the later firm of Bridgett, Bates & Beech (1875-81).

William Baker and John Bourne had both died before the dissolution of partnership in November 1833, which gave rise to the short-lived Bourne, Baker & Baker partnership (1833-35).

### G.F. BOWERS (& Co.), Tunstall, c.1840-68.

George Frederick Bowers is known mainly for his good quality porcelain and standard earthenware, but ironstone and white granite stone-type wares were also made, usually marked 'IRONSTONE CHINA. G.F. BOWERS' or with the initials 'G.F.B.' or 'G.F.B. & Co.' He succeeded the firm of Ambrose Wood & Co. as from 5 December 1840.

Frederick Thomas Bowers succeeded his father in 1868 but the new firm of Frederick Thomas Bowers failed in 1871. This concern may also have produced ironstone-type wares which could bear name or initial 'F.T.B.' marks.

PLATE 154. *A colourful and good quality Zachariah Boyle plate, the ironstone type body being termed 'Dresden China'. Printed mark incorporating the initials 'Z.B.' and the pattern number '154'. Diameter 10in. (25.4cm).*

**ZACHARIAH BOYLE (& Son or & Sons), Hanley & Stoke, c.1823-47.**

Zachariah Boyle produced a good range of earthenwares and some porcelains, firstly at Keelings Lane, Hanley (*c*.1823-30) and then at Church Street, Stoke, The earthenwares included ironstone-type wares. I have seen an impressed marked 'IRONSTONE CHINA' dessert service. The ornate printed mark incorporates the pattern number '163', the identifying initials 'Z.B.' and the trade-name 'Dresden China' – a strange name for ironstone! The design was a quite colourful Japan-type pattern coloured in over a printed outline. A plate of pattern 154 bearing a similar 'Dresden China' printed mark with the initials 'Z.B.' is here shown. Another colourful part-dinner service of pattern 155 bore a printed mark incorporating the description 'Improved

PLATE 155. *An impressed marked 'BOYLE' close copy of a standard shape Mason's ironstone 'Hydra' jug, decorated with a simple Japan pattern. 7in. (17.78cm) high. c.1825-35.*

Iron Stone China' with the initials 'Z.B.' below the cartouche. Mason-type Japan pattern jugs also occur (Plate 155). Boyle copied Mason's use of gilt and white enamel floral designs on a dark blue ground and of course the popular Japan patterns.

Zachariah Boyle died in December 1841 but the firm was continued under the old style, Zachariah Boyle & Sons. However, Joseph Boyle retired in November 1844, the firm then being continued by Samuel Boyle and the executors of his father's estate. This partnership was dissolved on 24 October 1847.

The initials 'Z.B.' relate to the 1823-28 period. The fuller marks 'Z.B. & S.' would relate to the post-1828 period but the singular form 'Zachariah Boyle & Son' was probably used c.1828-36, then 'Zachariah Boyle & Sons'. The basic name mark 'BOYLE' can also occur.

PLATE 156. *A Brameld (Rockingham) 'Fine Stone' ware dinner service plate, printed in underglaze-blue with the 'Parroguet' pattern. Blue-printed. 'B' initial mark, 'Brameld' impressed. Diameter 8½in. (21.59cm). c.1830-35.*

### BRADBURY, MASON & BRADBURY, Longton, c.1852-54.

The partnership between James Bradbury, Richard Mason and Thomas Bradbury at the Crown Works, Stafford Street, Longton, produced earthenwares and ironstone-type china in the approximate period 1852-1854. A slightly later partnership between James Bradbury, Richard Mason and James Broadhurst (trading as Bradbury, Mason & Broadhurst) was dissolved on 28 August 1854, by which date James Bradbury had died. This partnership probably also made ironstone wares, and was succeeded by James Broadhurst.

One printed mark incorporates the Royal Arms device with the helpful wording:

BRADBURY, MASON & BRADBURY
CROWN WORKS
IRONSTONE CHINA

### BRAMELD (& Co.) Swinton, Yorkshire, c.1806-42.

The Bramelds owned and managed the Swinton pottery (more popularly called 'Rockingham') from 1806 to its closure in 1842. The pottery is mostly known for its standard earthenware and fine porcelain, but ironstone bodies were also made (see Plate 156). Printed marks incorporate the name of the printed pattern such as 'Flower Groups' or 'India', with the description 'GRANITE CHINA', 'STONE CHINA' or 'FINE STONE'. The initial 'B' occurs rarely in these printed marks. The impressed name 'BRAMELD & CO.' may also appear on this Swinton or Rockingham ware. For information see *The Rockingham Pottery* by A.A. Eaglestone and T.A. Lockett, revised edition 1973, Alwyn and Angela Cox's *The Rockingham Works*, 1974 and the same authors' 1983 work *Rockingham Pottery & Porcelain 1745-1842* (Faber & Faber, London). Details of the closing auction sale held in May 1843 are given in Dr and Mrs Cox's paper 'The Closure of the Rockingham Works, Part II,' published in the *Journal of the Northern Ceramic Society*, Vol. 13, 1996.

The Bramelds' ironstone-type printed wares seem quite scarce, most of their less expensive table wares being in standard earthenware bodies. However, granite china and stone china articles included toilet articles, even bidets for mounting in mahogany stands. The marked ironstone and stoneware examples will post-date 1813.

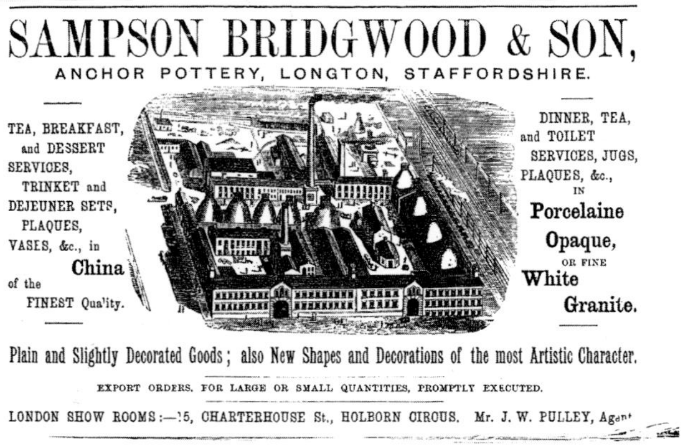


### SAMPSON BRIDGWOOD (& Son(s) (Ltd.), Longton, c.1822-1984.

The early Bridgwood earthenware is unmarked. In about 1853 the style became Sampson Bridgwood & Son. A large range of earthenware and porcelain was produced in the middle of the nineteenth century. In Jewitt's account of this firm, written in or before 1878, he wrote:

> In earthenware they produce largely the white granite for the United States, Australian and Canadian trade, and they also produce for the home market. One of their specialities is what is technically called 'Parisian Granite' (stamped 'Limoges'), which is of fine, hard, durable body and excellent glaze. In this ware, tea, breakfast, dinner and toilet services are largely produced; many are of excellent design... The Parisian granite bears the impressed stamp, an oval, with the word 'Limoges', and in the centre 'P.G.' (for Parisian

Granite). It also bears the printed mark of an elaborate shield of arms with mantling, sceptres, etc., and the words 'Porcelaine Opaque, Bridgwood & Son'.

But at this period the Bridgwood concern was out of the Bridgwood family hands.

Over the years the Bridgwood firm had employed many different impressed or printed marks. Most incorporate the firm's name in full or the initials 'S.B. & S.' An anchor device is included in many marks, relating to the Anchor Pottery at Longton. Some sample marks are here shown; the 'P.G' mark relates to the trade name 'Parisian Granite'.

Messrs Sampson Bridgwood & Sons was famous for its durable vitrified hotel ware and the firm is part of the large Churchill Group having been retitled Churchill Hotelware Ltd in 1984. The reader is referred to Rodney Hampson's specialist work, *Churchill China, Great British Potters since 1795* (University of Keele, Staffordshire, 1994).

**BRIDGWOOD & CLARKE, Burslem and Tunstall, c.1857-64.**

This firm produced ironstone or 'granite' ware mainly for the American market bearing the name in full or the initials 'B. & C.' with descriptions such as 'Opaque China' or 'Porcelain Opaque'. This firm was continued by Edward Clarke (& Co.).

**BRISTOL STONEWARE.**

This description was widely used for a type of clay-coloured stoneware mainly used for bottles, casks and other containers for liquids in the nineteenth century. Originally introduced in its glazed form in Bristol, the use of this general description spread to other ceramic centres.

For details of the various Bristol-based manufacturers the reader is referred to R.K. Henrywood's specialist book, *Bristol Potters, 1775-1906* (Redcliffe Press Ltd, Bristol, 1992). However, this type of clay-coloured stoneware should not be confused with the white-bodied stone china table ware featured in this work.

**BRITANNICUS DRESDEN CHINA mark, c.1820s.**

The wording 'Britannicus Dresden China' occurs printed in underglaze blue on good quality ironstone-type table ware of the 1810-25 period (Plate 157), but the maker has, as yet, not been positively identified. A typical blue printed mark is shown below but variations exist, one of which is rather more circular – as shown on the reversed dessert plate in Plate 157.

It has, however, been suggested (initially I believe by Richard Manwaring-White) that the similarity of the frame work and leafage to a standard mark attributed to Hicks & Meigh (see below) that the Britannicus Dresden china mark relates to that leading manufacturer.

In addition, Margaret Ironside in a paper on the slightly later Hicks, Meigh & Johnson porcelain has linked the pattern shown here with its 'Britannicus Dresden' mark to a shell-shape dessert dish which is stated to match known Hicks patterns, see *Northern Ceramic Society Newsletter*, No. 100, December 1995. The pattern here illustrated also occurs on a later marked 'Ashworth' plate, an important point when we

PLATE 157. *A good quality part stone china dessert service with printed 'Britannicus Dresden China' mark. Tureen 5¾in. (14.6cm) high. c.1815-25.*

remember that there is a link with the Hicks working materials, the engraved copper-plates, etc, and Ashworths. The quite rare marked 'Britannicus Dresden' examples are of good quality and could well have been produced by Hicks & Meigh (q.v.). However, we do not find the usual pattern number added to the 'Britannicus Dresden China' printed mark.

PLATE 158. *A blue printed earthenware soup plate probably depicting Trentham near Stoke. The clear sales enhancing printed mark reads 'BRITISH NANKEEN-CHINA'. Diameter 9¼in. (23.49cm). c.1810-20.*

**'BRITISH NANKEEN'.**
**'BRITISH NANKIN'.**
**'BRITISH NANKEEN CHINA.**

This description as used early in the nineteenth century presents problems. Obviously it was coined to describe English copies of blue and white Chinese porcelains – mainly dinner services – which had been for so many years the staple of the trade. The name was a trade marketing device and it may never have been used as a mark, unlike 'Ironstone' or 'Granite China'.

The description occurs in the Shrewsbury dealer Thomas Brocas' newspaper advertisements in March 1802:

> He has the satisfaction to inform them he has just received from Coalport Table Services of an entire new article called BRITISH NANKEEN, so exactly like the foreign, both as to shapes, colour &c., that few can distinguish it from Foreign [Chinese] blue & white china: and if there is any difference, it will be found the BRITISH NANKEEN excels both as to beauty and strength: he has two kinds of it, one an exact imitation of India [meaning Chinese] blue & white china, of a pale colour, which he offers at 18 guineas the Table service, manufacturer's price; the other exactly like the old fine dark blue stone ware or Nankeen, at 25 guineas. When it is considered the above ware will be equally durable with the foreign, more beautiful and comes at less than half the price of Foreign, he flatters himself it will be found an object worthy of consideration of those Families who, since the establishment of Coalport manufactory, have been pleased to countenance and encourage ingenuity and honest industry at Home rather than send their money abroad for an inferior article...

There seems little doubt that Thomas Brocas was advertising Coalport porcelain in the style of the popular blue and white Chinese porcelains. I show in Plate 13 a Coalport example of the type I believe was marketed as 'British Nankeen' by at least 1802.

This or a very similar trade description, however, was soon being advertised by Miles Mason, the former London dealer who was setting up as a porcelain manufacturer in the Staffordshire Potteries.

Mason's advertisement, which appeared in the *Morning Herald* of 15 October 1804, reads in part:

> MASONS' CHINA
>
> ...Miles Mason, late of Fenchurch Street, London, having been a principal purchaser of Indian porcelain... has established a manufactory at Lane

> Delph, upon the principle of Indian and Sève china. The former is now sold ... as British Nankin. His article is warranted from the manufactory to possess superior qualities to Indian Nankin china, being more beautiful as well as more durable, and not so liable to snip at the edges, more difficult to break and refusable or united by heat, if broken... N.B. The articles are stamped on the bottom of the large pieces to prevent imposition.

The impressed mark seems to have been only 'M. MASON' not 'British Nankeen'. The early Mason wares were seemingly printed in underglaze-blue with stock, mock-Chinese designs of the type shown in Colour Plate 11 and Plates 41 and 42.

There was some discussion between Brocas and Mason in later years about the introduction of British Nankeen or ironstone-type wares (see page 76) but clearly the descriptions were in use in the trade in the 1802-04 period. Also the term was being used by London auctioneers such as Harry Phillips who on 6 July 1804, sold:

> A Table service of blue and white china, British Nankin, containing 10 dishes in sizes, 2 soup tureens and stands, 4 sauce tureens and stands, 1 salad dish, 4 sauce boats, 4 vegetable dishes and covers, 4 baking dishes, 6 dozen meat plates, 2 dozen soup plates, 2 dozen pie plates and 2 dozen cheese plates.

This was apparently complete and perhaps new dinner service which sold for £15.4s.6d. The make-up and description of the four types of plates is interesting.

A further brief reference to British Nankin occurs in Mr Christie's February 1808 sale on the Cambrian Pottery retail premises at 64 Fleet Street, London. This closing-down sale included 'many services of Table, dessert and breakfast porcelain, British Nankin and Earthenware'. Not all of these goods would have been Welsh, but rather bought-in saleable goods from various manufacturers. Nevertheless the separation of British Nankin from porcelain and earthenware services is interesting.

None the less, some rather later standard blue printed earthenwares of pearlware-type do bear the printed mark 'BRITISH NANKEEN CHINA'. These pieces, seemingly of the 1810-1820 period, are almost certainly Mason but the examples seen by the author have not been of ironstone (see Plate 158).

## JAMES BROADHURST (& Sons) Longton, c.1855-70.

James Broadhurst succeeded the Bradbury, Mason & Broadhurst partnership and commenced potting under his own name at the Crown Works, Longton, c.1855. By 1856 he had taken at least some of his sons into partnership, then trading as James Broadhurst & Sons. This firm produced both porcelain and various types of earthenwares including ironstones and stonewares.

James Broadhurst died in February 1858 after which the pottery was continued by his widow and her sons. Mrs Broadhurst died in October 1861 after which unsuccessful attempts were made to sell the Crown Pottery. The two remaining sons, James and Samuel, dissolved partnership in December 1863, James Broadhurst continuing the Crown Pottery under his own name until c.1870, the pottery being auctioned in January 1871.

Various printed or impressed name marks occur, usually incorporating the address 'Broadhurst & Sons, Crown Pottery, Longton'. Initial marks 'J.B.' or 'J.B. & S.' also occur but not all necessarily relate to James Broadhurst at Longton. Further information is given in Rodney Hampson's book, *Churchill China Great British Potters since 1795* (University of Keele, 1994).

The Broadhurst name and production was to continue at Fenton – see the following entry.

## JAMES BROADHURST (& Sons) (Ltd.), Fenton (& Longton), 1870-1964.

James Broadhurst II, formerly of Longton, purchased the Portland Pottery, Victoria Road, Fenton, in 1870. Subsequently sons were taken into the business and the trading style was amended in about 1896 when the bill-heads stated that the firm were 'manufacturers of all kinds of earthenware'.

The now large and important Broadhurst firm became a Limited Liability Company in 1922. This firm was reformed in 1939 under the title 'James Broadhurst & Sons (1939) Ltd' and continued until c.1964. In these later years the Broadhurst firm was owned by the Roper family.

Early in 1964 James Broadhurst & Sons Ltd. acquired Messrs Sampson Bridgwood & Son Ltd. and the combined business was transferred to the larger Bridgwood Anchor Works, Longton. The hotel side of the trade was concentrated upon. Further acquisitions were made, including in 1974 the Crown Clarence Pottery. Later the combination became part of the Churchill Group. It is difficult to decide when the old Broadhurst company ceased to be an individual concern but for the purpose of this work I have terminated this outline at 1964.

Over the years many different types of name or initial marks occur on the various Broadhurst products, which included ironstone-type wares. Some but not all marks include late additions such as 'Ltd.'; indeed most post-1930 marks incorporate only the name 'Broadhurst'.

Very good details of the history of the Broadhurst firm is given in Rodney Hampson's specialist book, *Churchill China, Great British Potters since 1795* (University of Keele, 1994).

**BROADHURST & GREEN, Longton, c.1845-52.** This partnership between Job Broadhurst and William Green owned two potteries at Longton, the Anchor Works in Market Street and the New Street Pottery. The partnership was dissolved on 23 June 1852 after which William Green carried on alone.

Various earthenwares bear printed 'B. & G.' initial marks. Some of these probably relate to this mid-nineteenth century Longton partnership, although it must be borne in mind that other earlier and later firms also relate to these initials.

For further information on this Longton firm the reader is referred to Rodney Hampson's specialist study 'Longton Potters 1700-1865' *(Journal of Ceramic History*, Vol. 14, City Museum & Art Gallery, Stoke-on-Trent,1990).

**BROUGH & BLACKHURST, Longton, c.1872-95.** The partnership between Benjamin Brough and Thomas Blackhurst worked the Waterloo Pottery, Stafford Street, Longton from *c*.1872 until *c*.1895.

A general range of earthenwares was produced for the home trade as well as for export markets. Some ironstone or stoneware was produced and full name marks 'BROUGH & BLACKHURST' have been recorded. The initials 'B. & B.' may also have been employed by this partnership.

**BROUGHAM & MAYER, Tunstall, c.1853-60.** This partnership between James Brougham and John Mayer at Sandyford Works, Tunstall, was dissolved on 31 March 1860. The printed mark of the words 'Ironstone' and 'Brougham & Mayer' occurs, rarely, with a garter-shaped device.

Initial marks incorporating the initials 'B. & M.' may also relate to this partnership or to the earlier firm of Booth & Meigh, *c*.1828-37 (q.v.).

**T. & M.L. BROWN, London, c.1850s.** This sample entry relates to one of many retailers or wholesalers which stocked a large range of household ceramics.

The names of the larger long-lasting firms are recorded in some reference books such as my *Encyclopaedia of British Pottery & Porcelain Marks*, whilst others were in a small way of business in quite rural locations.

Messrs T. & M.L. Brown of 47 St Martin's Lane, London, exhibited at the Great Exhibition of 1851. Their stand included 'Dinner and dessert plates, specimens of enamelled and gilding on stone china, plates, entrée dishes and soup tureens, en suite' as well as porcelains and glass wares. Unfortunately the official Catalogue does not give the maker or illustrate any of these well decorated mid-nineteenth century stone chinas.

**WILLIAM BROWNFIELD (& Son(s) ), Cobridge, c.1850-92.** William Brownfield (d.1873) who succeeded Messrs Wood & Brownfield at Cobridge, as from 30 October 1850, produced large quantities of fine earthenware (and porcelain from 1871), and over 450 people were employed in 1861. The Brownfield pottery is not generally known for its ironstone, but such ware was certainly produced, indeed the firm's bill-head reads 'William Brownfield Manufacturer of Ironstone China & Earthenware'. William Brownfield's son was taken into partnership in 1871 and, from this period '& Son' was added to the firm's style and marks. The plural form dates from 1876. Marks comprise the name 'Brownfield', the initials 'W.B.' or 'W.B. & S.' (after 1871). From 1891-98 the firm was titled Brownfields Guild Pottery Society Ltd. (q.v.) and from 1898-1900 Brownfield Pottery Ltd.

The standard and excellent specialist book on the Brownfield history and products is Tim H. Peake's well-illustrated *William Brownfield and Sons(s)* (privately printed, 1995). Although the Brownfields are best known for their wide range of moulded jugs, they also produced dinner and dessert as well as toilet wares in stone china type bodies.

Mr Peake's book gives much helpful information including the approximate dates for the various pattern numbers. The number had exceeded sixteen thousand by 1863. It must be remembered, however, that like most large Staffordshire firms, the Brownfield pottery produced a wide range of ceramics. Advertisements of the mid-1870s headline 'China, Earthenware, Majolica, Parian, Ironstone, Stoneware, etc'. They had showrooms in London, Paris, Berlin and Vienna and enjoyed a large trade with north America.

**BROWNFIELD GUILD POTTERY SOCIETY Ltd., Cobridge, 1892-98.** This Guild Pottery Society or worker's co-operative arose from the closure of William Brownfield & Sons after voluntary closure in the summer of 1892. The early history of the new firm is told in Flora E. Haines' interesting little book *A Keramic Study* (privately published in the USA in 1895) and the Rheads provide comments on the novel venture in their joint work *Staffordshire Pots & Potters* (by G.W. & F.A. Rhead, Hutchinson & Co., London, 1906).

By this time the old firm was managed by Arthur Brownfield, who instigated the new co-operative venture at a period of great depression in the trade. The Guild was not, however, a success. Few new lines were introduced and it seems to have ceased trading in 1898, to be followed for a brief period by the Brownfield Pottery Company.

Tim Peake gives good information on the closing years of the Brownfield pottery but, by the late 1890s, the succeeding firm's production of ironstone-type wares must have been very small. However, Flora Haines related in her 1895 book how six plates were made especially for her, one of which was to be a 'P.G.' plate. We later learn that these initials were impressed into the clay together with the date numerals '3.93' and that P.G. related to the firm's 'Porcelain Granite' body. This almost certainly was a late form of granite ware of the earlier ironstone type and indicates that both Brownfields and the new Guild were still producing this type of ware into the early 1890s.

**HENRY BURGESS, Burslem, c.1864-92.**
Henry Burgess potted at the Kilncroft Works, Sylvester Square, Burslem. He enjoyed a large export trade, particularly to North America. Good ironstone-type wares were produced and bear clear name or 'G.H.' initial marks often with the Royal Arms device.

Jewitt recorded in 1878 that the firm produced white granite ware for the United States and for the Canadian markets.

The Burgess wares are one of many makes seemingly exclusively featured in American books such as Annise Doring Heaivilin's *Grandma's Tea Leaf Ironstone* (Wallace-Homestead Book Co., Des Moines, USA).

**BURGESS, DALE & GODDARD, Longton & USA, Merchants, etc. c.1850-58.**
This partnership between John Burgess, Robert Dale and John Hackett Goddard (b.c.1820) acted as merchants, wholesalers and agents.

Both Burgess and John Goddard had enjoyed previous experience as earthenware manufacturers and Robert Dale had been a ceramic colour manufacturer. The 1851 Staffordshire census includes John Hackett Goddard, then aged thirty-one, as an exporter of china and earthenware.

John Goddard remained resident in Longton, purchasing large quantities of Staffordshire earthenwares of all types for their American trade. The partnership had outlets in New York and various American cities and was able to influence the British potters by its large purchases and (rare) prompt payments.

The partnership was dissolved on 30 June 1858 and Messrs Burgess & Goddard (q.v.) succeeded.

The English side of these American partnerships traded under different styles – Goddard, Dale & Burgess and then Goddard & Burgess. The reader is referred to these entries.

**BURGESS & GODDARD, Longton & USA Merchants, Agents, Importers etc., 1858 to c.1890.**
This important American firm succeeded Burgess, Dale & Goddard from 30 June 1858. It had branches in New York, Boston, Philadelphia and Baltimore, shipped vast quantities of English (mainly Staffordshire) earthenwares into the United States of America. Some pieces made to their special order bear Burgess & Goddard name marks. A trade advertisement of the mid-1880s reads, in part:

> Representatives in the United States of some of the most celebrated manufacturers of White Granite, Semi-Porcelain, Printed ware and English China, including such names as John Edwards; Wedgwood & Co.; S. Bridgwood & Son; Burgess & Goddard; G.W. Turner & Sons; Dunn, Bennett & Co.; J.F. Wileman; Blair & Co...

Although the name Burgess & Goddard is included in this list of manufacturers and a Longton address is given in the advertisement, it seems that this partnership did not itself manufacture goods under this name. The reversed name Goddard & Burgess was, however, used in England. The partners in both the American and the Longton firms were John Hackett Goddard, John Burgess, William Burgess and John Wilson Burgess. John Burgess retired in October 1875, but the trading style continued as before until about 1890.

The reader is referred also to the Goddard & Burgess entry.

**BURGESS, LEIGH & Co., Burslem, c.1877-78.**
Llewellynn Jewitt in his *The Ceramic Art of Great Britain*, published in 1878, lists Messrs Burgess, Leigh & Co. as an alternative trade style for the partnership better known as Burgess & Leigh (q.v.) working the former Alcock Hill Pottery at Burslem. This contemporary authority, who may well have received information direct from the firm, also quotes the use of 'B.L. & Co.' initial marks.

**BURGESS & LEIGH (Ltd.), Burslem, c.1862-present day.**
This partnership between Frederick Burgess and William Leigh worked the Central Pottery, Market Place, Burslem, as well as the former Samuel Alcock Hill Pottery from the early 1860s. The firm was a large and important one, producing the various standard types of Staffordshire

earthenware useful wares. These goods included ironstone or granite goods, much of which was exported.

Various name or initial 'B. & L.' marks occur but the trade style was amended c.1889 when the firm became a Limited Liability Company. The trade brand-name 'BURLEIGH WARE' was much used, giving rise to marks such as:

BURLEIGH IRONSTONE
STAFFORDSHIRE

with, or without additions such as 'England'. From the late 1880s to the present day the firm, still run by the Leigh family, occupies the Middleport Pottery at Burslem.

**BURGESS & MEIGH**
One or more American authorities list the above firm as producing white ironstone wares. Such entries quoting 'Burslem 1867-89' are almost certainly erroneous and should refer to Burgess & Leigh (q.v.).

**BURLEIGH** – see Burgess & Leigh (Ltd.).

**J. BURN & Co., Newcastle upon Tyne, c.1852-60.**
Joseph Burn of the Stepney Bank Pottery, Ouseburn, Newcastle upon Tyne, produced various types of earthenware in the approximate period 1852-60.

Various printed or impressed marks incorporate the names 'J BURN & CO.', 'I. BURN & CO.' or 'BURN & CO.' Initial marks also occur – 'J.B. & CO.' or 'I.B. & CO.' – although these initials can also fit Staffordshire firms.

**SAMUEL & JOHN BURTON, Hanley, c.1832-45.**
This partnership at New Street, Hanley, produced general earthenwares, using the description 'Pearl China' as well as ironstone wares. Various marks incorporate the initials 'S. & J.B.' or the fuller style 'S. & J. Burton'.

**THOMAS & JOHN CAREY, Lane End, c.1823-42.**
John Carey commenced potting at Lane End in about 1813, trading as John Carey & Sons from c.1818. The partnership with Thomas commenced in about 1823 and was dissolved as from 22 January 1842. The Careys produced very good quality standard earthenware at their Anchor Works. The various earthenwares were usually decorated with fine blue printed designs. The standard mark is the word 'CAREY'S' with or without a fouled anchor, but at least one mark incorporates the description 'SAXON STONE CHINA'.

Some dinner wares bearing an impressed mark of a fouled anchor with the name 'CAREY'S' below have been noted with the pattern number 222. The shape of the six-sided tureens, with floral knobs, is very close to

PLATE 159. *A Carey's blue-printed stone china tureen stand of fine quality showing a view of York Minster. Printed mark 'Carey's Saxon Stone China' with impressed name mark with anchor device. 14½in. x 12¾in. (36.83cm x 32.38cm). c.1823-30.*

some Ridgway stone china dinner wares of the type shown in Plates 238 and 240. The Carey tureen-stand shown in Plate 159 is of this class.

Further information is given in Rodney Hampson's specialist work 'Longton Potters 1700-1865' (*Journal of Ceramic History*, Vol. 14. City Museum & Art Gallery, Stoke-on-Trent, 1990).

**JOHN CARR (& Co.) (or & Son or & Sons), North Shields, c.1847-c.1890.**
John Carr formerly worked the Low Lights Pottery at North Shields, Newcastle upon Tyne under the firm of Carr & Patton (q.v.).

The succession of the various related firms is somewhat uncertain but local directories suggest the following:

| | |
|---|---|
| John Carr | c.1847+ |
| John Carr & Co. | c.1850+ |
| John Carr & Son | c.1854+ |
| Carr Brothers | c.1856-75 |
| John Carr & Sons | c.1875-90 |

It would appear that, apart from these name-marks, the following initials can be incorporated in various printed marks: 'J.C.', 'J.C. & Co.' or 'J.C. & S.' These initials can be confused with those also used by Staffordshire firms. L. Jewitt records that a stag's head mark was used by John Carr but an impressed anchor device with the word 'London' is more often found on these North Shield's earthenwares.

**CARR & PATTON, North Shields, c.1838-47.**
This partnership succeeded Comfort, Carr & Patton at the Low Lights Pottery, North Shields, Newcastle upon Tyne from c.1838. They continued till about 1847 after which John Carr continued under his own name or as John Carr & Co., and later as John Carr & Son (q.v.). John Patton worked the Phoenix Pottery at Ouseburn.

Various printed marks incorporate the initials 'C. & P.', with such descriptions as 'Impressed Stone Ware'. The impressed anchor and 'London' device can also occur on such Carr & Patton ironstone wares. This device can also occur with 'J.C. & Co.' on marked John Carr & Co. earthenwares.

**CARTWRIGHT & EDWARDS (Ltd.), Longton and Fenton c.1859 into 1980s.**
Cartwright & Edwards worked the Borough Pottery at Longton from c.1859. The Victoria Works were taken in 1912 and the Heron Cross Pottery at Fenton in 1916. Advertisements of the 1880s mention 'IRONSTONE CHINA, AND EARTHENWARE of every description for the home, colonial and foreign markets'. Marks feature or include the initials 'C. & E.'. 'LTD.' was added to the firm's style and to some marks from c.1907.

A wide range of ware has been produced, including bone china which was the sole product from 1954.

In the latter part of the twentieth century this old firm had several owners – Alfred Clough Ltd., Federated Potteries Ltd., and Coloroll – but the factory was reported as being closed early in 1988.

For further information on this Longton firm the reader is referred to Rodney Hampson's specialist study 'Longton Potters 1700-1865' (*Journal of Ceramic History*, Vol. 14, City Museum & Art Gallery, Stoke-on-Trent, 1990).

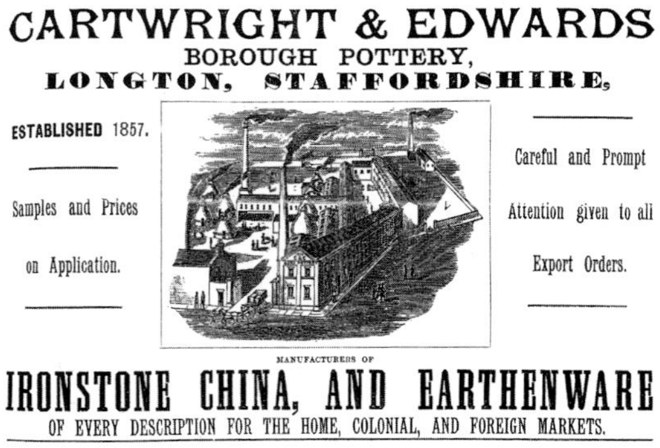

CARTWRIGHT & EDWARDS
BOROUGH POTTERY,
LONGTON, STAFFORDSHIRE,
ESTABLISHED 1857.
Samples and Prices
on Application.
Careful and Prompt
Attention given to all
Export Orders.
MANUFACTURERS OF
IRONSTONE CHINA, AND EARTHENWARE
OF EVERY DESCRIPTION FOR THE HOME, COLONIAL, AND FOREIGN MARKETS.


**CASE & MORT** – see Liverpool.

**C.C.**
Some British printed marks incorporate the initials 'C.C.'. In most cases these relate to the type of body, 'cream colour' or creamware, rather than the manufacturer.

**CHARLES CHALLINOR, Tunstall, c.1848-65.**
Charles Challinor potted in High Street, Tunstall. Name marks could relate to this firm or to the later firm of Charles Challinor & Co. (q.v.).

**EDWARD CHALLINOR, Burslem, c.1819-24.**
Various British ceramics occur with the name, or 'E.C.' initial mark, of Edward Challinor.

It should be understood that whilst a potter of this name potted at the Overhouse Pottery, Burslem, for some five years, most of these Challinor marks will relate to a later period and to the Tunstall potteries which were operational in the approximate period 1842-72. Certainly the American market stone china wares will have been produced at Tunstall during the later period – see the following entry.

**EDWARD CHALLINOR, Tunstall, c.1842-72.**
Various printed 'E. Challinor' name marks occur on ironstone and other wares. These seemingly simple marks present difficulties as the name occurs at different periods in connection with different potteries at Tunstall.

Staffordshire directories and rate records show Edward Challinor potting at the Pinnox Works, Woodland Street, Tunstall, c.1842-60, at High Street, Tunstall, c.1851-72 and at the Unicorn Pottery, Amicable Street, Tunstall, c.1862-67. The Unicorn and Pinnox works later passed to Woodwood & Co., which produced a large range of ironstone-type wares at these former Challinor potteries.

It is quite possible that 'E.C.' initial marks relate to Edward Challinor at Tunstall, who must have produced a large volume of earthenwares. He is not recorded as potting at Fenton under his own single name.

**CHARLES CHALLINOR & Co., Fenton, c .1892-96.**
This company succeeded E. & C. Challinor in 1892. Name marks occur on ironstone-type wares.

**E. CHALLINOR & Co., Fenton, c.1854-62.**
This Fenton firm produced good quality blue printed earthenware, examples of which are recorded with the name mark 'E. CHALLINOR & CO'. Various 'E.C. & Co.' initial marks will usually relate to this potter. However, it should be noted that Edward Challinor & Co. also potted at Tunstall in the approximate period 1851-54.

Challinor purchased Mason's former Patent Ironstone Manufactory in High Street, Lane Delph, Fenton in March 1854, and obviously continued the ironstone tradition there. Messrs E. & C. Challinor succeeded – see the next entry.

E. & C. CHALLINOR,
FENTON POTTERIES,
STOKE-UPON-TRENT,
MANUFACTURERS OF
IRONSTONE, WHITE GRANITE, PRINTED & COMMON
EARTHENWARE,
SUITABLE FOR THE
HOME, FOREIGN, AND COLONIAL MARKETS.
London Agent: JOHN BROOK, 10, Thavies Inn, Holborn, E.C. New York: MAYER BROS., Barclay Street.
PRICES AND PARTICULARS FORWARDED UPON APPLICATION.

**E. & C. CHALLINOR, Fenton, c.1862-91.**
This firm succeeded E. Challinor & Co. (see previous entry). Printed or impressed marks incorporate the name 'E. & C. CHALLINOR' or the initials 'E. & C.C.', sometimes below the Royal Arms.

The partnership's trade advertisements in the 1880s stated that they were 'Manufacturers of Ironstone, White Granite, printed and common earthenware suitable for the Home, Foreign and Colonial markets'. They had agents in London and New York.

**CHALLINOR & MAYER, Fenton, c.1887-88.**
This partnership potted at Market Street, Fenton in the brief period c.1887-88. Very little is known about this short-lived partnership but marked examples of granite ware have been reported by American collectors of their popular simple 'teaberry' pattern. One mark comprises a mock Queen's head device with the words 'Trade Mark. Warranted English Stone China. Challinor & Mayer. Fenton'.

**CHAMBERLAIN & Co., Worcester, c.1786-1852.**
As early as 1814 – one year after the original ironstone patent was granted – Chamberlain & Co., the Worcester porcelain manufacturers, had ordered ironstone ware from Mason.

It would appear that at least by the 1840s Chamberlain had themselves begun the manufacture of a similar type of hard, durable ware which they sold under the popular term 'Stone China'. However, this is now extremely scarce and was perhaps only made for a short period as an experiment.

A special printed mark has been recorded incorporating the name of an American importer:

MR. BILLSLAND, IMPORTER 447 BROADWAY.
CHAMBERLAINS
WORCESTER
MANUFACTURERS TO THE ROYAL FAMILY.
STONE-CHINA.

This printed mark would appear to be of the 1840-50 period. The trade name 'GRANITE CHINA' was also used.

Various references to less expensive bodies were made by the management in and about 1848:

> The dinner ware sent you is our opaque ware and is never so white as china, although it is more durable. (July, 1848)
>
> We are about bringing out some new patterns at earthenware prices. (August 1848)

At this period also there are a few interesting references to '22 body'. This was obviously a special mix and one which I believe relates to Chamberlain's 'opaque ware' or 'Stone China'. In order to further keep the price down these Chamberlain sets comprised coloured-in printed designs usually without ornate gilt borders or edging. The impressed mark:

CHAMBERLAIN'S
WORCESTER
22

has been reported. These '22 body' wares are much rarer than the Chamberlain porcelain services but they are not commercially as desirable.

The Chamberlain firm was succeeded by Kerr & Binns in 1852. For full details of the Chamberlain factory and its very varied porcelains the reader is referred to my standard book *Chamberlain-Worcester Porcelain 1788-1852* (Barrie & Jenkins, London, 1982). The long list of patterns given there in Chapter 8 includes from the 1840s several produced in the granite body, such as '2569 Granite dessert, 3 pink lines and gold line on rim. Pink and gold line on shoulder & gold centre ring'.

**DAVID CHETWYND, Burslem, Cobridge & Hanley, c.1850s-70s.**

David Chetwynd was born at Hanley in about 1851. Both he and his brother Elijah were well-known ceramic modellers supplying many popular new forms to various firms. David's son Elijah (b.c.1838) was apprenticed to him.

David and his brother Elijah later joined Charles Cockson in the manufacturing partnership of Cockson & Chetwynd, also known as Cockson, Chetwynd & Co., also with Charles Baker in the firm of Baker & Chetwynd.

Prior to 1866 David Chetwynd seemingly worked on his own account as a modeller and registered new designs in his own name before these models were sold on to various manufacturers. His Baltic-cum-Dallas shape was registered on 25 October 1855. His name is also associated with the very popular 'Ceres' moulded wheat-ear design.

Ceramic modelling and selling designs were common practices and pottery modellers were key personnel in the industry though largely unknown today. See also G.W. Reade.

**CHURCH GRESLEY. Derbyshire, Nineteenth century.**

The Church Gresley pottery in Derbyshire has been associated with the production of ironstone wares but, as Jewitt makes clear, this and nearby Derbyshire potteries were producing cane-coloured Derbyshire ironstone domestic articles, mixing bowls, etc., not conventional Staffordshire-type ironstone decorated wares.

**CHURCHILL HOTELWARE Ltd. and CHURCHILL TABLEWARE Ltd. c.1984 - present day.**

The relatively recent Churchill Group produced in the mid-1990s over one and a half million pieces of earthenware a week in its two main divisions – Hotelware and Tablewares – and employed well over a thousand persons. It can be justly claimed to represent Britain's largest family-owned pottery group.

The rather complicated story of Churchill China is well told in a recent book of this title, written by Rodney Hampson and published by the University of Keele in 1994. A study of this book will show how such modern groups have been built up over the years by the purchase of other potteries and firms. In this case the history is taken back to 1795 and takes in such famous potting names as the Broadhursts, the Bridgwoods, the Myotts and the Meakins.

However, the Churchill name only dates back to 1975 when 'Churchill China' was launched, producing in the main mugs and decorative figures. In 1984 the universally known Churchill name was adopted for the whole group of companies. The old respected firm of James Broadhurst & Sons Ltd. was retitled Churchill Tableware Ltd. and Sampson Bridgwood & Son Ltd. was renamed Churchill Hotelware Ltd. These companies continued to produce durable ironstone-type table wares under the new styles using clear Churchill name marks. Other firms were also included in the Churchill Group but they are not the concern of this work, although John Maddock Hotelware was added to the Churchill Group in 1985, and in 1991 Myott-Meakin was acquired. In October 1992 the Group became a Public Limited Company under the title Churchill China Plc., although its main products are durable earthenware-type bodies, comprising hotel wares and table wares. The various printed, impressed or relief-moulded marks incorporate or comprise the name 'Churchill' often with the trade name 'Sampsonite' (denoting a special durable, postwar, ironstone type body) and usually the description 'Vitrified Hotel Ware' or 'Super Vitrified'. Some marks incorporate the last two numerals of the year of manufacture, i.e. 9...5 for 1995. A British standard 'B.S.' number such as 4034, will also indicate a recent date.

For further details the reader is referred to Mr Hampson's standard book.

**EDWARD CLARKE (& Co.), Burslem and Tunstall, c.1865-87.**

This firm succeeded Bridgwood & Clarke (q.v.), at the Phoenix Works, Tunstall. Similar ware was produced – Jewitt, in or before 1870 noted: 'Mr Clarke produced

PLATE 160. *An impression from a J. Clementson copper plate showing the elaborate Royal Arms mark that would be transferred to the back of the plate. This includes, as was usual, the name of the pattern, the body description and the name of the manufacturer – each varies from pattern to pattern or for the different manufacturers. Public Record Office, London.*

'white granite' (porcelain opaque) in immense quantities and of the very best quality, for the American markets, where it successfully competed with French porcelain...'

Jewitt also noted that Edward Clarke owned the Churchyard Works at Burslem as well and potted there under his own name and formerly as Wood & Clarke (until 30 November 1872). Our Victorian historian noted that 'The productions of the Churchyard Works, while carried on by Mr Clarke, were opaque porcelain of the finest quality known as white granite, for the American market and ordinary earthenware...'

Edward Clarke also traded in partnership with Francis Joseph Emery, as Edward Clarke & Co. at the New Bridge Pottery, Longport, for a period prior to the dissolution of partnership on 13 November 1877.

Various marks incorporate the name 'Edward Clarke' or 'Edward Clarke & Co.', sometimes with the name of the town, Burslem or Tunstall. The latter indicates a period prior to 1877. I reproduce a typical printed mark.

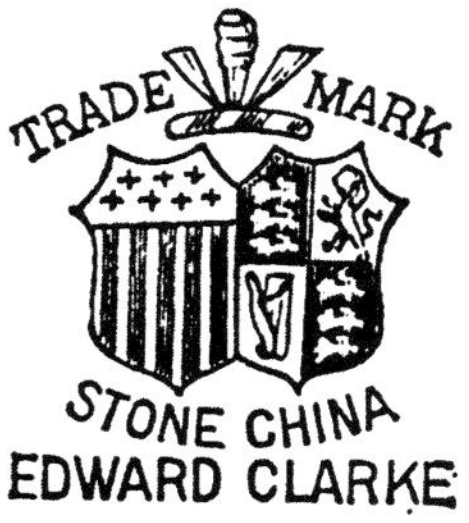


This example is obviously angled at the American market showing the Royal Arms and the stars and stripes, but similar devices were also used by American firms.

**JOSEPH CLEMENTSON, High Street (Shelton), Hanley, c.1839-64.**

Good quality ironstone and standard earthenware was made by Joseph Clementson (d.1871) who succeeded Read & Clementson as from 28 November 1839. One design registered in 1842 has a printed mark incorporating the initials 'J.C.' and the description 'GRANITE WARE'. Other ware is marked with the name in full, with or without the word 'IRONSTONE', 'STONE CHINA', 'STONE WARE' or 'GRANITE OPAQUE PEARL'. The standard impressed mark was:

J. CLEMENTSON
SHELTON

Joseph Clementson exhibited a good range of printed earthenware and presumably ironstone-type wares at the 1851 Exhibition, including 'flowered' wares which seemingly related to the flow or flown printing technique so popular in the export markets.

Joseph Clementson initially worked the Phoenix pottery at Hanley which he enlarged and in 1856 purchased the old Ridgway Bell Works. He enjoyed a large trade with North America and produced a good range of ironstone and white granite-type wares.

Various named patterns were included, which presumably were popular designs of the period and were produced in different colours – black, blue, brown, green, pink, mulberry. The patterns included Chusan, Leipsic, Japan beauty, Parisian flower groups, classical antiquities, Illenberg or Tillenberg, Tessino, Siam and Corea. Some of these pattern names will no doubt appear as part of various J. Clementson name or initial marks.

The extent of Clementson's export market is underlined in that the 1851 Exhibition listing included unhandled printed earthenware cups – very inexpensive goods. In 1861 Joseph Clementson's potteries gave employment to 149 men, 63 women, 146 boys and 76 girls.

Joseph Clementson retired in favour of four sons c.1864 and they continued working both potteries under the new style 'Clementson Bros.' – see the following entry. I show a typical Clementson printed mark as part of Plate 160, but many variations occur.

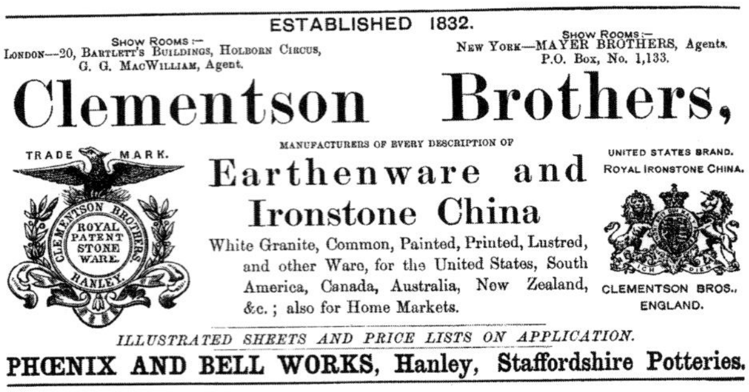


**CLEMENTSON Bros. (Ltd.), Hanley, c.1856-1916.**

Clementson Bros. succeeded Joseph Clementson, 1839-64 (as the preceding entry). Good quality ironstone and 'Royal Patent Stoneware' was made and sold with several marks incorporating the style 'Clementson Bros.' 'England' was added to most marks used between 1891 and 1916. The firm worked two major factories, the Phoenix and the Bell Works. Much Clementson ironstone was exported to North America and, from the 1840s, Francis Clementson of Burslem had an important retail establishment in Canada and one in New York.

I reproduce Messrs Clementson Bros.' trade advertisement which appeared in the 1882 *Pottery Gazette Diary*. The claimed date of establishment, fifty years earlier, relates to the Read & Clementson partnership (q.v.).

In the present century Clementson Brothers may largely have discontinued the production of the ironstone or granite-type bodies. William Scarratt, writing in *Old Times in the Potteries* (1906), noted:

> At one time Clementsons made a nice white granite body for the American market, of the then usual ponderous style peculiar to the trade. For many years past this style has been abandoned, and Messrs. Clementson, for the beauty of their pottery, its lightness of body and strength, are justly renowned.

However, Scarratt may have been referring to the change of style – the basic forms certainly were lighter – rather than the total discontinuance of the old granite body. Unfortunately, the firm does not seem to have advertised in the British trade magazine *Pottery Gazette* after 1900, so one cannot now be sure when Clementsons discontinued the granite body. It had certainly served them well in the nineteenth century.

PLATE 161. *A very good quality marked Clews stone china dinner service, including sauceboats and leaf-shape dishes. Impressed marked 'Clews Stone China Warranted' under a crown. Tureen 12½in. (31.75cm) high. c.1815-25. Messrs Christie's.*

**CLEMENTSON & YOUNG, Shelton, 1845-7.** This partnership between Francis Clementson and William Young carried on business at Broad Street, Shelton (Hanley), in succession to Clementson, Young and Jameson from September 1845 to 2 December 1847, when the partnership was dissolved. Francis Clementson was declared bankrupt in 1848.

A range of earthenware and ironstone-type wares were produced. These included flow blue-type patterns (such as 'Columbia') for the American market (see Colour Plate 29 and Plate 132). The partnership registered two sets of dinnerware forms on 22 October 1845, under the reference number 30701. The relevant diamond-shape Registration mark and reference number occurs on some marks.

Various impressed and printed marks occur featuring the firm's name, sometimes with the individual name of the pattern. Initial marks 'C & Y' may also have been used.

**CLEMENTSON, YOUNG & JAMESON, Shelton (Hanley), 1844-45.** This short-lived partnership at Broad Street, Shelton between Francis Clementson, William Young and William Jameson produced ironstone (as well as other earthenwares), as is proved by a design registered on 17 October 1844. A fluted jug shape was also registered on 15 January 1845. Marks incorporate the initials 'C.Y. & J.',[7] sometimes with the description 'Ironstone'. Flow-blue and other designs were produced for the North American market.

The partnership was dissolved on 2 September 1845, after which Francis Clementson and William Young continued under the style Clementson & Young (q.v.).

**RALPH & JAMES CLEWS, Cobridge, c.1814-34.** This partnership produced very good quality earthenware, often blue printed and from at least 1816 intended for the American market as well as for home consumption. Clews had earlier worked for Andrew Stevenson at Cobridge. Ironstone china was produced and this description is incorporated in several marks with the name 'Clews'. One early mark is a particularly close copy of the printed Spode mark reproduced on page 332, except that the name 'Clews' replaces 'Spode'. The term 'Dresden Opaque China' was also used as in the mark shown below. An 1823 printed bill-head lists the partnership as being 'Manufacturers of China, Ironstone & Earthenware'. The brothers were however bankrupt in 1834.

The standard impressed mark comprises 'Clews, Warranted Staffordshire', arranged in three lines under a crown and with the initials 'G.R.'. Other wording such as 'Clews, Stone China, Warranted' also occurs. Much American-market blue printed earthenware was produced and is actively collected in America.

**J.T. CLOSE (& Co.)**
**CLOSE & Co. Stoke, c.1861-69.**
John Theophilus Close is recorded at Brook Street, at High Street and at Church Street, Stoke, in the 1860s. The partner was apparently William Adams and several 'Close & Co.', 'J.T. Close' or 'J.T. Close & Co.' marks include the wording 'Late W. Adams & Sons'. Various earthenwares were produced including 'Stone china', 'Imperial French Porcelain', white granite etc. One set of relief-moulded dinner wares – titled 'Athenia' – was registered on 3 January 1866

Various printed or impressed marks occur; some include the Royal Arms device or, in the case shown below, the American Eagle device.

**R. COCHRAN & Co., Verreville and Britannia Potteries, Glasgow, Scotland, c.1847-96.**
Robert Cochran & Co., succeeded Kidston, Cochran & Co, at the Verreville Pottery, Glasgow in 1847. Robert Senior died in 1869 but the firm was continued by his son of the same name.

A good range of pottery was produced including ironstone type white and sponged wares as well as the standard printed wares. J. Arnold Fleming, in his 1923 book, *Scottish Pottery* (Maclehose, Jackson & Co., Glasgow), noted that in 1856 the Verreville Pottery ceased making chinaware:

> it was replaced by a new and more durable type of ware, 'Royal Ironstone China' or 'White Granite'. This was an imitation of the white heavy porcelain made then in France and was in great demand by the Americans, to which country this French porcelain was sent in large quantities. They largely lost this trade, for the British Ironstone China manufacturers produced cheaper and more serviceable ware.
>
> Ironstone china required a much larger proportion of ground calcined flint and Cornish stone than the old white earthenware bodies...

The Cochrans also owned and managed the separate Britannia Pottery at St. Rollox, Glasgow, from c.1855. Here also general earthenware and granite wares were produced for home and export. The Britannia Pottery was later owned by Messrs Cochran & Fleming – see the following entry. J. Arnold Fleming, having first-hand or at least family knowledge, remarked in his *Scottish Pottery* that both the Verreville and the Britannia Potteries managed by different brothers produced ware

> in quantities that totally eclipsed anything that ever had been dreamt of by the old potters. Britannia went for mass production. One thousand dozen of plates and as many cups and saucers were turned out daily, besides other articles. ...Royal Ironstone China or White Granite; fired hard and very durable, as its name implies, was the special feature...the ware was stained with oxide of cobalt till it possessed a distinct bluish hue to match the Continental porcelain.

Mr Fleming continued to give an interesting account of one particularly popular American market pattern or shape, 'Ceres'. This was moulded in relief with wheat motifs and was produced by many British potters for their overseas markets. Of Cochran's Scottish essays in this style Fleming reported:

> The greatest achievement was the 'Ceres' pattern. It was modelled by Chetwynd who was reckoned one of the finest modellers in Staffordshire. This pattern consists of sheaves of wheat and barley modelled in a raised conventional design round the brim of the articles. The pattern, used in a variety of domestic articles, was in demand by farmers and their folk wherever wheat was grown. In Spanish South America it was equally esteemed as 'Espiga', as with the Australian or Canadian wheat grower as 'Ceres,' or 'wheat.' When it was first introduced there were no railway lines like the Canadian Pacific Railroad. It was nothing strange in those pioneer days for a china merchant in Ontario to set out with his waggon of ware, and his farewell to his friends was, 'I will burst or make good', which really meant he was going 'out west' into the unknown and exposed Western States. The ware had to be, therefore, thick and hard-fired in the kiln, to stand all the abuse it was likely to get over the rough

prairie tracks those days. This class of ware was latterly used largely on ships, but it was too heavy to handle, and a finer quality gradually displaced this most useful, hard-fired class of ware, for it well deserved the name 'Ironstone China'.

It is difficult to conceive a pottery with six hundred operatives subsisting on one single pattern, such as 'Ceres', for fully fifteen years without a hitch in its prosperous career.

The Cochran marks can incorporate the initials 'R.C.' or 'R.C. & Co.' or the names 'R. Cochran & Co.' or 'Robert Cochran & Co.', with or without the names 'Verreville' or 'Britannia' and 'Glasgow' or the description of the body or design. Various descriptions of the body also occur incorporated in the marks 'Imperial Ironstone China', etc. Several marks incorporate the Royal Arms.

**COCHRAN & FLEMING, Glasgow, Scotland, c.1896-1920.**

This partnership, initially between Alexander Cochran (son of Robert) and James Fleming, owned the Britannia Pottery at Glebe Street, St. Rollox, Glasgow. This pottery was established by Robert Cochran in 1855 and traded under the style 'R. Cochran & Co.'

From c.1896 into the twentieth century the firm traded as Cochran & Fleming. The Pottery was sold to the Britannia Pottery Company Ltd. in June 1920. The last Cochran & Fleming partner was J. Arnold Fleming, who wrote an interesting book entitled *Scottish Pottery* (Maclehose, Jackson & Co. Glasgow, 1923) which includes several first-hand accounts of his experiences, his remarks on ironstone and granite wares are quoted in the previous entry.

Various types of ironstone or granite-type wares were produced and may bear various marks comprising or incorporating the initials

C & F<br>G

or the names in full. Some marks incorporate the description 'Royal Ironstone China'. The seated figure of Britannia graces some marks.

**COCKSON, CHETWYND & Co., Cobridge, c.1866-76.**

This partnership between Charles Cockson, Elijah Chetwynd and David Chetwynd (retired in April 1872) traded at the Cobridge or Globe Works at Cobridge from c.1866 as Cockson, Chetwynd & Co. The alternative title Cockson & Chetwynd was also used and from 1876 Cockson & Seddon (q.v.). Charles Cockson had previously traded under his own name but seemingly produced china rather than earthenwares.

A New York importer's catalogue of c.1875-6 features Cockson, Chetwynd & Co's. 'New Eagle Shape White Granite dinner service tureen' and makes the comment that this new and 'Beautiful design' was copied from a French porcelain model. The flowing graceful lines of this oval covered tureen certainly differ greatly from the chunky white granite designs of the 1840s.

Ironstone ware, marked with the Royal Arms and having the description 'Imperial Ironstone China' and the names of the partners, was produced between 1866 and 76. Initial marks 'C.C. & Co.' could also relate.

Both David and Elijah Chetwynd were well known and talented mid-Victorian ceramic modellers – see page 212. They were practising this craft from c.1850, supplying models and designs to many firms, before they joined the above manufacturing partnership. The popular 'Ceres' relief-moulded wheat motif design was introduced by the Chetwynds – see page 216.

**COCKSON & CHETWYND, Cobridge, c.1866-76.**

This partnership between Charles Cockson, Elijah Chetwynd and David Chetwynd (see page 212) worked the Cobridge or Globe Pottery at Cobridge. It also traded under the alternative trade name Cockson & Chetwynd.

Various name or initial ('C. & C.') marks are recorded, sometimes with the description 'Imperial Ironstone China'.

David Chetwynd left the partnership in April 1872 but Elijah continued until March 1876 when Cockson joined with Joshua Seddon to form the new Cockson & Seddon partnership.

David Chetwynd was also interested in the Baker & Chetwynd partnership (q.v.).

**COCKSON & SEDDON, Cobridge, c.1876-78.**

This partnership between Charles Edward Cockson and Joshua Seddon succeeded Cockson & Chetwynd at the Globe Works, Cobridge, from March 1876.

Various name or initial 'C. & S.' marks can occur on ironstone or granite-type wares.

**C. COLLINSON & Co., Burslem, c.1853-73.**
This partnership between Charles Collinson, George Guest and William Bloor worked the Fountain Place Pottery at Burslem with the approximate period 1853-1873. However, Collinson & Guest traded under these joint names for a short period in about 1860.

Various marks occur incorporating the name 'C. Collinson & Co.', with or without the place name 'Burslem'. The body description 'Imperial Ironstone China' was also incorporated in some marks, with the Royal Arms.

**COOMBS & HOLLAND, Llanelly, South Wales, c.1855-58.**
This short-lived partnership between Charles Coombs and William Holland worked the South Wales Pottery at Llanelly, in succession to the Chambers.

The standard book on this pottery is *Llanelly Pottery* by Gareth Hughes and Robert Pugh (Llanelli Borough Council, 1990). The authors report that some Coombs & Holland wares were produced in ironstone china and that these wares bear the impressed marks 'IRONSTONE CHINA' or merely 'IRONSTONE'. Other marks incorporate the partnership's initials 'C. & H.'

As Coombs & Holland produced some ironstone china it is very likely that the succeeding firm of W.T. Holland (c.1858-1868) produced similar wares (q.v.).

**T. COOPER, Hanley, c.1864-67.**
Thomas Cooper of the Royal Victoria Pottery, Broad Street, Hanley had formerly been in partnership with George Brammer, trading as Brammer & Co. He traded under his own name until c.1865, after which the pottery was carried on by his executors, who registered a dinner service design with formal key-design border in September 1865.

This moulded design has been reported on ironstone dinner wares by American authorities but pieces seen so far bear only the registration device, not the Cooper name or initials.

It would seem therefore that Cooper's Royal Victoria Pottery produced white and other ironstone wares for the American market but like the products of many other small or short-lived firms, his wares were not marked.

**W.T. COPELAND & Sons, Stoke, 1847-1970.**
William Taylor Copeland succeeded the Copeland & Garrett partnership (1833-47) at the Spode Works in the centre of Stoke. The new firm continued the old standard Spode lines including 'Stone China' of excellent quality.

Copeland's Art Director, Robert Abraham, reported to the American author Jennie Young, in or before 1878, that the Spode Stone China was their most celebrated ware; being of a slightly blue-grey tint it resembled Oriental porcelain. He observed that it was fired at a much higher temperature than earthenware and that Copeland's examples were fired in the high temperate kiln along with the porcelains. Whilst a large trade was carried out in making replacement pieces for old Chinese and other services, it was in the 1870s being revived as a standard Copeland durable body.

The new firm employed clear 'Copeland' marks; some later post-1870 items bear impressed potting marks, e.g. 'J.85' for January 1885. Information on the pattern number sequence is given in Chapter 8 of *Staffordshire Porcelain*. In 1970 the old Copeland trade name was changed to Spode Ltd. and in 1976 the company combined with Royal Worcester under the new style 'Royal Worcester Spode Ltd'.

Mr Robert Copeland's book *Spode & Copeland Marks* (Studio Vista, London, 1993, 2nd enlarged edition 1997) is helpful on marks and similar guides to period. This authority records impressed

Copeland
Ironstone

marks as well as printed 'New Stone' marks.

In 1960 a new, improved, body was introduced under the name 'Fine Stone'. This description was added to the standard Copeland-Spode mark. The trade name 'Alenite' was used for oven-proof articles in this new body.

Early versions of this mark have the letter 'X' added above as the example cited. In 1964 'A' replaced the 'X', then 'B' in 1965 and so on. These post-war examples are normally reissues of early nineteenth century Spode period patterns and examples can be found offered as antique! A further seldom-used method of dating the later Copeland wares relates to the pattern number or pattern prefix. New designs from 1939 bore the prefix 'W'; by 1960 the series had reached 'W.130'; by 1980 'W.160'. One can see that relatively few new stone-china patterns have been introduced in the post-war years.

**COPELAND & GARRETT, Stoke, March 1833-June 1847.**
The well-known partnership between William Taylor Copeland and Thomas Garrett at the Spode Works in the centre of Stoke was dissolved on 24 June 1847.

The partnership from March 1833 had taken over from Messrs Spode and continued that firm's fine quality porcelains, earthenwares and glass. The earthenwares included colourful and well-potted 'Stone China'.

The wares usually bear clear printed marks incorporating the name 'Copeland & Garrett' or the initials 'C & G'. Often the name of the durable ironstone-type body was added, e.g. 'Stone China', 'New Stone' or 'New Japan Stone'. Copeland & Garrett printed marks can occur added to impressed marked 'Spode New Stone' articles, formed but not decorated in the pre-March1833 Spode period.

Robert Copeland's book *Spode & Copeland Marks* (Studio Vista, London, 1997) is helpful on dating.

**CORK & EDGE, Burslem, c.1846-60.**
This firm produced at the Newport Pottery, Burslem, a large range of ornamental and useful earthenware, much of which was exported to North America. Trade terms 'Staffordshire Stone Ware' and 'Pearl White Ironstone' were employed on marks with the names 'Cork & Edge' or with the initials 'C. & E.'.

The mark reproduced is one of several which include the American eagle and motto as found on wares or patterns angled at the American market.

It should be noted that, whilst the initials 'C & E' usually relate to this partnership, the initials could also relate to Messrs Cope & Edwards of Market Street, Longton, in the 1844-1857 period.

E PLURIBUS UNUM
PEARL WHITE
IRONSTONE
CORK & EDGE.

**CORK EDGE & MALKIN, Burslem, c.1860-70.**
This partnership succeeded Cork & Edge at the Newport Pottery, Burslem, and produced a good range of ironstone-type wares under various names such as 'Pearl White Ironstone', 'White Granite', etc, Much of its output was exported and printed marks can feature the American eagle device.

The partners were Benjamin Cork, Joseph Edge, James Malkin and William Edge. Benjamin Cork retired on 30 June 1867 but the old style may have continued to 1870 or 1871, to be succeeded by Edge, Malkin & Co. (q.v.).

Various full name or initial marks 'C E & M' were used by Cork, Edge & Malkin.

**JOHN CORMIE, Burslem, c.1828-36.**
John Cormie is recorded at Queen Street, Burslem, in the 1828-34 period and at the Nile Street Works c.1834-36.

Mason type-ironstone dinner wares were made as well as – we may assume – other ironstone objects but marked examples are extremely rare.

One underglaze-blue printed mark can be likened to the Hackwood urn mark, with Ironstone China, but it has the surname 'CORMIE' added over the urn device.

IRON STONE
CHINA

**EDWARD CORN, Burslem, c.1853-64.**
Edward Corn of Navigation Road, Burslem commenced potting under his own name in about 1853. Various ironstone or white granite-type wares bear printed or impressed marks incorporating the name 'E. CORN' or 'EDWARD CORN'.

In about 1864 the trade name was amended to W. & E. Corn – see the following entry.

W. & E. CORN,
TOP BRIDGE WORKS,
Longport, Staffordshire,
MANUFACTURERS OF PLAIN AND EMBOSSED
White Granite, Ironstone China,
PRINTED AND ENAMELLED EARTHENWARE
IN GREAT VARIETY.
Makers of the Celebrated Ceres (Wheat) Ware,
Suitable for the
UNITED STATES, CANADIAN, SOUTH
AMERICAN, AND AUSTRALIAN MARKETS.
LITHOS AND PRICES ON APPLICATION.

**W. & E. CORN, Burslem & Longport, c.1864-1904.**
William and Edward Corn traded from Burslem from c.1864-91 and at the Top Bridge Works, Longport,

from 1891-1904. Jewitt, writing in or before 1878, noted that 'Messrs. W & E. Corn are exclusively devoted to the production of white granite ware for the United States and other foreign markets'. The firm's trade advertisements of the early 1890s read: 'Manufacturers of plain and embossed White Granite and Ironstone China, printed and enamelled earthenware in great variety. Makers of the Celebrated Ceres (Wheat) Ware, suitable for the United States, Canadian, South American and Australian markets'.

Various printed or impressed marks incorporate the Corn name or the initials 'W & E.C.' or 'W.E.C.' The trade name 'Porcelain Royale' was also used in marks from about 1900.

**CROWN MARKS.**

Very many printed marks found on ironstone-type wares incorporate a crown device and a few even comprise only a crown. In general these marks cannot be linked to an individual manufacturer unless a name or initials are also cited.

A series of *hand-painted* crown marks are found on ironstone table wares of the approximate period 1835-50. A pattern number can also be added below the painted crown, or perhaps Bishop's mitre device.

These wares were certainly made or decorated by one of the Staffordshire manufacturers. I show in Colour Plate 33 such a superb dinner set of hand-painted pattern 106. Being hand-painted, the marks vary slightly but I show below a typical example, taken from the service illustrated in Colour Plate 33.

**CROWN CLARENCE POTTERY, Longton, late 1960s.**

Ironstone wares were made by this firm of King Street, Longton, in the late 1960s before the firm was acquired by Jon Anton. The marks incorporate the trade-name 'Crown Clarence'.

**CYMRO, Swansea, c.1835-47.**

Various Swansea (Cambrian Pottery) moulded jugs of the approximate period 1835-47 bear a moulded mark with the wording 'CYMRO STONE CHINA'.

E. Morton Nance in his detailed work *The Pottery & Porcelain of Swansea & Nantgarw* (B.T. Batsford Ltd., London, 1942), noted that this mark had only been seen on Swansea jugs, not on other articles. Inscribed examples in his collection ranged between 1836 and 1847, although earlier or slightly later examples may exist. Various examples are illustrated by this specialist author.

These and other jug marks such as 'Imperial Stone' serve to underline the point that very many post-1820 moulded jugs were of a type of stoneware, related to the ironstone body.

PLATE 162. *A good quality Oriental-style vase of Mason type but bearing a 'D' initial mark with the words 'Japan Stone China'. 16in. (40.64cm) high. c.1825-40. Messrs Christie's.*

**'D' marks.**

As with most single initial marks, the initial can fit several possible firms. The natural inclination is to plump for the most commercially desirable!

The tall covered mock-Chinese porcelain vase shown here in Plate 162 is a case in point, being catalogued by a leading London firm of auctioneers as Dillwyn of Swansea. The ornate painted mark comprises a standing lion holding a flag or banner with the word 'JAPAN' with 'STONE WARE' in a scroll

PLATE 163. *An impressed marked 'Daniel's Ironstone' teapot with printed standard Mason's mark added over Daniel's maker's mark. See also page 95. 9½in. (24.13cm) high.* c.*1846-47.*

below and the cursive initial 'D'.

This mark is unlike any Dillwyn & Co. marks known to me and the shape is as yet unrecorded in fully marked Dillwyn pottery. It could just be Welsh but the whole feel of the piece suggests a Staffordshire origin. In addition, one would expect Dillwyn & Co. initial marks to read 'D. & Co.' rather than just 'D.'

This vase seems more likely to have been made perhaps at the Davenport or Dimmock factories, or even at the Daniel works. My main point, however, is to sound a warning regarding the attribution of single initial marks.

**HENRY DANIEL (& Co.), Shelton (Hanley) & Stoke, c.1823-34.**

Various 'H D & Co.' initial marks tend to be attributed to Henry Daniel & Co. However, such attributions need to be checked carefully, as the initials fit at least two other Staffordshire firms and the title Henry Daniel & Co. seems to have been employed for a very brief period *c.*1833-34.

The Stoke rate-records show Henry Daniel alone in the period July 1823-27 (then transferred to H. & R. Daniel). Other contemporary records including the rate records also show Henry Daniel at Bedford Row (or Captain's Lane), Shelton (Hanley) in the 1823-33 period. He worked two potteries from 1831. The Shelton rate records show the firm of Henry Daniel & Co. only in 1834.

Other Staffordshire firms that could have used the 'H.D. & Co.' marks, include:

| | |
|---|---|
| Hackwood, Dimmock & Co. | (*c.*1807-1825) |
| Henry Davenport & Co. | (*c.*1870) |

**RICHARD DANIEL (& Co.), Fenton & Stoke, c.1846-47 & c.1850-54.**

Richard Daniel (d.1884) had a unsuccessful, short-lived manufactory at Fenton in the mid-1840s. This was in fact Mason's former ironstone works, taken by Richard Daniel in September or October 1846. The stock was, however, sold by auction on 5 May 1847 after Richard Daniel's bankruptcy and included 'All the remaining valuable stock of Iron-Stone China, Earthenware materials...'

It is possible that in taking over C.J. Mason's factory at Fenton, Richard Daniel also purchased and used

PLATE 164. *A Richard Daniel ironstone jug bearing a rather poor quality printed design matching the teapot shown in Plate 163. Impressed 'Daniel's Ironstone' mark, overprinted with Mason's mark, as the teapot. 6¼in. (15.87cm) high. c.1846-47. Private collection.*

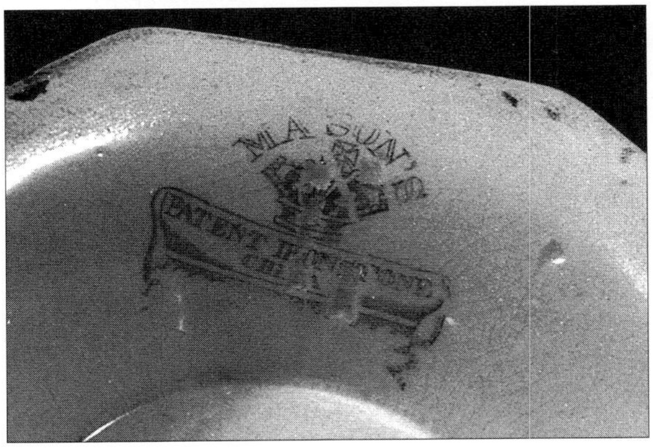

PLATE 165. *The printed Mason's Patent Ironstone China mark applied over the 'Daniel's Ironstone' impressed mark, as if to hide it.*

PLATE 166. *A Mason-type jug of the mid-1840s with blue printed 'Daniel Ironstone China' Royal Arms mark, linking with the over-printed Richard Daniel mark shown in the previous illustration. 7in. (17.78cm) high. c.1846-47. Private collection.*

Mason's copper-plates, moulds, etc., and that he then decorated his own blanks with Mason designs and added the Mason mark. The teapot illustrated as Plate 163 makes this possibility clear. It and a matching milk jug (Plate 164) both bear the impressed mark

DANIEL'S
IRONSTONE

but over this has been applied an on-glaze standard Mason mark of the mid-1840s type with the angular crown (Plate 165). The potting is bad and quite serious chips have been glazed or printed over. The pieces are very much in the nature of 'seconds' or 'thirds' but being showy and presumably inexpensive they suited a manufacturer who was in financial difficulties.

These pieces with their double marking could have been made by Richard Daniel before his bankruptcy and formed part of his stock which was sold in May 1847. Mason may then have purchased some 'seconds' or taken a consignment in payment of a debt and subsequently decorated the pieces himself with his own copper-plates – of an existing popular pattern and correctly used his own mark. These poorly potted and now much damaged pieces present several problems. It should be stated that although both the impressed and the printed marks incorporate the word 'Ironstone' the body appears to be a standard earthenware!

A Mason-type Fenton jug has also been reported with two forms of mark – 'Daniel. Real Ironstone' impressed with the printed mark 'Fenton Stone Works' within a double line frame. This jug was obviously made by Richard Daniel at the former Mason works in the 1846-47 period, perhaps using the Mason moulds and engraved copper-plates.

Richard Daniel's output must have been small and if marks were used they may well have comprised only the surname Daniel, so trading on the good name of the larger well-known firm of H. & R. Daniel. However, a printed mark incorporating the initials 'R.D. & Co.' has been recorded and attributed to Richard Daniel but he is only recorded using the trade style 'Richard Daniel & Co.' whilst at Boothen Road, Stoke, in the approximate period 1850-54.

It should be noted that Richard Daniel is recorded at various addresses in Fenton, Hanley, Burslem and Stoke in the period c.1840-54. For further information the reader is referred to *H. & R. Daniel 1822-1846* by Michael Berthoud (Micawber Publications, Wingham, 1980) and Rodney Hampson's contributions in the *Newsletters* of the Northern Ceramic Society, Nos. 22 (September 1976, p.16), 29 (March 1978, p.23), 68 (December 1987, p.36), and 75 (September 1989, p.7).

It is, however, not quite clear if Richard Daniel was working at Fenton under his own name or for the H. & R. Daniel partnership.

PLATE 167. *A Mason's Oriental-style vase (see Plate 32) but with rare impressed mark 'Daniel's Real Ironstone China'. 15¼in. (38.73cm) high. c.1846-47. Messrs Dreweatt Neate.*

Richard Daniel later (c.1860) superintended Copeland's decorating department and then was manager of the Hill Pottery at Burslem.

**H. & R. DANIEL, Stoke, Shelton and Fenton, c.1822-47.**

The Daniels produced very fine quality, richly decorated, porcelain of which few examples are marked. The firm, or Richard alone (for his father Henry died in 1841) also produced ironstone, stone china and some ordinary earthenwares. The rare impressed marks 'DANIEL'S REAL IRONSTONE', also 'DANIEL'S IRONSTONE', have been recorded; other marks incorporate the standard description 'Stone China'. Simeon Shaw, in his *History of the Staffordshire Potteries*, 1829, states that in 1826 Daniel produced their stone china in Shelton: '...the shapes and patterns being of the improved kind, so much preferred by the public...'.

The size, importance and quality of some of the pieces bearing the impressed mark 'DANIEL'S REAL IRONSTONE' and their obvious initial expense suggests that this imprecise name mark was used by H. & R. Daniel. Large Mason Oriental-style vases exist (see Plate 167) and Michael Berthoud illustrates as his Plate 95 a pair of Chinese style garden seats.

An existing pattern and price book confirms that Daniel produced stone china dinner, dessert and tea services as well as toilet sets. Recorded patterns reach number 1946. A typical entry reads: '1925. Japan groups of flowers blue outlines, blue & green leaves, gold fibres & gold lines'.

Printed tea-ware patterns mentioned by name include Birds, Broseley, Indian Figure, Peacock, Swiss Girl, Barbeaux, Fruit and Flowers, Strawberry. Printed dinner-ware designs were termed Chinese Scenery, Oriental Vases, Birds, Fruit and Flowers, Strawberry and Barbeaux.

It is interesting to note that articles made in stone china were more expensive than the same objects in the standard earthenware body.

Towards the end of 1846 Richard Daniel moved from the Stoke Works and the fixtures were sold by auction, 'Messrs Daniel having taken the extensive manufactory of Mr. Mason at Fenton but he was very soon bankrupt and his stock of 'Ironstone China' was sold in May 1847'. This Fenton aspect of the Daniel story is given by Rodney Hampson in his article

PLATE 168. *A good quality Daniel Stone China large drainer-platter from a blue printed dinner service. These 'Chinese Scenery' prints occur on shapes relating to H. & R. Daniel's porcelain. Printed scroll mark, with 'Stone China'. 'Chinese Scenery D'. 20¾in. x16½in. (52.7cm x 41.91cm). c.1825-35.*

PLATE 169. *An Ironstone China dessert service dish decorated with a printed outline, coloured-in, pattern. The Mason's style printed mark incorporates the initials H. & R.D. relating to H. & R. Daniel. 8in. (20.32cm) long.* c.1935-45.

'Richard Daniel at Fenton' published in *The Northern Ceramic Society Newsletter*, No. 68 of December 1987. See also the preceding entry – Richard Daniel (& Co.).

A Mason styled printed 'Ironstone China' mark has been reported bearing the initials 'H. & R.D.' (see above and *The Northern Ceramic Society Newsletter*, No. 68 of December 1987, page 37). The contributor dates this mark to the 1846-47 period on the assumption that it dates to Richard Daniel's occupancy of the Mason factory but these initials relating to Henry and Richard Daniel in partnership should (or might) not have been in use at this late period. Henry had died in 1841 and Richard continued the Stoke firm with Nathaniel Solomon up until 6 January 1846. It is not certain what style he traded under from this period but it may well have been R. Daniel, rather than the old R.R. Daniel style which should date to c.1822-41.

For further information on the Daniels the reader is referred to Chapter 19 of *Staffordshire Porcelain* and especially to Michael Berthoud's specialist book *H. & R. Daniel 1822-1846* (Micawber Publications, Wingham, 1980).

PLATE 170. *Marked 'Davenport Stone China' teawares of the same shape as was used for the more expensive Davenport bone china teasets. Simple 'Japan'-style pattern with overglaze enamels and enamel colours. Blue printed anchor mark, painted pattern number '659'. Teapot 10¾in. (27.3cm) long. c.1815-20.*

**DAVENPORT (Ltd.),**
**WILLIAM DAVENPORT & Co.,**
**Longport Staffordshire Potteries, c.1793-1887.**
This firm, which traded under various 'Davenport' trade names, produced a very fine range of porcelain, earthenware, stoneware and even glass. Neatly potted and tastefully decorated stone china was produced from c.1815 or before (see Plate 171). The exact date of the introduction of Davenport 'Stone China' is open to question. Davenport's 'Stone China' was certainly in production by January 1818, at which period a Scottish retailer (Child & Co. of Edinburgh) wrote to Davenports concerning Mason's Patent Ironstone China and Davenport's pattern 6. This dealer also requested Davenport's version of the popular blue printed Broseley pattern – a willow-pattern type of Oriental landscape design. The blue printed and colour-enhanced pattern 6 has also a distinct Oriental feeling and was a pattern also produced by Masons, although the potting of the Davenport pieces is finer and the forms were diverse – see Plates 171-174. Indeed some early Davenport stone china has almost the appearance of porcelain. It can also be painted with porcelain patterns and pattern numbers, although most stock stone china patterns were of a separate series ranging up to approximately 150.

The Davenport marked 'Stone China' teawares shown in Plate 170 are important but tantalizing. The shapes with these bifurcated handle forms rarely occur in Davenport bone china.[8] One would date the porcelains to c.1810 but this would pre-date the introduction of the ironstone body and presumably of stone china. It is, however, noteworthy that some porcelains of this shape bear the retailer's name 'J. Mist, N. 82 Fleet Street'. James Mist was trading alone at this London address from 1809 to 1815 when he became bankrupt. Davenports had taken over Mist's Fleet Street premises by 1818. James Mist had been burdened by financial difficulties by at least August 1812 when Mintons (and presumably other manufacturers) were being offered five shillings in the pound by Mist in settlement of his debts. With the potters only receiving a quarter of their dues, it might seem unlikely that they would continue to supply Mist with new goods. If this were the case the Mist-marked Davenport porcelains of these stone china shapes would predate the introduction of Mason's Ironstone in 1813.

Alas, all we can state is that those Davenport tea wares must be very early examples of this firm's stone china body and that it was being made to improve porcelain standards although, as was always the case, the basic production costs would have been lower and the price to the customer more attractive.

Various Davenport printed stone china marks occur and two early standard examples are here reproduced. All early examples include the name 'Davenport' with the name of the durable body – 'Stone China', 'Iron-

PLATE 171. *Representative pieces from an early 'Davenport Stone China' dessert service, including a rare basket and stand and a small handled dish. This printed outline design (number 6) was a standard Davenport design but Mason and other manufacturers produced very similar designs. Blue printed 'Davenport Stone China' and anchor mark. Basket 10½in. (26.67cm) long. c.1815-25.*

stone China' or 'Real Ironstone China'. Davenport toyed with such descriptive names as 'Improved Metallic Porcelain' and 'Davenport's Improved Ironstone', but these names were apparently not adopted. The stone china pieces appear superior in quality to the generally later ironstone wares and they were probably more costly to produce.

PLATE 172. *Representative pieces from a 'Davenport Stone China' dinner service of pattern number 6. A much-favoured Chinese styled design being a coloured-in printed outline. Tureen 13½in. (34.29cm) high. c.1815-25. Messrs Sotheby's.*

PLATE 173. *A rare and superbly potted marked 'Davenport Stone China' three-piece fruit-cooler decorated with Davenport's popular stone china pattern 6. 11¾in. (29.84cm) high. c.1815-25. Messrs Phillips.*

These marks, usually pre-1830, tend to occur in the colour of the outline print, normally in underglaze-blue.

A later impressed mark, as here shown, can occur from about 1850 onwards. A shape, size or potter's identification number was sometimes added below the anchor. Impressed month and year numbers can also occur, i.e. 1.60 for January 1860, indicating the date of manufacture.

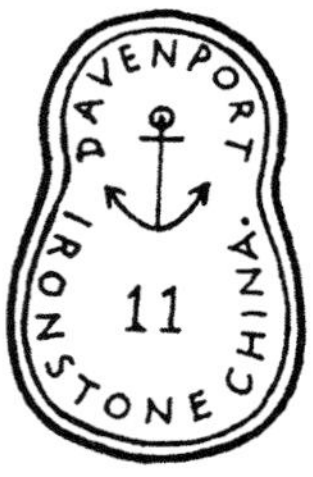


Although the firm's trade name was changed from time to time, for example being 'William Davenport & Co.' within the approximate period 1835-69, the marks tend to feature only the surname 'DAVENPORT'.

Direct copies of the Mason ironstone wares were seldom attempted, although a variation of the standard Mason jug shape (Plate 178) does occur with the Davenport name mark, and some Mason-type patterns appear mainly on dinner wares. Some rare ornamental wares can also occur, including large vases or urns.

Advertisements show that Davenport Ltd. produced ironstone-type ware up to the 1880s:

Ironstone ware. Plain and decorated in China Patterns, suitable for Barracks, Clubs, Hotels and Ships' uses.
White Granite, in great variety, suitable for Home Trade, north and south America and the Colonies.

An impressed mark of the 1840-70 period has the words 'Davenport Ironstone China' surrounding the anchor device. The date of manufacture of much of the mid-nineteenth century Davenport earthenware can be discovered by careful examination of the standard impressed 'Davenport' and anchor mark, for the last two numerals of the year were placed each side of the anchor. Other pieces sometimes have the month and year of manufacture impressed, i.e. 6.67 for June 1867.

The impressed marked 'Davenport Ironstone China' plate shown in Plate 181 was potted in 1860. It is interesting in that two distinct copper-plates have been used, one for the black English rural subject centre. The border (and mark) is printed in blue and it seems was originally made to accompany a Chinese design centre for the pattern which is titled 'Canton', a designation that can have no relation to the centre design on this two-colour plate. This example is a rare example of such multi-colour printing, a technique much favoured by the Davenport management. The majority of the Davenport ironstone and stone china wares are of a more conventional nature but the quality can be very high, often in my opinion superior to Mason's examples.

Some Victorian printed marks incorporate only the

PLATE 174. *A rare and highly finished marked 'Davenport Stone China' cheese dish and stand. Decorated with Davenport's popular stone china pattern 6, with well gilded handles. 12in. (30.48cm) high. c.1815-25.*

PLATE 175. *Representative pieces from a marked 'Davenport Stone China' dessert service of a rare pattern. The overall quality of this set is underlined by the intricately gilded feet and handles. Tureens 5¼in. (13.33cm) high. c.1815-25. Messrs Christie's.*

PLATE 176. *A blue printed Oriental-style plate from a marked 'Davenport Stone China' (and anchor device) dinner service. Diameter 6in. (14.24cm). c.1815-25.*

PLATE 177. *An impressed marked 'Davenport' over anchor mark plate. This plate is from a 'Friburg' blue printed dinner service. The impressed mark incorporates year numerals for 1844. Diameter 10½in. (26.67cm). 1844.*

single initial 'D'. These by no means always relate to the Davenport firm but the example here illustrated occurs with an impressed 'DAVENPORT' name mark. This is important as versions of this mark have been attributed to Dimmock, so underlining the difficulty of identifying single initial marks.

The standard book on this factory is *Davenport China Earthenware & Glass 1794-1887* by Terence A. Lockett and Geoffrey A. Godden, published by Barrie & Jenkins, 1989. Its Chapter 14 relates to the stone china wares. In this book Mr Lockett quotes an interesting mid-1820s letter from Henry Pontigny of the London establishment to Henry Davenport at Longport. The point is made that 'ironstone is not admitted in [to] France', presumably to protect the French manufacturers from British competition, although British porcelains were permitted. Hence Pontigny wrote 'I presume you make or can make in china all the patterns of Ironstone'. Such porcelains would of course have been more costly than the equivalent in ironstone. The final point is that a mutual friend is to be married and 'will have one of your new Ironstone Table (dinner) sets...'

The reader is also referred to Terence A. Lockett's earlier work *Davenport Pottery and Porcelain 1794-1887* (David & Charles, Newton Abbott, 1972) where further examples are featured.

PLATE 178. *A marked 'Davenport Stone China' jug, being a very close copy of a standard Mason shape (see Plates 38, 74 and 79) and pattern. Blue printed name and anchor mark. 5¾in. (14.6cm) high (various sizes occur). c.1820-40.*

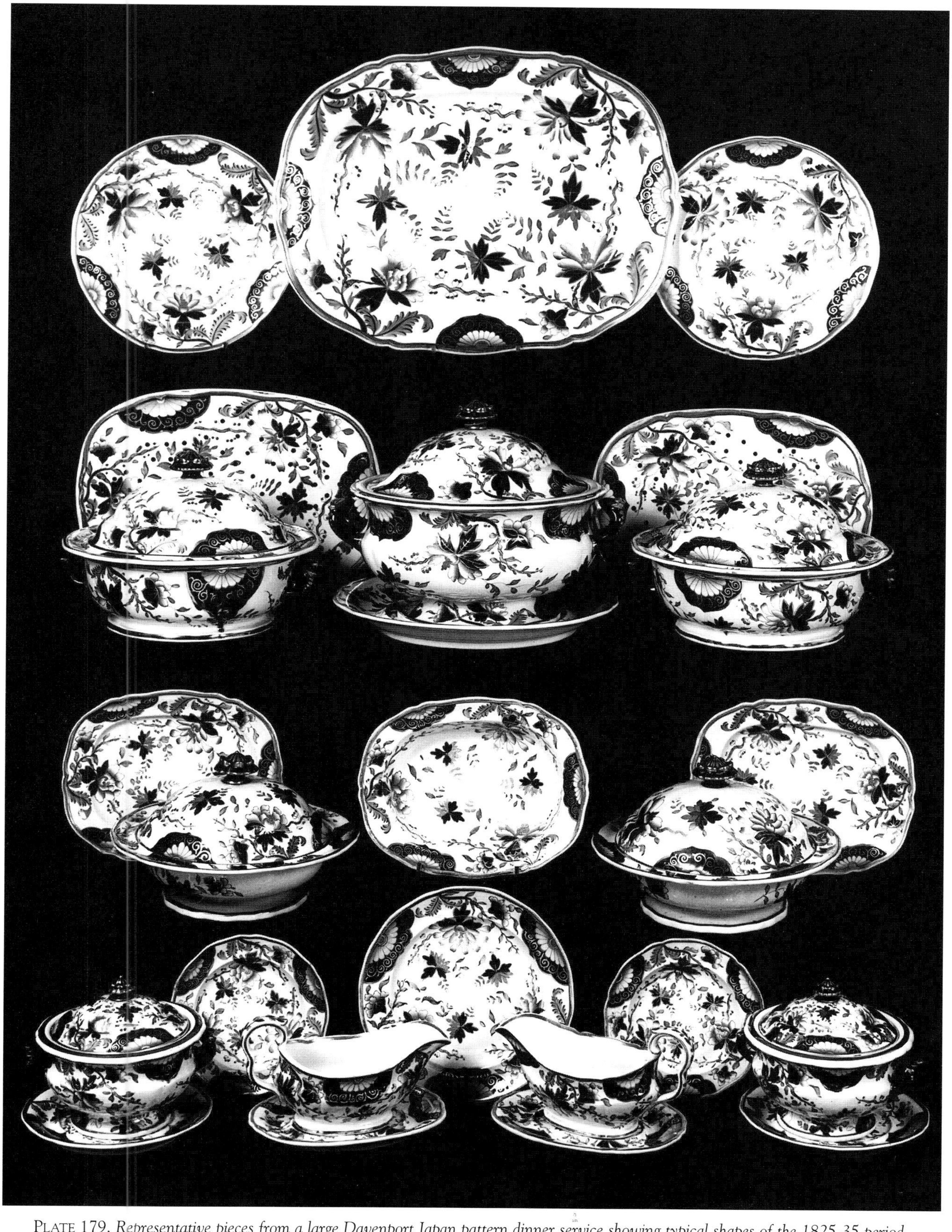

PLATE 179. *Representative pieces from a large Davenport Japan pattern dinner service showing typical shapes of the 1825-35 period. Printed 'Davenport Stone China' mark with anchor. Tureen 12¾in. (32.38cm) high. c.1825-35. Messrs Phillips.*

PLATE 180. *A rather heavily potted Davenport & Co. export-market handleless cup and stand. The basic faceted shape 'Niagara' was registered on 14 January 1853 and was used for a large range of useful wares. Registration and 'Davenport Ironstone' name mark. Cup 4in. (10.16cm) high. c.1853-57.*

PLATE 181. *An impressed marked 'Davenport Ironstone China' plate decorated with the 'Canton' pattern in two colours – black centre, blue printed border. The impressed name and anchor mark incorporates the year numerals for 1860. Diameter 7in. (17.78cm). 1866.*

**DAVENPORT BROTHERS.**
Thomas and James S. Davenport carried on a large importation and wholesaling business in New York from at least the early 1840s into the mid-1800s.

A typical blue printed mark reported by Arnold Kowalski and Frank and Paul Davenport from the States reads:

Manufactured
for
Davenport Bros.
203 Greenwich St.
N.Y.

These examples, which would include ironstone-type wares, were not necessarily all made by Messrs Davenport in the Staffordshire Potteries. Indeed, the mark cited above occurs on a Clementson ironstone plate with the printed 'Claremont' pattern. This was registered by J. Clementson of Shelton on 30 June 1856. Some examples with this registration device were being ordered by Davenport Bros. of New York, with their mark added incorrectly describing themselves as manufacturers. The American Eagle and Shield appears above the wording which is within a cartouche.

A certain S.W. Davenport was associated with the City Pottery at Trenton in the 1880s.

**J.H. DAVIS, Hanley, c.1875-91.**
John Heath Davis succeeded the J.H. & J. Davis partnership at the Trent Pottery, Kirkham Street, Eastwood, Hanley, from 13 July 1875. He continued to c.1891 and produced various types of useful earthenwares, including granite wares for the North American market.

Various impressed and printed name marks occur.

**J.H. & J. DAVIS, Hanley, c.1872-75.**
This partnership between John Heath Davis and James Davis succeeded Livesley & Davis at the Trent Pottery, Kirkham Street, Eastwood, Hanley, from 1872 but the partnership was dissolved on 13 July 1875, after which John H. Davis continued under his own name.

As Jewitt records, the Trent pottery produced white granite wares for the United States market as well as other useful wares for the home and other markets.

Various impressed and printed marks occur. These can include the Royal Arms and the description 'Royal Stone China' with the name 'J.M. & J. Davis'.

**WILLIAM DE MORGAN**
This entry at least illustrates that ironstone type wares were sometimes decorated by firms other than the manufacturers and that any type of decoration can, rarely, occur.

The well-known Victorian ceramic-decorator William De Morgan read a paper to the Royal Society of Arts which was republished in *The Pottery Gazette Diary* for 1894. The subject was his speciality -- the recreation of near-Eastern lustre effects on ceramics. Among lengthy descriptions of his experiments, he stated:

> The best of the first lustres I made on Staffordshire ware, were on ironstone or granite. The body was repellant in colour, but the glaze particularly good....

I have never come across any marked William De Morgan decorated ironstone-type ware – presumably plates or dishes – but such experimental efforts may still exist.

**DEAKIN & Son, Lane End, 1832-62.**
James Deakin & Son succeeded the Deakin & Bailey partnership at the Waterloo Pottery, Stafford Street, Lane End, as from 11 November 1832. The firm seemingly continued until c.1862, although the style Deakin & Co. is recorded in the 1846-51 rate records.

The firm produced various types of earthenware including stone china. Various 'D. & S.' initial marks are recorded, often with a lion crest. It should be noted, however, that these initials also fit Messrs Dimmock & Smith, c.1842-59 (q.v.).

However, other Deakin marks incorporate the name 'Deakin & Son' in full.

**DEAKIN & BAILEY, Lane End (Longton), c.1827-32.**
This partnership between James Deakin and John Bailey worked the Waterloo Pottery at Lane End in the approximate period 1827 up to the dissolution of partnership on 11 November 1832, after which James Deakin continued the concern, trading as Deakin & Son.

Staffordshire earthenwares bearing 'D. & B.' initial marks were probably produced by this short-lived partnership.

For further information on this firm the reader is referred to Rodney Hampson's specialist study 'Longton Potters 1700-1865' (*Journal of Ceramic History*, Vol. 14, City Museum and Art Gallery, Stoke-on-Trent, 1990).

**'DERBYSHIRE IRONSTONE'.**
The description 'Derbyshire Ironstone' is applied to a slightly cream-coloured earthenware body much used for thickly potted kitchen utensils such as mixing bowls.

In the context of this book such wares are not considered to be true ironstone but they enjoyed a long and continuing sale. Pigot's 1835 *Derbyshire Directory* lists in the Church Gresley section alone sixteen pottery firms under the heading 'Iron-stone and coarse earthenware manufacturers'.

The utilitarian Derbyshire Ironstone wares are seldom decorated or marked.

**L.L. DILLWYN (DILLWYN & Co.), Swansea, Wales, c.1831-50.**

Lewis Llewelyn Dillwyn owned the famous Swansea Pottery in Wales from 1831-50. Among the varied pottery he produced was some ironstone-type ware which bears descriptive marks. Various printed marks use the term 'STONE WARE' or 'IMPROVED STONE WARE' with the initial 'D' or 'D. & Co.' The full name 'DILLWYN & CO.' also occurs. The standard reference book on Swansea ceramics is E. Morton Nance's *The Pottery and Porcelain of Swansea and Nantgarw*, 1942.

The printed marks incorporating the single letter 'D' can be confused with the marks of other makers such as Dimmock.

Some moulded Swansea jugs bear the moulded mark 'CYMRO STONE CHINA' – see page 220.

**THOMAS DIMMOCK & Co. (Shelton), Hanley c.1828-59.**

Dimmock's were important producers of a large range of earthenware. Ironstone-type ware was made under the description 'Stone Ware' or 'Improved Stone Ware'. Printed marks incorporate the initial 'D' and can be mistaken for similar 'D' marks employed by Daniel, Davenports or by L. Dillwyn of Swansea. However, some Dimmock ware bears an impressed monogram device (see below) which is of great help in identifying this company's products.

**DIMMOCK & SMITH, Hanley, c.1842-59.**

Little is known of this partnership of Tontine Street, Hanley, but various 'Stone China' 'D & S' initial marks occur which could fit this firm. They are, however, more likely to relate to Deakin & Son, of Lane End (q.v.).

**DIXON, PHILLIPS & Co., Sunderland, c.1840-65.**

This partnership succeeded Dixon, Austin, Phillips & Co. at the Sunderland or Garrison Pottery at Sunderland in the 1840-1865 period.

The standard types of sponged, printed, painted and lustred wares were produced including, it is believed, ironstone type wares.

The few recorded marks include or comprise the names in full.

**D. & K.R.**

These initials are sometimes found on British mid-nineteenth century export-market wares, particularly those made for Russia. The initials seemingly relate to a foreign importer or wholesaler.

**D & S.**

Several printed marks occur incorporating the initials 'D. & S.', sometimes with the county name 'Staffordshire', with description of the body such as 'Stone China'. A lion crest sometimes appears above the wording.

These initials could link with the following Staffordshire firms:

| | |
|---|---|
| Deakin & Son, Lane End | c.1833-62 (see page 233) |
| Dean & Stokes, Burslem | c.1867-68 |
| Dimmock & Smith, Hanley | c.1826-33 |
| and | c.1842-59 |

**DU CROZ.**
**DU CROZ & CO.**
**DU CROZ & MILLIDGE, Retailers, London, c.1811-54.**

Many printed marks bear the name-marks of Du Croz, 'DUCROZ', 'DUCROZ & Co.' (c.1811-33) or the later partnership of Ducroz & Millidge (c.1833-54). William Millidge married a Du Croz (of Dutch extraction) in London in 1814. Various spellings occur, as one name Ducroz or separated Du Croz.

This London-based firm purchased ironstone and stone china type wares from several different manufacturers including Masons, Mintons and Hicks & Meigh or Hicks, Meigh & Johnson and John Ridgway. In some of their marks Du Croz (& Millidge) claimed to be the manufacturers of the wares, but this was not the case.

PLATE 182. *A Hicks, Meigh & Johnson stone china soup plate, part of a large order made for the Skinners' Company in 1827. Blue printed DuCroz retailer's name over a standard Hicks mark, with pattern number 51 added below – see mark. Diameter 10¼in. 26.03cm). 1827.*

Several elaborate printed marks occur incorporating these names and various London addresses, such as Skinner Street. The pre-Victorian Royal Arms are often featured in these marks. Several good quality services featuring armorial bearings are recorded with Du Croz marks and the partnership seems to have been well connected with City Companies.

The partnership between John Ducroz and William Millidge dates from November 1833. Millidge retired in May 1840. Ducroz & Millidge name marks can occur alone, without the Royal Arms. This partnership's marks are datable to 1833-40. Du Croz apparently continued alone, trading from a Regent Street address from 1842 using the old established trade name until c.1854. It is, however, difficult to date these marks from the name alone. The Du Croz mark here reproduced appears on stone china dinner wares made for the Salters' Company and was supplied to this London City Company in 1827 – a more colourful version was also made with coloured-over border design. The main part of the marks comprises a standard type of Hicks & Meigh and Hicks, Meigh & Johnson Royal Arms device, with the pattern number '51', one obviously in production by 1827 – see Plate 182 and mark detail.

The various Du Croz retailers' marks usually occur on good quality well-produced wares.

**JAMES DUDSON, Hanley, c.1845-82.**
James Dudson succeeded his father Thomas (d.July 1845) at the Hope Street Works at Hanley as from July 1845 (after a short-lived partnership between James and Charles Dudson).

Mrs Audrey M. Dudson, in her excellent specialist book, *Dudson. A Family of Potters since 1800* (Dudson Publications, Hanley, 1985), states that James Dudson advertised ironstone wares and that his recipe book included three different mixes for ironstone bodies.

None the less, I do not know of any marked or identifiable specimens. This may be because the ironstone articles were not table wares but conventional hard, stoneware-type, articles. At the 1862 Exhibition, for example, James Dudson showed 'Improved ironstone jugs and teapots with metal tops'.

**DUDSON BROTHERS (Ltd.), Hanley and Tunstall, 1899-1996.**
This important Staffordshire pottery firm succeeded James T. Dudson in December 1899. In May 1918, Dudson Brothers became a Limited Liability Company and the style was changed to Dudson Brothers Ltd. In June 1996 the trade style was amended to Dudson Ltd. The varied history of the firm is well told by Mrs Audrey M. Dudson in her book, *Dudson. A Family of Potters since 1800* (Dudson Publications, Hanley, 1985).

The company continues to produce ironstone-type vitrified stonewares and hotel type wares of good quality. Various printed marks incorporate the name 'Dudson'. The firm is now one of the largest producers of vitrified useful wares. So large were the orders for vitrified stoneware table wares between the wars that additional lines were produced by arrangement with Ridgways (Bedford Works) Ltd. After the Second World War new export markets were exploited and new factories taken to supply the very large demand for the Dudson vitrified wares. The old Hanley site ceased to be used for manufacturing in 1980 and was vacated in 1987, after which production was centred on Tunstall.

The reader is referred to the specialist book mentioned above for a comprehensive coverage.

**DUDSON Ltd., Burslem, 1996-present day.**
This trade name superseded the former Dudson Brothers Ltd. as from 1 June 1996. The Dudson Group comprises Dudson Ltd., Dudson Armorlite Ltd. and Dudson Duraline Ltd. The 'Dudson' trade name, with or without the initial 'D', occurs on several new style registered marks, as that here reproduced. Note the modern use of the BS (British Standards Institution) logo.

**DUDSON ARMORLITE Ltd., Burslem, 1996-present day.**
This firm superseded J.E. Heath Ltd. at the Albert Potteries, Hobson Street, Burslem, as from June 1996. It continues, as the new name suggests, to produce 'Armorlite' durable wares under the revised name. The new 1996 + standard mark is here reproduced.

**DUDSON DURALINE Ltd., Tunstall, 1996-present day.**
This new trade name superseded the former Duraline Hotel Ware Co. Ltd. as from 1 June 1996. The former lines continue to be produced in the strong 'Duraline' body under the Dudson name. A typical modern printed mark is reproduced.

**DUNN, BENNETT & Co. (Ltd.), Burslem, c.1875-present day. (as part of the Doulton Group).**
This firm, originally of the Boothen Works, Hanley, produced good ironstone ware. Jewitt, writing in the 1883 revised edition of his *Ceramic Art of Great Britain*, noted:

> Messrs. Dunn, Bennett & Co. here manufacture earthenware and ironstone china in all the usual services, both for the home and American markets.

Their productions are of a high quality, and having houses both in London and New York, they are in a position to cater successfully for both countries.

In 1887 they took over the large Royal Victoria Pottery[9] in Burslem. The firm's advertisement of the 1890s mentions 'Ironstone China', specially adapted for ships, hotels, restaurants and coffee house use. Early marks incorporated the initials 'D.B. & Co.', often with a bee-hive device. 'Ltd.' was added to marks late in 1907. Subsequent marks include the term 'Vitreous Ironstone' with the company's name in full. In about 1909 the firm introduced a near-miracle durable earthenware with a special printed mark:

Dunn Bennett's Patent.
Unchippable surface
Burslem.

The impressed mark on such wares was merely the word 'PATENT', usually with impressed month and year numbers – 11.09 for November 1909.

On 1 January 1938 the company moved to the famous Dale Hall Works, Newport Lane, Longport, Burslem, where they remained for many years, producing a good range of high quality 'Vitreous Ironstone' for the home and export markets. Dunn Bennett's wares still enjoy a large sale. In 1968 the company was merged with Doulton, now being part of Royal Doulton Tableware for the hotel and catering trades.

The name 'Royal Doulton Group' appears as part of most post-1968 marks. The firm is a large producer of 'Rocklite Vitrified Hotel Ware'.

## DURALINE HOTEL WARE CO. LTD., Tunstall, c.1979-96.

This company succeeded Grindley Hotel Ware Co. Ltd., at Tunstall. The specialities include vitrified tablewares for hotels, restaurants, hospitals, schools and canteens. The trade names include 'Duraline', 'Super-Vitrified' and 'Ultraline'.

The company was retitled and continued as Dudson Duraline Ltd. from 1996. New marks will reflect this change.

## D.W.

Various printed marks incorporate the initials 'D. W.', with or without the Royal Arms, and other initials or names.

These initials do not seem to relate to a British manufacturer but are more likely to relate to a foreign importer or agent. Most examples seem to relate to dinner wares produced in the approximate period 1840-60.

## EDGE, MALKIN & Co. (Ltd.), Burslem, c.1870-1903.

Edge, Malkin & Co. succeeded Cork, Edge & Malkin in 1870 or 1871 at the Newport and Middleport Potteries at Burslem. The partners up to November 1892 were Joseph Edge, James Malkin, William and John Edge. Advertisements of the 1880s mention 'IRONSTONE-CHINA AND EARTHENWARE, plain, printed, enamelled and gilt dinner, tea and toilet ware, in white ivory and other coloured bodies...'

The standard printed mark incorporates the initials 'E.M. & Co.' on a ribbon under a dog device but other initial or name marks can occur. The full name or initials also occur as impressed marks. The company had a very large output of good quality useful earthenwares, mainly table wares. The partnership enjoyed a profitable export trade, particularly to North America. Typical American designs and shapes are featured in standard books on American market ceramics.

## JAMES EDWARDS (& Son), Dale Hall, Burslem, c.1842-82.

From 1842, James Edwards traded under his own name until, in 1851, '& Son' was added to the style. James Edwards died in January 1867 but the firm continued to trade under the old name James Edwards & Son.

The firm was one of the leading exporters of ironstone and granite-type wares, concentrating on the North American trade. James Edwards, it was claimed, was one of the first to produce the granite body and bring it to perfection, enabling it to compete with the fashionable white French porcelains. Certainly the marked James Edwards ironstone and granite china is of very good quality and was seemingly much favoured in America. Llewellynn Jewitt, in his 1878 work, *The Ceramic Art of Great Britain*, gave a very flowery account of James Edwards' life but also helpfully noted:

> The productions consist of white graniteware for the American and steamship trade; ordinary earthenware for the home trade...Indian ironstone goods... These are all of the highest quality and are much in repute. In 'stone china', which is of good firm semi-transparent quality, many excellent patterns are made. Among these are the Bishop, Barley, Mediaeval, Rope, Tulip and Scroll.

In the 1870s the partners were Richard Edwards, Joseph Henry Edwards and Robert Edwards but Joseph continued alone from September 1878 and the firm closed in 1882. The firm had a London establishment at Hatton Garden.

The various printed or impressed marks comprise the

full name 'James Edwards' or 'James Edwards & Son' (or the abbreviation 'Jas.') or the initials 'J.E.' or 'J.E. & S.'. The place name 'Dalehall' often occurs as part of the mark. A simple mark

Edwards
D.H.

relates to this firm at Dale Hall.

Some marks also incorporate the name of the various bodies 'Stone China', 'Ironstone China'. An American eagle emblem was also incorporated in some marks on wares intended for the American market. A large export trade was carried on by this firm, which was succeeded by Messrs Knapper & Blackhurst.

**JOHN EDWARDS,**
Manufacturer of Porcelaine de Terre, Ironstone-China, and White Granite,
KING STREET, FENTON, STAFFORDSHIRE.
Samples and Quotations upon Application.
Agents in New York, U.S.:—Messrs. Burgess & Goddard, 26, Barclay Street. Agents for Boston, U.S.:—Messrs. A. French & Co., 151 & 153, Milk Street.

**JOHN EDWARDS (& Co.), Fenton, c.1847-1900.** John Edwards first potted at Longton, moving to King Street, Fenton, in about 1853. In 1861, 170 persons were employed. Jewitt noted in 1878: 'The goods produced are semi-porcelain and white granite for the American market'. The basic entry for the Edwards display at the 1878 Paris Universal Exhibition, read: 'John Edwards, white granite manufacturer, Fenton, Staffordshire. White granite, tea, dinner, toilet and jug services, white and ornamented'. Advertisements in the 1880s list 'Porcelaine de Terre, Ironstone China and White Granite'. John Edwards had agents in New York and Boston.

N.B. It should be noted that there was a firm of Liverpool shippers, agents, etc. by the name of John Edwards & Co., but as far as is known they were not connected with the Fenton potters of this name.

**T. EDWARDS, Burslem, c.1844-48.** An ornate printed mark incorporating the American eagle motif occurs with the British design registration device for 26 August 1847. The name 'T. Edwards' is added below, although the registration is in the name of James Edwards!

Thomas Edwards had left the J. & T. Edwards partnership in Sylvester Street, Burslem, on 1 April 1842. He then seems to have taken or built the Swan Bank Pottery – he is the first occupier listed by Jewitt. However, the first record of him at this address occurs in the British Registration files when on 3 April 1844 he entered various designs for fluted dinner wares – of export-market type.

Thomas Edwards is again recorded at the Swan Bank Pottery at Burslem in 1846 and he or another potter of this name is then recorded at the Waterloo Potteries, Burslem, in 1848, in which year he was declared bankrupt. The Waterloo works passed to T. & R. Boote. The Swan Bank Pottery was worked by Thomas Pinder from at least 1848.

Various printed and impressed 'T. Edwards' name marks are recorded and these should date to c.1842-48. 'T.E.' initial marks on wares of the 1840s should also relate to this potter.

**JAMES & THOMAS EDWARDS, Burslem, c.1839-42.** James and Thomas Edwards potted together at the Kilncroft Works, Burslem in c.1839-40 and then at Sylvester Street, Burslem. This partnership was dissolved on 1 April 1842. James Edwards (& Son) later worked the Dale Hall Pottery and Thomas subsequently worked the Swan Bank Pottery.

James & Thomas Edwards produced a good range of earthenwares including ironstone-type wares. Various name or initial 'J. &. T.E.' marks were used, sometimes with the town designation 'Burslem' or 'B'.

**ELKIN(s), KNIGHT & BRIDGWOOD, Foley, Fenton, c.1827-40**
See Knight, Elkin & Bridgwood

**LIDDLE ELLIOT (& Co.) (or & Son), Burslem c.1860-70.** Liddle Elliot succeeded Mayer & Elliot at the Dalehall Pottery, Longport, Burslem from 14 April 1860.

He, like the Mayers, produced a wide range of good quality earthenwares including ironstone-type wares.

The term 'Berlin Ironstone' occurs incorporated in some marks. The trade styles Liddle Elliot & Co. or Liddle Elliot & Son were also used, giving rise to the following range of initial marks:

L.E, L.E. & CO., L.E. & Son

Note, the initials L.E. in some other marks relate to the district Lane End – also that Liddle is the forename.

**ELSMORE & Son, Tunstall, c.1872-87.**
In about 1872 Thomas Elsmore was joined by his son (Henry) and the new firm of Elsmore & Son, or Thomas Elsmore & Son, continued the Clay Hills Pottery at Tunstall.

Ironstone-type wares were produced, much or all of which was exported to North America.

Various printed and impressed name marks occur and relate to this period.

**ELSMORE & FORSTER, Tunstall, c.1855-71.**
This partnership between Thomas Elsmore and Thomas Forster[10] succeeded Elsmore & Co. as from 31 January 1855. They worked the Clayhills Pottery at Tunstall where general earthenware as well as ironstone-type ware was produced. One of the best known lines has a raised wheat design. This basic 'Ceres' pattern was registered in November 1859. Its simple tasteful design proved extremely popular in North American markets; 'Ceres' and other relief moulded white ironstone useful wares proved highly popular overseas. Typical North American market Ceres-shape white ironstone table wares are shown in Plate 184.

PLATE 183. *A marked 'Elsmore & Forster. Warranted Ironstone China' jug with coloured-in theatrical prints. Royal Arms name mark. 8¾in. (22.22cm) high. c.1855-65.*

PLATE 184. *A selection of marked Elsmore & Forster's American market white Ceres-shape table wares, full size and child's size sets. Large coffee pot 11¼in. (28.57cm) high. c.1860-65. Dieringer's Arts & Antiques.*

This important partnership registered fifteen further forms, many of which were produced in ironstone-type bodies, and American authorities have recorded at least sixty-five variants or related patterns.

Most marks incorporate the name of the double partnership, often with the Royal Arms, but initial marks 'E. & F.' also occur. The body description 'Warranted Ironstone China' was often included in these marks, which can occur on decorative novelties such as the jug shown in Plate 183. Elsmore & Son succeeded the firm *c.*1872-87.

**FRANCIS JOSEPH EMERY, Burslem (or Cobridge), c.1878-93.**

Larry Freeman in his 1954 American book on *Ironstone China*, noted: 'F.J. Emery. For a short time, 1885-1893, this factory at Cobridge, England, turned out ironstone'.

Francis Emery is recorded at two addresses at Burslem, at the former W.E. Withinshaw's Church Works, Wood Street, *c.*1879 and then at the Bleakhill Works (Cobridge) Burslem, *c.*1880-1893. I have not seen any marked Emery ironstone-type wares although specimens may occur in American collections.

Francis Emery was connected with Edward Clarke, trading as Edward Clarke & Co. (q.v.) at the New Bridge Pottery, Longton, before 1877.

**ENGLISH IRONSTONE (POTTERY) Ltd., Shelton c.1972-74.**
**Title amended to ENGLISH IRONSTONE TABLEWARE Ltd. in 1974.**

This company, a branch of Washington Pottery (Staffordshire) Ltd., produced wares marked with this name in the early 1970s. Some wares include the full address, with the name of the pattern, i.e.

OLD WILLOW
ENGLISH IRONSTONE POTTERY
COLLEGE ROAD, SHELTON
STOKE-ON-TRENT
STAFFORDSHIRE
ENGLAND

**ENGLISH IRONSTONE TABLEWARE, Shelton, c.1974-c.1994.**

This new title succeeded English Ironstone (Pottery) Ltd. in 1974. As the title suggests, ironstone type table wares were produced under this name.

However, my endeavours to trace later details have been unsuccessful. My May 1994 letter to the Managing Director was unanswered and the *Daily Telegraph* of 17 September 1994 stated that receivers had made redundant 230 workers and that cuts were possible in regard to the remaining two hundred. It would seem therefore that sizeable production continued from 1974 to at least the middle of 1994. The trade journal *Tableware International* of December 1994 reported that the remaining assets of E.I.T. had been purchased by Harvergrange Plc. of Edgware. The Managing Director stated 'we plan to produce existing and new ranges of E.I.T. tableware products in a joint venture with Grindley Pottery in Tunstall. The products will continue to be marketed under the E.I.T. brand name...'

Standard printed ornate marks can include the following wording:

Staffordshire
underglaze
printing
Genuine Hand Engraved
dishwasher, detergent proof
micro-wave oven safe
made by
English
Ironstone
Tableware
Limited
England

**D.J. EVANS & Co.** – see EVANS & GLASSON.

**EVANS & GLASSON, Swansea, c.1850-70.**

The partnership between David Evans and John Evans Glasson worked the Cambrian Pottery at Swansea in the approximate period 1850-70, in succession to Lewis Llewelynn Dillwyn. John Glasson died in March 1852 and the later alternative mark was D.J. Evans & Co.

Various types of standard earthenware were produced but the finest days of Swansea ceramics had long passed and the post-1850 examples are basically of a utilitarian nature. These earthenwares included ironstone-type stoneware or 'Improved Stone Ware'.

Various printed and impressed marks incorporate the names 'Evans & Glasson' or 'D.J. Evans & Co.', with the name of the pattern and often the place name 'Swansea'.

**EVERARD, GLOVER & TOWNSEND, Longton, c.1837-45.**
This partnership between George Everard, James Glover and George Townsend (which also traded as Everard, Townsend & Co.) produced ironstone-type wares which were normally marked with printed marks incorporating the initials 'E G & T'. The style was changed to Everard, Colclough & Townsend in July, 1845.

For further information on this Longton firm the reader is referred to Rodney Hampson's specialist study 'Longton Potters 1700-1865' (*Journal of Ceramic History*, Vol. 14, City Museum & Art Gallery, Stoke-on-Trent, 1990).

**WILLIAM FAIRBAIRNS**
Printed marks occur comprising a reproduction of the British Royal Arms and supporters with the name 'William Fairbairns' below and 'Ironstone China' above.

I have, however, been unable to trace a British potter of this name. The mark may, therefore, relate to a mid-Victorian wholesaler, importer or exporter.

**JOHN FARRALL, Shelton. c.1854-55.**
John Farrall potted at Broad Street, Shelton (Hanley) for a short period from June 1854. He had earlier been a partner in the firm of Pearson, Farrall & Meakin which registered ironstone tableware forms in April 1854. He was soon involved in another short-lived partnership with William Freakley but this was dissolved in June 1854, after which John Farrall traded under his own name for a short period. He subsequently traded in partnership with Lewis (?) Meakin in 1855 but the firm was bankrupt in that year – see Meakin & Farrall.

Several printed marks occur incorporating John Farrall's name and the description 'ironstone china'. One mark includes a mock representation of the British Royal Arms, surmounted by the American eagle. This mark can also include the 11 April 1854 parcel number 5 diamond-shape registration device relating to the firm of Pearson, Farrall & Meakin. The John Farrall marks would date from June 1854 but could only have been used for less than a year.

Whilst 'J.F.' initial marks could relate to this potter, most such examples will have been used by larger firms, such as that of Jacob Furnival.

**THOMAS FELL (& Co. (Ltd.)),**
**Newcastle-upon-Tyne, c.1817-90.**
Thomas Fell established the St. Peter's Pottery at Newcastle upon Tyne in 1817. In 1869 it became a Limited Company but this did not affect the marks.

A wide range of earthenwares were produced, mainly in sponged and printed designs, and the various marks incorporate the names 'FELL' or 'FELL & Co.' The initials 'T F & Co.' or 'F & Co.' can also occur.

**FELSPAR CHINA.**
**FELSPAR PORCELAIN.**
It has been stated by at least one American author that Felspar China is 'another name for ironstone'.

This is certainly not the case as far as British porcelains are concerned. The Coalport, Minton and Spode companies (and several lesser firms) produced superb, highly translucent, porcelains including felspar from 1820 onwards. The major firms introduced special printed marks to distinguish their superior new body. These marks normally include the name Felspar (variations in spelling occur).

For further information on early nineteenth century English felspar porcelain the reader is referred to *Staffordshire Porcelain*, edited by Geoffrey Godden (Granada Publishing Ltd., London, 1983) or to Leonard Whiter's *Spode* (Barrie & Jenkins, London, 1970 and later editions).

**FERRYBRIDGE POTTERY, Yorkshire.**
The Ferrybridge Pottery was originally known as the Knottingley Pottery and as such it certainly dates back to the eighteenth century.

Several of the post-1815 firms no doubt produced useful wares in stone china or other ironstone china-type bodies such as granite. These firms or partnerships included:

| | |
|---|---|
| John Tomlinson | c.1815-26 |
| William Tomlinson | c.1826-28 |
| Edward Tomlinson | c.1828-30 |
| ? Wigglesworth | c.1830-31 |
| Reed & Taylor | c..1832-38 |
| Reed, Taylor & Co. | c.1838-43 |
| B. Taylor & Son | c.1843-47 |
| Edward Tomlinson | c.1848-50 |
| Lewis Woolf | c.1851-56 |
| Lewis Woolf & Sons | c.1856+ |
| Sydney Woolf | c.1860-84 |
| Poulson Brothers | c.1884-95 |
| Sefton & Brown | c.1895-1919 |

These dates are approximate only but the various owners used printed or, more rarely, impressed name or initial marks on their wares which included useful ironstone-type bodies. The most usually found initial marks are:

| | |
|---|---|
| R. & T. | Reed & Taylor |
| R.T. & Co. | Reed, Taylor & Co. |

| | |
|---|---|
| B.T. & S. | B. Taylor & Son |
| L.W.[11] | Lewis Woolf |
| L.W. & S. | Lewis Woolf & Sons |
| S .W. | Sydney Woolf |
| P.B. or P. Bros. | Poulson Brothers |

These initials may be followed by 'F.B.' indicating Ferrybridge Pottery. The single initial 'F' may also relate to Ferrybridge.

**FLACKET, CHETHAM & TOFT, Longton, c.1853.**

This short-lived partnership between Thomas Flacket, James Chetham and William Toft at the Melbourne Works in Church Street, Longton, produced general earthenwares. The partnership was dissolved on 8 December 1853. One mark incorporates the description 'Stone Ware' with the firm's initials 'F.C. & T.' The succeeding form of Flacket & Toft (1853-56) may well have produced similar wares marked with the initials 'F. & T.'

For further information on this Longton firm the reader is referred to Rodney Hampson's specialist study 'Longton Potters 1700-1865' (*Journal of Ceramic History*, Vol. 14, City Museum & Art Gallery, Stoke-on-Trent, 1990).

**STEPHEN FOLCH (& SONS), Stoke, c.1819-29.**

A long but damaged Folch Ironstone china dinner service was sold at Christie's in 1967. The shapes were very similar to the standard Mason Ironstone dinnerware forms.

The marks printed, in underglaze-blue on this service, took three forms. First, the key mark comprised an elaborate version of the Royal Arms with the Prince of Wales' feathers behind; under this device the wording 'GENUINE FOLCH'S STONE CHINA' appeared in a ribbon. Other pieces bore the same arms with two different styles of wording below – either 'IMPROVED IRONSTONE CHINA' or 'IMP$^{D}$ (or IMPRVD) IRONSTONE CHINA, STOKE WORKS'. These do not include the key word 'Folch's', but all pieces were clearly from the same service and the work of one manufacturer, so these marks can be added to those used by Stephen Folch during the period c.1819-30. Some other marks incorporate the longer title 'Folch & Sons', and sometimes the description 'New Cambrian China'. The impressed circular mark 'Imprvd Ironstone China' is also attributed to Folch. For a short period c.1821-22 Stephen Folch was working in partnership with Charles Scott – see the following entry.

According to a trade account dated October 1819, Folch's wares were modestly priced: covered soup tureens and stands at 11s., plates at 3½d. However, it

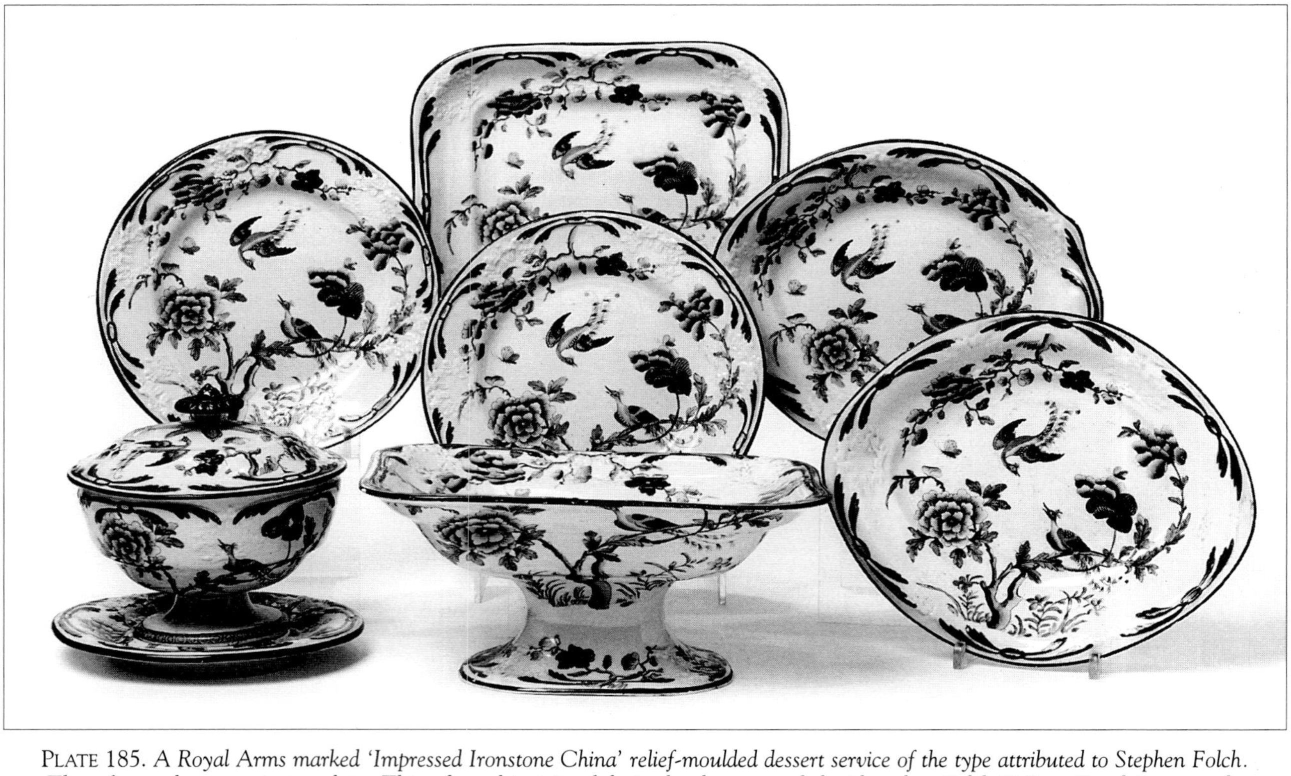

PLATE 185. *A Royal Arms marked 'Impressed Ironstone China' relief-moulded dessert service of the type attributed to Stephen Folch. These forms also occur in porcelain. This coloured-in printed design has been recorded with a clear Folch & Sons Royal Arms mark. Centrepiece 12½in. (31.75cm) long. c.1819-29.*

PLATE 186A. *A printed outlined Stephen Folch Ironstone China dessert service plate of typically good quality. Ornate Royal Arms mark with 'Improved Ironstone China' – see detail. Diameter 8in. (20.32cm). c.1819-29.*

PLATE 186B. *Finely engraved pre-Victorian Royal Arms mark featuring the Prince of Wales' three-feather device, with wording 'Improved Ironstone China'. This mark is tentatively attributed to Stephen Folch and appears on the plate shown in Plate 186A.*

would seem that Folch's Stoke factory (formerly owned by Thomas Wolfe) produced a wide range of decorative Mason style ironstone china, much of which has not been correctly attributed to this manufacturer. I have seen a very good quality marked Folch stone china jug, of the type illustrated by Mrs Jennifer Moody in the *Northern Ceramic Society's Newsletter* Number 78, page 24, and in *Antique Collecting* of June 1994.

Stephen Folch's works were advertised locally in March 1829 although some of his working materials had been advertised in February 1828.

For further information the reader is referred to Mrs Jennifer Moody's contribution, Number 13, to the *Northern Ceramic Society Newsletter,* Number 63 of September 1986. The position, however, appears to be complicated by the late Leonard King's contribution to the *Northern Ceramic Society's Newsletter*, Number 65 of March 1987, in which Mr King reported an example with a Folch-style printed Royal Arms mark and also an impressed Mason-type circular Patent Ironstone china mark. The practice of intertrading between different firms may explain this double marking, although the late Leonard King was of the opinion that Mason copied the Folch mark! Typical marked examples are shown in Plates 185 and 186.

**FOLCH & SCOTT, Stoke, c.1821-22.**
This short-lived partnership was between Stephen Folch and Charles Scott. Scott died in September 1822 and Stephen Folch continued. I do not know of any marked examples but it is likely that ironstone-type wares were made.

**FORD & CHALLINOR, Tunstall, c.1865-80.**
**FORD CHALLINOR & CO.**
Ford & Challinor (also listed as Ford, Challinor & Co.) occupied the Lion Works at Tunstall. The partners were Thomas Ford and William Challinor. Various types of earthenware, including ironstone-type wares were produced and sometimes bear name or initial marks – 'F. & C.' or 'F.C. & Co.'.

**FORESTER & HULME, Fenton, c.1887-92.**
This partnership between Thomas Forester and Joseph Hulme worked the Sutherland Pottery, High Street, Fenton, up to 31 December 1892.

Various earthenwares, including ironstone-type wares, were produced. Name and initial 'F. & H.' marks are recorded.

**WILLIAM FREAKLEY (& Co.), Shelton (Hanley), c.1852-53.**
This partnership between William Freakley and Samuel Harrison traded as William Freakley & Co. at Broad Street, Hanley, and is recorded in the dissolution of partnership notice of September 1853 as being 'Ironstone China Manufacturers', after which William Freakley was stated to have carried on alone. However, it would seem that he soon entered into a new partnership with John Farrall – see the following entry.

No marked specimens have as yet been recorded, but 'W.F. & Co.' initial marks could relate to this short-lived firm.

**FREAKLEY & FARRALL, Shelton (Hanley), 1853-54.**
This short-lived partnership between William Freakley and John Farrall at Broad Street, Shelton (Hanley), succeeded William Freakley & Co. 'Ironstone China Manufacturers'.

The new partnership was dissolved on 9 June 1854, after which John Farrall continued under his own name for a short period – see John Farrall. The situation is, however, complicated in that the Pearson, Farrall & Meakin partnership registered ironstone tableware shapes under their joint names on 11 April 1854. This triple partnership is not recorded in other available records and must have been very short-lived.

Whilst no name marks have as yet been reported, any 'F. & F.' initial marks will relate to this Staffordshire partnership between William Freakley and John Farrall.

**JACOB FURNIVAL (& Co.), Cobridge, c.1845-70.**
Jacob Furnival had previously been connected with Thomas & Jacob Furnival at Miles Bank, Hanley, and up to 13 February 1845 in the short-lived Cobridge partnership of Furnival & Wear. From this date he seems to have continued under the trade style Jacob Furnival & Co. This new firm registered a printed design on 30 April 1845.

Ironstone-type ware occurs with the initial mark 'J.F. & Co.' which probably relate to this firm. Fuller marks read 'J. Furnival & Co. Cobridge', often with descriptions of the body, 'Vitrified Ironstone China', etc.

The initial mark 'J.F.', as found on some mid-nineteenth century American-market ironstone wares, has been attributed to Jacob Furnival. It should be noted, however, that this potter does not seem to have worked on his own account – the printed name marks (and design registration entries) give the full title 'J Furnival & Co.' The reader is referred to my 'J.F.' entry.

**JACOB & THOMAS FURNIVAL, Hanley, c.1840-43.**
Ironstone-type stone china made by this firm bears the Royal Arms device with the initials 'J. & T.F.' The partnership at Miles Bank, Hanley, was succeeded from 29 December 1843 by Thomas Furnival & Co.

**THOMAS FURNIVAL & Co., Hanley, c.1840 and 1843-45.**
Thomas Furnival (Junior) with unknown partners potted at the former Reuben Johnson pottery in Miles Bank, Hanley in about 1840 using the trade name Thomas Furnival Jun. & Co. before joining with Jacob to trade as Jacob & Thomas Furnival. This joint partnership was dissolved on 29 December 1843 after which Thomas Furnival reverted to trading as Thomas Furnival & Co. Messrs Furnival & Clark succeeded for a short period, c.1845-46.[12]

This firm produced large quantities of ironstone and granite-type useful wares especially for the American market.

Various name and initial 'T.F. & Co.' (or perhaps 'T.F. Jun. & Co.') marks occur. These initial marks have been attributed in error to Thomas Ford & Co. or even to the early firm of Thomas Fell & Co. The design registration records show that some of these T.F. & Co. initial marks of the 1840s relate to Thomas Furnival & Co. of Hanley.

The abbreviated initials 'F. & Co.' may also have been used by this firm.

**THOMAS FURNIVAL & Son(s), Cobridge, c.1871-90.**
Thomas Furnival's pottery was in Elder Road, Cobridge. His early wares bear the impressed name mark 'FURNIVAL'. From c.1876 '& Sons' was added to the firm's style, replacing the singular 'Son'. Ironstone-type ware was made, advertised as 'white granite', as well as standard earthenware.

Jewitt, writing in or before 1878, noted that this firm occupied two factories at Cobridge and that the firm 'ranks high as manufacturers of white granite and vitrified ironstone... for the United States and Canadian markets, to which they ship large quantities of goods... For the home trade Messrs. Furnival & Sons produce, in their beautiful "patent ironstone", dinner and other services of various qualities in point of decoration'. Jewitt also describes and illustrates other Furnival wares but these do not appear to be of ironstone or the granite body.

Various marks incorporate the firm's name in full or the initials 'T.F.' or 'T.F. & S.' (or 'T.F. & Sons') after c.1876).

**FURNIVAL & CLARK, Hanley, c.1845-6.**
This partnership between Thomas Furnival and Richard Clark succeeded Thomas Furnival & Co. at Miles Bank, Hanley. The new firm registered a design for a toby-type moulded jug form on 30 December 1845. However, registrations for moulded edged table wares and a printed floral pattern were made on 21 November 1846 in the name of the firm of Thomas Furnival & Co.

This short-lived partnership may have used as yet unrecorded name or 'F. & C.' initial marks.

**FURNIVALS (Ltd.), Cobridge, c.1890-present day (as part of the Wedgwood Group).**
Furnivals succeeded Thomas Furnival (& Sons) – see previous entry. 'Ltd.' was added to the firm's style and to most marks in 1895. In January 1913 the style was changed to 'FURNIVALS (1913) LTD.', although the marks do not reflect this change of name. Good quality ironstone-type ware was made by all these firms.

In 1967 Furnivals was taken over by Barratts of Staffordshire Ltd., but the factory was closed in December 1968. The trade name and some patterns were purchased by Enoch Wedgwood (Tunstall) Ltd. early in 1969, which in turn joined the Wedgwood group. From the 1970s traditional popular Furnival patterns, such as 'Chelsea', 'Denmark' and 'Quail', have been produced by Wedgwood's Mason's Ironstone division at Hanley.

**FURNIVAL & WEAR, Tunstall & Cobridge, c.1844-45.**
This little-known partnership between Jacob Furnival and William Wear appears to have potted initially at Tunstall and subsequently at Cobridge. It was dissolved on 13 February 1845, at which period the address was Cobridge. Jacob Furnival was to pay all debts.

Apart from the official dissolution of partnership notice the firm does not show in other records and the partnership was presumably of short duration.

It is probable that typical ironstone-type wares of the period were produced and the 'F. & W.' initial marks may relate to this short-lived partnership.

**G.**

Whereas single letters always can relate to a number of different manufacturers or locations, it should be noted that various marks incorporating the initial 'G' were found on the Belle Vue Pottery site at Hull in 1970. The situation, however, is complicated by the appearance of impressed marks associated with the Swillington Bridge Pottery. The likely period of such pieces is *c.*1830-40.

See 'Hull Pottery' as reported in the *Northern Ceramic Society Newsletter* No. 99 of September 1995.

**THOMAS GATER & Co., Burslem, c.1885-94.**

Named marked examples of ironstone from this firm have been reported. Messrs Gater Hall & Co. succeeded and worked the Furlong Lane Pottery at Burslem (*c.*1895-98) and then the New Gordon Pottery, Tunstall, into the present century.

**GAUDY IRONSTONE,**
**GAUDY DUTCH,**
**GAUDY WELSH.**

These terms originated in America. They are widely used there and have spread to the British Isles, where they are little understood!

In very simple terms these 'Gaudy' designs are what we might regard as watered-down cottagey Japan patterns. By watered-down I mean they were repetitive, broadly-painted patterns seemingly produced by inexpensive labour, to set simple designs. They, like other more costly, intricate, Japan patterns, combine areas of underglaze-blue with overglaze enamels. Thin gilding was sometimes added to highlight the design. This inexpensive gilding can sometimes appear similar to a lustre.

The 'Gaudy' patterns were in the main unmarked and seldom bore even a pattern number. They are consequently difficult to attribute although known or probable makers include:

| | |
|---|---|
| William Adams | T. Walker |
| Davenport | E. Walley |
| Harvey | Wood |
| Riley | Enoch Wood & Sons |
| Rogers | |

Most Gaudy Dutch or Gaudy Welsh designs are tea wares made within the approximate period 1815-45. In my experience little of this type was produced on a true ironstone body but Americans use the term 'Gaudy Ironstone' when, to quote from Sam Laidacker, 'an opaque pottery or semi-porcelain was used'.

None the less, some hand-painted Gaudy or simple Japan-type designs do bear ironstone marks and the term 'Gaudy Ironstone' is certainly one used by American writers, dealers and collectors. It is as yet not used in the British Isles, perhaps because these wares are seldom seen in the country of their origin.

As the terms were coined in America and the Gaudy wares are very collectable there, it is relevant to list some of the specialist American books which will give illustrations and information about them.

*Anglo-American China*, Part 1, by Sam Laidacker (privately published, Bristol, PA, USA, 1st edition 1938, revised edition, 1954).
*Anglo-American China*, Part II (as above, 1951).
*The Collector's Encyclopedia of Gaudy Dutch & Welsh*, by John A. Shuman III (Collector Books, Paducah, USA, 1991).

**GELSON Bros., Hanley, c.1868-76.**

This firm produced various earthenwares including export-market white ironstone or 'Imperial White Granite' at the Cobden Works in High Street, Hanley. Thomas Gelson & Co. succeeded in the period February 1876-78. Name marks have been recorded. These include examples with the early use of 'England', well before 1891.

**GILDEA & WALKER, Burslem, c.1881-85.**

This partnership between James Gildea and John Walker succeeded Bates, Gildea & Walker (1879-81) and formerly T.J. & J. Mayer at the Dale Hall Pottery, Burslem. Various earthenware and ironstone-type wares were produced by this partnership.

Assorted impressed or printed name or initial 'G. & W.' marks were used.

James Gildea succeeded in January 1885 and continued to *c.*1889.

**WILLIAM GILL (& Sons), Yorkshire, c.1859-80.**

Marks incorporating the initials 'W.C.' may relate to William Gill who worked the Allerton Bywater Pottery, Castleford, Yorkshire, in the 1859-70 period and the Providence Pottery, Castleford, in the approximate period 1863-80. The firm later traded as William Gill & Sons.

**GODDARD & BURGESS, Merchants, Agents, Exporters, 1858-c.1890.**

This partnership between John Hackett Goddard (b.*c.*1820) and John Burgess succeeded Goddard, Dale & Burgess as from 30 June 1858.

Although these firms and the related American partnership, which traded as Burgess & Goddard (q.v.), were not themselves manufacturers, they played a very important part in the Staffordshire ceramic industry. They acted as purchasing agents or 'merchants' placing large orders with many firms. They were in a strong position to regulate American style forms and patterns and to control quality. As large cash customers their patronage was sought by large and small firms alike.

John Goddard, who was mainly resident in the potteries, kept a series of diaries (from 1851) which have fortunately been preserved in the family. These record countless transactions and the names of various suppliers. The long-running diary entries have been used to great advantage by Neil Ewins in his work on 'Staffordshire Ceramics and the American Market, 1775-1880' (*Journal of Ceramic History*, Vol. 15, 1997). The great influence held by such American purchasers is well explained, as is their trading methods, their preferences and the extent of their custom. The great depression in Anglo-American trade in the mid and late 1850s is also still felt via these diary notes. Mr Ewins rightly devotes twenty pages to the study of this American purchasing company and its activities in the Staffordshire Potteries. It is relevant and noteworthy that in 1881 John Goddard purchased the important firm of G.L. Ashworth & Bros. for his son, John Shaw Goddard. The firm thrived under the new owner and in later years was to be restyled Mason's Ironstone.

John Hackett Goddard died in the Potteries, at Longton Hall, in February 1885. The *Pottery Gazette* published a lengthy obituary notice of this 'very giant among men' and noted that it 'is impossible to estimate the loss such a gentleman as Mr Goddard entails upon a town like Longton'.

Further information on such Anglo-American partnerships is given in the 1997 *Journal of Ceramic Design* and in *Collecting Lustreware* by G.A. Godden and Michael Gibson (Barrie & Jenkins Ltd., London, 1991). The firm was continued by two of John Goddard's sons but it was not listed in 1892 local directories.

**A. GODFREY & SONS, Hanley, c.1886-90.**

This Hanley firm produced various earthenwares including white granite wares of export market-type during the approximate period 1886-90.

Printed name-marks have been recorded but 'A.G. & S.' initial marks may also have been used.

**JOHN & ROBERT GODWIN, Cobridge, c.1834-64.**

This partnership at Sneyd Street, Cobridge produced a range of various earthenwares, including 'Imperial Ironstone China'.

Various impressed and printed marks incorporate or comprise the initials 'J. & R.G.', sometimes with the Royal Arms device. The impressed initial mark sometimes has the additional initials 'B.B.' added above, perhaps for 'Best Body'.

**THOMAS GODWIN, Hanley, c.1834-54.**

Good-quality stone china ware occurs with the name 'THOS. GODWIN, BURSLEM' with or without the addition of a description of the body, e.g. 'Stone China', Thomas succeeded the former T. & B. Godwin partnership as from 15 January 1834.

**THOMAS & BENJAMIN GODWIN, Burslem, c.1890-34.**

T. & B. Godwin manufactured a wide range of earthenware decorated with fine-quality transfer-printed designs. Some ironstone-type ware was made under the description 'Stone China' after about 1820. Printed marks incorporate the initials 'T. & B.G.' The partnership was dissolved on 15 January 1834, after the death of Benjamin. Thomas then continued alone.

**GODWIN, ROWLEY & Co., Burslem, c.1828-31.**

This partnership between William Godwin, Thomas Rowley and others at the Market Place, Burslem, produced a range of earthenwares.

Blue printed useful wares bearing initial marks 'G.R. & Co' with the description 'Staffordshire Stone China' are believed to relate to this Burslem firm, although the initials could also refer to the earlier partnership of Godwin Rathbone & Co, at the same address.

Early in 1832 the Godwin and Rowley partnership was known as Godwin, Rowley & Johnson but this firm was dissolved on 25 April 1832. Marks incorporating the initials G.R. & J. could well relate to this short-lived partnership.

**GOODE & KENWORTHY, Tunstall, c.1879-88.**

The partnership between Frederick Lowndes Goode and Samuel Kenworthy potted at the Church Pottery, High Street, Tunstall, in the approximate period 1779-1888.

Ironstone-type earthenwares were produced and various initial 'G. & K.' and name marks occur, both printed and impressed.

**GOODE & WATTON, Tunstall, c.1888-90.**

This partnership between Frederick Lowndes Goode and William Watton at the Church Pottery, High Street, Tunstall, succeeded Messrs Goode & Kenworthy. The new partnership was dissolved on 18 January 1890, with Frederick Goode continuing.

Various earthenwares were produced and name or 'G. & W.' initial marks occur.

**THOMAS GOODFELLOW, Tunstall, c.1824-59.**
Thomas Goodfellow of the Phoenix Works, Tunstall made general earthenware, including ironstone-type ware bearing the name mark 'T. GOODFELLOW'. Various mark designs occur, sometimes incorporating the American eagle device or an anchor. The description 'Patent Ironstone China' has also been reported with his full name.

The estate was wound up by his executors in the 1860-61 period.

**JOHN GOODWIN, Longton, c.1841-51.**
John Goodwin (d.1857) of the Crown Pottery, Stafford Street, Longton, produced ironstone-type wares as well as the ordinary types of earthenware between 1841 and the end of 1851 before moving to the Seacombe Pottery, Birkenhead (Liverpool) in January 1852. Various printed marks occur incorporating the name of the pattern, the body description 'Ironstone' together with the name 'J. Goodwin'; the helpful place name 'Longton' or 'Seacombe Pottery, Liverpool', can also occur. One printed Royal Arms mark has been reported from America with the usual wording 'The Queen's Royal Ironstone' below the Royal Arms.

He most certainly produced ironstone wares when at Seacombe (q.v.) in the post-1852 period and this description occurs in several printed marks. For this period of his work see 'The Seacombe Pottery' by Helen Williams published in the *Journal of Ceramic History* No. 10, Stoke-on-Trent City Museums, 1978), the same authority's contribution 'The Goodwin Potteries at Longton and Seacombe' published in the *Journal of the Northern Ceramic Society*, Vol. 7, 1989, and Mrs Elizabeth Collard's article 'From Liverpool to Toronto' in *Collectors Guide* of November 1985.

For further information on this Longton firm the reader is referred to Rodney Hampson's specialist study 'Longton Potters 1700-1865' (*Journal of Ceramic History*, Vol. 14, City Museum & Art Gallery, Stoke-on-Trent, 1990).

**JOSEPH GOODWIN, Tunstall, c.1860.**
An impressed name mark, in oval surround, has been reported by American authorities; the mark includes the wording 'ironstone china'.

Yet it is difficult to confirm the link of this clear mark to a British potter of this name. There are many John and James Goodwins but only one Joseph.

A Joseph Goodwin, earthenware manufacturer, is included in the 1860 Post Office directory but he is not listed in Slater's 1862 *Directory of Staffordshire*. That name mark could relate to this Tunstall potter; I cannot suggest any other British contender.

**GEORGE GRAINGER, Worcester, c.1848-60.**
George Grainger, the Worcester porcelain manufacturer, introduced a thickly potted 'semi-porcelain' in about 1848. This or a similar body was called 'Chemical Porcelain'.

Although not really an ironstone-type body it can be mistaken for such and its main virtues are much the same – good looks, durability and low price. These virtues were cited in the *Art Journal* magazine of November 1848 when Grainger's semi-porcelain was first mentioned:

> ...for cleanness and beauty it is nearly equal to porcelain... it is vitrified throughout and has a sharp, clean fracture when broken... It combines the beauty of china with the economy of ordinary earthenware, as its price is little beyond the cost of the latter...

Some very decorative Grainger dessert services were made in this body in the 1848-60 period. Examples bear printed Grainger marks or the initials

GGW
SP

impressed into the body.

**WILLIAM GREEN, Longton, c.1849-56.**
William Green of the Anchor Works, Market Street, Longton, succeeded Broadhurst & Green from February 1849. Various printed marks occur incorporating the name 'W. GREEN' with descriptions such as 'Staffordshire Warranted Stone China'.

**THOMAS GRIFFITHS & Co., Lane End, Longton, c.1826-30.**
This firm potted at Flint Street, Longton in the 1826-30 period. They were succeeded by Messrs Griffiths, Beardmore & Birks, it being possible that one or both of these later partners were associated with Thomas Griffiths & Co.

As the short-lived Griffiths, Beardmore & Birks partnership certainly produced ironstone china, it is likely that the predecessors did also. 'T.G. & Co.' initial marks could therefore relate to this partnership.

**GRIFFITHS, BEARDMORE & BIRKS,**
**Lane End, Longton, c.1830.**
This partnership is listed in the Lane End (Longton) rate record for March, 1830. The names match the initials 'G.B. & B.' found on marked 'STAFFORDSHIRE IRONSTONE CHINA' with the pre-Victorian Royal Arms device.

The preceding firm at this Flint Street pottery, Lane End, was Thomas Griffiths & Co. (c.1826-30). It would appear that Messrs Beardmore & Birks succeeded in the 1831-43 period when the fuller address, St. Gregory's Works, High Street, Longton, is given.

For further information on this Longton firm the reader is referred to Rodney Hampson's specialist study 'Longton Potters 1700-1865' (*Journal of Ceramic History*, Vol. 14, City Museum & Art Gallery, Stoke-on-Trent, 1990).

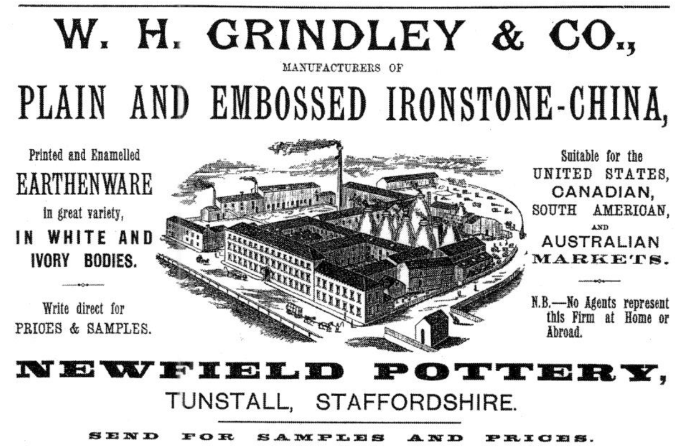


**W.H. GRINDLEY & CO. (LTD), Tunstall, c.1880-1991.**

This partnership was originally between William Harry Grindley (c.1867-1926) and Alfred Meakin at the Newfield Pottery, Tunstall, but Meakin left in March 1883 and W.H. Grindley continued alone. From c.1891 the address was the Woodland Pottery, Tunstall. The firm was a large concern producing plain and embossed ironstone 'in great variety... suitable for the Rome, United States and Colonial markets'. They were represented by Meakin & Taylor in New York. Much Grindley pottery is available and collected in America, especially the flow-blue patterns.

In post-war years the Grindley name has been taken over on several occasions being variously owned by Alfred Clough Ltd. (c.1960); by Royal Stafford China; by Federated Potteries; and was in 1991 reported as the largest failure in North Staffordshire since the early 1980s. In 1991 the Lambert Street factory at Tunstall employed some 320 persons. It was then purchased by Messrs Woodland Pottery (Holdings) and continued trading under the revised title Grindley Pottery Ltd.

Various impressed or printed marks occur incorporating the Grindley name in full, 'W.H. GRINDLEY & CO.' or simply 'Grindley' or 'Grindleys'. The names of various bodies – 'White Granite Vitrified', 'Satin-White', etc. also occur.

Whilst I doubt that the Grindley products are the subject of much interest in the country of their origin, I mention with pleasure the existence of a detailed privately published booklet on William Grindley and his potteries. This arose from a presentation by William H. Van Buskirk at the 1996 American Convention of the Flow Blue International Collectors Club Inc. It shows what can be done by dedicated enthusiastic collectors who set their minds to researching their pet subject. This is an example to us all! Not content with that the same American collector published a second booklet in June 1997 – *William H. Grindley*, Part II.

**GRINDLEY POTTERY Ltd., Tunstall, c.1986-present day.**

In the summer of 1986 Messrs Grindley of Stoke was acquired by Messrs Royal Stafford China and the old trade style was amended to Grindley Pottery Ltd., under which name it still trades.

Various marks incorporate this trade name. The trade description 'Satin White' has been continued from Grindley of Stoke and previously from W.E. Grindley & Co. Ltd.

**GRINDLEY HOTEL WARE Co. Ltd., Tunstall, c.1908-1979.**

This firm has produced a range of hotel wares including 'Duraline', a name which occurs on all marks. The Duraline Hotelware Co. Ltd. succeeded in 1979.

**GROSE & Co. Stoke, c.1867-69.**

Messrs Grose & Co. potted at the Bridge Pottery, Church Street, Stoke. Little is recorded of this small, short-lived concern but ironstone or stone china-type printed table wares have been reported. These bear a large British Royal Arms mark with 'Grose & Co. Stoke-upon-Trent' added below.

**HACKWOOD, Shelton and Hanley, c.1827-50.**

Several potters with the surname Hackwood worked in the Staffordshire Potteries in the nineteenth century producing good quality earthenware of various descriptions. A printed mark of an urn with a swag containing the words 'IRONSTONE CHINA' occurs on ware bearing the impressed name mark 'Hackwood', c.1830-50. These wares include octagonal Mason-type jugs, often with relief-moulded motifs. The body, however, appears to be a standard pottery rather than the heavier more compact ironstone.

The main possible manufacturers include:

William Hackwood, Eastwood, Hanley c.1827-43
Josiah Hackwood, Upper High Street, Hanley c.1842-43
William & Thomas Hackwood, New Hall Pottery, Shelton c.1843-50
Thomas Hackwood, New Hall Pottery, Shelton c.1850-55

Most authorities give only the surname Hackwood. They seem to be referring to William Hackwood of Eastwood, c.1827-1843. The preceding partnership was the lengthy one which traded as Hackwood, Dimmock & Co. in the approximate 1807-1827 period. See the following entry.

**HACKWOOD, DIMMOCK & Co., Hanley, c.1807-27.**

This partnership between William Hackwood, Thomas Dimmock and James Keeling, trading at Hanley, was dissolved on 11 November 1827.

It is very possible that some of the 'H.D. & Co.' initial marked earthenwares and stone chinas usually attributed to the short-lived firm of Henry Daniel & Co. (c.1834) were produced by Hackwood, Dimmock & Co.

**RALPH HALL (& Co.) or (& Son), Tunstall, c.1822-49.**

Ralph Hall produced a range of very good quality earthenware bearing fine printed designs, sometimes expressly made for the American market. Marks from 1822-41 incorporate the name 'R. Hall', 'R. Hall & Son' or 'R. Hall's'. From c.1841-49 the style became Ralph Hall & Co., during which time marks included the initials 'R.H. & Co.' or the fuller name 'R. Hall & Co.' Some ornate printed marks incorporate the description 'Stone China'. Podmore, Walker & Co. succeeded the firm (q.v.).

RALPH HAMMERSLEY,
OVER HOUSE POTTERY, BURSLEM,
AND BLACK WORKS, TUNSTALL,
MANUFACTURES
IRONSTONE, CHINA, & GENERAL EARTHENWARE,
EGYPTIAN BLACK, and ROCKINGHAM.
Specially adapted to the Home and Colonial Trade, also the United States of America and Continental Markets.
Real Ironstone China in shapes suitable for Hotels, Ships, &c. &c.
London Show Rooms—Mr. JOHN BROCK, 10, THAVIES INN, HOLBORN, E.C. *Prices and Particulars upon application.*

**RALPH HAMMERSLEY (& Son), Tunstall and Burslem, c.1859-1905.**

Ralph Hammersley took over Anthony Shaw's pottery in High Street, Tunstall, in about 1859 and seemingly continued to make similar ironstone and granite-type wares. The Burslem works date from c.1880.

Ralph Hammersley's advertisement lists 'IRONSTONE CHINA & GENERAL EARTHENWARE... specially adapted to the home and colonial trade, also the United States of America and continental markets. Real ironstone china in shapes suitable for Hotels, ships, etc. etc...' Early marks incorporate the initials 'R.H.' The firm's style was amended to Ralph Hammersley & Sons in 1803 and marks then incorporated the initials 'R.H. & S.'

The trade name 'IRONITE' was registered in January 1903. The Ralph Hammersley designs, etc., were sold to various buyers in March 1905.

**B.K.S. HANCOCK.**
The printed mark B.K.S. Hancock has been cited by American authorities. In giving and reproducing this mark the ampersand '&' has apparently been misread as 'K', making a simple 'B. & S. Hancock' marking into a non-existent B.K.S. Hancock. See B. & S. Hancock.

**B. & S. HANCOCK, Stoke, c.1876-1881.**
This partnership between Benjamin Hancock and Sampson Hancock worked the Bridge Pottery, Church Street, Stoke. from about 1876 until the dissolution of partnership on 31 December 1881, after which Sampson Hancock again traded under his own name (q.v.).

Name or initial 'B. & S.H.' marks occur.

**S. HANCOCK (& Sons), Tunstall and Stoke c.1858-1935.**
Sampson Hancock worked various potteries in Tunstall and Stoke and the succeeding firm of S. Hancock & Sons continued to the mid-1930s. Sampson Hancock's first pottery, of the 1858-68 period, was the Victoria Pottery, Tunstall. For a period c.1876-81 he potted in partnership with Benjamin at Stoke but then worked the Bridge Pottery at Stoke under his own name until 1891.

In 1891 the firm's style was amended to Sampson Hancock & Sons and in 1892 the firm moved to the Gordon Pottery, Wolfe Street, Stoke.

Various types of useful earthenware were produced including ironstone and granite-type wares, often of export type. Various name or initial 'S.H.' or 'S.H. & S.' marks occur.

**W. & G. HARDING, Burslem, c.1851-55.**
This partnership between William and George Harding worked the Furlong Pottery, Navigation Road, Burslem. The partnership was dissolved on 31 March 1855, after which William Harding continued.

Various types of earthenware were produced and marks incorporate the name 'W. & G. Harding' or the initials 'W.G.H.'

**W. & J. HARDING, Hanley, c.1863-69.**
This partnership between William and Joseph Harding of the New Hall Pottery, Hanley, succeeded the former Cockson & Harding partnership as far as it concerned earthenwares from 21 January 1863.

The Hardings produced various types of earthenwares including ironstone-type wares. Name or initial marks 'W. & J.H.' can occur.

**J.W. HARRIS, c.1835-50.**
Printed Royal Arms marks have been reported, with the description 'Ironstone China' and the name 'J.W. HARRIS'. Impressed marks 'I. HARRIS' have also been reported which could relate to the same potter, as 'J' was often rendered as 'I'.

However, I have been unable to trace any reference to a potter of this name. The wares included relief-moulded leaf-form dessert wares, and printed earthenwares of standard types of the approximate period 1835-50.

**C. & W.K. HARVEY (CHARLES HARVEY & Sons), Longton, c.1835-53.**
Charles and William Kenwright Harvey made good quality earthenware, including ironstone. The ironstone often bears the Royal Arms device with the description 'REAL IRONSTONE CHINA' and the initials 'C. & W.K. Harvey'. Holland & Green succeeded this firm (q.v.).

Some 'H' single-initial printed marks have been attributed to this firm. In some cases the attribution may well be correct but such 'H' initial marks could also have been used by other potters sharing H surnames.

For further information on this Longton firm the reader is referred to Rodney Hampson's specialist study 'Longton Potters 1700-1865' (*Journal of Ceramic History*, Vol. 14, City Museum & Art Gallery, Stoke-on-Trent, 1990).

**J. HAWTHORN, Cobridge, c.1879-82.**
John Hawthorn potted at the Abbey Pottery, Cobridge in the 1879-1882 period producing various types of earthenware, including ironstone-type wares. He registered two oval tureen forms, presumably for complete dinner services, on 19 March 1879. He may have continued at Liverpool Road, Burslem, until 1887.

Name or initial 'J.H.' marks occur sometimes with 'Cobridge'.

**JOSEPH HEATH, Tunstall, c.1841, 1845-53.**
Joseph Heath is recorded at the Newfield Pottery, Tunstall, in 1841 and at High Street, Tunstall, from 1845-53. Ironstone-type ware bearing the name 'J. Heath' probably relates to this Tunstall potter.

The American authority, George L. Miller, has noted that a Heath was shipping white granite wares to Philadelphia in about 1848.

It should be noted, however, that Joseph Heath traded as J. Heath & Co. (or Joseph Heath & Co.) during the earlier period, c.1828-41 – see the following entry.

**JOSEPH HEATH & Co., Newfield Pottery, Tunstall, c.1828-41.**
Good quality general earthenware was made, sometimes with North American transfer-printed views. Marks include 'J. Heath & Co.' – the initial 'J' can appear as 'I', this being a normal practice of the period. Simple initial marks 'J.H. & Co.' or 'I.H. & Co.' could relate to this potter, provided the piece is of this 1828-41 period.

The firm's bill-head shows an attractive engraving of the seated Britannia surrounded by crates of earthenware with shipping – underlining the firm's large export trade.

Printed patterns on a surviving 1839 written invoice included the following: 'Milanese', an (American?) 'Argllis', 'Indian Chief', 'Egyptian', 'Gothic', 'Jordan' and 'Persian'. The main colours were described as blue or purple.

**J.E. HEATH Ltd., Burslem, c.1950-96.**
J.E. Heath Ltd., of the Albert Potteries at Burslem, produce a good quality hotel-type ware, much of which is exported. The trade name 'Flintstone' was introduced in February 1963. The main trade name is 'Armorlite'. This occurs in most modern 'Heath' marks along with the 'BS' (British Standard) number '4034'. Messrs J.E. Heath Ltd, is part of the Dudson Brothers group.

The firm was retitled Dudson Armorlite Ltd. in 1996.

**HEATH & BLACKHURST, Burslem, 1859-77.**
John Heath and Abraham Blackhurst worked the Hadderidge Pottery, Bath Street, Burslem, from November 1859 in succession to W. & G. Harding. The partnership was dissolved on 26 July 1877, after which the works were continued by Blackhurst & Tunnicliffe.

Various types of earthenwares were produced mainly for the home market, but it would seem that granite-type wares were also produced.

Various name or initial 'H. & B.' marks were employed, usually within a garter-type surround.

The alternative trade title, Heath, Blackhurst & Co., was employed *c.*1866.

**HEATH, BLACKHURST & Co., Burslem, 1859-77.**
This is an alternative title for Messrs Heath & Blackhurst, presumably employed when there was a further partner in the concern. It was the title used by James Lidstone at the period of his 1866 *The Thirteenth Londoniad*.

John Heath and Abraham Blackhurst worked the Hadderidge Pottery, Bath Street, Burslem, in succession to W. & G. Harding from November 1859. The partnership was dissolved on 26 July 1877.

Various types of earthenware were made including granite-type wares.

The partnership, when trading under this extended title, probably used 'H.B. & Co.' initial marks, but the firm was more usually known as Heath & Blackhurst – see the preceding entry.

**HERCULANEUM POTTERY, Liverpool, c.1820-40.**
The Herculaneum pottery company (Samuel Worthington & Co.) at Toxteth Park, Liverpool (*c.*1796-1840), produced in the approximate period 1820-40 a good selection of earthenware table wares which were normally printed in underglaze-blue. Good decorative coloured-in printed outline patterns were also produced. A good export trade was enjoyed, particularly to North American markets.

Some printed marks incorporate the description 'Stone China', but the body is usually of normal earthenware type, not extra heavy or vitrified. The standard name-mark 'HERCULANEUM' can occur impressed or as part of various printed marks.

The standard book on this factory is *The Illustrated Guide to Liverpool Pottery* by Professor Alan Smith (Barrie & Jenkins, London, 1970). In recent years much research has been carried out on these nineteenth century Liverpool wares and several exhibitions held. An occasional newsletter, 'The Herculaneum Echo', is published by Peter Hyland of Berkhamsted.

The ownership of the pottery changed at various periods, the last being Messrs Mort & Simpson. The last partnership was dissolved as from 1 December 1840 and the Herculaneum Dock was built on the old factory site.

**HICKS & MEIGH, Shelton (Hanley), c.1803-22.**
This partnership between Richard Hicks (b.1765) and Job Meigh, potting at High Street (now Broad Street), Shelton (Hanley), was an extremely important one which produced a wide range of good quality earthenwares including stone china and later richly decorated porcelains.

Name or initial marks are extremely rare but the following basic types of printed marks are attributed to the Hicks & Meigh and to the succeeding Hicks, Meigh & Johnson partnership. The attribution was I believe first made by the late Alfred Meigh in his private researches and was published by the present writer. There has now been shown to be a helpful linkage of forms between these 'Stone China' marks and the Hicks porcelains – see Chapter 17 of *Staffordshire Porcelain*.

PLATE 187. A *Hicks & Meigh 'Stone China' dinner service plate decorated with printed outline coloured-in pattern 2. The eighteenth century standard Chinese export-market porcelain shape is still retained. Diameter 9¾in. (24.76cm). c.1813-22.*

PLATE 188. *The reverse side of the Hicks & Meigh plate in Plate 198 showing the Chinese-style of trimmed footrim and its printed 'Stone China' Royal Arms mark. The painter's initial mark appears near the footrim.*

If the Hicks stone china dates from approximately 1813, when Mason's Patent Ironstone China was introduced, then these marks will obviously date from that period onwards. The great (self-inflicted) problem is to determine which are Hicks & Meigh and which are Hicks, Meigh & Johnson marks used after 1822. This one feels is almost impossible as many of the same popular and colourful earlier patterns would have been continued by the succeeding partnership. The same pattern numbers and marks would also have been used. Further printed marks are shown on page 265. Some or all of these may have been used in the Hicks & Meigh period.

Messrs Hicks & Meigh was probably one of the first and amongst the leading manufacturers of stone china, with Spode and Davenport. The general quality is very

PLATE 189. *A typical good quality Hicks & Meigh marked 'Ironstone Warranted' tureen and cover (missing its stand) decorated with a printed outlined Japan pattern, number 5. 12in. (30.48cm) high.* c.*1813-22.*

high and the decoration usually comprised richly decorated so-called 'Japan' patterns, of the types shown in Plates 189-200.

Apart from dinner and dessert services, some stone china tea services (see Plate 199) were also made, although more often these were produced in the partnership's porcelain body. With the dinner and soup plates it is interesting to see that the footrim is turned

PLATE 190. *A typical and popular Hicks & Meigh's Chinese export-market form plate. Hicks printed outline pattern number 5. Crown and 'Ironstone Warranted' mark (as page 253). Diameter 9in. (22.86cm).* c.*1813-22.*

PLATE 191. *A standard, indented edged Hicks & Meigh 'Ironstone Warranted' plate. In this case the pattern number 5 is hand-painted near the footrim. Diameter 9¾in. (24.76cm).* c.*1813-22.*

PLATE 192. *Hicks and Meigh's colourful Japan pattern number 7, here shown on typical dessert wares. Centrepiece 13in. (33.02cm) long. c.1815-22.*

away in the manner of the Chinese examples and that sometimes the Hicks potters even went to the trouble of colouring the turned-away section to make them appear even more like the Chinese specimens. Such a Hicks example is shown in Plate 188. The edge of the plate is also often likewise tinted in the Chinese fashion, not gilt. The post-1815 Hicks tureens, however, are modelled to the British nineteenth century taste.

Although the partnership dates back to the early years of the nineteenth century, the ironstone bodies will date from c.1813 onwards. In 1822 the partnership was enlarged to take in the firm's chief traveller Johnson, which gave rise to the new style Hicks, Meigh & Co. or more usually Hicks, Meigh & Johnson (see following entry). However, it is extremely difficult to differentiate between the articles made by the pre-1822 firm and those made by the post-1822 enlarged partnership. The basic marks of the first period were almost certainly continued by the new firm – which continued production without change in designs or marks. Saleable early patterns continued in production for as long as they sold.

PLATE 194. *Detail showing the typical printed outline of pattern 8. These guidelines were then neatly coloured in by an enameller and sometimes gilding also was added.*

PLATE 193. *A Hicks & Meigh 'Stone China' soup plate from a dinner service. The typical printed outline coloured-in design (see Plate 194) is Hicks pattern number 8. The painter's tally-letter 'M' added in enamel. Diameter 9½in. (24.13cm). c.1813-22.*

The following basic printed marks occur incorporating the description 'Stone China'. These marks can occur printed in underglaze-blue or in overglaze colours, the colour being related to that used for the printed pattern or outline for the then painted-in design.

The early pattern numbers, perhaps below forty, will have been introduced by the first partnership Hicks & Meigh. The octagonal framed mark probably predates the Royal Arms device but as this mark was engraved as part of the original copper-plate the early mark will occur whenever the copper-plates were used.

PLATE 195. *A superb and typical Hicks & Meigh dinner service soup tureen decorated with pattern 8 (as Plates 193-196). Length 15in. (38.1cm). c.1813-22.*

PLATE 196. *Another form of Hicks & Meigh dinner service tureen bearing pattern number 8 as shown under the Royal Arms mark. 15in. (38.1cm) long.* c.1813-22.

PLATE 197. *Further Hicks & Meigh dinner service forms, decorated with pattern number 9. An attractive well-engraved design seemingly more favoured than Davenport's version (see page 261). Tureen 12½in. (31.75cm) high.* c.1815-22.

PLATE 198. *A Hicks & Meigh 'Stone China' Royal Arms marked soup plate bearing this colourful largely hand-painted pattern 13. See Plate 188 for reverse side. Diameter 9½in. (24.13cm). c.1815-22.*

The version of the Royal Arms used in marks is, of course, the pre-Victorian version with the inescutcheon or small inner shield. The type of hard, durable body 'Stone China' is given under the arms. Unusually the work's number for the pattern is incorporated under the mark. This prominent feature may well be unique to Hicks at this early period but some examples have the pattern number added by hand, often separate from the main mark. Painter's personal tally marks can also occur.

PLATE 199. *A rare Hicks & Meigh 'Stone China' Royal Arms marked teacup and saucer of pattern number 13. Hicks produced most tea sets in the porcelain body. Diameter of saucer 5½in. (13.97cm). c.1815-22.*

PLATE 200. *A colourful Hicks & Meigh dinner plate, mounted in metal to form a basket. Royal Arms 'Stone China' printed mark. Pattern number 20, a variation on pattern 13, shown previously. Diameter 10in. (25.4cm). c.1815-22.*

PLATE 201. *A blue printed Hicks & Meigh gadroon-edged soup plate of pattern 21. The design is engraved to show different shades of intensity of underglaze blue. Royal Arms 'Stone China' mark with 'No. 21' below. Diameter 10in. (25.4cm). c.1815-22.*

PLATE 202. *A rare footed cheese stand from a Hicks & Meigh dinner service with Royal Arms 'Stone China' mark with pattern number 23 below. The basic print is neatly coloured in by hand. Diameter 12in. (30.48cm), 2½in. (6.35cm) high. c.1815-22.*

PLATE 203. *A selection of pieces from a Hicks & Meigh Stone China dinner service, decorated with underglaze-blue printed pattern 21 but with gilt edge and trim. Large platter 16in. x 12½in. (40.64cm x 31.75cm). c.1815-22. Messrs Sotheby's, New York.*

PLATE 204. *Representative components from a Hicks & Meigh dinner service bearing the well-engraved basket of flowers pattern which was neatly overpainted by hand. Tureen 15in. (38.1cm) long. c.1815-22. Messrs Christie's.*

PLATE 205. *Representative dinner plates from a typical Hicks, Meigh & Johnson Stone China dinner service decorated with an intricate Japan pattern, rather similar to number 13. Royal Arms mark with 'LIV' below (54). Tureen 16in. (40.64cm) long. c.1832-35. Messrs Phillips.*

**HICKS, MEIGH & Co., Shelton (Hanley), c.1822-35.**

**HICKS, MEIGH & JOHNSON.**

In 1822 Richard Hicks and Job Meigh (of the previous Hicks & Meigh partnership), took their traveller or chief salesman, Johnson, into partnership. The resulting firm was variously called Hicks, Meigh & Co. or more usually Hicks, Meigh & Johnson.

From 1822 until c.1835 the firm produced a very good range of earthenware, stone china and fine quality porcelain but unfortunately relatively few examples bear a helpful name mark. Some printed marks normally found on printed earthenwares incorporate the initials 'H.M. & J.', usually appearing as 'H.M. & I.'

The standard marks on stone china appear to be versions of the following printed Royal Arms or crown marks. The pattern number was usually boldly added under the Royal Arms mark. In this way buyers, sellers and others could easily refer to the pattern, as was the case when Henry Davenport's London partner wrote in 1825, 'I am sorry to say everybody prefers Hicks & Co's no 9 to any of ours'. This design is shown in Plate 197. Whilst Davenport's own 'Stone China' wares were very good the Hicks specimens are normally rather richer in the colouring, particularly with regard to the bold Japan patterns.

The Hicks, Meigh & Johnson works were large and maintained to a high standard. The 1833 Government report stated that at that time six hundred persons were employed and that the Pottery was 'well conducted: great order and regularity are manifest all through the establishment. The hours are fewer here than in some other works; in summer from six to six, in winter from seven to six...'

It is very difficult to differentiate between the earlier, pre-1822, Hicks & Meigh Stone Chinas and the post-1822 Hicks, Meigh & Johnson products. Some shapes would have been continued as were, of course, the popular, still selling Hicks & Meigh patterns. I have featured in Plates 205-210 some of the numbered

PLATE 206. *A superbly engraved underglaze-blue printed dinner service meat platter. Royal Arms 'Stone China' mark with '61' added below. 13in. x 10¼in. (33.02cm x 26.03cm). c.1822-35.*

PLATE 207. *Hicks, Meigh & Johnson gadroon-edged Stone China dinner wares decorated with the very fussy pattern 66. Royal Arms mark. Vegetable tureen 12½in. (31.75cm) long. c.1822-35. Messrs Sotheby's.*

PLATE 208. *Representative pieces from a Hicks, Meigh & Johnson dessert service of pattern 69. The shapes link with Hicks porcelain dessert sets and some marked earthenwares (see Plate 209). Printed Royal Arms 'Stone China' mark with pattern number. Centrepiece 6in. (15.24cm) high. c.1822-35.*

patterns in excess of number 50. This division may well be arbitrary. However, Plate 211 shows an earlier numbered pattern but on a shape associated with 'H.M. & J.' initial marked examples.

The partnership was terminated in 1835, when Richard Hicks retired. The working materials, moulds, copper-plates, etc., were sold by auction in May 1835 and the pottery was taken over by Messrs Ridgway, Morley, Wear & Co. (q.v.). The works were subsequently taken over by G.L. Ashworth & Bros. (q.v.) and the present firm of Mason's Ironstone (part of the Wedgwood Group) now occupies the former Hicks & Meigh site. Some of the old Hicks pattern books are still preserved, having been handed down through the succeeding owners of the pottery.

The Hicks firm, with its various titles – Hicks & Meigh, Hicks, Meigh & Co., and Hicks, Meigh & Johnson – was undoubtedly one of the leading manufacturers of the colourful durable stone china wares of the 1810-35 period. Its tradition and standards were continued by later firms.

The following basic marks are believed to have been used by Hicks, Meigh & Johnson sometimes continuing earlier Hicks & Meigh marks. Many variations occur, as do different pattern numbers. It must be admitted, however, that some rival firms may have used very similar marks and that consequently some stone chinas at present attributed to Hicks &

PLATE 209. *A rare marked 'Oriental Shells [pattern name] H.M. & J.' dessert service footed dish, with upstanding handles. This and other initial marked earthenwares help to identify unmarked Stone China examples – as shown in Plate 208. 10¼in. x 8½in. (26.03cm x 21.59cm). c.1822-35.*

PLATE 210. *A well-engraved Hicks, Meigh & Johnson dinner service plate of typical gadrooned form. Coloured-in pattern 71 Royal Arms 'Stone China' mark. Diameter 10½in. (26.67cm). c.1822-35.*

PLATE 211. *A good quality Hicks, Meigh & Johnson Stone China dinner service tureen, decorated with earlier pattern number 23. This shape was also used on a smaller scale for dessert service tureens. Royal Arms 'Stone China' mark. 12in. (30.48cm) high. c.1822-35.*

Meigh or to Hicks, Meigh & Johnson could have been made by other potters.

The Hicks Stone China pattern numbers seem to have been quite different and much lower than those used for porcelain or standard earthenware designs. A note in the pattern book suggests that the Hicks, Meigh & Johnson Stone China pattern numbers did not exceed 128.

PLATE 212. *A Hicks, Meigh & Johnson stone china dessert dish, the edge with slight relief moulding. Royal Arms mark with '107', a variation on the earlier pattern 8 – see Plate 193. 8¼in. (20.95cm) long. c.1822-35. Messrs Phillips.*

**THOMAS HIGGINBOTHAM.**
**HIGGINBOTHAM, THOMAS & Co.**
**HIGGINBOTHAM & Son, Dublin, Ireland.**

Thomas Higginbotham was, like Donovan, a leading wholesaler and retailer of various types of ceramics, centred on Dublin.

His name marks occur on various types and makes of English ironstone-type table wares, not only Mason's.

Normally only his name appears as part of the mark so that this can be taken to be the manufacturer – a common occurrence with retailers' name marks.

Thomas Higginbotham was in business (at various Dublin addresses) from the 1790s. At one period in the c.1830s Thomas and Edward Higginbotham were in partnership with William Thomas, trading until April 1841 as Higginbotham, Thomas & Co. On William Thomas' retirement the firm seemingly traded as Higginbotham & Son. Many printed marks, however, use only the simple surname as a mark – such as

Higginbotham
Grafton Street,
Dublin

found on a Francis Morley & Co. ironstone dinner service of the 1845-58 period.

**P. HOLDCROFT & Co., Burslem, 1846-53.**

This firm worked the Lower Works, Fountain Place, Burslem from c.1846. Little is known of their product but the firm is associated with American market ironstone-type wares.

Peter Holdcroft apparently died before the partnership was dissolved in July 1853, when Mary Holdcroft was the main partner.

Name or initial 'P.H. & Co.' marks can occur.

**HOLDCROFT, HILL & MELLOR, Burslem, c.1860-70.**

This partnership is listed at the High Street Pottery, Burslem, in the approximate period 1860-1865 and then at Queen Street, Burslem, until 1870.

Various printed initial marks occur incorporating the initials 'H.H. & M.'

**JOHN HOLDEN, Burslem, c.1846.**

The name mark HOLDEN has been reported on American-market Spatterware. The American authorities, Earl and Ada Robacker, suggest that this simple mark could relate to an American potter, Jesse Holden of Sleubenville, Ohio.

It should be noted, however, that John Holden potted at the Knowl Pottery, Burslem, in the mid-1840s but was declared bankrupt in November 1847.

**W.T. HOLLAND, Llanelly, South Wales, 1858-68.**

William Thomas Holland succeeded Messrs Coombs & Holland at the South Wales Pottery, Llanelly from 21 May 1858.

As it is known that Coombs & Holland (page 218) produced some ironstone wares in 1855-58, it seems reasonable to assume that Holland also did so, using the former unhelpful simple impressed marks 'IRONSTONE CHINA' or merely 'IRONSTONE'. If printed marks also occur they will incorporate the initials 'W.T.H.'

W.T. Holland was joined by David Guest in 1868, giving rise to the Holland & Guest partnership, 1868-75 (not known to have produced ironstone).

**HOLLAND & GREEN, Longton, c.1853-80.**

Holland & Green succeeded C. & W.K. Harvey (q.v.). Elisha Holland had died by July 1800 and his executor Thomas Holland retired on 8 July leaving John Green's two executors to continue the works for a short period. The Holland & Green ironstone-type ware was marked with the Royal Arms and the firm's name or 'H. & G. late Harvey' (or Harveys). White Granite wares, presumably for the North American market, was especially mentioned in the partnerships advertisements in the mid-1860s. The descriptive term 'Real Ironstone China' was used, in various marks.

For further information on this Longton firm the reader is referred to Rodney Hampson's specialist study 'Longton Potters 1700-1865' (*Journal of Ceramic History*, Vol. 14, City Museum & Art Gallery, Stoke-on-Trent, 1990).

**HOLLINSHEAD & KIRKHAM, Burslem, c.1870-76.**
**Tunstall, c.1876-90 at Woodland Street Pottery, c.1890-1956 at Unicorn Pottery.**

The partnership between John Hollinshead and Samuel Kirkham worked several potteries firstly at Burslem and then, from 1876, at Tunstall.

This well-known firm produced a large range of earthenwares including ironstone. Some marks, both printed and impressed, incorporate the initials 'H. & K.' with the wording 'Late J. Wedgwood' relating to the Woodland Street Works which this firm occupied in the period 1876-90. It is noteworthy that the printed names WEDG WOOD are combined to read WEDGWOOD.

**HOLMES, PLANT & MADEW, Burslem, c.1876-84.**

The partnership between Edwin Holmes, Ralph Plant and Thomas Madew at the Sylvester Pottery, Burslem produced a range of earthenwares and ironstone-type wares from *c.*1876 until the retirement of Thomas Madew on 24 June 1884, after which the remaining partners traded as Holmes & Plant or as Holmes, Plant & Co.

Various name and initial, 'H.P. & M.', marks occur during the 1876-1884 period.

**HOPE & CARTER, Burslem, c.1862-78.**

This famous partnership between John Hope and John Carter produced a good range of earthenwares including ironstone-type wares at the Fountain Place Works which was later taken over by Ashworths. The partnership exhibited at the Philadelphia Exhibition in 1876, featuring decorative earthenwares as well as American market White Granite goods. John Hope joined Ashworths which claimed to have purchased the 'whole of Hope & Carter's pattern and description books' and were in a position to supply replacements to Hope & Carter's wares well into the 1880s. Full name or initial 'H. & C.' marks occur, sometimes including the Royal Arms device, with descriptions such as 'Stone China'.

**HORNE & ADAMS, Hanley, c.1872.**

Neil Ewins in the *Journal of Ceramic History*, Vol. 15 of 1997, records the Horne & Adams partnership at Hanley as having supplied white granite wares to a firm in Philadelphia, the source of this information being the Warshaw Collection in the Museum of American History, Washington, DC.

I am unable to trace this firm as a manufacturing partnership in Staffordshire. It is, however, possible that the firm of Stanway, Horne & Adams was involved – see that entry.

**HOTEL WARE – see also page 172.**

Masons and many other manufacturers obviously were in the market to produce and sell sturdy wares for hotel keepers, as for example Mason's 'white patent ironstone china, as used in the hotels of the United States of America', featured at the 1851 Exhibition.

However, the demand for specialist so-called hotel wares is of comparatively recent date. The market seems to be vast, for such usually thickly potted table wares are now sold to tens of thousands of hotels, restaurants and other eating places. Several large modern firms, such as Dudsons, successfully concentrate on this trade, and other large companies have specialist hotelware divisions.

Printed or other marks incorporating the words 'Hotel', 'Hotel ware', etc., will post-date 1950. Modern durable hotel wares, whilst obviously designed to withstand hard use, can be very tastefully designed and decorated, although they are clearly mass-produced.

**JOHN THOMAS HUDDEN, Longton, c.1860-85.**

John Thomas Hudden commenced potting at Stafford Street, Longton, in about 1860 and continued until *c.*1885. He also worked the British Anchor Works at Longton during the period 1874-84.

The Hudden earthenwares can bear name or initial 'J.T.H.' marks.

**ELIJAH HUGHES, Cobridge, c.1853-67.**

Various ironstone-type wares bear printed marks incorporating the initials 'E.H.'

Such marks could relate to Elijah Hughes of the Bleakhill Works at Cobridge in the approximate period 1853-67.

Other Staffordshire potters with these initials include Elijah Hodgkinson of Hanley *c.*1867-72.

**STEPHEN HUGHES (& Son), Burslem, c.1853-55.**

Stephen Hughes potted at Waterloo Road, Burslem, in the approximate period 1853-55. He registered ironstone or granite-type tableware forms on 17 April 1855 (Parcel number 4), using the style 'Stephen Hughes & Son' of Burslem.

Various 'S. Hughes' name marks are recorded and should relate to this Burslem potter, but the trade style 'Stephen Hughes & Co.' is not recorded in other available records. Initial marks 'S.H.' or 'S.H. & S.' may occur.

**S. & E. HUGHES, Cobridge, c.1846-53.**

Stephen and Elijah Hughes potted at Bleakhill, Cobridge, from April 1846 to the dissolution of the partnership on 1 January 1853. This partnership succeeded Stephen Hughes & Co. (q.v.).

Various initial marks 'S. & E.H.' relate to this Cobridge partnership which produced various types of earthenware. The Hughes had interests in wholesale and retail outlets in Canada.

**STEPHEN HUGHES & Co., Cobridge, c.1835-46**

This partnership between Stephen Hughes, John Hughes and Elijah Hughes, potting at the Bleakhill Works, Cobridge, produced a large range of earthenwares and ironstone-type wares. The partnership was dissolved on 25 April 1846 and was succeeded by S. & E. Hughes (q.v.).

Various name or initial 'S.H. & Co.' marks occur, but see 'S.H. & Co.'

**THOMAS HUGHES, Burslem, c.1866-94.**
Thomas Hughes of Waterloo Road, Burslem, and of the Top Bridge Works, Longport (Burslem), produced granite and ironstone china mainly for the North American market – see also page 170. His ware was marked with the name T. Hughes, Thos. Hughes or Thomas Hughes, often with the Royal Arms device. 'England' can occur on the later specimens. Other printed marks incorporate the American eagle device and the name of the durable granite-type body, such as 'Imperial French Porcelain'.

A Thomas Hughes mark unaccountably occurs with a registration device for April 1855 but the official entry is in the name of Stephen Hughes & Son (q.v.). There is also confusion concerning Thomas Hughes' starting date which is sometimes quoted as 1860 but, until at least December 1865, he was in partnership with Enoch Bennett, trading as Hughes, Bennett & Co.

In the late 1880s Thomas Hughes purchased Davenport's Unicorn Works, in Davenport Street, Longport, and continued to trade from the new address under the amended style Thomas Hughes & Son – see the following entry.

**THOMAS HUGHES & Son (Ltd.), Longport, c.1894-1957.**
This firm succeeded Thomas Hughes as from about 1894, having acquired the former Davenport Unicorn Works at Longport. It continued the old lines and produced a range of durable granite-type wares for the North American market.

Its wares are normally plainly marked with the full name. Thomas Hughes retired in December 1899; Allan Hughes then continued, retaining the old title. 'Ltd.' was added to the firm's style in about 1910 and this addition is featured in the post-1910 printed mark here reproduced. Earlier versions do not have 'Ltd.' 'England' will also occur instead of 'Made in England'.

After the firm's closure in 1957, the Unicorn Works were taken over by Arthur Wood & Son but in 1961 part of the old pottery was taken by Unicorn Pottery Ltd.

**T. HULME, Burslem, c.1860.**
Thomas Hulme is recorded at the Central Pottery, Market Place, Burslem in about 1860. The partnership of Hulme & Booth had earlier occupied this address. The important firm of Burgess & Leigh succeeded Thomas Hulme at the Central Pottery in 1861 or 1862 and later worked other potteries – see Burgess & Leigh (Ltd.).

Various 'T. Hulme' marks have been reported on ironstone-type wares. It is probable that 'T.H.' initial marks also relate to this potter.

**HULME & BOOTH, Burslem, c.1851-54.**
This partnership at the central Pottery, Market Place, Burslem, produced a range of earthenwares, including ironstone or granite-type wares, in the approximate period 1851-54. Name marks have been recorded, also various marks incorporating the initials 'H. & B.'

**HUMPHREYS BROTHERS, Tunstall, c.1893-1901.**
This partnership between Joseph Humphreys and John Humphreys potted at the Gordon Pottery, Tunstall. from October 1893 to c.1901.

Various types of pottery were produced including ironstone or granite-type wares. Marks include 'H. BROS.' as well as the name in full.

**IMPERIAL STONE, c.1820-30s.**
An applied circular pad mark occurs on some well-made moulded jugs, usually of a tinted body. Typical examples are shown in R.K. Henrywood's book, *An Illustrated Guide to British Jugs* (Swan Hill Press, Shrewsbury, 1997), Plates 302-306.

This entry, with others, underlines the point that various ceramic bodies were described as 'stone', particularly in regard to jugs, but they are dissimilar to the standard ironstone and stone china bodies as used for painted table services.

**J. JACKSON & Co., Rotherham, Yorkshire, c.1870-87.**
The name Jackson on ironstone-type wares can refer to various Staffordshire potters of this name but most references relate to J. Jackson & Co. of the Holmes Pottery, at Rotherham, Yorkshire, in the approximate period c.1870-87.

The Staffordshire wares are of a earlier period such as those of Job and John Jackson of the Church Yard Works at Burslem, who were bankrupt in 1835.

John Jackson & Co. of Rotherham produced various earthenwares which Jewitt in 1878 described as being of the 'commoner class'.

Various marks occur incorporating the initials 'J J & Co.' 'Jackson's Warranted' marks probably relate to the Staffordshire manufacturers.

**J. & J. JACKSON, Burslem, c.1831-35.**
Job and John Jackson worked the Churchyard Pottery at Burslem in the early 1830s. They were adjudged

bankrupt in 1835.

Various types of earthenware, including blue printed wares for the American market, occur variously marked 'Jackson', 'Jackson's Ware' or 'Jackson's Warranted'. These marks most probably relate to this Staffordshire partnership, although other potters with this surname are recorded in the approximate period 1810-40. It should be noted that J. Jacksons were also potting in Yorkshire and in Scotland.

**JAMES JAMIESON & Co., Bo'ness, Scotland, c.1836-54.**

James Jamieson worked the Bo'ness Pottery, in Scotland, from 1836. A good range of printed wares, white or sponged earthenwares were produced. These may include ironstone-type bodies.

Most marks incorporate or comprise the name but initial marks 'J.J. & Co.' also occur. Some marks incorporate the misleading description 'Porcelaine Opaque'.

Printed marks of the approximate period c.1840-50 bearing single initial 'J' marks could relate to this Scottish manufacturer. Some Mason-type faceted-bodied jugs, for example, bear an 'Indian Stone Ware' mark with the initial 'J'.

**J.B. mark, Staffordshire, c.1845-50.**

American writers, including Mrs Ellouise Baker Larsen in her standard book, *American Historical Views on Staffordshire China* (3rd edition, Dover Publications, New York 1975), have noted the initial mark 'J.B.' with the subject description 'Texian Campaigue'.

This American-Mexican conflict is of the 1846-48 period and later Texian designs bear an 'A. Shaw' mark. With the discovery of marked specimens of Shaw's manufacture, the 'J.B,' mark has been reclassified as that of the designer. This is almost certainly incorrect; designers or engravers did not use backstamps.

If we assume that J.B. represents a Staffordshire manufacturer, we have the following possible makers, working in the 1846-55 period when such pieces would have been made for the American market:

| | |
|---|---|
| James Beech, Tunstall | c.1834-89 |
| Joseph Birch, Hanley | c.1847-51 |
| John Banford, Hanley | c.1850-83 |
| Jesse Bridgwood, Burslem | c.1847-54 |

I have included a separate entry for James Beech of Tunstall.

**'J.F.' mark.**

The initial mark 'J.F.' appears on ironstone-type useful wares. Usually the initials are alone but sometimes they appear with the Royal Arms device and the description 'Ironstone China'.

This mark has been tentatively attributed to Jacob Furnival but that Cobridge potter seems only to have traded as Jacob Furnival & Co., not alone. American researchers, however, have linked wares bearing initial marks with seemingly related examples bearing the full 'J Furnival & Co.' name.

It should be remembered that these initials fit several Staffordshire potters including:

James Floyd of Market Street, Fenton c.1847-57
John Farrall of Broad Street, Shelton c.1854-55
Joseph Finney of Victoria Place, Longton c.1858-59
John Ferneyhough of Stafford Street, Longton c.1867-73

**J.M. & Co.**

Various initial marks occur comprising or incorporating these initials. It should be noted that these could relate to various firms that manufactured during the ironstone period:

| | |
|---|---|
| J. Morris & Co. | c.1818-23 |
| J. Machin & Co. | c.1828-30 |
| J. Magness & Co. | c.1829-41 |
| J. Mayer & Co. | c.1841 |
| J. Marshall & Co. (Scotland) | c.1854-99 |
| J. Maudesley & Co. | c.1862-64 |

In addition to these British firms, the same initials could relate to overseas manufacturers such as John Moses & Co. of Trenton, New Jersey, USA. That company was one of many American firms which used British style markings, including copies of the British Royal Arms – see page 364

**REUBEN JOHNSON, Hanley, c.1817-38.**

Printed marks occur depicting the name 'JOHNSON/HANLEY' over the description 'Stone China'. These are believed to relate to this potter and to Phoebe Johnson who continued from c.1823-c.1838. A typical blue printed name mark is here reproduced but several slight variations occur.

**JOHNSON Bros., Hanley and Tunstall, c.1883 to present day.**

From the mid-1880s Johnson Bros. expanded greatly, buying up other firms and potteries in Hanley and Tunstall. Their large Hanley pottery was built in 1888 and their other factories included the Charles Street Works, the Imperial Pottery (formerly J.H. Davis' Trent Pottery), the new Trent Works at Hanley, erected in 1898, and the Alexandra Pottery at Tunstall, formerly occupied by G.W. Turner & Sons. Henry Johnson learnt the trade at Meakins of Tunstall.

Johnson Bros.' output was clearly very large and large amounts of ironstone-type wares were produced for our home and export markets. The trade style was amended to Johnson Bros. (Hanley) Ltd. in about 1898 but this designation is seldom given in the marks, which usually incorporate the simple name 'Johnson Bros.' The description 'Royal Ironstone Ware' also occurs in several printed or impressed marks.

The firm continued producing durable wares up to 1 January 1969 when it was taken over by the Wedgwood Group, which continued the traditional run of Johnson earthenwares. Towards the end of 1997, however, Johnson Bros. separated from Wedgwood and occupied the Eagle Pottery at Hanley.

Most modern marks incorporate the wording 'Johnson Bros. England', with the name of the pattern 'Indian Tree' etc., and such recent claims as 'all decoration under the glaze Detergent & Acid resisting colours. A genuine hand engraving. IRONSTONE'.

**DAVID JOHNSTON.**

Various printed or impressed marks comprise or incorporate this name. These wares were made in the British fashion by David Johnston's factory at Bordeaux in France in the approximate period 1835-45 – see page 366. However, his successors may have continued using the Johnston name into the 1860s.

**F. JONES (& Co.), Longton, c.1864-76.**

Frederick Jones continued the Stanley Pottery in Stafford Street, Longton, after the dissolution of the Jones & Ellis partnership on 16 September 1864. However, by at least 1868 he had taken Emanuel Moritz into a new partnership to trade as Frederick Jones & Co. This firm is recorded at Chadwick Street and at Stafford Street, Longton, in the 1868-76 period. Moritz left in January 1869 but the firm seems to have continued under the same name until *c.*1876.

Various granite-type wares bear F. Jones name marks sometimes incorporating the Royal Arms with the description 'Pearl Ironstone China'. One set of forms termed 'Victor' was registered by this firm on 9 September 1868.

**GEORGE JONES (& Sons), (Ltd.), Stoke, c.1862-1951.**

George Jones (1823-93) learnt his trade, or at least the sales side of it, as a commercial traveller for Wedgwoods in the 1840s. In the 1850s he traded as a pottery Commission Agent and dealer,

He set himself up as a manufacturer in 1862 by taking Adams' former Bridge Pottery at Stoke. In the 1864-65 period he built himself a new works – the Trent Pottery at Stoke. This was later (in 1873) renamed the Crescent Pottery and a crescent became the firm's trade mark device.

The Trent Pottery opened in 1865 and here was produced a good and wide range of earthenwares and stonewares. Later, porcelains were added to the range. From the start good quality ironstone-type wares were produced, mainly for the American market. The trade name Royal Patent Ironstone was often used, although many marks included the standard description 'Stone China' with the company name or initials. Coded letter year marks can occur or more helpful month and year numbers.

Minton's Art Director, Léon Arnoux, writing in 1876 noted that Messrs George Jones was one of the largest manufacturers of white granite wares for the American market. By 1870 over five hundred persons were employed. Various Victorian writers, such as Jewitt, singled out George Jones' white granite wares made for the colonies and for North America.

Today the firm is better known for its highly collectable (and expensive) colourful majolica – glazed novelties, for its essays in *pâte-sur-pâte*, or for the tasteful bone china goods. Yet, as late as the 1920s the less expensive white granite export-market wares were being featured in trade reports.

Several different George Jones name or initial marks occur, the initials 'J.G.' being normally rendered in monogram form:

By December 1873 the firm's trading style changed to George Jones & Sons, giving rise to new initial marks, 'G.J. & S.', on newly engraved designs. George Jones' sons working in the firm were initially Frank and George, later joined by Frederick and Charles. In 1873 also the Crescent trade name and trade mark was registered. The Crescent device, however, seldom appears on ironstone or granite wares. The firm became a limited liability company in 1894 and the abbreviation Ltd. may subsequently appear in marks.

With several present century changes in ownership George Jones & Sons Ltd. continued production at Stoke until 1951. A good detailed study of the firm's history and productions was published by Robert Cluett in 1997.

**GEORGE JONES & Co., Stoke, c.1862-73.**
The trade style George Jones & Co. was the correct one for George Jones' initial manufacturing partnership at Stoke. However, it would seem that the shorter title George Jones was more often used. Even the design registration entries are in George Jones' sole name.

Initial marks 'G.J. & Co.' may exist and, if relating to the 1862-73 period, could relate to this firm. For details of this Stoke firm, see the preceding entry.

**JONES & ELLIS, Longton, c.1862-64.**
This partnership between Frederick Jones, Josiah Ellis Jones and William Ellis produced various standard earthenwares at their Stanley Pottery, Stafford Street, Longton from at least 1862 to 16 September 1864, when the partnership was dissolved. Frederick Jones then continued the pottery.

The Jones & Ellis partnership registered a vase-centred dinner service printed design on 31 July 1862, this being the first record of the firm.

Full name marks or 'J. & E.' initial marks will relate to this short-lived partnership.

**KEELE STREET POTTERY Co. (Ltd.), Longton, c.1915-67.**
This twentieth century firm produced ironstone-type wares as well as general earthenwares. The marks incorporate the initials 'K.S.P.'

**KENSINGTON POTTERY Ltd., Hanley and Burslem, c.1922 onwards.**
This company was founded at the Kensington Works, Hanley in 1922. Various 'Kensington', 'K.P.H.' or 'K.P.B.' initial marks.

The original company ceased trading in the early 1960s but production was continued within the Arthur Wood & Son group and some wares continued to be marketed under the old 'Kensington Ironstone' trade mark.

**KERR & BINNS (KERR & Co.), Worcester, 1852-62.**
The Kerr & Binns partnership succeeded Messrs Chamberlain & Co., at Worcester. While this firm is mainly known for its fine quality porcelains it seems that some Stone China was produced.

A sale notice issued in March 1862 relating to the clearance of old stock pending the take-over of the new Worcester Royal Porcelain Company (usually known as Royal Worcester) featured 'Breakfast, Dinner, Dessert, Tea and Toilet services in Fine Porcelain and Stone China'.[13] This sale took place at the Royal Porcelain Works suggesting that the articles were produced at this factory, not bought in from other manufacturers for sale at the firm's London or Dublin showrooms. Messrs Chamberlain & Co., had in the preceding period also produced 'Granite' wares, see page 211.

Kerr & Binns' stone china should bear marks incorporating the initials 'K. & B.', or Kerr & Co., or 'Kerr & Binns' and will have been produced within the period 1852-62.

**R.A. KIDSTON (& Co.) (KIDSTON, COCHRAN & Co.), Glasgow, c.1838-46.**
Robert Alexander Kidston succeeded John Geddes at the Verreville Pottery, Glasgow, in about 1838. He brought in many new workers, some from the Staffordshire Potteries, and added the production of china to the normal types of earthenware.

The Verreville pottery produced ironstone or stone china-type wares and various Royal Arms and other marks incorporate the initials 'R.A.K.' or, more usually, 'R.A.K. & CO'.

In 1846 Robert Kidston took into partnership Robert Cochran, giving rise to the firm of Kidston, Cochran & Co., but in the following year Robert Cochran took over the Verreville pottery and traded as Robert Cochran & Co. The 1846-47 Kidston, Cochran & Co. firm may also have produced ironstone-type wares. Any 'K.C. & CO.', initial marks would relate to this short-lived firm.

**KNAPPER & BLACKHURST, Tunstall and Burslem, c.1867-71 and c.1882-87.**
This partnership between Stephen Knapper and Jabez Blackhurst traded at Sandyford, Tunstall, from *c.*1862 until January 1871, after which Blackhurst continued alone. However, the partnership appears to have been reconvened in 1882 when Messrs Knapper & Blackhurst took over Messrs James Edwards & Son's Dale Hall Pottery at Burslem, which they continued until *c.*1887.

At this period, in the 1880s at least, Knapper & Blackhurst produced durable ironstone and granite type bodies in the Edwards' style but bearing name or initial 'K. & B.' marks.

**J.K. KNIGHT, Foley, Fenton, c.1846-53.**
John King Knight succeeded the Knight, Elkin & Co. Partnership. He made stone china as well as other earthenware. Marks incorporate the initials 'J.K.K.' or the name 'J.K. Knight' or sometimes 'I.K. Knight', sometimes with the place name 'Foley' and the name of the body 'Stone China' etc.

**KNIGHT, ELKIN & Co. and KNIGHT & ELKIN, Foley, Fenton, c.1826-46.**
These firms at King Street, Fenton, produced a wide range of earthenwares including stone china and other ironstone-type wares which can bear name or initial 'K.E. & Co.' or 'K. & E.' marks. Messrs Knight & Elkin succeeded Knight, Elkin & Co. from 13 October 1843. The partners were John King Knight, George Elkin and John King Wood Knight.

A typical printed mark depicts the British Royal Arms and supports with the wording 'Knight, Elkin & Co's. Ironstone China' added below, sometimes with a painted pattern number.

**KNIGHT, ELKIN & BRIDGWOOD, Foley, Fenton, c.1827-40.**
I have a printed bill-head giving the name of this partnership and an engraving of their Foley Pottery at Fenton. However, other records list the firm as Elkin(s), Knight & Bridgwood in the period 1827-40, in succession to Elkin, Knight & Elkin *c.*1822-27.

The firm was called Elkins, Knight & Bridgwood until November 1833 after which the first Elkin became singular – Elkin, Knight & Bridgwood.

Whilst most marks will include the initials 'E .K. & B.', it is possible in view of the bill-head that the initials 'K.E. & B.' were also used.

**KNIGHT, SPROSTON & KNIGHT, Tunstall, c.1807-09.**
This partnership between Thomas Knight, John Sproston and James Knight of Tunstall purchased ground ironstone from the Breeze grinding mill in the 1807-09 period. It is not known what type of earthenware was being produced from this material, before the introduction of Mason's Patent Ironstone China in 1813, as no marked specimens of Knight, Sproston & Knights' wares are recorded.

Thomas Knight and John Sproston had previously traded as Knight & Sproston (*c.*1801+) and both firms also traded under the short title 'Sproston & Co.'

**F. LEA, Fenton, c.1829-36.**
Frederick Lea produced various types of useful earthenware at Cross Lane Pottery, Fenton, from 1829.

Initial marks 'F.L.' on ironstone-type wares datable to this brief period could well relate to this potter.

**SAMUEL LEAR, Hanley, c.1877-86.**
Samuel Lear occupied two works at Hanley, one in Mayer Street, the other in the High Street.

Whilst he is mainly known as a porcelain manufacturer and decorator, and as a manufacturer of majolica and ivory-bodied earthenwares, marked examples of his, stated to be in a white ironstone body, have been reported by American specialists.

**'LEEK POTTERY'.**
This name was used by some mid-nineteenth century authorities to describe Mason's ironstone, or place its location.

Early editions of William Chaffers' *Marks & Monograms on Pottery & Porcelain* index Mason under 'Leek Pottery' and the brief entry commenced 'Leek. A recent manufacture belonging to Mr Mason'. The initial reason for this description is perhaps explained in pre-1881 editions of Frederick Litchfield's *Pottery & Porcelain, a guide to Collectors*, where it is stated 'Their works were near Leek, Staffordshire'. The pottery was, however, no nearer Leek than scores of other factories in the Staffordshire Potteries.

The error had been noted by Llewellynn Jewitt in 1867 who began his *Art Journal* account of Mason's Ironstone China: 'The ware usually but erroneously known as Leek Pottery…'.

**LIDDLE ELLIOT (& Son)** – see Elliot, as Liddle is the first name.

**LIVERPOOL, c.1830-40.**
The 'Herculaneum' factory at Liverpool produced good quality stone china-type ware during the closing years of its existence, during the management of Case & Mort (*c*.1833-36) and then of Mort & Simpson (*c*.1836-40). This Liverpool stone china ware may bear the impressed 'Liver bird' mark, and specimens will probably be found in North America and in the other export markets enjoyed by this great seaport factory. The full story of the important Herculaneum Pottery is given in Alan Smith's *Illustrated Guide to Liverpool Herculaneum Pottery*, 1970. See also my Herculaneum entry.

**LIVESLEY & DAVIS, Hanley, c.1868-71.**
This partnership worked the Trent Pottery at Kirkham Street, Eastwood, Hanley from *c*.1868-71. Messrs J.R. & J. Davis succeeded.

Various types of useful earthenware were produced including granite wares for the American market.

Printed Royal Arms marks have been recorded with the description 'Royal Stone China' and the Livesley & Davis names. L. & D. initial marks may also have been employed by this relatively small, short-lived partnership.

**LIVESLEY, POWELL & Co. Hanley, c.1851-65.**
This partnership between William Livesley, Edwin Powell and Frederick Bishop worked two potteries at Hanley. It was an important firm producing a wide range of china and earthenwares. At the 1862 Exhibition the partnership exhibited decorative dinner, dessert and toilet services 'which for quality of the ware and for beauty and freshness of design, will bear comparison with the productions of the first houses in the trade.' At that time Livesley Powell & Co. introduced a new form of lithographic printing in gold and silver but the firm also showed 'white granite for the American market'. Other types of ironstone or granite-type decorated wares were also produced for the home and export market and at this period over four hundred work-people were employed.

William Livesley retired on 1 December 1865 and the works continued under the new style Powell & Bishop (q.v.). Various printed and impressed marks occur incorporating the name in full, or the initials 'L.P. & Co.', often with the name of the body or pattern.

**JOHN LOCKETT (& Co.), Longton, c.1830-1960.**
John Lockett (b.*c*.1807) traded at several addresses in Lane End and Longton over a long period up to *c*.1879 and up to recent times as John Lockett & Co.

John Lockett's potteries produced a wide range of mainly unmarked porcelain and earthenwares. At the time of the 1861 census he employed sixty-nine men, sixty-eight women, nineteen boys and nine girls. At the 1862 exhibition he displayed 'china, earthenware and stoneware'. However, it seems probable that the stoneware articles were in the main very utilitarian items. A review of the exhibits mentions good porcelains, earthenwares including lustred wares and black jet goods plus 'stoneware morters, pestles and other chemical apparatus, garden pots and stands...'

A later John Lockett & Co. nineteenth century trade card also lists as specialities 'stone mortars and pestles, covered pots, bed pans and all kinds of Druggists' earthenware'.

John Lockett had died by, or in, 1879 and the firm was continued under the style John Lockett & Co. by John William Hancock and Robert Lockett Hancock, John retired in March 1880 and was replaced by Frederick Cresswell. The firm continued under the Hancock family into the middle of the present century producing chemists' sundries, sickfeeders, storage jars etc. but the Longton pottery was sold and demolished in 1960. The goodwill was purchased by Messrs Burgess & Leigh Ltd. of Burslem and many traditional Lockett lines were continued and sold under the Lockett name. However, by the 1980s such stonewares and earthenwares were being replaced by stainless steel or plastic articles.

For further information on this Longton firm the reader is referred to Rodney Hampson's specialist study, 'Longton Potters 1700-1865' (*Journal of Ceramic History*, Vol. 14, City Museum & Art Gallery, Stoke-on-Trent, 1990).

**J. & T. LOCKETT, Longton, c.1836-54.**
John and his brother Thomas Lockett traded together in succession to John Lockett & Son at King Street and Market Street, Longton, from the mid-1830s. The partnership ceased on Thomas' death in 1854, after which John continued trading under his own sole name.

Various types of earthenware (and china) were produced including ironstone-type useful wares of good quality. Initial marks 'J. & T.L.' can be considered to relate to this partnership.

Detailed information on the various members of the Lockett family and the names of many patterns are given in Rodney Hampson's 'Longton Potters 1700-1865' (*Journal of Ceramic History*, Vol. 14. City Museum & Art Gallery, Stoke-on-Trent).

PLATE 213. *A well-engraved Maddock(?) underglaze-blue printed 'Stone China' dinner service large platter of 'Fairy Villas' pattern. Ornate blue printed mark, incorporating the initial 'M'. 21½in. x 15½in. (54.61cm x 39.37cm). c.1842-50.*

**J. MADDOCK, Burslem, c.1842-55.**
John Maddock succeeded the Maddock & Seddon (c.1839-42) partnership. Good quality earthenware was produced with tasteful printed motifs, as Plate 213. Various impressed or fancy printed marks occur incorporating the name Maddock or with the initial 'M' introduced to one side. The description 'Stone China' usually occurs.

J. Maddock & Son(s) (q.v.) succeeded and used a similar basic printed mark.

**MADDOCK & Co., Burslem, c.1876-1903.**
The printed mark reproduced over first appeared with other Maddock marks in the *Pottery Gazette Diary* for 1907, prepared in 1906. However, it relates to the earlier firm of Maddock & Co., working part of the Dale Hall pottery at Burslem, in succession to Maddock & Gater.

The *Pottery Gazette* lists continued to list Messrs J. & J. Maddock or J. Maddock & Sons, as at Newcastle Street, Burslem, and at Dale Hall but other lists, such as the Kelly's 1877 Directory, give the separate title Maddock & Co. at the Dale Hall Pottery. I have not been able to trace this separate Maddock & Co. designation after an entry in the 1903 telephone directory; subsequent listings refer only to J. Maddock & Sons Ltd. The firm was always part of the J. & J. Maddock or J. Maddock & Sons firms at Burslem. However, ironstone-type 'Royal Stone China' was made at the Dale Hall pottery (as it had been by earlier owners) under the Maddock & Co. trade style.

Maddock & Co, printed marks have been reported from American sites, including West Coast settlements of the 1800s. I reproduce the standard mark as listed in the *Pottery Gazette* from 1907 onwards. This version with 'England' may have been continued by the main firm of J. Maddock & Sons Ltd., but it can date back to the mid-1870s.

**JOHN MADDOCK & Son(s) (Ltd.), (MADDOCK HOTELWARE), Burslem, c.1855-c.1982.**
This important firm produced a large range of durable earthenware. Jewitt, in his *Ceramic Art of Great Britain*, records that the firm 'Manufactures white granite ware for the American markets to a large extent'.

W. Percival Jervis in his interesting 1897 American work, *A Book of Pottery Marks*, recorded that James Maddock, then the head of this firm, visited America in 1876 and that 'upon his return home considerably enlarged the works, which give employment to over six hundred employees. His efforts have always been directed to the improvement of useful rather than ornamental goods, and being able to concentrate his energies on this, he has been happily successful... His nephew, John Francis, has been admitted as a junior partner by his uncle, and much of the present management of the firm devolves upon him...' This author, who obviously had good knowledge of the firm, further noted that the printed lion crest mark with 'vitrified' on a scroll was a then current mark on the firm's hotel ware.

Various marks have been employed over the years incorporating the name 'Maddock', 'John Maddock & Son' or 'John Maddock & Sons'. 'Ltd.' was added to the firm's style after 1896 although this feature was not always included in the company's marks.

Sample standard marks are reproduced below. Various name marks can incorporate the following descriptions 'Ironstone China', 'Royal Vitreous' and 'Stone China' as well as other descriptions for different non-ironstone bodies.

In the early 1980s the Maddock firm was retitled Maddock Hotelware (a division of Royal Stafford China Ltd.) and in 1985 was incorporated in Churchill Hotelware Ltd.

*Pre-war mark with registration number for 1925*

**MADDOCK & GATER, Dale Hall Pottery, Burslem, c.1874-76.**
Ironstone wares bearing the name marks of this Dale Hall partnership have been reported. M. & G. initial marks may also occur.

Messrs Maddock & Co. succeeded and continued the Dale Hall Pottery, as part of the John Maddock firm.

**MADDOCK & SEDDON, Burslem, c.1839-42.**
This partnership between John Maddock and Joshua Seddon produced good quality ware including 'Stone China'. Marks incorporate the initials 'M.&.S.' often placed one above the other at the side of a mark – similar in position to the 'M' on the later J. Maddock mark reproduced in that entry. The impressed mark

Ironstone
China

also occurs.

**E. MAGNESS (& Co.), Hanley, c.1825-37.**
Elijah Magness potted at the Hope Street Works, Hanley, from c.1825. In about 1829 he took Isaac Procter into partnership, then trading as E. Magness & Co. until February 1837.

Standard types of useful earthenware table wares were produced including some ironstone-type wares. Name and initial marks 'E,M,' or 'E.M. & Co.' have been reported.

**J. MAGNESS & CO., Lane Delph, c.1829-41.**
James Magness and Arthur Goddard traded at the Church Road Works, Lane Delph from *c.*1829 into the early 1840s.

Various types of standard useful earthenwares were produced, including ironstone-type wares.

Various printed marks such as the garter device include the initials 'J.M. & Co.' and possibly relate to this short-lived firm. It should be noted that these initials fit several pottery firms – see J.M. & Co.

**R. MALKIN (& Sons), Fenton, c.1865-94.**
Ralph Malkin worked the Park Pottery in Market Street, Fenton Culvert from the mid-1860s. He produced a good range of earthenwares including ironstone-type wares for export. Name and initial 'R.M.' marks occur.

The trade style was amended to Ralph Malkin & Sons in about 1882. By at least 1886 the firm was run by William, Frederick and Arthur Malkin but William retired on 31 December 1886. Initial marks at this period therefore comprised the initials 'R.M. & S.'

**MALKIN, EDGE & Co., Burslem, c.1870-98.**
**(Edge, Malkin & Co.)**
Various printed marks occur on ironstone-type wares which include the initials 'M.E. & Co.' Within the Staffordshire Potteries district these initials could fit Malkin, Edge & Co. *c.*1870-98 and Mann, Evans & Co. of *c.*1862.

Malkin, Edge & Co. of the Newport Pottery, Burslem traded in a large way in both the home and export markets. It undoubtedly produced some ironstone-type wares. Name or initial marks may occur, but the partnership was usually given as Edge, Malkin & Co, the partners being Joseph Edge, James Malkin, William Edge and John Wilcox Edge. The firm traded under the Edge, Malkin & Co. (Ltd.) name until 1903 (see page 237).

**MATT MARE, Shelton, c.1812-27**
This Shelton potter is recorded as having produced ironstone wares in the 1820s but I do not know of any marked examples.

Accounts quoted by the late Reginald Haggar in his contribution 'A Fragment of a pattern book' published in the *Newsletter* of the Northern Ceramic Society, No. 34, of June 1979, suggest that Mare's patterns included 'Amherst Japan', French-style sprig patterns, India vase pattern and bird patterns – not unique styles.

**MARPLE, TURNER & Co., Hanley, c.1851-58.**
Printed marks incorporating the initials 'M.T & Co.' occur and may relate to this firm, or alternatively to Mary Tipper & Co. (*c.*1851-60) or to Mellor, Taylor & Co. (*c.*1883-1904).

Messrs Marple, Turner & Co. comprised John Marple and George Turner, with William Ellis and John Tomkinson. They produced a range of earthenwares at their Upper Hanley Pottery and were succeeded at the end of 1858 by Marple, Ellis & Co. Turner & Tomkinson then formed a separate partnership at Tunstall.

**JACOB MARSH, Lane End, etc., c.1802-32.**
Several potters with the surname Marsh potted in Staffordshire in the nineteenth century. In particular Jacob Marsh is recorded at various addresses in Burslem, Fenton, Lane Delph and Lane End between 1802 and 1832. The Fenton pottery occupied by Marsh in the 1807-09 period was taken over by John Carey.

The impressed name mark 'MARSH' has been recorded in conjunction with a printed mark containing the description 'Opaque China Warranted'. These marks could well relate to Jacob Marsh, in the approximate period 1815-1825.

These marks are recorded on a strange shaped sauceboat shown on page 239 of *The Dictionary of Blue & White Printed Pottery 1780-1880* by A.W. Coysh and R.K. Henrywood (Antique Collectors' Club, 1982). This in its general form does appear to link with the stone china tureen and cover, which I have formerly attributed to Hicks & Meigh. It is certainly possible that the tureen form shown in Plate 214 in this book was produced by Jacob Marsh, with, of course, related dinnerware forms decorated in various styles.

It could well be that Jacob Marsh's potteries produced good quality stone china or ironstone-type wares of Hicks & Meigh type from *c.*1820. It will be worth searching for impressed 'Marsh' name marks.

**JOHN MARSHALL (& Co.) (Ltd.),**
**Bo'ness (Scotland), c.1854-99.**
John Marshall succeeded James Jamieson & Co. at the Bo'ness Pottery, Scotland from *c.*1854. In 1867 he took William McNay into partnership and traded as John Marshall & Co.

The firm's advertisements of the early 1890s featured printed earthenwares and sponged goods as well as 'wheatsheaf Granite for Home and Foreign Markets'. Such wheatsheaf designs were probably relief-moulded white granite useful wares, that were so popular in North America.

Various printed or impressed marks incorporate the name 'Marshall & Co.' or 'J. Marshall & Co.' or the initials 'J.M. & Co.', sometimes with the place-name 'Bo'ness.

The pottery was sold in September 1899 for reuse as a foundry.

PLATE 214. *A Hicks & Meigh-type covered tureen but possibly produced at Jacob Marsh's Lane End factory. 13½in. (34.29cm) high. c.1815-25.*

**MASON(S), Lane Delph (Fenton), c.1800-54.** Miles Mason produced good quality porcelains from the early 1800s. The first porcelain body was of the hybrid hard-paste type and many of the shapes and designs were similar to the popular Chinese export-market porcelains. In many ways these Miles Mason porcelains can be likened to the later developments in stone china and ironstone bodies. Mason also produced various standard earthenwares.

Miles Mason's son, Charles James Mason, patented the now famous 'Patent Ironstone China' body in 1813 – see Chapter III. For some forty years the Masons under various trade titles led the ironstone market and most pieces of their very large output bear a clear Mason name mark.

Charles James Mason was declared bankrupt in February 1848, but he proceeded to lease a works at Daisy Bank, Longton, from 11 November 1850 until 1853 (details of this late short-lived enterprise are contained in the *Mason Collectors' Club Newsletter* of August, 1982, and in the *Northern Ceramic Society Newsletter* of December 1983. Charles James Mason exhibited in the 1851 Exhibition and continued on a limited scale at Longton until 1854.

Several well-illustrated specialist books deal at length with the Mason wares. The reader is referred to: *The Masons of Lane Delph* by R.G. Haggar (Lund Humphries, London, 1952); *The Illustrated Guide to Mason's Patent Ironstone China* (Barrie & Jenkins, London, 1971); *Mason Porcelain & Ironstone 1790-1863* by R.G. Haggar and E. Adams; and *Godden's Guide to Mason's China and the Ironstone Wares* (Antique Collectors' Club, Woodbridge, 1980). A review of the factory and its site is contained in the City of Stoke-on-Trent Historic Buildings Survey (City Museum & Art Gallery, Hanley, 1985). The reader's attention is particularly drawn to Gaye Blake Roberts' 1996 publication *Mason's. The First Two Hundred Years* (Merrell Holberton Publishers Ltd., London). Some old Mason pattern books or parts thereof have survived – see the late Reginald Haggar's paper 'C.J. Mason, Pattern Books & Documents', published in the *Transactions of the English Ceramic Circle*, Vol. 9, part 3, 1975.

For fuller details of the Mason firms, their products and marks the reader is referred to Chapters III and IV in this book.

PLATE 215. *A good selection of Mason's traditional and new forms as produced in the 1990s bearing the 'Cathay', a still Oriental-inspired floral design. Messrs Mason's Ironstone.*

**WILLIAM MASON, Fenton, c.1812-c.1824(?).** William Mason was the eldest son of Miles Mason. He was born on 27 January 1785, and seemingly joined and assisted his father from perhaps *c.*1806, giving rise to the little-used trade style 'M. MASON & SON', up to *c.*1811.

William Mason, however, seems to have taken Sampson Bagnall's former pottery at Fenton in the approximate period *c.*1812-16. On Miles Mason's death, in 1822, William Mason took a pottery belonging to John Smith (and formerly worked by James Hancock) at Fenton Culvert. His name is given in rate records of 1823, but the record dated 29 May 1824 is marked 'Wm. Mason to Thomas Roden & Co.', indicating that William Mason had lately given up the works.

William Mason's short-lived factory at Fenton Culvert seems to have produced earthenware, but only a very few marked specimens are at present known; all are printed in underglaze blue. One of these is a fine platter, 20in. (50.8cm) long, from a dinner service decorated with an underglaze blue landscape within an ornate wide floral and scenic panelled border. This specimen from the late Alfred Meigh's collection is reproduced in Plate 389 of my *Illustrated Encyclopaedia of British Pottery and Porcelain*. Other examples are shown in Reginald Haggar's and Elizabeth Adams' book.

William Mason also had a retail establishment at Smithy Door, Manchester, where Wedgwood supplied creamware to him in January 1815, the order for which is still preserved. Later in 1815, he was unable to pay Wedgwood and his father, Miles, came to his aid, but in November 1828 three meetings were held for the 'Creditors of William Mason of Lane Delph' after which he moved to London where he acted as an auctioneer. William Mason does not seem to have

PLATE 216. *Traditional Mason's 'Double Landscape' design still proving popular at the end of the 20th century. Such modern issues will bear updated marks – see page 100. Messrs Mason's Ironstone.*

produced ironstone-type wares. It is, however, thought possible that he acted as a decorator and as such enhanced blanks obtained from his brothers or from other sources.

**MASON'S IRONSTONE (CHINA LTD), MASON'S IRONSTONE, Hanley,**
**1968-present day.**

From the spring of 1968 this new full trading title was adopted by the former firm of G.L. Ashworth & Bros. Ltd. (q.v.). The marks continue the old Mason tradition but with modern wording such as 'Guaranteed Detergent Proof and Acid Resisting Colouring'. The company has an interesting museum collection now housed at Messrs Wedgwood (see page 394) and still possesses some of the old Mason pattern books.

In April 1973 the firm joined the large Wedgwood Group and adopted the shorter trade name Mason's Ironstone, under which it trades to this day, on a large international scale.

The company's illustrated catalogues of the 1990s feature an interesting range of traditional shapes and patterns. The standard 'Hydra' shape jug is still available, made in at least four sizes. The simpler 'Fenton' shape jug is also still in production. For a selection of traditional and new forms see my Plates 215-217

It must not be thought, however, that the firm only produces reproductions of former shapes and patterns. The very decorative 'lustrous Decoupage range with its jewel colours' was introduced early in 1993. 'Java', a new old-style design, was introduced in 1994 and new patterns, such as 'Batik', appeared in 1996, the year in which Masons celebrated its two hundredth anniversary. New shapes and objects such as clock cases,

PLATE 217. *Traditional Mason's wares decorated with the coloured-in printed outline 'Oriental' designs now described on marks as 'printed and hand-painted'. These general Oriental styles have been popular over more than two hundred years. Messrs Mason's Ironstone*

made in six different shapes and decorated in many styles, have been added to the range in recent years.

The modern Mason wares bear clear printed modern trade marks – see page 100. The wares are well distributed amongst retailers and are, of course, included in Wedgwood displays and special rooms.

**J. MAUDESLEY & Co., Tunstall, c.1862-64.**
This partnership between Joseph Maudesley and William Cooper potted at Tunstall from March 1862 to December 1864 as J Maudesley & Co. or as Maudesley & Co. It was then continued as Cooper & Keeling.

Printed marks occur on ironstone-type stone wares with the initials 'J.M. & Co.' However, these initials also fit other Staffordshire partnerships, such as Joseph Machin & Co., c.1828-30 (not known to have produced ironstone).

**JOHN MAY, Burslem, c.1850s.**
Little is recorded about this potter. John Goddard recorded in his diaries (see page 247 purchasing cream-coloured wares and white granite from this potter.

Also, when R.H. Penman (& Co.) failed in 1856, he recommended that Penman should sell his American-market 'Senate' shape moulds to May.

In 1851 John Aubyn May was recorded at John Street, Tunstall. In 1860 he was at Hamil Road, Burslem. However, the *London Gazette* of 10 July 1866 refers to John Aubyn May as 'late of Burslem, earthenware manufacturer' then living at Astbury in Cheshire,

I do not know of any John May name marks but a 'J.M.' initial mark could relate to this potter, who seemingly produced American-market white granite wares.

**MAYER.**

The following four entries relating to different potters or firms sharing the surname Mayer should not be confused with some American firms bearing this name, several of which produced ironstone-type wares and sometimes used English-style marks. One such American firm was J. & E. Mayer, which sometimes used British Royal Arms style marks with the initials 'J. & E.M.'

**JOHN MAYER, Foley, Fenton, c.1833-41.**

Several printed marks have been seen and reported which feature the initials

I M
F

sometimes with a shape or pattern number added below the initials. The initial 'J' was normally rendered as an 'I' in the eighteenth and nineteenth centuries.

One seller of a Mason-type jug bearing such a mark interpreted the initials as standing for Ironstone Mason Factory. That dealer should go far!

These initials were I believe used by John Mayer of Fenton in the approximate period 1833-1841. His pottery had five kilns in 1836. He produced various types of earthenware including ironstone-type jugs and useful wares.

**THOMAS MAYER, Stoke and Longport, c.1826-38.**

Many different Mayers were potting in Staffordshire from the late eighteenth century onwards. Thomas Mayer of the Cliff Bank Works at Stoke (c.1823-35) and then at Brook Street, Longton (c.1836-38) produced very good quality earthenware, often transfer-printed with tasteful designs, many of which were made for the American market. The American eagle device appears in several marks. Ironstone-type ware was also made. Marks include the name 'T. Mayer', sometimes with the place name 'Stoke'.

The mark 'Thomas Mayer. New York' does not of course relate to this Staffordshire manufacturer.

**THOMAS & JOHN MAYER, Longport (Burslem), c.1841.**

Thomas & John Mayer are recorded at the Dale Hall Works, Longton, in 1841, but the partnership may well date back to 1838 when Thomas Mayer entries ceased at Longport. The partnership may have continued until 1843. The name mark 'T. & J. Mayer, Longport' occurs on ironstone.

**T.J. & J. MAYER, Longport (Burslem), c.1842-55.**

Thomas, John & Jos Mayer succeeded Thomas & John Mayer. A wide range of wares, including good parian and multi-colour printed earthenware, was produced and shown at the Exhibitions of 1851, 1853 and 1855. Ironstone-type articles bear marks 'T.J. & J. Mayer' or 'Mayer Bros.', often with the address 'Dale Hall Pottery, Longport'. Some printed marks incorporate the description 'Improved Ironstone China', others merely incorporate the description 'Mayer's Real Ironstone'. The description 'Improved Berlin Ironstone' can also occur on some printed marks. Wares made after May 1851 may include the wording 'Prize Medal 1851'. Wares made for the American market may also incorporate the address '86 Pearl Street, New York'. A large export trade was enjoyed, particularly to North America. Succeeding firms working this famous pottery were:

| | |
|---|---|
| Mayer Bros. & Elliot | c.1855~58 |
| Mayer & Elliot | c.1858-60 |
| Liddle[14] Elliot & Son | c.1860-70 |
| Bates, Elliot & Co. | c.1870-75 |
| Bates, Walker & Co. | c.1875-78 |
| Bates, Gildea & Walker | c.1878-81 |
| Gildea & Walker | c.1881-85 |
| James Gildea | c.1885-89 |

**MAYER (BROS.) & ELLIOT, Burslem, c.1856-60.**

Thomas Mayer and his brother Jos[14] with Liddle Elliot ran the famous Dale Hall Pottery at Longport, Burslem, in succession to T.J. & J. Mayer. As Longport was part of Burslem the double address was sometimes used, Burslem being the larger and better known town.

The new partnership continued to produce all Mayer's former lines including ironstone-type wares. Much of their output was exported and the firm had its own branch in New York. Printed Mayer & Elliot name marks occur, usually incorporating the Victorian Royal Arms. The old description 'Berlin Ironstone' was also continued.

The partnership was dissolved on 24 April 1858 and trade continued under the amended style Mayer & Elliot from April 1858 until 5 October 1860, after which Liddle Elliot continued the Dale Hall Pottery.

PLATE 218. *A Mason's ironstone-type Japan pattern Mayer & Newbold jug in the so-called 'New Opaque' body. Large 'M. & N.' blue printed initial mark. 5¾in. (14.6cm) high. c.1825-32.*

**MAYER & NEWBOLD, Lane End, c.1817-32.** This partnership between John Mayer and Richard Newbold at Market Place, Lane End (Longton) is known to collectors mainly because of their porcelains which sometimes bear the initials 'M. & N.'

However, the partnership also made earthenwares which include Mason-type jugs which can bear large blue printed marks incorporating the initials 'M. & N.' with a description of the body 'New Opaque' or 'Semi China' – see Plate 218. These earthenware bodies are admittedly rather softer than the best early ironstone but the intention was clearly to copy and perhaps undersell Mason's stock lines.

The partnership was dissolved on 12 September 1832.

For further information on this firm the reader is referred to Rodney Hampson's specialist study 'Longton Potters 1700-1865' (*Journal of Ceramic History*, Vol. 14, City Museum & Art Gallery, Stoke-on-Trent, 1990).

**ALFRED MEAKIN (Ltd.), Tunstall, c.1875-1974.** Alfred Meakin's advertisements of the 1880s feature 'IRONSTONE CHINA, WHITE GRANITE, suitable for North America, South America, West Indies, the Colonies, etc.'

William Scarratt recorded in his *Old Times in the Potteries* (privately printed, 1906) that at that time 'the productions are chiefly for the American market – the quality of the goods will maintain the celebrity the name has held for the past fifty years'. This Staffordshire historian also noted that Alfred Meakin learnt the trade with his elder brothers, James and George, at the Eagle Pottery at Hanley and that he became 'one of the notable commercial men at the latter end of the nineteenth century in Tunstall'.

Various self-explanatory marks were employed and 'Ltd.' was added to the title in about 1897. Marks include the trade description 'Royal Ironstone China'. From c.1913 the firm was retitled 'Alfred Meakin (Tunstall) Ltd.' but marks record only the name 'Alfred Meakin'.

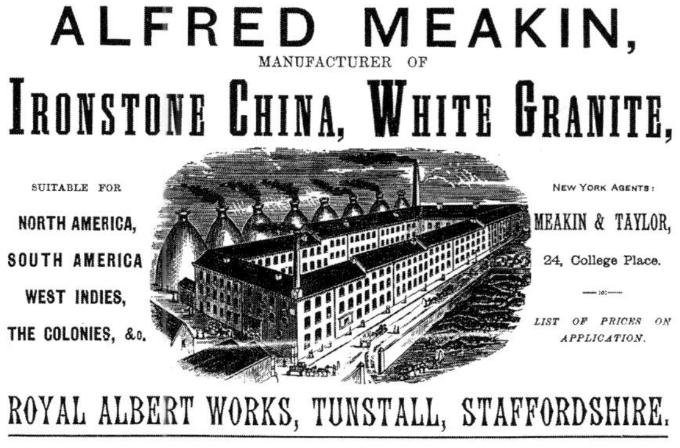

ALFRED MEAKIN,
MANUFACTURER OF
IRONSTONE CHINA, WHITE GRANITE,
SUITABLE FOR
NORTH AMERICA,
SOUTH AMERICA
WEST INDIES,
THE COLONIES, &c.
NEW YORK AGENTS:
MEAKIN & TAYLOR,
24, College Place.
LIST OF PRICES ON APPLICATION.
ROYAL ALBERT WORKS, TUNSTALL, STAFFORDSHIRE.


The firm was acquired in 1974 by Myott & Son. Co. Ltd. and retitled Myott-Meakin Staffordshire Ltd.

**CHARLES MEAKIN, Burslem and Hanley, c.1876-89.**

Charles Meakin worked the Trent Pottery at Burslem from *c.*1876-82 and the Eastwood Pottery at Hanley from 1883-89. His ironstone type granite ware was exported to North America. The mark comprises his name C. Meakin or Charles Meakin below the Royal Arms. The place name 'Burslem' usually occurs but this was superseded by 'Hanley' from 1883. This was sometimes replaced by the word 'England', especially on export wares.

**HENRY MEAKIN, Cobridge, c.1873-76.**

Henry Meakin made ironstone type earthenware at the Abbey Works in succession to Edward Pearson. It was marked with his name and initial below the Royal Arms device and the words 'IRONSTONE CHINA'. Jewitt writing in or before 1878 noted: 'White granite ware for the American markets only, has of late years been produced'.

Messrs Wood & Hawthorne succeeded Henry Meakin.

**J. & G. MEAKIN (Ltd.), Hanley, c.1851-present day; a division of the Wedgwood group from 1970.**

This important firm originally formed by James and George Meakin produced in the second half of the nineteenth century (245 persons were employed in 1861) a good range of ironstone-granite ware which was largely exported to North America. J. Arnold Fleming in his 1923 book, *Scottish Pottery* (Maclehose, Jackson & Co., Glasgow), especially noted that in the latter part of the nineteenth century 'The largest makers of ironstone chinaware were Messrs J. & G. Meakin in Staffordshire, their Eagle Pottery (built in 1859) being considered for a long time one of the largest and best equipped potteries in the world'.

Large as the Meakin factory undoubtedly was, it is said that demand often exceeded availability and that other firms such as George Jones helped to complete large orders. Bernard Holloway has written an interesting account of the firm, under the title *The Story of J. & G. Meakins*.

The marks are self-explanatory, including the firm's name and the description 'Ironstone China'. The registered trade name 'SOL' with a rising sun dates from 1912 and is used on many modern marks.

The firm became a limited company in about 1890 but this fact was certainly not shown in all marks. The presence or otherwise of 'Ltd.' does not therefore help the dating of a mark.

**LEWIS MEAKIN (& Co.?), Shelton (Hanley), c.1853-55.**

Lewis Henry Meakin potted at Cannon Street, Shelton, where he produced various earthenwares, of ironstone type. The name mark 'L.H. Meakin & Co.' has been reported by American authorities. This amended style may relate to the short-lived firm of Meakin & Farrall, which was bankrupt in 1855. John Farrall potted on his own account in the 1854-55 period.

**MEAKIN & FARRALL, Shelton (Hanley), 1855.**

This partnership between Lewis Meakin and John Farrall at Cannon Street, Shelton, was of very short duration and was probably related to Meakin & Co. – see the preceding entry.

Messrs Meakin & Farrall were bankrupt in 1855 but name or initial-marked ironstone-type wares may exist. John Farrall had earlier potted on his own account and with various partners – see page 241.

PLATE 219. *An impressed marked Charles Meigh 'Indian Stone china' dinner service tureen, cover and stand. Coloured-in printed Oriental-style pattern, number 422. 10½in. (26.67cm) high. c.1835-45.*

**MEAKIN Bros. (& Co.), Burslem or Cobridge, c.1862-76.**

This firm, variously styled 'Meakin Bros.' or 'Meakin Bros. & Co.', worked the Trent Pottery, Peel Street, Burslem, in the approximate period 1862-73. The firms are also recorded at the Elder Road Works at Cobridge and various marks incorporate their name 'MEAKIN & CO.' or 'MEAKIN BROS.', usually in conjunction with the place name 'Cobridge'. Royal Arms marks were employed.

The products of this firm were, according to Jewitt *(Ceramic Art of Great Britain)*, confined to white granite ware for the American market. He records that the works were capable of producing about 2,500 crates of ware per year for this market.

**CHARLES MEIGH, Hanley, c.1835-49.**

Charles Meigh succeeded his father Job at the Old Hall Works in 1835, although he had managerial command over these works before this date. A vast quantity of good quality earthenware, including ironstone-type ware, was produced. Various marks incorporate the name or the initials 'C.M.'An impressed lozenge or seal-type mark incorporates the description 'Improved Stone China' or 'Indian Stone China'.

This mark, which occurs with various slight variations, has been the subject of much discussion but it now seems to be agreed that the device was used by the Meighs, firstly by Job Meigh & Son and by the succeeding firm of Charles Meigh (& Son). The lettering in the top and bottom borders is never clear and was perhaps intended to look Oriental, but the

PLATE 220. *An impressed marked Charles Meigh 'Indian Stone china' dessert service dish, matching the dinner service tureen shown in Plate 219. Printed and coloured-in pattern, number 422. 12in. x 9½in. (30.48cm x 24.13cm). c.1835-45.*

lower border appears to represent the place name 'Hanley'. It should be noted that a similar but rather smaller (¾in. – 19mm long) version of this impressed mark was seemingly used by Mintons. Other potters may well have employed similar forms of impressed mark in the approximate period 1830-50. The description of various bodies, such as 'Improved Stone China' occur in the centre of this device.

**CHARLES MEIGH & Son, Hanley, c.1850-61.** This partnership between Charles Meigh and his son of the same name succeeded Charles Meigh Son & Pankhurst at the Old Hall Works, Hanley, from 6 July 1850.

A very large and good quality range of earthenwares were manufactured and the firm made a very good showing at the 1851 Exhibition.

Some superb exhibition pieces are preserved in the Stoke-on-Trent City Museum but the Meigh output also included more mundane useful table wares including white granite-type wares. In March 1861 Charles Meigh formed a new Limited Liability Company – The Old Hall Earthenware Company Ltd., to continue the famous Old Hall pottery.

Various printed marks incorporate the name or initials 'C.M. & S.' of the firm. The description 'Meigh's' was also used. The circular impressed mark 'Indian Stone China' also occurs, as does the description 'Impressed Stone China'.

I show in Colour Plate 43 a magnificent and highly decorative Charles Meigh earthenware plate which would seem to be of the quality included in the firm's stand at the 1851 Exhibition. This hand-painted example bears an impressed Charles Meigh 'Opaque

PLATE 221. *A superb quality Charles Meigh & Son hand-painted 'Opaque Porcelain' plate of 1851 Exhibition standard. Impressed mark overprinted with Royal Arms and 'Iron Stone' mark. Diameter 10¼in. (26.03cm). c.1850-55.*

Porcelain' mark but over this has been applied a Royal Arms mark with the description 'Ironstone China' incorporated in the ribbon below. I here reproduce this rare mark.

It would appear that some of the old Meigh moulds and patterns later passed into the hands of Messrs G.L. Ashworth & Bros. (q.v.) for Jewitt noted in his *The Ceramic Art of Great Britain* (1878):

> They [Ashworths] also manufacture Meigh's ironstone, from his old moulds, &c... This gentleman [Taylor Ashworth], who married the granddaughter of Mr Meigh, obtained by that alliance a vast deal of valuable information about the working of stoneware...

There is, however, a possibility that Jewitt or his informant was confusing the former Charles Meigh coloured stonewares, moulded jugs, etc., with the white bodied ironstone table wares.

Charles Meigh & Son enjoyed a large export market. Some special large orders included a personalized mark reported by American collectors – 'Ironstone China, manufactured for and imported by A. Reeves & Co., Louiville, Ky. Charles Meigh. Hanley', surmounted by the American eagle and shield device. Other such interesting marks no doubt exist.

N.B. American authorities have attributed 'M. & S.' initial marks to Charles Meigh & Son. This seems very unlikely. I believe the full initials 'C.M. & S.' were used. The 'M. & S.' initials are more likely to relate to Maddock & Seddon c.1839-42 (q.v.).

PLATE 222. *A superb quality blue printed dinner service meat platter. Impressed 'Improved Stone China' mark with printed pattern mark 'Vintage' with initials 'J.M. & S.' most probably relating to Job Meigh & Son. 18¼in. x 15¾in. (46.35cm x 40cm). c.1820-30.*

**C. MEIGH, Son & PANKHURST, Hanley, c.1848-50.**
This short-lived partnership between Charles Meigh senior, his son also Charles and the manager James Pankhurst preceded Charles Meigh at the Old Hall Pottery, Hill Street, Hanley. The partnership was dissolved on 6 July 1850 and Messrs Charles Meigh & Son succeeded. James Pankhurst set up on his own account, producing in the main white granite wares for the American market (q.v.).

Various printed marks incorporating the names or initials 'C.M.S. & P.' occur.

**JOB MEIGH & Son, Hanley, c.1812-34.**
This firm of the Old Hall Pottery, Hill Street, Hanley succeeded Job Meigh in c.1812 when Job took his son Charles into partnership. Whilst the earlier firm could not have produced ironstone or stone china, the new firm almost certainly did so although specimens are hard to identify – see Plate 222.

Some 'J.M. & S.' initial marks could well relate to Meigh, rather than to John Meir & Son but much will depend on the date of the article, as the Meir firm post-dates 1835.

Early examples of the lozenge-shape 'Improved Stone China' mark – see page 284 – could relate to Job Meigh & Son, rather than to the succeeding Meigh partnerships.

Messrs Charles Meigh, the '& Son' succeeded (q.v.).

**HENRY MEIR & SON, Tunstall, c.1850+.**
Henry Meir (b.1812) the son of John Meir, effectively ran his father's Greengates Pottery at Tunstall from at least the late 1840s.

While the firm continued to trade as John Meir & Son, some records list it as Henry Meir & Son.

The June 1876 registration for a printed design was made in the name of Henry Meir & Son, although the manufacturer's initials remain as the normal 'J.M. & S.' Several other versions of this garter mark occur – see the following entry.

PLATE 223. *An impressed marked 'MEIR & SON' cup and saucer of a design 'Chinese' registered on 27 December 1872. The printed mark incorporates the description 'Ironstone' and the initials 'J.M. & S.' (which also fit Job Meigh & Son. Diameter of saucer 8in. (20.32cm). c.1872-75.*

**JOHN MEIR & SON, Tunstall, c.1837-97.**
John Meir & Son of the Greengates pottery, Tunstall, produced a wide range of good quality earthenware (Plate 223) often decorated with underglaze-blue printed designs. The marks are numerous and comprise or incorporate the name 'MEIR', 'MEIR & SON', 'J. MEIR & SON', 'JOHN MEIR & SON', 'I. MEIR & SON' or the initials 'I.M. & S.', 'J.M. & S.' or 'J.M. & Son'. Descriptions such as 'Stone China', 'Ironstone China' or 'Ironstone' were used in most marks. The son was Henry Meir (born c.1812) who ran the firm for the greater part of its duration.

Some 'J.M. & S.' or 'I.M. & S.' initial marks could well relate to Job Meigh & Son, especially if they seem to predate 1835.

**MELLOR & Co.**
Various English-looking marks can occur on ironstone-type wares including the name 'Mellor & Co.' or even 'Mellor & Co. Etruria'. Although some Staffordshire firms or partnerships could have used this short title it would seem that such misleading marks were employed by an American firm – the Cook Pottery Company of Trenton, New Jersey. Certainly marked 'Mellor & Co.' wares found in America will not be of British origin.

**MELLOR, VENABLES & BAINES, Burslem, c.1850.**

This partnership is recorded in American reference works as producing white ironstone wares but the title does not appear, however, in available British records. It seems likely that it was an alternative trade style for Mellor, Venables & Co. after the retirement of Thomas Pinder in 1847 and before the Venables & Baines partnership came into being in June 1851 – see the following entry.

The partnership presumably worked the Hole House Pottery in Nile Street, Burslem. Any 'M.V. & B.' initial marks would link with the Mellor, Venables and Baines partnership.

**MELLOR, VENABLES & Co., Burslem, c.1834-51.**

This partnership between Charles Mellor, John Venables and Thomas Pinder potted at the Hole House Pottery, Nile Street, Burslem. Thomas Pinder retired on 28 January 1847 leaving Mellor and Venables to continue under the original name.

Mellor, Venables & Co. produced a fine range of printed earthenware, including ironstone-type ware. Much was exported to North America and several designs, including the arms of the different American States, were engraved.

Many different marks were employed incorporating the name 'Mellor Venables & Co.' or the initials 'M.V. & Co.' with descriptions such as 'Royal Patent Ironstone'. The partnership was dissolved on 30 June 1851, and was succeeded by Venables & Baines, 1851-52 (q.v.).

**MELLOR, TAYLOR & CO., Burslem, c.1880-1904.**

This partnership worked the Cleveland Works in Waterloo Road, Burslem, from c.1880. The firm continued with some changes in the partners to c.1904.

They produced a large range of ironstone stone china and white granite wares as well as the usual selection of 'semi-porcelains' or refined earthenwares.

Most printed marks incorporate the full name of the firm, as shown below, but 'M.T. & C°' initial marks may occur.

**J.H. MIDDLETON, Longton, c.1889-1911.**

Joseph Henry Middleton had been a partner in Messrs Middleton & Hudson (c.1877-88) in High Street, Longton, and at the Bagnell Street Works. In approximately 1889 he took over the Bagnell Street Works and traded there under his own name. This works was later renamed the Delphine Pottery.

Whilst Middleton and the succeeding firm of J.R. Middleton & Co. (c.1912-41) is mainly known for bone china, marketed under the Delphine trade name, some ironstone wares bear 'J.H.M.' initial marks which could well relate to the early period of J.R. Middleton potting under his own name.

The Royal Arms device and the description 'Royal Ironstone China' appear with these initials,

**W.R. MIDWINTER (Ltd.), Burslem, c.1910-c.1987.**

In recent years this firm has produced some very good modern designs in durable table wares. These bear clear Midwinter trade marks.

The Midwinter Pottery was a market leader in the post-war years, firstly with clean looking 'Stylecroft' shapes and designs, under Roy Midwinter, who died in 1990. The Midwinter company purchased the A.J. Wilkinson works in 1964 but J. & G. Meakin acquired Midwinter in 1968. Messrs Josiah Wedgwood acquired Meakins and the Midwinter company in 1970. In the spring of 1987 the Midwinter factory was closed, although some later Wedgwood products continued to bear the Midwinter name. Most of the Midwinter wares, however, are in a high grade standard earthenware body.

For further information the reader is referred to Alan Peal's paperback book *Midwinter, A Collectors' Guide* (Cameron & Hollis, Moffat, 1992), or to Steven Jenkins' *Midwinter Pottery, a revolution in British Tableware* (Richard Dennis, Shepton Beauchamp, 1997).

**HENRY MILLS, Hanley, c.1892.**

The mark shown is believed to relate to the short-lived works of Henry Mills, at Bryan Street, Hanley, although it is more likely to have been used by a Henry Mills who potted at George Street, Shelton, in the 1841-50 period.

**MINTON (various titles and partnerships), Stoke, c.1793-present day.**

The Minton firms are mainly known for their superb porcelain, but many different types of earthenware were also produced including 'White Ironstone'. Various impressed and printed marks can comprise or incorporate the description 'Stone', 'Stone China' or 'Improved Stone China' (Plate 224), with or without the initial 'M' or those given below. However, the description 'New Stone' as used by Mintons, often as an impressed mark, seems to relate to a standard earthenware body, not to an ironstone or stone china-type mix, as was the case at Spodes.

It is interesting to read in a Minton & Boyle letter written in August 1838 that the firm was still being asked to match presumably eighteenth century Chinese plates. This letter also makes the important point that for a run of plates the customer would be charged for the cost of engraving the copper-plates. This printing would, however, avoid the very high cost of hand-painting an intricate design. The letter reads, in part:

PLATE 224. *Detail of printed 'Amherst Japan (pattern) Stone China' printed mark with pattern number '62', with impressed lozenge-shape 'Improved Stone China' mark.*

> We have made an estimate of the Chinese plate alluded to in your letter. We cannot match the body precisely but our ironstone will be very near it... if the plate be printed we can charge it 5/-. The colours of course must be painted and it will be the outlines which will be printed. The expense of the engraving must be charged to you and will be 30/-... If the plate be painted throughout we shall have to employ one of our best hands to do it and the expense will be 16/- each, nor could any

PLATE 225. *Part of a Minton 'Improved Stone China' dinner service, decorated with coloured-in printed design. Ornate printed mark incorporating initial 'M', pattern number 964. Diameter of plates 9in. (22.86cm). c.1830-40. Messrs Sotheby's.*

PLATE 226. *Minton 'New Stone' dinner wares bearing a printed pattern designed by A.W.N. Pugin, pattern number A1140. Impressed marks 'B.B. New Stone' with year device for 1852. Diameter of plate 9in. (22.86cm). 1852. Messrs Sotheby's.*

less be charged whatever might be the extent of the order.

During this Minton & Boyle period (c.1836-41) marks incorporated the initials 'M. & B.' The initials 'M. & H.' occur on marks during the Minton & Hollins period (c.1845-68), but 'M. & C.' was widely used from c.1841-73. The single initial 'M' was incorporated in some single marks which are probably of Minton origin, such as 'Embossed Corinthian Stone China' which occurs on porcelain-like relief-moulded Minton tea wares of the 1825-35 period. The reader should, however, bear in mind that the single initial mark 'M' could relate to several leading makers of ironstone and stone china! Some marks tentatively attributed to Minton, such as the lion crested 'Berlin Chaplet' mark, do not incorporate an identifying initial or initials.

The later Minton post c.1860 products do not include the ironstone body. Minton is now part of the Royal Doulton Group. The study of Minton's productions has largely been concentrated on the fine porcelains. The three standard books on the factory – *Minton Pottery & Porcelain of the First Period 1793-1850* by G.A. Godden (Herbert Jenkins, London, 1968), *The Dictionary of Minton* by P. Atterbury and M. Batkin (Antique Collectors' Club, Woodbridge, 1990) and *Minton – The First Two Hundred Years of Design & Production* by Mrs Joan Jones (Swan Hill Press,

PLATE 227. *A Minton 'New Stone' tureen bearing the 'D'Orsay' Japan pattern which was registered on 4 December 1846. Registration device and impressed Minton marks 'B.B. New Stone'. 11in. (27.94cm) high. c.1846-49.*

Shrewsbury, 1993) – give very little information on the ironstone or stone china table wares which would have been decorated with standard relatively low-priced printed patterns.

**MOORE BROS., Cobridge or Burslem, c.1868-73.** Larry Freeman in his 1954 American book, *Ironstone China*, gives a brief entry for Moore Bros.: 'A Cobridge firm making much ironstone in the 1870s and 1880s...' It is recorded as producing a moulded ironstone design called 'Cambridge'.

Edward and Richard Moore traded together as Moore Bros. at the Bleakhill Pottery, Cobridge (Burslem), between c.1868 and 2 April 1873 when the partnership was dissolved. We also have the succeeding firm of Moore Bros. potting at St. Mary's Works, High Street, Longton, from 1873 to 1905.

The address of the Bleakhill Works (also given as Bleak Hill) is a little troublesome as it is variously given as Cobridge and Burslem. Jewitt in his 1878 *Ceramic Art of Great Britain* noted this pottery under Burslem and stated, 'The works formerly belonging to Messrs. Moore Brothers, who produced the white granite ware for the American markets...'

In the brothers' own dissolution of partnership notice of April 1873 they give the combined, correct, address 'Bleak Hill Pottery, Cobridge, in the parish of Burslem...'

Various name marks will occur.

**FRANCIS MORLEY (& Co.), Shelton (Hanley) c.1845-58.** Francis Morley of Broad Street, Shelton had great experience of the pottery trade. He married the daughter of William Ridgway, and a link exists between Francis Morley and Hicks, Meigh & Johnson, the celebrated producers of stone china (q.v.). Francis Morley acquired the Mason copper-plates, moulds and seemingly the right to use the description and marks 'Mason's Ironstone China' by private purchase, perhaps before the advertised April 1848 auction sale of the whole stock of Masons' 'Fixtures, Utensils, Stock &c,

belonging to the Estate of Mr C.J. Mason'. The auction sale apparently was never held but Morley and the succeeding partnership and firm of Morley & Ashworth and G.L. Ashworth & Son certainly had access to and used old Mason engraved designs and shapes and used or adapted the old Mason marks. It should be noted that the patent had long since run out but this did not stop Mason, Morley and later manufacturers from grandly referring to the 'Patent Ironstone China'.

Francis Morley used several types of 'Ironstone' and 'Stone China' marks incorporating his name or the initials 'F M' or 'F M & Co'. The description 'Real Stone China' was used in some marks. It is highly probable that he was producing stone china wares before his purchase of the Mason copper-plates and other working materials. Messrs Morley certainly should not be regarded as merely having purchased Mason's designs; the firm was a large scale manufacturer of stone china in its own right. It mainly traded as Francis Morley & Co. from c.1849 but Morley & Astbury is also recorded within the c.1847-1852 period – see the following entry.

An American wholesaler's advertisement of 1848, illustrated by Neil Ewins, features 'F. Morley & Co.'s celebrated vitrified white ironstone china, suitable for Hotel and steamboat services, when chipped, warranted not to stain in use or washing'. Its wares certainly enjoyed a wide and well deserved reputation. However, as in so many cases, the firm's decorative earthenwares found in Britain differ greatly from the more utilitarian and less expensive lines made for the American market.

Various printed and impressed marks were used by Francis Morley (& Co.). Most incorporate the firm's title or the initials 'F.M.' or 'F.M. & Co.' Sample printed marks are given below. High pattern numbers in third-series, fractional form occur as

3
1400.

PLATE 228. *An attractive, well-potted Francis Morley & Co. dinner service tureen of a form registered on 6 September 1853. Printed pattern number 3930. 11½in. (29.21cm) high. c.1853-56.*

**WILLIAM MORLEY, Fenton, c.1883-1906.**
William Morley who had previously traded at the Baltimore Works, Longton, with Alfred Steele as Morley & Co., moved to the Salopian Works, Fenton, in about 1883 and produced various types of earthenwares.

Various printed initial marks 'W.M.' or 'W.F.M.' most probably relate to this potter. Messrs Morley Fox & Co. succeeded.

**MORLEY & ASBURY, Shelton (Hanley), c.1847-52.**
This partnership between Francis Morley and Samuel Asbury at Brow Street, Shelton, usually traded under the simple style Francis Morley & Co. (see the previous entry) but some contemporary records give the full title of the partnership.

The firm undoubtedly produced a range of stone china wares, and marks incorporating the initials 'M & A' could relate to it although in most cases they will relate to the succeeding partnership of Morley & Ashworth – see the following entry.

**MORLEY & ASHWORTH, Hanley, c.1858-60.**
As related in the entry for G.L. Ashworth, the Morley & Ashworth partnership succeeded Francis Morley & Co. This partnership is a vital link in the preservation of the original Mason moulds, designs, etc., which Francis Morley had acquired. G.L. Ashworth succeeded this partnership from 4 August 1860. The standard marks incorporated the name in full or the initials 'M. & A.' The trade description 'Imperial Ironstone' was sometimes used as part of the mark.

**MORT & SIMPSON** – see Liverpool.

**G.T. MOUNTFORD, Stoke, c.1888-98.**
George Thomas Mountford of the Alexander Pottery, Stoke-upon-Trent, produced large quantities of ironstone and granite wares in the approximate period 1888-1898. His 1889 advertisement in the British trade journal, *Pottery Gazette*, includes the following claims:

> Manufacturer of earthenware, Ironstone china, and white granite for the Home Trade, the United States, and Colonial markets... Specialities in new shapes in granite for the United States. Specialities in Ironstone China for hotels and Restaurants.

Printed marks including the initials 'G.T.M.' with or without the place-name 'Stoke' occur.

**MYOTT MEAKIN LTD. (etc.) Cobridge, c.1974-1991.**
This post-1974 amalgamation between Myott, Son & Co. (Ltd.) and Alfred Meakin Ltd. of Tunstall produced ironstone-type wares under the 'Myott' or 'Myott-Meakin' trade names. A new firm, Myott Meakin (1982) Ltd., arose. After difficulties a revised title 'Myott Meakin Staffordshire Ltd.' (*c*.1989-91) was used until the firm was purchased by Churchill Tableware Ltd. in June 1991. Further details are given by Rodney Hampson in his book, *Churchill China, Great British Potters since 1795* (University of Keele, 1994), Chapter 12.

**NEALE, BAILEY & NEALE, London retailers, c.1808-1818.**
This partnership succeeded Neale & Bailey (*c*.1788-1800) at their retail (and wholesale) establishment or 'Original Staffordshire Warehouse' at 8 St Pauls Church Yard. The trade style reverted to Neale & Bailey for the period *c*.1819-34.

Some rare early Mason's ironstones were sold by this well-known London firm and some examples bear misleading marks such as:

Neale, Bailey & Neale
Patent Ironstone China

On one example in the Victoria & Albert Museum (number 54.1870) the third name is misspelt Neal.

**NEWBON & BEARDMORE, Longton, 1858-63.** This partnership between William Newbon and Thomas Beardmore succeeded Messrs Beardmore & Edwards from 24 April 1858 at 2 Commerce Street, Longton. The new partnership was in turn dissolved on 10 June 1863. Ironstone-type wares bearing the initial mark 'N. & B.' have been reported and no doubt relate to this five-year partnership.

**NEWBOLD & DAWSON, Longton, c.1864-66.** This partnership between William Newbon and James Dawson potted at Commerce Street, Longton, and seemingly succeeded Newbold & Beardmore. The blue-printed mark

Warranted Stone China
N & D

has been reported and these initials link only with this short-lived Longton partnership, dissolved on 19 January 1866, after which James Dawson succeeded.

**NEW BRIDGE POTTERY –**
see Edward F. Bodley & Co.

**NEW CAMBRIAN CHINA –**
see Stephen Folch (& Sons).

**NEW WHARF POTTERY Co., Burslem, c.1878-1908.**
This company situated in New Street, Burslem, produced various types of earthenware and 'White Granite, printed and decorated for the home and foreign markets'.

Various printed or impressed name or initial 'N.W.P. Co.' marks have been recorded.

There is a possible overlap of dates after 1894 when Messrs Wood & Son worked the New Wharf Pottery.

**OLD HALL EARTHENWARE Co. Ltd., Hanley, c.1861-86.**
This firm (the first limited liability company in the ceramic industry) was formed in March 1861 by Charles Meigh succeeding the firm of Charles Meigh & Son (q.v.). Good earthenwares were produced. Trade descriptive names used include 'Indian Stone China' – sometimes arranged in triangular form reading 'Stone China Indian' – 'Imperial Parisian Granite' and 'Opaque Porcelain', the last being used on normal earthenware and not on ironstone ware. Marks incorporate the initials 'O.H.E.C.' or 'O.H.E.C. (L)' or the full title of the company.

The firm was succeeded by the Old Hall Porcelain Works Ltd. (*c*.1886-1902).

**OPAQUE CHINA.**
This misleading description can occur as a mark or part of a mark. It is one of several, such as 'Semi Porcelain', which endeavour to upgrade earthenware to china or porcelain standards for sales purposes!

Opaque china is not china, porcelain or even ironstone; it is pottery or earthenware!

**W.E. OULSNAM (& Sons), Tunstall and Burslem, c.1867-92.**
William Emmerson (or Emerson) Oulsnam was in partnership with William Holdcroft trading as Oulsnam & Holdcroft *c*.1859-67. This partnership at Greenfields, High Street, Tunstall, was dissolved in August 1867, after which William Oulsnam continued alone.

In about 1871 he took his sons Thomas Mayer Oulsnam, William Ross Oulsnam and Joseph Hancock Oulsnam into partnership, trading as W.E. Oulsnam & Sons. At this period the firm moved from Tunstall to the Furlong Works, Newcastle Street, Burslem, where it continued to *c*.1892.

Various types of earthenware, including stone china, were produced but seemingly marks were seldom used. One, however, features the Royal Arms device with 'IRONSTONE. W.E. OULSNAM. TUNSTALL.' This should date to the 1867-71 period.

**OULSNAM & HOLDCROFT, Tunstall, 1858-67.** William Emerson Oulsnam and William Holdcroft succeeded Messrs Oulsnam, Holdcroft & Co. at their High Street Works, Tunstall. W.E. Oulsnam succeeded in 1867.

Various types of earthenware, including ironstone-type wares, were produced but no marked examples have as yet been reported.

**OULSNAM, HOLDCROFT & Co., Tunstall, c.1855-59.**

This Tunstall partnership between William Emerson Oulsnam, William Holdcroft and Ralph Unwin, trading as Oulsnam, Holdcroft & Co., was dissolved in December 1858, after which the firm continued as Oulsnam & Holdcroft (q.v.).

Various types of earthenware, including ironstone or stone china-type bodies, were produced. Initial marks 'O.H. & Co.' will relate to this firm.

**J.W. PANKHURST (& Co), Hanley, 1850-83.**

James William Pankhurst (1907-89) traded on his own account at the former William Ridgway, Charles Street Pottery, Hanley, in the 1850-52 period, after leaving the former firm of Charles Meigh, Son & Pankhurst. He subsequently traded in partnership with John Dimmock and then with James Meakin at Old Hall Street. The firm traded as J.W. Pankhurst & Co. from *c*.1852 until July 1883. Good quality ironstone-type stone china was made, mainly for the North American market, and was marked with the Royal Arms above the description 'Stone China' and the firm's name J.W. PANKHURST, J.W. PANKHURST & CO. or PANKHURST & CO. Initial marks such as 'J.W.P.' or 'J.W.P. & Co.' also occur. The firm may have reissued or continued William Ridgway patterns and pattern numbers.

This is one of several makes of ironstone collected and researched by American collectors. A good range of 'Pankhurst's Full ribbed & ribbed bud' moulded white wares are for example featured in *White Ironstone Notes*, Vol. 4, no. 2, Fall 1997 (Box 536, Bedding Rides, CT, US.A). The same issue of this American collectors' newsletter also contains a paper by Katey Banks of the City Museum & Art Gallery, Stoke-on-Trent, relating to Pankhurst shards found at Hanley.

**EDWARD PEARSON, Cobridge (and Burslem), c.1850-73.**

Edward Pearson of the Abbey Pottery, Sneyd Street, Cobridge, produced a range of 'white granite ware' mainly of export-market type. Various printed or impressed name marks occur, some of which incorporate the Royal Arms device and the place name 'Cobridge'. Other examples incorporate the American shield emblem. Edward Pearson is also recorded at Liverpool Road, Burslem, in the 1850-53 period but basically he was potting at Cobridge.

Strangely, forms registered in April 1854 and bearing the registration device with the name 'E. Pearson' were registered in the joint names of Pearson, Farrall and Meakin of Shelton, although such a potting partnership is not recorded in other contemporary records – see next entry. This registration could relate to a wholesaling or export-marketing partnership or to a short-lived one.

The Abbey Pottery was later worked by Henry Meakin, as recorded by Jewitt.

**PEARSON, FARRALL & MEAKIN, Shelton, c.1854.**

This Shelton partnership registered plate and tureen forms on 11 April 1854 under parcel number 5. It would appear that other related tableware forms were also produced in ironstone.

Yet this partnership is not recorded in the rate or other available records and the firm must have been of very short duration. I have not been able to trace a dissolution of partnership notice.

It would seem from other marked examples that John Farrall potted on his own account at a slightly later date – see John Farrall, also Meakin & Farrall. No marked Pearson, Farrall & Meakin wares have as yet been reported but any 'P.F. & M.' marks will relate to this 1854 firm.

**PEKIN.**

Various printed marks occur using the description 'Pekin'. Such marks include 'Pekin Stone China' and 'Pekin Japan Ironstone'.

It is probable that more than one maker used this fanciful description for the English ironstone-type wares that seem to have been produced in the approximate period 1820-40.

**R.H. PENMAN & Co., Armitage, Staffordshire, c.1850s.**

Little has been recorded about this firm situated at Armitage outside the main Staffordshire Pottery centre. It is not even mentioned in Jewitt's 1878 *Ceramic Art of Great Britain.* The firm is, however, mentioned in John Hackett Goddard's diaries (see page 247) and this firm of Anglo-American merchants seemingly had several dealings with this pottery.

The firm, comprising Robert Hedderwick Penman and Alexander Allan Laird, worked the Armitage Pottery under the title R.H. Penman & Co. It was visited by John Goddard and his partner John Burgess in July 1854, when it was seemingly in production as an order was placed for toilet wares.

John Goddard, as recorded by Neil Ewins (*Journal of Ceramic History*, Vol. 15, 1997), visited the Armitage Pottery on several occasions. In February 1856 he remarked on the high quality of the granite china and indicated that Penman would produce special American market forms. Goddard purchased cream-coloured standard earthenwares as well as granite china from R.H. Penman & Co.

The difficult trading conditions in the mid-1850s

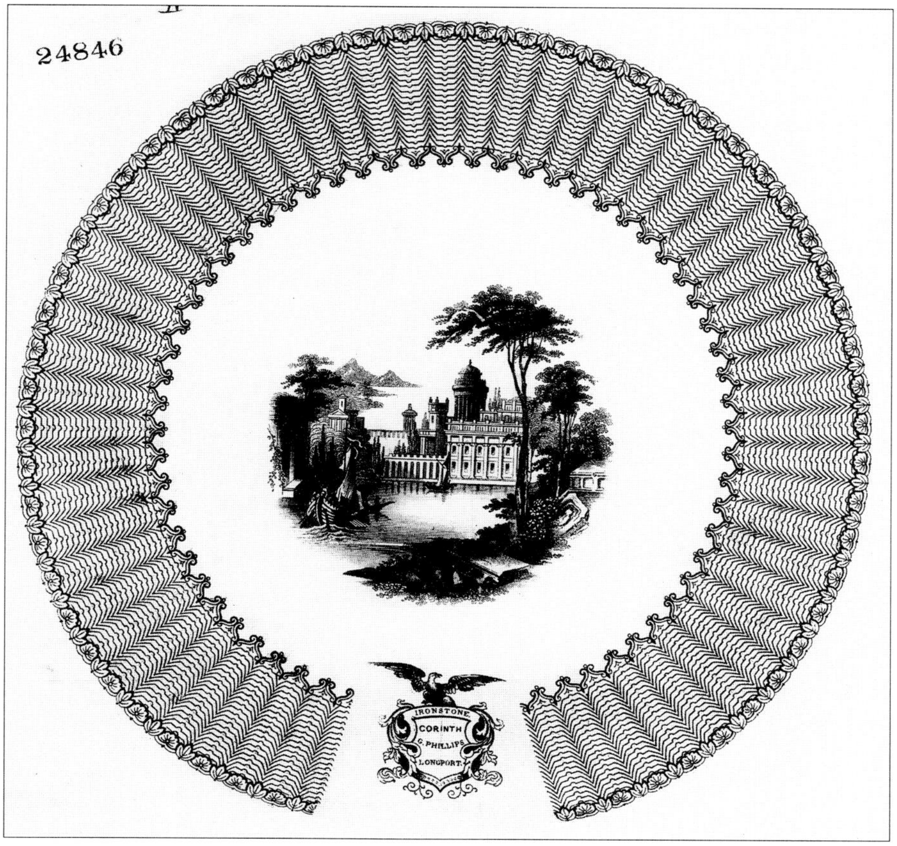


PLATE 229. *A pull from a G. Phillips engraved copper-plate showing the mark which was to be applied to the underside of the plate. The design 'Corinth' was registered on 11 January 1846. The printed mark incorporates the name of the body, that of the pattern and the name and place-name of the maker. Copyright Public Record Office.*

hastened the closure of this pottery towards the end of 1856, when it was advertised to be sold. It may have continued for a period, however, as the dissolution of partnership notice was dated 13 December 1858. Robert Hedderwick Penman (q.v.)moved to Scotland where he continued potting.

Various 'R.H.P. & Co.' initial marks have been reported by American authorities. These could relate to the Staffordshire period, in the mid-1850s, or to the slightly later Scottish period – see the following entry.

**R.H. PENMAN & Co., Glasgow (Scotland), c.1860s.**

Robert Hedderwick Penman, who previously worked the Armitage Pottery at Armitage in mid-Staffordshire, moved to Glasgow where he continued potting under the old style of R.R. Penman & Co. He initially retained the name Armitage Pottery, now situated at 295 Lobbie's Loan, Glasgow. The name was understandably soon changed to the Osley Pottery.

Scottish authorities, such as Henry E. Kelly (*Scottish Pottery* No. 16, 1994), state that the partner was Joseph Brown who left in 1865.

American collectors have reported both 'R.H.P. & Co.' initial marks and 'Penman, Brown & Co.' name marks. The initial marks can relate to the Staffordshire period or to this later Glasgow concern. The 'Penman, Brown & Co.' marks relate to the Glasgow pottery before the 1865 dissolution of partnership.

Robert Penman sold the Osley Pottery to Messrs David Smith & Co. in 1867.

**PENMAN, BROWN & Co. –**
see R.H. Penman & Co.

**EDWARD & GEORGE PHILLIPS, Longport (Burslem), c.1822-34.**

Edward and George Phillips potted in partnership at Longport from 1822 until 1834 when the partnership was dissolved on 12 June 1834 after the death of Edward. This partnership was much engaged in the American trade.

As George potting, in succession, produced ironstone-type wares it is presumed that this earlier partnership also produced this type of body. Marks incorporating the initials 'E. & G.P.' would obviously relate.

**GEORGE PHILLIPS, Longport (Burslem), c.1834-49.**

This potter produced good earthenware, including ironstone wares, between 1834 and 1847, in succession to Edward & George Phillips, *c.*1822-34 (q.v.). In 1843

PLATE 230. *A marked 'G. Phillips, Longport' ironstone soup plate bearing the 'Marine' printed design. This standard design is here amended to take the name of a London tavern, the Three Colts at London Wall. Diameter 10½in. (26.67cm). c.1840-45.*

George Phillips employed between four and five hundred persons, many of whom were of course young children. Those aged fourteen or fifteen received about seven shillings a week (35p) and even then Phillips stated 'being masters of these amounts before they know the real value of money, often squander it away at the ale-houses...' (Scriven Report on children's employment, 1843).

Marks often include his name with the place name 'LONGPORT'. The example reproduced relates to the pattern 'Friburg' registered in November 1846. Other marks are similar to the second here reproduced, with changing pattern names depending on the design (Plate 229). George Phillips produced wares of good quality for the home and export markets. He died in July 1847.

**THOMAS PHILLIPS & Son, Burslem, c.1845-46.** The name 'T. PHILLIPS & SON, BURSLEM' occurs on some marks found on earthenware of ironstone type. Other potters with this surname include Edward Phillips of Shelton (*c*.1855-62), Edward & George Phillips, Longport (*c*.1822-34) and George Phillips, Longport (*c*.1834-48).

**PINDER, BOURNE & Co., Burslem, 1862-82.** This partnership between Thomas Pinder and Joseph Bourne succeeded Pinder, Bourne & Hope (*c*.1851-62) of Nile Street, Burslem, from 13 January 1862. A large range of earthenware includes ironstone-type stoneware. The name 'IMPERIAL WHITE GRANITE' occurs on some marks, sometimes with the American eagle. The full name or the initials 'P.B. & Co.' were incorporated in marks. Doulton purchased the firm in 1878, but it was continued under the old style until 1882.

**PINDER, BOURNE & HOPE, Burslem, 1851-62.** This partnership at Nile Street and Fountain Place, Burslem, comprised Thomas Pinder, Joseph Bourne and John Hope. They produced a large range of good quality useful earthenware including ironstone-type wares.

Various name or initial marks 'P.B. & H.' occur.

The partnership was dissolved on 13 January 1862 after which Thomas Pinder and Joseph Bourne continued under the style Pinder, Bourne & Co. John Hope formed a separate partnership with John Carter (q.v.).

**PLYMOUTH POTTERY Co. Ltd., Plymouth, Devon, c.1856-63.** Jewitt, in his *Ceramic Art of Great Britain*, mentions this firm and the mark – the Royal Arms with the initials 'P.P. Coy. L.D.' and the description 'STONE CHINA' – but he was far from enthusiastic about the products.

Recent (1997) excavations on the factory site, reported by Mr J.C. Maynard, included blue printed wares and indeed most basic types of traditional inexpensive British earthenwares. The 'Stone China' mark reported by Jewitt occurred in an oval impressed form.

P.P. Coy L.D.
STONE CHINA.

**PODMORE, WALKER & Co., Tunstall, c.1834-59.** The products of this important firm were often marked with the name 'WEDGWOOD'. Enoch Wedgwood was, indeed, a partner and his name was found to be most useful. Good earthenware, including ironstone-type ware described as 'IMPERIAL IRONSTONE CHINA', 'IMPERIAL GRANITE' and 'PEARL STONE WARE' was made and exported to many countries. Many marks were employed with the initials 'P.W. & Co.', 'P.W. & W.', 'WEDGWOOD' or 'WEDGWOOD & Co.' A large export trade was enjoyed by the firm which employed 164 men, 133 boys, 60 women and 57 girls in 1851. From *c*.1860 the firm was retitled Wedgwood & Co. Ltd. (q.v.).

**JOHN POULSON, Hanley, c.1823-26.** The Hanley Rate Records list John Poulson as owning the 'Stone Works' or producing 'Stone Ware'. I do not know of any marked examples.

**POUNTNEY & Co. (Ltd.), Bristol, c.1859-1969.** Messrs Pountney & Co. succeeded Messrs Pountney, Edwards & Co. at the Bristol Pottery, the concern being continued by John Pountney's widow, Charlotte, until her death in 1872. The Bristol Pottery was then purchased by Mr Cobden of the local Victoria Pottery, and enlarged. The company became a limited company *c*.1889 and continued as Pountney & Co. Ltd. for a further seventy years.

From the 1870s the firm worked both the old Bristol Pottery and the more modern Victoria Pottery. The firm's advertisements in the early 1880s featured 'Dinner, Toilet, Tea and Breakfast Ware, White Granite, Rockingham, Mazarine, Jet, Green Glaze Ware, &c. suitable for Home and Export. Special facilities for shipping orders'.

Various printed and impressed marks include the name of the Company or the initials 'P. & Co.' or 'P. & Co. Ltd.' The place name 'Bristol' was often included. The trade name 'Vitrite' or 'Reinforced Vitrite' was used for hotel-type wares in the present century.

The firm was retitled 'Cauldon Bristol Potteries Ltd.' in November 1969 and moved to a new factory in Cornwall. The post-1905 history of the Company is well told by Sarah Levitt in her book, *Pountneys. The Bristol Pottery, 1905-1969* (Redcliffe Press, Bristol, 1990). R.K. Henrywood's book, *Bristol Potters 1775-1906* (Redcliffe Press Ltd., Bristol, 1992), is also helpful concerning all the Bristol manufacturers.

### J.D. POUNTNEY (& Co.) Bristol, c.1836 and c.1851-57.

John Pountney succeeded Messrs Pountney & Allies at the Bristol Pottery for a short period *c*.1836 before Messrs Pountney & Goldney took over in the approximate period 1837-1850.

John Pountney (d.1852) then continued trading as J.D. Pountney in the period *c*.1851-53. The firm then continued under the amended style J.D. Pountney & Co, during the period *c*.1854-57. Messrs Pountney, Edwards & Co. continued.

Marks incorporating the initials 'J.D.P.' or 'J.D.P. & Co.' would relate to these owners of the Bristol Pottery.

### POUNTNEY, EDWARDS & Co., Bristol, c.1857-58.

This short-lived partnership succeeded J.D. Pountney & Co. at the Bristol Pottery producing various types of pottery.

Marks have not as yet been recorded but any can be expected to incorporate the initials 'P.E. & Co.' or the firm's name in full.

Pountney & Co. continued.

### POUNTNEY & ALLIES, Bristol, c.1815-35.

Messrs Pountney & Allies worked the Bristol Pottery at Temple Backs, Bristol, in succession to Carter & Pountney.

Whilst most of their production comprised standard earthenwares, it is believed that some stone china was also produced there for the home and export markets.

Various impressed and printed marks comprise or incorporate the names or the initials 'P. & A.' sometimes with the description 'Improved Stone China'.

This partnership was succeeded for a short period *c*.1836 by J.D. Pountney and then by Messrs Pountney & Goldney (q.v.).

### POUNTNEY & GOLDNEY, Bristol, c.1837-1850.

The partnership between John Pountney and Gabriel Goldney succeeded Pountney & Allies and then J.D. Pountney at the Bristol Pottery.

The former range of standard earthenwares were produced plus some stone china-type wares.

The marks comprised the names or the initials 'P. & G.' or the partnership name in full, sometimes with the description 'Stone Ware' and the name of the individual pattern.

John Pountney succeeded from 24 June 1850.

### POWELL & BISHOP, Hanley, c.1865-78.

Edwin Powell and Frederick Bishop, from the former Livesley, Powell & Bishop partnership, established this new partnership in December 1865.

Two factories were in use. The Church Works at High Street, Hanley, were devoted to the manufacture of ironstone-type granite ware including 'white granite' which, according to Jewitt in *Ceramic Art of Great Britain*, 'they produce of excellent quality and in every variety of style, both plain, embossed, and otherwise decorated... for the United States and Canadian markets.' The partnership won medals at most international exhibitions of their period, including the 1876 Philadelphia Centennial Exhibition.

Marks incorporate the initials 'P. & B.' or the names of the partnership.

Messrs Powell, Bishop & Stonier succeeded.

### POWELL, BISHOP & STONIER, Hanley, c.1878-91.

This partnership succeeded Powell & Bishop at that firm's two potteries at Hanley, the additional partner, Stonier, being a china dealer from Liverpool.

Various types of earthenware and ironstone-type wares were produced of generally very good quality. Jewitt particularly noted the 'white granite' wares made for the North American markets.

Marks on these wares include the initials 'P.B. & S.' or the names in full.

### JOHN PRATT & Co. (Ltd.), Foley (Fenton), c.1850-78.

This firm succeeded John and William Pratt at the Lane Delph Pottery, Foley (Fenton) as from March 1850. The firm was a largish one employing some two hundred persons in 1861. Various types of earthenware were produced, including ironstone and granite-type wares. A large export trade was catered for.

Various initial 'J.P. & Co.' or name marks were used. 'Ltd.' can be added to the firm's style from 1872 onwards.

Messrs Pratt & Simpson succeeded and continued the Lane Delph Pottery.

**PRATT & SIMPSON,**

MANUFACTURERS OF

**SEMI-PORCELAINE, WHITE GRANITE**

**PRINTED, and all kinds of EARTHENWARE,**

**Suitable for COLONIAL and FOREIGN MARKETS**

**LANE DELPH POTTERY, FENTON, STAFFORDSHIRE.**

*PRICE LISTS AND SAMPLES ON APPLICATION.*

**PRATT & SIMPSON, Foley (Fenton), c.1878-82?**
This firm succeeded John Pratt & Co., at the Lane Delph Pottery, Foley, in about 1878. Its advertisements feature 'Semi-porcelain, white Granite, printed, and all kinds of earthenware, suitable for Colonial and foreign markets'. Ironstone, white as well as decorated, was produced mainly for overseas markets. Printed marks incorporate the initials 'P. & S.' or the name in full.

At the period of the dissolution of partnership in March 1882, the remaining partners were Joseph Gimson and Joseph Simpson. Joseph Gimson, and then Messrs Wallis Gimson & Co., continued the Lane Delph Pottery. Strangely, design registrations were made in the name of Pratt & Simpson in November 1882 and in April 1883.

**F. PRIMAVESI & Co.**
**F. PRIMAVESI & Son (s).**
Ironstones occur with one of several different Primavesi name marks, often with the place-name Cardiff, Swansea, Newport or London added.

This firm of wholesalers, shippers, agents, etc. was in business within the approximate period 1852-1915. The ironstone-type wares bearing the Primavesi mark are likely to be of British manufacture, but this firm probably ordered their wares from many different sources. Marked wasters have been discovered on Staffordshire sites.

**J. PROCTOR, Longton, c.1845-47.**
John Proctor, formerly of Messrs Meakin & Proctor, potted at the Dresden Works, Longton, in the 1845-47 period. He is listed by American authorities as producing ironstone wares but he is recorded as a porcelain manufacturer in contemporary Staffordshire records.

However, a later John Proctor potted at Tunstall and he may have been the maker of American market ironstone-type wares. See the following entry.

**J. PROCTOR, Tunstall, c.1873-97.**
John Proctor potted at Madeley Street, Tunstall, in the 1873-1897 period.

American authorities have listed a John Proctor of Longton c.1843-46 as producing ironstone wares, but this Longton potter is only recorded as producing porcelain. Any J. Proctor-marked ironstones were more probably produced by the Tunstall potter. It should be noted, however, that other potters of this name, or as John Proctor & Son, are recorded at Longton.

**PUBLISHED BY** – Marks – see Appendix II

**THOMAS RATHBONE & Co., Portobello, Scotland, c.1810-45.**
Excavations on or near the Rathbone factory site in Portobello have brought to light unglazed wasters of various types of earthenware. One waster bears the circular impressed mark 'Stone China. T.R. & Co.' with a crown device in the middle. This mark occurs on underglaze-blue printed earthenwares of willow pattern type and also 'The Font' pattern, known in its Spode version as 'The Girl in the Well' pattern. The pieces appear to be of the approximate period 1820-40.

The original information was contributed by Robin Armstrong Hill to the Scottish Pottery Society's *Archive News*, No. 4, 1979, and reprinted in the *Friends of Blue Bulletin*, No. 26,1979.

**RATHBONE, SMITH & Co., Tunstall, c.1883-95.**
Rathbone Smith & Co. (also listed as Rathbone, Smith & Binnall) of the Soho Pottery in High Street, Tunstall, produced a general range of earthenware including ironstone-type ware which was marketed under the description 'Imperial Stone'. The various marks incorporate the name in full or the initials 'R.S. & Co.' The partnership was dissolved on 31 December 1895.

**READ & CLEMENTSON, Shelton (Hanley), c.1833-39.**
This Shelton partnership at High Street between John Read and Joseph Clementson produced good quality richly decorated stone china ware (see Plate 231) as well as other types of earthenware then in demand in our home and export markets.

Joseph Clementson later claimed to have commenced in 1832 and certainly the partnership was paying rates in 1833.

The standard designs comprised printed useful table wares, and from the beginning this firm seems to have concentrated on North American export markets although much was made for the home and Irish trade.

Aspects of the firm's export trade is given in Mrs E. Collard's book, *Nineteenth Century Pottery and Porcelain in Canada*, and Mrs P.A. Halfpenny's paper 'Joseph

PLATE 231. *An initial-marked Read & Clementson plate decorated with an attractive coloured-in printed design 'Japan Beauty'. Diameter 10½in. (26.67cm) c.1833-39.*

Clementson: A Potter Remarkable for Energy of Character', *Northern Ceramic Society Journal*, Vol. 5, 1984.

The partnership was dissolved on 28 November 1839, after which Joseph Clementson continued on his own account. Printed marks, like the one shown, incorporate the initials 'R. & C.' or the names in full.

It is also possible that the partnership traded under the convenient short title Read & Co.

**READ, CLEMENTSON & ANDERSON, Shelton (Hanley), c.1836.**

This short-lived partnership between Jonah Read, Joseph Clementson and Robert Anderson (dealer in china and earthenwares at Galway, Ireland) was dissolved on 3 September 1836, after which Read & Clementson continued.

This partnership therefore falls with the longer working period of Read & Clementson (1833-1839). It is possible that this triple partnership related only to the Irish side of the wholesale trading business. Nevertheless printed marks occur with the partnership's initials 'R.C. & A.'

**READ & Co., Shelton (Hanley), c.1833-39.**

It would seem that the Read & Clementson partnership also traded under the convenient short title Read & Co.

**G.W. READE, Burslem, c.1850s.**
George William Reade was one of the many now unknown specialist modellers to the Staffordshire pottery industry. He is really only familiar to us today because he registered under his own name a set of 'Columbia' shape table wares on 29 October 1855. These forms have been recorded with the manufacturers' marks of 'I. [or J.] Meir & Son' and of 'Livesley & Powell', suggesting that Reade was an independent modeller to the trade. The 1855 registration was from Bleak Hill, Burslem.

**REED –** see Reed, Taylor & Co.

**REED & TAYLOR, Yorkshire, c.1830-38.**
This partnership seemingly worked three separate Yorkshire potteries:

| | |
|---|---|
| Mexborough Rock | c.1830-38 |
| Ferrybridge | c.1832-38 |
| Swillington Bridge | c.1833-38 |

Various printed or impressed marks incorporate the initials 'R. & T.', sometimes with the name of the body, 'Stone China', etc.

From c.1838 the new title Reed, Taylor & Co. was used giving rise to 'R.T. & Co.' initial marks. For further information see Heather Lawrence's *Yorkshire Pots & Potteries* (David & Charles, Newton Abbot, 1974).

**REED, TAYLOR & Co., Yorkshire, c.1838-43.**
This partnership succeeded Reed & Taylor at the Mexborough Rock Pottery, at Ferrybridge and at Swillington Bridge, during the period c.1838-43.

Various marks were used comprising or incorporating the initials 'R.T. & Co.'Other marks incorporate only the single surname 'REED'. Such marks are attributed to the Mexborough Rock Pottery during the period c.1844-70.

For further information see Heather Lawrence's *Yorkshire Pots & Potteries* (David & Charles, Newton Abbot, 1974).

**REGISTRATION MARKS OR NUMBERS –** see Appendix II.

**RIDGWAY.**
There were many firms and partnerships sharing this surname (without the so-often incorrectly added e), several of which produced good quality, well-decorated, ironstone or stone china-type table wares.

As the alphabetical arrangement of this list takes no account of the working period of the potters it would be helpful if I list here in chronological order the succession of Ridgway firms, most of which have separate entries and are listed in my specialist book *Ridgway Porcelain* (Antique Collectors' Club, Woodbridge, 1985).

*List A*
The Cauldon Place Works at Shelton (Hanley)

| | |
|---|---|
| Job Ridgway, Cauldon Place, Shelton | c.1802-08 |
| Job Ridgway & Sons, Cauldon Place | 1808-13 |
| John & William Ridgway, Cauldon Place | 1813-30 |
| John Ridgway (& Co.) Cauldon Place | 1830-56 |

N.B. In 1830 William Ridgway separated from his brother John, and worked several factories under various names – see List B.

The post-1855 firms working the Cauldon Place Works were:

| | |
|---|---|
| J. Ridgway, Bates & Co. | c.1856-58 |
| Bates, Brown-Westhead & Moore | c.1859-61 |
| Brown-Westhead, Moore & Co. | c.1862-1904 |
| Cauldon Ltd. | c.1905-20 |
| Cauldon Potteries Ltd. | c.1920-62 |
| Earthenware Division continued by Cauldon Bristol Potteries Ltd. | c.1962-71 |

All these firms produced a variety of ceramic bodies, not only ironstone-type wares, and in general clear name or initial marks were employed, for example John and William Ridgway usually employed various 'J. & W.R.' initial marks.

In November 1830 John and William Ridgway separated. John and his successors, as previously listed, continued the Cauldon Place Works at Shelton. From this period William Ridgway potted at various works in Shelton or Hanley, in partnership with his son Edward John Ridgway. They tended to trade under various titles at different potteries or at different times. The main divisions were:

*List B*

| | |
|---|---|
| William Ridgway, Bell Works, Shelton | c.1830-54 |
| William Ridgway & Co., Church Works, High St., Hanley | c.1834-54 |
| William Ridgway, Son & Co., Church Works Hanley | c.1838-45 |
| Ridgway & Robey, Hanley | c.1837-40 |

William Ridgway also had an interest in the separate firms of Ridgway, Morley, Wear & Co. (1836-42) (Wear was a talented engraver, and Morley was William Ridgway's son-in-law) and Ridgway & Morley (1842-45) of the Broad Street Works, Shelton – firms known especially for their 'Stone China' wares, see pages 316-7.

PLATE 232. *A superbly engraved large meat platter from a complete John Ridgway 'Stone Ware' dinner service of 'Giraffe' pattern. Ornate crowned garter mark 'Published Aug$^{st}$ 30th 1836. Agreeably to the Act', with 'J.R.' initials, as reproduced on page 306. 21¾in. x 18½in. (55.24cm x 46.99cm). c.1836-40.*

William Ridgway's son Edward John (1814-96), who had been trained under his father, was to continue the succession up to more recent times. The 'Son', in the style William Ridgway, Son & Co., marks Edward John's official entry into the ceramic industry at his father's Church Works at Hanley. He also used the trading style Ridgway & Abington (*c*.1835-60) and later traded as E.J. Ridgway (*c*.1860-67). It was during this period that he built the very famous Bedford Works at Vale Road, Shelton (Hanley). This was in 1866 when he closed the Old Church Works, and four years later he took his son John (b.1843) into partnership and traded as E.J. Ridgway & Son (*c*.1867-72). Later changes in partnership and title were:

| | |
|---|---|
| Ridgway, Sparks & Ridgway | Nov. 1872-June 1878 |
| Ridgways | *c*.1879-1920 |
| Ridgways (Bedford Works) Ltd. | *c*.1920-52 |
| Ridgways & Adderley Ltd. | |
| Booths & Colclough Ltd. | *c*.1952-55 |
| Ridgway, Adderley, Booths & Colcloughs Ltd. | |
| Ridgways Potteries Ltd. | *c*.1955-1946 |
| Allied English Potteries Ltd. | 1964-1972 |

The Allied English Potteries (A.E.P.) Group included in the 1960s and early 1970s 'Ridgways Steelite Hotelware' produced at the Vulcan Works at Hanley. The 'Steelite' body was used for various hotel wares and also for shipping lines. At the same time the generally more decorative Ridgway oven and table wares were being produced and generally marketed through A.E.P.'s retail chain, Messrs Lawleys. On 1 January 1973, however, Allied English Potteries Ltd. was merged with Royal Doulton and the Ridgway name was apparently phased out.

PLATE 233. *A well-engraved attractive early Victorian initial marked John Ridgway 'Stone Ware' 'Villa' pattern soup plate from a dinner service. Diameter 10¼in. (26.03cm). c.1840-45.*

**JOB RIDGWAY & Sons, (Shelton) Hanley, c.1808-13.**

Job Ridgway was the founder of several stone china firms which subsequently all produced very fine ironstone and stone china as well as other earthenware and porcelain. The sons mentioned in the firm's title were John and William, each of whom later owned separate factories (see subsequent entries and my specialist book, *Ridgway Porcelains*, Antique Collectors' Club, Woodbridge, 1985).

The early Job Ridgway & Sons ware was rarely marked. The impressed name 'RIDGWAY & SONS' occurs and also the initials 'J. R. & S.' or 'J.R. & Sons', sometimes with a beehive device. However, owing to the relative early period of Job's working it would seem unlikely that he produced ironstone or stonewares although his succeeding sons undoubtedly did so.

**JOHN RIDGWAY (& Co.), (Shelton) Hanley, c.1830-56.**

John Ridgway separated from his brother William in November 1830 and continued at his father's celebrated Cauldon Place Works where the finest porcelain and earthenware was produced. Many marks were used, often featuring the Royal Arms and incorporating the initials 'J.R.', 'J.R. – C.P.', J.R. & Co.' (from 1841) or the name in full. The descriptions 'Stone Ware', 'Real Ironstone China', 'Superior Stone China' or 'Imperial Stone China' were sometimes used and high pattern numbers often in excess of 5,000, according to the date of introduction of that pattern.

The general quality of even the Ridgway earthenwares is evidenced by the excellence of the printed 'Stone China', 'Giraffe' pattern large dinner-service platter shown in Plate 232. This bears an unusual dated 'Published by...' mark relating to 30 August 1836, also with the name 'Jno Ridgway' (see below) and would have been extremely costly.

The Cauldon Place Works produced some fine quality dinner and dessert services but the more delicate tea wares were normally produced in fine porcelains. A good range of John Ridgway wares are

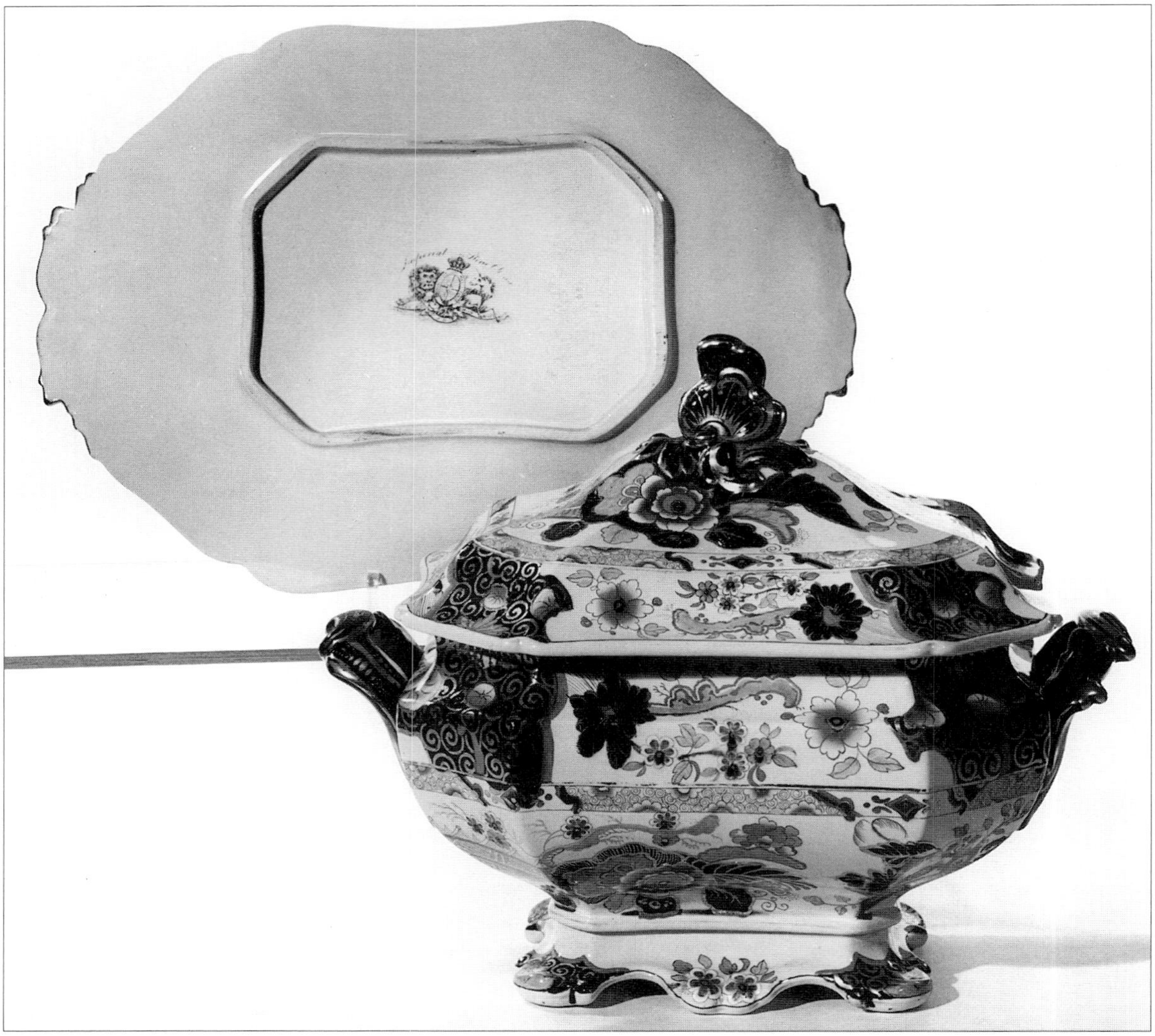

PLATE 234. *A Royal Arms initial-marked John Ridgway 'Imperial Stone China' colourful Japan pattern soup tureen and cover, the stand reversed to show the mark. 13in. (33.02cm) high. c.1835-40.*

featured in my specialist book, *Ridgway Porcelain* (Antique Collectors' Club, Woodbridge. 1985).

John Ridgway's ironstone-type ware, often dinner services, are usually of high quality with colourful decoration. At the 1851 Exhibition the firm showed a fine range of 'Fine Vitreous Earthenwares' including forty-five samples of dinner services in various colour combinations and patterns:

SPECIMEN TABLE SERVICES, FINE VITREOUS EARTHENWARE

| | | |
|---|---|---|
| 244 | Twelve Table Plates<br>One Dish, 16 inches<br>One Soup Tureen & Stand<br>Two Sauce ditto ditto<br>Two Dishes and Covers<br>One Salad Bowl | Cobalt Blue, Red and Gold |
| 245 | Twelve Table Plates<br>Two Dishes 16-14 inches<br>One Soup Tureen and Stand<br>One Sauce ditto ditto<br>One Dish and Cover<br>One Salad Bowl<br>One Cutlet Dish | Pale Coral and Gold |

PLATE 235. *A hand-painted John Ridgway initial-marked 'Imperial Stone China' plate of pattern 5053. Diameter 9¾in. (24/76cm). c.1835-40.*

246 Six Table Plates
One Dish 16 inches
One Soup Tureen and Stand
One Sauce ditto ditto
One Dish and Cover
} Fawn, &c. and Gold
247 One Table Plate ...
Coral, Flowers, Compartments and Gold
248 One ditto ... Coral Bands and Gold
249 One ditto ... Percy, Green, Pink, and Gold
250 One ditto ... ditto ditto ditto
251 One ditto ... ditto, Red and Blue
252 One ditto ... Cobalt Blue, Flowers, Buff, and Gold
253 One ditto ... Cobalt Blue, Fawn, and Gold
254 One ditto ... Blue India Border, Red and Gold
255 One ditto ... Blue and Red Foliage, and Gold
256 One ditto ... Blue, Fawn, Flowers and Gold
257 One ditto ... Ditto, Red, Green, and Gold
258 One ditto ... Ditto, Pink, and Gold
259 One ditto ... Ditto, Coral, ditto
260 One ditto ... Pompic Green, Fawn and Gold
261 One ditto ... Ditto, Bronze, Red, ditto
262 One ditto ... Ditto Chrome Green, Flowers and Gold
263 One ditto ... Ditto Mat Blue, Dresden, and Gold
264 One ditto ... Mat Blue Bands, Flowers and Gold
265 One ditto ... Azure ditto ditto
266 One ditto ... Marone ditto ditto
267 One ditto ... Sea Green, ditto ditto
268 One ditto ... Buff Flowers, and Gold Star
269 One ditto ... Red and Green Foliage, and Gold

PLATE 236. *A rather formalized Oriental Japan-type pattern shown on a tureen stand and dinner service platter. Printed Royal Arms 'Imperial Stone China' mark with 'J.R.' initials. Painted pattern number 5101. Platter 12in. x 10¼in. (30.48cm x 26.03cm). c.1845-50. Messrs Sotheby's, New York.*

270 One ditto ... Pink, ditto, ditto, ditto
271 One Table Plate
... Red and green Border and Gold
272 One ditto ... Mulberry Songsters, Red and coloured Edge
273 One ditto ... Coloured ditto, Green ditto
274 One ditto ... Mulberry, Lily, Green ground and Gold
275 One ditto ... Olive ditto, Pink ditto
276 One ditto ... Blue ditto, Coral
277 One ditto ... Azure, Band, Flowers and Gold
278 One ditto ... Sea Green and Gold
279 One ditto ... India Green band, Coloured Flowers and Gold
280 One ditto ... Sky Blue, Flowers and Gold
281 One ditto ... Azure Border, and Gold Star
282 One ditto ... Mat Blue, Wild Flowers and Gold
283 One Cover Dish
... Tiger Lily, Green, Pink and Gold
284 One Table Plate
... Ditto Red ditto
285 One ditto ... Dresden, Coloured Flowers
286 One ditto ... India Blue, Red, and Gold
287 One ditto ... Ditto Coloured, Pink, ditto
288 One ditto ... Ditto, Green and Gold
289 One ditto ... Blue and Green Band

Apart from dinner service wares or sample plates there was also a selection of dessert wares in 'Fine Vitreous Earthenware'. The designs seem to have been quite rich with gilding although, of course, the basic price would have been less than that required for a porcelain service.

## FINE VITREOUS EARTHENWARE DESSERT SERVICES

290 One Specimen Suite
... Blue, Fawn, Flowers and Gold
291 One ditto ... Green Landscape ditto
292 One Dessert Plate
... Pink and Green, Foliage

PLATE 237. *A superbly engraved underglaze-blue printed John & William Ridgway 'Stone China' dinner service platter. Printed mark incorporating the initials 'J.W.R.' and 'India Temple'. 21in. x 18in. (53.34cm x 45.72cm). c.1815-25.*

293 One ditto ... Cobalt Blue, Flowers and Gold
294 One ditto ... Marine Flowers, and Gold
295 One ditto ... Sea Green, Landscape and Gold
296 One ditto ... Mat Blue, Straw and Gold
297 One ditto ... Chrome Green, Landscape and Gold
298 One ditto ... Fawn Ground, Ribbon ditto
299 One ditto ... Azure, Landscapes, Compartments and Gold
300 One ditto ... Yellow, Green Bands and Gold
301 One ditto ... Fawn and Gold
302 One ditto ... Sea Green, Flowers and Gold
303 One ditto ... Adelaide, ditto

J. Ridgway, Bates & Co. succeeded (q.v.).

**JOHN & WILLIAM RIDGWAY, (Shelton) Hanley, c.1814-30.**

Job Ridgway's two sons, John and William, took over their father's Cauldon Place Works, and also the Bell Works. Their various kinds of ware are very diverse in design but are always of good quality. Many marks incorporate the initials 'J.W.R.', 'J. & W.R.' or 'J. & W. Ridgway'. The various printed marks usually incorporate the name of the pattern and of the 'stone china', 'opaque china', etc.

The two brothers dissolved the partnership on 13

PLATE 238. *A blue printed 'India Temple' patterned 'Stone China' dinner service sauce tureen and cover with its now rare ladle. Shield-shaped 'J. & W.R.' initial mark. Tureen 6in. (15.24cm) high. c.1815-25.*

*Plate 239. Representative parts of an initial-marked John & William Ridgway 'Stone China' dinner service. Painted formal Oriental-style floral pattern – number 1200. Platter 16½in. x 12½in. (41.91cm x 31.75cm). c.1815-25. Messrs Christie's.*

*Plate 240. A printed marked 'Fancy Stone China. J.W.R.' soup tureen, cover and stand with upturned sauce tureen (as Plate 238). Painted pattern number 1289. Soup tureen 11in. (27.94cm) high. c.1815-25.*

November 1830 and continued separately, John at the Cauldon Place Works – see John Ridgway & Co.

The Ridgway brothers produced exceedingly fine quality 'Stone China' often using the more expensive porcelain shapes, as in Plates 237-242. As the large bedroom jug and basin of 'Columbia' pattern (Plate 243) shows, that the Ridgways' output was by no means restricted to stone china dinner and dessert services. These two pieces also show that the Ridgway pattern numbers had climbed to at least 1362 before the brothers separated in 1830.

In addition to the helpful initial marks, various rather softer bodied earthenwares attributed to this partnership bear blue printed 'Opaque China' marks, reading, for example 'Japan Opaque China' or 'Dresden Opaque China'. As previously explained I do not regard such marks as denoting a high-fired or dense ironstone-type body. However, other similar wares seemingly linking with moulded form J. & W. Ridgway porcelain shapes do bear simple 'IRONSTONE CHINA' or 'STONE CHINA' wording enclosed within a double line frame, or within a scrolled cartouche, with or without a crown above. It is not clear why such marks do not bear the usual Ridgway brothers' initials 'J. & W.R.' If a painted pattern number appears with these marks it should be in the approximate range 750 to 1100, fitting in with the Ridgway dessert and dinner service series. Plate 244 shows typical dessert ware shapes which can bear marks of the above type, other wares have moulded grape and vine leaf mouldings.

PLATE 241. *An initial marked John & William Ridgway 'Stone China' dessert service handled plate of a characteristic shape. Printed outline flower sprigs and light green border – pattern 1230. 9¼in. x 8¾in. (23.5cm x 22.2cm). c.1815-25.*

PLATE 242. *An initial marked blue printed John & William Ridgway 'Stone China' dessert dish of 'Bandana' shape. 10¾in. x 9¼in. (27.3cm x 23.5cm). c.1820-30.*

PLATE 243. *A rare jug and basin from a rare toilet service. Blue printed, shield-shaped 'J.W.R.' initial mark with pattern name 'Columbia' and body description 'Stone China'. Pattern number 1362. Jug 10½in. (26.67cm) high. c.1815-25.*

PLATE 244. *J. & W. Ridgway dessert wares showing typical shapes which can occur with 'Stone China' or 'Ironstone China' blue printed marks. Pattern 767 with cursive 'Japan Opaque China' mark. Centrepiece 12in. (30.48cm) long. c.1820-25.*

The fine porcelains and the history of the Ridgway family are illustrated and explained in my specialist book, *Ridgway Porcelains* (Antique Collectors' Club, Woodbridge, 1985). The reader is also referred to Mr K. Church's article 'J. & W. Ridgway – Anonymous Marks' published in the *Northern Ceramic Society's Newsletter,* No. 107, September 1997.

**WILLIAM RIDGWAY (& Co.), (Shelton) Hanley, 1830-54.**

William Ridgway, after the separation from his brother John in November, 1830, worked the Bell Works and the Church Works at Shelton. Fine earthenware and stoneware was produced. The hand-painted ornamental ware was often unmarked, but the transfer-

PLATE 245. *An impressed marked 'W.R. & Co.' William Ridgway colourful Japan pattern dinner plate of typical type. Diameter 10½in. (26.67cm). c.1835-45.*

*A William Ridgway printed Royal Arms mark – sometimes found alone but here with the impressed 'W.R. & Co. Opaque Granite China' shield-shaped device. The body description can vary in this mark which was closely copied by other firms. c.1830-54.*

printed useful wares bear marks including the name 'W. Ridgway' or 'W. Ridgway & Co.' (from c.1834) or the initials 'W.R. & Co.' (from c.1834). Descriptive names such as 'Granite China', 'Improved Granite China', 'OPAQUE GRANITE CHINA' and 'QUARTZ CHINA' were used. An impressed mark occurs comprising the Royal Arms, supporters and a shield with the initials 'W.R. & Co.', as here shown.

William Ridgway and the succeeding firm of W. Ridgway, Son & Co. and Ridgway, Morley, Wear & Co. had an important agency in America, managed by Charles Cartlidge (& Co.) and R.Q. Ferguson (& Co.) from c.1841. Cartlidge & Co., later became important manufacturers of porcelain at Green Point, NY.

PLATE 246. *An impressed marked shield-shaped 'Opaque Granite China. W.R. & Co.' dessert dish bearing a version of the ever popular Willow pattern. 12½in. x 9¾in. (31.75cm x 24.76cm). c.1835-45.*

**WILLIAM RIDGWAY, Son & Co., Hanley, c.1838-45.**

This variation of the William Ridgway company produced the same types of earthenware as the parent or main firm. As from 11 November 1845 the firm became E.J. Ridgway & Abington.

Some fine transfer printed dinner and dessert services were produced in durable bodies sometimes termed 'Granite China' or 'Imperial Stone'. The ornate granite china mark found on the dinner plate shown in Plate 248 bears the pattern number 1471 and the initials 'W R S & Co.' These initials, rather than the name in full, occur as part of most marks.

**J. RIDGWAY, BATES & Co., (Shelton) Hanley, 1856-58.**

John Ridgway in partnership with William Bates and Thomas Brown-Westhead worked at the celebrated Cauldon Place Works in succession to J. Ridgway & Co.

Ironstone-type wares and other ceramics bear various

PLATE 247. *A printed Royal Arms mark relating to William Ridgway's 'Imperial Stone' body with initials 'W.R.S. & Co.' added below, as used in the 1838-45 period. These fragments were found on the New Melones archaeological site in America.*

PLATE 248. *A marked 'W.R.S. & Co.' 'Granite China' dinner service plate of high quality, printed in brown with blue border. Pattern 1471. Diameter 10in. (25.4cm).* c.*1838-45.*

marks comprising or incorporating the name:

J. RIDGWAY, BATES & CO.

Messrs Bates, Brown-Westhead & Co. succeeded on John Ridgway's retirement in June 1858.

**RIDGWAY & CLARKE.**

The American author, Mrs Jean Wetherbee,[16] includes the firm of Ridgway & Clarke in her list of 'English Ironstone Potters... whose marks have been found on white ironstone Made in England in the nineteenth century'.

I cannot trace any such British partnership, nor have I seen such a name mark. Details of such a mark would be most welcome but the names may relate to an American importer or retailer rather than British manufacturers.

**RIDGWAY & MORLEY, (Shelton) Hanley, c.1842-44.**

The Ridgway & Morley partnership between William Ridgway and Francis Morley succeeded Ridgway, Morley, Wear & Co. on 24 June 1842 (see next entry). Good quality earthenware was produced, which included 'Improved Granite China' and 'Stone Ware'. Francis Morley continued on his own from 1 January 1845. He purchased most of Mason's moulds and designs in about 1848, passing them on through the Morley & Ashworth partnership to the present holders, the Ashworth firm later retitled 'Mason's Ironstone China Ltd.'

The various Ridgway & Morley marks incorporated the initials 'R. & M.' or the names in full. However, some Royal Arms marks, added below the initialled marks, are believed to have been used by this partnership.

Ridgway & Morley's use of the description 'Patent Ironstone China' in a mark, closely copying a Mason design featuring the factory, in the early 1840s is

China' was used. The partnership was dissolved on 24 June 1842, when Messrs Ridgway & Morley succeeded. Very good quality stone china useful wares were produced by this important partnership.

The firm's ornately printed bill-head includes the device of an anchor overlaid by a shield containing a sailing ship; certainly the partnership carried on a large export trade. The firm was also described as 'Earthenware & Ironstone China Manufacturers'. Several standard 'Japan' type patterns were supplied printed in different colours, as 'Japan Flowers' which was available printed in pink, purple, lavender, blue, green, brown or black. The pattern numbers tend to be far higher than those found on Mason's wares; the Ridgway partnerships could well exceed a thousand and sometimes a fractional series was employed.

interesting. The original patent protection had long since run out – it expired in 1827 – and Morley would not at this period have acquired the Mason moulds or any related Mason rights. C.J. Mason was still in business producing his own Patent Ironstone China. He was not bankrupt until 1848 and his Fenton works and materials were not advertised for sale until April 1848, some years after Ridgway & Morley used a Patent Ironstone mark.

It should be noted that the various Ridgway-Morley partnerships were large-scale manufacturers of stone china useful wares over a long period. They represented one of Mason's major competitors in the 1835-44 period and at this time the quality of their products exceeded the standard late Mason ironstones.

The pattern numbers tended to be high and were often of third-series fractional form, such as 3/1402. Some of the original Ridgway & Morley pattern book entries are still preserved by Messrs Mason.

**RIDGWAY, MORLEY, WEAR & Co. (Shelton) Hanley, c.1835-42.**
This partnership between William Ridgway, Francis Morley and William Wear succeeded to the Shelton Works of Hicks, Meigh & Johnson (q.v.). The new partnership continued to produce very good quality stone china richly decorated in the Mason style. Many different marks incorporate the initials 'R.M.W. & Co.' or the name in full. The description 'Improved Granite China' was used.

Many of the original Ridgway, Morley & Wear and Ridgway & Morley patterns and engravings are preserved at the present Mason's factory at Hanley.[17] The related crest book includes pulls of many of the partner's marks. Those relating to ironstone-type wares include the descriptions: Imperial Patent, Stone Ware, Improved Granite China, Real Stone China and Royal Stone China.

This partnership obviously produced a huge quantity of above average, decorative ironstone type table and other wares. It was rightly proud to mark its wares which, as stated, can bear various styles of 'R.M.W. & Co.' initial marks.

**J. & R. RILEY, Burslem, c.1796-1828.**
This partnership between the brothers John and Richard Riley potting principally at the Hill Works, Liverpool Road, Burslem, produced a good range of porcelain and various types of earthenware in the first quarter of the nineteenth century. The output both for the home and American markets was relatively large and of good quality but, as few examples are marked, the wares were little known until the publication in 1988 of Roger Pomfret's researches 'John & Richard Riley, China & Earthenware Manufacturers' (*Journal of Ceramic History*, Vol. 13, City Museum & Art Gallery, Stoke-on-Trent).

Entries in the factory recipe book show that various attempts had been made to produce ironstone or stone china bodies and one dated 1820 is described as 'the very best of any from a great number of trials'. Various printed 'Riley' or 'Riley's' marks incorporate standard descriptions such as 'Semi China' or 'Opaque China' but these are of soft-fired earthenware bodies. Nevertheless, Riley ironstone or stone china was made and is awaiting discovery.

**ELIZABETH RING (& Co.), Bristol, c.1795-1834.**

Elizabeth Ring of Bristol was a dealer rather than a manufacturer. She occupied various addresses at different periods and had a large business, purchasing pottery, porcelain and glass from many different manufacturers.

I have included this retailer in this book as her advertisement in Matthews' local directory of 1834 includes Elizabeth Ring & Co's advertisement for 'Earthenware, China, Glass &c, from the first [leading] manufacturers. Services of Earthenware, China & Glass to pattern, also of the newly invented Stone China...'.

It is interesting to note that she used this term rather than Patent Ironstone. It would also be helpful if any reader can trace an earlier advertisement featuring 'Stone China'.

**J. ROBINSON, Burslem, c.1876-1901.**

It should be noted that most, if not all

J R
B

initial marks relate to Joseph Robinson of the Knowl Works, Burslem, not to John Ridgway, Bates & Co., as has been stated by some authorities.

**ROBINSON & HOLLINSHEAD, Burslem, 1872-74.**

This partnership between Joseph Robinson and John Hollinshead succeeded Messrs Robinson, Kirkham & Co, at the New Wharf Pottery, Burslem from 3 September 1872. This partnership was dissolved on 7 November 1874 after which John W. Hollinshead succeeded and traded at the New Wharf Pottery as Hollinshead & Kirkham.

Some 'R & H' initial marks on Staffordshire earthenwares and ironstone-type wares could relate to this short-lived partnership.

**ROBINSON, KIRKHAM & Co., Burslem, c.1868-72.**

This partnership between Joseph Robinson, Samuel Kirkham and John Hollinshead, trading as Robinson, Kirkham & Co., worked the Overhouse Pottery, Wedgwood's Place, Burslem, in the approximate period 1868-69. They subsequently worked the New Wharf Pottery at Burslem until the dissolution of partnership on 3 September 1872. Messrs Robinson & Hollinshead succeeded.

Various 'R.K. & Co.' initial marks have been reported on North American market blue printed wares. In some instances the mark also incorporates the address 'Wedgwood's Place. Burslem'. These initials seem to fit only this Staffordshire partnership.

**ROBINSON & WOOD, Shelton, c.1832-36.**

This partnership between Noah Robinson and John Wood at Broad Street, Shelton, produced a good range of earthenwares including 'Stone China'. They had four ovens in 1836 and their wares normally bear marks which incorporate the initials 'R. & W.', or the name in full, as shown on page 377 of A.W. Coysh and R.K. Henrywood's *The Dictionary of Blue and White Printed Pottery. 1780-1880* (Antique Collectors' Club, Woodbridge 1982). Messrs Robinson, Wood & Brownfield succeeded and worked the former R. & J. Clews works at Cobridge.

**ROBINSON, WOOD & Co., Cobridge, c.1837.**

This title may have been used as an alternative or short-lived variation for Messrs Robinson, Wood & Brownfield (q.v.). The abbreviated name occurs in the Bourne & Hudson accounts for the supply of ground bones in 1837. This name could well have been taken from the firm's letter or bill-head, as other names of potters or partnerships appear to have been accurately recorded. Transcripts of the accounts are given by Roger Pomfret in his paper 'My Bones are Burned as a Hearth. The Origins of Jesse Shirley & Son Ltd.' (*Northern Ceramic Society Journal*, Vol. 5, 1984).

**ROBINSON, WOOD & BROWNFIELD, Cobridge, c.1836-41.**

This partnership, initially between Noah Robinson, John Wood and William Brownfield, succeeded Robinson & Wood in 1838, working the former Stevenson and R. & J. Clews Cobridge Works which had been erected in 1808. Noah Robinson died in September 1837. He was replaced by John Robinson who was seemingly Noah's father. Tim Peake, the Brownfield specialist, has written in his standard book *William Brownfield & Son(s)* (privately published in 1995) that from Noah's death in 1837 the firm traded as Wood & Brownfield. However, the official dissolution of partnership notice dated 16 July 1841 refers to the firm as Robinson Wood and Brownfield. John Robinson had died by this date, a fact that could well have caused the dissolution although his widow, Dorothea, had succeeded him and was named as the surviving partner. The dissolution notice states that the '... firm of Robinson, Wood & Brownfield has been and stands dissolved and put an end to upon and from the 12th day of March now last past...', that is from March 1841.

There is also the important point that the firm's own impressed full name marks of 'Published by ...' type include one with the date 1 September 1839. Clearly the full triple partnership name was in use at this period, as would have been related 'R.W. & B.' initial marks. However, another 'Published by ...' mark of 1 January 1841 gives only the names 'Wood & Brownfield'. The date of the official change in the firm's name is therefore open to some doubt.

As the firm occupied the former Cobridge pottery of Andrew Stevenson and of Ralph and James Clews, a pottery described by John Ward in 1843 as 'the large works', it can be assumed that the firm enjoyed a large trade with existing home and overseas customers and that good quality earthenwares were produced. The range certainly included ironstone-type wares. Recorded marks include the description 'Stone Ware'.

Dinner and other durable wares including toilet wares were produced. Enamel as well as underglaze blue designs were produced, mainly printed patterns. The wares are relatively rare as the partnership's duration was a mere five years, the first of which was restricted by a widespread strike of the Staffordshire workforce.

Various printed or impressed name or initial 'R.W. & B.' marks occur, often with an added pattern number. Information on pattern numbers and illustrations of typical wares are given in Tim H. Peake's privately published 1995 book, *William Brownfield and Son(s)*.

Mr Peake has kindly reported an impressed lozenge-shaped mark, similar to those used by Charles Meigh and by Minton (see pages 284 and 290). This device with the central wording 'Ironstone China. Pearl

PLATE 249. *An initial-marked Robinson, Wood & Brownfield 'Opaque Stone China' dinner service platter, decorated with coloured-in printed pattern, number 24. Printed crowned mark. 19½in. x 15½in. (49.53cm x 39.37cm). c.1836-41.*

PLATE 250. *An initial marked Robinson, Wood & Brownfield 'Stone Ware' cup and saucer decorated with a well-engraved early Victorian design 'Mansion'. Ornate printed crowned mark. Diameter of saucer 6in. (15.24cm). c.1836-41.*

White' appeared on an Amo pattern jug of pattern 53 with workmen's marks found on other Robinson, Wood & Brownfield wares. This rare but indistinct lozenge shape mark may also have been employed by succeeding firms such as Wood & Brownfield.

**ROGERS Bros., Hanley, c.1903-04.**
Mrs Jean Wetherbee in her American book, *White Ironstone: A Collector's Guide* (Antique Trader Books. Dubuque, USA, 1996), lists Rogers Bros. as a name recorded on nineteenth century British white ironstone made for the American market. No details of the mark are given nor are examples illustrated.

The only Staffordshire manufacturer of this name is the little-known firm of Rogers Bros. of the Nelson Place Works at Hanley. The approximate period of their activity was c.1903-04. It is not at present known if the white ironstones found in America were in fact produced by this Edwardian firm.

**J. ROGERS & Son, Dale Hall, Longport, c.1814-36.**
John Rogers succeeding John & George Rogers (c.1784-1814) produced a good range of mainly blue printed earthenware which normally bears the simple impressed name mark 'Rogers'.

It seems probable that the firm in the 1820s up to c.1836 also produced some 'Ironstone' and 'Stone China'-type wares. The following rather neutral 'Stone China' mark has been reported on pieces bearing the impressed 'Rogers' mark.

**ROWLAND & MARSELLUS Co., Agents, late 19th - early 20th centuries.**
Various printed name or initial monogram marks occur mainly on printed Staffordshire earthenwares made especially for the American market. A typical mark is reproduced below.

Although the marks generally include the place name 'Staffordshire' and, after 1891, the country of origin, Messrs Rowland & Marsellus seemingly did not own its own Staffordshire pottery but merely ordered special designs from established Staffordshire manufacturers. Indeed the firm does not seem to be listed in British directories, although it was responsible for the manufacture of much earthenware imported into North American markets under its name.

**ROYAL CAULDON.**
The position regarding the trade name 'Royal Cauldon' is complicated.

The ceramic association dates back to Job Ridgway's building of his new factory on the banks of the Cauldon Canal at Shelton (now Hanley) in 1802. He later took into partnership his two sons John and William. John continued the Cauldon Place Pottery after 1830 and became Potter to Queen Victoria.

After several succeeding partnerships Messrs Cauldon Ltd. took over the pottery in 1905 and used as trade names and marks 'Cauldon' and 'Royal Cauldon'. In 1920 the firm was retitled 'Cauldon Potteries Ltd'. This later took in several other firms including G.L. Ashworth & Bros. and Grindley Hotel Ware Co. but up to 1962 the 'Royal Cauldon' trade name was probably not used on ironstone-type wares.

However, late in 1962 the Royal Cauldon Company was acquired by Messrs Pountney & Co. Ltd. of Bristol. From at least 1967 this Bristol firm which moved to Cornwall in 1969 used the printed marks incorporating the main wording 'Royal Cauldon Bristol Ironstone'.

For further details the reader is referred to *Pountneys. The Bristol Pottery. 1905-1969* by Sarah Levitt (Redcliffe Press, Bristol, 1990).

**ROYAL DOULTON (UK) Ltd., ROYAL DOULTON – HOTELWARE, Burslem, modern.**
The very large Royal Doulton group has many divisions. An important one is the Hotelware Group which produces a large range of table wares. The special durable body is named 'Steelite' and the marks are clear and self-explanatory.

**ROYAL VITRESCENT ROCK CHINA, c.1820s.**
An elaborate printed mark occurs comprising an angel with trumpet holding a scroll on which is written 'Royal Vitrescent Rock China'. The Riley pattern book on page 44 relates Felspar to Vitrescent clay and notes that the 'Vitrescent of Felspar Clays burn much whiter when vitrified...' As yet the ironstone or stone china made by J. & R. Riley have not been identified although this rare mark could relate to the Rileys. It has been suggested by The Friends of Blue (*Bulletin* 96, Summer 1997) that this mark may relate to Machin & Potts but one might expect this partnership to use its own name or initials in a mark.

The rare examples of Royal Vitrescent marked wares (Plate 251) are of good quality stone china, decorated with well-engraved underglaze blue prints. The examples have the appearance of emanating from one of the top firms and they seem to relate to the 1820-30 period.

**ROYAL WORCESTER, Worcester, 1862-present day.**
The Worcester Royal Porcelain Company, which was founded in 1862 in succession to Messrs Kerr & Binns (1852-62), is not known for its ironstone or stone china wares. It is rightly associated with very fine quality porcelains.

However, from about 1870, the Company did produce a strong vitreous body, sometimes termed 'Crownware'. Henry Sandon in his standard book *Royal Worcester Porcelain from 1862 to the Present Day* (Barrie & Jenkins, London, 1973 and later editions), noted:

> The glaze on Worcester bone china made about 1870 had a tendency to craze... and about this date they brought out Crownware, or, as it became known, Vitreous ware, a heavy earthenware found to be extremely durable and made from about 1870 until 1930 for hotel and domestic ware. This ware, of course, is opaque and not translucent.

Later in the same book the terminal date was amended! – 'at the end of the war, in 1918, production of the "vitreous" earthenware body, long used for hotel

PLATE 251. *A large, deep circular dish bearing well-engraved underglaze-blue printed designs. Printed mark 'Royal Vitrescent Rock China' without an indication of the maker. c.1820s.*

and domestic ware, was given up'. This body was normally used for table wares – usually dinner services.

A good range of these Royal Worcester 'Vitreous' dinner services were featured in the Silber & Fleming's catalogue discussed on page 386. These late Victorian wares were described in this London wholesaler's catalogue as 'Best English Stoneware'. In an effort to investigate these Royal Worcester stonewares I wrote to Mr Harry Frost, the Curator of the Works Museum. He replied, in part:

> Royal Worcester made a number of these services for large households, colleges or institutions. They are usually extensive and decorated with modest patterns... The body has excellent durability, I have never seen it craze. It is a compact grey colour, it rarely chips but it is not translucent... When fractured, it makes a clean break. I believe this body was made until about the First War when it was superseded by an earthen ware body. This was not a great success and was, in turn, succeeded by our current Hard Porcelain which became a resounding success.

Mr Frost also kindly enclosed a copy of a 1912 price list for Royal Worcester Vitreous dinner services. These were then available in four sizes. Firstly sets of 101 pieces ranging in price from £25.12s.0d. to £12.10s.0d., according to the cost of the added pattern. Other lower-priced sets comprised 96, 67 or 52 pieces. Each component was also available individually. Single dinner plates ranged from 2s.9d. to 1s.2d. each, whilst the most expensive object was the soup tureen. These ranged in price from £2.1s.6d. to £1.1s.9d. for a simple narrow-bordered design. Two of the six featured patterns were formal Oriental floral designs of the basic type favoured by Mason and other leading makers of ironstone services.

The Royal Worcester 'Crownware' or 'Vitreous' bodied table wares normally bear an impressed Royal Worcester crowned circular mark, often with year numbers or letters added below. One would also expect a Royal Worcester printed mark of the type reproduced below. The word 'England' in this case denotes a post-1890 dating.

The Royal Worcester Company's official guide book published *c.*1909 quoted extracts from the American Judges' award made at the Chicago Exhibition of 1893: 'The Vitreous Ware also is specially worthy of notice. It has a fine hard body, is well glazed and calculated to wear well in use.'

The Company's list of current products included 'badged ware for hotels, restaurants, steamers, yachts clubs, regimental messes, etc.' Much of this type of table ware would have been in 'Vitreous Ware'.

**RALPH SCRAGG, Hanley, c.1850s.**

Ralph Scragg of the 'Pottery Observatory', Hanley, registered a set of tableware forms under his own name on 18 April 1856.

Examples of these 'mobile' forms bearing Scragg's registration mark have been reported with G. Bower's maker's mark, suggesting that Scragg was an independent modeller to the trade.

**SEACOMBE POTTERY, Seacombe, near Liverpool, c.1852-70.**

This little-known pottery was established by the Staffordshire potter John Goodwin in 1852. The first kiln was fired in June 1852 and good general earthenware as well as 'Ironstone China' was produced, mostly decorated with underglaze-blue prints in the Staffordshire tradition. In fact, Goodwin took with him to Liverpool engraved copper-plates he had previously used in Staffordshire. The works had closed by October 1871. Marks include the name 'J. Goodwin' or 'Goodwin & Co.' with the address 'Seacombe Pottery, Liverpool'. A typical Ironstone mark is reproduced, and it is interesting to see that the registration mark relates to a printed design registered by John Goodwin in 1846, while he was working the Crown Pottery at Longton. This fact suggests that similar ironstone-type ware was produced by John Goodwin in Staffordshire prior to 1851 – but such examples would not, of course, bear the Liverpool address. A large export business was carried out and in the 1850s the firm had a retail establishment in Toronto. The printed design 'Lasso' was a very popular one in the American markets.

The *Journal of Ceramic History*, No. 10 of 1978, Stoke-on-Trent City Museums, contains a very detailed paper on the Seacombe Pottery by Helen Williams.

**SEMI CHINA.**
**SEMI PORCELAIN.**

These are misleading descriptions used by various potters in an endeavour to upgrade their earthenwares in the eye of the buyer, via the descriptive mark.

The so-called Semi Chinas or Semi Porcelains are usually neither ironstone nor granite wares but are lower-fired earthenwares and are consequently less expensive to produce.

Blue-printed Staffordshire and other earthenwares of the approximate period 1810-1850 can bear various types of blue printed 'Semi China' or 'Semi porcelain' marks.

**S.H. & Co. initial marks, c.1820-50.**

As with the previous entry relating to 'B. & H.' initial marks, the several printed marks comprising or incorporating the initials 'S.H. & Co.' have given difficulty.

Some American authorities have linked these marks to 'Sampson Hancock & Co.' of the Bridge Pottery, Stoke. I cannot, however, trace any reference to Sampson Hancock (working c.1858-70 at Tunstall) having traded under this style – as a company. Nor can I trace any reference to such a firm at a period that would link to these wares.

The most likely firm to have employed these initials was Stephen Hughes & Co. of Cobridge, working in the approximate period 1835-46. Less likely firms are Samuel Heath & Co. of Lane End, c.1831, or Samuel Hamilton & Co. of Lane End, c.1840.

**'S & H' initial marks.**

Various marks have been recorded which incorporate the initials 'S.&H.' As with any initial mark, great problems arise in attributing the initials to a potter, partnership or firm.

The assumption is usually made that the piece is British and indeed of Staffordshire origin. This is not necessarily the case. Porcelains made between about 1870 and the 1930s bearing these initials with a crown and crossed batons will be Derby, to quote one example.

However, assuming that the problem piece is Staffordshire, then very much depends on the accurate dating of the piece. Once this is established (no easy task), one can narrow the possible manufacturers down to one or a few. This also assumes that the marks relate to the manufacturer, rather than a wholesaler or retailing firm.

In the case of 'S. & H.' marks we have, for example, the following Staffordshire firms to consider:

| | | |
|---|---|---|
| Shorthose & Heath | Hanley | c.1795-1815 |
| Sheridan & Hewitt | Lane End | c.1805-1808 |
| Sheridan & Hyatt | Lane End | c.1808-1811 |
| Shaw & Hallam | Lane End | c.1827-1829 |
| Sneyd & Hill | Hanley | c.1845-1846 |
| Shelley & Hartshorn | Longton | c.1856-1891 |
| Stanway & Horne | Hanley | c.1862-1866 |
| Stubbs & Hall | Longton | c.1889-1902 |
| Smith & Hodgkinson | Tunstall | c.1910-1912 |

If we are only concerned with ironstone or granite-type articles, then we are obviously only considering post-1813 partnerships. We could further disregard Shelley & Hartshorn who are recorded as china manufacturers.

After that it is a case of a personal choice, mainly depending on the likely period of the article. These general remarks relate to all initial marks that do not include a surname or the town of origin.

**SHARPE BROTHERS & Co. (Ltd.), Swadlincote, c.1838 into the present century.**
Thomas Sharpe and his successors, Sharpe Brothers & Co., produced at Swadlincote, near Burton-on-Trent a class of domestic thickly potted earthenware which was described as 'Derbyshire Ironstone caneware'.

This normally has a slightly creamy or yellowish tint and was much used for traditional kitchen ware such as baking and pudding dishes or bowls, made over a very long period.

By the late 1840s Sharpe's 'ironstone cane ware' was being exported to America and featured in importers' advertisements along with leading makes of Staffordshire earthenwares. This firm exhibited such wares at the 1851 Exhibition, the Official Catalogue entry reading:

> Specimens of fire-proof baking-dishes and other articles of Derbyshire ironstone caneware... The characteristics of ironstone caneware are, its capability of enduring the action of fire, its strength and its general usefulness.

Such wares are seldom decorated, although they can have simple surface moulding, and are not to be confused with the decorative Mason's ironstone and stone china-type table and ornamental wares.

**ANTHONY SHAW (& Sons, & Son or & Co.), Tunstall and Burslem, c.1850-1900.**
Jewitt, writing in his *Ceramic Art of Great Britain*, revised 1883 edition, noted:

> The Mersey Pottery [Burslem] was established in 1850 by Anthony Shaw, and is now, since 1882, carried on as 'Anthony Shaw & Sons'. Goods, specially adapted for the various American markets are made, the specialities being white granite ware and cream-coloured wares for the United States... In 1855 Mr. Shaw was awarded a medal at the Paris Exhibition. The mark formerly used was the Royal Arms, with ribbon bearing the words STONE CHINA, and beneath, in three lines, WARRANTED, ANTHONY SHAW, BURSLEM. That at the present time has the words WARRANTED. ANTHONY SHAW & SONS, OPAQUE STONE CHINA, England. The works were rebuilt on a very extensive scale in 1866.

James Torrington Spencer Lidstone's *Londoniad*, privately published in 1866, includes a poem on Anthony Shaw's products with the following lines:

> While the inventive mind of men could scarce divine a
> Series of more classical shapes for his Iron Stone China...
> General Earthenware of all clines, and, too, of all kinds,
> As well as for Texas, Crockett's clime, the inquirer finds.
> His Egg Cups took my fancy and his peculiar Mugs, Jugs, Toilets, which are known well thro many nations far.
> Here Dinners, Teas and Breakfasts, like himself, withouten flaw,
> Are hail'd by the nations from the eminent Anthony Shaw...

The dates originally given in my *Encyclopaedia of British Pottery & Porcelain Marks* have caused some confusion. The dates given for the two separate factories – Tunstall c.1851-56 and Burslem c.1860-1900 – were based on rate records. No payment was seemingly made between 1856 and 1860. It now appears, however, that Anthony Shaw was potting at Tunstall until at least February 1858 when he made a Board of Health payment and that he was at Burslem by at least 25 May 1858 when he registered a printed design 'Castanette Dance' from Burslem. The old pottery in High Street, Tunstall, apparently was taken over by Ralph Hammersley from 1859. The occurrence of these town names or the initials 'T' or 'B' in marks obviously assist the dating of the piece.

Anthony Shaw's wares are particularly collected in the United States of America and he or his pottery is acknowledged as the first manufacturer to have introduced the very popular so-called 'Tea Leaf' design. This is an extremely simple pattern comprising a copper-lustre three-leaf and bud motif within a line border. This design on fashionable mid-nineteenth century shapes rather thickly potted was exported in vast quantities, presumably because it was expensive, but it is practically unknown in the British Isles. Numerous American articles and books feature these Shaw wares. It is interesting to note that several post-1945 manufacturers copied this mid-Victorian pattern, which had been produced at the time by over twenty British potteries.

Anthony Shaw's pottery also produced a lengthy range of transfer- printed wares, some of which were made especially for the north American market. These include 'Texian Campaigue' prints but the firm was a large one and many other printed designs were produced. These can occur printed in colours other than underglaze-blue.

Various name marks were used: 'SHAW', 'SHAW'S', 'A. SHAW', or 'ANTHONY SHAW', with various devices, Royal Arms, etc., and different wording such as 'Stone China'. From 1882 '& Son' or '& Sons' may be added to the name; but from *c.*1898 to 1900 '& Co.' takes the place of '& Sons'. The all-embracing name 'Shaws' also occurs.

Good examples of the Shaw export-market shapes are shown in American works such as Annise Doring Heaivilin's *Grandma's Tea Leaf Ironstone* (Wallace Homestead Book Co., Des Moines, USA, 1981). Typical marks are also featured but these are self-explanatory.

**C. & J. SHAW, Staffordshire, c.1830s.**
Printed 'Stone China' marks have been reported with the clear initials and name 'C. & J. Shaw', or 'C. & J. Shaw, Junr.'

I have been unable, however, to find a record of such a Staffordshire partnership. Taking the initials individually we can trace Mrs Catherine (or Kitty) Shaw of Lane End in the approximate period 1829-36, and Charles Shaw who was a junior partner in Messrs Goodwin, Taylor & Co. which was dissolved in November 1825. Charles signed the dissolution agreement with a cross. He then entered into a new partnership with John Taylor; this was dissolved in October 1826. Charles then entered into a short-lived partnership, *c.*1827, with William Hallam or Hallum.

There were several Shaws with the initial J. Those that could relate to the C. & J. Shaw partnership include Jesses Shaw of Fenton (*c.*1835-38), John Shaw of Green Dock, Lane End (*c.*1825-38). John and Jesse worked in partnership for a period in the mid-1830s. The Lane End rate-records also list J. Shaw & Co. in the mid-1820s.

I have in the preceding remarks assumed that the 'C. & J. Shaw' marks relate to a manufacturing partnership. This is by no means certain. A Charles Shaw was a dealer in Staffordshire wares having businesses in Birmingham, Liverpool and London, while he lived in the Staffordshire Potteries. This Charles Shaw, who died in his eighty-eighth year in 1851, had a son John. Charles and John Shaw were listed together as earthenware dealers in the 1830s. I assume, therefore, that this mark relates to the dealers or Staffordshire merchants rather than to the makers.

**SHROPSHIRE IRONSTONE –**
**see Wrekin Ironstone Company.**

**W. SMITH & Co., Stockton-on-Tees, c.1825-55.**
William Smith's 'Stafford Pottery' at South Stockton, Stockton-on-Tees (Co. Durham) was an important pottery producing a wide range of earthenwares and enjoying a large export trade. There was a branch factory in Belgium.

The vast majority of the output comprised printed and sometimes multi-colour printed earthenwares of standard types often termed 'Opaque China' or 'Semi China' but some 'Stone China' was also produced, from about 1826.

William Smith employed several misleading or deceptive marks. Up to July 1847 the description 'Wedgwood' or 'Wedgewood' was much used. After an injunction by Messrs Josiah Wedgwood & Sons, the Stockton firm tended to use the description 'Queen's Ware'.

William Smith also used the description 'Stafford', seemingly to pass his wares off as being produced in the Staffordshire Potteries. This practice gave rise to printed marks such as

In this case the number 14 relates to the pattern, an underglaze-blue printed Willow pattern. This basic printed mark occurs with various other pattern numbers.

Other makers used the trade name 'W. Smith & Co.' and the initials 'W.S. & Co.' also occur. Some printed marks incorporating the designation 'S. & Co.' may well relate to this firm.

Another mark incorporates the wording 'Warranted Stafford Pottery. Stone China', with a castle and anchor crest, or rarely with 'Tees'. These marks are believed by Mr and Mrs John Cockerill, the specialist W. Smith collectors, to have been used by W. Smith junior who manufactured independently at the Stafford Pottery within the approximate period 1841-45 before transferring to the new North Shore Pottery at Stockton.

In 1855 the Stafford Pottery was acquired by George Skinner & Co. and subsequently passed to several new owners who seemingly did not produce ironstone or stone china-type wares. By 1905 the old Smith factory was owned by the Thornaby Pottery Co. as South Stockton was by then known as Thornaby.

The Stockton earthenwares produced by William Smith & Co. were generally inexpensive mass-produced printed wares but they can be charming – especially the colour-printed children's plates. Such Smith non-stone wares are very collectable.

**SMITH, FORD & Sons.**

These names have been reported by American authorities but I have been unable to trace a British firm with this title.

It could be a mis-reading of Smith, Ford & Jones or a hitherto unrecorded variation on Smith & Ford. However, the succeeding firm was S. Ford & Co., suggesting that Ford did not have sons trading with him.

Wares attributed to Smith, Ford & Sons, if they exist, would seem to date to the 1890s.

**SMITH, FORD & JONES, Burslem, 1889-94.**

This partnership between William Smith, Samuel Ford and Frederick Jones produced various types of useful earthenwares at the Lincoln Pottery, Burslem, from 1889 until the dissolution of partnership in May 1894. Messrs Smith & Ford succeeded.

Various marks occur incorporating the names or the initials 'S.F. & J.' The year of the firm's establishment was sometimes added to the mark.

**SMITH & FORD, Burslem, 1894-98.**

This partnership between William Smith and Samuel Ford succeeded Messrs Smith, Ford & Jones at the Lincoln Pottery, Burslem, from the end of May 1894. The firm continued until the end of June 1898, after which Samuel Ford continued under the new style Samuel Ford & Co.

Printed name or 'S. & F.' initial marks occur, but not necessarily on ironstone-type wares.

**SOUTH WALES POTTERY, Llanelly, Wales, c.1839-58.**

W. Chambers established the South Wales Pottery in 1839, producing a wide range of earthenware including 'PEARL WHITE IRONSTONE'. Marks include the name 'Chambers', 'South Wales Pottery' or the initials 'S.W.P.' From 1854 to 1858 the pottery was continued by Coombs & Holland (q.v.), then by Holland & Guest, and finally by Guest & Dewsberry to *c.*1927.

These Welsh wares can be very collectable, at least by specialists, but in the case of most printed designs the engraved copper-plates were supplied by engravers in the Staffordshire Potteries.

**SPODE, Stoke, c.1784-1833.**

Josiah Spode was possibly the second potter to have produced 'Stone China'-type wares, and the first to coin the description 'Stone China' for this new type of compact, durable body so well-adapted to produce dinner services. He is said to have purchased Turner's 1800 patent rights on the then newish body in about 1805 (see page 64), but Leonard Whiter in his book, *Spode: A History of the Family. Factory and Wares from 1733-1833*, suggests that this Spode stone china body was introduced in 1814. This view is at least partly supported by letters in the Wedgwood archives housed at Keele University and quoted by Robin Reilly in Volume II of his work *Wedgwood* (Macmillan London Ltd., 1989). The 1814 date is supported by Robert Copeland in his book, *Spode & Copeland Marks*, Studio Vista, 1997. The first mention of Spode's 'Stone China' was, I believe, in a letter written by Josiah Byerley in London to Josiah Spode on 19 March 1814. This stated in part:

> Everyone enquires for the stone china, made by Spode and Mason and it has a great run. I presume you know what it is – it is a thick course china body, not transparent, with china patterns...
> (Wedgwood 13.12081)

A week later, on 16 March 1814, Josiah Byerley returned to the subject of the now available and seemingly popular new durable wares. Having sent a sample of Mason's Patent Ironstone China back from London to Wedgwood in the Potteries, he noted:

> ...it [the Mason sample] is not equal to Spode's in quality I believe... I will endeavour to get one of Spode's.... (Wedgwood 13.02083)

Most present-day collectors would agree with this view. The Spode stone china is neater and more thinly potted than the rather heavily potted Mason ironstone. The Spode patterns too are of far better quality. One forms the opinion that Spode, with his London retail showroom, was aiming for a socially higher clientele than Mason.

Spode certainly succeeded in this aim when on 2 July 1817 Queen Charlotte visited his Portugal Street, London, showrooms where, to quote from *The Times* of 4 July:

> The newly invented china, called stone china, by Mr Spode, was exhibited to the Queen; it so closely resembles India [meaning Chinese] china, that it is with great difficulty that the difference can be discovered. Her Majesty bought a service for herself, and a variety of articles for presents...

It may seem strange that as late as the summer of 1817 the Spode stone china should be written of' as 'newly invented' when Josiah Byerley had stated it 'has a great run' in March 1814. No doubt the Queen was told the goods she was viewing were new, as opposed to old, and indeed the patterns could have been newly introduced. It was also more newsworthy to speak of the Queen's purchases as novel or new rather than standard products.

Certainly, the Spode printed bill-head in use before the Queen's visit described the then partnership as 'Porcelain, Stone China, Earthenware & Glass Manufacturers to his Royal Highness the Prince Regent'. The Queen's visit to the Spode showrooms and the subsequent publicity gave an added impetus to the sale of Spode's stone china. Wedgwood's London sales manager reported back to Etruria in October 1817:

> ...Since the Queen went to Mr. Spode, the stone china is much required for and is got more into repute – indeed a dealer cannot be without it, and a great deal is sold.

The Spode firm produced very fine stone china certainly by 1814, proving that this hard, durable body could be finely potted and decorated in tasteful designs fit for any drawing or dining room. Superb dessert and dinner services were made by Spode and decorated with Chinese-type patterns. One gains the impression that Spode was striving to capture the large market formerly served by imported Chinese porcelains, the importation of which certainly fell sharply as the new English stone china came into prominence. It must be admitted that this change was assisted by the still high import duties on Chinese porcelains and that little was being imported but, at the same time, Spode stone china was finer in the potting and far less liable to chip than the Oriental porcelain. Spode made many replacements and additions to existing Chinese porcelain services and these have withstood the passing of time better than the originals.

The early Spode stone china, so suitable for dinner and dessert services, is thinly potted and excellently finished. Many fine Spode pieces were made: ice pails, trays, baskets and bowls, as well as the more normal components of dinner, dessert and tea services. Many of the new Spode shapes were new to the market and did not copy Oriental shapes which were becoming old-fashioned.

The London showrooms of the Spode firm traded under the joint names Spode & Copeland. An interesting printed standard list of their service for twenty-four persons is reproduced in Barbara Horn's English Ceramic Circle paper 'Ceramic Bills – discoveries of 1987' as published in the *Transactions of the English Ceramic Circle*, Vol. 14, part 1, 1990. The related Spode & Copeland account of 1821 relates to a dinner service of pattern 2118. The printed (and slightly amended by hand) list reads:

SPODE & COPELAND'S
STONE CHINA
SUPERIOR TO INDIA
SERVICE FOR TWENTY-FOUR PERSONS.

1 large dish
1 less (i.e. smaller)
2 less
4 less
4 less
4 less
60 large plates
24 soup
24 pie (plates)
2 soup tureens (covers) and stands
4 sauce tureens (covers) and stands
1 square salad bowl
1 large fish dish
1 baking dish
2 less
4 square covered vegetable dishes

The reference to the claimed inferior 'India' services, relates, of course to the Chinese export-market porcelain dinner services. The 1821 purchaser, William Hay, in fact amended the standard list, deleting the twenty-four pie plates, the pair of sauce tureens and stands and one of the two large soup tureens. For this amended stone china service of pattern 2118, he was charged £29.6s.0d. Mr Robert Copeland has recorded that the first special stone china pattern was number 2053 which, he states, may have been introduced about May 1814.

Even at this post-1813 period Spode enjoyed a large trade in matching or making replacements for eighteenth century Chinese European market dinner services. Such individual orders included fine armorial designs (see Colour Plate 2) as well as more standard blue and white Oriental patterns. These individual matchings did not bear a Spode pattern number and usually they are hand-painted. The Spode name mark may also be hand-painted, not printed as would have been the case with standard patterns, which were usually printed, at least, in outline.

The Spode company also used its popular and durable body for a wide range of what we would now term hotel wares. Such crested or named wares include

PLATE 252. *A marked 'Spode Stone China' blue printed plate from a dinner service. The plate shape and the border design, as well as the main pattern, are very much in the style of 18th century Chinese export-market porcelains. Blue printed designs seldom bear pattern numbers. Diameter 10¼in. (26cm). c.1813-20.*

various inn, hotel or college sets as well as a wide range of army mess table wares – 26th Regiment (pattern 3504 of c.1822), 44th Regiment (pattern 4074 of c.1824) or the 16th Lancers (pattern 3988 of c.1824) to name but three special military orders. Such sets would have been large and sometimes included the double-walled, hot-water plates for retaining the heat.

The mark 'SPODE STONE CHINA' or 'SPODE'S STONE CHINA' is often impressed or more often printed with an Oriental-style square mark, as reproduced. The impressed mark 'SPODES/NEW STONE' is also often found, as are the impressed initials 'N.S.', both of which date from c.1820. Copeland & Garrett succeeded from March 1833-47 (some Spode pieces will be found bearing a printed mark of this partnership and such pieces were decorated in the new period. Messrs Copeland continued from 1847 to 1970 when the style 'Spode Ltd.' was adapted to underline the continuous link with original Spode works and traditions – indeed Spode-type stone china can be found with the name marks of Copeland & Garrett (1833-47) and of Copeland (1847-1970) with the firm then returning to use the Spode name – see the following entry. In 1960 a new recipe was introduced under the revised name 'Fine Stone'.

A standard reference book is *Spode and his Successors* by A. Hayden, 1924, a work superseded by Leonard Whiter's *tour-de-force*, *Spode* (Barrie & Jenkins, London, 1970, and subsequent revised editions). Other helpful books on the very varied Spode wares include, *Spode's Willow Pattern & other designs after the Chinese* by Robert Copeland (Studio Vista/Christie's, London, 1980), *Spode Printed Ware* by David Drakard and Paul Holdway (Longman Group Ltd., London, 1983) and

PLATE 253. *A typically well-potted good quality 'Spode Stone China' marked dinner service tureen and cover. Decorated with the popular printed outline design number 2054 (see also Plate 12). Tureen 11½in. (29.21cm) high. c.1815-25.*

PLATE 254. *A large and magnificent marked 'Spode Stone China' covered vase. Decorated in the style and up to the quality of a fine porcelain vase, but less expensive in Stone China. Pattern number 2247. 24in. (60.96cm) high.* c.*1815-20. Messrs Christie's.*

*Spode & Copeland Marks* by Robert Copeland (Studio Vista, London, 1997). This latest work gives the key to various Copeland and later Spode Ltd. year-codes.

The following Spode marks, which are usually printed in blue or the colour of the printed design, occur, often with the painted pattern number. Robert Copeland attributed the first mark to c.1812. The half-mark version (without the section above the word 'Spode') he attributes to c.1815 onwards. As previously stated, the name 'New Stone' denotes a revised, later, mix. I have arranged my

PLATE 255. *A marked 'Spode Stone China' dessert service centre dish, decorated with a Chinese-inspired printed outline design, pattern 2647. 13½in. (34.29cm) long, 4in. (10.16cm) high. c.1813-20.*

PLATE 256. *A marked selection of 'Spode Stone China' dessert wares, decorated with the Oriental-style pattern 2647. The baskets and tureen ladles are rarely found today. Centrepiece 15in. (38.1cm) long. c.1815-25. Messrs Sotheby's.*

PLATE 257. *A fine large marked 'Spode New Stone' dinner service tureen, cover and stand of Chinese-style pattern number 1038. This piece also bears the retailer's mark of 'James Kerr & Sons, Dublin'. 12in. (30.48cm) high. c.1820-25.*

PLATE 258. *Impressed and printed marked 'Spode New Stone' dinner wares bearing the popular Chinese-inspired* Famille Rose*-type design, number 2115. This, like most such patterns, is a coloured-in printed outline. Platter 20¼in. (51.43cm) long. c.1820-25. Messrs Sotheby's, New York.*

PLATE 259. *A rare, marked 'Spode New Stone' chamber pot decorated with* Famille Rose*-style pattern number 2118. A great variety of shapes – useful as well as decorative objects – would bear such popular Oriental-style designs. 5¼in. (13.33cm) high. c.1820-25.*

illustrations to show marked 'Spode Stone China' before the 'New Stone' examples but pattern numbers on the New Stone pieces may relate to earlier still-popular designs. Painted 'Stone China' marks occur but very rarely.

PLATE 260. *An impressed marked 'Spode New Stone' dinner service tureen, cover and stand decorated with a colourful Japan pattern. 14½in. (38.83cm) high. c.1820-25.*

PLATE 261. *Representative pieces from a superb quality and extremely colourful marked 'Spode New Stone' dinner service of pattern 2375, which has gilt handles and trim. Tureen 12¾in. (32.38cm) high. Impressed and printed seal marks. c.1820-25. Messrs Sotheby's, New York.*

PLATE 262. *Representative pieces from a marked 'Spode New Stone' dinner service, decorated with one of many colourful Japan patterns, in this case pattern number 3248 and one used at the Coronation of George IV in July 1821. Tureen 14½in. (36.83cm) high. c.1821-25. Messrs Christie's.*

PLATE 263. *A rare marked 'Spode New Stone' three-piece vegetable dish with bottom container for hot water. Pattern number 3248 as the preceding illustration. 12in. (30.48cm) long. c.1821-25.*

PLATE 264. *Representative parts of a 'Spode New Stone' dinner service decorated with an unusual Oriental-style printed outline pattern – Spode's number 3425. Platter 19in. (48.26cm) long. c.1822-27.*

PLATE 265. *Representative pieces from a marked 'Spode New Stone' dinner service, decorated with an Oriental-inspired pattern, number 3873. It is interesting to find such 18th century-style Chinese export-market forms being used on Spode patterns of the 1820s. Platter 17in. (43.18cm) long. c.1824-30. Messrs Christie's.*

PLATE 266. *Marked 'Spode New Stone' dinner wares bearing the printed outline design 4363, with some gilt enrichments. The sauceboats and stands are rarely found today. Tureen 11¾in. (29.84cm) high. c.1825-33. Messrs Christie's.*

**SPODE (Ltd.), Stoke, 1970 to present day.**
I have here separated the modern firm of Spode from the eighteenth and nineteenth century parent, although both are related, via Messrs Copeland & Garrett (*c*.1833-47) and Messrs W.T. Copeland (& Sons Ltd.) (*c*.1847-1970).

In 1970 the Copelands reverted to the old style by renaming the Company 'Spode Ltd.' In 1976 the company merged with the Worcester Royal Porcelain Company and traded as Royal Worcester Spode Ltd. which underwent several changes of ownership. However, in 1989 the two firms separated and the title 'Spode Ltd.' continued until 1993 when the style reverted to the original 'Spode'. With all these changes, the present company still occupies the original (now enlarged) Spode factory site in the middle of Stoke.

The post-1970 Spode firm continued to produce its 'Fine Stone' body particularly for the American market until c.1992 when production was discontinued. The American-market articles tended to copy old so-called 'Chinese Lowestoft' (Chinese export-market) shapes and designs which have proved popular over a long period, the twentieth century Copeland-Spode range being termed 'Spode' s Lowestoft'.

From about 1978 various 'Oven to Tableware' marks were employed and *c*.1981 a new range of 'Imperial Cookware', 'Stone China oven to Table' articles.

For further information on the Spode products and marks the reader is referred to Robert Copeland's *Spode & Copeland Marks* (Studio Vista, Cassell, London, second enlarged edition, 1997).

**'STAFFORD', 'WARRANTED STAFFORD', 'STAFFORD POTTERY'**

Marks incorporating the name 'Stafford' or 'Stafford Pottery' are mostly misleading in that the name relates to Messrs William Smith & Co.'s Stafford Pottery at Stockton-on-Tees in Yorkshire. A typical 'Stone China' mark is here reproduced. The same piece bears the impressed mark 'W S & Co's WEDGEWOOD', this firm also using or misusing the name 'Wedgewood' until the main Wedgwood Company took out an injunction against Smith in 1847 – see page 325.

**STAFFORDSHIRE POTTERIES Ltd., Meir Park, c.1964-90.**

This firm produced under the registered trade name 'Kilncroft' a range of table wares which bear clearly printed marks including the description 'English Ironstone'.

**STANWAY & HORNE (STANWAY, HORNE & CO.), Hanley, c.1862-65.**

This partnership, which also traded as Stanway, Horne & Co., owned a pottery in Joiner's Square, Hanley, in the approximate period 1862-65. It was later known as the Trent Works. The partnership, and in particular the succeeding firm of Stanway, Horne & Adams, are mainly known as manufacturers of inexpensive parian goods.

Jewitt wrote at some length of the firm (in the late 1870s) and mentioned that they also produced 'useful goods of an improved design in stoneware and ordinary earthenware...' It is, therefore, possible that some 'S. & H.' or 'S. & Co.' initial-marked earthenwares of the 1860s were produced by this Hanley firm.

In about 1865 Messrs Stanway, Horne and Adams succeeded but this partnership was dissolved in April 1880 – see the following entry.

**STANWAY, HORNE & ADAMS, Hanley, c.1865-80.**

This partnership between William Stanway, Thomas Horne and Thomas Adams (with others) succeeded Stanway & Horne at the Trent Pottery, Hanley.

While the partnership is mainly known for its parian wares, Jewitt recorded in his 1878 *Ceramic Art of Great Britain* that it also produced 'useful goods of an improved design in stoneware and ordinary earthenware'. These table wares may well have included ironstone or granite-type articles.

Thomas Horne died possibly in the 1870s and was succeeded as a partner by his widow (William Stanway's sister). She too had died by 1880, when the partners were William Stanway, John Stanway, Jonathan Snow and James Wood. The partnership was dissolved on 23 April 1880.

Thomas Adams continued the Trent Pottery under his own name during the approximate period 1880-1885. He may have traded, however, in partnership with James Wood as Adams & Wood for a short period.

**'STEELITE', Staffordshire Potteries, 1968+.**

This extremely significant trade name for a modern durable ceramic body was first used for Allied English Potteries Hotel Ware marketed in Australia. In 1968 this name was used by Allied English Potteries but was coupled with the Ridgway name. Hence in the 1968-73 period marks incorporating the description

Ridgway Steelite
Vitreous China Hotelware

were in use.

The same trade name can, however, relate to Royal Doulton and to Steelite International Plc. (q.v.).

In 1973 Messrs S. Pearson, the owners of A.E.P., purchased Doultons, and the Steelite products came under the new Royal Doulton Tableware Group. The word 'China' was dropped from the old marks which were adapted to Steelite Vitreous Hotelware. Later markings underlined the Doulton connection, giving rise to printed marks incorporating the words 'Royal Doulton Hotelware, England, Steelite'. This form of Doulton mark was used between 1976 and March 1983 when a new separate company was formed to produce and market Steelite – see the following entry.

**STEELITE INTERNATIONAL plc., Stoke-on-Trent, 1983 to present day.**

This company was formed on 16 March 1983 from what was originally part of the Hotelware Division of Royal Doulton Tablewares.

The trade name 'Steelite' has similar commercial connotations to Mason's original 'Ironstone China' and the new high-alumina body is claimed to be 'exceptionally strong and incredibly durable' and 'the strongest name in tableware'.

The forms are pleasingly clean and simple, enhanced with attractive designs. The new wares, angled at the hotel and catering trade, have won world-wide acclaim and the name 'Steelite' may well, like 'Ironstone', become a household word. A new translucent body was introduced early in 1994 under the name 'Albalite'.

The mark incorporates the trade name 'Steelite' above the words 'International' and 'England', all below a portcullis device. Year numbers usually occur to show the year of production.

PLATE 267. *An impressed marked Stevenson dessert basket and stand, decorated with a hand-painted formal Japan pattern – similar to the so-called 'Gaudy' wares. This shape of fruit basket was also produced by other potters such as Ridgways. 8¼in. (20.95cm) long.* c.1815-25.

**STEVENSON, Cobridge, c.1810-36.**
A printed mark, closely based on the standard Mason printed 'Patent Ironstone China' mark, has been reported. It comprises the wording:

STEVENSON'S
PATENT IRONSTONE
CHINA

under the crown device.

This mark may have been used by Andrew Stevenson (c.1810-32) at the Lower Manufactory at Cobridge. Ralph Stevenson was also in partnership with Augustus Aldborough Lloyd Williams – see the following entry.

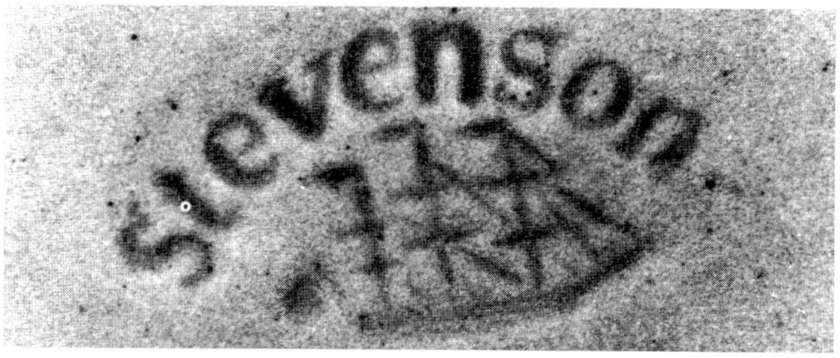


Some earthenwares and, rarely, ironstone-type wares bear an impressed mark comprising the simple name 'STEVENSON' over a representation of a sailing vessel. This mark has been attributed to Ralph Stevenson (c.1810-32) and sometimes to the

PLATE 268. *A printed Royal Arms marked Stevenson & Williams 'Royal Stone China' plate of characteristic shape. The mark (as shown) incorporates the initials 'R.S. & W.' Diameter 9½in. (24.13cm). c.1825-7.*

Greenock Pottery in Scotland. It is also noteworthy that Ralph Stevenson and his brother Andrew were in partnership together in Glasgow prior to 5 July 1799, at a date before that of the wares here under discussion.

The 'Stevenson' and ship mark is now attributed to Andrew Stevenson of Cobridge (*c*.1810-36) although it could also have related to the earlier partnership between James and Andrew Stevenson (*c*.1806-10) also at Cobridge. The ironstone-type dessert wares shown in Plate 267 and bearing this impressed mark are very similar in form to a range of Ridgway dessert shapes of the approximate period 1815. At about this period Messrs Chamberlain & Co., the Worcester porcelain manufacturers, purchased some earthenwares from 'Andrew Stevenson, Cobridge' (also listed as 'Stevenson & Co.'). One purchase dated 21 January 1814 was for 'Blue printed Abbey pattern'. These blue printed items were most probably of earthenware rather than ironstone and it must be mentioned that some of Andrew Stevenson's earthenwares bear a clear impressed mark reading 'A Stevenson. Warranted Staffordshire' around a crown device. The significance of the sailing ship device on the problem mark has not as yet been satisfactorily explained unless it merely suggests that a large export trade was carried on by this firm. Blue printed

STEVENSON'S
STONE CHINA

marks also occur on wares seemingly of the 1815-25 period. Such wares could have been produced by either Andrew or Ralph Stevenson, both of whom had large potteries at Cobridge at that period.

**STEVENSON & WILLIAMS, Cobridge, c.1825-27.**

Printed marks incorporating the initials 'R.S.W.' or 'R.S. & W.' are believed to relate to the partnership between Ralph Stevenson and Augustus Williams, which is mentioned in a mortgage deed of 1825. The partnership was dissolved on 18 November 1827.

A sample printed initial mark is reproduced below. This description 'Royal Stone China' appears with the initials 'R.S.W.' on printed dinner and dessert wares (Plates 268-270) which are well potted and of unusual forms. The description 'Nankin Stone China' also appears on some 'R.S.W.' printed marks.

This partnership was much engaged in the American trade.

PLATE 269. *An initial marked Stevenson & Williams 'Royal Stone China' dessert service showing the characteristic forms used by this short-lived partnership. Centrepiece 14½in. (36.83cm) long. c.1825-27.*

PLATE 270. *A rare initial-marked Stevenson & Williams 'Royal Stone China' dinner service tureen of characteristic form. 12½in. (31.75cm) high. c.1825-27.*

## STOKE CHINA.

This impressed name or description rarely occurs on early nineteenth century Spode china of an experimental or transitional type. It has the surface appearance of china, or of Spode's celebrated bone china, but is usually rather thicker in the potting and can display little or no translucency.

It was, like other bodies of this period, an undoubted effort to produce durable porcelain-looking wares at or near the cost of earthenwares, the basic object being, of course, to compete commercially with the importations from the East or from the Continent.

Spode's 'Stoke China' can, I believe, be classed as an early form of refined stone china but it is certainly nearer to porcelain than to earthenware. The probable period of the 'Stoke China' was c.1800-05 but the impressed mark is rarely found.

## 'STOKE WORKS' with Royal Arms mark, c.1813-25.

One of many types of an as yet unidentified good quality group of early ironstone bears a very well engraved ornate version of the pre-Victorian Royal Arms device.

The wording below the Royal Arms reads 'IMP$^{d}$. [Improved] IRON STONE CHINA, Stoke Works'. The use of the words 'Iron Stone' suggests a date after 1813, but the identity of the manufacturer has not as yet been discovered. William Adams had works at Stoke (as well as at Tunstall) from 1811-30, and he may be regarded as a possible producer of the fine early ironstone ware which bears this printed mark. However, these same ornate Royal Arms, with the Prince of Wales' feathers above and the motto 'Ich Dien' below, are shown on page 243, where the same ornate printed design occurs with the words 'Genuine Folch's Stone China'. As related under Stephen Folch (& Sons) entry, this 'Stoke Works' mark occurred on a dinner service together with matching pieces with the Folch name mark. It seems highly probable that this is a Folch mark.

## SWIFT & ELKIN, Longton, c.1840-43.

This Staffordshire partnership between John Swift and Samuel Elkin succeeded Swift, Elkin & Nicholls from 25 September 1840. The firm produced 'Staffordshire Stone China' as well as normal earthenware. Printed marks include the initials 'S. & E.'

From September 1843 John Swift carried on this Longton pottery with James Brindly under the style Swift & Brindly but this short-lived partnership was dissolved on 9 September 1844.

It is possible that Swift, Elkin & Nicholls and Swift & Brindly also produced stone china but as yet no name or initial ('S.E. & N.' or 'S. & B.') marks have been recorded.

## SWILLINGTON BRIDGE, near Leeds, Yorkshire, c.1820-50.

Excavations by Mr Christopher Gilbert on the site of a pottery at Swillington Bridge, some six miles south-east of Leeds, have shown that this small Yorkshire pottery produced 'Ironstone China' and 'Opaque

Granite China' during the 1820-50 period.

Good quality blue printed ware was made, as well as brown printed and enamelled earthenware. Excavated factory wasters show that an impressed crown mark was used, as well as a shield mark incorporating the words 'Opaque Granite China', the shield supported by a lion and a unicorn, an example of which is reproduced. The same basic mark, but with the initials 'W.R. & Co.', was used by William Ridgway of Shelton.

Blue printed ironstone bears the printed mark with crown, reproduced. The discovery of these fragments on the site of the small, little-known factory suggests that other small Yorkshire potteries may well have made ironstone ware.

For further information see Mr Gilbert's article in *Country Life* of 1 September 1966 and Heather Lawrence's *Yorkshire Pots and Potteries* (David & Charles, Newton Abbot, 1974).

**SWINNERTONS Ltd., Hanley. c.1907-71.**
Messrs Swinnertons Ltd. worked the Vulcan Pottery from c.1907, later adding the Washington and Victoria Pottery – all at Hanley – to their joint ownership.

The firm was a large producer of good quality useful earthenwares including ironstone-type wares. The various printed marks incorporate the firm's name, usually without the addition of 'Ltd.' A typical ironstone mark is here reproduced.

In the 1970-71 period Messrs Swinnertons Ltd. became part of Ridgway Potteries Ltd. and the Allied English Potteries group.

**JOHN TAMS (& Son) (Ltd.), Longton, c.1875 to present day.**
John Tams worked the Crown Pottery at Longton from c.1875. Early marks incorporate the name 'J. Tams' or 'Tams' with a crown above and the description 'ROCK STONE'. Other marks incorporate the initials 'J.T.', often joined. Several marks incorporating the initials 'J.T.' with the descriptive term 'stone ware' are believed to relate to John Tams, and the name of the patterns – 'Orleans', 'Peacock', etc. – are also included. From 1903-12 '& Sons' was added to the firm's style, and initial marks 'J.T. & S.' occur. From 1912 the style has been 'John Tams Ltd.', but most marks include only the name 'Tams'.

This Longton potter does not seem to be related to the mystery firm 'S. Tams & Co.' which produced blue-printed American market earthenwares earlier in the century.

**WILLIAM TAYLOR, Hanley, c.1860-73.**
L. Jewitt, writing in *Ceramic Art of Great Britain* of William Taylor and the Pearl Pottery, Brook Street, Hanley, stated: 'In 1860 the works passed into the hands of William Taylor, who commenced making white granite and common coloured and painted ware, but he discontinued, and confined himself to white granite-ware for the United States and Canadian markets, of both qualities -–the bluish tinted for the provinces and the purer white for the city trade. He was succeeded in 1881 by Wood, Hines & Winkle...'

**GEORGE & SAMUEL TAYLOR, Hunslet New Pottery, Leeds, Yorkshire, c.1837-66.**
William Taylor built the Hunslet Pottery prior to 1823 and was succeeded by his sons George and Samuel in the late 1830s.

Various printed 'Iron Stone China' marks, which incorporate the initial 'G & S.T.', probably relate to this partnership. Many willow pattern useful wares seem to have been made. Basic details are given in Heather Laurence's *Yorkshire Pots and Potteries* (David & Charles, Newton Abbot, 1974).

**TAYLOR BROTHERS (& Co.), Burslem and Hanley, 1859-71.**
This Burslem firm potted at Market Street, Hanley from May 1859 and produced a good range of earthenwares, including granite-type export wares. Various marks include the styles:

TAYLOR BROS.
HANLEY
or
TAYLOR BROS & CO.
HANLEY

The two brothers were William Taylor and James Taylor.

**JOHN THOMSON (& Sons), Glasgow, Scotland, c.1826-75.**

John Thomson established his Annfield Pottery at Glasgow in 1826, having travelled up from the Staffordshire potteries, bringing with him Staffordshire workers and traditions.

A wide range of earthenwares (and perhaps some china) was produced, including black and Rockingham glazed wares. Certainly ironstone-type wares were produced both for the home and export markets. Various printed marks incorporate body descriptions such as 'granite' or 'stone ware'. Some inexpensive sponged designs were on the granite body and the impressed mark incorporates an anchor device.

In, or slightly before, 1865 John Thomson took his two sons James and William into partnership and the firm then traded as 'John Thomson & Sons'. The basic marks incorporate the initials 'J.T.', after 1865 'J.T. & S.' or 'J.T. & Sons', or the firm's name. The place names 'Annfield' and/or 'Glasgow' can also occur along with the name of the pattern. Most of the printed copper-plates were supplied by specialist engraving firms in the Staffordshire Potteries.

An interesting article, 'The Annfield Pottery' by Gerald Quail, is incorporated in the *Scottish Pottery Historical Review,* No. 8. (1984). Finds on a Canadian site are discussed by Synne Sussman in *Scottish Pottery 17th Historical Review* (1995). This authority reports pre-1854 marks, including an impressed anchor with 'John Thomson' and 'Granite'. Other marks found in Canada comprise an impressed shield containing the words 'Stone Ware' and the initials 'J.T.'

The starting and closing dates of this pottery are open to debate. The earlier writers stated that the pottery dated back to 1816 but Mr Quail favours 1826, a date quoted in a near contemporary directory advertisement.

Various dates are suggested for the closure. Former works have quoted 1884 but Mr Quail, having noted that John Thomson died in 1873, stated that his sons 'continued to manufacture earthenware until 1888, when, due to the competition from cheaper English and foreign goods, the pottery ceased production. The moulds and plant were dispensed at an auction sale...'

However, the first (1878) edition of Jewitt's *Ceramic Art of Great Britain,* which would have been prepared before 1878, treated the pottery in the past tense and stated 'The works have been closed for some time'. Also the first *Pottery Gazette Diary* (that of 1882, prepared in 1881) carries a John Thomson & Son advertisement but purely relating to its activities as 'Grinders of Flint and Cornish Stone'.

It should be noted that John Thomson & Sons registered a new printed design titled 'Oaknut' on 11 May 1874. The firm was obviously in production at that time and the sons were then, no doubt, looking ahead to continue the pottery. For the above stated reasons I regard the closure of John Thomson & Sons' Annfield pottery as an earthenware manufactory to have been c.1875.

**THOMAS TILL & Son(s), Burslem, c.1850-1928.**

Thomas Till formerly potted at the Sytch Pottery, Burslem, in the firm of Barker, Sutton & Till (c.1834-42) and then in the firm of Barker & Till (q.v.). This partnership was dissolved on 15 April 1850 after which Thomas Till and his son continued on their own account.

Thomas Till & Son of the Sytch Pottery, Burslem, exhibited at the 1851 Exhibition and their wares included 'pearl white granite':

> Albany shape dishes, baker and plates; pearl white granite,
> Virginia shape set, teapot, sugar, cream jug, cup and saucer, in pearl white granite. Set of jugs, pearl white granite.
> Albany shape soup tureen, complete, and sauce tureen,
> complete, white granite, gold bands... Virginia shape, set tea cup and saucer and teapot, white granite, gold band.

At that period, 61 men, 34 women, 46 boys and 33 girls were employed. Till's various earthenware pieces are normally marked with the name in full. The trading style had been amended to Thomas Till & Sons at least by March 1869.

The firm was engaged to a large degree in the export market, particularly for the less expensive types of ironstone and granite wares. Various printed and impressed marks incorporate the name or the initials 'T.T. & S.'

Pearl Pottery (Burslem) Ltd. worked Till's old Sytch Pottery from 1929.

**TOMKINSON Bros. & Co., Hanley, c.1869.**

The name mark Tomkinson Bros. & Co. has been recorded on American market white granite wares but neither the rate records nor the directories include this exact trade style. However, the name does occur in the

PLATE 271. *A marked 'Tonquin China' dessert service dish bearing a typical printed outline Japan pattern. 11½in. x 8in. (29.21cm x 20.32cm). c.1820s.*

design registration records as having registered dinnerware forms on 4 August 1869, the address being given as Columbia Works, Hanley. The only Hanley-based firm given in directories of the period is T. Tomkinson & Co. of Clarence Street, Hanley (formerly Tomkinson & Phillips, *c.*1868). It is probable that the Tomkinson Bros. & Co. marked wares were produced by the short-lived firm of T. Tomkinson & Co., *c.*1869.

**TONQUIN CHINA mark.**
Blue printed marks incorporating the description 'Tonquin China' occur on good quality ironstone-type ware of the 1820 period (see Plate 271). The name of the manufacturer is as yet not known.

**GEORGE TOWNSEND, Longton, c.1850-65.**
George Townsend succeeded Sampson Bridgwood at St. Gregory's Pottery, High Street, Longton from *c.*1850. He is also recorded at Chadwick Street, Longton.

Various printed marks occur usually including the Royal Arms and the description 'Staffordshire Ironstone China' plus the name 'G. Townsend'. Initial marks 'G.T.' probably also relate to this Longton potter.

For further information on this Longton firm the reader is referred to Rodney Hampson's specialist study 'Longton Potters 1700-1865' (*Journal of Ceramic History*, Vol. 14, City Museum & Art Gallery, Stoke-on-Trent, 1990).

**T.P.** see Trachtenberg & Panthes.

**TRACHTENBERG & PANTHES, Odessa, mid-19th century.**
Various British ironstones bear Royal Arms and other marks incorporating the initials 'T.P.'

These initials relate to Trachtenberg & Panthes of Odessa in Russia, a firm which seemingly ordered large quantities of British useful wares. Some of these goods were printed with Russian views.

One such printed pattern was registered by Wedgwood & Co. of Tunstall on 17 September 1867. The mark comprises the British Royal Arms and supporters with the initials 'T.P.' prominently placed, one each side. The additional British wording 'Patent Paris White Ironstone' appears on these Russian-market articles.

**E.T. TROUTBECK, Tunstall, c.1844-46.**

Edmund Twemlow Troutbeck produced various earthenwares at Sandyford, Tunstall in the mid-1840s.

Various name and initial ('E.T.T.') marks have been recorded on blue printed or Spatterware-type wares. The place name 'Tunstall', sometimes with an anchor device, can occur with these rare Troutbeck markings.

Rodney Hampson gave an account of Troutbeck's rates of pay and discontent over these in the *Northern Ceramic Society Newsletter*, No. 91 of September 1993. Troutbeck assigned this stock to trustees in April 1846.

**TRUBSHAW, HAND & Co., Longton, c.1878-85.**

This partnership between John Trubshaw, Richard Hand and Thomas Hulme at the Albert Pottery, High Street, Longton was a china manufacturer but its trade advertisements in the early 1880s stated that the partnership was 'also dealers in stone, jet and granite wares'. This serves to remind us that several firms traded in types of ceramic that they did not necessarily manufacture.

**G.R. TURNBULL, Newcastle upon Tyne, c.1840-72.**

Various blue printed earthenwares have been reported bearing impressed and printed marks reading, in various forms, 'TURNBULL', 'STEPNEY POTTERY' or incorporating the helpful initials 'G.R.T.'

Such marks relate to G.R. Turnbull of the Stepney (Bank) pottery at Newcastle upon Tyne. This potter succeeded Dalton & Burn and was in turn succeeded by John Wood in the early 1870s. Although most examples are of standard earthenware, Turnbull may well have produced some stone china.

It should, of course, be noted that Stepney does not in these cases refer to the London district of Stepney.

**G.W. TURNER (& Sons), Tunstall, c.1873-94.**

This firm succeeded Messrs Turner & Tomkinson at the Victoria Works in High Street, Tunstall. As from 1 July 1873 George Wardle Turner continued and was joined by his sons. It seems they also potted at the Alexandra Works in Scotia Road, Tunstall. Printed initial 'G.W.T.' or 'G.W.T. & S.' marks have been reported on ironstone-type wares.

**JOHN TURNER (TURNER & Co.), Lane End, c.1762-1806.**

John Turner produced extremely fine earthenware – cream-coloured ware, Wedgwood-type jasper and basalt ware and, later, fine stoneware-type jugs, etc.,

PLATE 272. *A well-potted, marked 'Turner's Patent' dessert service centrepiece decorated with Oriental-inspired willow pattern-type design printed in underglaze-blue. See also Plate 8. 13½in. (34.29cm) long. c.1800-05.*

PLATE 273. *A marked 'Turner's Patent' oval centrepiece painted with a popular Turner Oriental floral design. See Plate 9 for a similar dessert service. 12in. (30.48cm) long. c.1800-05. Mrs Frank Nagington.*

with relief motifs – as well as porcelain. The standard reference book on John Turner and his ware is *The Turners of Lane End – Master Potters of the Industrial Revolution* by Bevis Hillier, 1965.

So far as this book is concerned the most important section of Turner's varied products is his 'Patent' stone china-type body, which bears the painted mark 'TURNER'S PATENT' or the impressed mark 'TURNER'.

The abstract of the 1800 patent reads:

> A new method, or methods of manufacturing porcelain and earthenware, by the introduction of a material not heretofore used in the manufacturing of these articles. The material is known in Staffordshire by the names 'Tabberner's Mine Rock', 'Little Mine Rock' and 'New Rock'. It is generally used as follows: ground, washed, dried in a potter's kiln, commonly called a slip kiln, afterwards mixed with a certain proportion of growan or Cornish Stone, previously calcined, levigated, and dryed, a small quantity of flint similarly prepared is also added, but in different proportions, according to the nature of the ware, and the heat required in burning it.

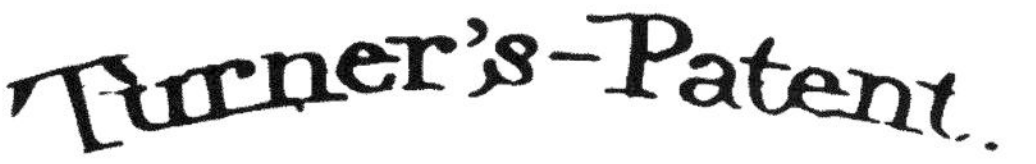


The resulting ware bears the painted mark 'Turner's Patent' and, although the first of the stone chinas, it is often slightly translucent. Fine quality dessert services, mugs, jugs, bowls, etc. were made (see Plates 8, 9, 273-277), the favourite pattern being a neat but bold formal floral pattern in the Chinese style (see Plates 9 and 273) similar in general effect to the later Mason 'Japan' patterns. Other rarer examples show finer styles of decoration. I have seen some apparent pattern-plates with blue painted reference numbers added below the standard red painted 'Turner's Patent' mark – 'No 10', 'No 14', and so on. These plates bore unusual patterns that I have not otherwise seen in services or other articles.

The Turner's Patent wares can be of very fine quality and they can be regarded as the first of the British ironstone-type bodies, the patent dating from 1800.

In February 1804 John Glover and Charles Simpson

*Plate 274. A rare marked 'Turner's Patent' punch bowl very much in the style of 18th century imports from China. Diameter 10½in. (26.67cm). c.1800-05.*

joined the Turners, but the new partnership was of short duration for in November of that year John Turner withdrew and in March 1806 the remaining partners dissolved their association. In July 1806 the Turners were declared bankrupt and in June of the following year 'a large and elegant assortment of Earthenware and china, comprising the different articles... consisting of cream colour, china glazed blue

PLATE 275. *A rare impressed marked 'TURNER' stone china-type plate, hand painted in the Oriental manner with underglaze blue and overglaze enamels. Diameter 9in. (2.86cm).* c.1800-05.

PLATE 276. *Two views of a superb quality 'Turner's Patent' jug with underglaze blue ground. The hand-painted decoration combines Oriental and European features.8½in. (21.59cm) high. c.1800-05. City Museum &Art Gallery, Stoke-on-Trent.*

edge, china glaze printed and painted, Egyptian black (basalt), Cane, Stone, Jasper, Pearl and Patent China... of Messrs Turner & Co...' was offered for sale. The reference to 'Patent China' obviously refers to the 1800 patent.

According to tradition, Josiah Spode purchased the rights to the 'Turner Patent' body. However, no reference is made to it in the marks used by Spode on his own 'Stone China', which was probably a new variation of Turner's patent, using the basic raw materials with additions. It is now thought that Spode did not buy up the Turner Patent rights on the bankruptcy in 1806 but rather that Spode's 'Stone China' was not introduced until about 1813. See Leonard Whiter's *Spode*, Chapter 10 and my page 64. However, Whiter did suggest that William Turner may have produced some patent wares when potting at Lane End on his own account up to about 1829. No late-looking marked 'Turner' stone chinas have, however, been reported.

Do note that the Staffordshire Turners are not related to Thomas Turner, the eighteenth century manufacturer of porcelains at Caughley in Shropshire. Some authors tend to confuse the situation!

PLATE 277. *A rare 'Turner's Patent' blue-ground mug matching the jug shown in the preceding illustration. Note the concave top to fit the lips. 5½in. (13.97cm) high. c.1800-05. City Museum &Art Gallery, Stoke-on-Trent.*

**TURNER, GODDARD & Co., Tunstall, c.1868-74.**
This partnership between George Turner, John Goddard and John Bargen trading as Turner, Goddard & Co. worked the Royal Albert Pottery in Parsonage Street, Tunstall, in the 1868-74 period. Albert Meakin later took over this pottery.

Turner, Goddard & Co. produced some ironstone or granite-type wares. Various marks incorporate their joint names. The partnership was dissolved on 1 June 1874.

**TURNER & TOMKINSON, Tunstall, c.1858-73.**
As recorded by Jewitt, John Tomkinson built the Victoria Works at Tunstall in 1858. He was joined by G.W. Turner and the two traded as Messrs Turner & Tomkinson prior to John Tomkinson's retirement in 1873. The firm was then continued as G.W. Turner & Sons.

Various types of ironstone or granite wares were produced and different printed or impressed marks incorporate the full name Turner & Tomkinson or the initials 'T & T.' The description 'Pearl Ironstone China' occurs as part of some marks.

**JOSEPH TWIGG & Bros., Kilnhurst Pottery, Yorkshire, c.1839-84.**
Benjamin, Joseph and John Twigg of the Newhill Pottery near Swinton leased the Kilnhurst Pottery in 1839. Various types of earthenware were made some of which is marked 'TWIGGS' and some stone china was also produced. Various printed marks incorporate the initial 'T', sometimes with 'K P' for Kilnhurst Pottery – see *Yorkshire Pots and Potteries* by H. Laurence (David & Charles, 1974).

**THOMAS & CHRISTOPHER TWYFORD, Hanley, c.1858-9.**
This partnership between Thomas and Christopher Twyford at Bath Street and New Street, Hanley, produced a range of useful earthenwares and ironstone-type stone china wares.

The partnership was dissolved on 9 July 1859, from which date Thomas Twyford continued alone at the Bath Street Works and Christopher Twyford took over the New Street works.

Printed marks incorporating the initials 'T & C T' have been recorded, some with the description 'Stone Ware'.

It is probable that Christopher and Thomas used their own initial marks, 'C.T.' and 'T.T.' after the July 1859 dissolution of their partnership. The initial mark

T.T.
H

has been recorded as being used by Thomas Twyford but not necessarily on ironstone type wares.

**U. & C., U. & Cie.**
Various ironstone wares have been reported as bearing 'U. & C.' or 'U. & Cie.' marks. As it is sometimes assumed that these are of British manufacture I should point out that these initial marks usually relate to Utzschneider & Cie. of Sarrequemines on the Franco-German border. This large firm produced a wide range of wares in the nineteenth century, many of which emulated British styles.

**UNICORN TABLEWARE, Hanley, c.1979-to present day.**
After 1979 when Messrs Josiah Wedgwood & Sons Ltd. acquired the firm of Enoch Wedgwood (Tunstall) Ltd., that company continued to produce some popular traditional Enoch Wedgwood patterns such as 'Asiatic Pheasants', 'Oriental Pheasants' and 'Woodland' under the trade name 'Unicorn' or 'Unicorn Tableware'.

**V. & B.**
Whilst marks comprising or incorporating the initials 'V. & B.' could relate to Messrs Venables & Baines of Nile Street, Burslem in the 1851-52 period, it is much more likely that they relate to the large Continental firm of Villeroy & Boch.

This German complex, that could be likened to Doulton's, produced a very large range of earthenwares and stonewares at their several factories. The main Villeroy & Boch works were at Dresden, Mettlach and Septfontaines (Luxemburg), and these names or the initial of these place-names can occur with 'V. & B.' marks.

**THOMAS BOLTON VENABLES.**
On 21 January 1854 Thomas Bolton Venables took out a provisional patent for improvements in the manufacture of earthenware by dispensing with the use of flint and Cornwall stone and replacing these ingredients with 'Staffordshire Granite slip'.

Such a mix would presumably have produced a durable ironstone, granite china-type body, but the patent was not proceeded with and T.B. Venables is not recorded as a Staffordshire manufacturer. However, a Thomas Venables paid the rates on Meakins Pottery in Cannon Street, Shelton, in 1858.

**J. VENABLES & Co., Burslem, c.1854-60.**
It is difficult to date precisely the period of this firm which appears also to have traded as Venables, Mann & Co.

Certainly in 1860 it was trading as John Venables & Co., the then partners being John Venables, Thomas Martyn and John Hooper (who retired on 20 August 1860). For a short period from then to April 1861 it traded as Venables & Martyn.

These firms produced various types of earthenware as well as china, and had a wholesale outlet in London. Printed Royal Arms and name marks are recorded.

The American authority Sam Laidacker, in his book *Anglo-American China* Parts I & II, quotes a pattern registration for J. Venables & Co. on 7 January 1852. I have not been able to trace this in the British records.

**VENABLES, MANN & Co., Burslem, c.1853-56. (J. VENABLES & Co.)**
This partnership at Nile Street, Burslem, between John Venables, Arthur Mann, Francis Nicholls and Henry Gasett, succeeded Venables & Baines (q.v.). Francis Nicholls retired in June 1853 but the partnership continued to trade under the original name.

John Venables and Arthur Mann jointly took out several patents for novel forms of ceramic decoration in 1854 and 1855.

Various types of earthenwares including ironstone-type wares were produced and printed marks incorporate the title of the partnership or the initials 'V.M. & Co.'

It is possible that the firm also traded for at least part of its period as John Venables & Co. (q.v.).

**VENABLES & BAINES, Burslem, 1851-52.**
This short-lived partnership between John Venables and Charles Baines appear to have succeeded Messrs Mellor Venables & Co. at the Hole House Pottery in Nile Street, Burslem from 30 June 1851. The new partnership was dissolved from 30 June 1852.

Various types of blue printed and other earthenwares were produced including ironstone-type wares. A scenic-centred, American-market, design was registered by Venables & Baines on 17 February 1852 (Parcel number 1). This and related prints with a panelled border occur on octagonal dinner service forms in the ironstone body. Similar designs were produced by the preceding partnership of Mellor Venables & Co. Messrs Venables, Mann & Co. (also known as J. Venables & Co.) succeeded in 1853.

Impressed or printed marks incorporate the name Venables & Baines or the initials 'V & B'. Please note, however, that these initials can relate to the large Continental firm of Villeroy & Boch – see my 'V. & B.' entry.

**VENABLES & NICHOLS, Stoke, c.1863-64.**
This short-lived partnership between John Venables and Samuel Nichols potted at Stoke-on-Trent for a short period prior to the dissolution of partnership on 12 June 1864.

Ironstone-type wares bearing 'V. & N.' initial marks would relate to this firm.

**'VICTORIA', 'VICTORIA WARE', 'VICTORIA IRONSTONE'.**
This British-sounding trade name was in fact used by several foreign manufacturers. Whilst hard-paste porcelains will be of German origin some 'Victoria' earthenwares and ironstones were produced by the C.C. Thompson Pottery Company of East Liverpool, Ohio, USA from c.1890 into the twentieth century. This manufacturer, like other American firms, used near copies of the British Royal Arms as the main feature of the mark. These American products are unlikely to be found today in the British Isles.

As the market abounds with Mason-style wares bearing marks incorporating the word 'Victoria', it should also be noted that Messrs Blakeney Art Pottery of Stoke (q.v.) has used the 'Victoria' trade name on post-war products which in many cases reflect nineteenth century shapes and patterns. It would appear that some 'Victoria' ironstone type products are being sold at antiques fairs and similar outlets as old. As one correspondent reported in 1995: '...my wife and I found a suspicious number of exactly similar wares, bearing the above mark... to my mind they are all well fashioned reproductions, with a misleading mark, indicating they are at least one century older than they are in fact'.

The printed marks on reproductions of Victorian wares usually feature a version of the British Royal Arms. Trade names such as 'Victorian Ironstone' were used. I do not know of any nineteenth century British ironstone which incorporates the name 'Victoria' in the mark in the manner of the reproductions which abound in the 1990s.

**'W. & C.' marks.**
Various British printed marks occur incorporating these initials. One crowned scroll 'Stone China' Lily pattern example is shown in Serry Wood's interesting and early (1959) study *English Staffordshire* in the China Classics series of thin books (Century House, Watkins Glen, NY, USA).

Having shown an obviously post-1840 example with this 'W & C' mark, the author stated: 'The only

Staffordshire firm to which the initials applies is Wood & Caldwell, operating from 1790-1818. But the plate scarcely seems to be this early, being typical of the wares of the 1845 period instead ... There is no other known Staffordshire firm with the initials 'W. & C.' or 'W & Co'.

In fact apart from Wood & Caldwell there were at least eight Staffordshire partnerships entitled to use 'W. & C.' initial marks. There were also at least twelve pre-1900 firms using 'W & Co.' marks.

Of the 'W. & C.' firms that produced ironstone or stone china wares in the 1840s, the most likely is Wood & Challinor (q.v.). Later manufacturers of granite-type wares include Walker & Carter (*c*.1867-89) or Wade & Colclough (1870-85).

However, Leslie Bockol in her 1995 book *Willow Ware. Ceramics in the Chinese Tradition* (Schiffer Publishing Ltd., USA) illustrates a 'W. & C.' Stone Ware scroll mark with 'England' added, indicating a post-1890 date. Furthermore the Willow pattern plate with advertising motifs matches one marked 'Wedgwood & Co. Ltd.' in full. We must therefore assume that Wedgwood & Co. may on occasions have used (or reused) 'W. & C.' initial marks.

**WADE & COLCLOUGH, Burslem, c.1870-85.**
Little is known of this partnership between John Wade and James Colclough at Bournes Bank, Burslem.

Standard types of Staffordshire export-market earthenwares were produced and some granite type wares bearing 'W. & C.' initial marks may have been produced by this Burslem firm.

**THOMAS WALKER, Tunstall, c.1845-51.**
Thomas Walker worked the Lion Pottery at Tunstall. A good range of earthenware was produced, much of which was intended for the American markets. Marks include the name 'T. WALKER' or 'THOS. WALKER', sometimes with the American eagle device. In some instances the place name 'Tunstall' was added to distinguish the ware from that produced by other potters of the same name, such as Thomas Walker of Longton (*c*.1856-57) and Thomas Henry Walker of Longton (*c*.1846-49).

Other 'Stone Ware' or 'Pearl Ironstone China' marks incorporate only the initials 'T.W.' These initials, when on Staffordshire wares of the 1840s, almost certainly relate to Thomas Walker. A typical T. Walker printed mark is here reproduced.

**THOMAS HENRY WALKER, Lane End, c.1845-49.**
Thomas Henry Walker, formerly of Batkin, Walker & Broadhurst, started on his own account at Church Street, Lane End (Longton), from November 1845. He seems, however, to have potted for only a few years. He was bankrupt in 1849.

Printed marks incorporating the initials 'T.H.W.' seem only to fit this Staffordshire potter. Such initial marks can incorporate the wording 'Staffordshire Warranted Stone China'.

**WALKER & CARTER, Longton & Stoke, c.1865-89.**
This partnership between Thomas Walker and William Carter succeeded Messrs Walker & Bateman at the British Anchor Pottery, Anchor Road, Longton, from July 1865. In about 1872 the partnership moved to the Anchor Works at Stoke, where they continued to *c*.1889.

Various types of standard Staffordshire useful wares were produced. Some 'W. & C.' initial marks may relate to this partnership at Longton or Stoke.

**WALLEY, Staffordshire Potteries, c.1830-60.**
Various impressed and printed marks occur incorporating the surname Walley, without other identification. One mark includes the description 'Paris White Ironstone China'.

It is probable that most Walley marks on ironstone-type wares were produced by Edward Walley of Cobridge – see the following entry. However, other Walleys potting at the same approximate period include: George Walley, Longton, John Walley, Burslem and Hanley, and William Walley, Burslem and Hanley.

**EDWARD WALLEY (& Son), Cobridge, 1845-62.**
Edward Walley, successor to Jones & Walley at the Villa Pottery, Cobridge, from February 1845. He produced general earthenware, including ironstone which often bore the impressed mark 'Ironstone China. E. Walley'. Various other printed or impressed marks include the initials 'E.W.' or the name in full. Bold hand-painted designs were employed as well as private patterns.

Seemingly the firm of Edward Walley & Son (also listed as E. & W. Walley) succeeded Edward Walley in about 1857 but there is a dearth of records to confirm this before 1860. The new firm continued up to the dissolution of partnership on 30 January 1862. Edward was then responsible for the debts. Local directories do not show any further occupiers of the Villa Pottery until Keate's 1869-70 directory when Wood, Son & Co. is

PLATE 278. *A marked 'Edward Walley. Ironstone China' 'Sidney's Patent measure jug' in a blue tinted body. The portholes are filled with glass to show the level of the liquid. 6in. (15.24cm) high. c.1845-55.*

listed. Edward Walley was an important manufacturer of American-market ironstone-type wares in the period *c.*1868-79.

The Villa Pottery under Edward Walley, and under the later firm of Edward Walley & Sons, enjoyed a large export trade, particularly to North America. Its wares are well known to American collectors and are featured in American books. Edward Walley also produced the American market 'Tea Leaf' patterns, some of which are described as lustred. The so-called hand-painted 'Cauldy' patterns were also produced.

Edward Walley registered a series of moulded dinner, tea ware and toilet ware in rather angular forms on 29 November 1856 (nos. 107783-5). The firm gave the name 'Niagara' to these shapes which proved very popular. The registration device and the name appear on some examples which may be in their white undecorated state or embellished with simple export patterns.

The strange marked 'Walley Ironstone China', 'Sidney Patent' measure-jugs with glass windows (Plate 278) were made in various sizes, with different measures, i.e. 'Quart', and can be found decorated in different styles. But the main Walley output lay in American market, inexpensive useful wares. Several forms closely follow this Gothic form measure-jug.

**E. & W. WALLEY, Cobridge, c.1858-59.**
This entry originates from the British design registration files where shapes were entered in the name of E. & W. Walley. These entries would have been based on the letterhead or form of signature sent to London with the drawings. It seems therefore that in the approximate period 1858-59, the old firm of Edward Walley of the Villa Pottery, Cobridge (as used in the registration of 29 November 1856), traded as E. & W. Walley, rather than as Edward Walley & Son, a

form of title used by at least 1860.

The E. & W. Walley registrations were entered on 29 January 1858 and 7 May 1859. They relate to a fluted jug form, a vine-patterned jug and one featuring dead game.

The reader is referred to the main, preceding, entry for Edward Walley (& Son). However, the E. & W. Walley partnership may have worked a separate pottery at Bleak Street, Cobridge, rather than the Villa Pottery.

Various marks incorporating the initials 'E. & W.W.' will relate to this firm. The fuller mark 'E. & W. Walley' also occurs.

**JAMES WARREN, High Street, Longton, c.1841-53.**

A printed 'Stone China' mark with a lion crest above and the name 'Warren' below has been reported.

This mark could have been used by James Thomas Warren of the Victoria and Park Place Works at Longton in the approximate period 1841-1853. However, James Warren is recorded as a china manufacturer, rather than an earthenware or ironstone maker.

Other marks include or comprise the initial and name 'J. Warren'. Initial marks 'J.W.' could also relate to this Longton potter.

**WASHINGTON POTTERY (STAFFORDSHIRE) Ltd., Shelton, c.1946-c.1983.**

This company of College Road, Shelton, produced 'an international range' of ironstone table wares marked with the Washington Pottery trade name. One mark incorporates the description 'English Ironstone Tableware'.

**(J.H.) WEATHERBY & SONS Ltd., Hanley, Staffordshire Potteries, 1891 to present day.**

John Henry Weatherby, having dissolved his partnership in Whittaker & Co. in August 1891, rented a factory in Pinnox Street, Tunstall, to commence trading on his own account. In 1892 or 1893 he purchased the Falcon Pottery in High Street (now Old Town Road), Hanley. This can always have been a family business and the present managing director is a great-grandson of the founder.

The firm mainly produced standard earthenwares but hotel-type wares and ironstone-type bodies have been produced. After Messrs A.J. Wilkinson Ltd. ceased production *c*.1970, Messrs Weatherby took over its popular relief-moulded white wheat designs which were mainly exported to North America. These wares bear a printed mark including the basic wording:

ROYAL CROWNFORD IRONSTONE
WHITE WHEAT
WEATHERBY, HANLEY, ENGLAND

with the last two numerals of the year added below, i.e. 87 for 1987.

**'WEDGEWOOD'.**

Marks on stone china and ironstone-type wares incorporating the name 'Wedgewood' – with the middle 'e' – do not relate to the main Staffordshire firm founded by Josiah Wedgwood.

In most cases these wares were produced by William Smith & Co. of the Stafford Pottery, Stockton-on-Tees, Co. Durham. Smith's marks incorporating the name 'Wedgewood' should pre-date 1848. See page 325.

**J. WEDGWOOD.**

Wares bearing this name mark, in any form, will not relate to the main firm founded by Josiah Wedgwood, the subject of the next entry.

In most cases they relate to nineteenth century earthenwares produced by John Wedge Wood or by John Wedge Wood & Co. (q.v.).

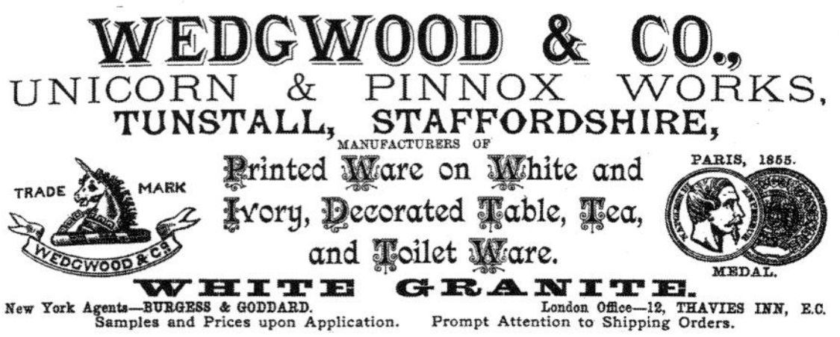
WEDGWOOD & CO.,
UNICORN & PINNOX WORKS,
TUNSTALL, STAFFORDSHIRE,
MANUFACTURERS OF
Printed Ware on White and Ivory, Decorated Table, Tea, and Toilet Ware.
TRADE MARK
WEDGWOOD & CO.
PARIS, 1855.
MEDAL.
WHITE GRANITE.
New York Agents—BURGESS & GODDARD.
London Office—12, THAVIES INN, E.C.
Samples and Prices upon Application.
Prompt Attention to Shipping Orders.

**WEDGWOOD & Co. (Ltd.), formerly Tunstall, later Hanley, c.1860-1979.**
**ENOCH WEDGWOOD (Tunstall) Ltd., from 1965.**

Wedgwood & Co. succeeded Podmore, Walker & Co. (q.v.), a firm which had already used the name Wedgwood in its marks. Quotations from Jewitt's standard work *Ceramic Art of Great Britain* show the standing of the company and its products in the 1870s:

> The works, which are very extensive, and give employment to six or seven hundred persons, occupy an area of about an acre of ground, and are among the most substantially built and best arranged in the pottery district. The goods produced are the higher classes of earthenware… The quality of the 'Imperial Ironstone China' – the staple production of the firm, is of remarkable excellence, both in body and in glaze, and the decorations are characterized by pure taste, artistic feeling, and precision of execution… they associate durability of quality in body and a perfect glaze with purity of outline in form, chasteness of decoration, and clearness and harmony of colour, adapting their designs and styles of decoration to the

PLATE 279. *Representative pieces from a marked 'Wedgwood's Stone China' dessert service decorated with a printed outline coloured-in design. Pattern number 1156. Centrepiece 11½in. (29.2cm) long. c.1821-29.*

National tastes of the people in the various climes to which the goods are sent. One of the most successful of their original ordinary printed designs is the pattern known as 'Asiatic Pheasants', which has become so popular as to be considered one of the standard patterns of this country and the colonies. They also supply large quantities of ironstone china specially made for the use of ships, restaurants, hotels, etc.... The Unicorn Works (as opposed to the Pinnox Works) is entirely devoted to the production of plain white granite ware for the American trade...

The 'Asiatic Pheasants' pattern referred to is shown in Plate 280. It was indeed popular, for I have seen the design and special 'Asiatic Pheasants' mark with the name or initials of more than twenty firms.

Wedgwood & Co.'s trade advertisements in the early 1890s make special reference to 'White Granite, lustre and decorated earthenware for the American markets'. The company also had an agency in New York.

Owing to the confusion between Josiah Wedgwood & Sons Ltd. and Wedgwood & Co. Ltd. the latter was changed to Enoch Wedgwood Tunstall Ltd. in 1965 but, in the winter of 1979, Messrs Josiah Wedgwood & Sons Ltd. purchased the Tunstall firm. From this period the old style was discontinued although some popular designs continued under the Unicorn name.

The various marks incorporate the name 'Wedgwood & Co.' while 'Ltd.' was often added from c.1900. The use of the '& Co.' distinguishes the marks from the one-word 'Wedgwood' impressed into the ware made by Josiah Wedgwood & Sons Ltd. Standard descriptive names include 'Stone-Ware', 'Stone China', 'Imperial Ironstone China' and 'Patent Paris White Ironstone' or 'Stone-Ware. Wedgwood & Co.'

PLATE 280. *A marked 'Wedgwood & Co.' (of Tunstall) blue printed dinner service plate bearing a version of the popular 'Asiatic Pheasant' design. This was copied by a host of other manufacturers. Diameter 9in. (22.86cm). c.1860-70.*

**JOSIAH WEDGWOOD (& Sons Ltd.), Etruria (now at Barlaston, to the south of Stoke), c.1759 to present day.**

This famous firm should not be confused with Wedgwood & Co. (Ltd.) (see previous entry). Josiah Wedgwood & Sons Ltd. is mainly known for its fine coloured jasper ware with white relief motifs and for its fine cream-coloured or Queen's ware.

In 1817, experiments were begun to produce stone china to compete with Spode's 'Stone China' body successfully marketed under that name. A letter of 1817 from Josiah Bateman, Wedgwood's salesman, is quoted in the Spode entry, and may have been responsible for sparking off the experiments. Examples are mainly in underglaze-blue 'WEDGWOOD'S/ STONE CHINA' but examples are seldom found today. A dessert set with typical 'Japan' style design is illustrated in Plate 279.

Research in the Wedgwood archives carried out by Robin Reilly[18] suggests that the new body was not produced commercially before the latter part of 1821. Although some other authorities suggest that Wedgwood's 'Stone China' was produced up to 1861, this is open to serious doubt. No orders have I understand been discovered for these wares subsequent to October 1829, although trials for stone china-type bodies were produced up to the end of 1853.

As one would expect, the general quality of Wedgwood's stone china is very good and the impressed or printed marks will comprise or incorporate the name 'WEDGWOOD'. Examples are, however, scarce and whilst the designs are tasteful, they are not as colourful as most Mason, Davenport, Hicks or Spode examples. For further information the reader is referred to Robin Reilly's 1989 work, *Wedgwood.*

In later years this great firm also produced strong-bodied useful wares although they were by no means its main concern. In 1994 the company introduced a new 'Vitro-China' being 'A strong durable body, containing no animal bone. It is high-fired for extra strength and is an amalgam of vitreous products with flux, to give translucency'.

Wedgwood's Vitro-China is also claimed to be 'dishwasher, microwave and freezer safe, and can be warmed in a conventional oven'. The initial designs were tasteful and simple – trellis flower, blue Delphi and a bird design harping back to the early nineteenth century – and were launched under the group name 'Infinity'.

A range of cookware (oval roasting dishes, circular casseroles, etc.) is also produced in this Vitro-China, which like other Wedgwood products bears a clear name mark. The Company also, in the 1990s, produces superior quality Hotel Ware for cruise lines and high class establishments. These wares carry various Hotel Ware marks but always including the Wedgwood name.

The reader should note, however, that 'J. Wedgwood', 'Wedgwood & Co.' and 'Wedgewood' marks do *not* relate to the main Wedgwood company.

**G. WESTON, Lane End, c.1807-29.**
Blue printed marks have been recorded incorporating a crown device and the wording 'IRON STONE CHINA. G. WESTON'. This potter is recorded at High Street, Lane End, within the period c.1807-29. His ironstone wares may date from about 1815. Examples are rare. Initial marks 'G.W.' may also have been used.

**WHITEHAVEN.**
Several potters produced various types of earthenware at Whitehaven in Cumberland. Many of their products were exported but few examples bear helpful marks.

Some marks incorporate the initials 'W.P. Co.', 'I.W.' or 'J.W.' with or without the place name 'Whitehaven' and 'Stone China' or 'Warranted Stone China'.

The standard work on the Whitehaven potters is *The History of the West Cumberland Potteries* by Florence Sibson (privately published, 1991).

**HENRY WILEMAN, Foley, Fenton, 1857-64.**
I have a trade card relating to this manufacturer. This lists his specialities as 'Earthenware, Ironstone, China, Egyptian Black, Stoneware &c. &c.' The address is given as 'The Foley Potteries, Staffordshire'.

The works were later continued by J. Wileman & Co. and then by James Francis Wileman.

Name marks should occur but I have not seen any examples.

**JAMES F. WILEMAN, Foley, Fenton, c.1869-92.**
Various members of the Wileman family worked the Foley Pottery (formerly occupied by Elkin, Knight & Bridgwood), and James Francis Wileman succeeded James and Charles Wileman (who also traded as J. Wileman & Co.) in about 1869[19], James concentrating on earthenwares.

L. Jewitt, commenting on the contemporary products, wrote 'The goods produced are the usual granite ware, printed wares, lustres, Egyptian and shining black and cream-coloured wares... the great bulk of the trade are exported to the United States, Panama, Australia, South Africa, Ceylon, Java and India'.

Printed or impressed marks incorporate the initials 'J.F.W.' or the name in full.

**A.J. WILKINSON (Ltd.), Burslem, 1882-1964.**
Arthur James Wilkinson, trading as A.J. Wilkinson (Ltd.) at the Royal Staffordshire Pottery (formerly the Central Pottery), Burslem, produced good quality 'Royal Patent Ironstone' for the home and American markets from 11 November 1882 onwards, in succession to Wilkinson & Hulme (q.v.). Marks are full and self-explanatory; an example is here reproduced. The trade name 'Royal Staffordshire Pottery' is also used. Some marks include the additional wording 'Late R. Alcock'[20] but this would have been discontinued before 1900. Much export-market ware was produced including the popular 'white Wheat' relief-moulded wares – a line taken over by Messrs J.H. Weatherby & Sons Ltd. Messrs Midwinter took over the main Wilkinson concern in November 1964.

Wilkinson were still producing 'White Granite' as well as semi-porcelain earthenware bodies and hotel wares in the 1920s and had agencies in New York, Argentina, Brazil, Cuba, Greece, South Africa and Australia.

Sample Wilkinson printed marks are shown below. 'Ltd.' was added to the firm's style and marks from c.1896 when the old Central Pottery was retitled the Royal Staffordshire Pottery.

**JOHN WILKINSON, Whitehaven, Cumberland, c.1829-68.**
John Wilkinson took over the Whitehaven Pottery from Woodworth in 1829. He continued it until his death in 1868, after which it was carried on by his widow and then by his son Randle, trading as Wilkinson's Pottery Company, which ceased c.1887.

John Wilkinson produced a wide range of earthenwares, including some stone china. Many of the modest wares were exported. Impressed marks incorporate the name and place, i.e. 'Wilkinson, Whitehaven', but some printed marks incorporate the initials 'I.W .' (the J usually being rendered as I at this period).

For further information on the Whitehaven earthenwares the reader is referred to *West Cumberland Potteries* by Mrs F. Sibson (privately published, 1991).

**WILKINSON & HULME, Burslem, c.1881-02.**
This short-lived partnership between Arthur J. Wilkinson and Joseph B. Hulme succeeded Richard Alcock at the Central Pottery, Market Place, Burslem.

Various earthenwares including 'Royal Patent Ironstone' were produced for the home and export markets.

The partnership was dissolved on 11 November 1882, after which A.J. Wilkinson continued the pottery – see A.J. Wilkinson (Ltd.).

The printed Wilkinson & Hulme marks incorporate the Royal arms, the name of the body, the partnership name together with the basic address 'Burslem. England', the last word being a very early use of the country of origin designation.

**I. WILSON & Co., Middlesbrough, Yorkshire, 1852-87.**
Isaac Wilson, the former manager of the Middlesbrough Pottery near Stockton-on-Tees, took over the pottery (which had been built in 1834) in 1852.

He traded as Isaac Wilson & Co. until the closure in 1887. General earthenwares were produced for the home and export markets. Reputedly a quarter of a million items were exported in 1852.

Most printed or impressed marks incorporate the initials 'I.W. & Co.'. The place name 'Middlesbro', 'Middlesborough' or 'Middlesborough Pottery' were sometimes added. The full name mark 'Isaac Wilson & Co.' has also been recorded.

**WOOD, c.1820-50.**
The simple impressed mark WOOD occurs on generally inexpensive types of British earthenware of the approximate period 1820-50.

It should be borne in mind that this mark is unlikely to relate to the well-known and important firm of Enoch Wood & Sons but rather to a lesser potter endeavouring to pass his wares off as originating from the large Burslem firm.

Within the Staffordshire Potteries the following two potters could have used this 'WOOD' surname mark.

| | |
|---|---|
| Ephraim Wood, Burslem | c.1818-42 |
| John Wedge Wood (& Co.), Burslem & Tunstall | c.1825-58 |

There are in addition many Wood partnerships that may have found it advantageous to have used the single name Wood, rather than the full name of a little-known partnership.

We must also remember that there were many potters working elsewhere, north of Staffordshire.

**E. WOOD (& Sons), Burslem, c.1818-30.**
Ironstone-type wares bearing printed or other marks incorporating the simple initial, and name 'E. Wood', present some difficulties even when the place name 'Burslem' is added.

Such marks could well be attributed to the famous Enoch Wood of the large Fountain Place Works at Burslem but, at the probable period of such wares, Enoch Wood was using the trade style 'Enoch Wood & Sons' and most marks incorporate this style or the initials 'E.W. & S.' The Enoch Wood periods may be summarized as follows:

| | |
|---|---|
| Enoch Wood | c.1783-92 |
| Wood & Caldwell | c.1792-1818 |
| Enoch Wood & Sons | c.1818-46 |

The 'E Wood' marks could just relate to Enoch Wood Junior who is recorded as being at the Big House, Burslem, in 1829 but it is probably more likely that the mark relates to Ephraim Wood of Hole House, Burslem, who potted there between about 1818 and 1830. At least one 'E. Wood, Burslem' printed mark incorporates the description 'Dresden Ironstone China'.

Some post-1818 'E.W. & S.' initial marks also incorporate the description 'Celtic China', which is a form of durable vitrified stone china.

Many 'pulls' from original Enoch Wood & Sons' copper-plates are in the Pennsylvania Museum. The standard book on the Ralph Woods, and on Enoch Wood, is Frank Falkner's 1912 classic *The Wood Family of Burslem* (Chapman & Hall Ltd., London).

**EDMUND THOMAS WEDG WOOD, Tunstall, c.1858-77.**
Tunstall health-rate records show that Edmund T.W. Wood took over the former John Wedg Wood, Woodland Street Pottery at Tunstall from at least February 1858, John Wedg Wood having died in 1857.

It would seem that Edmund continued to use the misleading name mark 'WEDGWOOD' or even 'J. WEDGWOOD' as used by his predecessor John Wedg Wood – see the following entry. Messrs Hollinshead & Kirkham took over the pottery in c.1877 and some 'H. & K.' marks incorporate the statement 'Late J. WEDGWOOD'.

**JOHN WEDGWOOD, Burslem and Tunstall, c.1837-58 or c.1876.**
This potter, working in succession to John Wedg Wood & Co. (see next entry), used misleading 'J. Wedgwood' marks as the example reproduced. It should be noted that the marks of Josiah Wedgwood & Sons Ltd. do

not include the initial 'J'.

The John Wedg Wood marks should correctly display a slight gap between the names 'Wedg' and 'Wood', but this is seldom clear and such pieces are still often attributed to the main Wedgwood firm, in error. The Tunstall Woodland Street works were taken over by Edmund Thomas Wedg Wood from *c.*1858 but he seemingly continued to use the former J. Wedgwood mark and the J. Wedg Wood trade style until *c.*1876. A registration for a printed design was made in the name of John Wedg Wood in August 1860, when the firm was under E.T. Wedg Wood. In October 1863 registrations were in Edmund T. Wood's name.

Some John Wedg Wood factory ledgers are preserved in the Staffordshire County Record Office at Stafford (refs. D4842/1 6/4/3 and D4842/4/1). These cease in 1876 and are quoted by Neil Ewins in *The Journal of Ceramic History*, Vol. 15 (City Museum & Art Gallery, Stoke-on-Trent, 1997). These documents are of the greatest interest and good use is made of them by Neil Ewins.

Messrs Hollinshead & Kirkham took over the Woodland Pottery, Woodland Street, Tunstall, *c.*1877. Their marks can include the wording 'H. & K. late J. WEDGWOOD'.

**JOHN WEDGWOOD & Co., Burslem, later at Tunstall, c.1830s-37.**

John Wedg Wood, working in partnership with Edward Challinor at Burslem, seems to have used the misleading name 'John Wedg Wood & Co.' and such a name and initials were probably used in marks – 'J WEDGWOOD' or 'J WEDGWOOD & Co.'

The partnership was dissolved on 25 March 1837, after which John Wedg Wood continued on his own account – see the previous entry. However, it is extremely difficult to untangle the J Wedg Wood & Co. dates or to discover the partnership's year of foundation in the 1830s. It is possible that various trade styles were employed – the Wedg Wood misleading name and mark being favoured when Wood & Challinor would have been more accurate.

A circular mark comprising the wording 'Wedgwood & Co. Stone Granite' probably relates to this firm although Wedg and Wood are run together. There is of course another Wedgwood & Co. of Tunstall and John Wedg Wood moved to the Woodland Street pottery in about 1845.

**WOOD & Son(s) (Ltd.), Burslem, c.1865-1982.**

Wood & Son produced good quality general earthenware and ironstone ware. Marks are invariably clear and self-explanatory – for example, the Royal Arms with the wording 'Royal Patent Ironstone. Wood & Son. England'. Impressed month and year numerals can occur. From *c.*1907 '& Son' was changed to '& Sons' and from 1910 'Ltd.' was added to the firm's official title.

**WOOD & Sons (1982) Ltd., Burslem, 1982-89.**
**WOOD & Sons (Ltd.), Burslem, c.1990 to present day.**

This firm succeeded Wood & Sons Ltd. A similar range of 'Vitrex' hotel ware and other vitrified wares were produced. In about 1990 the trading style reverted to Wood & Sons. Ltd, but from *c.*1991 the trade listings give only Wood & Sons. Their products include catering and hotel wares.

**WOOD & BROWNFIELD, Cobridge, c.1841-50.**

This partnership between John Wood and William Brownfield potted at the old Clews Works, Cobridge, in succession to Robinson, Wood & Brownfield (q.v.). As related under the entry for the former partnership, there is some doubt as to the exact date of the change in title. The official dissolution of partnership notice dated 16 July 1841 refers to the date of dissolution as being 'from the 12th day of March' 1841. However, one 'Published by' mark of 1 January 1841 gives the names as Wood & Brownfield. It is possible that the name was amended on jugs of this model produced after March 1841.

The Wood & Brownfield partnership was dissolved on 30 October 1850 after which William Brownfield continued on his own account – see William Brownfield & Son(s).

The 1841-1850 partnership produced a wide range of

earthenwares, table services and especially jugs. A good range of shapes and patterns are reviewed in Tim Peake's specialist book, *William Brownfield and Son(s)* (privately printed, 1995).

The ironstone and stone china-type wares normally bear one of many types of printed mark incorporating the initials 'W. & B.' or more rarely the names in full. The wares are usually of above average quality and were produced within a ten-year period. The impressed lozenge shape 'Ironstone China. Pearl White' device reported as being found on Robinson, Wood & Brownfield wares could also have been used by Wood & Brownfield.

**WOOD & CHALLINOR, Brownhills, Tunstall, c.1824-37.**
This partnership between John Wedg Wood and Edward Challinor (also of the Burslem firm of John Wedg Wood & Co.) existed at both Burslem and Tunstall during the approximate period 1824-1837. The Burslem partnership was dissolved on 25 March 1837, after which John Wedg Wood continued alone.

The partnership was a large business having seven kilns in 1836. Various standard types of Staffordshire useful wares were produced including ironstone and stone china wares.

Various printed marks on ironstone and other earthenwares made in the 1820s and 1830s, incorporating the initials 'W. & C.', almost certainly relate to this partnership. The names may also occur in full.

**WOOD & CLARKE, Burslem, c.1871-72.**
The partnership between Josiah Wood and Edward Clarke potted at the famous Churchyard Works at Burslem for a short period in the early 1870s. Edward Clarke continued alone from 30 November 1872. Clarke produced good quality white granite wares mainly for the American market and it can be assumed the preceding partnership produced similar wares.

Apart from clear name marks, initial marks incorporating 'W. & C.' may well relate to this short-lived partnership. However, several other partnerships used these initials – see 'W. & C.' and Wood & Challinor.

**WOOD & HAWTHORNE, Cobridge, c.1882-84+.**
This partnership between William Wood and John Hawthorne potted at the Abbey Works, Cobridge. They produced white granite ware or ironstone exclusively for the American market. The partnership was dissolved on 31 December 1884, but William Wood may have continued under the original name until 1887. The standard mark includes the description 'Ironstone China' and the name 'WOOD & HAWTHORNE, ENGLAND' beneath the Royal Arms.

**WOOD & HULME, Burslem, 1882-1905.**
This partnership worked the newly built Garfield Pottery in Waterloo Road, Burslem, from 1882. Various standard types of Staffordshire earthenwares were produced.

Name or initial 'W. & H.' marks can occur on ironstone-type wares.

**WOOD, RATHBONE & Co., Cobridge, c.1868.**
Marked ironstone from this short-lived company has been reported. From 6 November 1868, the firm was continued by Messrs Wood, Son & Co.

**L. WOOLF (& Sons), Ferrybridge, Yorkshire, c.1856-84.**
Lewis Woolf and his sons, Sydney and Henry, worked the Ferrybridge Pottery in Yorkshire from at least 1856 into the 1880s. Lewis Woolf & Sons also built and worked the nearby Australian Pottery – so-named because most of the output was made for that market.

A wide range of earthenwares were produced including ironstone or granite-type bodies.

Various marks incorporate the name or the initials 'L.W.', 'L.W & S.', with or without the Royal Arms. Body names such as 'Opaque Granite China' or 'Iron Stone China' occur incorporated in various marks. Sydney Woolf owned the Australian Pottery in the approximate period 1877-87, and used his own 'S.W.' marks.

It should be noted that the large-scale German manufacturer, Ludwig Wessel, also incorporated the initials 'L.W.' or 'L.W.P.' in his marks. Some of these German wares included blue printed British-style wares which have been mistaken for Ferrybridge specimens.

**S. WOOLF, Ferrybridge, Yorkshire, c.1860-87.**
Lewis Woolf of the Ferrybridge Pottery gave the new Australian pottery to his elder son Sydney to manage in 1860. Sydney became the owner in 1877 and continued the pottery to c.1887.

Various types of useful earthenwares including ironstone-type wares were made mainly (but not exclusively) for the Australian market. Various marks incorporate the initials 'S.W.'

**G. WOOLISCROFT (& Co.), Tunstall, c.1851-53 and 1860-63.**
George Wooliscroft potted at High Street and Wall Street, Tunstall, during the 1851-53 period and at the Sandyford Potteries, Tunstall, c.1860-63. The style George Wooliscroft & Co. was also used, the partner being Henry Galley.[21] This partnership was dissolved on 7 November 1863. George Wooliscroft registered printed designs for table wares on 10 February 1853 and a further scenic-centred plate design on 24 June 1853. During his second period he registered an oval tureen form on 19 November 1862. All these entries were made under his own name, George Wooliscroft, not that of the company.

Marks normally incorporate the name of the body – 'Ironstone' etc. – the pattern and the full surname or the initials 'G.W.' or 'G.W. & Co.'

**WREKIN IRONSTONE CHINA.**
The Wrekin is a high and well-known landmark in Shropshire, and the description 'Wrekin Iron-stone or Wrekin Ironstone China' occurs in various newspaper advertisements issued by Thomas Brocas, a leading china dealer in Shrewsbury. Brocas had connections with the reasonably local Coalport porcelain works but he also stocked Wedgwood and other makes of earthenware as well as Oriental and Continental porcelain. By 1815 Brocas was selling Mason's Patent Ironstone wares and claimed to be the only retailer of such in Shropshire.

Yet early Brocas advertisements relate to Wrekin Ironstone in a manner which suggests to us today that it was of local Shropshire manufacture – 'table services of the Wrekin or Shropshire iron-stone china'. I have not, however, noted any marked Wrekin examples and it is difficult to suggest where in Shropshire such ironstone wares would have been made. Brocas' advertisements of the 1801-02 period mention only seemingly porcelain dinner services, the blue printed Oriental styled types he described as 'an entire new article called BRITISH NANKEEN, so exactly like the foreign (Chinese) both as to shapes, colour & that few can distinguish it from Foreign blue and white china...'. The later Wrekin Ironstone wares were presumably less expensive than the Coalport porcelain services, although these were priced between 18 and 25 guineas a complete service.

**WREKIN IRONSTONE COMPANY, Shropshire, c.1815.**
Michael Messenger, in his catalogue of *Pottery & Tiles of the Severn Valley* (Remploy Ltd., London, 1979) illustrates a Mason-type ironstone vase which he suggests may have been produced by the 'little-known Shropshire factory of the Wrekin Ironstone Company which flourished c.1815'. This authority continued: 'They are known to have made very close copies of Mason's Ironstone... and a number of pieces featuring this mark have occurred in Shropshire'.

The mark referred to, however, seems to be only the description 'IRONSTONE CHINA'. This can occur on various makes and does not seem to offer evidence that the piece illustrated has a Shropshire origin. I have been unable to trace a pottery company of this name although the description Wrekin Ironstone was certainly used. Thomas Brocas, the Shrewsbury retailer, stated in *Eddowes Journal* of 20 November 1816: '...in the china warehouse a variety of Coalport. Also Wrekin Ironstone which they have sold for many years and which lately has been so highly approved of'. In another advertisement, 'he [Brocas] now has by him a number of tea and breakfast services also table (dinner) services of the Wrekin or Shropshire Iron-stone china'.

**YATES & CO., Hanley, c.1801-03.**
As related on page 67, John Yates and Thomas Baggeley traded as Yates & Co. up to the dissolution on 12 March 1803. I have also quoted an intriguing early reference to Yates & Co. as 'stoneware' manufacturers in 1801, see page 65. This early reference to Staffordshire 'Saxon Blue stoneware' dinner wares available in Scotland is extremely interesting and puzzling! The dissolution of partnership notice includes reference to the payment for a set of table plates, which was to be settled by Lady Day 1804.

**JOHN YATES, Shelton and/or Fenton, c.1784-1835.**
John Yates produced a wide range of earthenware. The early examples would seem to have been unmarked, but ware of the 1820-35 period occurs with the mark 'J.Y. Warranted Stone China, Fenton'. The initials are believed to relate to this potter, although no potter with the Yates surname is recorded at Fenton. Messrs Yates & May succeeded (q.v.).

**YATES & MAY, Shelton (Hanley), c.1835-43.**
Messrs Yates & May succeeded John Yates at Broad Street, Shelton (Hanley), in about 1835. The partnership was listed as owning seven kilns in 1836.

The partnership produced various types of Staffordshire earthenwares which almost certainly included ironstone-type wares.

Various 'Y. & M.' initial marks are recorded and no doubt relate to this Shelton partnership.

PLATE 281. *A Welsh Ynysmedw Pottery blue printed ironstone dinner service dish of 'Rio' pattern. Impressed initial mark 'Y.M.P.' with blue printed crowned Williams mark. 10in. long (25.4cm). c.1854-60. D. Harper Collection.*

**YNYSMEDW POTTERY, Nr. Swansea, Wales, c.1840-70+.**

Recent excavations by Mr D. Harper on the site of this little-known Welsh pottery have proved that its production included 'Ironstone' china. A blue printed platter is shown in Plate 281.

Marks include the impressed initials 'Y.M.P.' or 'Y.P.' or the name in full, 'YNISMEDW POTTERY. SWANSEA VALE' (note alternative spelling of Ynysmedw). Printed marks incorporate the name 'WILLIAMS' (c.1854-60), the initials 'L. & M.' (c.1860-70) or the initials 'W.T.H.', denoting the last proprietor, W.T. Holland, c.1870+.

This last entry underlines the point that ironstone-type ware was made by potteries large and small throughout the British Isles, and it was by no means limited to the Staffordshire potteries.

# CHAPTER VII

# The Non-British Manufacturers

While most, or all, successful ceramic bodies or styles were soon taken up by commercial rivals, probably none was as widely copied as the English ironstone-type wares of the Victorian period, especially in the United States of America.

The American, and some European, manufacturers copied not only the thickly potted durable body, but also the English shapes and used very close copies of the original marks, even the British Royal Arms device!

## NORTH AMERICA

The story of the American ironstone and granite wares is a large subject and there are several specialist American books that deal with it, see page 366. I can (without doubling the size of this work) only make a few basic points, for my subject is the wares that inspired the copies, not the copies themselves.

Although British collectors will not find examples of the American wares on their home islands, they should be aware of their existence in other countries. The copyists were not in business to praise British pottery by emulation, they were endeavouring to cut the British out of their market and to undersell the imports. In this commercial aim they were not surprisingly helped by their own governments which imposed high duties on imported pottery and porcelains. Even British Dominions or Commonwealth countries, Newfoundland and Canada, for example, levied 40 per cent and 30 per cent duties respectively. The Americans were not backward in imposing their own high import duties, which varied from time to time. To such added expenses, the imports had to bear shipping, handling and packing costs plus the percentage charged by various middle-men in the long chain between the manufacturers in inland Staffordshire and the ultimate buyer in North or South America or in the Southern Hemisphere.

America entered the ceramic industry rather hesitantly. No earthenware manufacturer sent samples of his wares to the 1851 Great Exhibition at the Crystal Palace in London, although a floating church and thousands of other non-ceramic articles were sent across the Atlantic. The Official Catalogue, in its introduction to the United States section, merely states in regard to the ceramics, 'Of earthenware the coarser varieties only are produced in any considerable quantities. Of the finer earthenware and porcelain the whole supply is imported'.

Yet in the next twenty-five years the situation was to change drastically as many American manufacturers sought to take on the British and European firms. In this they had to a great extent been helped by British manufacturers, for in times of difficulty in the Potteries many highly-trained British operatives had emigrated to North America to seek their fortune. Few in fact prospered but the Americans were to benefit from such knowledge.

By at least the 1870s the growing American production of ironstone and granite useful wares was affecting the Staffordshire potters. The Secretary of the American National Potters' Association reported in 1878, that 'during the past year the English and French manufacturers have adopted a new class of goods, called unselected or run of the kiln, for the especial purpose of competing unfairly with the American manufacturer'. This obviously suited the makers who did not have to sort the goods and sell the 'seconds' or 'thirds' at greatly reduced prices. The sorting, if any was carried out, was done by the American buyer.

The published report of the Fourth Annual Convention of the United States Potters' Association held at Pittsburgh in January 1878, made some interesting points concerning the American trade and the importation of European wares. First, we learn how the demand for ceramics (nearly all wares would have been of a useful nature, mainly table wares) had increased over a ten-year period. The quoted official figure for the importations into the United States in 1863 was in value just over two and a quarter million dollars, whereas in 1873 the importations had risen to be valued at just over six million dollars, representing a vast quantity of low-priced objects.

In the years following 1873 the value of the importations did drop but was usually calculated between four and five million dollars. The American potters attributed this decrease in the imports to their own increasing production of white granite, cream-coloured earthenware and some china wares. In 1877 they put the value of this home production at $2,975,000. The committee of statistics in 1877 calculated that there were 777 potteries in the US employing 6,116 hands, and the yearly wages bill was $2,247,173 (approximately £560,000).

As a result the committee was able to report early in 1878 that 'almost incredible strides have been taken in the past fifteen years, or, more properly speaking, since the tariff of 1861, so that today we have in operation potteries enough of all grades to produce twice the quantity imported from Europe and Asia last year'. The Secretary continued:

> It may be asked, in what way have the people of the United States been benefitted? This question can be very easily answered by presenting the following invoices of white granite ware sold, the one in 1860 under the 25 per cent tariff, the other, in 1877, under the 40 per cent tariff. These will show that goods are being sold today by first class jobbers in crockery about 18 per cent. cheaper than they were in 1860. This shows only the actual apparent difference between the prices of the two periods, to say nothing about the increase in sizes and improved quality of the ware by the more careful selection.

I will not reproduce the lists of prices for 1860 and for 1878 but the list of 'white granite' articles may be of interest. In each case these comprised:

| | |
|---|---|
| Jugs, in four sizes – | 4s, 6s, 12s & 24s |
| Tea cups | (at $1.05 a dozen) |
| Tea cups, unhandled | (at 90 cents a dozen in 1878) |
| Dishes, in six sizes | |
| Bakers, in four sizes | |
| Plates | |
| Bowls | |
| Covered dishes | |
| Sugars | |
| Ewers and basins | |
| Chambers, in two sizes | |
| Soap dishes and trays | |

It is interesting that in both 1860 and 1878 unhandled teas were being made and sold, the cost difference being fifteen cents per dozen cups or little more than a cent each.

The object of the two listings was to show that the price of American-produced white granite standard objects had dropped over this period. The total bill in January 1860 was $90.44; for the same goods in 1878 the total was $73.69.

The report also showed that the American manufacturers were having labour difficulties. The President of their Association stated:

> It is the broad labor question they should consider, not what you pay your workmen – in Trenton, East Liverpool, Cincinnati and New York – or I pay mine, but the most direct means to get rid of the large mass of our turbulent labor, and the best means to avoid the labor strikes...

The American manufacturers certainly had to pay their work-people at higher rates than was normal in Great Britain or on the Continent. They also apparently had difficulties over the basic raw material – the clay. In this regard the President[1] noted in 1878:

> There is one thing that stares us in the face, and that is the production of clays, for we have got to make better and better goods all the time. There is scarcely an even American clay that we can buy... The only clay we are able to get at present, is from Pennsylvania, and all know that these clays are not good. They are refractory, unyielding to the fire; they do not fire easily. We need a better clay. We do not get a regular article. You cannot depend upon the quality being at all times uniform.

A special committee was in being to look into the question of materials, their quality and price. The Chairman reported that although basic costs had dropped:

> ...clays, flint and spar have not yet, in the opinion of your committee, reached that point which will enable us to compete successfully with foreign manufacturers... we must procure these articles at less prices than we are now paying. In the fierce fight now going on between the American and English for control of the American market, it is of the utmost importance that the production cost of our goods should be reduced... so long as imported English clays can be sold in our markets at less prices than our own American clays, we shall certainly labor under great disadvantages.

The President then underlined the cheapness of the

imported English clay and its superiority over their native materials:

> I think we had better have a discussion on these matters, especially in reference to foreign clays, which can be put down in New York tide water cheaper than you can buy Pennsylvannia clay by about fifteen per cent, although paying a duty... You can import clay superior to anything we have now, to the very best Pennsylvannia clays, yielding and coming down far better to the fire and always reliable. A brand of clay which once being understood is always the same, which is very far from being the case with our clays... The transportation from England in the latter season being no greater than the fare from Philadelphia to New York...

In answer to questions the President stated that he purchased his English clays in New York from the importers or their agents, the best quality costing some $17.50 a long ton of 2,240 lbs. We must always remember that the Americans suffered high transport costs for raw materials and finished wares within their own vast country, with distances unheard of in the British Isles.

Whilst the American potters could obviously very easily obtain British shapes and patterns to copy by merely going to the nearest store, they also debated the proposition that they send a representative to the 1878 Paris Exhibition to report back on the latest developments in Europe. Or as the President stated:

> Is there not something there which we might get by sending a competent individual, who might look out and see what is there and make sketches and gain some valuable information for the potters, and get knowledge of the different moulds and machinery... There is a great fund of information that could be picked up, and of much value to the association...

It was duly resolved:

> That it is the opinion of this Association that a thoroughly practical man be recommended to the President of the United States, for the purpose of visiting the Paris Exhibition, with the view of securing designs, drawings and artistic and utilitarian suggestions upon the most meretorious exhibits, for the purpose of general distribution among the manufacturers of this country, and that a committee of three be appointed to act in the premises.

Official commercial spying, paid for by the State!

It should be noted that the traffic was one way. Only three American potters exhibited their wares at this important Paris exhibition,[2] hence the need to send a special delegate – to use a polite description. In fact an official Report by the 'United States Commissioners to the Paris Universal Exposition' was issued in 1880.

The American potters exhibiting at Paris in 1878 were concerned with the finer quality decorative wares, not with the American home market stonewares or granite ware table wares. The exhibitors were James Carr, showing pottery and parian goods, Ott & Brewer, with vases, busts, etc., in true porcelain and Louise McLaughlin with painted porcelains. The report stated that the Paris display,

> ...was wholly disproportioned to the extent of the pottery interests of the country... but our pottery interests are not declining... they are, on the contrary, expanding with great rapidity and strength. Fostered and encouraged by the duties laid upon the importation of foreign ware, they have been protected in their infancy; capitol has been encouraged to lend its aid, and as a result we now have well-established potteries producing, at the present time, enough to supply two-thirds of the demand. The quality also has been improved until our stone china ware is fully equal to, if not superior to, any of the same grades made in England.

Whilst trade was reported as being extremely difficult in Britain 'the home trade is extremely unsatisfactory, and travellers report an increasing difficulty in obtaining orders or the settlement of accounts'. Yet at the same period the American potteries were expanding; thirty new kilns were brought into use in 1879 and most potteries were being enlarged for the demand of the home trade. In contrast to the British potters, the manufacturers were not concerned with exporting; their vast and growing home market absorbed all their output.

At this period the potters' President, Thomas C. Smith, was a lone voice in requesting that the American potters cease the practice of closely copying British marks and emblems. He started the discussion by stating:

> I would like to see you gentlemen leave off the British lion, and come out under your own colors... Gentlemen, the adoption of foreign trade marks is truckling, and cringing. You dare not stand upon your manhood if you put on a miserable deceptive trade mark that makes people buy your

wares under deception. Why even some folk follow the analogy of name, by putting on their initials, if they happen to be the same as a foreign manufacturers... I do insist that we can rise to the standard of making and calling our ware what it is...

The American manufacturers, or most of them, favoured British style marks for sound commercial reasons. Their buyers, trade and private, favoured British type pottery because over such a long period it had built up a great reputation. The great bulk of ceramics pouring into this rapidly expanding New World market had been of British origin which out-sold the Chinese imports and also those of the great and famous German and French porcelain manufacturers. British-styled ceramics bearing the once-despised British Royal Arms device (or the supporters) sold better than American wares – a strange but true position. I show a few typical examples of American potters' marks produced in the British manner.

These representations of American ironstone china marks in the British fashion were taken, I must acknowledge, from Lois Lehner's monumental and extremely helpful work, *Lehner's Encyclopedia of U.S. Marks on Pottery, Porcelain & Clay* (Collector Books, PO Box 3009, Paducah, KY, USA, 1988. ISBN 0 89145 365 2).

It must be remembered, however, that earlier in the nineteenth century some British potters had employed the American eagle device in some of their marks. Such Anglo-American marks are mainly associated with patterns made especially for the North American markets. In some cases these patterns were expressly ordered by American merchants. The use of American devices was not, however, made to pass off the Staffordshire earthenwares as being of American manufacture; they were popular in their own right. Even in the 1870s and 1880s some British firms still used versions of the American flag or national shield.

We must always remember the vast export trade enjoyed by the British potters. Llewellynn Jewitt's monumental work *The Ceramic Art of Great Britain*, the first edition of which was being type-set when the American convention was sitting, illustrates the British dependence on export trade well. After visiting all the manufacturers or obtaining their publicity material and catalogues, he mentioned that there was probably not a Staffordshire manufacturer that did not between 1850 and 1900 sell goods to America, and many firms seemingly were entirely dependent on this trade. British earthenware potters were more geared to American requirements than they were to the home trade and depressions or difficult trading times across the Atlantic affected life in Staffordshire just as much as they did in North America.

The American manufacturers and their work-people also shared many of the same commercial problems. The Americans at that 1878 meeting returned to the old thorny problem of regulated sizes and common prices for standard lines. Obviously agreed prices could be undercut if one manufacturer gave more goods for the money than another. They endeavoured to introduce the 'American measure'. As the President noted:

> When one man makes a jug, calling it twelve to the dozen, another man, fourteen to the dozen, there is no sense in it, or in calling seven jugs of a certain size to a dozen, and twenty four of another...You have a dish that you call four inches, which measures six inches, and you have one that you call six inches, that measures five. If that is not an asinine operation, I don't know what is...

The Americans, of course, here followed the British fashion. They formed a committee to investigate the problem and report back in the following year. In fact the United States Potters' Association's last By-law, Article XIII, stated:

> No change in the standard Selling Price List of White Granite or Cream Color ware shall be made by any member or members of this association; neither shall sizes be regulated or established different from those now in vogue, without first being considered by a Standing Committee of five and a favorable report presented by them to the annual Convention.

It is interesting too that the American manufacturers were experiencing labour difficulties and that wages had drifted, or been forced, downward. The potters' Committee on Labor reported in January 1878:

> ...at the period of the commencement of the formidable strike which took place over a year ago,

at Trenton, the wages of all other manufacturing interests had suffered heavy reductions, whilst the manufacturers of pottery ware were compelled to lower the prices of their goods to such an extent as to leave them nearly without profit, and in several instances positively without any. After a hard fought battle the manufacturers were victorious, and the result was a drop equal as a whole to 12½ per cent.

> The East Liverpool white ware potters obtained also a reduction of about 10 per cent, and after a short strike the Cincinnati manufacturers also obtained a nominal reduction of 10 per cent, but actually less, as some kinds of labor, viz., apprentices, females and laboring hands were not reduced.
>
> Your committee cordially desire that our people, particularly skilled laborers, should be fully remunerated... But all experience shows that in the main, human nature is selfish – so that representations of suffering manufacturers when appealing to their men to join them in tiding over the rocks and shoals of disastrous times, seldom meet with any sympathy, and this leads us to say that we are of opinion that the rates now paid for the manufacture of cream colored, White Granite, Rockingham and Yellow ware are fully high as compared with the low rates at which we are compelled to sell our goods. In saying this your committee... are of opinion that if there is not a change either in the price of goods – by way of advance, or else a reduction in the price of materials and other expenses incident to our business, we think that such abatement of prices of labor will eventually take place.

It would seem that even at the then current reduced wage levels the American rates were higher than those paid in the UK and therefore higher also than those paid by the European manufacturers. With this fact in mind the American committee was of the 'opinion that the cost of labor in this country ought to be based on the price of English labor, as early as possible, adding the advantages of tariff protection, whether high or low.'

The committee referred again to the vexed question of potters' sizes:

> ...we desire to say that considerable injustice has been done to the hands, and still more to those manufacturers retaining average sizes, by raising sizes to the extent of a full size, without paying the workmen anything additional.

From this observation we can deduce that the American operatives were paid on a piece-rate basis, not per hour, day or week.

In conclusion the American potters' committee made the universally correct observation:

> In conclusion, we simply desire to say that it is both the duty and the interest of the employer to remunerate his people fairly and honestly, and it is equally the duty and interest of the employee to deal in like manner by his employer by not demanding of him such remuneration as his business is incapable of affording.

The members of the United States Potters' Association were, of course, not entirely concerned with the production of British-style ironstone or granite wares. A few produced hard-paste porcelains, many produced 'C.C.' or cream coloured earthenwares or the dark-glazed so-called 'Rockingham' wares or the utilitarian 'yellow wares' such as the traditional mixing bowls. But at this period in the middle of the nineteenth century most would have produced what was termed 'White Granite'. This was the usually thickly potted durable table ware that was so closely related to the British ironstone wares.

Returning to the subject of comparative wages and costs between the British and American manufacturers, *The Staffordshire Times* of 30 December 1876 printed interesting tables. In regard to wages, it was then stated that the ordinary labourer earned in England some \$5 to \$6 (£1.5s.0d. to £1.10s.0d.) a week, whereas in America the wages varied between \$9 and \$10 (£2.5s.0d. to £2.10s.0d.). British child labour was paid 4s.to 6s. a week but American boys and girls were paid 15s. to £1. Individually the differences may not now seem great but the industry was workmen-orientated with teams of three or four needed for most operations. Also the cost of all basic materials was far higher in North America than in Staffordshire. The cost of the all-important coal in America was quoted in 1876 as some £15.0s.0d. a ton, against our 15s. In America china clay was priced at the equivalent of £4.5s.0d. to £4.10s.0d. a ton; in Britain £1.10s.0d. to £1.15s.0d. a ton. Flint in America was some £4 or more a ton; in Britain £2.10s.0d.

This book is, of course, concerned with British ironstone and ironstone-type bodies, such as white granite. I do not therefore propose to list the many American firms that produced similar wares for their home market. These firms and their products are well covered by American specialists having the advantage of good source material. These wares and marks are also available to them, whilst they are not found in the British Isles.

An early and little known American book contains interesting information on mid-nineteenth century America potters. This is *The Ceramic Art. A Compendium of the History and Manufacture of Pottery and Porcelain* by Jennie J. Young, published by Harper Brothers of New York in 1879.

In her introduction to the sections on the United States ceramic industry, the author repeats many of the points made in the 1878 Report of the United States Potters' Association. These facts were deemed of great importance and I assume both the potters and the author of this book on world ceramics were seeking to air the problems facing the home manufacturers.

Jennie Young noted some of the obstacles in the way of the American manufacturers who were seeking to produce the type of ceramics traditionally imported from Europe. She stated, for example, that even with a 'high protective tariff the home manufacturer is barely enabled to compete with the foreign producer in plain domestic wares. The import duty does not cover the greater expense of working in this country. Statistics show that in the item of labor and material the American manufacturer, as compared with the European, labors under a disadvantage of about one hundred per cent'. She was particularly concerned about the low import tariff on the imported white granite wares. So, turning the situation around, the British and other European goods enjoyed a price advantage.

This 1879 author also wrote at length on the traditional high reputation of the imported goods and the slowness of her home buyers to accept the relatively new American productions – 'the foreign competitor comes branded as a genius… American art may be good, even equal to the best, but unfortunately it is American'.

She continued, 'It has been said that, as a rule, Americans take a pride in their own manufacturers. That of pottery is an exception. Almost anywhere granite-ware can be seen bearing as a mark the royal arms of England… It is a curious mark for an American potter… the explanation is simple. The dealers will not buy it without that mark… Their customers look for the English mark, and finding it are satisfied…'.

No wonder the American buyers sailed over to Staffordshire to see the latest British goods and to order their desirable and relatively inexpensive durable goods. No wonder that several English manufacturers specialized in supplying this vast market.

Returning to the subject of American reference books, the main examples known to me are the following (a fuller listing is given in the Bibliography): *Lehner's Encyclopaedia of U.S. Marks on Pottery, Porcelain & Clay* by Lois Lehner (Collector Books, Paducah, KY, USA, 1988) and *DeBolt's Dictionary of American Pottery Marks* by Gerald DeBolt (Collector Books, Paducah, KY, USA, 1994). Whilst these two books are mainly concerned with factory markings, they do give at least basic details of the many American pottery firms, many of which produced British-style ironstone-type wares.

## EUROPE

Apart from the many North American producers of British-style ironstone or granite-type wares, other European or Scandinavian manufacturers also entered the market enjoyed by the British exporters. I obviously cannot list all such firms and certainly the wares are not found in the British Isles. In general the marks will include the relevant foreign name or town. The later products too should include in the mark the country of origin: France, Germany, etc.

It should be remembered that many European and North American potteries were set up or staffed by British workmen. They were trained in Britain and sought to gain their fortune overseas. This exportation of British labour was especially strong in the first half of the nineteenth century. They greatly helped the overseas manufacturers to produce British-style earthenwares to compete with the so-popular imports. As we have seen with the American manufacturers, they also employed British-style ceramic marks (see page 364) and even when they only used a name mark this often was or seemed English.

### David Johnston

A classic, but little-known case is David Johnston potting in France at Bordeaux. Johnston (b.1789) founded an English-style pottery in about 1834. He seemingly imported a number of workmen (perhaps whole families) from Staffordshire. David Johnston may not have been a practising potter himself. He was, I understand, born in France in 1789 and served as Mayor of Bordeaux in the 1838-42 period. It appears that the key man in the pottery venture was Thomas Potter. His recipe book dated 1839 has survived. This includes a mass of interesting notes relating to various ceramic bodies and glazes as well as details on techniques and comments on the results – 'Green glazes - a good one', 'Fire at the top of Glost oven…' or 'This stands the fire well & works well'.

In addition there are references to the bodies and materials used by various Staffordshire potteries, such as John Ridgway or Mintons, suggesting that Thomas Potter had working experience gained in the Staffordshire Potteries before joining David Johnston in France in the late 1830s. It is interesting to read that most of the raw materials came from British sources.

The basic recipes include some for ironstone bodies. Number 70 reads:

| | |
|---|---|
| 300 lbs | Cornish Stone |
| 250 do. | Cornish clay |
| 100 do. | Flint |
| 200 do. | Blue clay |
| 1 do. | Blue calx. |

The 1839 book gives some prices for British working materials – 'the silk lawns are 4/6$^{d}$ each in England at Mr Smith's, the lawn weaver'. These lawns were hand-made silk sieves for sifting various colours or other ceramic materials. The British were supplying the world with various specialist tools and materials.

Thomas Potter's recipe book, as used at David Johnston's Bordeaux pottery, included details of most colours used in printing, including the Anglo-Chinese Broseley pattern of willow-pattern style underglaze-blue design.

Although the Johnston English-style printed (and other) types of earthenware are little known in Britain, they would have supplied the French market and perhaps exported their products to countries which favoured such British-type wares and patterns. Reputedly the factory also produced good quality bone china, and certainly the 1839 book contains many references to china bodies and glazes. The pieces seen by the author have, however, been of pottery and have even, when marked, been mistaken for English wares.

It is believed that the Johnston factory at Bordeaux only lasted for ten or eleven years, being taken over by Jules Vieillard in 1845, although Johnston may have retained an interest in the enterprise for some years. The Johnston name marks could have been continued until at least the 1860s. Later in the century the works employed over a thousand hands. The factory seemingly closed in the mid-1890s.

Various printed or impressed name marks occur. These typically include, or comprise, the name 'David (or 'D') Johnston', with the place name 'Bordeaux'. The amended title 'D. Johnston & Cie' may also have been used, probably in the 1844-45 period when he had taken on Jules Vieillard as what may be called Art Director and technical adviser.

Another rather complicated mark comprises the basic wording within three interlaced crescents. Two blue-printed examples of Bordeaux earthenware (not ironstones) are illustrated in *The Dictionary of Blue and White Printed Pottery 1780-1880*, Vol II, by A.W. Coysh and R.K. Henrywood (Antique Collectors' Club, Woodbridge, 1989).

In its products and in at least some of its work-people and working materials (including the engraved copper-plates which were almost certainly obtained from Staffordshire), the Bordeaux factory could be considered almost to be the foreign outpost of the British industry; it was probably not alone in this regard.

**Arabia of Finland**

Even the Arabia company in Finland produced from about 1873 a range of British-style ironstone wares, including the Willow pattern. These Arabia wares may well have been exported, as well as used in their home market.

Various printed or impressed marks occur, comprising or including the name 'ARABIA', often with the place name 'HELSINGFORS'. This Finnish firm was a branch of the better-known Rörstrand firm in Sweden.

It should be noted that many of these non-British firms may well have obtained their engraved copper-plates and other materials from British sources. There were many Staffordshire firms supplying sets of engraved copper-plates to foreign as well as British manufacturers.

**Petrus Regout (& Co.) of Maastricht**

That important point, which perhaps partly explains the similarity of continental designs to standard British patterns and styles of mark, applies particularly to the Dutch firm of Petrus Regout (& Co.) of Maastricht. This firm produced a wide range of usually English-style earthenwares from *c*.1836 into the present century.

Petrus Regout wares bear marks incorporating the two names of the later title Petrus Regout & Co. Later marks incorporate the initials 'S.M.' standing for Sphinx-Maastricht. Yet the English style-printed marks include English language descriptions such as 'ironstone china', 'Royal Ironstone China', 'White Stone' or 'White Granite'.

We can assume, therefore, that many of these continental productions were intended for English-language countries, in the main the United States of America. They are outside the scope of this book on British ironstone-type wares but they do exist. They obviously owe their origin to the British ironstone manufacturers and their world-wide markets for such durable useful and decorative wares. They, too, were made to be used, were very fit for their purpose and were relatively inexpensive. The object of these general remarks is to record the fact that not every British-style mark or wording should be taken as proof that a piece is British, though the likelihood is certainly so.

## THE FAR EAST

Lastly, in this section on non-British manufacturers of ironstone-type wares I could well mention again the reproductions of antique Mason's ironstone wares which seem to originate from far-eastern sources. These colourful wares, closely copying Mason shapes and patterns, are available in the UK and I assume elsewhere. They are the stock lines of importers and wholesale firms. One centred near Birmingham describes itself as 'Specialist suppliers to the Antique and reproduction trade'.

Many of these obviously commercially viable lines are being offered at the smaller antique and collectors fairs, at some auction sales and by the less specialist traders. These goods, although heavily potted and often clumsily decorated, are decorative and are available, on wholesale terms at least, at very reasonable prices. They are being made, shipped around the world and sold through several hands because they are very saleable. Curiously, the forms are usually of objects that we no longer use for their original purpose. A selection of illustrated examples before me described as a 'special purchase' comprises large jugs and basins, chamber pots and two-handled slop-bowls – forms originally made for Victorian bedrooms in the days before modern plumbing. Today they can be classed only as decorative articles.

For decoration they are perfectly acceptable, especially as the original articles are hard to find and will be expensive. The difficulty comes over their mode of sale. They bear a close approximation of the standard nineteenth century Mason trade mark. Why one may ask? The mark (usually) blue-printed comprises the crown with the magic words IRONSTONE CHINA below. They seem, however, to be made of a hard porcelain body, covered with a very glossy glaze. Many modern examples being marketed in the 1990s have a circled reference number in addition to the main mark. This feature does not occur on genuine English ironstone. The pieces do not bear a country of origin mark.

If the seller is not prepared fully to describe his wares – as perhaps Antique Mason (or at least English) ironstone china – or is not prepared to issue a detailed receipt, you can draw your own conclusion. You are probably buying modern foreign reproductions, not genuine old English ironstone china. This is fine if you only want decorative articles but not if you seek the genuine article and are paying a related price. There is, of course, nothing wrong with reproductions or reissues – the present Mason's company is producing its own traditional styled articles, but they bear modern marks and cannot be classed as fakes.

APPENDIX I

# Check-List of Manufacturers' Initial Marks and Trade Names

In this Appendix I list, in alphabetical order, the various initials that were used by British ironstone, stone china and granite ware manufacturers, as part of their various impressed or printed marks.

This list of manufacturers' initials relates only to those found on ironstone-type wares and does not relate to other earthenware or porcelain manufacturers. The listing will, however, assist the reader to find the likely maker of British ironstones which bear an initial mark. Some early nineteenth century British marks include the first initial I. In most cases this refers to the initial J, so that the initials 'I.B.' might refer to, say, James Brown rather than to Ian or Ivor Brown. From page 372 I give under a separate heading an alphabetical list of trade name or ceramic body descriptions as found on many marks. Again these will assist identification.

Great attention, however, should always be given to the working period of the person or firm listed and to the period of the piece, remembering always to note the latest feature of a mark. For example a mark bearing the word 'England' will not relate to a manufacturer who had ceased by 1840!, See my list of Godden pointers, pages 174-5.

## INITIAL MARKS

| | |
|---|---|
| A. Bros. | G.L. Ashworth & Bros. |
| A.B. & G. | Allerton, Brough & Green |
| A.G. & S. | A. Godfrey & Sons. |
| B. | Brameld |
| B.B. | Barker Bros. |
| B.B. & B. | Bourne, Baker & Baker |
| B.B. & B. | Bourne, Baker & Bourne |
| B.B. Ltd. | Barker Bros. Ltd. |
| B. & B. | Bates & Bennett |
| | Beardmore & Birks |
| | Brough & Blackhurst |
| B. & C. | Bridgwood & Clarke |
| B. & Co. | Bodley & Harrold |
| B. & D. | Beardmore & Dawson |
| B. & E. | Beardmore & Edwards |
| B. & G. | Broadhurst & Green |
| B. & H. | Beech & Hancock |
| | Bodley & Harrold |
| B.H. & Co. | Beech & Hancock |
| B.L. & Co. | Burgess, Leigh & Co. |
| B.& L. | Burgess & Leigh |
| B. & M. | Booth & Meigh |
| | Brougham & Mayer |
| B. & S.H. | B. & S. Hancock |
| B.S. & T. | Barker, Sutton & Till |
| B. & S | Baker & Son |
| | Barker & Son |
| | Bishop & Stonier |
| B. & T. | Barker& Till |
| B.W. & B. | Batkin, Walker & Broadhurst |
| B.W. & Co. | Bates, Walker & Co. |
| C.C. | See C.C., page 210 |
| C. & C. | Cockson & Chetwynd |
| C.C. & Co. | Cockson, Chetwynd & Co. |
| C. & E. | Cartwright & Edwards |
| | Cork & Edge |
| C. & E. Ltd. | Cartwright & Edwards Ltd. |
| C.E. & M. | Cork, Edge & Malkin |
| C. & F. | Cochran & Fleming |
| C. & F. G | Cochran & Fleming |
| C. & G. | Copeland & Garrett |
| C. & H. | Coombs & Holland |
| C.M. | Charles Meigh |
| C.M. & S. | Charles Meigh & Son |
| C.M.S. & P. | C. Meigh, Son & Pankhurst |
| C. & S. | Cockson & Seddon |
| C.T. | T. & C. Twyford |
| C. & Y. | Clementson & Young |
| C.Y. & J. | Clementson, Young & Jameson |
| D. | See 'D marks', page 220 |
| | Davenport |
| | L.L. Dillwyn |
| | T. Dimmock & Co. |
| D. & B. | Deakin & Bailey |
| D.B. & Co. | Dunn, Bennett & Co. |
| D. & Co. | L.L. Dillwyn |
| D. & K.R. | See page 234 |
| D. & S. | Deakin & Son and page 234 |
| D.W. | See page 237 |
| E.C. | E. Challinor |
| E.C. & Co. | E. Challinor & Co. |
| E. & C.C. | E. & C. Challinor |
| E. & F. | Elsmore & Forster |

| | |
|---|---|
| E.F.B. & Co. | E.F. Bodley & Co. |
| E.F.B. & S. | E.F. Bodley & Son |
| E.F.B. & Son | " |
| E. & G.P. | E. & G. Phillips |
| E.G. & T. | Everard, Glover & Townsend |
| E.H. | Elijah Hughes |
| E.K. & B. | Knight, Elkin & Bridgwood |
| E.M. & Co. | Edge, Malkin & Co. |
| E.W. | E. Walley |
| E.W. & S. | E. Wood |
| | |
| F. | Ferrybridge Pottery |
| F.B. | " |
| F. & C. | Ford & Challinor |
| F. & Co. | T. Fell |
| F.C. & Co. | Ford & Challinor |
| F.C. & T. | Flacket, Chetham & Toft |
| F. & F. | Freakley & Farrall |
| F. & H. | Forester & Hulme |
| F.L. | F. Lea |
| F.M. | Francis Morley |
| F.M. & Co. | " |
| F. & T. | Flacket, Chetham & Toft |
| | |
| G. | See page 246 |
| G. B. & B. | Griffiths, Beardmore & Birks |
| G.F.B. | G.F. Bowers |
| G.F.B. & Co. | " |
| G.G.W. | George Grainger |
| S.P. | |
| G.H. | H. Burgess |
| G.J. | G. Jones |
| G.J. & S. | G. Jones |
| G. & K. | Goode & Kenworthy |
| G.L.A. & Bros. | G.L. Ashworth & Bros. |
| G.R. & Co. | Godwin, Rowley & Co. |
| G.R. & J. | Godwin, Rowley & Co. |
| G.R.T. | G.R. Turnbull |
| G. & S.T. | G. & S. Taylor |
| G.T. | George Townsend |
| G.T.M. | G.T. Mountford |
| G.W. | G. Weston |
| | G. Wooliscroft |
| G.W. & Co. | " |
| G.&.W. | Gildea & Walker |
| | Goode & Watton |
| G.W.T. | G.W. Turner |
| | |
| H. | C. & W.K. Harvey |
| H.A. & Co. | H. Alcock & Co. |
| H. Bros. | Humphreys Bros. |
| H.B. & Co. | Heath, Blackhurst & Co. |
| H.& B. | Heath & Blackhurst |
| | Hulme & Booth |
| H. & C. | Hope & Carter |
| H.D. & Co. | Hackwood, Dimmock & Co. |
| | H. Daniel |
| H. & K. | Hollinshead & Kirkham |
| H.M. & I. | Hicks, Meigh & Co. |
| H.M. & J. | Hicks, Meigh & Co. |
| H.P. & M. | Holmes, Plant & Madew |
| H. & R.D. | H. & R. Daniel |

| | |
|---|---|
| I.B. & Co. | J. Burn & Co. |
| I.H. & Co. | J. Heath & Co. |
| I.M. | J. Mayer |
| F | |
| I.M. & S. | J. Meir & Son |
| I.W. | Whitehaven |
| | J. Wilkinson |
| I.W. & Co. | I. Wilson & Co. |
| | |
| J. J. | Jamieson & Co. |
| J.B. | J. & M.P. Bell & Co. |
| | J Broadhurst |
| J.B. & Co. | J. Burn & Co. |
| J.B. & S. | J. Broadhurst |
| J.C. | J. Clementson |
| J.D.B. | J.D. Bagster |
| J.D.P. | J.D. Pountney |
| J.D.P. & Co. | " |
| J.E. | J. Edwards |
| J.E. & S. | J. Edwards |
| J. & E. | Jones & Ellis |
| J. & E.M. | Mayer |
| J.F. | See page 269 |
| | J. Farrall |
| | J. Furnival |
| J.F.W. | J.F. Wileman |
| J. & G. A. | J.& G. Alcock |
| J.H. | J. Hawthorn |
| J.H. & Co. | J. Heath & Co. |
| J.H.M. | J. Middleton |
| J.J. & Co. | J. Jackson & Co. |
| | J. Jamieson & Co. |
| J.K.K. | J.K. Knight |
| J.M. & Co. | J. Magness & Co. |
| | John Marshall |
| | J. Maudesley & Co. |
| J. & M. P.B. & Co. | J. & M.P. Bell & Co. |
| J.M. & S. | Job Meigh & Son |
| | H. Meir & Son |
| | J. Meir & Son |
| J.R. | John Ridgway |
| J.R. – C.P. | " |
| J.R. | J. Robinson |
| B | |
| J.R. & Co. | John Ridgway |
| J. & R.G. | J. & R. Godwin |
| J.R. & S | Job Ridgway & Sons |
| J.R. & Sons | " |
| J.T. | John Tams |
| | John Thomson |
| J. & T.E. | J. & T. Edwards |
| J & T.F. | J & T. Furnival |
| J. & T.L. | J. & I. Lockett |
| J.T. & S. | John Tams |
| J.T. & Sons. | John Thomson |
| J.V. & Co. | Venables, Mann & Co. |
| J.W. | J. Warren |
| | Whitehaven |
| J.W.P. (& Co.) | J.W. Pankhurst (& Co.) |
| J.W.R. | J. & W. Ridgway |
| J. & W.R. | J. & W. Ridgway |
| J.Y. | John Yates |

| | |
|---|---|
| K. & B. | Knapper & Blackhurst |
| K.C. & Co. | R.A. Kidston |
| K.E. & B. | Knight, Elkin & Bridgwood |
| K.E. & Co. | Knight, Elkin & Co. |
| K. & E. | Knight, Elkin & Co. |
| K.P.B. | Kensington Pottery Ltd. |
| K.P.H. | Kensington Pottery Ltd. |
| K.S.P. | Keele Street Pottery |
| L. & D. | Livesley & Davis |
| L.E. | Liddle Elliot |
| L.E. & Co. | " |
| L.E. & Son. | " |
| L. &M. | Ynysmedw Pottery |
| L.P. & Co. | Livesley, Powell & Co. |
| L.W. | Ferrybridge Pottery |
| L.W. & S. | L. Woolf |
| M. | J. Maddock |
| | Minton. |
| M. & A. | Morley & Asbury |
| | Morley & Ashworth |
| M. & B. | Minton |
| M. & Co. | Minton |
| M. & G. | Maddock & Gater |
| M. & H. | Minton |
| M.J.B. | Blakeney |
| M.& N. | Mayer & Newbold |
| M. & S. | Maddock & Seddon |
| M.T. & Co. | Marple, Turner & Co. |
| | Mellor, Taylor & Co. |
| M.V. & Co. | Mellor, Venables & Co. |
| N. & B. | Newbon & Beardmore |
| N. & D. | Newbon & Dawson |
| N.S. | Spode |
| N.W.P. Co. | New Wharf Pottery Co. |
| O.H. & Co. | Oulsnam, Holdcroft & Co. |
| O.H.E.C. | Old Hall Earthenware Co, Ltd. |
| O.H.E.C. (L.). | " |
| P. & A. | Pountney & Allies |
| P.B. | Ferrybridge Pottery |
| P. & B. | Powell & Bishop |
| P. Bros. | Ferrybridge Pottery |
| P.B. & Co. | Pinder, Bourne & Co. |
| P.B. & H. | Pinder, Bourne & Hope |
| P.B. & S. | Powell, Bishop & Stonier |
| P. & Co. | Pountney & Co. |
| P. & Co. Ltd. | " |
| P.E. & Co. | Pountney, Edwards & Co. |
| P.F. & M. | Pearson, Farrall & Meakin |
| P.G. | S. Bridgwood |
| | Brownfield Guild Pottery |
| P. & G. | Pountney & Goldney |
| P.H. & Co. | P. Holdcroft & Co. |
| P.P. Coy. LD. | Plymouth Pottery Co. |
| P. & S. | Pratt & Simpson |
| P.W. & Co. | Podmore, Walker & Co. |
| P.W. & W. | Podmore, Walker & Co. |
| R.A.K. | R.A. Kidston |

| | |
|---|---|
| R.A.K. & Co. | R.A. Kidston |
| R.B. | R. Beswick |
| R.C. | R. Cochran |
| R.A. & Co. | R. Cochran & Co. |
| R. & C. | Read & Clementson |
| R.C. & A. | Read, Clementson & Anderson |
| R.H. | Ralph Hammersley |
| R.H. & Co. | R. Hall |
| R.H. & S. | R. Hammersley |
| R & H. | Robinson & Hollinshead |
| R.K. & Co. | Robinson, Kirkham & Co. |
| R.M. | R. Malkin |
| R.M. & S. | R. Malkin |
| R. & M. | Ridgway & Morley |
| R. & M. Co. | Rowland & Marsellus & Co. (monogram) |
| R.M.W. & Co. | Ridgway, Morley, Wear & Co. |
| R.S. & Co. | Rathbone, Smith & Co. |
| R.S. & W. | Stevenson & Williams |
| R. & T. | Ferrybridge Pottery |
| | Reed & Taylor |
| R.T. & Co. | Ferrybridge Pottery |
| | Reed, Taylor & Co. |
| R.T. & S. | Ferrybridge Pottery |
| R. &W. | Robinson & Wood |
| R.W. & B. | Robinson, Wood & Brownfield |
| S.A. & Co. | S. Alcock & Co. |
| S. & B. | Swift & Elkin |
| S.B. & S. | S. Bridgwood |
| S.B. & Son | " |
| S. & E. | Swift & Elkin |
| S. & E.H. | S. & E. Hughes |
| S.E. & N. | Swift & Elkin |
| S. & F. | Smith & Ford |
| S.F. & S. | Smith, Ford & Jones |
| S.H. | S. Hancock |
| | Stephen Hughes |
| S.H. & Co. | Stephen Hughes & Co. |
| S.H. & S. | S. Hancock |
| | Stephen Hughes |
| S. & J.B. | S. & J. Burton |
| S.W. | Ferrybridge Pottery |
| | S. Woolf |
| S.W.P. | South Wales Pottery |
| T. | J. Twigg & Bros. |
| T.B. | Thomas Barlow |
| T.B. & Co. | T. Booth & Co. |
| T.B. & S. | T. Booth & Co. |
| T. & B.C. | T. & B. Godwin |
| T. & C.T. | T. & C. Twyford |
| T.E. | T. Edwards |
| T.F. | T. Furnival & Son |
| T.F. & Co. | T. Fell |
| | T. Furnival & Co. |
| T.F. & S. | T. Furnival & Son |
| T.F. & Sons | " |
| T.G.B. | T.G. Booth |
| T.G. & Co. | T. Griffiths & Co. |
| T.G. & F.B. | T.G. & F. Booth |
| T.H. | T. Hulme |
| T.H.W. | T.H. Walker |

| | |
|---|---|
| T.K.P. | J. Twigg & Bros. |
| T.M. | Blakeney |
| T. & R.B. | T. & R. Boote Ltd. |
| T.R. Co. | T. Rathbone & Co. |
| T.T. | T. & C. Twyford |
| T. & T. | Turner & Tomkinson |
| T.T.<br>H | T. & C. Twyford |
| T.T. & S. | Thomas Till |
| U. & C. | See page 348 |
| U. & Cie. | " |
| V. & B. | See page 348<br>Venables & Baines |
| V.M. & B. | Venables, Mellor & Baines |
| V.M. & Co. | Venables, Mann & Co. |
| V. & N. | Venables & Nichols |
| W.A. & Co. | William Adams |
| W.A. & S. | William Adams |
| W.B. | W. Brownfield |
| W. & B. | Wood & Brownfield |
| W.B. & S. | W. Brownfield |
| W. & C. | See page 349<br>Wade & Colclough<br>Walker & Carter<br>Wood & Challinor<br>Wood&Clarke |
| W. Co. | See page 350 |
| W.E.C. | W. & E. Corn |
| W. & E.C. | W. & E. Corn |
| W.F. & Co. | W. Freakley |
| W.G. | W. Gill |
| W.G.R. | W. & G. Harding |
| W. & H. | Wood & Hulme |
| W. & J.R. | W. & J. Harding |
| W.M. | W. Morley |
| W.M.<br>F. | W. Morley |
| W.P. Co. | Whitehaven |
| W.R. & Co. | William Ridgway |
| W.R.S. & Co. | William Ridgway Son & Co. |
| W.S. & Co. | William Smith & Co.<br>Stafford |
| W. & T.A. | William Adams<br>W. & T. Adams |
| W.T.H. | W.T. Holland<br>Ynysmedw Pottery |
| Y. & M. | Yates & May |
| Y.M.P. | Ynysmedw Pottery |
| Y.P. | Ynysmedw Pottery |
| Z.B. | Z. Boyle |
| Z.B. & S. | Z. Boyle & Sons |

## CHECK-LIST OF IRONSTONE TYPE TRADE NAMES AND DESCRIPTIONS

The following list should enable marks to be correctly attributed by reference to the manufacturers listed. However, no such listing can be complete, not all possible marks have been reported and published, and you might happen upon a 'new' marking.

I have not included marks incorporating common body descriptions such as Ironstone, Stone China, Stone Ware, Granite, Hotel Ware or simple variations of these standard descriptions. Every manufacturer will on occasions have used marks incorporating such names and it would be a useless exercise to list all possible manufacturers who used the description 'Ironstone'.

Even the more precise description 'Patent Ironstone China' was used by several firms but in reality only the Mason partnerships were entitled to use this description. Likewise the prefix 'Royal' or the British Royal Arms device was used indiscriminately!

Except in a very few cases it is dangerous to rely too heavily on body descriptions incorporated in marks to identify the maker. Personal names or initials are far more reliable. Initials have been previously listed and the manufacturers' names are given in alphabetical order in Chapter VI.

The abbreviated simple names have been used in this section for the cross-references, such as 'J. Tams', whereas the full entry will give all the alternatives, 'John Tams (& Son) (Ltd)', but the simple names will lead the reader to the correct entry in Chapter VI.

| | |
|---|---|
| Armorlite | J.E. Heath |
| Berlin Ironstone | Liddle Elliot, Mayer & Elliot |
| Best Ironstone China | H. Alcock & Co |
| Burleigh Ironstone | Burgess & Leigh |
| Burleigh Ware | Burgess & Leigh |
| Celtic China | J.D. Bagster<br>E. Wood |
| Chemical Porcelain | G. Grainger |
| Corinthian Stone China | Minton |
| Crownware | Royal Worcester |
| Cymro Stone China | L.L. Dillwyn |
| Dresden China | Z. Boyle |
| Dresden Opaque China | J. & R. Clews |
| Duraline | Duraline Hotel Ware<br>Grindley Hotel Ware |
| English Ironstone Tableware | Washington Pottery (Staffordshire) Ltd. |
| Flintstone | J.F Heath Ltd. |
| Genuine Ironstone (china) | E.F. Bodley & Co.<br>Bodley & Harrold |
| Granite Opaque Pearl | J. Clementson |
| Hotel Ware | see page 267 |
| Imp$^{d}$ Ironstone China | S. Folch |
| Imperial French Porcelain | J.T. Close & Co. |
| Imperial Granite | Podmore, Walker & Co. |

| | |
|---|---|
| Imperial Ironstone | Morley & Ashworth |
| Imperial Ironstone China | J. Alcock |
| | H. Alcock & Co. |
| | Baker & Chetwynd |
| | Birks Brothers & Seddon |
| | P. Cochran & Co. |
| | C. Collinson & Co. |
| | J. & R. Godwin |
| | Podmore, Walker & Co. |
| | Wedgwood & Co. Ltd. |
| Imperial Parisian Granite | Old Hall Earthenware Co. |
| Imperial Stone | Rathbone, Smith & Co. |
| | W. Ridgway, Son & Co. |
| Imperial White Granite | Pinder, Bourne & Co. |
| Improved Berlin Ironstone | T.J. & J. Mayer |
| Improved Granite China | Ridgway & Morley |
| | Ridgway, Morley, Wear & Co. |
| | Ridgway, Morley & Wear |
| Improved Ironstone China | S. Folch |
| Improved Stone China | C. Meigh |
| Improved Stone Ware | L.L. Dillwyn |
| | T. Dimmock & Co. |
| Indian Ironstone | S. Alcock |
| Indian Stone China | C. Meigh & Son |
| | Old Hall Earthenware Co. |
| Ironite | R. Hammersley |
| Ironstone China. Pearl White | Robinson, Wood & Brownfield |
| | Wood & Brownfield |
| Ironstone Warranted | Hicks & Meigh |
| Japan Stone Ware | see 'D', page 220 |
| Kensington Ironstone | Kensington Pottery Ltd. |
| Limoges | S. Bridgwood |
| Mason's Vitrified | G.L. Ashworth & Bros. |
| Micratex | W. Adams |
| New Cambrian China | S. Folch |
| New Stone | Minton |
| | Spode |
| Opaque China Warranted | J. Marsh |
| Opaque Granite China | W. Ridgway |
| | Swillington Bridge |
| Opaque Porcelain | Old Hall Earthenware Co. |
| Opaque Stone China | A. Shaw |
| Oriental Stone | J. & G. Alcock |
| | J. & S. Alcock |
| Parisian Granite | T.G.. & F. Booth |
| | S. Bridgwood |
| Patent Paris White Ironstone | Wedgwood & Co. Ltd. |
| Pearl China | S. &. J. Burton |
| Pearl Ironstone China | F. Jones |
| | Turner & Tomkinson |
| Pearl Stone Ware | Podmore, Walker & Co. |
| Pearl White Ironstone | Cork & Edge |
| | Cork, Edge & Malkin |
| Porcelain Royale | W. & E. Corn |

| | |
|---|---|
| Quartz China | W. Ridgway |
| Queen's Royal Ironstone | J. Goodwin |
| Real English Ironstone | W. Adams |
| Real Ironstone China | G.L. Ashworth & Bros. |
| | Davenport |
| | C. & W.K. Harvey |
| Real Iron Stone China | G.L. Ashworth & Bros. |
| Real Stone China | G.L. Ashworth & Bros. |
| Reinforced Vitrite | Pountney & Co. |
| Rock Stone | J. Tams |
| Royal Crownford Ironstone | Weatherby & Sons Ltd. |
| Royal Ironstone China | H. Alcock & Co. |
| | W. Baker & Co. |
| | R. Cochran & Co. |
| | Cochran & Fleming |
| | Johnson Bros. |
| | Alfred Meakin |
| | Mellor, Taylor & Co. |
| Royal Patent Ironstone | R. Alcock |
| | T. & R. Boote |
| | Mellor, Venables & Co. |
| | Turner, Goddard & Co. |
| Royal Patent Stone Ware | Clementson |
| Royal Stone China | G.L. Ashworth & Bros. |
| | J. & M.P. Bell & Co. |
| | J.H. & J. Davis |
| | F. Morley |
| | Ridgway, Morley, Wear & Co. |
| | Stevenson & Williams |
| Royal Tudor Ware | Barker Bros. Ltd. |
| Royal Vitreous J. | Maddock & Son |
| Royal Vitrescent Rock China | see page 321 |
| Satin White | W.H. Grindley & Co. |
| | Grindley Pottery Ltd. |
| Saxon Stone China | T. & J. Carey |
| Sol | J. & G. Meakin |
| Stafford Stone China | W. Smith & Co. |
| Staffordshire Ironstone China | Griffiths, Beardmore & Birks |
| Staffordshire Stone China | Godwin, Rowley & Co. |
| | Swift & Elkin |
| Staffordshire Warranted Stone China | W. Green |
| Steelite | see page 336 |
| Stoke Works | S. Folch |
| Stone China Indian | Old Hall Earthenware Co. |
| Super-Vitrified | Duraline Hotel Ware |
| Superior Stone China | J. Ridgway |
| Tonquin China | see page 343 |
| Tudor Ware | Barker Bros.Ltd. |
| Turner's Patent | J. Turner |
| Ultraline | Duraline Hotel Ware |
| Victoria | see page 349 |
| Vitrite | Pountney & Co. |
| Vitro China | Josiah Wedgwood |
| Warranted Stafford Stone China | W. Smith & Co. |
| White Granite Vitrified | W.H. Grindley & Co. |
| Wrekin | see page 359 |

APPENDIX II

# Registered Marks, Patterns or Forms British Ironstone Manufacturers in 1885 and 1900

The first form of copyright protection to affect British ceramics relates to the *Sculpture Copyright Act* of 1797 as amended in 1814. Under this act any sculptured or modelled form could enjoy protection against copyists merely by the artist, sculpture, modeller or indeed the manufacturer marking the design with his name, address and the date of publication.

This required information was usually preceded by the words 'Published by' followed by the relevant name, address and date. Such marks often found on moulded jugs (see Plate 282) and the like are known as 'Published by marks'. They conveniently show the name of the maker and the earliest possible date of production. There is no central register of such forms.

From 1839 to 1842, however, designs that were to be protected by such copyright had to be registered with the British Board of Trade and these records are preserved at the Public Record Office at Kew. As each registered design still had to bear the name of the maker and the date one does not need to consult these original records; the mark should record the basic facts.

The British system was, however, both enlarged and simplified in 1842 when the new *Design Copyright Act* came into being and covered added designs, normally printed patterns as well as the basic shapes. Under this system various porcelains and earthenwares including some ironstone, stoneware or granite-type ceramics bear the new diamond-shape basic registration mark as here shown.

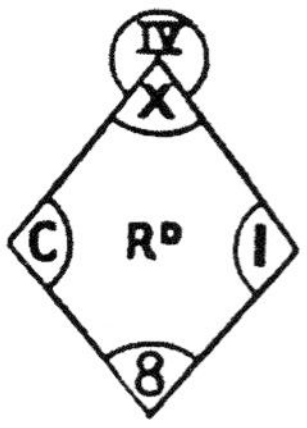


Under this system the manufacturer or designer would send a drawing or photograph of the object or a pull from the engraved copper plate, with the required fee, to the Office of Registry of Designs in London. The prototype was obviously in being at this stage. On receipt of the design the clerks would enter the details in a large ledger or 'register' under a 'parcel number' or individual number for that day's business. It could

PLATE 282. *A moulded stoneware jug of the type protected by 'Published by...' marks, giving details of the name and address of the manufacturer or designer and the date of publication. This relates to E. Jones of Cobridge, a design of 1 September 1838. 7in. (17.78cm) high.*

PLATE 283. *A typical drawing of the type submitted to the 'Office of Registry of Designs' in London. This relates to fluted dinner ware forms entered by James Edwards of Burslem on 30 May 1842. Public Record Office, London.*

happen, especially in the early years, that a clerk entered more than one article from a given manufacturer under the same parcel number, so that a few duplicate entries occur when the device is decoded. The clerk would then allocate a coded version of the official diamond-shape mark to that design and send this back to the manufacturer. This then had to be added to the mould, to the engraved copper plate, or be otherwise affixed to every copy of that now registered shape or design. This official registration gave copyright protection to new designs for an initial period of three years. The period of copyright could be extended by paying a further fee when usually a new registration mark was allocated.

With the first system of coding, in use from 1842 to 1867, the year letter was added at the top inner angle below the 'Class Number', that for ceramics being IV. The day of the month appears on the right, the coded month letter at the left and the parcel, or entry, number at the bottom. The registration devices do not include a direct reference to the person or firm who registered the design, although in some rare cases the manufacturer did add his name or incorporated the device in his standard trade mark.

A revised system was employed from 1868 to 1883 when the positions within the diamond were changed. The day of the month, of the official entry, now appears at the top, the month letter at the bottom, the year letter at the right and the parcel number on the left. These positions are shown below.

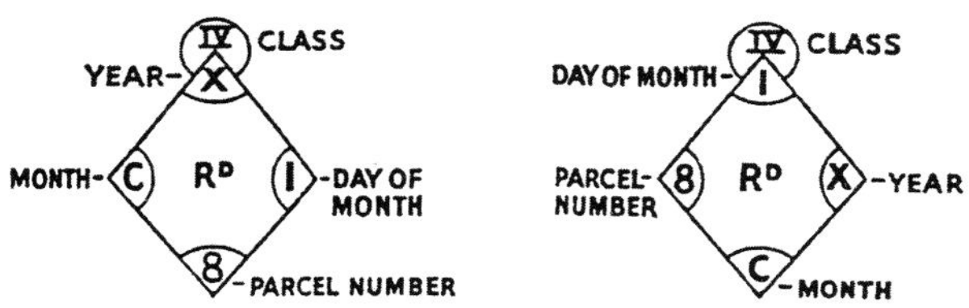


As the original records are still preserved, one can discover the name and address of the person or firm who registered the article, and this is not always the manufacturer. The records are housed at the Public Record Office, Ruskin Avenue, Kew, Surrey, under

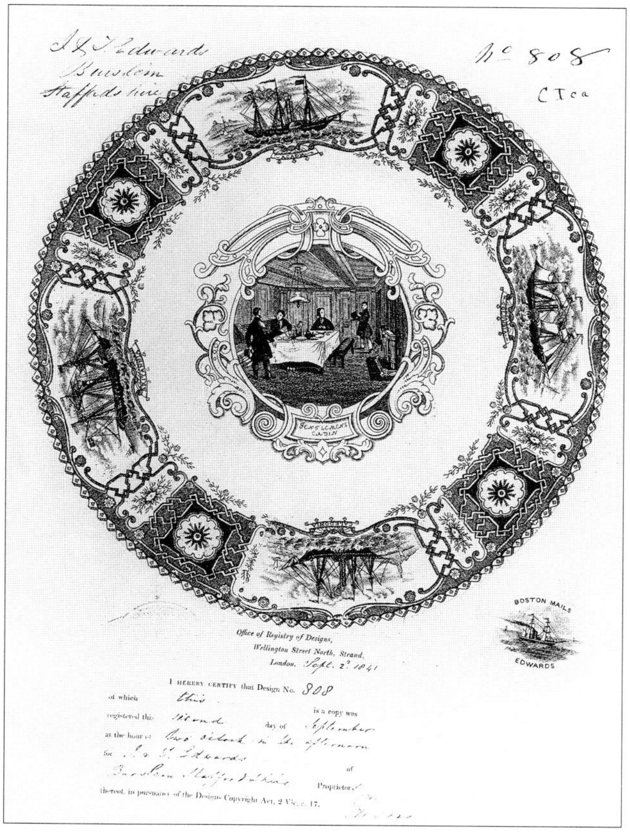


PLATE 284. *A pull from a J. & T. Edwards engraved copper-plate for the 'Boston Mails' subject, shown with the 'Edwards' printed mark which was part of the engraved copper-plate. This was entered in the Registry of Designs records on 2 September 1841. Public Record Office, London.*

reference BT43 (Representations, i.e. the shape of pattern) and BT44 (Registers, i.e. the dated entries). Many large files are indexed and unless the searcher has the precise details taken from a clear registration device the search is likely to be very time-consuming. It would be as well to ascertain that the Public Record Office is open at the time and date that you intend calling: it is not open on Saturday or Sunday and may be closed at some other times for internal reasons. (The British telephone number is 0181 876 3444.) I list from page 377 the registrations that seem to relate to ironstone-type wares but a shape or pattern could originally have related to a porcelain object and was subsequently employed on ironstone-type wares – this would not affect the registration which remained whatever ceramic body was used.

A further complication can arise when the registered design was sold on to another firm, as might be the case with a change of partnership or when a pottery was sold with all its working materials. The official entry obviously shows only the original depositor and the earliest possible date of manufacture.

In general terms moulded or impressed registration mark devices will relate to the basic shape of the object. Printed marks usually relate to the added pattern. It should be borne in mind, however, that whilst only a plate shape might have been registered, the whole dinner service would follow the basic shape or moulding. Also, with teasets the teapot form may have been registered but all the components would be newly designed to match. It could also happen that a shape was registered for one type of article but was unofficially extended to embrace different types, i.e. a dinner service registration appears on tea wares.

Also, when a new shape was registered it could bear any number of added patterns. Alternatively a registered pattern could be added to many different shapes or objects.

In a few cases the registration diamond-shaped device will be added to a maker's mark or otherwise enhanced with the manufacturer's name for that shape or pattern. Such bonuses are rare, but all registered objects were mass-produced for general sale and will not represent unique articles.

The code for 1842-1883 is here given. In all over 408,000 entries were made under this system before the end of 1883. Although the registration mark should not have been used after the three-year copyright period had expired it seems that in some cases the device was not removed from moulds or from engraved copper-plates so that the device continued in, illegal, use.

## TABLE OF REGISTRATION MARKS 1842-83

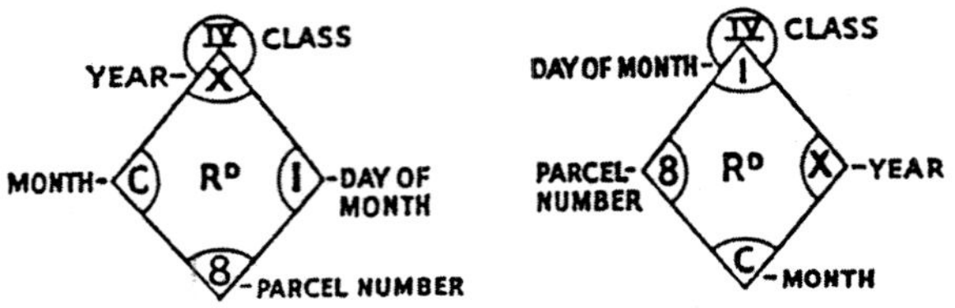


Above are the two patterns of Design Registration Marks that were in current use between the years 1842 and 1883. Keys to 'year' and 'month' code letters are given below.

The left-hand diamond was used during the years 1842 to 1867. A change was made in 1868, when the right-hand arrangement was adopted.

## INDEX TO YEAR AND MONTH LETTERS

### YEARS

| 1842-67 | | | | 1868-83 | | | |
|---|---|---|---|---|---|---|---|
| Year Letter at Top | | | | Year Letter at Right | | | |
| A = | 1845 | N = | 1864 | A = | 1871 | L = | 1882 |
| B = | 1858 | O = | 1862 | C = | 1870 | P = | 1877 |
| C = | 1844 | P = | 1851 | D = | 1878 | S = | 1875 |
| D = | 1852 | Q = | 1866 | E = | 1881 | U = | 1874 |
| E = | 1855 | R = | 1861 | F = | 1873 | V = | 1876 |
| F = | 1847 | S = | 1849 | H = | 1869 | W= | (Mar.1-6) |
| G = | 1863 | T = | 1867 | I = | 1872 | | 1878 |
| H = | 1843 | U = | 1848 | J = | 1880 | X = | 1868 |
| I = | 1846 | V = | 1850 | K = | 1883 | Y = | 1879 |
| J = | 1854 | W = | 1865 | | | | |
| K = | 1857 | X = | 1842 | | | | |
| L = | 1856 | Y = | 1853 | | | | |
| M = | 1859 | Z = | 1860 | | | | |

### MONTHS (BOTH PERIODS)

| | | |
|---|---|---|
| A = December | G = February | M = June |
| B = October | H = April | R = August (and |
| C or O = January | I = July | 1-19 September |
| D = September | K = November | 1857) |
| E = May | December 1860) | W = March |

As from 1 January 1884, a new system of denoting registered designs or shapes was employed, replacing the former diamond-shaped registration device. This relates to the *Patents, Designs and Trade Mark Act* of 1883.

Under the new Board of Trade system, only a number was used to denote the entry in the official records.

This number was very often prefixed by the abbreviation R$^{D}$.N$^{O}$. for Registered Number. The simple progressive system included all types of manufactured article; the first ceramic object was number 130, registered in the name of J. Dimmock & Co. of Hanley on 10 January 1884. By May 1888, after less than four and a half years, 100,000 entries had been registered.

The following list of numbers reached by the January of each year from 1885 to 1997 will enable owners to discover the year of registration and even the approximate month within that year. Reference to this listing will therefore show the earliest possible date of that object.

By reference to the original records and indexes the reader may discover the name under which the registration was entered. However, this is not necessarily the manufacturer as some designs were registered by agents, wholesalers or retailers.

The early original records are housed at the Public Record Office at Kew, but entries for registered design number 548920 of September 1909 onwards are held at the Design Registry at Cardiff. Prior application to The Patent Office (Designs Registry), Cardiff Road, Newport, Gwent, NP9 1RH (Tel 01633 811146) may save delay or a wasted journey should the position have changed since this section was written.

This table shows the approximate number reached by January of each year.

## TABLE OF REGISTRATION NUMBERS 1884-1999

| | | | |
|---|---|---|---|
| 1 = 1884 | 612431 = 1913 | 839230 = 1942 | 950046 = 1971 |
| 19754 = 1885 | 630190 = 1914 | 839980 = 1943 | 955342 = 1972 |
| 40480 = 1886 | 644935 = 1915 | 841040 = 1944 | 960708 = 1973 |
| 64520 = 1887 | 653521 = 1916 | 842670 = 1945 | 965185 = 1974 |
| 90483 = 1888 | 658988 = 1917 | 845550 = 1946 | 969249 = 1975 |
| 116648 = 1889 | 662872 = 1918 | 849730 = 1947 | 973838 = 1976 |
| 141273 = 1890 | 666128 = 1919 | 853260 = 1948 | 978426 = 1977 |
| 163767 = 1891 | 673750 = 1920 | 856999 = 1949 | 982815 = 1978 |
| 185713 = 1892 | 680147 = 1921 | 860854 = 1950 | 987910 = 1979 |
| 205240 = 1893 | 687144 = 1922 | 863970 = 1951 | 993012 = 1980 |
| 224720 = 1894 | 694999 = 1923 | 866280 = 1952 | 998302 = 1981 |
| 246975 = 1895 | 702671 = 1924 | 869300 = 1953 | 1004456 = 1982 |
| 268392 = 1896 | 710165 = 1925 | 872531 = 1954 | 1010583 = 1983 |
| 291241 = 1897 | 718057 = 1926 | 876067 = 1955 | 1017131 = 1984 |
| 311658 = 1898 | 726330 = 1927 | 879282 = 1956 | 1024174 = 1985 |
| 331707 = 1899 | 734370 = 1928 | 882949 = 1957 | 1031358 = 1986 |
| 351202 = 1900 | 742725 = 1929 | 887079 = 1958 | 1039055 = 1987 |
| 368154 = 1901 | 751160 = 1930 | 891665 = 1959 | 1047479 = 1988 |
| 385180 = 1902 | 760583 = 1931 | 895000 = 1960 | 1056075 = 1989 |
| 403200 = 1903 | 769670 = 1932 | 899914 = 1961 | 2003720 = 1990 |
| 424400 = 1904 | 779292 = 1933 | 904638 = 1962 | 2012047 = 1991 |
| 447800 = 1905 | 789019 = 1934 | 909364 = 1963 | 2019933 = 1992 |
| 471860 = 1906 | 799097 = 1935 | 914536 = 1964 | 2028115 = 1993 |
| 493900 = 1907 | 808794 = 1936 | 919607 = 1965 | 2036116 = 1994 |
| 518640 = 1908 | 817293 = 1937 | 924510 = 1966 | 2044227 = 1995 |
| 535170 = 1909 | 825231 = 1938 | 929335 = 1967 | 2053121 = 1996 |
| 552000 = 1910 | 832610 = 1939 | 934515 = 1968 | 2062140 = 1997 |
| 574817 = 1911 | 837520 = 1940 | 939875 = 1969 | 2071420 = 1998 |
| 594195 = 1912 | 838590 = 1941 | 944932 = 1970 | 2080159 = 1999 |

It should be noted that registration marks covering designs and shapes are quite different from patented novel techniques or objects. One sometimes find 'Patent' wording and the date of the patent on ceramic objects. These may relate to British patents or to American patents or to those of any nation. Again they may indicate the earliest possible date of manufacture but the Patent Office records are quite different from those kept by the old Design Registration Office and the reference numbers do not link one with the other.

In practice few British ceramics were covered by patent rights and fewer bear wording relating to a patent. Llewellynn Jewitt gave at the end of Volume 11 of the 1878 edition of his *The Ceramic Art of Great Britain* (Virtue & Co. Ltd., London) a list of British ceramic patents granted between 1676 and 1877. The given name of the patentee, is not, however, necessarily the name of the manufacturer of the object.

## BRITISH REGISTERED DESIGNS OR FORMS RELATING TO IRONSTONE-TYPE WARES 1842-1883

The bracketed number relates to the parcel (or entry) number.

**1842**

| | | |
|---|---|---|
| December 2nd | (3) | J. Clementson, Shelton<br>Printed design 'Lucerne' |
| December 2nd | (3) | J. Clementson, Shelton<br>Printed design 'Rustic Scenery' |
| December 30th | (2) | J. Edwards, Burslem<br>Fluted jug or toiletware forms |

**1843**

| | | |
|---|---|---|
| August 30th | (8) | J. Edwards, Burslem<br>Eight-sided dinner service forms |

**1844**

| | | |
|---|---|---|
| April 3rd | (3) | T. Edwards, Burslem<br>Faceted dinner service forms |
| May 7th | (4) | T. Dimmock junr. & Co., Shelton<br>Printed design 'Rhine' |
| June 29th | (3) | T. Dimmock junr. & Co., Shelton<br>Printed design 'Lily' |
| July 20th | (5) | J. Ridgway & Co., Shelton<br>Eight-sided dinner and teaware forms |
| July 20th | (5) | J. Ridgway & Co., Shelton<br>Printed design 'Doria' |
| September 19th | (4) | J. Ridgway & Co., Shelton<br>Dinner service forms |

| | | |
|---|---|---|
| October 17th | (3) | Clementson, Young & Jameson, Shelton<br>Printed design 'Aleppo' |
| November 11th | (5) | James Edwards, Burslem<br>Printed design – scenic centre |
| December 16th | (6) | W. Ridgway, Son & Co., Hanley<br>Printed designs. 'Catskill Moss' border design.<br>Various scenic centres |

**1845**

| | | |
|---|---|---|
| January 11th | (6) | G. Phillips, Longport<br>Printed design 'Corinth' |
| February 27th | (3) | G. Phillips, Longport<br>Dinner ware forms |
| April 26th | (3) | T. & R. Boote, Burslem; Edward Walley, Cobridge; E. Jones, Hanley.<br>Dinner ware forms,<br>registered in joint names |
| June 19th | (1) | G. Phillips, Longport<br>Printed design 'Lobella' |
| July 5th | (1) | G. Phillips, Longport<br>Six shape designs |
| July 26th | (1) | W. Adams & Sons, Stoke<br>Printed design 'Habana' |
| August 28th | (3) | J. Clementson, Shelton<br>Printed design incorporating portrait panels |
| October 22nd | (2) | Clementson & Young, Shelton<br>Dinner service forms (Plate 132) |
| December 29th | (2) | J. Clementson, Shelton<br>Design for twelve-sided plate form |

**1846**

| | | |
|---|---|---|
| January 7th | (2) | J. Clementson, Shelton<br>Printed design 'Tessine' |
| January 24th | (2) | Jacob Furnival & Co., Cobridge<br>Printed dinnerware design, scenic centre |
| May 21st | (3) | H. Minton & Co., Stoke<br>Toilet ware forms |
| July 16th | (1) | W. Ridgway, Son & Co., Hanley<br>Moulded forms, jugs etc. |
| September 3rd | (2) | G. Phillips, Longport<br>Printed design, scenic centre |
| October 26th | (1) | Francis Morley & Co., Shelton<br>Dinner ware forms |
| November 5th | (2) | G. Phillips, Longport.<br>Printed design 'Friburg' |
| November 21st | (2) | T. Furnival & Co., Hanley<br>Printed design – American eagle motif |
| December 29th | (2) | Edward Challinor, Tunstall<br>Printed design, scenic centre |

**1847**

| | | |
|---|---|---|
| January 9th | (4) | J. Ridgway & Co., Shelton<br>Dinner ware forms |
| June 11th | (4) | J. Edwards, Burslem<br>Dinner ware forms |
| June 25th | (2) | J. Edwards, Burslem<br>Dinner ware forms |
| July 16th | (5) | J. Edwards, Burslem<br>Dinner, tea and other useful ware moulded forms |
| July 27th | (3) | T.J. & J. Mayer, Burslem<br>Dinner ware forms but these so-called 'classic Gothic' forms occur on other non-dinner service shapes |
| September 25th | (5) | J. Wedg Wood, Tunstall<br>Fluted teaware forms |
| October 8th | (4) | J. Wedg Wood, Tunstall<br>Fluted dinner ware forms |

**1848**

| | | |
|---|---|---|
| March 27th | (8) | J. & S. Alcock, junior, Cobridge<br>Various dinner ware forms, eight- sided tureen, etc. |
| June 30th | (3) | Ridgway & Abington, Hanley<br>Moulded wheat ear and leaf pattern |
| August 23rd | (2) | J. Wedg Wood, Tunstall<br>Printed design, scenic centre and panels |
| September 30th | (7) | J. Ridgway & Co., Shelton<br>Dinner ware forms, six-sided tureen, twelve-sided plates |
| December 16th | (3) | J. Edwards, Burslem<br>Three dinner ware forms |

**1849**

| | | |
|---|---|---|
| March 13th | (2) | J. Clementson, Shelton<br>Printed design, Etruscan figure subjects |
| April 2nd | (5) | Podmore, Walker & Co., Tunstall<br>Printed design 'California', with misleading 'Wedgwood' name |

| | | |
|---|---|---|
| April 16th | (6) | C.J. Mason, Longton<br>Eight-sided Patent Ironstone plate form.<br>see Plates 34 and 35 |
| **1850** | | |
| February 13th | (3) | J. &. M.P. Bell & Co., Glasgow<br>Printed design 'Ionia' |
| April 8th | (1) | J. Clementson, Shelton<br>Printed design 'Siam' |
| July 16th | (5) | T.J. & J. Mayer, Burslem<br>Three designs for dinner ware forms, 'Florentine' |
| September 21st | (1) | Mellor, Venables & Co., Burslem<br>Design for eight-sided tureen form |
| **1851** | | |
| April 26th | (3) | Edward Walley, Cobridge<br>Moulded wheat ear jug etc, ' Ceres' |
| July 21st | (7) | T. & R. Boote, Burslem<br>Tea ware designs |
| September 2nd | (4) | T.J. & J. Mayer, Longport<br>Dinner ware forms |
| September 19th | (3) | T. & R. Boote, Burslem<br>Dinner ware forms |
| September 29th | (4) | J. Edwards, Longport<br>Dinner ware forms, hexagonal |
| September 30th | (3) | J. Edwards, Longport<br>Dinner ware forms |
| October 10th | (6) | T. & R. Boote, Burslem<br>Dinner ware forms, ten-sided plates |
| December 2nd | (2) | Messrs Mayer, Burslem<br>Relief moulded jug form |
| December 5th | (5) | J. Ridgway & Co., Shelton<br>Dinner ware forms, eight-sided plates |
| **1852** | | |
| October 23rd | (4) | Davenports & Co., Longport<br>Five designs for dinner wares etc, ten-sided plates |
| **1853** | | |
| January 14th | (3) | Davenports & Co., Longport<br>Various tea, breakfast and toilet set forms, 'Niagara' |
| January 18th | (2) | Davenports & Co., Longport<br>Various tea and toilet set forms, 'Plain French' |
| February 4th | (9) | J. Pankhurst & J. Dimmock (James Pankhurst & Co.) Hanley<br>Design for tureen form |
| April 23rd | (2) | W. Adams & Sons, Tunstall<br>Designs for dinner ware forms |
| May 7th | (5) | John Alcock, Cobridge<br>Seventeen designs for dinner and tea ware forms, 'Hebe' |
| July 18th | (4) | John Edwards, Longton<br>Design for moulded tea wares, 'Tuscan' |
| August 8th | (1) | Anthony Shaw, Tunstall<br>Printed design 'Peruvian Horse Hunt' |
| September 3rd | (2) | T. & R. Boote, Burslem<br>Designs for dinner ware forms, 'Sydenham' |
| September 21st | (2) | James Edwards, Burslem<br>Designs for dinner ware forms |
| October 5th | (2) | Venables, Mann & Co., Burslem<br>Eighteen designs for dinner and tea ware forms |
| October 10th | (3) | Barrow & Co,, Longton<br>Design for covered dish, apple knob |
| October 12th | (3) | James Edwards, Burslem<br>Design for dinner ware forms |
| October 12th | (4) | Livesley, Powell & Co., Hanley<br>Designs for dinner and tea ware forms |
| October 22nd | (1) | T.J. & J. Mayer, Burslem<br>Designs for two tureen forms |
| November 24th | (2) | Thomas Till & Son, Burslem<br>Designs for dinner ware forms |
| **1854** | | |
| March 31st | (1) | Holland & Green, Longton<br>Designs for various moulded wares 'Gothic' |
| April 11th | (5) | Pearson, Farrall & Meakin, Shelton<br>Designs for moulded dinner wares |
| June 21st | (5) | T. & R. Boote, Burslem<br>Designs for toilet ware forms, 'Sydenham' |

| | | |
|---|---|---|
| July 18th | (2) | T. & R. Boote, Burslem<br>Designs for moulded teaware forms, 'Sydenham' |
| September 5th | (3) | S. Alcock & Co., Burslem<br>Design for moulded edge plate form |
| October 6th | (4) | Davenports & Co., Longport<br>Designs for moulded teawares |

**1855**

| | | |
|---|---|---|
| January 15th | (4) | Brougham & Mayer, Tunstall<br>Designs for dinner, tea and toilet wares, 'Virginia' |
| January 30th | (1) | John Edwards, Longton<br>Design for moulded dinner wares, 'President' |
| February 3rd | (4) | J. & M.P. Bell & Co., Glasgow<br>Printed design, 'Anemone' |
| February 7th | (2) | John Alcock, Cobridge<br>Designs for moulded edge dinner wares, 'Flora' |
| March 5th | (3) | Elsmore & Forster, Tunstall<br>Designs for moulded teawares, 'Columbia' |
| April 17th | (4) | S. Hughes & Son, Burslem<br>Designs for dinner service forms |
| April 28th | (7) | Venables,Mann & Co., Burslem<br>Designs for dinner service forms, leaf border |
| June 7th | (4) | John Alcock, Cobridge<br>Designs for dinner service forms, 'Trent' |
| July 24th | (1) | Charles Meigh & Son, Hanley<br>Eight designs for dinner and teawares |
| August 8th | (6) | James Edwards & Son, Burslem<br>Designs for lobed dinner ware forms |
| August 27th | (2) | Barrow & Co., Fenton<br>Seven designs for table and toilet ware forms 'Adriatic' |
| October 25th | (3) | David Chetwynd, Cobridge<br>Design for tureen form, 'Baltic' |
| October 29th | (6) | G.W. Reade, Burslem<br>Three designs for dinner wares, made by several manufacturers and termed 'Columbia' |

**1856**

| | | |
|---|---|---|
| January 5th | (3) | John Edwards, Longton<br>Designs for toilet wares, 'President' |
| April 7th | (2) | Anthony Shaw, Tunstall<br>Four designs for dinner and teawares |
| April 18th | (3) | Ralph Scragg, Hanley<br>Design for covered dish |
| June 30th | (7) | Joseph Clementson, Shelton<br>Printed design, 'Claremont' |
| July 28th | (3) | Edward Challinor, Tunstall<br>Printed design, 'Dora' |
| August 22nd | (4) | T. & R. Boote, Burslem<br>Five designs for dinner, tea and toilet wares |
| November 14th | (9) | Davenports & Co., Longport<br>Five designs for dinner ware forms |
| November 27th | (3) | Davenports & Co., Longport<br>Eight designs for teaware forms |
| November 29th | (1) | Edward Walley, Cobridge<br>Ten designs for dinner, tea and toilet wares, 'Niagara' |
| December 18th | (2) | Mayer Brothers & Elliott, Longport<br>Design for oval tureen forms |
| December 23rd | (4) | Mayer Brothers & Elliott, Longport<br>Design for circular dinner ware tureens |

**1857**

| | | |
|---|---|---|
| February 4th | (5) | John Meir & Son, Tunstall<br>Five designs for dinner ware forms, 'Menmon' |
| February 23rd | (9) | Podmore, Walker & Co., Tunstall & Hanley<br>Design for moulded form, 'Athens' |
| March 20th | (4) | John Alcock, Cobridge<br>Nine designs for two sets of teawares |
| April 16th | (1) | John Alcock, Cobridge<br>Seven designs for fluted dinner ware forms |
| October 17th | (2) | T.& R. Boote, Burslem<br>Designs for teawares, etc. |

**1858**

| | | |
|---|---|---|
| April 22nd | (5) | T. & R. Boote, Burslem<br>Three designs for dinner ware forms, 'Atlantic' |

| | | |
|---|---|---|
| May 25th | (4) | Anthony Shaw, Tunstall<br>Printed design, 'Castanete Dance' |
| May 31st | (1) | Holland & Green, Longton<br>Designs for dinner, tea and toilet ware forms |
| May 31st | (4) | W. Adams, junior, Tunstall<br>Four designs for dinner ware forms |
| September 6th | (5) | James Edwards, Longton<br>Four designs for dinner ware forms |
| September 10th | (6) | Bridgwood & Clarke, Burslem<br>Six designs for dinner ware forms |
| December 8th | (11) | T. & R. Boote, Burslem<br>Three designs for various moulded forms |
| December 8th | (12) | Joseph Clementson, Hanley<br>Four designs for moulded teaware forms, 'New York' |

**1859**

| | | |
|---|---|---|
| February 2nd | (3) | T. & R. Boote, Burslem<br>Designs for dinner ware forms |
| October 12th | (4) | W. Adams, junior, Tunstall<br>Three designs for dinner ware forms |
| November 2nd | (3) | Elsmore & Forster, Tunstall<br>Seventeen designs for dinner, tea and toilet wares, fluted, 'Ceres' and 'Laurel wreath' |

**1860**

| | | |
|---|---|---|
| January 23rd | (7) | Mayer & Elliot, Longport<br>Design for tureen form |
| May 2nd | (2) | J. Meir & Son, Tunstall<br>Design for ivy-leaf bordered dinner wares |
| May 30th | (10) | Edward Corn, Burslem<br>Design for moulded bordered plate |
| October 19th | (4) | Joseph Clementson, Shelton<br>Eleven designs for dinner, tea and toilet wares |
| October 19th | (5) | Holland & Green, Longton<br>Designs for dinner, tea and toilet wares |
| November 23rd | (9) | T. & R. Boote, Burslem<br>Design for toilet ware forms, 'Garibaldi' |

**1861**

| | | |
|---|---|---|
| February 15th | (3) | F. Furnival & Co., Cobridge<br>Design for fluted dinner ware forms |
| February 27th | (5) | James Edwards & Sons, Longton<br>Designs for dinner ware forms |
| April 12th | (3) | Davenport & Co., Longport<br>Eleven designs for dinner and teaware forms, 'Erie' |
| November 18th | (3) | J. Clementson, Shelton<br>Five designs for moulded dinner tea and toilet wares, wheat ear or 'Prairie' designs |

**1862**

| | | |
|---|---|---|
| March 13th | (7) | W. Adams, junior, Tunstall<br>Designs for half-fluted dinner and teaware forms |
| March 22nd | (9) | T. & R. Boote, Burslem<br>Design for vine moulded forms, 'Venetia' |
| July 12th | (4) | J. Clementson, Shelton<br>Design for moulded teawares |
| July 19th | (6) | J. Clementson, Shelton<br>Design for moulded dinner wares |
| September 17th | (6) | Hope & Carter, Burslem<br>Designs for dinner ware forms |
| September 26th | (1) | Hope & Carter, Burslem<br>Designs for dinner, tea and toilet ware forms |
| October 23rd | (8) | W. Baker & Co., Fenton<br>Eleven designs for dinner, tea and toilet wares |

**1863**

| | | |
|---|---|---|
| January 30th | (3) | T.& R. Boote, Burslem<br>Designs for dinner ware forms, 'Prairie Flower' |
| February 17th | (1) | T.& R. Boote, Burslem<br>Designs for toilet wares, 'Prairie Flower' |
| May 11th | (3) | Edward Pearson, Cobridge<br>Four designs for dinner and tea ware forms |
| August 21st | (1) | J. Clementson, Hanley<br>Design for tureen form |
| November 3rd | (5) | J. Meir & Son, Tunstall<br>Design for dinner ware form |
| November 4th | (7) | T. & R. Boote, Burslem<br>Five designs for dinner ware forms 'Mocho' |
| December 2nd | (5) | J.W. Pankhurst & Co., Hanley<br>Designs for dinner ware forms |

**1864**

| | | |
|---|---|---|
| March 3rd | (4) | G.L. Ashworth & Bros., Hanley<br>Design for tureen form |
| April 23rd | (11) | G.L. Ashworth & Bros., Hanley<br>Printed design, Indian view to centre |
| September 16th | (6) | G.L. Ashworth & Bros., Hanley<br>Two designs for dinner ware forms |
| November 10th | (2) | Elsmore & Forster, Tunstall<br>Nine designs for moulded dinner and teaware forms, 'Olympia' |

**1865**

| | | |
|---|---|---|
| April 28th | (4) | Hope & Carter, Burslem<br>Two designs for tureen forms |
| June 6th | (6) | J.T. Hudden, Longton<br>Printed designs, 'Pelew' and 'Orleans' |
| September 18th | (6) | Liddle Elliot & Son, Longport.<br>Design for tureen form |
| November 10th | (4) | Anthony Shaw and Pinder Bourne & Co., Burslem<br>Design for moulded edge dinner wares |

**1866**

| | | |
|---|---|---|
| January 3rd | (6) | J.T. Close & Co., Stoke<br>Three designs for dinner service forms |
| April 14th | (7) | G.L. Ashworth & Bros., Hanley<br>Eight designs for dinner, tea and toilet wares, 'Nile' |
| May 1st | (4) | J. Furnival & Co., Cobridge<br>Two designs for tureen forms |
| June 12th | (1) | John Edwards, Fenton<br>Eight designs for dinner, tea and toilet wares |
| September 15th | (8) | G.L. Ashworth & Bros., Hanley<br>Printed design, 'St Petersburgh' |

**1867**

| | | |
|---|---|---|
| April 4th | (9) | Elsmore & Forster, Tunstall<br>Seven designs for dinner, tea and toilet wares |
| May 22nd | (6) | Clementson Bros., Hanley<br>Designs for dinner and jug forms |
| June 11th | (6) | Clementson Bros., Hanley<br>Designs for teaware forms |
| July 8th | (3) | G.L. Ashworth & Eros., Hanley<br>Printed pattern 'Seasons' |
| July 12th | (5) | George Jones, Stoke<br>Design for tureen form |
| November 7th | (4) | J. Edwards & Son, Burslem<br>Three designs for dinner ware forms |

**1868**

| | | |
|---|---|---|
| January 7th | (11) | Cockson Chetwynd & Co., Cobridge<br>Five designs for dinner, tea and toilet ware forms |
| January 8th | (5) | T. & R. Boote, Burslem<br>Seven designs for teaware shapes, 'Classic' |
| January 13th | (2) | G.L. Ashworth & Bros., Hanley<br>Printed design, 'Daisy' |
| April 16th | (7) | G.L. Ashworth & Bros., Hanley<br>Printed design |
| August 15th | (8) | J. Edwards & Son, Burslem<br>Designs for dinner, tea and toilet wares |
| December 31st | (6) | G.L. Ashworth & Bros., Hanley<br>Moulded toilet ware forms |

**1869**

| | | |
|---|---|---|
| May 13th | (16) | J. Edwards & Son, Burslem<br>Design for dinner ware forms |
| September 8th | (6) | Pinder, Bourne & Co., Burslem<br>Printed design, ship in ice |
| September 21st | (7) | Gelson Bros., Hanley<br>Designs for dinner, tea and toilet wares |
| October 29th | (4) | Powell & Bishop, Hanley<br>Ten designs for dinner, tea and toilet wares |
| November 2nd | (12) | Edward Clarke, Tunstall<br>Five designs for table and toilet wares |
| December 18th | (2) | Powell & Bishop, Hanley<br>Five designs for table and toilet wares |
| December 24th | (1) | Gelson Bros., Hanley<br>Design for tureen form |

**1870**

| | | |
|---|---|---|
| May 21st | (12) | J. Edwards & Son, Burslem<br>Designs for toilet ware forms |
| August 22nd | (4) | T. & R. Boote, Burslem<br>Six designs for dinner and toilet ware forms |

| | | |
|---|---|---|
| September 27th | (4) | Elsmore, Foster & Co., Tunstall<br>Four designs for dinner ware forms |
| November 26th | (9) | T. & R. Boote, Burslem<br>Eight designs for dinner, tea and toilet wares |
| **1871** | | |
| January 2nd | (2) | Gelson Bros., Hanley<br>Design for tureen form |
| January 30th | (2) | Gelson Bros., Hanley<br>Design for tureen form |
| February 20th | (2) | Elsmore & Forster, Tunstall<br>Twelve designs for dinner and toilet ware forms |
| May 24th | (10) | John Meir & Son, Tunstall<br>Two designs for tureen forms |
| **1872** | | |
| June 18th | (3) | G.L. Ashworth & Bros., Shelton<br>Designs for fluted table wares |
| July 24th | (2) | W. & T. Adams, Tunstall<br>Printed design, Armorial |
| July 29th | (7) | J. Dimmock & Co., Hanley<br>Two designs for tureen forms |
| **1873** | | |
| July 28th | (8) | J. Meir & Sons, Tunstall<br>Printed design, Russian scene |
| **1874** | | |
| January 23rd | (5) | J. Meir & Sons, Tunstall<br>Two designs for tureen forms |
| August 1st4 | (9) | Cockson & Chetwynd, Cobridge<br>Three designs for teaware forms |
| **1875** | | |
| February 12th | (6) | J. Maddock & Sons, Burslem<br>Two designs for tureen forms |
| December 1st | (9) | Gelson Bros., Hanley<br>Five designs for dinner service forms |
| **1876** | | |
| March 2nd | (8) | Thomas Gelson & Co., Hanley<br>Four designs for table ware forms |
| September 18th | (10) | G.L. Ashworth & Bros., Hanley<br>Printed design |
| November 14th | (8) | Clementson Bros., Hanley<br>Five designs for table wares |
| **1877** | | |
| March 20th | (3) | Clementson Bros., Hanley<br>Seven designs for dinner, tea and toilet wares, 'Canada' |
| June 9th | (3) | Baker & Co., Fenton<br>Six designs for dinner and teaware forms |
| June 13th | (2) | Baker & Co., Fenton<br>Design for animal form but reported from America as occurring on 'Dominion' shape table wares |
| July 23rd | (2) | John Edwards, Fenton<br>Three designs for dinner and teaware forms |
| **1878** | | |
| January 14th | (3) | W. Adams, Tunstall<br>Three designs for dinner and teaware forms |
| March 7th | (4) | John Edwards, Fenton<br>Design for oval tureen form |
| April 20th | (2) | Thomas Furnival & Sons, Cobridge<br>Two designs for dinner and teaware forms, 'Lorne' |
| July 17th | (9) | W. Adams, Tunstall<br>Design for oval tureen form |
| September 13th | (5) | G.L. Ashworth & Bros., Hanley<br>Designs for toilet ware forms |
| November 23rd | (2) | E. & C. Challinor, Fenton<br>Printed design, 'Lorne' |
| December 7th | (2) | Anthony Shaw, Burslem<br>Design for oval tureen form |
| **1879** | | |
| February 1st | (13) | Clementson Bros., Hanley<br>Design for jug form |
| February 24th | (3) | W.& T. Adams, Tunstall<br>Three printed designs – figure subjects |
| March 14th | (9) | Edward Clarke, Longport<br>Design for oval tureen form |
| March 19th | (2) | John Hawthorn, Cobridge<br>Design for oval tureen form |
| October 17th | (2) | G.L. Ashworth & Bros., Hanley<br>Design for tureen form |
| October 29th | (7) | Clementson Bros., Hanley<br>Design for moulded-edged table wares |

December 10th (9) Clementson Bros., Hanley
Design for oval tureen form

**1880**

February 25th (18) Clementson Bros., Hanley
Design for tureen form

September 15th (6) G.L. Ashworth & Bros., Hanley
Design for teaware forms

**1881**

January 21st( 11) W. & T. Adams, Tunstall
Printed device or mark – American eagle emblem

May 24th (5) G.L. Ashworth & Bros., Hanley
Designs for toilet wares

August 29th (7) W.T. Adams, Tunstall
Printed device or mark, crowned garter emblem

**1882**

January 7th (2) W.H. Grindley & Co., Tunstall
Printed design for table wares

March 23rd (2) W. & T. Adams, Tunstall
Printed device or mark, crowned garter emblem

No ironstone or granite china entries seem to have been made in 1883. The new system of Registered Numbers was then commenced at 'R$^{D}$. No.1' – see pages 376-7.

PRODUCERS OF IRONSTONE AND GRANITE WARE ADVERTISING IN *POTTERY GAZETTE 1885 DIARY*

**Geo. L. Ashworth & Bros.,** Hanley ... Sole manufacturers of Real Ironstone-china and Mason's Patent Ironstone-china Patterns and shapes

**Baker & Co.,** Fenton ... Manufacturers of white Granite...

**E.F. Bodley & Son,** New Bridge Pottery, Longport ... Manufacturers of Genuine Ironstone china and earthenware...

**T.G. & F. Booth,** Tunstall ... Best Ironstone for Hotels and Ship's use...

**E. & C. Challinor,** Fenton ... Manufacturers of Ironstone, white Granite...

**Clementson Bros.,** Phoenix & Bell Works, Hanley ... Earthenware and Ironstone china...

**Davenports Limited, Longport** ... Ironstone ware, plain and decorated, in china patterns, suitable for barracks, clubs, hotels and ship uses. White Granite, in great variety suitable for home trade, North & South America and the Colonies...

**J. Dimmock & Co.,** Albion Works, Hanley ... Earthenware and Ironstone china, for home, colonial and export ... originators of the celebrated flowing blue...

**Edge, Malkin & Co.,** Newport Works, Burslem ... Ironstone china and earthenwares...

**John Edwards,** Fenton, Manufacturer of Porcelain de Terre, Ironstone-china and white Granite...

**Thomas Furnival & Sons,** Cobridge ... Manufacturers of white Granite...

**W.H. Grindley & Co.,** Tunstall, Manufacturers of plain and embossed Ironstone china...

**Ralph Hammersley & Son,** Overhouse Pottery, Burslem. Manufacturers of Ironstone china and general earthenware ... Real Ironstone china in shapes suitable for Hotels, Restaurants, Steamships, etc. with crests or monograms...

**Alfred Meakin,** Tunstall ... Manufacturers of Ironstone china, white Granite...

**Powell, Bishop & Stonier,** Hanley, Manufacturers of china and earthenware ...White Granite for the United States...

**Wedgwood & Co.,** Unicorn & Pinnox Works, Tunstall ... white Granite...

The list for the year 1900 is substantially the same:

'Ltd.' is added to Baker & Co.'s style
Messrs T.G.& F. Booth are restyled 'Booths Ltd.'
Messrs Thomas Furnival & Sons are restyled 'Furnivals Ltd.'
'Ltd.' is added to A. Meakin's style

and the following firms were listed as producers of 'Ironstone china' or 'White Granite':

**Cochran & Fleming,** Britannia Pottery, Glasgow ... Manufacturers of Royal Ironstone china and Porcelain Granite...

**W. & E. Corn,** Longport ... white Granite.

**Dunn Bennett & Co.,** Burslem ... Ironstone china, specially adapted for ships, hotels, restaurants and coffee house use...

**Thomas Hughes & Son,** Longport ... White Granite.

**Anthony Shaw & Co.,** Burslem, Earthenware and Ironstone china.

**T. Till & Sons,** Burslem ... ironstone china...

**Wood & Son,** Burslem ... white granite...

APPENDIX III

# The Silber & Fleming Trade Catalogue

It is a perhaps natural but understandable minor ceramic tragedy that so few British manufacturers', retailers' or wholesalers' catalogues have survived or are known to collectors and writers.

From about the middle of the nineteenth century many manufacturers, large and small, issued catalogues or illustrated price lists detailing their most saleable or new lines. The advertisements given in the British trade journal *Pottery Gazette* from 1879, and in its annual *Pottery Gazette Diary* from 1882 onwards, abound with advertisements, the closing lines begging buyers to write for 'illustrated Pattern sheets and Lists of Prices' or for 'Illustrated Catalogues'.

As such lists quickly became out-dated or were superseded by new lists, or as the buyers cleared up their offices or went out of business, so such ephemera were discarded – to our great loss.

Some large manufacturers seemingly issued their own catalogues of wares shown at Victorian national and international exhibitions. Perhaps the only such document surviving from the 1851 exhibition is the John Ridgway catalogue, now preserved in the Bodleian Library at Oxford. I have quoted interesting information from this in my specialist book, *Ridgway Porcelains* (Antique Collectors' Club, Woodbridge, 1985), and in the John Ridgway (& Co.) section of the present study. This manufacturer's own catalogue also serves to show how basic is the listing given in the widely quoted *Official Descriptive and Illustrated Catalogue of the Great Exhibition, 1851*.

Most of the manufacturers' price lists would have been flimsy affairs, having a decidedly short life, but some large retailers and wholesalers issued more solid catalogues. Late publications of this type include the various Army & Navy Stores or the Harrods illustrated catalogues featuring a host of household goods as well as clothing, luxury or utilitarian objects, in bewildering variety. American readers have highly interesting early mail-order catalogues to consult.

As far as the present study of ironstone-type wares is concerned, a series of hard-covered catalogues issued late in the nineteenth century by the London-based wholesalers Messrs Silber & Fleming, occupying huge premises in Wood Street, Cheapside in London's EC district, between St. Pauls and Guildhall, is of great interest. This firm, or at least Albert Silber, dates back to the 1850s but by the 1880s it had expanded to become a large-scale importer of Continental and Oriental goods and a leading firm of London wholesalers.

A series of Silber & Fleming catalogues from 1872 into the 1880s is preserved in the National Art Library at the Victoria & Albert Museum. One undated issue of about 1883 was reprinted by Studio Editions (of London) in 1983, with an introductory foreword by Dorothy Bosomworth. This publication was retitled *The Victorian Catalogue of Household Goods* and claimed to be 'a complete Compendium of over five thousand items to furnish and decorate the Victorian home'. A further reissue was made by Wordsworth Editions Ltd. of Ware, in 1990.

My own large-size original Silber & Fleming illustrated catalogue can also probably be dated to the early 1880s although it is different from the 1983 reissue. I am also fortunate in having a separate price list which adds interest and further information to the illustrations in the main catalogue. The large hard-back 'Illustrated Pattern Book of English China & Earthenware…' included, in brief, china and earthenware, pressed, engraved and cut glass, coloured and decorated glass, sterling silver goods, electro-plated goods, cutlery, oil lamps, etc., but we are really mainly concerned with the first section which comprised 'Dinner services in stoneware, china and ironstone'.

Unfortunately the Silber & Fleming catalogue does not detail the manufacturers of the sets being sold because the company did not wish its customers to go direct to the manufacturers but, in several cases, we can identify the patterns or shapes featured as Minton, Wedgwood and Ashworth Bros. The prelims, explanations or trade terms do give us a helpful insight into what was available in the 1880s and how such goods were sold by the larger firms and wholesalers.

The dinner services were supplied in four sizes – first, with fifty-four pieces for six persons, then of seventy-three pieces for eight persons, of 120 pieces for twelve persons and lastly of 168 pieces for eighteen persons. Each piece was included in the count, so that a tureen with a cover, stand and ladle was counted as four pieces. The dinner service for six persons comprised:

Two sauce tureens, covers and stands plus ladles
Two covered vegetable dishes
One 16in. [40.64cm] platter
One 14in. [35.56cm] platter
Two 9in. [22.86cm] platters
Twelve meat plates
Twelve tart plates
Twelve cheese plates

No large soup tureen or soup plates were included, although both these lines were included in the seventy-three piece set. The largest size, for eighteen persons comprised:

One soup tureen, cover and stand plus ladle
Four sauce tureens, complete
Four covered vegetable dishes
Two pie dishes 11in. [27.94cm]
Two ditto, 9in. [22.86cm]
One salad bowl
One cheese stand
One fish drainer
One gravy dish or platter, 20in. [50.8cm]
One flat platter, 20in. [50.8cm]
One ditto. 18in. [45.72cm]
Two ditto. 16in. [40.64cm]
Two ditto. 14in. [35.56cm]
Four ditto. 12in. [30.48cm]
Four ditto. 10in. [25.4cm]
Fifty-four meat plates
Eighteen soup plates
Twenty-four tart plates
Eighteen cheese plates

These represent standard British market sets but of course other customers might well amend their requirements, as could anyone, depending on their habits, taste or pocket!

Extra articles, such as hot-water plates, vegetable drainers, cheese stands with covers, butter boats, pickle trays, hash dishes with hot-water pan or beef-steak dishes could also be supplied to match any service. Monograms, crests, Masonic devices, regimental, hotel or other badges could also be printed (or painted) on any wares, to special order.

'Best English Stoneware' dinner services decorated with single colour narrow borders and lines and devoid of gilding had the lowest prices. All net prices were given per set and also at a discounted rate for crates of not less than six sets, for this was a wholesaler's catalogue. However, the prices for bulk purchases were described as 'at the potteries', so such amounts may well represent the price charged by the manufacturer to individual retailers. They in turn may expect a 25 per cent to 33per cent mark-up.

The simple banded sets, available with maroon, green or light blue border, ranged from 16s.6d. for the fifty-four piece service to £3.17s.6d. for the largest set of 168 pieces for single sets or 14s.6d. to £3.5s.0d. per set when six were ordered. This works out at a mere 4.64 old pence or less than three new pence per piece. Simple gilding increased the basic price by over fifty per cent, to £1.3s.0d. for fifty-four pieces and to £4.17s.6d. for 168 pieces.

Moving on to printed stoneware or ironstone dinner services decorated with printed Japanese style basically floral designs which were so popular in the 1880s, we find the prices have increased about 25per cent. The smallest set without gilding was priced at 18s., while the largest set of 168 pieces was £3.17s.0d. With gilt enrichments the prices had risen to £2.10s.0d. and £9.12s.6d., or to £11.11s.0d. for a single service.

More colourful Japanese-style designs printed in more than one colour, or hand-enamelled over a printed base and with gilt edges, were obviously more costly. An average pattern produced by an unnamed good, but not leading, manufacturer would cost £2.17s.6d. for the small sets to £12.12s.0d. for the largest size.

All the sets and prices previously cited have been for 'fine stone ware' or 'Best English Stoneware', which we might now consider to be a standard granite-type body of the period. The Royal Worcester services produced in the 'Crownware' or the 'Vitreous' body introduced in about 1870 (see page 321) are also featured in this London retailer's catalogue under the heading 'Best English Stoneware'. Simple printed bordered sets with oval tureens of the 'Imperial shape' range from ungilt small services at £2.12s.0d. to £10.8s.6d. to slightly gilt £3.18s.6d. to £15.5s.6d. per set, at the lowest bulk order rates. More ornately printed Royal Worcester 'Vitreous' dinner services, described as 'Fine Stone ware, decorated with game, fish etc; handles of tureens &c., in bronze gilt', were quoted at £6.16s.6d. to £26.10s.0d. for the large sets of Elephant shape, so named on account of the elephant-head handles. The 'Vitreous' bodied Royal Worcester services were amongst the cheapest produced by this leading firm. The porcelain services were often hand-painted and always much more expensive.

One page in the Silber & Fleming catalogue features four Ashworth ironstone dinner service patterns (Plate 285). In this case the description 'Best English Real

PLATE 285. *A colour printed page from the London wholesaler Silber & Fleming's trade catalogue of* c.1880. *This page shows Messrs Ashworth's Mason's ironstone-type dinner service patterns, with three different tureen forms readily available at that period.*

Ironstone' is used, 'Real Ironstone' being the trade description favoured by Ashworths. All these sets were very expensive when compared with the sets made by other makers in perhaps not true ironstone bodies.

The Ashworth designs were far more colourful than most other patterns and they are decidedly of superior quality. It is noteworthy that this one page, in a single catalogue available at one time, showed four different basic shapes, all of which were available from stock. The prices for these *c.*1880 Ashworth dinner services were quoted per set and 'By crate of not less than two sets. Price at the potteries'. The official descriptions and the wholesaler's reference number were as quoted:

No 3064. Real Ironstone, white ground, enamelled in colours, dark green and coral with Chinese decoration, and richly gilt.

| | |
|---|---|
| 54 piece set | £12. 8.0 |
| 73 piece set | £19.11.0 |
| 120 piece set | £34. 2.0 |
| 168 piece set | £47.16.0 |

No 3065. Real Ironstone, white ground, with black band, decorated with richly enamelled flowers and gilt.

| | |
|---|---|
| 54 piece set | £ 9. 2. 6 |
| 73 piece set | £14. 7. 6 |
| 120 piece set | £25.12. 0 |
| 168 piece set | £36.15. 0 |

No 3066. Real Ironstone, white ground, decorated with flowers, vases, and fancy borders – old Derby pattern, and richly gilt.

| | |
|---|---|
| 54 piece set | £ 8.10. 6 |
| 73 piece set | £13.10. 0 |
| 120 piece set | £23. 9. 6 |
| 168 piece set | £32. 8. 6 |

No 3067. Real Ironstone, white ground, decorated with dark green borders almost covering the ware and Japanese figures, flowers &c in colours, very richly gilt.

| | |
|---|---|
| 54 piece set | £11.10. 0 |
| 73 piece set | £18. 2. 0 |
| 120 piece set | £31.13. 0 |
| 168 piece set | £44. 3. 0 |

Apart from the standard net prices requoted here from the *c.*1880 catalogue, it would appear that slightly faulty or 'seconds' were available at a lower price. The slightly strange wording – which reads as if such faulty pieces had to be made to order – was:

> Most of the Patterns of Dinner Services illustrated in this catalogue can be supplied of an inferior or mixed quality, when ordered in quantities, at lower prices than quoted in our price list. As we do not keep these qualities in stock, two or three months are required to execute such orders.

All the Silber & Fleming dessert and tea services were described as china, rather than ironstone or stone china. This is to be expected at this late period when the main articles made in ironstone-type bodies were dinner services. The major exceptions were toilet services for bedrooms, before the advent of piped hot water and good plumbing.

Most of the many and varied 'Toilet Services' featured were described as 'English Stoneware' or 'Best English Stoneware', descriptions which may apply to various ironstone-type mixes or even to slightly above average quality earthenwares. However, the standard make-up of such sets may be of interest, as few complete sets survive today.

Once again Messrs Silber & Fleming sold such standard sets in various sizes comprising five, six or nine pieces, although the make-up could be amended to suit individual customer's requirements. The standard sets comprised:

Ewer (water jug)
Basin
Chamber
Soap box
Brush tray

The six-piece set included an extra chamber pot. The so-called 'Double Toilet Service' comprised:

Two Ewers
Two Basins
Two Chambers
One Soap box
One Brush tray
One Sponge bowl

In addition extra articles, such as foot-bath, large slop-jar, supply jug, covers to chamber pots, mouth ewers and basins, would be purchased to match any pattern.

It is difficult to quote prices for the patterns are so varied. However, sets decorated with an underglaze-blue printed hawthorn design were priced at 9s.9d., 11s.6d. and 18s.6d. per set, depending on the number of pieces, as cited above. Supplied in crates of not less than twelve sets the prices dropped to 8s., 9s.3d. and 15s.6d.

Obviously, the more elaborately decorated toilet sets were much more costly. For example, a relief-moulded mock-Japanese design produced by Messrs Josiah

Wedgwood & Sons and registered in March 1879, was described and costed as:

> Toilet Service, fine stone-ware, ivory coloured ground, decorated with a coloured fan, turquoise handle, and turquoise bird embossed, per set.
> £2.0.6 £2.7.6 £3.17.0

The same registered moulded design was available in several different colour combinations. Apart from the Wedgwood sets, designs registered by Messrs Mintons and by Messrs Powell & Bishop can be identified.

This late Victorian wholesaler's catalogue contains twelve pages illustrating sixty-seven different bedroom or toilet services. It must be remembered that at this period these services, which were often extremely decorative, were the main line produced by most English earthenware manufactories; some completely specialized in such articles. Every middle-class home would have a toilet set in every bedroom. They were needed far more than a dinner or dessert service.

Many of the ceramic articles supplied by Messrs Silber & Fleming bear a printed initial and Staffordshire knot device, as here shown. The initials relate to the senior partner and founder of the business, Albert Marcuis Silber. The firm dealt in a wide range of Continental, Oriental and British goods, of which I have only been interested in the ironstone-type dinner services and toilet sets.

# Notes

**Preface**
1. For a discussion of creamware and its developments the reader is referred to *Creamware & Pearlware by* T.A. Lockett and P.A. Halfpenny, being the catalogue to the 1986 exhibition held at the City Museum, Stoke-on-Trent.
2. For further information on bone china see *Staffordshire Porcelain* (Granada Publishing, 1983) and in particular Reginald Haggar's Chapter 7.
3. See Appendix I for a list of such differing names.

**Introduction**
1. Source material from records at the India Office, London.
2. Further details are given in my out-of-print book *Chinese Export Market Porcelain* (Granada Publishing, London, 1979).
3. The potters were partly successful as the new rate was settled at 80 per cent, see page 61
4. Perhaps 'stand in need' was intended. Author.

**Chapter I**
1. Typical examples of Turner's jugs are illustrated in my *British Pottery, an illustrated guide* (Barrie & Jenkins, London, 1974), Plates 240-250, and in the specialist work *The Turners of Lane End: Master Potters of the Industrial Revolution* (Cory, Adams & MacKay, London, 1965).
2. The salvaged cargo was from the English East India Company vessel *Diana*, trading between Canton and India. She sank off Malacca on 4 March 1817, carrying cargo including over eleven tons of mainly blue and white export-market porcelain that would have been produced in 1816. See Dorian Ball's book, *The Diana Adventure* (Malaysian Historical Salvors, Kuala Lumpur, 1995).
3. *Chamberlain-Worcester Porcelain 1877-1852* (Barrie & Jenkins, London, 1982).
4. *Chinese Armorial Porcelain* (Faber & Faber Ltd., London, 1974).

**Chapter II**
1. The full title is F. Knapp, *Chemical Technology – or Chemistry Applied to its Arts and to its Manufacturers*, Hippolyte Vailliere, Paris and London, 1848.
2. Thomas Brocas (1756-1818) became an important 'Chinaman' in Shrewsbury. He recorded in November 1804 that he had dealt with the leading Staffordshire manufacturers for sixteen years. His pre-1816 Journals are preserved in the Shropshire Record Office, Shrewsbury.
3. Wedgwood archives, 34-25470, of 3 April 1819, as quoted by Robin Reilly.

**Chapter III**
1. 'From the Urals to the Pyrenees the civilized world was banded against England and closed to her shipping and her goods' (G.M. Trevelyan, *History of England*, Longman Group. 1973 edition).
2. It is possible, however, that the old trading styles – C & G Mason or C & G Mason & Co. – continued in use until May 1832 for the dissolution announcement did not appear in the *London Gazette* until this later date.
3. The impressed name-mark 'M. MASON & SON' has been noted but was very rarely employed.
4. Quoted by T.A. Lockett in *Davenport China, Earthenware & Glass, 1794-1887* by T.A. Lockett and G.A. Godden (Barrie & Jenkins, London, 1989).
5. Andrew Lamb's study of the disagreement between worker and master is published in the *Journal of Ceramic History*, no 9 (Stoke-on-Trent Museums, 1977).
6. Some old designs transferred from original copper-plates will in most cases include the earlier form of mark but newly introduced copper-plates will have the revised one.

**Chapter IV**
1. See *Godden's Guide to Mason's China and the Ironstone Wares*.
2. He died at Newcastle-under-Lyme, Staffordshire, on 26 April 1822.
3. It is of course possible that these were unsold lots from the earlier sales, rather than new lots not previously offered.

**Chapter V**
1. Specialist books, such as *The Staffordshire Potter* by Harold Owen (1901 and 1970 reprint by Kingsmead Reprints, Bath) and *A History of the Potters' Union* by F. Burchill and R. Ross (Ceramic and Allied Trades Union, Hanley, 1977), give good information on conditions in Staffordshire and on the emigration of workers.
2. Standard reference books on British creamwares include *English Cream Coloured Earthenware* by Donald C. Towner (Faber & Faber, London, 1957, revised edition 1978), *Creamwares and other English Pottery at Temple Newsam House, Leeds* by Peter Walton (Manningham Press, 1976) and *Creamware* by P.A. Halfpenny and T.A. Lockett (City Museum, Stoke-on-Trent, 1986 exhibition catalogue).
3. Export-type English white ironstone or white granite wares were purchased by the City of Stoke-on-Trent Museum as late as 1997 and then this important type was represented by four examples.

**Chapter VI**
1. This section is an enlarged version of his article in *The Art Journal* in 1867.
2. The description 'Indian' very often meant at this period and in these contexts Chinese designs!
3. Not Baxter, as given by some authorities.
4. Jewitt appears to give the name Barker in error for Baker.
5. Some marks appear to give the middle initial 'B', rather than 'G'.
6. The partnership also traded, or is listed, under the alternative titles Bourne & Baker and Bourne, Baker & Co.
7. Full name marks may also occur.
8. See *Davenport China, Earthenware & Glass, 1794-1887* (Barrie & Jenkins, London, 1989), Colour Plate XVI and Plate 201.
9. This may have been the old Hill Works, renamed the Royal Victoria Works by Dunn, Bennett & Co, the incoming firm. The *Pottery Gazette* noted that Dunn, Bennett & Co of Boothen Works, Hanley, had taken the Hill Works, Burslem, but the firm's advertisements refer to the grandly titled Royal Victoria Pottery.
10. This surname is sometimes incorrectly given as Foster.
11. Some 'L.W.' marks relate to Ludwig Wessel of Poppelsdorf in Germany.
12. As noted under Furnival & Clark, shape and printed pattern registrations were made under Thomas Furnival & Co.'s name in November 1846.
13. See *Porcelain in Worcester, 1751-1951, an Illustrated Social History*, Ray Jones (Parkbarn, Worcester, 1993).
14. Liddle is a christian name.
15. Jos Mayer was seemingly so christened; it is not an abbreviation!
16. *White Ironstone: A Collector's Guide* (Antique Trader Books, Dubuque, .SA, 1996).
17. Details of the archives were given by the late Reginald G. Haggar in his paper, printed in the *English Ceramic Circle Transactions* Vol. 9, part 3, 1975, pp. 276-286.
18. Quoted in his two-volume work *Wedgwood* (Macmillan London Ltd., 1989).
19. The first mention of James alone was his registration of a new moulded jug form on 24 March 1869.
20. This relates to Richard Alcock who worked the Central Pottery, Burslem, before Messrs Wilkinson & Hulme took over c.1881-82 to be succeeded by A.J. Wilkinson using the new name 'Royal Staffordshire' pottery.
21. For a short period c.1862 the trade style Wooliscroft & Galley seems to have been used. Note there was only one 'l' in the surname Wooliscroft.

**Chapter VII**
1. Thomas C. Smith of the Union Porcelain Works, Greenpoint, New York.
2. Some American manufacturers had exhibited at the 1876 World's Fair at Philadelphia, on their own soil, but their displays were very poor and badly displayed in relation to the imported European goods. The 1878 President referred to it as 'the old sore of the centennial' when suggesting (incorrectly) that no member would be exhibiting in Paris.

# Select Bibliography

This bibliography is divided into two sections. First, the works originally published in the British Isles. These are concerned with Mason's Ironstone or with home market products.

Secondly, there are now a wealth of American books angled at American collectors and which feature, in the main British export market ironstone and granite china wares produced by very many of our potters. In most cases such export market wares are all but unknown to British collectors as the pieces were made only for overseas markets.

The extent to which the British manufacturers exported their products on a world-wide basis can be gauged by consulting Llewellynn Jewitt's late Victorian work *The Ceramic Art of Great Britain*. This monumental study was originally published in two volumes by Virtue & Co. in 1878 with an updated, single-volume revised edition published in 1883. Jewitt visited hundreds of potteries or corresponded with the owners and obtained catalogues or reviews of their products and markets. I published an abridged version of the nineteenth century Jewitt work in 1972 under the title Jewitt's *Ceramic Art of Great Britain 1800-1900* (Barrie & Jenkins Ltd., London, 1972). All these three versions are now out of print and difficult to obtain. This is also the case with most other elderly reference books.

As a general guide to the types of British earthenware made for North America the reader should consult Mrs E. Collard's *Nineteenth Century Pottery & Porcelain in Canada* (McGill University Press, Montreal, Canada, 1967).

Desirable out of print works often command a premium over the original price, as the demand for such helpful works exceeds the supply. Various firms or individuals specialize in locating and supplying such books. Several of these advertise in collectors' magazines or exhibit at fairs. Some, such as Barrie Lamb's 'Reference Works' (12 Commercial Road, Swanage, Dorset BB19 1DF), issue helpful detailed catalogues of available stock.

If you are unable to locate a desired out of print book, your local Public Library or Reference Library may well have a copy which you can borrow or consult in the reference section. The library staff, or a good specialist book dealer, should also be able to tell you if a given title is in print and available new, or if it is out of print and no longer available from the publisher.

As the British ironstone and stone china bodies were originally introduced to emulate, match and compete with the large importations of Chinese porcelain, the reader who wishes to learn of the Oriental prototypes should consult my (out of print) work *Oriental Export Market Porcelain and its influence on European Wares* (Granada Publishing, London, 1979).

## BRITISH SPECIALIST BOOKS ON IRONSTONE-TYPE WARES


*The Masons of Lane Delph* by Reginald G. Haggar, Lund Humphries, London, 1952.

*The Illustrated Guide to Mason's Patent Ironstone China* by Geoffrey Godden, Barrie & Jenkins, London, 1971.

*Mason Porcelain & Ironstone 1796-1853* by Reginald Haggar and Elizabeth Adams, Faber & Faber, London, 1977.

*Godden's Guide to Mason's China and the Ironstone Wares* by Geoffrey Godden,. Antique Collectors' Club, Woodbridge, 1980. This is an enlarged edition of my 1971 book with additional illustrations. This work is now also out of print The ISBN reference number is 0 902028 86 3.

*The Masons of Lane Delph. Porcelain, Stoneware & Ironstone China*, 1974 Exhibition catalogue published by the City Museum & Art Gallery, Stoke-on-Trent, 1974.

*Mason, a Family of Potters* edited by Deborah Skinner, City Museum & Art Gallery, Stoke-on-Trent, 1982.

*Masons Pottery Factory...* Historic Buildings Survey, City Museum & Art Gallery, Stoke-on-Trent, 1985

'Longton Potters 1700-1856' by Rodney Hampson, *Journal of Ceramic History*, Vol. 14, City Museum & Art Gallery, Stoke-on-Trent, 1985.

*Mason's. The First Two Hundred Years* by Gaye Blake Roberts. Merrell Holberton Publishers Ltd., London, for Josiah Wedgwood & Sons Ltd., 1996.

In addition the present Mason's Ironstone Company issues sales and publicity material, catalogues of current productions, etc. These should be available from Messrs Josiah Wedgwood & Sons, Ltd., Barlaston, Stoke-on-Trent, ST12 9ES.

Other relevant material may be found in John Vivian Goddard's work *The Mason Family and Pottery,* first published in 1910, and in Alfred Meigh's unpublished manuscript 'The Masons of Lane Delph' completed in 1937. Reginald G. Haggar's paper entitled 'C.J. Mason. Pattern Books and Documents' was published in the *Transactions of the English Ceramic Circle*, Vol. 9, Part 3, 1975.

It is also relevant to list the leading works on British ceramic marks. These really fall into two families, those prepared by John P. Cushion and published by Faber & Faber Ltd. and those written by myself and published by Barrie & Jenkins, being part of the International Random House Group. These books have been published in various editions and printings and in all cases one should consult the latest edition!

In alphabetical order we have John Cushion's *Pocket Book of British Ceramic Marks* and his *Handbook of Pottery and Porcelain Marks*. Then my own *Encyclopaedia of British Pottery and Porcelain Marks* and the related smaller *Handbook of British Pottery & Porcelain Marks*.

In addition my *Encyclopaedia of British Porcelain Manufacturers* (Barrie & Jenkins, London, 1988) gives details of many manufacturers of ironstone as well as British porcelain makers.

Several books give good detailed information on British nineteenth century printed earthenwares which enjoyed very wide sales both at home and abroad. Of these special mention must be made of the two joint-author dictionaries listed below. However, relatively few of these designs appear on ironstone-type bodies; they are, in the main, standard lower-fired earthenwares of pearl-ware type.

*The Dictionary of Blue & White Printed Pottery 1780-1880*, Vol. I, by A.W. Coysh and R.K. Henrywood, Antique Collectors' Club Ltd., Woodbridge, 1982.

*The Dictionary of Blue & White Printed Pottery 1780-1880*. Vol. II, by A.W. Coysh and R.K. Henrywood Antique Collectors' Club Ltd., Woodbridge, 1989.

In a similar manner some types of ironstone are shown and discussed in *An Illustrated Guide to British Jugs* by R.K. Henrywood (Swan Hill Press, Shrewsbury, 1997). Chapter 9 of this work discusses Stone China and certainly the manufacturers of mid-nineteenth century moulded jugs often referred to them as 'Stone Jugs', although the body varied greatly.

Readers interested in manufacturing processes in general should seek out Revd. Malcolm Graham's 1908 book *Cup and Saucer Land* (Madgwick, Houlston & Co. Ltd., London.). The processes described and illustrated by the Vicar of Burslem also relate to the nineteenth century techniques. William Scarratt's 1906 privately printed work *Old Times in the Potteries* gives interesting information on many firms then supplying the American market. Another interesting work for the researcher is James Torrington Spencer Lidstone's now rare book of poems entitled *The Thirteenth Londoniad... giving a full description of the Principal Establishments in the Potteries*, privately published in 1866. I have quoted relevant passages from this strange work at various points in the main section on the manufacturers.

A most helpful insight into the vast Anglo-American trade is given in Neil Ewins' research paper 'Supplying the Present Wants of our Yankee Cousins – Staffordshire Ceramics and the American Market 1775-1880'. published in Vol. 15 of the *Journal of Ceramic History* (City Museum & Art Gallery, Stoke-on-Trent. 1997).

Other, non-British, books relating to American market ceramics include the following. Unfortunately not all will be available in British public libraries or otherwise easily available outside North America.

It should also be noted that some attributions given by American authors differ from those given by modern British writers. Certainly some dates given in earlier books are at variance with facts uncovered by recent researchers and therefore differ from manufacturers' dates given in this book.

Nevertheless, the following mainly American books are helpful in showing a wide range of British wares which in the main were made expressly for our export trade. These are often lines not found in the country of their origin!

The works I have consulted include:

*American Historical Views on Staffordshire China* by Ellouise Baker Larsen. First published in 1939. Revised edition 1950 (Doubleday & Co. Inc., NY), republished 1975 by Dover Publications Inc., NY.

*Anglo-American China*, Part I, by Sam Laidacker, privately published, Bristol, USA, 1938. Second edition 1954.

*Anglo-American China*, Part II, by Sam Laidacker, privately published, Bristol, USA, 1951.

*China Classics IV. Ironstone China* by Larry Freeman, Century House, Watkins Glen, N.Y., 1954.

*The American Antique Collector* Vol III, No. 9, Sam Laidacker, privately printed magazine, Bristol, USA, 1956.

*China Classics VI. English Staffordshire* by Serry Wood, Century House, Watkins Glen, NY, 1959.

*Spatterware and Sponge...* by Earl F. and Ada F. Robacker, A.S. Barnes & Co. Inc., Cranbury, USA,1978.

*Grandma's Tea Leaf Ironstone* by Annise Doring Heaivilin, Wallace-Homestead Book Co., Des Moines, USA, 1981.

*The Collector's Encyclopaedia of Flow Blue China* by Mary Frank Gaston, Collector Books, Paducah, KY, USA, 1983.

*A Second Look at White Ironstone* by Jean Wetherbee, Wallace-Homestead Book Co., Lombard, USA, 1985.

*The Wheat Pattern, An Illustrated Survey* by Lynne Sussman, Wallace-Homestead Book Co., Lombard, USA, 1985.

*White Ironstone Body Styles, Copper & Gold Lustre Decorated 1840-1900* by Jean Wetherbee, Tea Leaf Club International, USA, 1990.

*The Collector's Encyclopedia of Gaudy Dutch & Welsh* by John A. Shuman III, Collector Books. Paducah, KY, USA, 1991.

*Mulberry Ironstone. Flow Blue's Best Kept Little Secret* by Ellen H. Hill. Mulberry Hill, Madison, NJ, USA, 1993.

*Historic Flow Blue* by Jeffrey B. Snyder, Schiffer Publishing Ltd., Atglen, P., USA, 1994.

*Collector's Encyclopedia of Flow Blue China* by Mary Frank Gaston, Gaston Books, Paducah, KY, USA, 1994.

*A Pocket Guide to Flow Blue* by Jeffrey B. Snyder, Schiffer Publishing Ltd., Atglen, PA, USA, 1995.

*Historical Staffordshire. American Patriots & Views* by Jeffrey B. Snyder. Schiffer Publishing Ltd., Atglen, PA, USA, 1995.

*White Ironstone. A Collector's Guide* by Jean Wetherbee, Antique Trader Books, Dubuque, Iowa, USA, 1996.

*Flow Blue China. Additional Patterns and new information* by Norma Jean Hoener, Flow Blue International Collectors Club Inc., USA, 1996.

*White Ironstone. A Survey of its many Forms...* by Dawn Stoltzfus & Jeffrey B. Snyder, Schiffer Publishing Ltd., Atglen, PA, USA, 1997.

*Romantic Staffordshire Ceramics* by Jeffrey B. Snyder, Schiffer Publishing Ltd., Atglen, PA, USA, 1997.

*Fascinating Flow Blue* by Jeffrey B. Snyder, Schiffer Publishing Ltd., Atglen, PA, USA, 1997.

*Anglo-American Ceramics*, Part I by D. & L. Arman, Oakland Press, USA, 1998.

Specialist books giving details of American pottery firms and their marks include:

*Lehner's Encyclopedia of U.S. Marks on Pottery, Porcelain & Clay* by Lois Lehner, Collector Books, Paducah, KY, USA, 1988.

*DeBolt's Dictionary of American Pottery Marks, Whiteware & Porcelain* by Gerald DeBolt, Collector Books, Paducah, KY, USA, 1994.

In addition there are various reports on archaeological digs on old settlement sites. These can include details of British ceramics and marks found in a nineteenth century context. Such publications include *Ceramic Marks from Old Sacramento*, California Archaeological Report 22 of 1983 published by the State of California, Department of Parks and Recreation.

Further helpful information on British ceramics found in North America and the researches of American collectors are to be found in the publications of specialist societies. Publications of this nature sent to me are:

*Blue Berry Notes* published by the Flow Blue International Collectors Club. The current (1999) editor is Pamela Krainik, Box 204, Baraboo, WI, 53913, USA.

*White Ironstone Notes*, published by the White Ironstone China Association, Inc., edited by Ernie and Bev Dieringer, Box 536, Redding Ridge, CT, 06876, USA.

The Tea Leaf Club International also publish helpful information for club members. My contact is Dale Abrams, 960 Bryden Road, Columbus, OH 43205, USA.

I have been sent the first issues of a further American collectors' journal entitled *The China and Glass Quarterly*, first issue dated January/February 1997. This publication is edited by David and Linda Arman and is published by The Oakland Press, PO Box 39, Portsmouth RI, 02871, U.S.A. The annual subscription is $60. The contents, including news of new discoveries, will certainly be of interest to American collectors, although in this first issue there is little information on ironstone-type wares. The main ceramic interest seems to be in blue printed Staffordshire earthenwares.

Specialist sources of information such as the official catalogue of the 1851 Exhibition, or articles or papers on individual factories, are listed in the relevant place in the main text.

Good representative collections of Mason porcelain and ironstone china are available for study at the City of Stoke-on-Trent Museum at Hanley. This collection includes the bequest made by the late Reginald and Dorothy Haggar. A prior appointment should be made to see pieces not on display but held in the reserve or study section. The museum telephone number is 01782 202173.

Likewise, a good collection is housed at Keele University, just outside Newcastle- under-Lyme. Again a prior appointment should be made with the university authorities to view the Raven collection, telephone number 01782 621111. The current contact is Professor Francis Frascina in the Visual Arts Department.

A further important collection (the old Mason's Works' collection) is now housed at the Wedgwood Museum at Barlaston, to the south of Stoke. Enquiries should be made to the Company, Josiah Wedgwood & Sons Ltd., Barlaston, Stoke-on-Trent, Staffs, TT12 9ES, telephone 01782 204141.

Specialist dealers, such as Valerie Howard, have also held interesting sales exhibitions of mainly Mason's ironstones at their business addresses. Valerie Howard, now of Campden Street, London W8, also issues helpful, illustrated, catalogues of these displays. Another specialist dealer is Janice Paul of Kenilworth. These and other specialists advertise in collectors' magazines.

Collectors of antique Mason porcelains and the earthenwares should consider joining the British-based Mason Collectors' Club which, apart from holding meetings, also publishes a private (members only) newsletter containing information on new discoveries and on members' research. The club can be contacted by writing to Mason's Collectors' Club, c/o The City Museum & Art Gallery, Hanley, Stoke-on-Trent, Staffs., ST1 3DW. This has now been retitled The Potteries Museum.

# Acknowledgements

Over the very long period during which I have been preparing this book, or at least gathering material for the project, I have received help from very many auctioneers, collectors, dealers, museum officials and others. In some cases I fear that I may have neglected to have noted their names – I crave their pardon. I gladly acknowledge the kind assistance of the following persons:

Dale Abrams, Mrs Elizabeth Adams, Dr and Mrs G. Barnes, Mrs M. Barritt, Francis Baxendale, Harry Ford Blackburn, Messrs. Bonhams, Mrs J. Bradley, Geoffrey Stafford Charles, Messrs Christie's staff (all branches), Mrs Cleggett, Robert Copeland, Mrs Y. Eldridge, Jennie Evans, Mr and Mrs G. Fisk, Harry E. Frost, Christopher Gilbert, Mr and Mrs A.E. Grove, Mrs P.A. Halfpenny, Rodney Hampson, Derek Harper, Ellen R. Hill, Bevis Hillier, Valerie Howard, Mrs S. Hulme, Ronald E. James, Arnold Kowalsky, Barry Lamb, Mark Law, Dr J. Leibrick, Terence A. Lockett, Dr Teresita Majewski, Trevor Markin, J.C. Maynard, George L. Miller, Mrs J. Moody, C.D. Moore, Carl Morgan, Ron Morley, Mrs Frank Nagington, Messrs Neales, Mark Newstead, Mrs Janice Paul, Messrs Phillips staff (all branches), Roger Pomfret, Public Record Office, London and Kew, Mrs Betty Reed, Mrs Liane Richards, Miss Gaye Blake Roberts, Miss Letitia Roberts, Bill Saks, Henry Sandon, Mrs Debbie Skinner, Professor Alan Smith, Messrs Sotheby's staff (all branches), Stoke-on-Trent City Museum, Mrs P.A. Timms, Mrs Jean Ward, Dr R.E. Webb, Miss R. Weller, Mr and Mrs E.J. Wenharn, Jean Wetherbee, Mrs J. Wilkie, Worthing Reference Library staff.

My special gratitude is extended to the Directors of Messrs Christie, Manson & Woods Ltd. and of Messrs Phillips, Son & Neale Ltd., the well-known London fine art auctioneers, for permitting me to quote from their early nineteenth century catalogues of sales of Mason's wares in 1818 and in 1822.

Other contemporary records held in the Public Record Office, at the Guildhall Library, at the India Office and the National Newspaper Library have been consulted with the assistance of their helpful staff. I am also indebted to the researches of the late Alfred Meigh and Reginald G. Haggar and to the more recent researches and help of the very much with us Rodney Hampson., The illustrations drawn from a variety of sources are individually acknowledged in the captions, except that uncredited items are from the former Godden stock or records. The objects depicted, however, are not now necessarily in the same ownership, which can be regarded as relating to the photograph. The photographs of Godden examples have been professionally taken by Messrs Walter Gardiner, Photographers, of Worthing. I regret that I do not have information on the photographers responsible for the other illustrations but I am happy to acknowledge their professional services.

I am also indebted to a host of collectors and dealers who over the years have reported interesting and often hitherto unrecorded marks which have led to the identification of new manufacturers. I trust they will all enjoy the fruits of their labour.

# Index


A. Bros., 98, 192
Abbott & Newbury, 63, 64
A.B. & G., 181
Adams, 177-8
Adams & Co., 177
Adams, G. & Sons, 178
Adams, J. & Co., 177
Adams, W. (& Co.), 63, 177-8
Adams, W. & Son(s), 177-8. Plate 133
Adams, W. & T., 177-8
Adams & Bromley, 177
Albalite, 336
Albion, 197
Alcock, H. & Co (Ltd.), 179
Alcock, J., 178-9
Alcock, J. & G., 178-9
Alcock, J. & S., 179
Alcock, R., 179
Alcock, S. & Co., 179. Plates 135-7
Alcock's Indian Ironstone, 179. Plates 135-7
Alenite, 218
Allerton, Brough & Green, 181
American manufacture, 361-6
American market, 391
American subjects, 391
Amherst Japan, 181-8
A.S.M. in knot, 389
Anton, J. (Ltd.), 182, 220
Arabia, 367
Arnoux, L., 168, 169
Asbestos China, 182
Ashworth, G.L. & Bros. (Ltd.), 97-8, 182-192, 286. Colour Plates 31, 32. Plates 138-152, 285
Ashworth & Morley, 182
auction sales, 84-8, 93-4, 107-154

B., 202
B. & Co., 199
Bagnall, S., 82, 83
Bagshaw & Meir, 193
Bagster, J.D., 193. Plate 153
Bailey, W. & D. (& Co.), 193
Bailey & Bevington, 193
Bailey, Bevington & Co., 193
Baker & Co. (Ltd.), 194
Baker & Son, 194
Baker, C., 193
Baker, W. & Co., 194
Baker, W. & Son, 194
Baker & Chetwynd, 194
Barker Bros., 194
Barker Bros. Ltd., 194
Barker & Son, 194
Barker, Sutton & Till, 195
Barker & Till, 195
Barlow, T., 195
Barlow, T.W. (& Son), 195
Barlow, T.W. Ltd., 195
Barrow & Co., 195
Bates, Walker & Co., 195-6
Batkin, Walker & Broadhurst, 196
B.B., 194, 247
B.B. Ltd., 194
B. & B., 196, 207
B.B. & B., 200
B. & C., 203
B. & D., 196
B. & E., 196
Beardmore & Co., 196
Beardmore & Birks, 196
Beardmore, Birks & Blood, 196
Beardmore & Dawson, 196
Beardmore & Edwards, 196
Beck, Blair & Co., 196
Beech, J., 197
Beech, Hancock & Co., 197
Beech & Hancock, 197
bell (device – mark), 197
Bell Bros., 197
Bell & Co., 172
Bell, J. & M.P. & Co. (Ltd.), 197
Belleek, 197-8
Beswick, R., 198
B. & G., 207
B.H. & Co., 197
B. & H., 197, 198, 199
Birks Brothers, 198
Birks, Bros. & Seddon, 198
Bishop & Stonier, 198
B.L. & Co., 208
B. & L., 209
Blakeney (Pottery Ltd.), 198
Blakeney Art Pottery, 198, 349
B. & M., 193, 207
Bodley & Co., 199
Bodley, E.F. & Co., 198-9
Bodley, E.F. & Son, 199
bones – calcined, 9
bone china, 8-10
Boote, 170
Boote, T. & R. (Ltd.), 199. Plate 125
Booth, G. & W., 199
Booth, T. & Co., 200
Booth, T. & Son, 200
Booth, T.G., 199
Booth, T.G. & F., 199
Booth & Meigh, 200
Bordeaux, 366-7
Bourne, J., 200
Bourne, S., 74-5, 117. Colour Plates 5, 6, 13. Plates 17, 54-6
Bourne, W., 200
Bourne, Baker & Baker, 200
Bourne, Baker & Bourne, 200
Bowers, G.F. (& Co.), 200
Boyle, Z. (& Sons), 201. Plates 154-5
Bradbury, Mason & Bradbury, 202
Brameld (& Co), 202
Brammer & Co., 218
Breeze, 72
Bridgwood, S. & Son Ltd., 202-3, 206, 212
Bridgwood & Clarke, 203
Bristol, 57
Bristol stonewares, 203
Britannicus Dresden China, 203-4. Plate 157
British marks copied, 363-4
British Nankeen, 68-9, 70, 205-6, 359
British Nankin, 205
Broadhurst, J. (& Sons) (Ltd.), 206, 212
Broadhurst & Green, 207
Brocas, T., 68-9, 70, 76-7, 80, 205-6, 359
Brough & Blackhurst, 207
Brough & Mayer, 207
Brown, T. & M.L., 207
Brownfield, W. (& Sons), 207
Brownfield Guild Pottery Society, 207-8
B.S. (number), 175
B. & S., 194, 198
B. & S. H., 251
B.S. & T., 195
Burgess, H., 208
Burgess, Dale & Goddard, 208
Burgess & Goddard, 208
Burgess, Leigh & Co., 208
Burgess & Leigh (Ltd.), 208-9
Burgess & Meigh, 209
Burleigh (Ware), 209
Burn & Co., 209
Burn, J. & Co., 209
Burton, S. & J., 209
B.T. & S., 242
B. & T., 195
B.W. & Co., 196
B.W. & B., 196

C within circle, 100
Cambrian Pottery, 206
Carey, J. & Sons, 209
Carey, T. & J., 209. Plate 159
Carr, J. (& Co.), 210
Carr, J. & Son(s), 210
Carr & Patton, 210
Cartwright & Edwards (Ltd.), 210
C.C., 13, 210, 365
C.C. & Co., 217
C. & C., 217
C. & E., 210, 219
Celtic China, 193, 356. Plate 153
C.E. & M., 219
C. & F., 217
C. &G.F., 217
C. & G., 219
C. & H., 218
Challinor, C., 210
Challinor, C. & Co., 211
Challinor, E. (& Co.), 210, 211
Challinor, E. & C., 211
Challinor & Mayer, 211
Chamberlain & Co., 211
Chemical Porcelain, 248
Chetwynd, D., 212, 216, 217
china glaze, 8
Christie's, 107, 108
Church Gresley, 212
Churchill China (plc), 212
Churchill Company, 172
Churchill Hotelware Ltd., 203, 206, 212
Churchill Tableware Ltd., 212
C.J.M. & Co., 101
Clarke, E. (& Co.), 212-3
clays, 362-3
Clementson Bros., 214
Clementson, J., 171, 214. Plates 130, 160
Clementson & Young, 215. Colour Plate 29
Clementson, Young & Jameson, 215
Clews, R. & J., 215. Plate 161
Close, J.T. (& Co.), 216
C.M., 284
C.M. & S., 285
C.M.S. & P., 287
Coalport, 67-9, 70, 76-7. Plate 13
Cochran, R. & Co., 216
Cochran & Fleming, 217
Cockson & Chetwynd, 217
Cockson, Chetwynd & Co., 217
Cockson & Seddon, 217
collections, 392-3
Collinson, C. & Co., 218
colour printing, 166-8. Colour Plate 30
Coombs & Holland, 218
Cooper, T., 218
Copeland, W.T. (& Sons), 218
Copeland & Garrett, 219, 328, 335
copper-plates, 290
Copper Tea Leaf design, 164
copyright, 175
Cork & Edge, 219
Cork, Edge & Malkin, 219
Cormie, J., 219
Corn, E., 219
Corn, W. & E., 219-220
Coronation Ware, 195
country of origin marks, 175
C. & P., 210
creamware, 172
crown mark, 220
Crown Clarence Pottery, 220

Crownware, 322, 386
C. & S., 217
C.T., 348
C. & Y., 215
C.Y. & J., 215
Cymro, 220, 234

D., 220-1, 230, 234, 236. Plate 162
D. & Co., 221, 234
Daniel, H. (& Co.), 221
Daniel, H. & R., 95, 224-5. Plates 168, 169
Daniel, R. (& Co.), 94-5, 221-2. Plates 163-6.
date markings, 98, 100, 174, 191, 212, 218, 228
Davenport, 104, 226-232. Plates 170-181
Davenport Brothers, 233
Davis, J.H., 233
Davis, J.H. & J., 233
D. B. & Co., 237
D.B. & Co. Ltd., 237
Deakin & Son, 233
Deakin & Bailey, 233
dealers, 293
De Morgan, W., 233
Derbyshire Ironstone, 200, 233
Dillwyn (& Co.), 234
Dimmock, T. & Co., 234
Dimmock & Smith, 234
dissolution of partnerships, 105-6
Dixon, Phillips & Co., 234
D. & K.R., 234
Dresden China, 201
Dresden Opaque China, 215
D. & S., 233, 234
Du Croz & Co., 234-5. Plate 182
Du Croz & Millidge, 234-5
Dudson, J., 236
Dudson Armorlite Ltd., 236
Dudson Brothers (Ltd.), 236
Dudson Duraline Ltd., 236
Dudson Ltd., 236
Dunn, Bennett & Co. (Ltd.), 236
Duraline, 250
Duraline Hotelware, 237, 250
D.W., 237

East India Company, 10, 11, 13, 14, 15, 60
E.C., 210, 211
E.C. & Co., 211
E. & C.C., 211
Edge, Malkin & Co. (Ltd.), 237
Edwards, J., 170. Plate 283
Edwards, John (& Co.), 238
Edwards, J. (& Son), 173, 237
Edwards, J. & T., 238. Plate 284
Edwards, T., 238
E. & F., 240
E.F.B. & Co., 198
E.F.B. & S., 199
E.F.B. & Son, 199
E. & G.P., 297
E.G. & T., 241
E.H., 267
E.K. & B., 272
Elsmore & Son, 239
Elsmore & Forster, 239-240. Plates 183-4
E.M., 275
E.M. & Co., 237, 275
Emery, F.J., 240
England (in marks), 100
English Ironstone Ltd., 240
English Ironstone (Pottery) Ltd., 240
English Ironstone Tableware, 240
E.T.T., 344
Evans, D.J. & Co., 240
Evans & Glasson, 240
Everard, Glover & Townsend, 241
E.W., 350-2
E.W. & S., 356
E.W.W., 352
exhibition of 1851, 96-7, 100, 104, 171-2, 214, 306-9, 324, 385. Colour Plate 8. Plates 32, 33, 34, 36
export wares and markets, 173

Fairbairns,W., 241
Faraday, S.B., 82, 85-6, 92, 106
Farrall, J., 241
F.B., 242
F. & C., 244, 245
F.C. & Co., 244
F.C. & T., 242
Fell & Co., 241
Fell, T. (& Co.), 241
Felspar, 241
Fenton Stone Works, 101, 105
Ferrybridge Pottery, 241
F. & F., 244
F. & H., 244
Fine Stone, 218, 335
F.L., 272
Flacket, Chetham & Toft, 242
Flow Blue, 164-6. Colour Plate 29. Plates 131-2
Flown Blue – *see* Flow Blue
F.M., 293
F.M. & Co., 293
Folch, S. (& Sons), 242-4. Colour Plate 35. Plates 185-6
Folch & Scott, 244
Ford & Challinor, 244
Ford, Challinor & Co., 244
Forester & Hulme, 244
Freakley, W. (& Co.), 244
Freakley & Farrall, 244
French wares, 169
F. & T., 242
F.T.B., 201
Furnival, J. (& Co.), 244
Furnival, J. & T., 244
Furnival, T. & Co., 245
Furnival, T. (& Sons), 245
Furnival & Clarke, 245
Furnival & Wear, 245
Furnivals (Ltd.), 245
F. & W., 245

G., 246
Gater, T. & Co., 246
Gaudy Dutch, 246
Gaudy Ironstone, 168
Gaudy Welsh, 246
G.B. & B., 248
Gelson Bros., 246
G.F.B., 201
G.F.B. & Co., 201
G.G.W., 248
G.S.G.p.W., 248
Gildea &Walker, 246
Gill, W. (& Sons), 246
G.J. & Co., 271
G.J. & S., 271
G. & K., 247
G.L.A. & Bros., 98
Goddard & Burgess, 246-7
Godfrey, A. & Sons, 247
Godwin,J. & R., 247
Godwin, T., 247
Godwin, T. & J., 247
Godwin, Rowley & Co., 247
Goode & Kenworthy, 247
Goode & Watton, 247
Goodfellow, T., 248
Goodwin, J., 248
Goodwin, J. (& Co.), 323
G.R., 216
G.R. & Co., 247
G.R. & J., 247
Grainger, G., 248
granite body, 101, 168-9
granite china or ware, 101, 168-9
Green, W., 248
Griffiths, T. & Co., 248
Griffiths, Beardmore & Birks, 248
Grindley Hotelware, 172, 250
Grindley Pottery Ltd., 249
Grindley, W.H. & Co., 249
Grose & Co., 250
group letters, 191
G.R.T., 344
G. & S.T., 341
G.T., 343
G.T.M., 294
G.W., 359
G.W. & Co., 359
G. & W., 246-7
G.W.T., 344
G.W.T. & S., 344

H., 251
H.A. & Co., 179
Hackwood, 250
Hackwood, Dimmock & Co., 250
Hall, R. (& Co.), 250
Hall, R. (& Son), 250
Hammersley, R. (& Son), 250
Hampson, R., 65, 93, 94
Hancock, B.K.S., 251
Hancock, B. & S., 251
Hancock, S. (& Sons), 251
hard paste porcelain, 9-11
Harding, W. & G., 251
Harding, W. & J., 251
Harris, J., 251
Harris, J.W., 251
Harvey, C. & W.K., 251
Hawthorn, J., 251
H. Bros., 268
H.B. & Co., 252
H. & B., 252, 268
H. & C., 267
H.D. & Co., 221, 250
Heath, J., 251. Plate 1
Heath, J. & Co., 252
Heath, J.E. Ltd., 252
Heath & Blackhurst (& Co.), 252
Herculaneum Pottery, 252
H.H. & M., 266
Hicks & Meigh, 235, 252-260. Colour Plates 36-41. Plates 187-204
Hicks, Meigh & Johnson, 261-265. Colour Plates 34, 42. Plates 205-212
Higginbotham, T. (& Co.), 266
Higginbotham & Son, 266
H. & K., 266, 356-7
H.M. & I., 261, 263
H.M. & J., 261
Holdcroft, P. & Co., 266
Holdcroft, Hill & Mellor, 266
Holden, J., 266
Holland, W.T., 266, 360
Holland & Green, 266
Hollinshead & Kirkham, 266
Holmes, Plant & Madew, 267
Hope & Carter, 170, 267
Horne & Adams, 267
hotel ware, 15, 172-3, 267
H.P. & M., 267
H. & R.D., 96. Plate 169
Hudden, J.T., 267
Hughes, E., 267
Hughes, S. (& Son), 267
Hughes, S. & Co., 267
Hughes, S. & E., 267
Hughes, T., 169-170, 172, 268
Hughes, T. & Son (Ltd.), 268
Hulme,T., 268
Hulme & Booth, 268
Hulse,Nixon & Adderley, 97
Humphreys Bros., 268
Hydra jug, 102-4. Plate 38

I.B. & Co., 209
I.D.B., 193
I.H. & Co., 252
Imari – style, 109
I.FM., 281
I.M. & S., 288
Imperial Cookware, 335
Imperial Stone, 268
import duties, 14, 15, 61-2
Improved Ironstone China, 100
Improved Stone China, 284-5, 287
Indian Stone China, 284-5
initial marks, 369-372
Ironite, 251
Ironstone, 72, 74, 174
I.W., 355
I.W. & Co., 356

J., 269
Jackson, J. & Co., 268
Jackson, J. & J., 268-9
Jamieson, J. & Co., 269
Japan patterns, 74, 109
J.B., 197, 206, 269
J.B. & Co., 269
J.B. & S., 206
J.C., 210, 214
J.C. & Co., 210
J.C. & S., 210
J.D.B., 193. Plate 153
J.D.P., 300
J.E., 238
J. & E., 271
J.E.M., 281
J.E. & S., 238
J.F., 241, 244, 269
J.F. & Co., 244
J.F.W., 355
J.G. monogram, 270-1
J. & G.A., 179
J.H., 251
J.H. & Co., 252
J.H.M., 289
J.J. & Co., 268
J.K.K., 272
J.M., 281
J.M. & Co., 269, 276, 280
J.M. & S., 287, 288

J. & M.P.B. & Co. (Ltd.), 197
Johnson Bros., 270
Johnson, R., 269
Johnston, D., 270, 366
Jones, E., Plate 282
Jones, F. (& Co.), 270
Jones, G. & Co., 271
Jones, G. (& Sons), 270
Jones & Ellis, 271
J.P. & Co. (Ltd.), 300
J.R., 305
J.B.R., 318
J.R. & Co., 305
J. & R.G., 247
J.R. & S., 305
J.R. & Sons, 305
J.T., 341, 342
J. & T.E., 238
J.T.H., 267
J. & T.L., 273
J.T. & S., 341, 342
J.T. & Sons, 342
J.W., 352, 355
J.W.P., 296
J.W.P. & Co., 296
J.W.R., 309, 311
J. & W.R., 309
J.Y., 359

K. & B., 271
K.C. & Co., 271
K. & E., 272
K.E. & B., 272
K.E. & Co., 272
Keele Street Pottery Co. (Ltd.), 271
Kensington Pottery Ltd., 271
Kerr & Binns, 271
Kerr & Co., 271
Kidston, R.A. & Co., 271
Kidston, Cochran & Co., 271
Kilncroft, 336
Knapper & Blackhurst, 271
Knight, J.K., 272
Knight, Elkin & Bridgwood, 272
Knight, Elkin & Co., 272
Knight & Elkin, 272
Knight, Sproston & Knight, 72, 272
K.P., 348
K.P.H., 271
K.S.P., 271

labour problems, 88
L. & D., 273
L.E., 239
L.E. & Co., 239
L.E. & Son, 239
Lea, F., 272
Lear, S., 272
Leek Pottery, 272
Liddle Elliot (& Co.), 238
Liddle Elliot (& Son), 238
Lidstone, J., 178, 324, 391
Limpus & Mason, 105, 106
Liverpool, 273
Livesley & Davis, 273
Livesley, Powell & Co., 273
Livesley & Powell, 303
L. & M., 360
Lockett, J. (& Co.), 273
Lockett, J. & T., 273
London (and anchor), 210
L.P. & Co., 273
Ltd., 175
L.W., 242, 358
L.W.P., 358
L.W. & S., 242, 358

M., 274, 290
M. & A., 294
Maastricht, 367
Maddock, J. (& Son), 274, 275. Plate 213
Maddock & Co., 274-5
Maddock Hotelware, 275
Maddock & Gater, 275
Maddock & Seddon, 275
Made in England – in mark, 100, 175
Magness, E. (& Co.), 275
Magness, J. & Co., 276
Malkin, R., 276
Malkin, Edge & Co., 276
mantelpieces, 155. Plate 30
Mare, M., 276
marks – general points, 174-6
Marple, Turner & Co., 276
Marsh, J., 276. Plate 214
Marshall, J. (& Co.), 276
Mason factories, 104-5
Mason, C.J. (& Co.), 74, 81-3, 88, 92-3, 97, 171
Mason, G. & C. (& Co.), 72, 81-2, 88, 98, 100-1, 106
Mason, G.M. & C.J., 100-1
Mason, M., 70, 81, 98, 205-6
Mason, M. & Co., 106
Mason, M. & Son, 278
Mason marks, 77, 98-102
Mason, W., 82, 104, 278
Mason & Wolfe, 105-6
Mason Collectors' Club, 393
Mason's Ironstone body, Chapters II, III and IV, 10, 65, 71-160, 277. Colour Plates 3-28. Plates 14-19, 22-124
Mason's Ironstone China Ltd., 279-280. Plates 215-217
Mason's London shop, 112, 146-154
Mason's patent, 71-3
Mason's Patent Ironstone China Ltd., 98, 100
Maudesley, J. & Co., 280
May, J., 280
Mayer, J., 281
Mayer, T., 281
Mayer, T. & J., 281
Mayer, T.J. & J., 281
Mayer (Bros.) & Elliot, 281
Mayer & Newbold, 282. Plate 218
M. & B., 291
M.E. & Co., 276
Meakin Bros (& Co.), 284
Meakin & Co., 284
Meakin Ltd., 166
Meakin, A. (Ltd.), 282. Plate 129
Meakin, C., 283
Meakin, H., 283
Meakin, J. & C., 283
Meakin, L. (& Co.), 283
Meakin & Farrall, 283
Meigh, C. (& Son), 284-6. Colour Plate 43. Plates 219-221
Meigh, C., Son & Pankhurst, 287
Meigh, J. & Son, 287
Meir, 194
Meir, H. & Son, 287
Meir, J. & Son, 288, 303. Plate 223
Mellor & Co., 288
Mellor, Taylor & Co., 289
Mellor, Venables & Co., 289
Mellor, Venables & Baines, 289
M. & G., 275
M. & H., 291
Micratex, 178
Middleton, J.H., 289
Midwinter, W.R. (Ltd.), 289
Mills, H., 289
Minton, 290-2. Plates 224-227
Minton & Boyle, 78, 290-1
Minton & Hollins, 291
Mist, J., 64, 226
M.J.B., 198
M. & N., 282
Moore Bros., 292
Morley, F. (& Co.), 97, 292-3. Plates 227-8
Morley, W., 294
Morley & Asbury, 294
Morley & Ashworth, 97-8, 294
Mountford, G.T., 294
M. & S., 275, 286
M.T. & Co., 289
Mulberry Ironstone, 166
M.V. & Co., 289
M.N. & B., 289
Myott Meakin Ltd., 294

Nankeen, 14
N. & B., 295
N. & D., 295
Neale, Bailey & Neale, 294
New Stone, 290
New Stone China, 101
New Wharf Pottery Co., 295
Newbold & Dawson, 295
Newbon & Beardmore, 295
N.S., 328
N.W.P. Co., 295

O.H. & Co., 296
O.H.E.C. (L.), 295
Old Hall Earthenware Co. Ltd., 295
Opaque China, 171, 295
Oriental imports, 10, 11-4, 60-2, 69, 70. Colour Plate 1. Plates 2, 5-7, 13
Oriental reissues, 368
Oulsnam, W.E. (& Sons), 295
Oulsnam & Holdcroft, 295

P. & A., 300
Pankhurst & Co., 170
Pankhurst, J.W. (& Co.), 296
Parisian Granite, 203
patent, 377
Patent Ironstone China, 98
pattern numbers, 175
P.B., 242
P.B. & Co., 299
P. & B., 300
P.B. & H., 299
P.B. & S., 300
P. Bros., 242
P. & Co., 299
P. & Co. Ltd., 299
P.E. & Co., 300
Pearl, 162-3
Pearl Granite, 169
pearl ware, 8, 11, 13
Pearl White, 162-3
Pearson, E., 296
Pearson, Farrall & Meakin, 296
Pekin, 296
Penman, R.H. & Co., 296-7
Penman, Brown & Co., 297
P.F. & M., 296
P.G., 203, 208
P. & G., 300
P.H. & Co., 266
Phillips, E. & G., 297
Phillips, G., 297-8. Plates 229, 230
Phillips, H., 63, 107, 112
Phillips, P.W., 103
Phillips, T. (& Son), 299
Pinder, Bourne & Co., 299
Pinder, Bourne & Hope, 299
P.L.C., 175
Plymouth Pottery Co. Ltd., 299
Podmore, Walker & Co., 299
Porcelaine Opaque, 169
*Pottery Gazette Diary*, 384-5
Poulson, J., 299
Pountney & Co. (Ltd), 299
Pountney, J.D. (& Co.), 300
Pountney & Allies, 300
Pountney, Edwards & Co., 300
Pountney & Goldney, 300
Powell & Bishop, 170, 300
Powell, Bishop & Stonier, 300
P.P. Co. Ld., 299
Pratt, J. & Co. (Ltd.), 300
Pratt & Simpson, 301
prices, 387-9
Primavesi, F. & Co., 301
Primavesi, F. & Son, 301
printed outlines, 78. Plate 20
Proctor, J., 301
P. & S., 301
Pt. Iron China, 98
Public Record Office, 374-7
published by, 374. Plates 282-4
Pugin, A.W.N., Plate 226
P.W. & Co., 299
P.W. & W., 299

Queen"s Ware, 8, 13, 325

R in circle, 100, 175
R.A.K., 271
R.A.K. & Co., 271
Rathbone, T. (& Co.), 301
Rathbone, Smith & Co., 301
R.B., 198
R.C., 217
R.C. & Co., 217
R. & C., 302
R.C.A., 302
R.D. & Co., 223
R$^{D}$. N$^{o}$...., 175
Read & Co., 302
Read & Clementson, 301-2. Plate 231
Read, Clementson & Anderson, 302
Reade, G.W., 303
Real Ironstone China, 98
Real Stone China, 192
recipes, 72-4, 165-8, 170
Reed, 303
Reed, Taylor & Co., 303
Reed & Taylor, 303
reference books, 390-2
registered designs, 377-384
registered shapes, Plates 34, 35
registration marks, 175, 374-7
registration numbers, 175, 377
Regout, P. (& Co.), 367
reproductions, 103, 368

retailers' marks, 176
R.H., 250
R.H. & Co., 250
R.H. & S., 250
R. & H., 318
R.H.P. & Co., 297-8
Ridgway, 303
Ridgway, Job & Sons, 44, 305
Ridgway, John (& Co.), 44, 304-9, 385. Plates 232-6
Ridgway, J. & W., 309-313. Plates 237-244
Ridgway,W. (& Co.), 313-4. Plates 245-6
Ridgway, W., Son & Co., 315. Colour Plate 45
Ridgway, Bates & Co., 315-6
Ridgway & Clarke, 316
Ridgway & Morley, 97, 316-7
Ridgway, Morley & Wear, 97, 171, 317
Ridgway, Morley, Wear & Co., 317
Riley, J. & R., 317-8
Ring, E. (& Co.), 64, 318
R.K. & Co., 318
R. & M., 316, 321
R.M. & S., 276
R.M.W. & Co., 317
Robinson, J., 318
Robinson & Hollinshead, 318
Robinson, Kirkham & Co., 318
Robinson & Wood, 318
Robinson, Wood & Brownfield, 318, 319. Colour Plate 46. Plates 249, 250
Robinson, Wood & Co., 318
Rocklite Vitrified, 237
Rogers Bros., 320
Rogers, J. & Son, 320
Rowland & Marsellus Co., 321
Royal ... (prefix), 175
Royal Arms,175
Royal Cauldon, 321
Royal Crownford, 352
Royal Doulton, 321, 336
Royal Terra Cotta Porcelain, 102
Royal Tudor Ware, 194
Royal Vitrescent Rock China, 321
Royal Worcester, 321, 386
Royal Worcester Spode Ltd., 218, 335
R.S. Co., 301
R.S.W., 338, 339
R. & T., 241, 303
R.T. & Co., 241, 303
R. &W., 318
R.W. & B., 319

S. & Co., 325, 336
S.A. & Co., 179. Plate 136
salt-glaze wares, 57, 162. Plate 4
Sampsonite, 212
Satin White, 249
Saxon Blue Stoneware, 65
Saxon Stone China, 209
S. & B., 340
S.B. & S., 203
S.B. & Son, 203
Scragg, R., 323
S. & E., 340
Seacombe, 248, 323
S. & E.H., 267
Semi-China, 173, 322, 323. Plate 21
S.E. & N., 340
S. & F., 326
S.F. & J., 326
S.H., 251, 267
S.H. & Co., 267, 323
S.H. & S., 251, 267
S. & H., 323, 336
Sharpe Brothers & Co. (Ltd.), 324
Shaw, A. (& Co.), 164, 170, 324-6. Plate 128
Shaw, A. (& Son), 324-6
Shaw, C. & J., 325
Silber, A., 385
Silber & Fleming, 322, 385
Silicon China, 200
S. & J.B., 209
S.M., 367
Smith, W. & Co., 325-6, 335
Smith, Ford & Sons, 326
Smith, Ford & Jones, 326
Smith & Ford, 326
Sol, 283
source material, 176, 390-2
South Wales Pottery, 326
Spatter Ware, 171-2
Spode, 8-10, 62-5, 74, 326-334. Colour Plates 2, 47, 48. Plates 10-12, 262-266
Spode Ltd., 335
Spode & Copeland, 327
Spode ('s) New Stone, 219
Stafford, 325, 335
Stafford Pottery, 335
Staffordshire Potteries, 174
Staffordshire Potteries Ltd., 336
Stanway & Horne, 336
Stanway, Horne & Co., 336
Stanway, Horne & Adams, 336
Steelite, 336
Steelite International PLC., 336
Steelite Vitreous Hotelware, 336
Stevenson, 337. Plate 267
Stevenson & Williams, 338. Plates 269, 270
Stockton, 90
Stoke China, 9, 340
Stoke Works, 340
Stone China, 57-60, 320
Stone Ware, 57-60
Super Vitrified, 212
S.W., 242, 358
Swift & Elkin, 340
Swillington Bridge, 340-1
Swinnertons Ltd., 341
S.W.P., 326

T., 348
Tams, J. (& Son), 341
Taylor, G. & S., 341
Taylor, W., 341
Taylor Brothers (& Co.), 341
T.B., 195
T.B. & Co., 200
T.B. & S., 200
T.B. & Son, 200
T. & B.G., 247
T. & C.T., 348
T.E., 238
Tea Leaf Design, 163-4. Plates 128-9
Tea Leaf Lustre, 164
T.F., 245
T.F. & Co., 245
T.F. Jun. & Co., 245
T.F. & S., 245
T.F. & Sons, 245
T.G. & Co., 248
T.G.B., 199
T.G. & F.B., 199
T.H., 268
Thomson, J. (& Sons), 342
T.H.W., 350
Till, T. & Son(s), 171, 342
tin-glazed wares, 13. Plate 3
T.M., 198
toilet sets, 388
Tomkinson Bros. & Co., 342-3
Tonquin, 343. Plate 271
Townsend, G., 343
T.P., 343
T.R. & Co., 301
Trachtenberg & Panthes, 343-4
trade names, 372-3
trade mark, 175
T.R.B., 199
Troutbeck, E.T., 344
Trubshaw, Hand & Co., 344
T.T., 348
T.H.T., 348
T. & T., 348
T.T. & S., 342
Tudor Ware, 194
Turnbull, G.R., 344
Turner (& Co.), 344-5, 347
Turner, G.W. (& Sons), 344
Turner, J., 58-9, 62, 71, 344-7. Plates 272-7
Turner, W. & J., 62
Turner, Goddard & Co., 348
Turner & Tomkinson, 170, 348
Turner's Patent, 63-4, 71, 344-7. Plates 8, 9, 272-7
T.W., 350
Twigg, J. & Bros., 348
Twyford, T. & Co., 348

U. & Co., 348
U. & Cie., 348
Ultraline, 237
Unicorn Pottery Ltd., 268
Unicorn Tableware, 348
U.S. Potters' Association, 361-5
Utzschneider & Cie., 348

V. & B., 348-9
Venables, J. & Co., 349
Venables, T.B., 348-9
Venables & Baines, 349
Venables, Mann & Co., 349
Victoria (Ware), 349
Victoria Ironstone, 349
Victorian (mark), 198
Villeroy & Boch, 348
Vitrified Hotel Ware, 212
Vitreous ware, 322
V.M. & Co., 349

W.A. & Co., 177-8
W.A. & S., 177
Wade & Colclough, 350
wage rates, 90
Walker, T., 350
Walker, T.H., 350
Walker & Carter, 350
Walley, 350
Walley, E. (& Son), 350. Plate 278
Walley, E. &W., 351
Warren, J., 352
Washington Pottery, 352
W.B., 207
W.B. & S., 207
W. & B., 358
W.C., 246
W. & C., 349, 350, 358
W. & Co., 350
Weatherby (J.H.) & Sons Ltd., 352
W.E.C., 220
W. & E.C., 220
Wedgewood, 325, 335, 352, 354
Wedgwood, J., 8, 13, 57-8, 62-3
Wedgwood, J. & Sons Ltd., 391
Wedgwood, John (& Co.), 356-7
Wedgwood, Josiah (& Sons Ltd.), 299, 325, 354. Plate 279
Wedgwood & Co. (Ltd.), 299, 352-3, 354
Wessel, L., 358
Weston, G., 355
W.F. & Co., 244
W.F.M., 294
W.G., 162
W.G.H., 251
W. & H., 358
White Granite, 168-9
White Ironstone, 160-3, 392. Plates 125-7
Whitehaven, 355
Wileman, H., 355
Wileman, J.F., 355
Wilkinson, A.J. (Ltd.), 355
Wilkinson, J., 355
Wilkinson & Hulme, 356
Williams, 360
Wilson, I. & Co., 356
W. & J.H., 251
W.M., 294
Wolfe,Thomas & Co., 105
Wood, 356
Wood, E. (& Sons), 14, 356
Wood, E.T.W., 356-7
Wood, J. Wedge, 352, 356-7
Wood & Sons (Ltd.), 357
Wood & Brownfield, 357-8
Wood & Caldwell, 75
Wood & Challinor, 358
Wood & Clarke, 358
Wood & Hawthorne, 358
Wood & Hulme, 358
Wood, Rathbone & Co., 358
Woolf, L. (& Sons), 358
Woolf, S., 358
Wooliscroft, G. (& Co.), 359
Worcester Royal Porcelain Co., 271, 321, 386
W.P. Co., 355
W.R. & Co., 314, 341
Wrekin Ironstone,359
W.R.S. & Co., 315. Plate 247
W.S. & Co., 325, 335
W. & T.A., 177-8
W.T.H., 266, 360

Yates, J., 359
Yates, J. & W., 67-8
Yates & Co., 359
Yates & Baggeley, 67-8
Yates & May, 359
Y.M.P., 359
Y. & M., 359
Ynysmedw, 360
Y.P., 359

Z.B., 201
Z.B. & S., 201A. Bros., 98, 192